# READINGS IN
# RUSSIAN FOREIGN POLICY

# *Readings in* RUSSIAN FOREIGN POLICY

*Edited by*

ROBERT A. GOLDWIN

with GERALD STOURZH

and MARVIN ZETTERBAUM

*1922*

*New York* OXFORD UNIVERSITY PRESS 1959

Printed in the United States of America

# PREFACE

The purpose of this volume of readings is threefold: to serve the college and university student as primary or supplementary course material, to offer the general reader an opportunity to acquaint himself systematically with the best thought on a wide range of the fundamental problems, and to function as the basic reading material for organized programs of adult education discussion groups.

Several unique features distinguish this book from other books of readings and affect the ways in which it can best be used. Its main characteristic is the plan of selection and editing. The articles are grouped in sections, each about 50 to 75 pages long, intended to be read as a unit. The selections have the continuity of a debate; opposing views are deliberately juxtaposed and the reader must judge the merits of each argument. The articles within each unit will be most instructive, therefore, if they are read in the order in which they appear. The sections are also best taken up in order, for the materials in later sections assume knowledge of the issues discussed in earlier sections.

This book has no index; although it contains a great deal of historical information, it is not a book for "looking up" isolated facts or events. It is a book of political argument. Although the readings present clear and forceful statements of a variety of positions—some quite partisan, others more detached and analytical—the collection as a whole is not meant to represent or support any particular viewpoint. Readers should not assume that any author in these pages is the spokesman of the editors. Nor is this volume intended to be comprehensive. The aim is rather to provoke thought on a limited number of highly significant problems and to provide a sound basis for further study.

Although final responsibility for selection rests, of course, with us, we are indebted to the following distinguished authorities for valuable advice and suggestions: Max Beloff, Reader in the Comparative Study of Institutions, University of Oxford; George B. Carson, Jr., Director, Service Center for Teachers of History of the American Historical Association, Washington, D. C.; Harold H. Fischer, Chairman of the Hoover Institute and Library, Stanford University; Abram L. Harris, Professor of Economics, University of Chicago; Chauncy D. Harris, Professor of Geography, University of Chicago; J. B. Hoptner, Director of Studies, Mid-European Studies Center; Paul L. Horecky, Slavic Division, Library of Congress; Bert F. Hoselitz, Director of Studies, Committee on International Relations, University of Chicago; Simon Kaplan, Tutor, St. John's College; Hans J. Morgenthau, Professor of Political Science, University of Chicago and Director, Center for the Study of American Foreign and Military Policy, University of Chicago; Philip Mosely, Director of Studies, Council on Foreign Relations; William L. Neumann, Professor of Diplomatic History, Goucher College; Frederick L. Schuman, Woodrow Wilson Professor of Government, Williams College; Leo Strauss, Professor of Political Philosophy, University of Chicago; Kenneth W. Thompson, Associate Director of Social Sciences, Rockefeller Foundation; Julian Towster, Associate Professor of Political Science, University of California; Quincy Wright, Professor Emeritus of International Law, University of Chicago; and Sergius Yacobson, Chief, Slavic Division, Library of Congress.

These readings were originally prepared by members of the staff of the American Foundation for Continuing Education for use in discussion programs for the education of adults. The AFCE devotes itself primarily to the development of materials (such as this book) in many subject-matter fields and to the development of leadership training programs. The Foundation seeks to cooperate with persons or organizations interested in conducting discussion programs and welcomes requests for assistance or advice on training or promotion. Inquiries may be addressed to the Executive Director, American Foundation for Continuing Education, 19 South La Salle Street, Chicago 3, Illinois.

THE EDITORS

*Chicago, Illinois*
*April 1959*

# ACKNOWLEDGMENTS

The editors wish to acknowledge the kind permission of the publishers listed below to reproduce materials from their copyrighted publications, as follows:

McGraw-Hill Book Co., Inc.: for the maps "Rivers of Russia" and "Railways in the U.S.S.R., 1940" from *The Basis of Soviet Strength,* by George B. Cressey; copyright, 1945. Also for the maps "The Medieval State System," "Emergence of the Modern State System," "Europe in 1740," "The Napoleonic Empire," "The State System Restored," "Europe in 1914," "The Zenith of German Power," "Europe after Versailles," "Europe on September 1, 1939," and "Europe on January 1, 1941" from *International Politics,* 3rd edition, by Frederick L. Schuman; copyright, 1941.

Alfred A. Knopf, Inc.: for the maps "Political Divisions of the U.S.S.R.," "Industrial Areas of the U.S.S.R.," and "Natural Resources of the U.S.S.R." from *A History of Russia,* 4th edition, by Bernard Pares; copyright, 1926, 1928, 1937, 1944.

Harvard University Press: for the maps "Russia's Territorial Gains in the West," "Across the Pole," and "U.S.S.R." from *The United States and Russia,* by Vera M. Dean; copyright, 1947, 1948.

D. Van Nostrand Co.: for the maps "Expansion of the Russian Empire," and "Soviet Union," and the table "Rulers of Russia" from *An Introduction to Russian History and Culture,* by Ivar Spector; copyright, 1949. Also for the "Chronological Table" from *Russia, Past and Present,* by Anatole G. Mazour; copyright, 1951.

Charles Scribner's Sons: for the map "Russia" from *The Aftermath, The World Crisis 1918-1928,* by Winston Churchill; copyright, 1929.

# CONTENTS

## I. THE RUSSIAN PEOPLE

1. Roger Dow, *Prostor*     3
2. Feodor Dostoievsky, *The Utopian Conception of History*     18
3. Nicolas Berdyaev, *Religion and the Russian State*     25
4. Geoffrey Gorer, *The People of Great Russia*     34
5. Alexander Herzen, *The Russian People and Socialism*     47
6. Alexander Blok, *Scythians*     61

## II. CZARISM AND THE RUSSIAN REVOLUTION

1. Rostislav A. Fadieev, *What Should Be the Policy of Russia?*     67
2. Friedrich Engels, *The Foreign Policy of Russian Czarism*     74
3. *Documents on the Beginnings of Soviet Foreign Policy*     93
4. Winston S. Churchill, *The Nameless Beast*     112

## III. WORLD REVOLUTION AND NATIONAL INTEREST

1. Joseph Stalin, *The October Revolution*     133
2. Leon Trotsky, *The Permanent Revolution*     146
3. *Documents on the Question of United States Recognition of the Soviet Union*     155
4. Raymond Robins, *Recognition of Russia and World Peace*     164
5. John Spargo, *The Soviet Union: The Question of Recognition*     171
6. Michael T. Florinsky, *Soviet Foreign Policy*     181

IV. ASPECTS OF THE THEORY OF COMMUNISM:
PRO AND CON

1. Joseph Stalin, *Dialectical and Historical Materialism*   195
2. Karl Federn, *The Materialist Conception of History*   214
3. V. I. Lenin, *Imperialism—The Highest Stage of Capitalism*   236
4. Joseph A. Schumpeter, *Imperialism and Capitalism*   250

V. RUSSIA AND THE EAST

1. Feodor Dostoievsky, *Geok-Tepe. What Is Asia to Us?*   269
2. Albert J. Beveridge, *The Russian Advance*   279
3. Andrei Lobanov-Rostovsky, *Some Aspects of the Far Eastern Crisis*   294
4. Mao Tse-tung, *On the People's Democratic Dictatorship*   307
5. Mao Tse-tung, *Let a Hundred Flowers Bloom*   320
6. G. F. Hudson, *New Phase of Mao's Revolution*   332

VI. IDEOLOGY AND THE BALANCE OF POWER

1. *The Comintern: The Twenty-one Conditions of Admission into the Communist International*   349
2. Maxim Litvinov, *The Organization of Peace*   356
3. Franz Borkenau, *World Communism*   364
4. Joseph Stalin, *We Stand for Peace*   379
5. *Documents on Russia as a Neutral*   390
6. Winston S. Churchill, *The Soviet Nemesis*   402
7. *The Dissolution of the Comintern*   417

VII. THE COLD WAR

1. Hans J. Morgenthau, *The Real Issue Between the United States and the Soviet Union*   423
2. Joseph Stalin, *The Inevitability of Wars*   433
3. Nikita S. Khrushchev, *The International Position of the Soviet Union*   439

4. Nikita S. Khrushchev, *The Task of Surpassing the U.S.A.*                                                      450

5. Dean Acheson, *Power Today*                                      464

6. George F. Kennan, *Russia's Economic Progress*      477


VIII. THE "CAMP OF SOCIALISM": YUGOSLAVIA

1. *The Soviet-Yugoslav Dispute*                            489

2. Roy Macridis, *Stalinism and the Meaning of Titoism*    502

3. *The "Normalization" of Soviet-Yugoslav Relations*      517

4. Nikita S. Khrushchev, *Crimes of the Stalin Era*        522

5. *Declaration of 12 Communist Parties*                   529

6. Richard Lowenthal, *The Logic of One-Party Rule*        539

7. *The Soviet-Yugoslav Dispute Renewed*                   548


IX. THE "CAMP OF SOCIALISM": HUNGARY

1. Jozsef Revai, *Our People's Democracy*                  577

2. Paul Kecskemeti, *Decompression in Hungary*             587

3. *Hungary, 1956*                                         602

4. Josip B. Tito, *Our Tragedy*                            622

5. Milovan Djilas, *The Storm in Eastern Europe*           630

6. Nikita S. Khrushchev, *Soviet-Hungarian Friendship*     638

7. *The Execution of Imre Nagy*                            643

8. Wladyslaw Gomulka, *The Rout of the Counterrevolution*  650


X. WHAT GUIDES RUSSIAN FOREIGN POLICY?

1. Michael Karpovich, *Russian Imperialism or Communist Aggression?*                                              657

2. Peter Meyer, *The Driving Force Behind Soviet Imperialism*                                                 667

3. Arnold J. Toynbee, *Russia and the West*                680

4. R. S. Tarn, *Continuity in Russian Foreign Policy*      689

5. Edward Crankshaw, *Russia's Imperial Design*            705

# APPENDIX

TABLES

Rulers of Russia (A.D. 1328-1917)                                    723

Chronological Table of Russian History (A.D.
    1147-1958)                                                       725

MAPS

The Soviet Union: Special Map for This Volume                       752

The U.S.S.R. and the U.S. (A Comparison of Areas and
    Densities of Population)                                        754

The Soviet Union                                                    756

Political Divisions of the U.S.S.R.                                 758

Industrial Areas of the U.S.S.R.                                    759

Natural Resources of the U.S.S.R.                                   760

Rivers of Russia                                                    761

Railways in the U.S.S.R., 1940                                      762

Russian Expansion to 1914                                           764

Russia's Territorial Gains in the West to 1947                      766

The Changing Map of Europe:
    1360A.D. and 1648                                               768
    1740 and 1810                                                   769
    1815 and 1914                                                   770
    1918 and 1919                                                   771
    1939 and 1941                                                   772

The Anti-Bolshevik Armies in Russia, 1919                           773

East Central Europe                                                 774

Across the Pole (A Polar View of the U.S.S.R. and
    the U.S.)                                                       775

# THE AUTHORS

ROGER DOW (b. 1906), Supervisor of Central and Eastern European History, Harvard University, 1938–42; Research Analyst, Office of Strategic Services, 1942–46; since 1946, with the Department of State.

FEODOR DOSTOIEVSKY (1821–1881), Russian novelist.

NICOLAS BERDYAEV (1874–1948), Russian philosopher and religious thinker, lived in exile in Western Europe after the Russian Revolution.

GEOFFREY GORER (b. 1905), British anthropologist, author of *The American People*.

ALEXANDER HERZEN (1812–1870), Russian revolutionist and exile; author, editor, and publisher.

ALEXANDER BLOK (1880–1921), Russian poet.

ROSTISLAV A. FADIEEV (1824–1884), Major General in the Russian Imperial Army and author of works on military and political subjects.

FRIEDRICH ENGELS (1820–1895), German economist and historian; collaborator with Marx.

WINSTON S. CHURCHILL (b. 1874), British statesman and historian; Prime Minister, 1940–1945, and 1951–1955.

JOSEPH STALIN (1879–1953), virtual ruler of the Soviet Union from 1928 until his death; Secretary of the Central Committee of the Communist Party of the Soviet Union and in his last years also Chairman of the Council of Ministers.

LEON TROTSKY (1879–1940), Communist leader and associate of Lenin; first Commissar of Foreign Affairs of the Soviet Government; exiled from Russia in 1929, murdered in Mexico.

RAYMOND ROBINS (1873–1954), lecturer and writer; head of American Red Cross mission in Russia, 1917–1918.

JOHN SPARGO (b. 1876), author, prominent in Socialist party until 1917; most recently Director-Curator, Historical Museum and Art Gallery, Bennington, Vermont.

MICHAEL T. FLORINSKY (b. 1894), Russian-born American economist and historian; Professor of Economics, Columbia University.

KARL FEDERN (1868–1942), Austrian writer, last resident in England.

V. I. LENIN (1870–1924), leader of the Bolshevist revolution, October–November 1917; President of the Council of People's Commissars until his death.

JOSEPH A. SCHUMPETER (1883–1950), Austrian economist and one-time Finance Minister of Austria; from 1932 to his death, Professor at Harvard University.

ALBERT J. BEVERIDGE (1862–1929), U.S. Senator from Indiana, 1899–1911; biographer of Lincoln and Chief Justice John Marshall.

ANDREI LOBANOV-ROSTOVSKY (b. 1892), Russian-born American historian; Professor at the University of Michigan since 1945.

MAO TSE-TUNG (b. 1893), Chairman of the Central Committee of the Chinese Communist Party.

G. F. HUDSON (b. 1903), British political analyst and writer on Chinese affairs, Director of the Center for Far Eastern Studies at St. Antony's College, Oxford.

MAXIM LITVINOV (1876–1951), Commissar for Foreign Affairs of the Soviet Union, 1930–1939; Ambassador to the United States, 1941–1943.

FRANZ BORKENAU (1900–1957), Austrian-born historian, last resident in Zurich, Switzerland; author of many books and studies on International and Soviet Communism.

HANS J. MORGENTHAU (b. 1904), Professor of Political Science and Director of the Center for the Study of American Foreign and Military Policy, University of Chicago.

NIKITA S. KHRUSHCHEV (b. 1894), First secretary of the Communist Party of the Soviet Union since 1953 and Chairman of the Council of Ministers since 1958.

DEAN ACHESON (b. 1893), Secretary of State from 1949 to 1952, now practices law in Washington, D. C.

GEORGE F. KENNAN (b. 1904), a U.S. foreign service officer from 1927 to 1952; Ambassador to the Soviet Union in 1952; since 1952 a member of the Institute for Advanced Study, Princeton.

ROY MACRIDIS (b. 1918), Professor of Political Science at Washington University, St. Louis, Missouri.

RICHARD LOWENTHAL (b. 1908), political analyst and writer on international affairs for the London *Observer*.

JOZSEF REVAI (b. 1898), leading member of the Hungarian Communist Party under Rakosi; now also in a leading position in the Kadar regime.

PAUL KECSKEMETI (b. 1901), formerly with the Office of War Information and the War Department, now Senior Research Associate with the RAND Corporation.

JOSIP BROZ TITO (b. 1892), President of Yugoslavia.

MILOVAN DJILAS (b. 1910 or 1911); Vice-President of Yugoslavia until his break with Marshal Tito's regime; author of *The New Class* (1957), a criticism of Communist society; now serving a prison term for the publication of both the article reprinted in this volume and of his book.

WLADYSLAW GOMULKA (b. 1905), First Secretary of the Polish United Workers' Party Central Committee.

MICHAEL KARPOVICH (b. 1888), Russian-born American scholar; until his recent retirement, Professor at Harvard University.

PETER MEYER (1902–1953), author; authority on Soviet affairs.

ARNOLD J. TOYNBEE (b. 1889), British historian; until his retirement, Research Professor of International History, University of London, and Director of Studies, Royal Institute of International Affairs.

R. S. TARN is a pseudonym.

EDWARD CRANKSHAW (b. 1909), noted British authority on Soviet affairs; author of *Cracks in the Kremlin Wall* and other books.

# I

# THE RUSSIAN PEOPLE

# PROSTOR*

BY

## ROGER DOW

[1941]

In size and continental character, Russia and the United States possess a common trait which has dictated that their expansion and cohesion into nations should follow parallel lines. In both countries the most important geopolitical factor has been space, and the chief result has been colonialism. The interrelation of these two has produced a frontier on a vast scale and a species of regionalism differing from those in any other modern empire, and has given the two nations certain national attitudes, national characteristics, and national policies of striking similarity.

The origins and historical development of Russia and the United States followed lines laid down by the logic of geography. The American Republic began as a handful of colonies scattered along the broad reaches of the Atlantic seaboard which, after winning their independence and achieving formal unity at the end of the eighteenth century, proceeded to send pioneers pushing westward across the plains for thousands of miles until the continent was spanned and lands annexed.

Russia's march to the Pacific across the vast area of Siberia was accomplished with the same rapidity and in exactly the same way. Neither waited to settle. California's admission to the Union in 1850 found her separated from her nearest sister state by many a lonely mile, as the establishment of Nikolayevsk-on-Amur made it an isolated outpost of empire far removed from the mother country.

Russian expansion properly begins with Ivan IV [1553-84] and the establishment of the Tsardom of Moscow. Ivan inherited a cluster of principalities near the Baltic and Black Sea watershed, which had been gradually acquired by purchase, by pacts, and by

* "Prostor: A Geopolitical Study of Russia and the United States" in *The Russian Review*, November 1941, Vol. I, No. 1. Reprinted by permission.

conquest, and welded into an independent state by his predecessors. The realm of their former suzerains, the Tartars, on the other hand, had gradually disintegrated until it was split into several dissociated khanates of which Kazan was the nearest and most dangerous to Muscovy.

Holding high the cross of Dmitri Donskoi and shouting "Lord! In Thy Name we go forth!" Ivan's warriors stormed the walls of Kazan [1552] and, in taking the city and its territory, found themselves the heirs to a vast territory beyond. For the city of Kazan sits astride the Volga near its junction with the turbulent Kama, and it commands the river-routes and roads to the north, east, and south as St. Louis controls the Mississippi, the Missouri, and the road to the west.

With Kazan in his hands, Ivan moved rapidly down the Volga to seize the khanate of Astrakhan with the Volga delta and a stretch of Caspian Sea coast. These conquests, together with the final pacification of Novgorod, are comparable in Russian history to the American acquisition of the Ohio country in the final settlement with Great Britain after the War of Independence. When Tsar Michael [1613-45] added the region between the Volga and the Ural rivers, he rounded off the tsardom somewhat as the Florida cession had rounded off the United States on the southeast. In strategic value, however, it was less like Florida than, perhaps, the Gadsden Purchase, for the Floridas completed the vital break in the seacoast that gave the Americans complete mastery of their southern and eastern maritime approaches from New Orleans to Maine. The Caspian, on the other hand, is a landlocked sea.

Throughout her history Muscovy's imperative need was an outlet to the sea, for while the United States held the keys to her front and side-doors almost from the beginning, Muscovy never really got her keys. The conquest of Novgorod brought access to the White Sea during part of the year, and had Ivan IV been able to break through to the Baltic, he might have gained a foothold there, but his long and disastrous Livonian Wars ended in tragic failure.

Since the Caspian was no good, the Baltic could not be reached, and the White Sea was inaccessible for several months each year, Ivan's successors pushed towards the warm waters of the south. In three waves, extending over more than a century, the Muscovites conquered South Russia and reached the Black Sea. The first wave under Tsar Alexis [1645-76] brought in the ancient cradle of the Russian people, once the center of a great civilization, but since the coming of the Tartars and the endless civil wars a blood-drenched land known as the *Moskovskaya-Ukraina*—the Muscovite Frontier. It is still called Ukraine by many, though the Muscovites eventually dubbed it Little Russia in distinction from Great, or metropolitan, Russia. The next wave under Empress Anna [1730-40] added a real "New Muscovy," and completed the pacification of the Dnieper Valley to the rapids, and finally Catherine the Great [1762-96] reached the Sea with "New Russia," the *Zaporozhie,* or lands beyond the rapids.

This was Russia's Louisiana Purchase. Louisiana doubled the area of the United States, gave her control of the essential Mississippi Valley with its delta and New Orleans, removed any potential danger from France as Ohio had removed the potential danger from Britain, and brought the United States for the first time to the Gulf and into irritating proximity with Mexico. Russia's southern conquests gave her vast and fertile new lands with the control of the essential Dnieper Valley, protection of the mouth of the Don, and her first Black Sea coast, removed any further danger from the Tartars, and brought her into irritating proximity with Turkey.

Here again, as with the approaches to the Atlantic, geography was a friend to the United States and an enemy to Russia, for the Black Sea emptied through a narrow channel held by a strong state, and the Russian equivalent of New Orleans, Constantinople, lay not at the mouth of the Dnieper but many miles beyond. The United States would have faced an analogous situation had the Gulf of Mexico been closed and open on the west only through one narrow channel at the isthmus of Panama, with New Orleans on both sides of this channel and Great Britain determined that it should never fall into American hands. The United States' position vis-à-vis Mexico would then have been identical with

Russia's vis-à-vis Turkey, and a major part of American foreign policy would have been directed toward conquering or immobilizing this Mexican Constantinople. Instead of a Mexican War there would have been several Mexican Wars.

Since New Orleans did not lie in Mexico, the United States contented herself with the annexation of Texas, New Mexico, the rest of Colorado, Arizona, Utah, Nevada, and California, the central and southeastern parts of which are equivalent in some ways to Catherine the Great's partitions of Poland and Alexander I's annexation of Bessarabia and the Grand Duchy of Warsaw. Unfortunately for Russia, her Polish lands were full of Poles who were allergic to Russian sovereignty, whereas the Mexican annexations had fewer Mexicans in proportion to the colonists from the United States. Thus, San Antonio never became a focus of insurrection as Warsaw did, though the United States prudently kept its greatest army post there.

With all these annexations Russia would have remained an inland country and prey to foreign marauders had Peter I [1689-1725] not justly earned his title of Great and founded the Russian Empire by finally breaking through to the Baltic. Peter's window on the west at St. Petersburg could be paralleled in American history only by supposing America to be joined to Europe below New Jersey, and that in the settlement after the Revolution, Canada had managed to retain New Jersey, New England, and the Hudson Valley. Inevitably the desperate need of the United States for access to the sea would have forced her to break through these artificial bands as Russia broke through hers.

## II

In her conquests bordering on Europe and the Caucasian highlands, Russia added alien populations, but elsewhere her annexations were chiefly of lands colonized from Muscovy or Kiev. The trail-breakers were the Cossacks, sometimes of Great Russian and sometimes of Little Russian origin, but like the American frontiersmen a social and not an ethnic group. Both of them got pretty mixed up in the course of time, the Cossacks mating with the Tartars or Kirghiz or other Mongoloid peoples, and the American hunters and fur-trappers with Indians, but in the beginning they were simply men flying before dissatisfaction at home—fugitive serfs, bankrupts, criminals, or simply men who were tired of civilization and looking for roominess and adventure of the frontier.

At first this frontier—this *Moskovskaya Ukraina*—lay right at Moscow's door, but it was pushed back until the land still called the Ukraine had no more to do with the frontier than Indiana has to do with Indians. Beyond the Ukraine they came to really new lands where the names they gave indicate the colonialism—New Muscovy *(Novomoskovsk)*, and still farther south New Russia *(Novorossiisk)*, "as felicitiously named," says Leroy-Beaulieu, "as New England." But it was a New England that was an overland and not an overseas extension of the mother country, an extension more like Ohio and Kentucky, eldest daughters of New England and Virginia.

The important point is the colonial character of these lands, a point that Leroy-Beaulieu perfectly understood when he emphasized and re-emphasized that "Russia is a colonial country, a fact which should not for a moment be lost sight of. Russia is a colony one or two centuries old." It was a point that Russia's greatest historian, Kluchevsky, never lost sight of, and which he stressed in the opening pages of his monumental history: "Colonialism is the fundamental fact of Russian history." And it was a characteristic that she shared with the United States and no other modern power.

The dates of city settlements in New Russia are a striking example of this. Rostov-on-Don was founded in the same decade as Harrodsburg and Boonesboro, first settlements in Kentucky, and Ekaterinoslav within two years of Ohio's Marietta. Nikolaev and Cincinnati were born in the same year, and Odessa, capital of New Russia, in the year that Ohio entered the Union. Boston and New York and Williamsburg, with their nearly two centuries of existence, are ancient capitals beside these fruits of the wilderness, and the towns of Europe are lost in the mists of prehistoric times.

Colonialism manifested itself most noticeably in the newest parts of the country, in the American West and the Russian East. The spanning of Siberia was as rapid as America's march to the

Pacific. While the ruins of Kazan were still smoking the Cossacks were on their way eastward, not as soldiers or officials or government representatives, but as free souls like the American pioneers. Later, others went as agents of the Stroganovs, the great merchant family of Russia and Siberia, as some American frontiersmen were trappers for Astor's American Fur Company, but most were independent. Tobolsk, the Siberian Westport, was founded in 1587, Tomsk in 1604, Yeniseisk in 1618, and Yakutsk far up the Lena River, in 1632. Four years later the Cossacks had reached the Sea of Okhotsk and were looking greedily towards Kamchatka and the lands beyond. Strung out behind them for four thousand miles was the line of isolated settlements that would become Siberia's Omahas, Denvers, and Salt Lake Cities of tomorrow.

Behind them, too, lay hecatombs of slaughtered natives, for the Cossack had Jim Bridger's attitude towards the Tunguses, Samoyeds, Yakuts, Kalmycks, Buryats, Chukchees, and dozens of other Mongolian or Mongoloid tribes—good only when dead. And in their wake came the same sort of people who followed the Jim Bridgers of America—more fur-trappers, hunters, gold-seekers, all the types of prospectors or *promyshlenniki* that human society has developed: soldiers to build and defend the forts and keep the roads open; officials to collect taxes and maintain the posting stations and give the barest suggestion of administrative unity to the sprawling empire; and the dispossessed and unhappy from every walk of life.

Among the latter was one element that the American West never had, the unwilling migrants in the convict trains, a steady trickle for hundreds of years that might rise in times of stress to a pouring stream, but which in the total migration to Siberia has reached more fame than its numbers justify. Many contemporary Sibiryaks have convict origins but they no more account for the bulk of the population in Siberia than Oglethorpe's settlers accounted for the bulk of colonial Georgia. Siberia was settled by free peasants or fugitive serfs moving eastward in search of open land as New Englanders moved westward to Kansas. Siberia is still sparsely settled, even by the rather broad standards of

European Russia, but then so is Kansas by the standards of Massachusetts.

## III

The vastness of Russia and America has inevitably bred regionalism, but regionalism essentially different from the European type. The only region in Russia comparable to those of France or Germany, or Great Britain was the Ukraine, where the languages, customs, and traditions made the Ukrainian differ as markedly from the Muscovite as the Scot from the Sassenach or the Catalonian from the Castilian. But elsewhere in Russia, and throughout the United States, there were no clearly distinguished regions.

In the United States the popular mind identifies such areas as the "North," the "South," or the "Midwest," but they are largely fictitious divisions. It was the Civil War that emphasized, if it did not actually draw, the line between the two chief zones—the "North," where the culture was essentially New England or New York-Philadelphian; and the "South," where the culture was essentially Virginian or Carolinian. But in the first place these were zones of external colonization.

Each of these centers sent its own cultural pattern along with its colonizers as they moved westward, the New England pattern into Ohio and Illinois and Kansas (where Lawrence's very name marked it an outpost of New England), and the Virginian into Kentucky and Arkansas and Texas (where the classic white-columned houses are pure Virginian). But while the streams moved westward, there were also cross-currents and eddies, from Ohio and Illinois into Texas, from Tennessee and Arkansas into Kansas, until the two streams were fused into a generalized American pattern that was neither midwestern nor southwestern, New England, nor Virginian. American regions are, in a very real sense, hardly more than geographical expressions, and they express fewer cultural and linguistic differences than are to be found in a hundred-mile trip in Germany or Italy.

The same was true, with one exception, in Russia also, for the only regional differences of the European pattern—aside from the areas which were not Russian at all in their culture—were those

between Great and Little Russia, between the Muscovite and
Kievan cultural patterns. This was far greater than the differences
between New England and Virginia, and in many ways—linguistically, for example—than between America and England. But
as these two centers expanded to the east and southeast, different
as they were, they tended to fuse into a type that was neither
Muscovite nor Ukrainian, though the numerical superiority of the
Great Russian made it more like the former than the latter.

In both the United States and Russia, always excepting the
Ukraine itself, the differences tended to be fleeting and superficial.
Linguistically, it was confined to a few words peculiar to one
region or another, a half-dozen vowels lengthened or shortened,
and the stress or elision of a consonant or two.

This fusion was a consequence of the rapidity with which the
frontier was pushed back. Until the nineteenth century Siberia
and the American West—and to a great extent European Russia
also—were simply voids to be filled, and they were filled so rapidly
and the districts integrated into the fabric of the metropolitan area
so soon, that there was no opportunity for regional cultures to develop. The frontier was officially closed in the United States at
the end of the nineteenth century and in Russia it was pushed back
towards the frigid and torrid zones in Siberia by the penetration of
the Trans-Siberian Railroad. But while the frontier lasted, it
acted as a zone of Americanization or Russianization, "a melting
pot which effected the fusion of divers racial elements and their
absorption by the Russian element," as P. Bizilli has phrased it.

There was no place for racial or ethnic pride on the frontier.
Muscovites, Ukrainians, Poles, and Tartars lived contentedly together in Siberia and were assimilated in a Russian pattern as
quickly as were the immigrants of German, Italian, or Jewish
origin in the American West. As fear of native reprisals gradually
died away, the natives were also partially included in the melting
pot, the Tunguses and Kamchadals in Siberia and the Indians in
Oklahoma. This was an attribute of the frontier as such and had
little to do with colonialism, for it was equally true in Caucasia,
where the upper classes became thoroughly Russianized, and in
southern Texas and Louisiana where the Creole aristocracy lost all

but the sentimental attributes of its Spanish, French, or Mexican origins.

The melting pot worked because the bulk of the immigration represented the dominant ethnic strain of the metropolitan areas, Anglo-Saxon in America and Great Russian in Siberia. The others who followed were in a minority and so hopelessly divided that it was easy to accept the ethnic values of the majority. The ease with which this occurred on the frontier and in the colonized areas suggested that its failure in the older parts was due chiefly to the innate obstinacy of the minorities. Archibald Cary Coolidge has remarked: "Many an American who has condemned the iniquity of trying to Russianize the Finns or the Armenians believes as a matter of course that the English language should be imposed as soon as possible on the Puerto Ricans"—or the Filipinos, or the Texas Mexicans.

Siberia, like the American West, was a land of farms where there were no manorial estates, and the aristocracy was represented only by the impermanent army officers or government officials. Everyone had to work together to harvest the crops, or raise the barns, or keep away marauding natives, and in this democratic milieu Peter the Great's Table of Ranks was as irrelevant as John Locke's Grand Model. The Sibiryaks paid no more attention to it than the Carolinians did to the imported caciques and land-graves.

Independence and isolation also instilled a tendency to make and execute one's own laws. "The Yankee farmer and the Russian peasant," John Quincy Adams III once remarked in the course of a diplomatic dinner, "are the only rustic people on earth who are capable of holding town-meetings, and do so instinctively and practically." This was an overstatement and does more credit to Mr. Adams' courtesy than to his knowledge, for originally the Yankee town-meeting and the Russian *mir* were probably products of the frontier, and rustic people have always tended to develop such institutions instinctively and practically when they lived on the frontier.

Neither the town-meeting nor the *mir* reached full maturity in the colonized regions, for the national governments arrived before there was any opportunity for such local institutions to develop very far, but their elementary forms were present in the rough, drumhead justice prevalent on the two frontiers. Acts harmful to the community or to a member of the community were punished with speed and dispatch by the community as a whole or by the individual member, and the evildoer would be dead and buried and the earth above his grave smoothed nonchalantly down before a policeman could get from St. Louis or Irkutsk.

The frontier was not peculiar to Russia and the United States, for it has played an enormous role in the development of most countries. Much of the European Middle Ages can be understood only by reference to the frontier conditions that prevailed. But its role in the development of Russia and the United States is of greater importance than elsewhere, partly because emergence from the frontier period has been so recent and partly because the frontier extended over such a vast area. . . .

## IV

Looked at from Washington or St. Petersburg, the mere task of traversing so much territory, even without native tribes to bar the way, was a task of appalling dimensions. The task of civilizing and integrating it into a unified nation was a job that staggered the imagination. Henry Adams found the America of the 'sixties crude in comparison with England and France, but looking back on it after forty years he was amazed that it had been no cruder than it was, and he realized that there had been more important things to do than import a few pictures or bric-a-brac.

"Doubtless the country needed ornament—needed it very badly indeed—but it needed energy still more, and capital most of all, for its supply was ridiculously out of proportion to its wants. On the new scale of power, merely to make the continent habitable for civilized people would require an immediate outlay of money that would have bankrupted the world. And yet, no portion of the world except a few narrow stretches of western Europe had ever been tolerably provided with the essentials of comfort and convenience; to fit out an entire continent with roads and the decencies of life would exhaust the credit of the entire planet."

And vast as America was, Siberia was vaster. Rude and uncivilized as the West was, the Russian East was ruder and more uncivilized, with a harsher climate and more rigorous demands on humanity. America was so big that two-and-seventy warring sects could set up Utopias from New Harmony to the Great Salt Lake and not interfere with each other or with the conservatives, so big that communities could be mislaid and forgotten for years. In Siberia a community could get mislaid for three centuries. April 19, 1931, *The New York Herald Tribune* reported the finding of a village of five hundred souls on the Indigirka River in northern Siberia whose ancestors had been dropped off there by the *promyshlenniki* in the reign of Ivan the Terrible. In the confusion of the civil wars that followed, they were lost sight of and forgotten and when the inquisitive archaeologists turned them up once more, they were speaking a language that no living Russian had ever heard and had been seen only in old documents and literary histories, as strange to twentieth-century ears as the Elizabethan dialects spoken in the Appalachian highlands.

But vast as the areas were, they were conquered and, in part at least, civilized. In Henry Adams' day the pony express was already carrying American goods, American news, American ideals to the outermost parts of the land, and in Siberia the Imperial Russian Post linked the scattered settlements from the Urals to the Amur. "From the southern end of the peninsula of Kamchatka to the most remote village in Finland, from the frozen, windswept shores of the Arctic Ocean to the hot, sandy deserts of Central Asia, the whole empire is one vast network of post routes," wrote George Kennan in the 'sixties. "You may pack your portmanteau in Nizhni-Novgorod, get a *podorozhnaya* from the postal department, and start for Petropavlovsk seven thousand miles away with the full assurance that there will be horses, reindeer, or dogs ready and waiting to carry you on, night and day, to your destination."

When the pony express gave way to the railroad, the development came more rapidly. In 1903, when Albert Beveridge visited Irkutsk, he found a thriving city with its own museum, a first-class theater producing plays with excellent casts, and a fine opera house built with money raised in one week by public subscription. Siberia had gotten its first things first. Now it was getting its ornaments.

Illimitable space has been the birthright of Russians and Americans and it has colored their lives and their ways of thinking. In Old Russia a word was often heard on the lips of her people that expressed this feeling—*prostor*. It is a word not easily translated, for there are other words for "distance" or "vastness" as such. *Prostor* is illimitable distance, vastness beyond statistical measurement, mile upon mile of rolling plain and steppe that flows away into the distance as far as the eye can see. When the Russian tried to describe *prostor* for a foreigner he could only throw out his arms, a gesture he always used when he thought of *prostor*. When he was called to serve in the Caucasus amid the breath-taking beauties of lofty mountains and towering peaks, he grew homesick for the flat level plains of Tula or Kaluga. "One can't *see* anything in the mountains," he would complain.

Americans have no word for it, but westerners have the feeling itself, and they have also the same characteristic gesture of throwing their arms wide when they think of it. The plainsman's feelings when he finds himself in the narrow, crooked, winding streets of the old seaboard cities would be perfectly understood by a Russian. Down every street a dead-end of stifling walls, on every side crowded buildings—nowhere to turn, no *prostor*.

Americans and Russians have had a certain love of vastness for its own sake. When the Russians built their railroads they insisted that the tracks must have a wider gauge than elsewhere—"Russia is so much bigger," they explained to the harassed engineers. It is exemplified in the reports of Russian resources, for great as they are, they never quite equal the optimism of the official statistics. It is exemplified in America's constant reference to her inexhaustible supplies and her boundless wealth, in her tall tales of the frontier, in the sagas of Paul Bunyan, and the magnificent lies of Mark Twain. When Twain was travelling in Russia he got into a discussion with Baron Ungern-Sternberg, the Minister of Railways, who all but overwhelmed him with statistics. At one point, the minister said there were ten thousand convicts working on railway gradings and right-of-ways, at which point the American sized him up for a minute and then blandly replied that in the United States there were *eighty thousand* convicts working on the railways, and that every one was under sentence of death for first-degree murder! "That closed *him* out," he said happily.

Mark Twain felt right at home in Russia, and he reported that the people were not only like home-folks, but even the towns had a familiar look until he came to the Russian church. St. Petersburg delighted him as a model of what a city should be, and its wide streets and spacious squares appealed to his midwestern heart. Here there was space to breathe.

Other Americans have also been struck with the outward resemblances between Russian and American towns, and particularly between the towns of Siberia and the West. Among many others, Senator Beveridge, who said Siberia was like the Kansas he had seen in the 'eighties "with all its rawness and newness," and William Boyce Thompson, who wrote to an American friend that he was vividly reminded of the West he had known as a boy. Ivan Golovin said he disliked Switzerland very much because of its "colossean grandeur," but that America was more to his liking because he could see so far in all directions.

The resemblance was no accident, for the towns of Siberia and the West were in the zones of internal colonization, where there was no need to encompass them with fortifications or pack the citizens in a restricted area. There was more land than anything else, and the houses could sprawl contentedly across the plain. The national capitals were themselves of the same type, both laid out on an enormous scale, both deliberately founded as the capitals of great nations. And both of them, at first, only grandiose and somewhat ridiculous hopes for the future.

This common passion for vast concepts has influenced their national policies, and to it can be traced the most characteristic political expressions of both countries. Russia and America were big, each was a world within itself, and each thought of itself in hemispheric terms. No other nation has ever developed theories of splendid isolation quite like the Monroe Doctrine or Slavophilism, or global notions quite like Pan-Americanism and Pan-Slavism.

"The Monroe Doctrine had its philosophical roots in a notion that there was a difference between the American and European sphere," writes Henry Steel Commager, "between the New World young, buoyant, healthy, moral, and the Old decadent and depraved." And Slavophilism was based on a belief in the uniqueness of the Slavic culture, the universality of Russia, and a similar feeling that between the Russian and the European there was a gap that could not and should not be bridged. Leroy-Beaulieu called Slavophilism "one of the most curious phenomena of Russian life in the nineteenth century," and added wonderingly, that while the number of self-admitted Slavophiles was small and mostly regarded as cranks, "one not unfrequently stumbles on some Slavophile dogma or superstition among people of the world, or writers who make it a point to have nothing to do with such idolatry."

There are few self-admitted isolationists or "hundred-per-cent" Americans and most of these are on the lunatic fringe, but one not infrequently finds, among worldly people or among writers, a steady belief in Anglo-Saxon uniqueness, in the United States' special position in the world, and in a moral heritage peculiarly American. No wonder a Frenchman like Leroy-Beaulieu or an Englishman like George Curzon neither understood nor very much liked them. Even in their milder aspects these notions seem to the European like "nationalism gone mad," in the expressive phrase of William L. Langer—but the Hawley-Smoot tariff bill was not put over, nor participation in the League of Nations wrecked, solely by a little group of willful men divorced from the currents of American life, however blind they may have been to external reality.

Pan-Slavism and Pan-Americanism are by no means the same things as Slavophilism or "hundred-per-cent" Americanism, though they stem from the same roots, nor are they just a more polite way of saying Pan-Russianism or Pan-United-States-ism, though these things, too, they have often tended to be in practice.

It is not easy to say precisely what they are in all of their protean manifestations, but they have more in common than a Greek prefix. Their origins lie deep in the minds and hearts of two space-loving people. They are expressions of the idea that here are worlds so rich and so inexhaustible in their own resources that they can prosper without other lands or other cultures; lands so vast and so varied that either of them is to all lands as one world to another. It may be called Americanism, or Slavophilism, or Pan-something-or-other-ism. It may be called anything you like, but it is really Russian *prostor*.

# THE UTOPIAN CONCEPTION OF HISTORY*

## BY

## FEODOR DOSTOIEVSKY

### [1876]

Throughout these hundred and fifty years after Peter we have done nothing but live through a communion with all human civilization, affiliating ourselves with their history and their ideals. We have learned, and trained ourselves, to love the French, the Germans and everybody, as if they were our brethren—notwithstanding the fact that they never liked us and made up their minds never to like us. However, this was the essence of our reform—the whole Peter cause; we have derived from it, during that century and a half, an *expansion* of our view, which, perhaps, was unprecedented, and cannot be traced in any other nation, whether in the ancient or in the new world. The pre-Peter Russia was active and solid, although politically she was slow to form herself; she had evolved unity within herself and she had been ready to consolidate her border regions. And she had tacitly comprehended that she bore within herself a treasure which was no longer existent anywhere else—Orthodoxy; that she was the conservatrix of Christ's truth, genuine truth—the true image of Christ which had been dimmed in all other religions and in all other nations. This treasure, this eternal truth inherent in Russia and of which she had become the custodian, according to the view of the best Russians of those days, as it were, relieved their conscience of the duty of any other enlightenment. Moreover, in Moscow the conception had been formed that any closer intercourse with Europe might even exercise a harmful and corrupt influence upon the Russian mind and the Russian *idea;* that it might distort Orthodoxy itself and lead Russia along the path to perdition "much in the same way as

*From *The Diary of a Writer*, Vol. I, by Feodor Dostoievsky, translated and annotated by Boris Brasol. Copyright 1949 by Charles Scribner's Sons. Reprinted by permission of the publisher.

all other peoples." Thus ancient Russia, in her isolation, was getting ready to be unjust—unjust to mankind, having taken the resolution to preserve passively her treasure, her Orthodoxy, for herself, to seclude herself from Europe—that is, mankind—much as our schismatics who refuse to eat with you from the same dish and who believe it to be a holy practice that everyone should have his own cup and spoon. This is a correct simile because prior to Peter's advent, there had developed in Russia almost precisely this kind of political and spiritual relation with Europe. With Peter's reform there ensued an unparalleled broadening of the view, and herein—I repeat—is Peter's whole exploit. . . . Now, what is this "expansion of the view," what does it consist of, and what does it signify?—Properly speaking, this is not enlightenment, nor is it science; nor is it a betrayal of the popular Russian moral principles for the sake of European civilization. No, this is precisely something inherent only in the Russian people, since nowhere and at no time has there ever been such a reform. This is actually, and in truth, almost our brotherly love of other peoples, which was the result of the hundred-and-fifty-year-long living experience of our intercourse with them. This is our urge to render universal service to humanity, sometimes even to the detriment of our own momentous and immediate interests. This is our reconciliation with their civilization; cognition and *excuse* of their ideals even though these be in discord with ours; this is our acquired faculty of discovering and revealing in each one of the European civilizations—or, more correctly, in each of the European individualities—the truth contained in it, even though there be much with which it be impossible to agree. Finally, this is the longing, above all, to be just and to seek nothing but truth.

Briefly, this is, perhaps, the beginning of that active application of our treasure—of Orthodoxy—to the universal service of mankind to which Orthodoxy is designated and which, in fact, constitutes its essence. Thus, through Peter's reform our former idea—the Russian Moscow idea—was broadened and its conception was magnified and strengthened. Thereby we got to understand our universal mission, our individuality and our role in humankind; at the same time we could not help but comprehend that this mission and this role do not resemble those of other nations since, there, every national individuality lives solely for, and within, itself. We, on the other hand, will begin—now that the hour has come— precisely with becoming servants to all nations, for the sake of general pacification. And in this there is nothing disgraceful; on the contrary, therein is our grandeur because this leads to the ulti- mate unity of mankind. He who wishes to be first in the Kingdom of God must become a servant to everybody. This is how I under- stand the Russian mission *in its ideal*. After Peter the first step of our new policy was revealed of its own accord; it had to consist in the unification of the whole Slavdom, so to speak, under Russia's wing. And this communion is to be effected not for the sake of usurpation, not for the sake of violence, nor for the purpose of the annihilation of Slavic individualities in the face of the Russian colossus—but with the object of their own regeneration, so that they may be placed in a proper relation to Europe and to mankind, and that they may finally be given an opportunity to compose and repose themselves after their never-ending secular plight, to restore their spirit, so that when they shall have perceived their new strength—they be given a chance to contribute their own mite to the treasury of the human spirit and to utter their word to civiliza- tion.

Oh, of course, you might laugh at all these "fancies" about the Russian mission; however, tell me: do not all Russians desire the resurrection of the Slavs precisely on this basis—precisely for the sake of their full individual liberty and the resurrection of their spirit—and not at all for the purpose that Russia may politically acquire them and, through them, increase her political power? Yet it is exactly of this that Europe suspects us. Indeed, isn't this so?—And thus, at least partly, are my "fancies" substantiated. Of course, it is for the same purpose that, sooner or later, Constanti- nople must be ours. . . .

God, what a sceptical smile would appear on the face of some Austrian or Englishman, were he to peruse all the above *fancies*. and suddenly read the passage concerning the *positive* deduction: "Constantinople, the Golden Horn, this most important political spot in the whole world . . . isn't this seizure?"

Yes, the Golden Horn and Constantinople—they will be ours, but not for the purpose of seizure, not for the sake of violence— I would reply. To begin with, this will come to pass of its own accord, precisely because the hour has come, and even if it has not yet arrived, indeed it will come in the near future; all symptoms point to this. This is a natural solution—so to speak, the word of nature herself. If this has not occurred before, it has been precisely because the time has not yet been ripe. In Europe, people believe in some "Testament of Peter the Great." It is nothing but a forged document, written by the Poles. However, even had the thought then occurred to Peter to seize Constantinople, instead of founding Petersburg, I believe that, after some deliberation, he would have abandoned this idea—granted that he was powerful enough to crush the Sultan—since in those days the time was inopportune and the project could even have brought ruin to Russia.

If in Finnish Petersburg we did not elude the influence of the neighboring Germans who, though useful, had paralyzed Russian progress before its genuine path had been ascertained, how then in Constantinople—so enormous and original, with her remnants of a most powerful and ancient civilization—could we have managed to elude the influence of the Greeks, men far more subtle than the coarse Germans, men who have infinitely more points in common with us than the Germans who do not resemble us at all —numerous courtiers who would promptly have surrounded the throne and who, ahead of the Russians, would have become educated and learned, who would have captivated Peter himself, not to speak of his immediate successors, taking advantage of his weak spot by their skill in seamanship.

Briefly, they would have captured Russia politically; they would forthwith have dragged her along some new Asiatic path—again into a seclusion of some sort—and the Russia of those days, of course, could not have endured this. Her Russian strength and nationality would have been arrested in their development. The mighty Great Russian would have remained in estrangement in his grim, snowy North, serving merely as material for the regenerated Constantinople, and, perhaps, in the long run, he would have made up his mind not to follow her at all. At the same time the

Russian South would have been captured by the Greeks. Moreover, there might have occurred a schism in Orthodoxy itself
which would have been divided into two worlds—the regenerated
world of Constantinople and the old Russian. . . . In a word, this
would have been a most untimely event. At present things are
quite different.

Today, Russia has already visited Europe and is herself educated. More important still: she has become conscious of her
strength—and is, indeed, strong. She has also learned wherein
she is strongest. Now Russia understands that Constantinople may
be ours not at all as her capital, whereas had Peter, two centuries
ago, captured Constantinople, he could not have helped but transfer thither his capital—and this would have spelt ruin, since
Constantinople is not Russia and *could not* have become Russia.
Even if Peter might have avoided this error, his immediate successors would not have eschewed it. However, if Constantinople
may be ours, not as the capital of Russia, it may be ours not as a
capital of Slavdom as a whole—as some people are dreaming.
Slavdom without Russia would exhaust itself there in its struggle
with the Greeks, even in the event that it might succeed in forming from its parts some political whole. But, for the Greeks alone
to inherit Constantinople is at present altogether impossible: it is
impossible to surrender to them so important a spot on the globe;
this would be something altogether out of proportion. Slavdom
with Russia at its head is a wholly different proposition, but
whether or not it is a good proposition is again a question. Would
it not resemble a political seizure of the Slavs—a thing we do not
need at all? Thus, in the name of what, by virtue of what *moral*
right could Russia claim Constantinople? Relying upon what sub-
lime aims could Russia demand Constantinople from Europe?—
Precisely as a leader of Orthodoxy, as its protectress and guardian
. . . a role which unquestionably revealed itself only after Peter the
Great, when Russia perceived in herself the strength to fulfill her
mission and factually became the real and sole protectress of Orthodoxy and of the people adhering to it. Such is the ground,
such is the right to ancient Constantinople, which would be intelligible and not offensive even to the Slavs most sensitive to their

independence, even to the Greeks themselves. Besides, thereby would be revealed the true essence of those political relations which inevitably must develop between Russia and all other Orthodox peoples—whether Slavs or Greeks makes no difference. Russia is their guardian, or even their leader, perhaps, but not their sovereign; their mother, but not their mistress. Even if she were to become their sovereign some time in the future, it would be only by their own election and subject to the preservation of everything by which they themselves would define their independence and individuality. So that eventually, and in the long run, such a union could even be joined by non-Orthodox European Slavs who would see for themselves that common unity under the protection of Russia is merely the assurance to each of his independent personality, whereas in the absence of this immense unifying force, they would, perhaps, again exhaust themselves in mutual strife and discord, even if they should some day become politically independent of the Mohammedans and Europeans to whom they now belong.

What's the use—it may be said—of juggling with words: what is this "Orthodoxy"? And wherein, here, is there a peculiar idea —a special right to the unification of the peoples? And would it not be a purely political union like all other similar ones, founded upon the broadest principles, akin to the United States of America —or even broader? Such may be the questions propounded to me. And these I will answer.—No, this would not be the same, and this is not verbal jugglery: here there is *in reality* something peculiar, something unheard-of. This would not be merely a political union and, of course, not one for the sake of political usurpation and violence—this seems to be the only way Europe can conceive the proposition. And it would be a union not for mercantile pursuit, personal gain—those invariable and eternal deified vices, under the guise of official Christianity which is believed by no one but the *plebs*. No, this would be a genuine exaltation of Christ's truth, preserved in the East, a new exaltation of Christ's Cross and the final word of Orthodoxy, which is headed by Russia. This would precisely constitute a temptation to the mighty of this world, to those who thus far have been triumphant in it and who have always looked upon such "expectations" with disdain and derision; to those who are even unable to understand that one may seriously believe in the brotherhood of men, in the general reconciliation of the nations, in a union founded upon the principles of common service to mankind, and, finally, in man's regeneration based on the true principles of Christ. And if the belief in this "new word" which may be uttered by Russia, heading united Orthodoxy, is a "Utopia" worthy of nothing but ridicule, let people class me, too, among these Utopians, while the ridicule—leave that to me.

"But"—it may perhaps be argued—"that Russia will ever be *permitted* to head the Slavs and to enter Constantinople, is in itself a Utopia. One may be dreaming about it, and yet these are but dreams!"

In truth, is this so? But, aside from the fact that Russia is strong and, maybe, much stronger than she herself realizes— aside from this, have there not arisen before our eyes, during recent decades, immense powers which have reigned in Europe, one of which has been reduced to dust, swept away by God's tempest in a day, and in its place a new Empire has come into being—an Empire which, seemingly, has never before been surpassed in strength? And who, in good time, could have predicted this? And if such sweeping changes, which have already occurred before our eyes in our day, are possible, can the human mind unmistakably predict the fate of the Eastern question? Where are the real grounds for despair in the resurrection and unity of the Slavs? Who knows the ways of Providence?

# RELIGION AND THE RUSSIAN STATE[*]

BY

## NICOLAS BERDYAEV

[1937]

## I

Russian Communism is difficult to understand on account of its twofold nature. On the one hand it is international and a world phenomenon; on the other hand it is national and Russian. It is particularly important for Western minds to understand the national roots of Russian Communism and the fact that it was Russian history which determined its limits and shaped its character. A knowledge of Marxism will not help in this. The Russian people in their spiritual make-up are an Eastern people. Russia is the Christian East, which was for two centuries subject · to the powerful influences of the West, and whose cultured classes assimilated every Western idea. The fate of the Russian people in history has been an unhappy one and full of suffering. It has developed at a catastrophic tempo through interruption and change in its type of civilization.

In spite of the opinion of the Slavophils it is impossible to find an organic unity in Russian history. The Russians held sway over too vast an expanse of territory—the danger from the East, from the Tartar invasions (from which it protected the West as well), was too great. And the danger from the West itself was also great.

We distinguish five different Russias in history: the Russia dominated by Kiev [beginning in the 9th century], the Russia of the Tartar period [1238-1462], the Russia of the Moscow period [1462-1711], the imperial Russia of Peter [1711-1917] and finally the new Soviet Russia. It would not be true to say that Russia is a land of new culture, that not long ago she was still half barbarous; in a definite sense Russia is a land of ancient cul-

[*] From *The Origin of Russian Communism.* Copyright 1937 by Charles Scribner's Sons. Reprinted by permission.

ture. The Russia of the Kiev period gave birth to a higher culture than that of the contemporary West. Already in the fourteenth century there existed in Russia a classically perfect ikonography and a remarkable architecture. Russia of the Moscow period developed a very high culture in the plastic arts with an organic integrated style and highly finished forms of life. This was an Eastern culture—the culture of the Christianized Tartar Empire.
. . .

The inconsistency of the Russian spirit is due to the complexity of Russian history, to the conflict of the Eastern and Western elements in her. The soul of the Russian people was moulded by the Orthodox Church—it was shaped in a purely religious mould. And that religious mould was preserved even to our own day, to the time of the Russian nihilists and communists. But in the Russian soul there remained a strong natural element, linked with the immensity of Russia itself, with the boundless Russian plain.

Among Russians "Nature" is an elemental power, stronger than among Western peoples, especially those of the most elaborated, *i.e.*, Latin, culture. The nature-pagan element entered even into Russian Christianity. In the typical Russian two elements are always in opposition—the primitive natural paganism of boundless Russia, and an Orthodox asceticism received from Byzantium, a reaching out towards the other world. A natural dionysism and a Christian asceticism are equally characteristic of the Russian people.

A difficult problem presents itself ceaselessly to the Russian—the problem of organizing his vast territory. The immensity of Russia, the absence of boundaries, was expressed in the structure of the Russian soul. The landscape of the Russian soul corresponds with the landscape of Russia, the same boundlessness, formlessness, reaching out into infinity, breadth.

In the West is conciseness; everything is bounded, formulated, arranged in categories, everything (both the structure of the land and the structure of the spirit) is favorable to the organization and development of civilization. It might be said that the Russian people fell a victim to the immensity of its territory. Form does not come to it easily, the gift of form is not great among the Russians. Russian historians explain the despotic character of Russian government by this necessary organization of the boundless Russian plain. Kluchevsky, the most distinguished of Russian historians, said, "The state expands, the people grow sickly." In a certain sense this remains true also of the Soviet-Communist government, under which the interests of the people are sacrificed to the power and organization of the Soviet state.

The religious formation of the Russian spirit developed several stable attributes: dogmatism, asceticism, the ability to endure suffering and to make sacrifices for the sake of its faith whatever that may be, a reaching out to the transcendental, in relation now to eternity, to the other world, now to the future, to this world. The religious energy of he Russian spirit possesses the faculty of switching over and directing itself to purposes which are not merely religious, for example, to social objects. . . .

After the fall of the Byzantine Empire [1453], the Second Rome, the greatest Orthodox state in the world, there awoke in the Russian people the consciousness that the Russian people was the only nation who professed the Orthodox Faith. It was the Monk Filofei who expounded the doctrine of Moscow as the Third Rome. He wrote to the Tsar Ivan III [1462-1505]: "Of the third new Rome" . . . "Of all kingdoms in the world, it is in thy royal domain that the holy Apostolic Church shines more brightly than the sun. And let thy Majesty take note, O religious and gracious Tsar, that all kingdoms of the Orthodox Christian Faith are merged into thy kingdom. Thou alone, in all that is under heaven, art a Christian Tsar. And take note, O religious and gracious Tsar, that all Christian kingdoms are merged into thine alone, that two Romes have fallen, but the third stands, and there will be no fourth. Thy Christian kingdom shall not fall to the lot of another."

The doctrine of Moscow the Third Rome became the basic idea on which the Muscovite state was formed. The kingdom was consolidated and shaped under the symbol of a messianic idea. . . . Profession of the true, the Orthodox Faith, was the test of belonging to the Russian kingdom. In exactly the same way profession of the true communist faith was to be the test of belonging to

Soviet Russia, to the Russian communist state.  Under the symbolic messianic idea of Moscow as the Third Rome there took place an acute nationalizing of the Church.  Religion and nationality in the Muscovite kingdom grew up together, as they did also in the consciousness of the ancient Hebrew people.  And in the same way as messianic consciousness was an attribute of Judaism it was an attribute of Russian Orthodoxy also.  But the religious idea of the kingdom took shape in the formation of a powerful state in which the Church was to play a subservient part.  The Moscow Orthodox kingdom was a totalitarian state. . . .

In the seventeenth century there took place one of the most important events in Russian religious history, the Old-ritualist schism.

It is a mistake to think that this religious schism was the outcome simply of the Russian people's beliefs about ceremonial and that the struggle was waged merely over the question of making the sign of the cross with two or with three fingers, and over other details in the ordering of divine worship.  There was something deeper than that in the schism.  The question was this: is the Russian kingdom a true Orthodox kingdom, *i.e.*, is the Russian people fulfilling its messianic vocation? . . .

Both among the Russian masses and among the Russian intelligentsia will be found the search for a kingdom founded on justice.  In the visible kingdom injustice reigns.  In the Muscovite kingdom, aware of itself as the Third Rome, was mingled the Kingdom of Christ, a kingdom of justice, with ideas of a mighty state ruling by injustice.  The schism was the exposure of the inconsistency, the result of the mingling.  But the popular mind was unenlightened, often superstitious; in it Christianity was mingled with paganism.  The schism gave the first blow to the idea of Moscow as the Third Rome.  It showed that all was not well with the Russian messianic consciousness.  The second blow was given by the reform of Peter.

## II

Peter's reform was a fact so decisive for all subsequent Russian history that our currents of thought in the nineteenth century were distinguished by the value they assigned to it. One must now regard as equally untrue and out of date both the Slavophil and the Western points of view about Peter's work. The Slavophil saw in it the betrayal of the original national basis of Russian life, a violation and interruption of its organic development. The Westerners saw nothing original and distinctive whatever in Russian history; they considered Russia as only a backwater in enlightenment and civilization. The Western European type of civilization was for them the only type, and must be universal. Peter showed Russia the ways of Western enlightenment and civilization.

The Slavophils were wrong, because Peter's reform was absolutely inevitable. Russia could no longer exist as a closed country, in a backward condition both military and naval, and economic, without education and technical civilization. In such circumstances the Russian people not only could not fulfil its great mission, but its very independence was exposed to danger. The Slavophils were wrong for this reason too, that it was precisely in the Petrine period of its history that Russian culture bloomed, Pushkin and the great period of Russian literature appeared, thought awoke and the Slavophils themselves became possible. Russia was obliged to break out of its isolation and join in the swirling life of the world. Only in such ways could the Russians make their contribution to the life of the world.

The Westerners were wrong, because they denied any original distinctive character to the Russian people and Russian history, they clung to naively simple views of the progress of enlightenment and civilization, and saw no mission of any sort for Russia, except the necessity of catching up with the West. They did not see, what for that matter even the Slavophils saw, the violation of the soul of the people, which Peter perpetrated. Peter's reform was unavoidable, but he achieved it in a way which did terrible violence to the soul of the people and to their beliefs. And the people answered this violence by founding a legend of Peter as Anti-christ.

Peter was a revolutionary from above; and not without reason is he considered a bolshevik in type. Peter's methods were absolutely bolshevik. He wanted to destroy the old Muscovite Russia,

to tear up by the roots those feelings which lay in the very foundation of its life. With that object in view he did not stop at the
execution of his son, who held to the old-fashioned ways. The
methods adopted by Peter in dealing with the Church and the old
religion are very reminiscent of the methods of the bolsheviks. He
did not like the old Muscovite piety and was especially severe on
the adherents of the old rites and on the Old Believers. Peter
ridiculed the religious feelings of the old days; he organized a
mock Council with a mock Patriarch. This very much recalls the
anti-religious activities of the godless in Soviet Russia. Peter
founded a synodal regime to a large extent copied from the German Protestant form, and he brought about the final subjection of
the Church to the State. . . .

A comparison might be made between Peter and Lenin, between
the Petrine and the bolshevik revolutions. They display the same
barbarity, violence, forcible application of certain principles from
above downwards, the same rupture of organic development, and
repudiation of tradition, . . . the same formation of a privileged
bureaucratic class, the same centralization, the same desire sharply
and radically to change the type of civilization. But the bolshevik
revolution, by terrible violence, liberated forces that were latent in
the masses and summoned them to take their share in making history; therein lies its significance. While Peter's revolution, having
strengthened the Russian State and urged Russia along the way of
Western and world enlightenment, widened the gulf between the
people and the upper classes, the cultured and ruling class, Peter
secularized the Orthodox kingdom and guided Russia into the way
of enlightenment. This process took place in the upper levels of
Russian society, among the nobility and civil servants, while at the
same time the people went on living by the old religious beliefs
and feelings. The autocratic power of the Tsar, in fact, assuming
the form of a Western enlightened absolutism, kept in the people's
eyes its old religious sanction as a theocratic authority. . . .

The influence of the West struck primarily at the masses and
strengthened the privileged classes. . . . Only in the nineteenth
century did the influence of the West on the Russian educated
intelligentsia give birth to love of the people and to liberationist

movements.  But even then the educated and cultured classes seemed alien to the people.  Nowhere, apparently, was there such a gulf between the upper and lower classes as in Petrine, imperial Russia, and not another single country lived at the same time in such different centuries, from the fourteenth to the nineteenth and even to the coming twenty-first century.

Russia of the eighteenth and nineteenth centuries lived a completely inorganic life.  In the soul of the Russian people a struggle between East and West was waged, and that struggle is continuing in the Russian revolution.  Russian communism is a communism of the East.  The influence of the West during the two centuries of its action failed to subdue the Russian people. . . .

The Empire founded by Peter grew outwardly; it became the largest in the world.  It had an outward enforced unity, but there was no inward unity; inwardly it was broken into fragments.  Government and people were rent apart, people and intelligentsia, and the nationalities which were gathered together in the Russian Empire were sundered from each other.  The Empire with its Western type of imperial absolutism less than anything realized the idea of the Third Rome.  The very title "Emperor" substituted for "Tsar" was, in Slavophil opinion, a betrayal of the Russian idea. . . .

The fundamental opposition was between the idea of an Empire, a mighty State of the military-police type, and the religious, messianic idea of a Tsardom which descended to become the possession of the masses, and then, under a transformed aspect, reached the intelligentsia.  The conflict between the idea of Empire as expressed by the Government and the outlook of the intelligentsia was to be fundamental for the nineteenth century.  The Government was to make itself more and more alien from the intelligentsia among the cultured classes of society, in which a revolutionary temper was to begin to grow.  The nobility, which was the leading and specially cultured class at the beginning and even in the middle of the nineteenth century, in the second half of the century was to sink in cultural level, become reactionary, and be forced to give way to an intelligentsia drawn from many classes who would bring with them another and new type of culture. . . .

The bulk of the Russian people—the peasantry—lived in the grip of serfdom. Inwardly they lived by the Orthodox Faith and that gave them power to bear the sufferings of life. The people always considered serfdom as a wrong and an injustice, but they assigned the blame for this injustice not to the Tsar, but to the ruling class, the nobility. The religious conception of the Tsar's authority was so strong among the people that they lived in the hope that the Tsar would protect them and put an end to the injustice when he learned the whole truth.

In accordance with their own ideas of property, the Russian peasantry always thought it wrong that the nobles should possess vast tracts of land. Western ideas of property were alien to the Russian people; they were but feebly understood even by the nobility. The soil was God's, and all who toiled and labored at it might enjoy the use of it. A naive agrarian socialism was always an accepted principle among the Russian peasants.

To the cultured classes—to the intelligentsia—the mass of the people remained a sort of mystery of which the secret was yet to be discovered. They believed that in the still silent inarticulate people lay concealed a great truth about life, and the day would come when the people would say their say. . . . By the nineteenth century Russia had assumed the form of an immense, unbounded peasant country, enslaved, illiterate, but with its own popular culture based on a faith; with a ruling noble class, idle and with little culture, which had lost its religious faith and its sense of nationality; with a Tsar at the top, in relation to whom a religious belief was retained; with a strong bureaucracy and a very thin and fragile layer of culture.

Social classes in Russia have always been weak, subjected to the State; they were even formed by state authority. The only vigorous elements were the monarchy, which had taken the form of Western absolutism, and the masses. The cultured layer felt itself crushed by these two forces. The intelligentsia of the nineteenth century stood over an abyss which at any moment might open and swallow it. The best, the most cultivated part of the Russian nobility was aware of the abnormality, the wrongness of its position, the blame attaching to it in the face of the masses. By the nineteenth century, the Empire was very sick, both spiritually and economically. . . .

Russia and the Russian people can be characterized only by contradictions. On the same grounds the Russian people may be characterized as imperial-despotic and anarchic freedom-loving, as a people inclined to nationalism and national conceit, and a people of a universal spirit . . . cruel and unusually humane; inclined to inflict suffering and illimitably sympathetic. This contradiction is established by all Russian history and by the eternal conflict of the instinct of imperial might with the instinct of the people's love of freedom and justice.

In spite of the opinion of the Slavophil, the Russian people were endowed with political sense. This remains true even for the Soviet State, and at the same time it is a people from whom issued constantly the Cossack freebooters, . . . a revolutionary intelligentsia, anarchic, a people who sought for a kingdom of righteousness not of this world. That righteousness was not to be found in the vast Empire State founded through terrible sacrifices. This was felt by the masses and by the best part of the nobility and by the newly-educated intelligentsia.

Russia of the nineteenth century was self-contradictory and unhealthy; in it there was oppression and injustice, but psychologically and morally it was not a bourgeois country and it set itself against the bourgeois countries of the West. In this unique country political despotism was united with great freedom and breadth of life, with freedom in manner of life, with absence of barriers, imposed conventions and legalism.

# THE PEOPLE OF GREAT RUSSIA*

BY

## GEOFFREY GORER

[1949]

\*   \*   \*

From all the evidence we can get, it seems as though [Russian] peasants accept the birth of a child as an inevitable portion of human life, rather than welcome it with very deep emotion. . . .

When a child is born it is normally very well treated, and protected from hunger, cold, and all other unpleasant physical experiences to the greatest possible extent, often at the cost of considerable parental sacrifice; but the attitude of the parents seems to be one of succoring protection, rather than of great emotional attachment. . . .

From the day of its birth onwards the baby is tightly swaddled in long strips of material, holding its legs straight and its arms down by its sides. When Russians are asked why they swaddle their babies in this way, they give a considerable variety of reasons, but they all have one common theme: the baby is potentially so strong that if it were not swaddled it would risk destroying itself or doing itself irreparable harm, and would be impossible to handle. For one mother an unswaddled baby would risk developing a hunchback or crooked spine, others fear it would break its arms or legs or back by thrashing about, and would certainly have crooked limbs, others again that it would scratch out its eyes or ruin its nose. In the Ukraine (which of course may be different) in 1947 John Fischer was told by pediatricians, "If a baby's hands were left untrammelled, he would wave them in front of his face, thus getting a fright which might permanently upset the nervous system."[1] All Russians are agreed that an unswaddled baby is impossible to handle, and would jump out of constraining arms;

---

*Excerpts from *The People of Great Russia: A Psychological Study* by Geoffrey Gorer and John Rickman. Published by the Chanticleer Press, Inc., New York. Reprinted by permission.
[1]John Fischer, *Why They Behave Like Russians.*

Russians exposed to Occidental practices justified swaddling on the ground that Russians had no perambulators. . . .

The usual method of swaddling is very impersonal and involves little contact between the baby and the swaddler. The infant is laid on its back on a table or other flat surface, and lifted from the ankles as the cloths are wrapped round. It seems possible that the concept of the baby's great and destructive strength is in some way communicated to the infant by the manner in which the adults handle it during the swaddling.

This swaddling is maintained on the average for about nine months though there may be variations according to the season. The baby is unswaddled, and wrapped in a loose shawl, for nursing unless the mother is too busy, and for occasional bathing in carefully adjusted tepid water, but for no other reason. In careful families the swaddling is removed gradually, the shoulders, chest, and arms being freed before the rest of the body; in more slatternly households all the swaddling is taken off at the same time. Informants say that the unswaddled baby crawls on all fours "like a bear" before it can stand and walk. . . .

In contrast to peasant children, upper-caste children were *always* expected to be unswaddled for nursing; and they were usually left unswaddled for half an hour before the evening bath when they could kick and exercise their limbs. After about 1900 a new style of wrapping up children became fashionable: they were put in "envelopes"—large squares of material stuffed with down and typically quilted, which were fastened over both sides and from the bottom; the child's head and neck were supported by a pillow. This style allowed the child a little lateral movement of its limbs.
. . .

From the age of two or three, and often till they had passed adolescence, upper-caste children were put in the charge of a variety of maids, governesses, and tutors of almost any Occidental nationality except Russian, often two or three at a time, to teach them manners and various accomplishments, especially foreign languages. These foreign instructors were frequently changed. . . .

The chief contrasts so far discovered between the typical experiences of children from the upper castes and from the peasant caste seem to have been the following: upper-caste children were not expected to manifest responsibility or to contribute early to the comfort or wealth of the household; and the presence of governesses and tutors of non-Russian culture often produced emotional conflicts, either by their demands, their attitudes or their sudden removal, which accentuated tendencies in later life to neuroses and character problems similar to those found in Occidental society, and different in form and content from those found among Russians not early exposed to non-Russian influence. . . .

Under normal conditions the Russian infant is not exposed to conditions which might be expected to give rise to any of the painful internal physiological feelings which often form part of the infantile experience of members of other societies. He is not expected to be hungry or cold, and no demands for the control of elimination direct his early attention on his gastro-intestinal tract. But except during the short periods when he is being fed or bathed he is completely inhibited in the free movement of his limbs; he cannot explore the external universe through the use of his hands or through carrying things to his mouth; the only way he can express emotion of any sort is through his eyes or by screaming; and the latter may be impeded by "plugging" the baby with the comforter.

These facts are observable and verifiable; their incidence could easily be established statistically. The deductions which follow are unverified hypotheses, though verification could be obtained.

When human infants are not constrained they move their limbs and bodies a great deal, especially during the second six months of life; it seems probable that much of this movement is physiologically determined, as an aspect of biological maturation. Infants tend to express emotion with their whole body and not merely their face, for example arching their back or thrashing about or hugging. They also explore their own body and the universe around them with their hands and their mouth, gradually discovering what is edible and what inedible, what me and what not-me. While they are swaddled in the Russian manner, Russian infants can do none of these things; and it is assumed that this inhibition of movement is felt to be extremely painful and frustrating and is responded to with intense and destructive rage, which cannot be adequately expressed physically. This rage, it is assumed, is directed at the constraint, rather than at the people who constrain the infant. Since the infant's exploration of the universe is very limited it would seem that the identification of the people who constrain him is impeded; the more so since, as has already been pointed out, the actual swaddling is done in a very impersonal manner with little contact between the swaddler and the infant who is handled and turned around almost as though it were a rigid and inanimate object. . . .

Psychoanalysis has coined the phrase "omnipotence of thought" to describe the typical mental processes of infants and young children before they can distinguish between wish and reality. If this is the case the assumed destructive rage would appear to give the infant a feeling of overwhelming destructive strength; and this may well be one of the sources for the rationalizations given by adults for swaddling their children.

A second very primitive thought mechanism is technically known as "projection"; this is acting as though the thoughts or wishes emanating from the self (whether conscious or unconscious) were emanating from persons other than the self. It is assumed that this mechanism is regularly employed by Great Russian infants who project on to the vague figures in their environment their own hostile wishes; in consequence they feel that they risk being bitten or devoured if they were to gratify their destructive wishes (or in retaliation for having gratified them in fantasy). It is worth noting that swaddling prevents the gross muscular movements of the limbs which accompany "temper tantrums" in unswaddled children; and as a consequence fantasies of rage and destruction will not normally be accompanied by fantasies which involve the voluntary use of the large muscles. This may help account for the emphasis given by many Russians to the workings of the soul and the inner nature.

Because of this projection of their hostility and fear the painful restraints which exacerbate the destructive rage become at the same time an essential protection both for the Russian infants themselves and for those around them; for the restraint prevents the full gratification of the destructive wishes, and so saves the infants from the fantasied perils of retaliation. . . .

These feelings of rage and fear are probably made endurable, but also given emphasis, by the fact that the baby is periodically loosed from the constraints, and suckled and petted while unswaddled. This alternation of complete restraint without gratifications, and of complete gratifications without restraint, continues for at least the first nine months of life. It is the argument of this study that the situation outlined in the preceding paragraphs is *one* of the major determinants in the development of the character of the adult Great Russians.

It is *not* the argument of this study that the Russian manner of swaddling their children produces the Russian character; and it is not intended to imply that Russian character would be changed or modified if some other technique of infant training were adopted. Swaddling is one of the devices which Russian adults employ to communicate with the child in its first year of life, to lay the foundation for those habits and attitudes which will subsequently be developed and strengthened by all the major institutions in Great Russian society. . . .

For several months, at least, the Russian infant experiences intense but relatively undirected rage and fears derived from his projection of this rage on to the external world; as a result of this he develops a feeling of pervasive though unfocused guilt. So pervasive is this unfocused guilt for some Russians that they can (or did) feel responsible for the sins and miseries of the whole world, an emotion most graphically and beautifully described by Dostoievsky in his major novels. This feeling of diffuse guilt presumably underlies the Orthodox dogma of the universal sinfulness of human beings, and accounts for the admission in confession of sins one is not conscious of having committed; it would also help account for the great feeling of psychological relief which accompanies confession and absolution for the devout, and also for the role which confessions outside religion have continuously played in Russian public life. The sensational confessions of the purge trials of 1936-38 and the recantations of error in communist self-criticism are modern examples. . . .

A trait of Great Russian character which has been frequently commented on by Russians and non-Russians alike are the sudden switches and alternations from one type of behaviour to another in complete contrast to the first. . . .

These switches from kindness to cruelty, from brutality to gentleness could be endlessly illustrated. They are very disconcerting to most non-Russians. There is a frequently repeated prototype to this dramatic and sudden change of feeling in the infantile experience of most Great Russians. At one moment they are lonely, filled with rage, constricted by the swaddling; the next moment their limbs are free, they are held in warm and strong arms and given the bountiful breast. Then this freedom and bliss in its turn comes to an end; the babies are wrapped up as though they were unfeeling parcels and left alone with their emotions. . . .

\*　　\*　　\*

If the arguments advanced . . . are correct, it will follow that the majority of Great Russians have a diffuse feeling of guilt, which is largely or entirely unconscious, and a diffuse feeling of fear, derived from the projection of their infantile hostility. This fear would appear to take the form of an emotional conviction that there exists in the external world an enemy (or enemies) who plan to constrict and destroy them, but no sort of certainty concerning the identity of the enemy.

The theory and practice of the Orthodox Church took these feelings into consistent account, and gave relief to them; the malicious enemy was identified as the devil and his minions, and minute ritual instructions were given for warding him off; the pervading sense of guilt could be at least temporarily assuaged by a full confession (or, more properly, admission of guilt) followed by ritual absolution. . . .

When, however, Great Russians ceased to practice Orthodox Christianity they had no technique left (with the possible exception of the orgy) for ridding themselves even temporarily of the oppression of unconscious guilt; and consequently they could not admit that others could be absolved, however completely they confessed and repented. If one's own guilt cannot be alleviated, then an enemy who has been identified appears to be irremediably wicked, and almost without human qualities, as though he were an incarnation of the scriptural devil no longer consciously believed in. . . .

The most straightforward identification of dark forces in the real (as contrasted with the supernatural) world is the contemporary secular authority or forces responsible for existing constraints. Russian history, up till recent years, contains a considerable number of conspiracies to assassinate and actual assassination of figures of authority. Perhaps even more revealing is the fact that Russians in positions of authority seem to expect those they control to attempt assassination and take very elaborate precautions to ward off this eventuality.

If it is believed that authority is evil, suspicious, and pervasive, attempts to overthrow it must be masked with very elaborate techniques of conspiracy. These techniques are gradually becoming known to the non-Russian world through the imitative practices of contemporary communist parties. Besides secretiveness and dissimulation, they include the testing of aspirant members by ordeal instead of by investigation, public and covert authorities, and the use of *agents provocateurs*. These techniques on conspiracy seem to be Russian rather than specifically communist. . . .

At about the turn of the twentieth century (if not earlier) the Russian authorities extended the employment of a technique for diverting from themselves the . . . unfocused hostility of the mass of the population. This technique consisted in pointing out to the masses that there were other groups who were planning to oppress, constrain, and destroy them, with the implication (usually tacit) that the removal of existing authorities would lay the masses open to even greater constrictions. These malevolent dark forces can be discovered anywhere; they may be any foreign nation, Jews, Trotskyists, fascists, capitalists, and so on endlessly. . . .

Once an enemy has been "unmasked" and identified, what should be done? . . .

It would seem as though an attack of rage had a somewhat cathartic effect (perhaps similar to the "righteous anger" recognized by Anglo-Saxons) and is not avoided; and that violence— especially emotional violence—becomes valued *as an instrument* in liberating one temporarily from the diffuse unconscious guilt and fear and destroying the confusions produced by the dark forces. . . .

In so far as violence is positively valued as an instrument for liberating one from the feelings of guilt and fear, it tends to be treated like directly physical pleasures in which quantity becomes of great psychological importance. It seems as though Russians felt a continuous psychological compulsion to go all the time to the limit of their strength and endurance. One can only know that one has gone to the limit of one's strength (done all that one should do) by a feeling of complete exhaustion, or by coming against an indestructible barrier and being repulsed and pushed back. This may be an analogue of the infantile situation in which depression is warded off by constant pushing against the constraining bonds of swaddling. It is probably this feeling which makes the tactical retreat so acceptable to Russians, Czarist and Soviet alike.[1] . . .

Since the later middle ages, and with a certain amount of interruption in the earlier years of the Soviet regime, political authority in Russia appears to have possessed two components: a Leader who is held to be all-wise and all-knowing, the embodiment of Truth and Foresight, and a minutely graded hierarchy of officials to carry out the wishes, plans, and revelations of the Leader and to transmit and interpret them to the mass of the population. . . .

---

[1]It should be noted that although the notion of being pushed back, after one has exerted all one's strength, is acceptable, the notion of weakness, of not having the strength to exert, is almost intolerable. I have never interviewed willing informants from any other society who were so incapable of recalling incidents from their own childhood; it is as though all memories of the period of physical weakness were suppressed.

It would seem as though this very great idealization of the Leader were a psychological necessity to the mass of Great Russians. With the all-pervasive unconscious hostility and guilt engendered by their infantile experiences, their psychological well-being (perhaps on a certain level even their sanity) depends on preserving in the external world at least one figure completely uncontaminated by the all-pervading suspicion and fear, a figure which has no human frailities, which stands as a safeguard against their own guilt and its consequences. . . .

This hypothesis is not merely of theoretical importance. If it is correct it would imply that it would be psychologically intolerable for Great Russians to live for any length of time without an idealized Leader, that a Leader is necessary to save them from political anarchy and personal disintegration. . . .

The Leader and his associates . . . cannot indulge in . . . emotions for their own sake; for to do so would distract them from their occupation in the most important activity of mankind—the gradual discovery and application of the Truth, *pravda*.[1] In the Russian conception of the universe, their concept of Truth holds an extremely important place.

The concept of Truth can be likened to a circle which surrounds one; it is analogous to the horizon which bounds the limitless and featureless Russian steppe. This steppe is, for very many Great Russians, the "typical" Russian landscape, no matter what sort of country or town they may actually have been reared in; and it is often used, both by them and by non-Russians, as an illustration and explanation of Russian character. . . .

In actual material fact, the great plains of Russia are not—at least to the casual traveller—more immense or featureless than the plains of the Middle West United States, or large areas of India, China, Indo-China, or Argentina; but Great Russians (and, as already said, very many non-Russians) consider this featureless landscape relevant to the understanding of the Russian character, in a fashion quite different to the relevance commonly attributed

---

[1] Much of this analysis of *pravda* is founded on concepts developed by Dr. Margaret Mead and Mr. N. Calas.

to the other areas named in the formation of the character of their inhabitants. Possibly a connection can be traced between the belief in the relevance of the limitless plain bounded by the horizon and the fact that in the typical childhood experience intense feeling is diffused (not concentrated) on the periphery of the body where it is bound by the swaddling, and the interior of the body is felt to be "featureless" without objects on which the attention can fasten.

The concept of Truth can be likened to a circle which surrounds one. Truth exists, one and indivisible, and it can be discovered and applied. There is not a "core" or "heart" of Truth with a series of applications which may be more or less correct. Truth is rather a system of interconnected items, arranged in a hierarchy, but in such a way that the destruction of one item jeopardizes the whole system. There is no concept of relative truths or of the possibility of various "aspects" or "versions" of truth. As a consequence compromise is inadmissible (except perhaps as a tactic); and there is no possibility of a "loyal opposition." All men of good will must recognize the Truth when it is pointed out to them; if they refuse to recognize it, this shows their wicked characters and evil intentions. . . .

The Leader and the hierarchy of authority under him see the Truth more clearly than the led, and they impart their discoveries and applications to the latter. But all Great Russians, however ignorant and however humble, feel that they are part of the Pentecostal Congregation . . . and so live in the Truth and follow it to the extent of their capacities. It is this conviction that they live in the Truth and pursue it as do the people of no other nation which gives the mystical overtones to the phrase "Holy Russia" and the newer form "Soviet Motherland." It is this conviction which binds the Russians in the sure belief of their righteousness and superiority and gives them their seeming unyielding rigidity, whether the present aspect of the Truth be Orthodox Christianity, or the latest version of Leninism-Stalinism.

If the views expressed . . . are correct, the following statements can be made about Great Russians. Most important of these per-

haps is the fact that there are very marked differences in character
between the Soviet élites on the one hand, and the mass of the
population on the other. The mass of the population is oppressed
by diffuse feelings of guilt and hostility, but shows very little anxiety. They tend to oscillate suddenly and unpredictably from one
attitude to its contrary, especially from violence to gentleness. . . .
They have deep warmth and sympathy for all whom (at a given
time) they consider as "the same as" themselves; they direct their
vague and unconscious hostility on all whom they consider "different to" themselves, paying little attention to which figure is
momentarily the focus of their hostility. They seem to expect
hostility from all who are "different." They consider themselves
superior to the rest of the world, because they and their country
are the special repository of the Truth, one and indivisible; it is
their duty to make this Truth prevail. . . . They submit unwillingly
but resignedly to firm authority imposed on them from above, and
merge themselves willingly with an idealized figure or Leader.

The intelligentsia and élites seem to share the diffuse guilt and
hostility and to see potential enemies all around them, including
the mass of the people they control. . . . They consider themselves
to be in possession of the Truth to a greater degree than the mass
of the population, and would appear to have esoteric versions of
the Truth which cannot safely be communicated to outsiders.

All Great Russians seem to feel the psychological compulsion
to exert their strength to the limit, and to place value on violence
as a means of liberation and producing order out of confusion. . . .

On the basis of these generalizations, it would seem possible to
derive the following political maxims:

(I) It is useless to try to make friends with, or win the sympathy of, the mass of the Great Russian people, in the hopes of
producing transformations of policy. The mass of the people
never have had, and (in any foreseeable future) are not likely to
have any appreciable influence on the policies their leaders adopt.
Policy, both foreign and domestic, is determined by a very small
group.

(II) The leaders suspect that those they lead are hostile towards
them, and they seek to divert this hostility on to other figures. If

the leaders were to feel convinced that the mass of the population (or a sizeable portion of it) were becoming disaffected from them and favouring some outside power, this might well exacerbate the leaders' fears and induce them to precipitate a war, as the most efficacious way of diverting hostility from themselves.

(III) No techniques are yet available for eradicating the all-pervasive suspicion which Great Russians, leaders and led alike, feel towards the rest of the world. This suspicion springs from unconscious and therefore irrational sources and will not be calmed, more than momentarily, by rational actions.

(IV) Great Russians, leaders and led alike, will continue to go all the time to the limit of their strength. They will expand their boundaries like a flooded lake, and this flood will only be contained by the political equivalent of a firm and solid dike. To continue the analogy one step further, the Great Russians will always seek out weak places or gaps in this dike; and if they find them they will exploit them. . . .

(VI) It should be remembered that the strategical retreat is a highly acceptable maneuver to Great Russians. (We have no information as to how this is viewed by the other peoples of the U.S.S.R.) To be forced back means that one has gone to the limit of one's strength and endurance, done one's utmost. It is not necessarily a humiliation. . . .

(VIII) Ideological arguments, notes of admonition and disapproval, and the like, are a complete waste of time and energy, as far as the Great Russians are concerned. With the Great Russian concept of Truth, *pravda,* it is impossible for them to admit error in any one instance, for that would destroy their whole system of Truth, and their self-esteem. If one action or attitude is wrong (incorrect) then all are wrong; and such an admission is only forthcoming in a religious conversion or political purge trial. Neither of these is likely to happen on an international scale.

(IX) There is no likelihood of Great Russians voluntarily engaging their country in any form of international organization which might conceivably give to other countries the possibility of constraining them. . . . There is no possibility of the development of a "world state," as now conceived, except under complete Russian domination, while the U.S.S.R. is an independent power with Great Russians in most of the positions of authority.

(X) Although the Russians will resist every encroachment, while themselves encroaching to the greatest possible degree, there would seem to be no necessity for war between the Western Powers and the U.S.S.R. The one situation which might evoke war (apart from the Western Powers "compressing" Russia) would be if the Western Powers manifested such weakness, or such alterations between strength and weakness, that the Russians would feel compelled to advance to such a degree that the Western powers would feel that the menace was intolerable. If Russia is faced with *permanent* strength, firmness, and consistency there would appear to be no reason why a tolerable and durable *modus vivendi* should not be maintained indefinitely.

# THE RUSSIAN PEOPLE AND SOCIALISM*

BY

ALEXANDER HERZEN

[1851]

Dear Sir—You hold so high a position in the esteem of all thinking men, and every word which comes from your noble pen is received by the European democracy with such complete and deserved confidence, that I cannot keep silent in a matter that touches upon my deepest convictions. I cannot leave unanswered your description of the Russian people. . . .

Poor Russian people! There is no one to raise a voice in its defense! Judge whether I can in duty be silent.

The Russian people, my dear sir, is alive, strong, and not old; on the contrary, indeed, very young. . . .

The past of the Russian people is obscure, its present is terrible, but it has claims on the future. It does not *believe* in its present position; it has the temerity to expect the more from time, since it has received so little hitherto. . . .

The Russian question is assuming immense and fearful proportions; it is the object of interest and anxiety to all parties; but I think that too much attention is paid to Imperial Russia, to official Russia, and too little to the Russia of the people, to voiceless Russia. . . .

Some tell us only of the unlimited power of the Tsar, of the capricious tyranny of his Government, of the slavish spirit of his subjects; others assert, on the contrary, that the Imperialism of Petersburg has nothing in common with the people, that this people, crushed under the twofold despotism of the Government and the landowners, bears the yoke, but is not resigned to it, that it is not crushed, but only unfortunate, and at the same time de-

---

*Excerpts from a letter to J. Michelet, the famous French historian. From A. Herzen, *My Past and Thoughts,* copyright 1928 by Chatto and Windus. Reprinted by permission.

clare that it is this very people which gives unity and power to the
colossal Tsardom that crushes it. Some add that the Russian people
is a *contemptible rabble of drunkards and knaves;* others maintain
that Russia is inhabited by a competent and richly gifted race.   It
seems to me that there is something tragic in the senile heedless-
ness with which the old world mixes up the different accounts it
hears of its antagonist.   In this confusion of contradictory opinions
there is apparent so much senseless repetition, such distressing
superficiality, such petrified prejudice, that we are involuntarily
moved to a comparison with the days of the fall of Rome.

Then, too, on the eve of catastrophe, on the eve of the victory
of the barbarians, men loudly proclaimed the eternity of Rome,
the impotent madness of the Nazarenes, and the insignificance of
the movement that was arising in the barbarian world.

You have performed a great service you first in France have
spoken of the Russian people, you have, unawares, touched on the
very heart, the very source of life.   The truth would have been
revealed to your eyes at once, if you had not, in a moment of anger,
pulled back your outstretched hand, if you had not turned away
from the source because its waters were not clear.

I read your bitter words with deep distress, with melancholy,
with anguish in my heart.   I confess I looked in vain in them for
the historian, the philosopher, and, above all, the tender-hearted
man whom we all know and love.   I hasten to explain, I fully understood the cause of your indignation; sympathy for unhappy
Poland prompted your words. We, too, deeply cherish this feeling
for our Polish brothers, and in us the feeling is not merely one of
pity, but of shame, and pangs of conscience.   Love for Poland!
We all love her, but is it necessary to combine with that feeling
hatred for another people as unhappy, a people forced to aid with
its fettered hands the misdeeds of its savage Government? . . .

At this point we are inevitably brought by logic to a question of
primary importance.   Assuming that the Slav world can hope in
the future for a fuller development, are we not forced to enquire
which of the elements that have found expression in its undeveloped state gives it grounds for such a hope?   If the Slavs believe
that their time has come, this element must be in harmony with
the revolutionary idea in Europe.

You indicated that element, you touched upon it, but it escaped you, because a generous sentiment of sympathy for Poland drew your attention away from it.

You say that "the fundamental basis of the life of the Russian people is *communism*," you maintain that "their strength lies in their agrarian law, in the perpetual re-division of the land."

What a terrible *Mene Tekel* has dropped from your lips! . . . Communism—the fundamental basis! Strength resting on re-division of the land! And you were not alarmed at your own words?

Ought we not here to pause, to take thought, to look more deeply into the question, and not to leave it before making certain whether it is a dream or truth?

Is there in the nineteenth century an interest of any gravity which does not involve the question of communism, the question of the re-division of the land?

Carried away by your indignation you go on: "They (the Russians) are without any true sign of humanity, of moral sensibility, of the sense of good and evil. Truth and justice have for them no meaning; if you speak of these things—they are mute, they smile and know not what the words signify." Who may those Russians be to whom you have spoken? What conceptions of *truth and justice* appeared beyond their comprehension? This is not a superfluous question. In our profoundly revolutionary epoch the words "truth and justice" have lost all absolute meaning identical for all men.

The *truth and justice* of old Europe are falsehood and injustice to the Europe which is being born. Nations are products of Nature, history is the progressive continuation of animal development. If we apply our moral standards to Nature, we shall not get very far. She cares nought for our blame or our praise. Our verdicts and the Montyon prizes[1] for virtue do not exist for her. The ethical categories created by our individual caprice are not applicable to her. It seems to me that a nation cannot be called either bad or good. The life of a people is always true to its

---

[1]A philanthropist, Baron de Montyon, endowed prizes for virtue and literary distinction to be distributed by the Institut in Paris.—(Translator's note.)

character and cannot be false.  Nature produces only what is prac-
ticable under given conditions: all that exists is drawn onwards by
her generative ferment, her insatiable thirst for creation, that thirst
common to all things living.

There are peoples living a prehistoric life, others living a life
outside history; but once they move into the broad stream of history, one and indivisible, they belong to *humanity*, and, on the
other hand, all the past of humanity belongs to them.  In history
—that is, in the life of the active and progressive part of humanity
—the aristocracy of facial angle, of complexion, and other distinctions is gradually effaced.  That which has not become human
cannot come into history: so no nation which has become part of
history can be reckoned a herd of beasts, just as there is no nation
which deserves to be called an assembly of the elect. . . .

Nature never sta' s all her fortunes on one card.  Rome, the
Eternal City, wh n had no less right to the hegemony of the
world, tottered, fell into ruins, vanished, and pitiless humanity
strode forward over its grave.

On the other hand, unless one looks on Nature as madness in-
carnate, it would be hard to see nothing but an outcast race, nothing
but a vast deception, nothing but a casual rabble, human only
through their vices, in a people that has grown and multiplied
during ten centuries, that has obstinately preserved its nationality,
that has formed itself into an immense empire, and has intervened
in history far more perhaps than it should have done.

And such a view is the more difficult to accept since this people,
even judging from the words of its enemies, is far from being in
a stagnant condition.  It is not a race that has attained social forms
approximately corresponding to its desires and has sunk into slumber in them, like the Chinese; still less, a people that has outlived
its prime and is withering in senile impotence, like the people of
India.  On the contrary, Russia is a quite new State—an unfinished
building in which everything smells of fresh plaster, in which
everything is at work and being worked out, in which nothing has
yet attained its object, in which everything is changing, often for
the worse, but anyway changing.  In brief, this is the people whose
fundamental principle, to quote your opinion, is communism, and
whose strength lies in the re-division of land. . . .

With what crime, after all, do you reproach the Russian people? What is the essential point of your accusation?

"The Russian," you say, "is a liar and a thief; he is perpetually stealing, he is perpetually lying, and quite innocently—it is in his nature."

I will not stop to call attention to the sweeping character of your verdict, but will ask you a simple question: who is it that the Russian deceives, from whom does he steal? Who—if not the landowner, the Government official, the steward, the police officer, in fact the sworn foes of the peasant, whom he looks upon as heathens, as traitors, as half Germans? Deprived of every possible means of defense, the peasant resorts to cunning in dealing with his torturers, he deceives them, and he is perfectly right in doing so.

Cunning, my dear sir, is, in the words of Hegel, the irony of brute force.

Through his aversion for private property in land, so correctly noted by you, through his heedless and indolent temperament, the Russian peasant has gradually and imperceptibly been caught in the snares of the German bureaucracy and of the landowners' power. He has submitted to this humiliating disaster with the resignation of a martyr, but he has not believed in the rights of the landowner, nor the justice of the law-courts, nor the legality of the acts of the authorities. For nearly two hundred years the peasant's existence has been a dumb, passive opposition to the existing order of things. He submits to coercion, he endures, but he takes no part in anything that goes on outside the village commune.

The name of the Tsar still stirs a superstitious sentiment in the people; it is not to the Tsar Nicholas that the peasant does homage, but to the abstract idea, the myth; in the popular imagination the Tsar stands for a menacing avenger, an incarnation of Justice, an earthly providence.

Besides the Tsar, only the clergy could possibly have an influence on orthodox Russia. They alone represent old Russia in governing spheres; the clergy do not shave their beards, and by that fact have remained on the side of the people. The peasantry listen with confidence to the monks. But the monks and the higher clergy, occupied exclusively with life beyond the grave, care little for the people. The village priests have lost all influence through their greed, their drunkenness, and their intimate relations with the police. In their case, too, the peasants respect the idea but not the person. . . .

Apart from the Tsar and the clergy every element of government and society is utterly alien, essentially antagonistic to the people. The peasant finds himself in the literal sense of the word an outlaw. The law-court is no protector for him, and his share in the existing order of things is entirely confined to the twofold tribute that lies heavy upon him and is paid in his toil and his blood. Rejected by all, he instinctively understands that the whole system is ordered not for his benefit, but to his detriment, and that the aim of the Government and the landowners is to wring out of him as much labor, as much money, as many recruits as possible. As he understands this and is gifted with a supple and resourceful intelligence, he deceives them on all sides and in everything. It could not be otherwise; if he spoke the truth he would by so doing be acknowledging their authority over him; if he did not rob them (observe that to conceal part of the produce of his own labor is considered theft in a peasant) he would thereby be recognizing the lawfulness of their demands, the rights of the landowners and the justice of the law-courts.

To understand the Russian peasant's position fully, you should see him in the law-courts; you must see his hopeless face, his frightened watchful eyes, to understand that he is a prisoner of war before the court-martial, a traveller facing a gang of brigands. From the first glance it is clear that the victim has not the slightest trust in the hostile, pitiless, insatiable robbers who are questioning him, tormenting him and fleecing him. He knows that if he has money he will be acquitted; if not, he will be found guilty.

The Russian people speak their own old language, the judges and the attorneys write in a new bureaucratic language, hideous and barely intelligible; they fill whole folios with ungrammatical jargon, and gabble off this mummery to the peasant. He may understand it if he can and find his way out of the muddle if he knows how. The peasant knows what this performance means, and maintains a cautious demeanor. He does not say one word too much, he conceals his uneasiness and stands silent, pretending to be a fool.

The peasant who has been acquitted by the court trudges home, no more elated than if he had been condemned. In either case the decision seems to him the result of capricious tyranny or chance.

In the same way, when he is summoned as a witness he stubbornly professes to know nothing, even in face of incontestable fact. Being found guilty by a law court does not disgrace a man in the eyes of the Russian peasant. Exiles and convicts go by the name of *unfortunates* with him.

The life of the Russian peasantry has hitherto been confined to the commune. It is only in relation to the commune and its members that the peasant recognizes that he has rights and duties. Outside the commune everything seems to him based upon violence. What is fatal is his submitting to that violence, and not his refusing in his own way to recognize it and his trying to protect himself by guile. Lying before a judge set over him by unlawful authority is far more straightforward than a hypocritical show of respect for a jury tampered with by a corrupt prefect. The peasant respects only those institutions which reflect his innate conception of law and right.

There is a fact which no one who has been in close contact with the Russian peasantry can doubt. The peasants rarely cheat each other. An almost boundless good faith prevails among them; they know nothing of contracts and written agreements.

The problems connected with the measurement of their fields are often inevitably complicated, owing to the perpetual re-division of land, in accordance with the number of taxpayers in the family; yet the difficulties are got over without complaint or resort to the law-courts. The landowners and the Government eagerly seek an opportunity of interference, but that opportunity is not given them. Petty disputes are submitted to the judgment of the elders or of the commune, and the decision is unconditionally accepted by all. It is just the same thing in the *artels*. The *artels* are often made

up of several hundred workmen, who form a union for a definite
period—for instance, for a year. At the expiration of the year
the workmen divide their wages by common agreement, in accordance with the work done by each. The police never have the satisfaction of meddling in their accounts. Almost always the *artel*
makes itself responsible for every one of its members.

The bonds between the peasants of the commune are even closer
when they are not orthodox but dissenters. From time to time the
Government organizes a savage raid on some dissenting village.
Peasants are clapped into prison and sent into exile, and it is all
done with no sort of plan, no consistency, without rhyme or reason,
solely to satisfy the clamor of the clergy and give the police something to do. The character of the Russian peasants, the solidarity
existing among them, is displayed again during these hunts after
heretics. At such times it is worth seeing how they succeed in
deceiving the police, in saving their comrades and concealing their
holy books and vessels, how they endure the most awful tortures
without uttering a word. I challenge any one to bring forward a
single case in which a dissenting commune has been betrayed by
a peasant, even by an orthodox one.

The peculiarity of the Russian character makes police enquiries
excessively difficult. One can but heartily rejoice at the fact. The
Russian peasant has no morality except what naturally, instinctively
flows from his communism; this morality is deeply rooted in the
people; the little they know of the Gospel supports it; the flagrant
injustice of the landowner binds the peasant still more closely to
his principles and to the communal system.

The commune has saved the Russian people from Mongol bar-
barism and Imperial civilization, from the Europeanized landlords and from the German bureaucracy. The Communal system,
though it has suffered violent shocks, has stood firm against the
interference of the authorities; it has successfully survived *up to
the development of socialism in Europe.* This circumstance is of
infinite consequence for Russia.

The Russian Autocracy is entering upon a new phase. Having
grown out of an anti-national revolution, it has accomplished its
destined task. It has created an immense empire, a formidable

army, a centralized government. Without real roots, without tradition, it was doomed to ineffectiveness; it is true that it undertook a new task—to bring Western civilization into Russia; and it was to some extent successful in doing that while it still played the part of an enlightened government.

That part it has now abandoned.

The Government, which severed itself from the people in the name of civilization, has lost no time in cutting itself off from culture in the name of autocracy.

It renounced civilization as soon as the tri-colored phantom of liberalism began to be visible through its tendencies; it tried to turn to nationalism, to the people. That was impossible—the people and the Government had nothing in common; the former had grown away from the latter, while the government discerned deep in the masses a new phantom, the still more terrible phantom of the Red Cock.[1] Of course, liberalism was less dangerous than the new Pugatchovism, but the terror and dislike of new ideas had grown so strong that the Government was no longer capable of making its peace with civilization.

Since then the sole aim of Tsarism has been Tsarism. It rules in order to rule, its immense powers are employed for their mutual destruction, for the preservation of an artificial peace. But autocracy for the sake of autocracy in the end becomes impossible; it is too absurd, too barren. . . .

From all this you see how fortunate it is for Russia that the village commune has not perished, that personal ownership has not split up the property of the commune; how fortunate it is for the Russian people that it has remained outside all political movements, outside European civilization, which would undoubtedly have undermined the commune, and which has today reached in socialism the negation of itself.

Europe, as I have said in another place, has not solved the problem of the rival claims of the individual and the State, but has set herself the task of solving it. Russia has not found the solution either. It is in this problem that our equality begins.

[1]To "let fly the Red Cock" is the popular Russian phrase for arson.— (Translator's note.)

At the first step towards the social revolution Europe is confronted with the people which presents it with a system, half-savage and unorganized, but still a system, that of perpetual re-division of land among its cultivators.   And observe that this great example is given us not by educated Russia, but by the people itself, by its actual life.   We Russians who have passed through European civilization are no more than a means, a leaven, mediators between the Russian people and revolutionary Europe.   The man of the future in Russia is the peasant, just as in France it is the workman.

But, if this is so, have not the Russian peasantry some claim on your indulgence, sir?

Poor peasant!   Every possible injustice is hurled at him: the Emperor oppresses him with levies of recruits, the landowner steals his labor, the official takes his last rouble.   The peasant endures in silence but does not despair, he still has the commune.   If a member is torn from it, the commune draws its ranks closer.   One would have thought the peasant's fate deserved compassion, yet it touches no one.   Instead of defending him, men upbraid him.

I will say no more about the peasants, but beg you to listen to a few more words about educated Russia.

Your view of the intellectual movement in Russia is no more indulgent than your opinion of the popular character; with one stroke of the pen you strike off all the work hitherto done by our fettered hands!

One of Shakespeare's characters, not knowing how to show his contempt for a despised opponent, says to him: "I even doubt of your existence!"   You have gone further, for it is not a matter of doubt to you that Russian literature does not exist.

Next to the communism of the peasants, nothing is so deeply characteristic of Russia, nothing is such an earnest of her great future, as her literary movement.

Between the peasantry and literature there looms the monster of official Russia.   "Russia the deception, Russia the pestilence," as you call her.   This Russia extends from the Emperor, passing from gendarme to gendarme, from official to official, down to the lowest policeman in the remotest corner of the Empire.   Every step of the ladder, as in Dante, gains a new power for evil, a new degree of corruption and cruelty. This living pyramid of crimes, abuses, and bribery, built up of policemen, scoundrels, heartless German officials everlastingly greedy, ignorant judges everlastingly drunk, aristocrats everlastingly base: all this is held together by a community of interest in plunder and gain, and supported on six hundred thousand animated machines with bayonets. The peasant is never defiled by contact with this governing world of aggression; he endures its existence—only in that is he to blame.

The body hostile to official Russia consists of a handful of men who are ready to face anything, who protest against it, fight with it, denounce and undermine it. These isolated champions are from time to time thrown into dungeons, tortured, sent to Siberia, but their place does not long remain empty, fresh champions come forward; it is our tradition, our inalienable task. The terrible consequences of speech in Russia inevitably give it a peculiar force. A free utterance is listened to with love and reverence, because among us it is only uttered by those who have something to say. One does not so easily put one's thoughts into print when at the end of every page one has a vision of a gendarme, a troika, and, on the far horizon, Tobolsk or Irkutsk. . . .

Cast into oppressive surroundings, and armed with a clear eye and incorruptible logic, the Russian quickly frees himself from the faith and morals of his fathers. The thinking Russian is the most independent man in the world. What is there to curb him? Respect for the past? . . . But what serves as a starting-point of the modern history of Russia, if not the denial of nationalism and tradition?

Or can it be the tradition of the Petersburg period? That tradition lays no obligation on us; on the contrary, that "fifth act of the bloody drama staged in a brothel" sets us completely free from every obligation.

On the other hand, the past of the Western European peoples serves us as a lesson and nothing more; we do not regard ourselves as the executors of their historic testaments.

We share your doubts, but your faith does not cheer us. We share your hatred, but we do not understand your devotion to what your forefathers have bequeathed you; we are too downtrodden, too unhappy, to be satisfied with half-freedom. You are restrained by scruples, you are held back by second thoughts. We have neither second thoughts nor scruples; all we lack is strength. This is where we get the irony, the anguish which gnaws us, which brings us to frenzy, which drives us on till we reach Siberia, torture, exile, premature death. We sacrifice ourselves with no hope, from spite, from boredom. . . . There is, indeed, something irrational in our lives, but there is nothing vulgar, nothing stagnant, nothing bourgeois.

Do not accuse us of immorality because we do not respect what you respect. Can you reproach a foundling for not respecting his parents? We are independent because we are starting life from the beginning. We have no law but our nature, our national character; it is our being, our flesh and blood, but no means a binding authority. We are independent because we possess nothing. We have hardly anything to love. All our memories are filled with bitterness and resentment. Education, learning, were given us with the whip.

What have we to do with your sacred duties, we younger brothers robbed of our heritage? And can we be honestly contented with your threadbare morality, unchristian and inhuman, existing only in rhetorical exercises and speeches for the prosecution? What respect can be inspired in us by your Roman-barbaric system of law, that hollow clumsy edifice, without light or air, repaired in the Middle Ages, whitewashed by the newly enfranchised petty bourgeois? I admit that the daily brigandage in the Russian lawcourts is even worse, but it does not follow from that that you have justice in your laws or your courts. . . .

We are held in too many chains already to fasten fresh ones about us of our own free will. In this respect we stand precisely on a level with our peasants. We submit to brute force. We are slaves because we have no possibility of being free; but we accept nothing from our foes.

Russia will never be Protestant, Russia will never be *juste-milieu*.

Russia will never make a revolution with the object of getting rid of the Tsar Nicholas, and replacing him by other Tsars—parliamentary representatives, judges, and police officials. We perhaps ask for too much and shall get nothing. That may be so, but yet we do not despair. . . .

I confidently hope that you will forgive the passages in which I have been carried away by my Scythian impetuosity. It is not for nothing that the blood of the barbarians flows in my veins. I so longed to change your opinion of the Russian people, it was such a grief, such a pain to me to see that you were hostile to us that I could not conceal my bitterness, my emotion, that I let my pen run away with me. . . . In my turn I confess that I fully understand the impression the very name of Russia must produce on every free man. We often ourselves curse our unhappy Fatherland. You know it, you say yourself that everything you have written of the moral worthlessness of Russia is feeble compared with what Russians say themselves. . . .

Unhappily, free speech in Russia arouses terror and amazement. I have tried to lift only a corner of the heavy curtain that hides us from Europe, I have indicated only the theoretical tendencies, the remote hopes, the organic elements of our future development. . . .

Heavy and dreadful is the yoke of years of slavery with no struggle, no hope at hand! In the end it crushes even the noblest, the strongest heart. Where is the hero who is not overcome at last by weariness, who does not prefer peace in old age to the everlasting fret of fruitless effort?

No, I will not be silent! My words shall avenge those unhappy lives crushed by the Russian autocracy which brings men to moral annihilation, to spiritual death. . . .

A fable very widely known in Russia tells how a Tsar, suspecting his wife of infidelity, shut her and her son in a barrel, then had the barrel sealed and thrown into the sea.

For many years the barrel floated on the sea.

Meanwhile, the Tsarevitch grew not by days but by hours, and his feet and his head began to press against the ends of the barrel. Every day he became more and more cramped. At last he said to his mother: "Queen-mother, let me stretch in freedom."

"My darling Tsarevitch," answered the mother, "you must not

stretch, the barrel will burst and you will drown in the salt water."

The Tsarevitch thought in silence for a while, then he said: "I will stretch, mother; better stretch for once in freedom and die."

That fable, sir, contains our whole history.

Woe to Russia if bold men, risking everything to stretch in freedom for once, are no more to be found in her. But there is no fear of that.

* * *

# SCYTHIANS*

## BY

## ALEXANDER BLOK

### [1918]

Of you there are millions.
   Of us—hordes, and hordes, and hordes.
Just try to measure your strength with us!
Yes, we are Scythians. Yes, we are Asiatics,
With slant and avaricious eyes!

For you whole ages—for us a single hour.
Like obedient serfs, we held
The shield between two hostile races
Of Mongols and of Europe!

For ages and ages your ancient furnace forged,
And deafened the thunder of an avalanche.
As a wild tale seemed to you the downfall
Of Lisbon and Messina!

Hundreds of years you gazed upon the East,
Gathering and conveying on sea our pearls.
Scoffing, you only awaited the day
For big guns to open fire.

Now the time has come. Calamity beats her wings.
Each day multiplies humiliations.
The day may come when not a trace
Will remain of your proud old cities.

O old world! Before your doom does come,
While still in throes of raptured anguish,
Pause, O world, as wise as Oedipus,
Before the Sphinx with ancient riddle!

---

*Translated from the Russian by John Cournos. Copyright 1953 by the
American Foundation for Political Education.

Russia is a Sphinx!  Exultant and afflicted,
Drenched in blackest blood.
She gazes, gazes, gazes into you,
Yes, with hatred, and with love!

Yes, to love as our blood loves,
None among you has loved thus since aforetime!
You have forgotten, there is a love
Which burns and consumes!

We love *all*—the heat of cold numbers,
The gift of godlike visions.
We comprehend *all*—the sharp Gallic mind,
The morose German genius. . .

We remember *all*—the Hades of Paris streets,
The cool Venetian breezes,
The remote aroma of lemon groves,
The dusky towering piles of Cologne. . .

We love the flesh—its taste, its color,
The oppressive smell of mortal flesh. . .
Is the fault ours, if your skeleton should crunch
In the embrace of our clumsy tender paws?

We have learned to grasp the reins
Of spirited rearing steeds,
To break their stubborn backs,
To subdue the will of refractory beasts. . .

Come to us!  From horrors of war
Come to a peaceful embrace!
Before it is too late—restore sword to sheath.
Comrades!  Let us become brothers.

If not—we have nothing to lose,
We too can be perfidious!
Ages, ages—shall curse you,
O ailing, tardy generation!

Through thickets and woods
We shall appear before the gates of comely Europe.
We shall scatter far and wide!   Then turn toward you
Our ugly Asiatic mugs!

Come one, come all!   Come to the Urals!
We shall clear the field for battle
Of steel machines—where breathes the strength
Of a savage Mongol horde!

As for us—no longer shall we be your shield,
Henceforth we shall stand aside.
As the mortal combat seethes, we shall look on
With narrowed eyes.

We shall not stir when the savage Hun,
Ghoul-like, rifles the pockets of the dead,
Burns towns, crowds churches with human droves,
And roasts the flesh of his white brothers! . . .

For the last time—old world, be warned!
We call you to a fraternal feast of peace.
For the last time—you are summoned to a radiant feast,
O listen to the barbarian's clarion call!

II

# CZARISM AND THE RUSSIAN REVOLUTION

# WHAT SHOULD BE THE POLICY
# OF RUSSIA?*

BY

ROSTISLAV A. FADIEEV

[1869]

Russia's chief enemy is by no means Western Europe, but the German race with its enormous pretensions. The victory will be on the side of him who first gets the upper hand in that disputed ground—Slavonic by race and German by political geography—which divides two powerful nations. When the unity of the German race is completed in the bounds it has proudly assigned to itself, and when it begins to Germanize the Slavonians by Prussian measures, it will be too late to go to law. The Slavs outside of the boundaries of Russia will be its sacrifice. At the same time the fate of the last great Aryan race will be sealed, with all that it promised for humanity, together with the fate of those political fragments of the orthodox world still preserved outside of Russia, and the import of Russia's history, with which no nation can part with impunity.

I shall speak my mind frankly: contemporary Russia has already grown out of the limits of race which give legality and firmness to the existence of a State, but has not yet attained that higher legality, of being the center of her own special Slavonic and orthodox world. Russia cannot be consolidated in her present state; political, like natural, history does not eternize undefined, unfinished phases. All depends now on the way in which the Slav Question is decided. Russia must either extend her pre-eminence to the Adriatic or withdraw again beyond the Dnieper. She has hitherto steadily advanced towards the solution of the historic problem which is before her.

---

*From a pamphlet entitled "Opinion on the Eastern Question," first published at St. Petersburg, "with the permission of the censorship," December 4, 1869. Translated by T. Michell, British Consul at St. Petersburg, and published in London by Edward Stanford, 1871.

At the time when the Slavonian and orthodox world began to be threatened with thraldom, the Muscovite Empire grew out of a Norman Principality and gathered round it the kindred Great-Russian race, and, later, all the branches of the Russian people, receiving in that process of absorption the legacy of the moral inheritance of the expiring Empire of the East, until at last it crossed the confines of a Slavonian world of alien origin. It is now either too early or too late to stop. Russia might have remained a great Power, without leaving in the West the boundaries of her race, and without taking upon herself the mission, now converted into a duty, of regenerating the Christian East; but she has done it, and it may be confidently asserted that she could not have done otherwise. As the head of a great race, gradually reasserting itself in her person, and as a refuge of all the Orthodox, Russia has never enclosed herself within strictly defined boundaries, and has indeed been compelled to step beyond them. . . . The idea of the community of the Slav race has always existed in Russia, in the form of a tendency to union with kindred by blood—first with the people of Great Russia, next with the Russian race in general, including all its transitional forms; and it is therefore natural that that idea should have at last grown to its present significance. A similar tendency has never been manifested in Poland, which has always regarded herself in the light of a State, not a people, and she has therefore never been of importance to her kindred neighbors. Russia now stands amidst a Slavonian world that is not Russian, and that is divided by an arbitrary line between her own dominion and that of Germany. At the same time, the consciousness of the identity of race on either side of that line, and a comprehension of the community of material and moral requirements, are rapidly ripening. This is the decisive hour that can never return, and that admits of no long hesitation. One of two courses must be adopted. Russia must either acknowledge herself to be a State in the sense of old Poland, and nothing more than a State, alien in her heart to everything outside the boundaries which have been accidentally given to her, and proceed in a decisive manner to root out every independent feature of the races of which she is composed or which are still to enter into her composition; she must in such a case sincerely and openly renounce all thought of Slavism or of the Orthodox East, and that community with them which envenoms her relations with Europe, casting them away from her and regarding them in the same manner as Prussia or France; in fact, shutting herself up at home and maintaining her borders by force, until in the course of centuries they become merged with the body of the Empire; or, leaving to the Russian people their inalienable pre-eminence in the Slavonian world, and to the Russian language its undoubted right to be the political and connecting tongue of that world, Russia must open her arms to all those who are nearer akin to her than to Europe, receiving them as younger but independent members of the same great family.

The *first* of these two decisions would be opposed to history—a dangerous road! But that is not all. Although such a decision might have been possible under the reign of Catherine II, it is at present almost impossible. We have gone too far: tribal affinities have been aroused, the Eastern Question has been raised, divided Poland has become an apple of discord between the Germanic and Russian races; the general connection of all these difficulties has visibly asserted itself, and bears a well-defined name. . . . The *first* consequence of such a course will be that the Black Sea will be entirely taken away from Russia, and that a hostile predominance will be established on it. The *second* will be the hatred of the forty millions of Slavs and Orthodox whom Russia will have repelled, and who will certainly in such a case join the ranks of the enemy—a course which they will not be able to avoid. The *third* will be the excessive and crushing power of the German race, neighboring Russia. The *fourth* will be a dispute about Poland, with all its possible results; the united Germans will not voluntarily present their flank to Russia when they might protect it, nor make a present to Russia of a soil so well adapted to receive the seeds of Germanism in the future; they will not let slip an opportunity of keeping Russia constantly on the alert; they will have an account to settle with us on the shores of the Baltic. The *fifth* consequence will be "additional articles" relative to Finland, Livonia, Bessarabia, the Crimea. By renouncing her historical destiny, Russia at the same time renounces the only allies on whom she can ever depend. We may gain a battle by our own efforts, and in our own

name, but we cannot attain any objects.   And at the same time
we shall have to carry on a fight with the same obstacles and with
the same enemies—a defensive, not an offensive struggle, not in
order to terminate that struggle with a triumph, but merely to
neutralize as much as possible its unfavorable issue.   The historical
move of Russia from the Dnieper to the Vistula, was a declaration
of war to Europe, which had broken into a part of the Continent
that did not belong to her.   Russia now stands in the midst of the
enemy's lines—such a condition is only temporary: she must either
drive back the enemy or abandon her position.

But besides the two lines of action which have just been passed
in review, there is a third—a middle course.   This is the worst of
all.   It consists in irritating the whole world against us without
doing anything in reality, and without making positive preparations for anything.   The Lord forbid that Russia should enter upon
such a course.

A war for the independence of any people or State, can only
have that independence in view; there is nothing to be said to the
contrary.   As far as Russia is concerned, there is no sensible reason,
moral, politico-economical, or military, for desiring new annexations in Europe; in the Russian mind there is no idea of con-
verting kindred countries into subject provinces. . . . When the
races allied to Russia by blood shall have been completely liberated,
the country watered by the Vistula becomes no longer ours.   In
the Slavonian and Orthodox countries which surround Russia,
there are six or eight principal centers of gravitation (this has not
yet become sufficiently clear); and it is around these that the
national units must collect.

If Russia continues to pursue her historical path, her peaceful
efforts in favor of those who are nearest to her should not be in-
discriminate, but in strict conformity with the peculiar conditions
and requirements of each center, taken separately.   In addition to
these natural groups, there is yet another place on the earth immeasurably important to Russia, having no national character, but
from its exceptionable position too important to belong to any
small people—Constantinople, with the surrounding suburbs,
country, and straits.   The most positive interests of Russia render it

desirable that that city, far more eternal than Rome, should become the free city of a tribal union.

If there be any sense in history and the liberation of the Slavs be effected, their mutual relations toward each other and towards Russia will be determined by the force of things. The independence of each member of the liberated family in his internal affairs, a separate Ruler and separate political institutions, as may be most convenient to each—all this is already settled by history. But independence in an international and military point of view is quite a different question. It is not enough to be freed, it is necessary to remain free. In the present state of Europe there is no room for a heap of small nations, disposing of their own small armies, declaring war, making peace and alliances—each in its own person. And where?—Between the Russian and the future German Empire. And what, we ask, are those nations? Rejected races, not recognized by Europe, whose masters of yesterday will long continue to regard them as rebel subjects, and await a fitting opportunity for enslaving them anew.

To create such a condition of chaos, pregnant as it would be with quarrels, disorders, and internecine strife—a condition of which even tomorrow's existence would be uncertain, and which would be burdensome to all, and to the liberators in particular—would be taking upon oneself not the restoration, but the destruction of legitimate rights and of order in Europe, and holding up to derision one of the greatest of all questions in which the world is concerned. Affairs would, moreover, soon return to the same issueless condition. The liberated East of Europe, if it be liberated at all, will require: a durable bond of union, a common head with a common council, the transaction of international affairs and the military command in the hands of that head, the Tsar of Russia, the natural Chief of all the Slavs and Orthodox.

It is necessary that the citizens of each nation in the Union should have the full rights of a citizen of the entire Union. There is no necessity to place all the military forces of the confederate nations under the banner of Russia, after the model of the North Germanic Confederation; it will be sufficient if the active army, whether on a peace or a war footing, and whether at home or

abroad, according to circumstances, should, together with the federal fortresses and the entrances into the Black Sea, be at the entire
disposal and under the sole government of the head of the Union.
The great confederate family, independent in each of its separate
parts, will thus form but one State as regards the rest of the world.

. . . When the great Eastern family shall have arisen, its union
can only be consolidated by a community of family thrones in one
dynasty.   Every Russian, as well as every Slav and every Orthodox
Christian, should desire to see chiefly the Russian reigning House
cover the liberated soil of Eastern Europe with its branches, under
the supremacy and lead of the Tsar of Russia, long recognized, in
the expectation of the people, as the direct heir of Constantine the
Great.   The isolation of the Eastern world of Europe, of which
the foundations were laid in days of antiquity, is only now bearing
fruit, after the lapse of fifteen hundred years. . . . Russia grew up
apart from the Union, which therefore remained fruitless.

I know that many will consider my conclusions mere poesy.  But
I have already expressed my conviction, based on a sufficient series
of proofs; should my poesy not be realized, notwithstanding that
the history of a thousand years leads irresistibly to its realization,
Russia will scarcely remain, as a State, within its present limits.
Nationalities have now begun to form into groups; ill-defined
boundaries have become unstable; revolutions are effected with an
astounding rapidity.   The spirit of the age, in conjunction with
the actual sense of the position of Russia, admits but of two solutions: either Russia as a local empire of the Russian race, or Russia
as a concentration of the Slav and Orthodox world.

As regards the present, those two solutions may be expressed by
two verbs: to await or to act.

At first the action of Russia can only be moral.  The open recognition of her right to be the representative of a kindred world, and
the bringing back under the parental roof, at the first opportunity,
of the last enslaved remnants of the Russian race, and an unanimous impulse on both sides towards the common object—these
should precede political unification.   There will then be no lack of
favorable opportunities; the nineteenth century is not an age of
peace and tranquil prosperity in Europe.

But however great may be the unanimity, and however favorable the opportunity, this great question can only be settled by force, and at first by Russian force alone. Now, more than ever, Russia requires an army commensurate in its numbers and its quality with the magnitude of the task which she has before her—an army that shall be Russian, not in an abstract sense, but an army that shall be educated by military commanders who understand the spirit of Russian soldiers and Russian regiments. With half-a-million such troops on the western frontier . . . the task can be fulfilled. This can be as easily proved as that twice two make four.

Events cannot be averted by expectation; it is only the hour that will be chosen, not by Russia, nor for her convenience; the rest will remain unchanged. Russia will come into collision with the same adversaries, Prussia not excepted, and with the same number of soldiers and guns, on the subject of the inaccessible Eastern Question and its inevitable supplement—the insoluble Polish Question, as well as in respect to the accessible Pan-Slavist Question.

Many will, doubtless, find my sincerity indiscreet. I have more than once been blamed for it, but I nevertheless retain my conviction that a Russian should speak as openly of the affairs of his country as foreigners speak of them. Language is, in the present day, a weapon, and the unarmed cannot fight with the armed. I apprehend that the States and nations of which I speak are quite indifferent to my personal opinions on the Eastern Question. When, however, the idea of Pan-Slavism becomes a State idea, it will dazzle all like lightning; there will then also be no need for secrecy. Russian affairs will be in a fair way, only when the peasant women on the banks of the Moldau or on the slopes of the Balkans shall hush their children to sleep, saying, "Don't cry, the Russians are coming soon to help us, and they will bring you lollipops."

# THE FOREIGN POLICY OF RUSSIAN CZARISM*

## FRIEDRICH ENGELS

[1890]

We, the West-European labor parties, have a twofold interest in the victory of the Russian revolutionary party. First, because the Russian Czarist empire forms the greatest fortress, reserve position and at the same time reserve army of European reaction, because its mere passive existence already constitutes a threat and a danger to us. Second, however—and this point has still not been sufficiently emphasized on our part—because it blocks and disturbs our normal development through its ceaseless intervention in Western affairs, intervention aimed moreover at conquering geographical positions which will secure it the mastery of Europe, and thus make impossible the liberation of the European proletariat.

. . . Many revolutionaries are so scornful of the Czarist government that partly due to its narrowness, partly due to its corruption, they consider it incapable of doing anything rational. So far as internal politics are concerned this is indeed correct; here the impotence of the Czarist regime lies exposed to the light of day. However, it is necessary to know not only the weaknesses of the enemy, but also his elements of strength. And foreign policy is unquestionably the side on which Czarism is strong, very strong. The Russian diplomatic corps forms, so to speak, a modern Jesuit order, powerful enough in case of necessity to overcome even the whims of the Czar and to become master of the corruption within Russia, in order to disseminate it abroad the more plentifully. . . . It is this secret society, recruited originally from foreign adventurers, which has raised the Russian empire to its present plenitude

*From Marx and Engels, *The Russian Menace to Europe,* translated and edited by Paul W. Blackstock and Bert F. Hoselitz. Copyright 1952 by the Free Press. Reprinted by permission.

74

of power. With iron perseverance, eyes set fixedly on the goal, not shrinking from any breach of faith, any treason, any assassination, any servility, distributing bribes lavishly, never over-confident following victory, never discouraged by defeat, over the dead bodies of millions of soldiers and at least one Czar, it is this gang —as talented as it is without conscience—rather than all the Russian armies put together which has extended the Russian boundaries from the Dnieper and Dvina beyond the Vistula, to the Pruth, the Danube and the Black Sea, from the Don and Volga beyond the Caucasus and to the source of the Oxus and Iaxartes Rivers; it is this gang which has made Russia great, powerful and feared, and has opened up for it the way to world domination. . . .

But how could such a gang of adventurers ever gain a position in which they could wield such a powerful influence over European history? Quite simply. They have not created something new out of nothing; they merely knew how to exploit correctly an already present factual situation. For all its successes Russian diplomacy has a palpable material basis.

Let us look at Russia in the middle of the last century. An already gigantic territory inhabited by a race of unusual homogeneity. A sparse, but rapidly increasing population thus assuring a steady increase of power by virtue of the mere passage of time. This population, intellectually stagnating, without initiative, but within the limits of its traditional mode of existence unconditionally available for any use; tough, brave, obedient, inured to all hardships, incomparable soldier material for the wars of that time, when closed masses decided the battle. The country itself, turned toward Europe on one side only, was thus open to attack only at that point; it was without a vital center, the conquest of which could force a peace. Because of its lack of roads, its expanse, its poverty of resources, it was almost absolutely protected from conquest. Here was an unassailable power position made to order for those who understood how to take advantage of it, and who, from this position, could with impunity, permit themselves actions which would have drawn any other power into war after war.

Strong to the point of being unassailable on the defensive, Russia was correspondingly weak on the offensive. The mustering, organization, equipping and movement of its armies internally ran up against the greatest obstacles, and in addition to all these material difficulties was still added the boundless corruption of civil servants and officers. . . .

These weaknesses have never been a secret to the Russian diplomats; accordingly they have at all times avoided war wherever possible, have admitted it only as a last resort, and then only under the most favorable circumstances. The only wars which can suit their purpose are those in which Russia's allies bear the brunt of the burden, sacrifice their territory to the devastation of the battlefield, provide the great bulk of the fighting men—wars in which Russian troops, assigned the role of reserves, are spared from most engagements, but to whom in all great battles the honor of the final decision is reserved with relatively slight sacrifices entailed— as in the war of 1813-15. However a war under such favorable circumstances is not always to be had, and therefore Russian diplomacy prefers to utilize, for its own ends, the conflicting interests and greediness of the other powers, to set these powers against each other and exploit these enmities to the advantage of the Russian policy of conquest. Only against decidedly weaker powers such as Sweden, Turkey or Persia does Czarism wage war on its own account—and in these cases it also need not share the booty with anyone.

But let us return to the Russia of 1760. This homogeneous, unassailable country had for neighbors only countries which either apparently or actually were falling into ruin, which were nearing dissolution and hence were pure raw material for conquest. In the North was Sweden, whose power and prestige had fallen precisely because Charles XII had sought to invade Russia; he had thereby ruined Sweden and made evident the unassailability of Russia. In the South were the Turks. . . . The Turkish power to attack had been broken for 100 years, their defensive power was still considerable, but likewise declining. The best sign of this growing weakness was the beginning of rebellious convulsions among the subject Christians, the Slavs, the Rumanians and the Greeks, who formed the majority of the population of the Balkan peninsula. . . . And then here in the South there beckoned to the greedy conqueror a prize of victory compared to which Europe could produce no equal: the old capital of the Eastern Roman Empire, the metropolis of the whole Greek-Catholic world, the city whose Russian name already proclaimed mastery of the East and the prestige which in the eyes of Eastern Christianity surrounds its possessor—Constantinople—Czarigrad.

Czarigrad as the third Russian capital city beside Moscow and Petersburg—that would mean not only moral dominion over Eastern Christendom but would also be the decisive step toward domination over Europe. That would mean a single sovereign authority over the Black Sea, Asia Minor and the Balkan peninsula. That would mean, whenever the Czar wished it, the closing of the Black Sea to all except Russian merchant and war ships, its transformation into a Russian naval base and an exclusive maneuver area for the Russian fleet, which from this secure reserve position could sally forth through the fortified Bosphorus and retreat back to it as often as it pleased. Then Russia would need to achieve only the same control, direct or indirect, over the Sound and the Danish Belts and it would be unassailable also from the sea.

Domination over the Balkan peninsula would bring Russia to the edge of the Adriatic Sea. And this boundary in the Southwest would be untenable unless the whole Russian frontier, especially in the West, were advanced correspondingly and its power sphere significantly extended. Here, moreover, the circumstances were almost more favorable:

First, Poland, in complete disintegration, a republic of nobles founded on the fleecing and suppression of the peasants, with a Constitution which made any unified national action impossible and accordingly made the country into a prize to be taken with impunity by its neighbors. . . .

On the other side of Poland lay a second country which seemed to be falling irreparably to pieces—Germany. Since the Thirty-Years War the Holy Roman Empire had not been a state except in name. The territorial sovereignty of the princes was gradually approaching ever closer to full sovereignty; their power to defy the Emperor . . . was expressly provided for in the Peace of West-phalia under French and Swedish guarantee. Any strengthening of the central government was thus made dependent on the consent of foreign powers, who had every reason to prevent this strengthening. . . .

This was the situation in Germany at the time of Peter the Great. . . . He did everything possible to become a German prince through acquisition of German territory but in vain: he could only inaugurate the system of marital alliances with the German princes and the diplomatic exploitation of internal German dissensions.

Since the time of Peter this situation has developed considerably more in favor of Russia, due to the rise of Prussia. With this development there grew up within the Empire itself a rival to the German Emperor of almost equal power who perpetuated and exacerbated the division of Germany. And at the same time this rival was always sufficiently weak that he had to rely on the support of either France or Russia—mostly on Russian support—with the result that to the extent to which he emancipated himself from vassallage to the German Empire he fell all the more surely under the bondage of Russia.

Thus there remained in Europe only three powers yet to be reckoned with: Austria, France and England. And to incite these against one another, or to bribe them with the bait of territorial acquisitions was not a difficult art. England and France were still rivals on the sea: France could be had through the prospect of falling heir to territory in Belgium and Germany; Austria was lured by alleged gains at the expense of France, of Prussia, and . . . of Bavaria. Here were to be had strong, indeed overwhelmingly strong allies for every diplomatic action of Russia provided their conflicting interests were clearly exploited. And now, confronting these disintegrating neighboring states, and confronting these three Great Powers which were embroiled in continuous quarrels due to tradition, conditions of economic survival, political and dynastic interests or greed for conquest, and occupied constantly with attempts to outwit each other, stood the unified, homogeneous, youthful, rapidly growing Russia, hardly assailable and fully unconquerable; an unwrought, almost unresistant, plastic raw material—what an opportunity for men of talent and ambition who were striving for power, no matter where or how, provided only that it was real power, a real field for exercising their talent and ambition! And the "enlightened" eighteenth century produced quantities of such men . . . —a noble-bourgeois rationalist International "without fatherland." . . . It was from the rank of this International that . . . Catherine II of Russia drew the elements for her Jesuit order of the Russian diplomatic corps. . . .

Let us now see how this Jesuit order works, how it uses the continually changing goals of the competing Great Powers for the attainment of its own single, never-changing, never lost-sight-of objective: the domination of the world by Russia. . . .

\* \* \*

I shall not go into the details of the first partition of Poland [1772]. However, it should be noted that it was carried out—against the will of the old-fashioned Maria Theresa—mainly by the three great pillars of European enlightenment, Catherine, Frederick and Joseph. The last two, proud of the shining political wisdom with which they cast aside the superstitious faith in established international law, were so shortsighted as not to see how they were binding themselves to Russian Czarism by their participation in the dismemberment of Poland.

Nothing could have been more advantageous to Catherine than these enlightened, princely neighbors. Enlightenment was the slogan of Czarism in Europe during the 18th century as was National Liberation in the nineteenth. There was no land-grab, no outrage, no repression on the part of Czarism which was not carried out under the pretext of enlightenment, of liberalism, of the liberation of nations. And the childish Western European liberals believed it, right down to Gladstone, while the equally simple conservatives believed just as tenaciously in phrases about the protection of legitimacy, the maintenance of order, of religion, of the European balance of power, of the sanctity of treaties—slogans which official Russia simultaneously utters. Russian diplomacy had managed to take in both the great bourgeois parties of Europe. Russian diplomacy alone was allowed to be legitimist and revolutionary, conservative and liberal, orthodox and enlightened in the same breath. One can understand the contempt with which a Russian diplomat looks down on the "educated" West. . . .

Turkey was not forgotten. Russian wars against the Turks always fall in periods when Russia has peace on its Western borders, and, if possible, when Europe is occupied in other quarters. Catherine led two such wars. The first [1768] brought the conquest along the sea of Azov and the independence of the Crimea, which four years later was converted into a Russian province. The second [1787] advanced the borders of Russia from the Bug to the Dniester. In both wars Russian agents had incited the Greeks to revolt against the Turks. Naturally, the insurgents were finally left in the lurch by the Russian government. . . .

The outbreak of the French Revolution [1793] was a new stroke of luck for Catherine. Far from fearing the spread of revolutionary ideas toward Russia, she saw in it only a new opportunity to spread discord among the European states in order that Russia might thereby obtain a free hand. . . . The Revolution gave Catherine the opportunity—under the pretext of fighting Republican France—of chaining Prussia and Austria to Russia again; and at the same time, while they were occupied at the French frontiers, of making new conquests in Poland. Both of them, Austria and Prussia, fell into the trap. And even though Prussia . . . changed its mind in good time, claiming a larger share of Poland, and although Austria likewise had to be paid off with a part of Poland, Catherine was still able once again to collect the biggest prize: almost all of White Russia and the Ukraine were now united with Great Russia. . . .

In Catherine's policy we already find sharply drawn all the essential lines of the Russian foreign policy of today: the incorporation of Poland—even though to begin with, a part of the booty had to be left to the neighbors; . . . Constantinople the great main objective—never to be forgotten, however slowly it must be conquered; . . . the incitement of uprisings by the Christian rayahs in Turkey; finally the happy uniting of liberal and legitimist phrases, so that whenever necessary, the Western European "educated" philistine who believes in phrases, the so-called public opinion can be made a fool of.

At Catherine's death [in 1796] Russia already possessed more than even the most exaggerated national chauvinism could have desired. Everything which bore a Russian name—even including the few Ukranians under Austrian rule—stood under the scepter of her successor, who with full justice could now call himself Autocrat of all the Russians. Not only had access to the sea been won, but on the Baltic as well as the Black Sea Russia possessed an extensive coastline and numerous harbors. Not only Finns, Tartars and Mongolians, but also Lithuanians, Swedes, Poles and Germans stood under Russian dominion. What more did he want? For any other nation that would have been the conclusion. For the Czarist diplomatic corps—the nation was not asked—that was only laying the foundation, in order now to get started in earnest.

The French Revolution had spent its fury and had created for itself a master—Napoleon. It had apparently proven the superior wisdom of Russian diplomacy, which had not let itself be intimidated by the gigantic popular upheaval. Now the rise of Napoleon offered it an opportunity for a new success: Germany was ripening toward the same fate as Poland. But Catherine's successor, Paul [1796-1801], was headstrong, capricious, unpredictable. He crossed the action of the diplomats at every moment. He was unbearable; he had to be removed. To accomplish this end the necessary officers of the guard were easily found. The successor to the throne, Alexander [1801-1825], was in on the conspiracy and covered it up. Paul was strangled to death, and soon began a new campaign for the greater glory of the new Czar, who, because of the manner in which he ascended the throne, had become the life-long servant of the diplomatic Jesuit gang.

Thus it was left to Napoleon to shatter completely the German Empire and to drive the state of dismemberment to its zenith. However, when it came time to settle accounts Russia again stepped forward. . . . Russia and France were both laying claim to the inheritance of the German crown. France had crushed the old Empire by force of arms, it pressed against the tiny states as a direct neighbor along the entire length of the Rhine; the glory of Napoleon's victories and the French army did the rest to cast the petty German princes at his feet. And Russia? Now when it could almost seize the goal sought after for a century, now when Germany lay there helpless and perplexed in full disintegration, and exhausted to the point of death, at just this point was Russia to allow the Corsican upstart to snatch away the booty from under its nose?

Russian diplomacy at once began a campaign to gain supremacy over the petty German states. It was self-evident that this was impossible without a victory over Napoleon. Hence it was of the utmost importance to win over the German princes and so-called German public opinion, in so far as it could be said to exist at all at that time.

The princes were belabored with diplomacy, the philistine public with literature. While Russian cajolery, threats, lies and bribes were lavished on the courts, the public was deluged with mysterious pamphlets in which Russia was praised as the only power which could save and effectively protect Germany. . . . And when the war of 1805 broke out it must have been clear to anyone with his eyes even half-open that only one issue was at stake—whether the petty states were to be formed into a French or into a Russian Rhine Confederation. Fate protected Germany. The Russians and Austrians were defeated at Austerlitz and the new Rhine Confederation thus did not become an outpost of Czarism. The French yoke was at least a modern one, which forced the German petty states to do away with the most crying abuses of their former way of life.

After Austerlitz came the Prussian-Russian alliance . . . and the Peace Treaty of Tilsit in 1807. Here was again evident what a monstrous advantage Russia had from its strategically secure position. Defeated in two campaigns, it won new territory at the expense of its former ally and the alliance with Napoleon for the partition of the world—for Napoleon the West, for Alexander the East!

The first fruit of this alliance was the conquest of Finland. Without even so much as a declaration of war, but with the consent of Napoleon, the Russians marched in. The incompetence, disunity and venality of the Swedish generals assured an easy victory. The bold crossing of the frozen Baltic by Russian units forced a violent change on the throne in Stockholm, and the cession of Finland to Russia. . . .

But Finland was only a prelude. What Alexander was after

was, as always, Czarigrad.   At Tilsit . . . Moldavia and Wallachia
were firmly promised to him by Napoleon, and a division of Turkey was envisaged in which, however, Constantinople was to have
been excluded.   Since 1806 Russia had been at war with Turkey.
This time not only the Greeks but also the Serbs had revolted. But
what was merely irony with reference to the Poles proved to be the
actual truth in the case of the Turks—disorder held them together
The indestructible common soldier, the son of the imperturbable
Turkish peasant, found precisely in this disorder an opportunity to
repair the damage done by the corrupt pashas.   The Turks could
be defeated in a battle but not annihilated, and the Russian armies
advanced but very slowly toward Czarigrad.

However, the price for this "free hand" in the East was adherence to Napoleon's Continental System, the breaking off of all
trade with England.   And at the time that meant commercial ruin
for Russia. . . . The commercial blockade became unbearable.
Economics proved mightier than diplomacy and the Czar put together.   Commerce with England was secretly resumed, the Tilsit
agreements were violated, and war broke out in 1812.

Napoleon, with the combined armies of the entire West, crossed
the Russian borders.   The Poles, who were able to judge the situation, advised him to halt on the Dvina and Dnieper, to reorganize
Poland, and to wait there for the attack of the Russians. A general
of Napoleon's stature must have perceived that this plan was the
right one.   But Napoleon, on the dizzy heights and uncertain base
on which he was standing, could not fight any more long drawn-
out campaigns.   Quick successes, dazzling victories, peace won by
storm were indispensable to him.   He cast the Polish counsel to
the winds, went to Moscow, and by this very action, brought the
Russians to Paris.

The annihilation of the great Napoleonic army on the retreat
from Moscow gave the signal for a general uprising against French
domination in the West. . . . Scarcely eighteen months after
Napoleon's entrance into Moscow, Alexander entered Paris—the
lord and master of Europe.

Betrayed by France, Turkey had concluded the Peace of Bucharest in 1812, and had sacrificed Bessarabia to the Russians.   The

Congress of Vienna brought Russia the Kingdom of Poland, so that now almost nine-tenths of the former Polish territories were united with Russia.  However, the position in Europe which the Czar now obtained was worth more than all that.  He no longer had any competitors on the European continent.  Austria and Prussia had been taken into his tow.  The French Bourbon dynasty had been restored by him and was likewise obedient to him. Sweden had received Norway through him as security for a pro-Czarist policy. . . .

Never before had Russia occupied such a powerful position. But it had also taken a further step beyond its natural boundaries. Although Russian chauvinism may still have had a few pretexts— I will not say justifications—for the conquests of Catherine II, this was certainly no longer true for the conquests of Alexander.  Finland is Finnish and Swedish.  Bessarabia is Rumanian, and Congress Poland is Polish.  There is no longer any question of the uniting of scattered and related ethnic groups which can all be called "Russian"; here we are dealing with the naked conquest by force of foreign territories, with robbery pure and simple.

\* \* \*

With Nicolas [1825-1855] a Czar came to the throne who couldn't have been better suited to the wishes of the Russian diplomatic corps—a mediocre second-lieutenant's nature to whom the *semblance* of overlordship was all-important, and who therefore with this semblance could be managed for any end. . . .

Russian diplomacy had already survived, not only undamaged but with direct profit, so many Western European revolutions, that it was in a position to greet the outbreak of the February Revolution of 1848 as an exceedingly favorable occasion.  That the revolution spread to Vienna and thereby not only removed Metternich, Russia's chief opponent, but also roused the Austrian Slavs— prospective allies of Czarism—out of their slumber; that it struck Berlin and thereby cured of his longing for independence from Russia Frederick William IV, whose aspirations were matched only by his incompetence—what could be more welcome?  Russia was safe from all contagion and Poland was so heavily occupied that it could not budge. And when the revolution spread even to the Danubian provinces, Russian diplomacy had what it wanted: an excuse for a new invasion of Moldavia and Wallachia in order to restore order and to establish Russian domination there more and more firmly.

But this was not enough. Austria, Russia's toughest, most stubborn rival on the borders of the Balkan peninsula, was brought to the brink of ruin by the Hungarian and the Viennese uprising. But a victory of Hungary would have meant the renewed outbreak of the European revolution, and the numerous Poles in the Hungarian army were an assurance that this revolution would not stop again at the Polish frontier. Nicolas feigned magnanimity. He invaded Hungary with his armies, suppressed the Hungarian troops with superior forces, and thereby sealed the defeat of the European revolution. And when Prussia still continued to make attempts at utilizing the revolution to dissolve the German Confederation and at least to subject the North-German petty states to Prussian hegemony, Nicolas called Prussia and Austria before his tribunal in Warsaw and decided in favor of Austria. Prussia was thanked for its many years of submission to Russia, by being shamefully humiliated because momentarily it showed a feeble desire to resist. . . . Not only Hungary, all Europe lay at the feet of the Czar, and that as a direct consequence of the revolution. Was Russian diplomacy not right in being secretly enthusiastic about revolutions in the West?

But the February revolution was nevertheless the first death knell of Czarism. The little mind of the narrow Nicolas could not support such undeserved good fortune. He was too hasty with his advance toward Constantinople; the Crimean War broke out [1853]; England and France came to the aid of Turkey, and Austria was burning with the desire "to stun the world by the magnitude of its ingratitude." . . .

The Crimean War was one single colossal comedy of errors in which at every moment the question was asked: "Who's being swindled here?" But this comedy cost untold treasure and over a million human lives. The first allied troops had hardly landed in Bulgaria, when the Austrians occupied the Danubian provinces, and the Russians withdrew across the Pruth.  By this move Austria interposed itself between both the warring parties on the Danube; a further continuation of the war in this region was possible only with its consent.  But Austria was willing to participate in a war at the Western frontier of Russia. It knew that Russia would never forgive her this brutal ingratitude; accordingly it was willing to side with the allies, but only in return for a serious war, one which would restore Poland and push back the Western borders of Russia appreciably.  Such a war would also have drawn into the alliance Prussia, through whose territory Russia drew all its supplies; a European coalition would have blocked Russia on land and water, and would have attacked with such overwhelming strength that victory would have been beyond doubt.

But this was by no means the intention of England and France. On the contrary, both were happy to be rid of all danger of a serious war by Austria's advance.  What Russia was hoping for— that the allies would turn toward the Crimea and get stuck fast there—was suggested by Palmerston, and Louis Napoleon, over-joyed, grasped the proposal with both hands.  To sally forth from the Crimea into the interior of Russia would have been strategic madness.  Thus the war was happily transformed, into a sham war, and all the chief participants were satisfied.  However, in the long run the Czar Nicolas could not tolerate a situation in which enemy troops entrenched themselves firmly on Russian soil on the edge of his Empire; for him the sham war soon became serious again. However, what in the case of a sham war was for him most favor-able ground was more dangerous for a real war.  Russia's elements of defensive strength, the vast expanse of its thinly populated terri-tory, lacking in roads and poor in raw materials—were turned to Russia's disadvantage as soon as Nicolas concentrated all his com-bat forces at Sebastopol, this single point on the periphery.  The south-Russian steppes, which would have been the grave of any attacker, became the grave of the Russian armies which Nicolas drove one after the other, with a stupid, brutal recklessness peculiarly his own—at last in the dead of winter—into the Crimea. And when the last of these armies, hastily mobilized, barely sup-plied with necessities, and poorly fed, had lost two-thirds of their

effectives on the march—whole battalions perished in the blizzards
—and the survivors were in no condition seriously to attack the
enemy, the inflated empty-headed Nicolas collapsed pitifully, and
he fled from the consequences of his own Caesarist megalomania
by taking poison.

The peace which his successor [Alexander II] now quite hastily
concluded, turned out to be very indulgent. But the internal consequences of the war were all the more serious. In order to be able
to govern absolutely at home, Czarism had to appear outwardly
more than invincible, it had to appear constantly victorious, in
order to be in a position to reward unconditional obedience by the
chauvinistic intoxication of victory, by ever new conquests. And
now Czarism had collapsed miserably just in its externally most
imposing aspect; it had compromised Russia before the world, and
thereby compromised itself before Russia. There followed a terrible disillusionment. The Russian people were too much aroused
by the colossal sacrifices of the war, the Czar had had to rely too
much on their devotion, to be brought back without further ado to
the passivity of unthinking obedience. For gradually even Russia
had developed further both economically and intellectually; beside
the nobility there now stood the beginnings of a second educated
class, the bourgeoisie. In short the new Czar had to play the liberal, but this time *at home*. However, this gave a start to the internal history of Russia, to a movement of minds within the nation
itself and its reflex, public opinion, which henceforth could be less
lightly disregarded, which, although still feeble, was making itself
felt more and more, and thus arose an enemy against which Czarist
diplomacy was to founder. For this sort of diplomacy is possible
only as long as the people remain unconditionally passive, have no
will except that imposed by the government, no function except to
provide soldiers and taxes to achieve the objectives of the diplomats. Once Russian internal development, with its internal party
struggles, had begun, the winning of a constitutional framework
within which this party struggle could be fought without forcible
convulsions, was only a question of time. But in such a situation
the former Russian policy of conquest is a thing of the past; the
changeless constancy of diplomatic objectives is lost in the struggles
of the parties for control; the ability unconditionally to dispose of

the forces of the nation is lost—Russia remains difficult to attack and relatively weak on the offensive, but in other respects it becomes a European country like any other, and the peculiar strength of its former diplomacy is forever broken.

. . . The war had shown that Russia needed railroads and heavy industry, if only for purely military considerations. Consequently the government set about raising a Russian capitalist class. But such a class cannot exist without a proletariat, and to provide the elements of the latter, the so-called emancipation of the serfs had to occur. The peasant paid for his personal freedom by making over the best part of his landed property to the nobles. What remained to him was too little to live on and too much to die on. While the Russian peasant community was thus stricken at its root, the great new bourgeoisie developed at the same time as in a hot-house through railway privileges, protective tariffs and other favors; and thus in city and country a full-scale social revolution was ushered in, in which, once it had been set in motion, could no longer let the minds be at rest. The young bourgeoisie was reflected in a liberal-constitutional movement; the proletariat, which was just coming on the plain, in the movement which is usually called Nihilism. . . .

And here we come to the crux of the matter. The internal development of Russia since 1856 supported by governmental policy has had its effect; the social revolution has taken gigantic steps forward; Russia is becoming daily more westernized; heavy industry, railroads, the conversion of all charges in kind into money payments and the accompanying loosening of the old bases of society are developing with increasing rapidity. But the incompatibility of absolutist Czarism with the newly evolving society grows in the same proportion. Constitutional and revolutionary opposition parties are being formed and the regime can dominate them only through increased brutality. And the Russian diplomatic corps sees with consternation approach the day when the Russian people will take part in the debate and when the settling of its own internal affairs will not leave enough time or inclination to keep it occupied with such trifles as the conquest of Constantinople, India, and world domination. The revolution which in 1848 halted at the Polish frontiers, is now knocking at Russia's gates, and it already has enough allies in the interior, who are merely waiting for the occasion to open the gate.

To be sure, if one reads the Russian papers, one could believe that all Russia is enthusiastically supporting the Czarist policy of conquest; there all is chauvinism, Panslavism, emancipation of the Christians from the Turkish and of the Slavs from the German-Magyar yoke.  But in the first place, everyone knows in what chains the Russian press lies bound; in the second place the regime has nourished this chauvinism and Panslavism for years in all the schools; and thirdly, those papers which express an independent opinion at all are voicing the sentiments of the city population, that is, the newly-formed bourgeoisie, which is naturally interested in new conquests as an expansion of the Russian market.  But this city population forms a vanishing minority in the whole country. As soon as a national assembly gives the vast majority of the Russian people, the peasant population, an opportunity to raise voice, very different things will be heard. . . . A Russian National Assembly, if only to overcome the most urgent internal difficulties, will soon find itself forced to put a decisive barrier in the way of all drives toward new conquests.

The European situation today is governed by three facts: (1) the annexation by Germany of Alsace-Lorraine; (2) the drive of Russian Czarism toward Constantinople; (3) in all countries, the struggle between the proletariat and the bourgeoisie, which is burning with an increasing intense heat, as measured by the thermometer of the socialist movement, which is on the upswing everywhere.

The first two factors determine the current grouping of Europe into two great armed camps.  The German annexation of Alsace-Lorraine makes France an ally of Russia; the Czarist threat to Constantinople makes Austria and even Italy allies of Germany. Both camps are arming for a showdown fight, for a war such as the world has never seen, in which ten to fifteen million armed men will be pitted against each other. . . .

This entire danger of a world war will vanish on the day when the situation in Russia permits the Russian people to draw a thick line through the traditional policy of conquest of the czars, and to attend to their own vital interests at home—interests which are threatened in the extreme—instead of phantasies of world conquest.

On that day Bismarck will lose all the anti-French allies which the Russian threat has driven into his arms. Neither Austria nor Italy will then take the slightest interest in pulling Bismarck's chestnuts out of the fire of a gigantic European war. . . . Then also the mutual rapprochement of Russia—struggling for its freedom—and republican France will not only correspond to the position of both countries, but will no longer endanger the general European situation. Then Bismarck, or whoever succeeds him, will also think three times before he starts a war with France in which neither Russia will cover his flank against Austria, nor Austria his flank against Russia, but in which both of them will rejoice in any defeat he may suffer, and in which it is highly questionable that he can finish with the French alone. Then all sympathies would be on the side of France, and if the worst came to pass, it would be assured against the further loss of territory. Thus rather than unleashing a war, Germany probably would find isolation so unbearable that it would seek an honest settlement with France, and then all the frightful danger of war would be removed; *Europe could disarm*, and of all countries Germany would have gained most.

On the same day Austria will lose its single, historical justification for existence—that of a barrier against the Russian drive toward Constantinople. Once the Bosphorus is no longer threatened by Russia, Europe loses all interest in the continuance of this motley complex of peoples. Then the whole so-called Eastern Question will be equally a matter of indifference—the continuation of Turkish hegemony over the Slavic, Greek and Albanian territories, and the fight for possession of the entrance to the Black Sea, which no one will then be able to monopolize against Europe. Magyars, Rumanians, Serbs, Bulgars, Arnauts, Greeks, and Turks will then finally be in a position to settle their own mutual disputes without the intervention of foreign powers, to settle among themselves the boundaries of their individual national territories, to manage their internal affairs according to their own judgments. It can be seen at a glance that the great obstacle to the autonomy and free grouping of the peoples and ethnic fragments between the Carpathian mountains and the Aegean sea has been nothing but the very Czarism which has used the alleged liberation of these peoples as a cloak for its own plans for world domination.

France will be freed from the unnatural, forced position in which the alliance with the Czar has bound it. If the alliance with a republic is repugnant to the Czar, the bond with the despot, the muzzler of Poland and Russia, is even more repugnant to the revolutionary French people. . . . But if instead of the mighty Czar there were in Russia a National Assembly, then the alliance of the newly emancipated Russia with the French Republic would be a self-evident and natural one. Such an alliance would further instead of blocking the revolutionary movement in France, it would be a gain for the European proletariat struggling for its emancipation. Thus France would also profit by the fall of the Czarist autocracy.

At the same time all pretexts would vanish for the mad armaments race which is turning all Europe into an armed camp, and which makes war seem almost a relief. Even the German Reichstag would then soon block the incessantly increasing demands for military expenditures.

At this point, undisturbed by foreign diversions and intervention, the West would be in a position to occupy itself with its present historical mission: with the conflict between the proletariat and the bourgeoisie, and the transforming of the capitalist into the socialist society.

But the fall of the Czarist autocracy in Russia would also directly accelerate this process. On the day when the Czarist power falls— this last, powerful fortress of the entire European reaction—on that day a totally different wind will blow throughout all of Europe. For the reactionary governments of Europe know one thing for sure: in spite of all their quarrels with the Czar over Constantinople, etc., the moment may come when they will toss in his lap everything he has so far demanded—Constantinople, the Bosphorus, the Dardanelles, and anything else he asks—if he will only protect them against the Revolution. Therefore, on the day when this main fortress itself passes into the hands of the Revolution, then the last spark of self-assurance and security will die in the reactionary governments of Europe. They will then be thrown back on their own resources, and will soon discover what a difference that makes. Perhaps they may be in a position to order out their armies to restore the authority of the Czar—what an irony of history!

These are the reasons why Western Europe generally, and the Western European labor parties specifically, are interested, very deeply interested in the victory of the Russian revolutionary party and the fall of the Czarist absolutism. As if on an inclined plane, Europe is sliding with increasing speed into the abyss of a world war, a war of as yet unheard-of extent and violence. Only one thing can now halt it: a change of the regime in Russia. This must come within a few years, of that there can be no doubt. Let us hope that it may yet come in time, before the otherwise unavoidable happens.

# DOCUMENTS ON THE BEGINNINGS OF SOVIET FOREIGN POLICY*

[1917-1918]

1. DECREE OF PEACE, PASSED BY THE SECOND ALL-RUSSIAN CONGRESS OF SOVIETS OF WORKERS', SOLDIERS', AND PEASANTS' DEPUTIES—8 NOVEMBER 1917

The Workers' and Peasants' Government, created by the revolution of 24-25 October [6-7 November], and based on the Soviets of Workers', Soldiers', and Peasants' Deputies, proposes to all belligerent peoples and their Governments the immediate opening of negotiations for a just and democratic peace.

An overwhelming majority of the workers and the labouring classes of all the belligerent countries, exhausted, tormented, and racked by war, are longing for a just and democratic peace—a peace which in the mose definite and insistent manner has been demanded by the Russian workers and peasants since the overthrow of the Tsarist monarchy. By such a peace the Government understands an immediate peace without annexations (i.e. without seizure of foreign territory, without the forcible incorporation of foreign nationalities), and without indemnities.

The Government of Russia proposes to all belligerent nations to conclude such a peace immediately. It expresses its readiness to take at once, without the slightest delay, all the decisive steps pending the final ratification of all the terms of such a peace by the plenipotentiary assemblies of the representatives of all countries and all nations.

By annexation or seizure of foreign territory the Government understands, in accordance with the sense of justice of democracy in general, and of the labouring classes in particular, the incorporation into a large or powerful State of a small or weak nationality, without the definitely, clearly, and voluntarily expressed consent and desire of this nationality, regardless of when this forcible incorporation took place, regardless also of the degree of

---

*From *Soviet Documents on Foreign Policy*, Vol. I, selected and edited by Jane Degras. Oxford University Press 1951. Reprinted by permission.

development or backwardness of the nation forcibly annexed or forcibly retained within the frontiers of the given State, and finally, regardless of whether this nation is located in Europe or in distant lands beyond the seas.

If any nation whatsoever is retained as part of a given State by force, if, despite its expressed desire—whether expressed in the press, in popular assemblies, in the decisions of political parties, or by rebellions and insurrections against national oppression, it has not the right of choosing freely—the troops of the annexing or, generally, the more powerful nation being completely withdrawn and without any pressure being brought to bear—the constitutional forms of its national existence, then its incorporation ¬ annexation, that is, seizure and coercion.

Government considers it the greatest crime against humanity tinue this war for the sake of dividing among the powerful and wealthy nations the weaker nationalities which they have conquered, and the Government solemnly declares its determination to sign immediately terms of peace which will put an end to this war, on the conditions here stated, which are equally just for all nationalities without exception. At the same time the Government declares that it does not regard these conditions as in the nature of an ultimatum; that is, it is ready to consider any other terms of peace, insisting, however, that they be proposed as soon as possible by any one of the belligerent countries and that they be presented with the utmost clarity and to the absolute exclusion of any ambiguity, or any secrecy.

The Government abolishes secret diplomacy and on its part expresses the firm intention to conduct all negotiations absolutely openly before the entire people; it will at once begin to publish in full the secret treaties concluded or confirmed by the Government of landowners and capitalists from February to 25 October [7 November] 1917. The Government denounces absolutely and immediately all the provisions of these secret treaties designed, as they were in the majority of cases, to secure profits and privileges for Russian landowners and capitalists, and to retain or increase the territories annexed by the Great Russians.

While proposing to the Governments and peoples of all countries to start immediately open negotiations for the conclusion of peace the Government expresses its readiness to conduct these negotiations by written communications, by telegraph, as well as by negotiations with representatives of the different countries, or at a conference of such representatives. To facilitate such negotiations the Government is appointing a plenipotentiary representative in neutral countries.

The Government proposes to all the Governments and peoples of all the belligerent countries to conclude an armistice immediately, and it considers it desirable that this armistice should be concluded for a period of not less than three months—that is, a period quite long enough to complete the peace negotiations with the participation of the representatives of all peoples and nationalities, without exception, drawn into the war or compelled to take part in it, as well as to convene the plenipotentiary assemblies of people's representatives of all countries for the final ratification of the terms of peace.

While addressing this proposal of peace to the Governments and peoples of all the belligerent countries, the Provisional Workers' and Peasants' Government of Russia appeals also in particular to the class-conscious workers of the three most advanced nations of the world and the three mightiest States taking part in the present war—England, France, and Germany. The workers of these countries have been of the greatest service to the cause of progress and socialism. The great example of the Chartist movement in England, the series of revolutions, of universal historic importance, made by the French proletariat, and finally, the heroic struggle against the anti-Socialist law in Germany and the prolonged, stubborn, disciplined work—setting an example to the workers of the world—of creating mass proletarian organizations in Germany—all these examples of proletarian heroism and historic creative work serve as a pledge that the workers of these countries will understand the duty which now rests upon them of saving mankind from the horrors of war and its consequences, that these workers by their resolute and vigorous activity will help us to bring to a successful end the cause of peace, and, together with this, the cause of the liberation of all who labour and are exploited from every kind of slavery and exploitation.

2. EXTRACTS FROM A STATEMENT BY TROTSKY ON THE INTER-
   NATIONAL SITUATION AT THE CENTRAL EXECUTIVE COM-
   MITTEE—21 NOVEMBER 1917

Our policy in the field of international relations is dictated by the decree on peace adopted by the All-Russian Congress of Soviets. The very fact of its adoption was unexpected for the old routine habits of thought of the European bourgeois world, and the decree was first taken as a party declaration rather than as a definite act of State power. It was not until the lapse of some time that the ruling classes of Europe began to realize that they were dealing with a proposal emanating from a State which represented many millions of people. The bourgeoisie of the Allied countries adopted an extremely hostile attitude towards this decree. The attitude of the Governments of the enemy countries was ambiguous, and could not have been otherwise. On the one hand, the revolution interested them as a means of aggravating the confusion in Russia and of improving their own military prospects, and this was a cause for rejoicing. On the other hand, in so far as they understood that they were dealing not with an ephemeral phenomenon, capable only of disorganizing, in so far as they saw that the Soviet Government was supported by the large armed masses, to that extent they could not fail to recognize that the victory of the Soviets was a fact of the greatest international importance. In this respect the attitude in Germany towards the news of the victory over Kerensky is significant. Our broadcast from Tsarskoe Selo was picked up by the Austrians, but the Hamburg radio tried to jam the broadcast of the telegram. The ambiguity in the German attitude consists in the fact that as Germans they are ready to rejoice; as bourgeois propertied classes they see that they have cause to fear. . . .

In western Europe the mood was one of waiting. There was lack of confidence in the new Soviet Government. The mass of the workers had confidence in the Government, but there was fear that it would not be able to survive. Now the Government has been established as a reality in both capitals of the country, in many important provincial centres, among the vast majority of the army, and it is attracting the peasant masses. These facts are indisputable. . . .

Now even the most hardened European diplomats appreciate that it is impossible to smash the Soviet Government either in a day, or in a week. They are confronted with the complete political helplessness of the bourgeoisie in Russia, in spite of its enormous economic power. They have to reckon with the Soviet Government as a fact, and to establish certain relations with it. These relations are being formed empirically, in practice; the agents of the European Powers are compelled to approach us with all sorts of questions concerning current matters, such as questions of leaving or entering the country, etc. With regard to political relations, this is not uniform on the part of the various Powers. Probably the most hostile of them is the Government of Great Britain, the country whose upper bourgeoisie risk losing less than anybody else from the war, and hope to gain most. The drawn-out nature of the war is not in the least inconsistent with British policy. As to France, the majority of the petty-bourgeois democracy are peacefully inclined, but they are helpless. The petty-bourgeois Cabinet is dependent on the Stock Exchange. The small French shopkeeper is a pacifist and does not personally know anything about those secret treaties and imperialist aims for which he sheds his blood. France had suffered most from the war. France feels that the prolongation of the war threatens it with degeneration and death. The struggle of the working class against war is growing. The acuteness of the situation in France and the growth of the opposition on the part of the working class within the country has led to France reacting to the creation of Soviet power by forming the Clemenceau Ministry. Clemenceau is a radical of the extreme jacobin chauvinist wing. In the course of three years of war he could not form his own Ministry; the Clemenceau Ministry now formed without the participation of the socialists and directed against the socialists is a convulsion of the French petty-bourgeois democracy, terror-stricken by the setting up of the Soviet Government. Petty-bourgeois France considers us to be a Government in alliance with Wilhelm, and perhaps a Government of struggle against France.

The scanty news from Italy speaks about the enthusiasm with which the working class greeted the Soviet Government. Italy hesitated for nine months which camp it would be more advantageous to join, and in the course of those nine months the working class of Italy had an opportunity of recognizing the fatal effect of collaboration of the proletariat with the bourgeoisie.   As to the middle classes and the peasantry, they became disillusioned in this war, and this disillusionment provided a favourable sounding-board for the protesting voice of the proletariat.

The United States began to intervene in the war after three years, under the influence of the sober calculations of the American Stock Exchange.   America could not tolerate the victory of one coalition over the other.   America is interested in the weakening of both coalitions and in the consolidation of the hegemony of American capital.   Apart from that, American war industry is interested in the war.   During the war American exports have more than doubled and have reached a figure not reached by any other capitalist State.   Exports go almost entirely to the Allied countries. When in January Germany came out for unrestricted U-boat warfare, all railway stations and harbours in the United States were overloaded with the output of the war industries.   Transport was disorganized and New York witnessed food riots such as we ourselves have never seen here.   Then the finance capitalists sent an ultimatum to Wilson: to secure the sale of the output of the war industries within the country.   Wilson accepted the ultimatum, and hence the preparations for war and war itself.   America does not aim at territorial conquests; America can be tolerant with regard to the existence of the Soviet Government, since it is satisfied with the exhaustion of the Allied countries and Germany. Apart from that America is interested in investing its capital in Russia.

As to Germany, its internal economic situation forces it to take up an attitude of semi-tolerance towards the Soviet Government. The peace proposals made by Germany are partly feelers: partly they were dictated by the anxiety to lay responsibility for the continuation of the war on the other side.

All the news we have about the impression made in Europe by the decree on peace proves that our most optimistic assumptions were justified.   The German working class is fully aware of what is happening in Russia at present; perhaps it appreciates these events even better than people in Russia itself.   The actions of the working class in Russia are more revolutionary than their consciousness; but the consciousness of the European working class has developed over decades; and, starting from a class analysis of the events now taking place in Russia, the proletariat of the West understands that power has not been seized here by a handful of conspirators with the support of the Red Guard and the sailors, as the bourgeois press tries to make out; it understands that here a new epoch in the history of the world is beginning. The working class have taken the machinery of state into their own hands, and this machinery must necessarily become the instrument of the struggle for peace. A fatal blow was dealt to war on the historic night of 25 October [7 November]. War as a colossal enterprise of the various classes and groups is dead. The European Governments are no longer concerned with the realization of their initial aims, but with the liquidation of this enterprise with the least possible damage to their rule. It is not possible for either side to think of victory; and the intervention of the working class in this conflict is a factor of immeasurable importance. The decree on peace is being widely broadcast throughout Europe. The war is at its last gasp and it is the task of the Soviet Government to deal it a final blow by the formal proposal of peace negotiations.

The secret treaties are in my possession. The senior officials of the Ministry, Neratov and Tatishchev, have handed them to me voluntarily, as far as one can speak at all of voluntary consent. These are not treaties written on parchment; they are in essentials diplomatic correspondence and coded telegrams exchanged between Governments. I shall begin their publication tomorrow. They are even more cynical in their contents than we supposed, and we do not doubt that when the German Social Democrats obtain access to the safes in which the secret treaties are kept, they will show us that German imperialism in its cynicism and rapacity yields in nothing to the rapacity of the Allied countries.

3. STATEMENT BY TROTSKY ON THE PUBLICATION OF THE
   SECRET TREATIES—22 NOVEMBER 1917

In publishing the secret diplomatic documents from the foreign policy archives of Tsarism and of the bourgeois coalition Governments of the first seven months of the revolution, we are carrying out the undertaking which we made when our party was in opposition.  Secret diplomacy is a necessary tool for a propertied minority which is compelled to deceive the majority in order to subject it to its interests.  Imperialism, with its dark plans of conquest and its robber alliances and deals developed the system of secret diplomacy to the highest level.  The struggle against the imperialism which is exhausting and destroying the peoples of Europe is at the same time a struggle against capitalist diplomacy, which has cause enough to fear the light of day.  The Russian people, and the peoples of Europe and the whole world, should learn the documentary truth about the plans forced in secret by the financiers and industrialists together with their parliamentary and diplomatic agents.  The peoples of Europe have paid for the right to this truth with countless sacrifices and universal economic desolation.

The abolition of secret diplomacy is the primary condition for an honest, popular, truly democratic foreign policy.  The Soviet Government regards it as its duty to carry out such a policy in practice.  That is precisely why, while openly proposing an immediate armistice to all the belligerent peoples and their Governments, we are at the same time publishing these treaties and agreements, which have lost all binding force for the Russian workers, soldiers, and peasants who have taken power into their own hands.

The bourgeois politicians and journalists of Germany and Austria-Hungary may try to make use of the documents published in order to present the diplomacy of the Central Empires in a more advantageous light.  But any such attempt would be doomed to pitiful failure, and that for two reasons.  In the first place, we intend quickly to place before the tribunal of public opinion secret documents which treat sufficiently clearly of the diplomacy of the Central Empires.  Secondly, and more important, the methods of secret diplomacy are as universal as imperialist robbery.  When the German proletariat enters the revolutionary path leading to the secrets of their chancelleries, they will extract documents no whit inferior to those which we are about to publish.  It only remains to hope that this will take place quickly.

The workers' and peasants' Government abolishes secret diplomacy and its intrigues, codes, and lies.  We have nothing to hide.  Our programme expresses the ardent wishes of millions of workers, soldiers, and peasants. We want peace as soon as possible on the basis of decent co-existence and collaboration of the peoples. We want the rule of capital to be overthrown as soon as possible. In exposing to the entire world the work of the ruling classes, as expressed in the secret diplomatic documents, we address the workers with the call which forms the unchangeable foundation of our foreign policy: "Proletarians of all countries, unite."

4. APPEAL FROM THE PEOPLE'S COMMISSARIAT FOR FOREIGN AFFAIRS TO THE TOILING, OPPRESSED, AND EXHAUSTED PEOPLES OF EUROPE—19 DECEMBER 1917

An armistice has been signed at Brest-Litovsk. Military operations on the eastern front have been suspended for twenty-eight days. This in itself is a tremendous victory for humanity. After nearly three and a half years of uninterrupted slaughter, with no issue in sight, the workers' and peasants' revolution in Russia has opened the way to peace.

We have published the secret treaties. We shall continue publishing them in the immediate future. We have declared that these treaties will in no way bind the policy of the Soviet Government. We have proposed to all nations the way of open agreement on the principle of the recognition for each nation, great or small, advanced or backward, of the right freely to determine its own destiny. We do not attempt to conceal the fact that we do not consider the existing capitalist Governments capable of making a democratic peace. The revolutionary struggle of the toiling masses against the existing Governments can alone bring Europe nearer to such a peace.

Its full realization can only be guaranteed by the victorious proletarian revolution in all capitalist countries.

While entering into negotiations with the existing Governments, which on both sides are permeated through and through with imperialist tendencies, the Council of People's Commissars has never for a moment deviated from the path of social revolution. A truly democratic people's peace will still have to be fought for. The first round in this struggle finds in power, everywhere except in Russia, the old monarchist and capitalist Governments which were responsible for the present war, and which have not yet accounted to their duped peoples for the waste of blood and treasure. We are forced to begin negotiations with the Governments which are now in existence, just as, on the other hand, the monarchist and reactionary Governments of the Central Powers are forced to carry on negotiations with the representatives of the Soviet Government, because the Russian people have confronted them with the fact of a workers' and peasants' Government in Russia. In negotiating for peace the Soviet Government has set itself a double task: first, to bring to an end as quickly as possible the disgraceful and criminal slaughter which is laying Europe waste; and second, to use all the means at our disposal to help the working class in all lands to overthrow the rule of capital and to seize political power in order to reconstruct Europe and the whole world on democratic and socialist lines.

An armistice has been signed on the eastern front. But on the other fronts the slaughter is still going on. Peace negotiations are only just beginning. It should be clear to socialists in all countries, but especially to socialists in Germany, that there is an irreconcilable difference between the peace programme of the Russian workers and peasants and that of the German capitalists, landowners, and generals. If there were nothing but the clash of these two policies, peace would obviously be impossible, for the Russian people have not overthrown the monarchy and bourgeoisie in their own lands merely to bow before the monarchs and capitalists of other lands. Peace can only be brought nearer, realized and guaranteed, if the voice of the workers makes itself heard firmly and resolutely, both in Germany and in the lands of its allies. The German, Austro-Hungarian, Bulgarian, and Turkish workers must oppose to the imperialist programme of their ruling classes their own revolutionary programme of agreement and co-operation between the labouring and exploited classes in all countries.

An armistice has been signed on one front only. Our delegation, after a long struggle, wrung from the German Government, as one of the conditions of the armistice, an undertaking not to transfer troops to other fronts. Thus, those German troops which are stationed between the Black Sea and the Baltic are to have a month's respite from the gruesome nightmare of war. The Rumanian army also, against the will of the Rumanian Government, adhered to the armistice. But on the French, Italian, and all other fronts the war is still going on. The truce remains partial. The capitalist Governments fear peace, because they know they will have to render an account to their people. They are trying to postpone the hour of their final bankruptcy. Are the nations willing to go on patiently enduring the criminal activities of Stock Exchange cliques in France, Great Britain, Italy, and the United States?

The capitalistic Governments of these countries conceal their abject and greedy calculations under fine talk about eternal justice and the future society of nations. They do not want an armistice. They are fighting against peace, but you, peoples of Europe, you, workers of France, Italy, England, Belgium, Serbia, you, our brothers in suffering and struggle, do not you, together with us, want peace—an honourable, democratic peace among nations?

Those who tell you that peace can only be guaranteed by victory are deceiving you. In the first place, they have been unable, in the course of nearly three and a half years, to give you victory, and show no signs of doing so should the war go on for years longer. And in the second place, if victory should appear possible for one side or the other, it would only mean further coercion of the weak by the strong, thus sowing the seeds of future wars.

Belgium, Serbia, Rumania, Poland, the Ukraine, Greece, Persia, and Armenia can only be liberated by the workers in all belligerent and neutral countries in the victorious struggle against all imperialists, and not by the victory of one of the imperialist coalitions.

We summon you to this struggle, workers of all countries! There is no other way. The crimes of the ruling, exploiting classes in this war have been countless. These crimes cry out for revolutionary revenge. Toiling humanity would be forswearing itself and its future if it continued meekly to bear on its shoulders the yoke of the imperialist bourgeoisie and militarists, their Governments and their diplomacy.

We, the Council of People's Commissars, empowered by the Russian workers, peasants, soldiers, sailors, widows, and orphans, we summon you to common struggle with us for the immediate cessation of hostilities on all fronts. May the news of the signing of the armistice at Brest-Litovsk ring like a tocsin for the soldiers and workers in all the belligerent countries.

Down with the war! Down with its authors! The Governments opposing peace and the Governments masking aggressive intentions behind talk of peace must be swept away. The workers and soldiers must wrest the business of war and peace from the criminal hands of the bourgeoisie and take it into their own hands. We have the right to demand this from you, because this is what we have done in our own country. This is the only path to salvation for you and for us. Close up your ranks, proletarians of all countries, under the banner of peace and the social revolution!

5. DECREE OF THE COUNCIL OF PEOPLE'S COMMISARS APPROPRIATING TWO MILLION RUBLES FOR THE INTERNATIONAL REVOLUTIONARY MOVEMENT—26 DECEMBER 1917

Taking into consideration that the Soviet Government is based on the principles of the international solidarity of the proletariat and on the brotherhood of the toilers of all countries; that the struggle against war and imperialism can be brought to a completely successful conclusion only if waged on an international scale, the Council of People's Commissars considers it necessary to offer assistance by all possible means, to the left internationalist wing of the labour movement of all countries, regardless of whether these countries are at war with Russia, in alliance with Russia, or neutral.

For this purpose the Council of People's Commissars decides to allocate two million rubles for the needs of the revolutionary international movement and to put this sum at the disposal of the foreign representatives of the Commissariat for Foreign Affairs.

6. THESES BY LENIN ON THE QUESTION OF A SEPARATE PEACE WITH GERMANY—20 JANUARY 1918

1. The position of the Russian revolution at the present moment is that nearly all the workers and the vast majority of the peasants are undoubtedly in favour of Soviet government and of the Socialist revolution which it has started. To that extent the Socialist revolution in Russia is assured.

2. At the same time, the civil war, provoked by the frantic resistance of the wealthy classes, who fully realize that they are faced with the last, decisive fight for the preservation of private ownership of the land and means of production, has not yet reached its climax. The victory of Soviet government in this war is assured, but some time must inevitably elapse, no little exertion of effort will inevitably be demanded, a certain period of acute economic disruption and chaos, such as attend all wars, and civil war in particular, is inevitable, before the resistance of the bourgeoisie is crushed.

3. Furthermore, this resistance, in its less active and non-military forms—sabotage, corruption of the declassed elements and of agents of the bourgeoisie, who worm their way into the ranks of the Socialists in order to ruin their cause, and so on and so forth— has proved so stubborn and capable of assuming such diversified forms, that the fight to counter it will inevitably still take some time, and, in its main forms, is scarcely likely to end before several months. And unless the passive and covert resistance of the bourgeoisie and its supporters is definitely crushed, the Socialist revolution cannot possibly succeed.

4. Lastly, the organizational problems of the Socialist reformation of Russia are so immense and difficult that their solution—in view of the abundance of petty-bourgeois fellow-travellers of the Socialist proletariat, and of the latter's low cultural level—will demand a fairly long time.

5. All these circumstances taken together are such as to make it perfectly clear that for the success of Socialism in Russia a certain amount of time, not less than several months at least, will be necessary, during which the hands of the Socialist Government must be absolutely free for the job of vanquishing the bourgeoisie in our own country first, and of arranging widespread and far-reaching mass organizational work.

6. The situation of the Socialist revolution in Russia must form the basis of any definition of the international tasks of our Soviet state, for the international situation in the fourth year of the war is such that it is quite impossible to calculate the probable moment of outbreak of revolution or overthrow of any of the European imperialist governments (including the German). That the Socialist revo-

lution in Europe must come, and will come, is beyond doubt. All our hopes for the *final* victory of Socialism are founded on this certainty and on this scientific prognosis. Our propagandist activities in general, and the organization of fraternization in particular, must be intensified and extended. But it would be a mistake to base the tactics of the Russian Socialist Government on an attempt to determine whether the European, and especially the German, Socialist revolution will take place in the next six months (or some such brief period), or not. Inasmuch as it is quite impossible to determine this, all such attempts, objectively speaking, would be nothing but a blind gamble.

7. The peace negotiations in Brest-Litovsk have by this date—7 [20] January 1918—made it perfectly clear that the upper hand in the German government (which leads the other governments of the Quadruple Alliance by the halter) has undoubtedly been gained by the military party, which has virtually already presented Russia with an ultimatum (and it is to be expected, most certainly to be expected, that any day now it will be presented formally). The ultimatum is as follows: either the continuation of the war, or an annexationist peace, i.e., peace on condition that we surrender all the territory we occupy, while the Germans retain *all* the territory they occupy and impose upon us an indemnity (outwardly disguised as payment for the maintenance of prisoners)—an indemnity of about three thousand million rubles, payable over a period of several years.

8. The Socialist government of Russia is faced with the question—a question which brooks no postponement—of whether to accept this annexationist peace now, or at once to wage a revolutionary war. Actually speaking, no middle course is possible. No further postponement is now feasible, for we have *already* done everything possible and impossible artificially to protract the negotiations.

9. Examining the arguments in favour of an immediate revolutionary war, the first we encounter is the argument that a separate peace at this juncture would, objectively speaking, be tantamount to an agreement with the German imperialists, an "imperialistic deal," and so forth, and that, consequently, such a peace would be

at complete variance with the fundamental principles of proletarian internationalism.

But this argument is clearly incorrect. Workers who lose a strike and sign terms for the resumption of work which are un-favourable to them and favourable to the capitalists, do not betray Socialism. Only those betray Socialism who barter to secure ad-vantages for a section of the workers in exchange for advantages to the capitalists; only such agreements are impermissible in principle.

Whoever calls a war with German imperialism a defensive and just war, but actually receives support from the Anglo-French imperialists, and conceals from the people secret treaties concluded with them, betrays Socialism. Whoever, without concealing any-thing from the people, and without concluding any secret treaties with the imperialists, agrees to terms of peace which are unfavour-able to the weak nation and favourable to the imperialists of one group, if at the given moment he has no strength to continue the war, does not betray Socialism in the slightest degree.

10. Another argument in favour of immediate war is that, by concluding peace, we, objectively speaking, become agents of Ger-man imperialism, for we afford it the opportunity to release troops from our front, surrender to it millions of prisoners, and the like. But this argument too is clearly incorrect, for a revolutionary war at the present juncture would, objectively speaking, make us agents of Anglo-French imperialism, by providing it with forces which would promote its aims. The British bluntly offered our commander-in-chief, Krylenko, one hundred rubles per month for every one of our soldiers provided we continued the war. Even if we did not take a single kopek from the Anglo-French, we never-theless would be helping them, objectively speaking, by diverting part of the German army.

From that point of view, in neither case would we be entirely escaping some sort of imperialist tie, and it is obvious that it is impossible to do so entirely without overthrowing world imperial-ism. The correct conclusion from this is that the moment a Social-ist government triumphs in any one country, questions must be decided, not from the point of view of whether this or that im-perialism is preferable, but exclusively from the point of view of the conditions which best make for the development and consolidation of the Socialist revolution which has already begun.

In other words, the underlying principle of our tactics must not be, which of the two imperialisms is it more profitable to aid at this juncture, but rather, how can the Socialist revolution be most surely and reliably ensured the possibility of consolidating itself, or, at least, of maintaining itself in one country until it is joined by other countries.

11. It is said that the German Social-Democratic opponents of the war have now become "defeatists" and are requesting us not to yield to German imperialism. But we recognized defeatism only in respect to *one's own* imperialist bourgeoisie, and we always discountenanced victory over an alien imperialism, victory attained in formal or actual alliance with a "friendly" imperialism, as a method impermissible in principle and generally obnoxious.

This argument is therefore only a modification of the previous one. If the German Left Social-Democrats were proposing that we delay concluding a separate peace for a *definite* period, and guaranteed revolutionary action in Germany in this period, the question *might* assume a different aspect for us. But far from saying this, the German Lefts formally declare: "Stick it out as long as you can, but decide the question from the standpoint of the state of affairs in the *Russian* Socialist revolution, for we cannot promise you anything positive regarding the German revolution."

12. It is said that in a number of party statements we positively "promised" a revolutionary war, and that by concluding a separate peace we would be going back on our word.

That is not true. We said that in the era of imperialism it was *necessary* for a Socialist government to *"prepare for and wage"* a revolutionary war; we said this as a means of countering abstract pacificism and the theory that "defense of the fatherland" must be completely rejected in the era of imperialism, and, lastly, as a means of countering the purely egoistical instincts of a part of the soldiery, but we never gave any pledge to start a revolutionary war without taking account of how far it is possible to wage it at any given moment.

Unquestionably, even at this juncture we must *prepare* for a revolutionary war. We are carrying out this promise, as we have in general carried out all our promises that could be carried out at once; we annulled the secret treaties, offered all nations a fair peace, and several times did our best to drag out peace negotiations so as to give other nations a chance to join us.

But the question whether it is possible to wage a revolutionary war *now and at once* must be decided exclusively from the standpoint of whether material conditions permit it, and of the interests of the Socialist revolution which has already begun.

13. Having weighed up the arguments in favour of an immediate revolutionary war, we are forced to the conclusion that such a policy might perhaps answer the human yearning for the beautiful, dramatic and striking, but that it would absolutely ignore the objective relation of class forces and material factors in the present stage of the Socialist revolution which has begun.

14. There can be no doubt but that our army is absolutely in no condition at the present moment, and will not be for the next few weeks (and probably for the next few months), to resist a German offensive successfully; firstly, owing to the extreme fatigue and exhaustion of the majority of the soldiers, coupled with the incredible chaos in the matter of victualling, replacement of the overfatigued, etc.; secondly, owing to the utter unfitness of our horses, which would doom our artillery to inevitable destruction; and thirdly, owing to the utter impossibility of defending the coast from Riga to Reval, which affords the enemy a certain chance of conquering the rest of Livonia, and then Esthonia, and of outflanking a large part of our forces, and lastly, of capturing Petrograd.

15. Further there is not the slightest doubt that the peasant majority of our army would at the present juncture unreservedly declare in favour of an annexationist peace, and not of an immediate revolutionary war; for the Socialist reorganization of the army, the merging of the Red Guard detachments with it, and the like, have only just begun.

With the army completely democratized, to wage war in defiance of the wishes of the majority of the soldiers would be sheer recklessness, while to create a really staunch and ideologically-strong Socialist workers' and peasants' army will require months and months, at least.

16. The poor peasants in Russia are capable of supporting a

Socialist revolution led by the working class, but they are not capable of a serious revolutionary war immediately, at the present juncture. To ignore this objective relation of class forces in the present instance would be a fatal error.

17. Consequently, the situation at present in regard to a revolutionary war is as follows:

If the German revolution were to break out and triumph in the coming three or four months, the tactics of an immediate revolutionary war might perhaps not ruin our Socialist revolution.

If, however, the German revolution does not eventuate in the next few months, the course of events, if the war is continued, will inevitably be such that a smashing defeat will compel Russia to conclude a far more disadvantageous separate peace, a peace, moreover, which would be concluded, not by a Socialist government, but by some other (for example, a bloc of the bourgeois Rada and the Chernovites or something similar). For the peasant army, which is unendurably exhausted by the war, will, after the first defeats—and very likely within a matter not of months but of weeks—overthrow the Socialist workers' government.

18. Such being the state of affairs, it would be absolutely impermissible tactics to stake the fate of the Socialist revolution which has begun in Russia merely on the chance that the German revolution may begin in the immediate future, within a period measurable in weeks. Such tactics would be a reckless gamble. We have no right to take such risks.

19. And the German revolution will not be jeopardized, as far as its objective foundations are concerned, if we conclude a separate peace. Probably the chauvinist intoxication will weaken it for a time, but Germany's position will remain extremely grave, the war with Britain and America will be a protracted one, and the aggressive imperialism of both sides has been fully and completely exposed. A Socialist Soviet Republic in Russia will stand as a living example to the peoples of all countries, and the propaganda and revolutionizing effect of this example will be immense. There—the bourgeois system and an absolutely naked war of aggrandizement of two groups of marauders. Here—peace and a Socialist Soviet Republic.

20. In concluding a separate peace we free ourselves *as much*

*as is possible at the present moment from* both hostile imperialist groups, we take advantage of their mutual enmity and warfare—which hamper concerted action on their part against us—and for a certain period have our hands free to advance and consolidate the Socialist revolution. The reorganization of Russia on the basis of the dictatorship of the proletariat, and the nationalization of the banks and large-scale industry, coupled with exchange of products in kind between the towns and the small peasants-consumers' societies, is economically quite feasible, provided we are assured a few months in which to work in peace. And such a reorganization will render Socialism invincible both in Russia and all over the world, and at the same time will create a solid economic basis for a mighty workers' and peasants' Red Army.

21. A really revolutionary war at this juncture would mean a war waged by a Socialist republic on the bourgeois countries, with the aim—an aim clearly defined and fully approved by the Socialist army—of overthrowing the bourgeoisie in other countries. However, we *obviously* cannot set ourselves this aim at the *given* moment. Objectively, we would be fighting now for the liberation of Poland, Lithuania and Courland. But no Marxist, without flying in the face of the principles of Marxism and of Socialism generally, can deny that the interests of Socialism are higher than the interests of the right of nations to self-determination. Our Socialist republic has done all it could, and continues to do all it can to give effect to the right of self-determination of Finland, the Ukraine, etc. But if the concrete position of affairs is such that the existence of the Socialist republic is being imperilled at the present moment on account of the violation of the right to self-determination of several nations (Poland, Lithuania, Courland, etc.), naturally the preservation of the Socialist republic has the higher claim.

Consequently whoever says, "We cannot sign a shameful, indecent, etc., peace, betray Poland, and so forth", fails to observe that by concluding peace on condition that Poland is liberated, he would only *still further* be strengthening German imperialism against England, Belgium, Serbia and other countries. Peace on condition of the liberation of Poland, Lithuania, and Courland would be a "patriotic" peace *from the point of view of Russia,* but would none the less be a peace with the *annexationists,* with the German imperialists.

# THE NAMELESS BEAST*

BY

## WINSTON S. CHURCHILL

[1929]

At the beginning of the war France and Britain had counted heavily upon Russia. Certainly the Russian effort had been enormous. Nothing had been stinted; everything had been risked. The forward mobilization of the Imperial Armies and their head-long onslaught upon Germany and Austria may be held to have played an indispensable part in saving France from destruction in the first two months of the war. Thereafter in spite of disasters and slaughters on an unimaginable scale Russia had remained a faithful and mighty ally. For nearly three years she had held on her fronts considerably more than half of the total number of enemy divisions, and she had lost in this struggle nearly as many men killed as all the other allies put together. The victory of Brusilov in 1916 had been of important service to France and still more to Italy; and even as late as the summer of 1917, *after the fall of the Czar,* the Kerensky Government was still attempting offensives in aid of the common cause. The endurance of Russia as a prime factor, until the United States had entered the war, ranked second only to the defeat of the German submarines as a final turning-point of the struggle.

But Russia had fallen by the way; and in falling she had changed her identity. An apparition with countenance different from any yet seen on earth stood in the place of the old Ally. We saw a state without a nation, an army without a country, a religion without a God. The Government which claimed to be the new Russia sprang from Revolution and was fed by Terror. It had denounced the faith of treaties; it had made a separate peace; it had released a million Germans for the final onslaught in the West. It had declared that between itself and non-communist society no good

* From *The World Crisis—1918–1928: The Aftermath.* Copyright 1929 by Charles Scribner's Sons, New York. Reprinted by permission.

faith, public or private, could exist and no engagements need be respected. It had repudiated alike all that Russia owed and all that was owing to her. Just when the worst was over, when victory was in sight, when the fruits of measureless sacrifice were at hand, the old Russia had been dragged down, and in her place there ruled "the nameless beast" so long foretold in Russian legend. Thus the Russian people were deprived of Victory, Honor, Freedom, Peace and Bread. Thus there was to be no Russia in the Councils of the Allies—only an abyss which still continues in human affairs.

*    *    *

A retrospect is necessary to explain how this disaster had come upon the world, and to enable the reader to understand its consequences.

The Czar had abdicated on March 15, 1917. The Provisional Government of Liberal and Radical statesmen was almost immediately recognized by the principal Allied Powers. The Czar was placed under arrest; the independence of Poland was acknowledged; and a proclamation issued to the Allies in favor of the self-determination of peoples and a durable peace. The discipline of the fleets and armies was destroyed by the notorious Order which abolished alike the saluting of officers and the death penalty for military offences. The Council of Soldiers and Workmen's Deputies at Petrograd so prominent in the revolution, the parent and exemplar of all the soviets which were sprouting throughout Russia, maintained a separate existence and policy. It appealed to the world in favor of peace without annexations or indemnities; it developed its own strength and connections and debated and harangued on first principles almost continuously. From the outset a divergence of aim was apparent between this body and the Provisional Government. The object of the Petrograd Council was to undermine all authority and discipline; the object of the Provisional Government was to preserve both in new and agreeable forms. On a deadlock being reached between the rivals, Kerensky, a moderate member of the Council, sided with the Provisional Government and became Minister of Justice. Meanwhile the extremists lay in the midst of the Petrograd Council, but did not at first dominate it. All this was in accordance with the regular and conventional Communist plan of fostering all disruptive movements, especially of the Left and of pushing them continually further until the moment for the forcible supersession of the new government is ripe.

The Provisional Ministers strutted about the Offices and Palaces and discharged in an atmosphere of flowery sentiments their administrative duties. These were serious. All authority had been shaken from its foundation; the armies melted rapidly to the rear; the railway carriages were crowded to the roofs and upon the roofs with mutinous soldiers seeking fresh centers of revolt and with deserters trying to get home. The soldiers' and sailors' Councils argued interminably over every order. The whole vast country was in confusion and agitation. The processes of supply, whether for the armies or for the cities, were increasingly disjointed. Nothing functioned effectively and everything, whether munitions or food, was either lacking or scarce. Meanwhile the Germans, and farther south the Austrians and the Turks, were battering upon the creaking and quivering fronts by every known resource of scientific war. The statesmen of the Allied nations affected to believe that all was for the best and that the Russian revolution constituted a notable advantage for the common cause.

In the middle of April the Germans took a sombre decision. Ludendorff refers to it with bated breath. Full allowance must be made for the desperate stakes to which the German war leaders were already committed. They were in the mood which had opened unlimited submarine warfare with the certainty of bringing the United States into the war against them. Upon the Western front they had from the beginning used the most terrible means of offence at their disposal. They had employed poison gas on the largest scale and had invented the "Flammenwerfer." Nevertheless it was with a sense of awe that they turned upon Russia the most grisly of all weapons. They transported Lenin in a sealed truck like a plague bacillus from Switzerland into Russia. Lenin arrived at Petrograd on April 16. Who was this being in whom there resided these dire potentialities? Lenin was to Karl Marx what Omar was to Mahomet. He translated faith into acts. He devised the practical methods by which the Marxian theories could be applied in his own time. He invented the Communist plan of campaign. He issued the orders, he prescribed the watchwords, he gave the signal and he led the attack.

* * *

At the time of the [fall of the Czar] France, Britain and the United States were engaged in supplying munitions to Russia on a gigantic scale. These munitions had been purchased by Russia, Czarist and Revolutionary, upon loans. More than 600,000 tons of military material, apart from an equal quantity of coal, had been landed at Archangel and Murmansk. . . . The Bolshevik Government repudiated all the loans by which they had been purchased. They were therefore in equity the property of the Allies. But a far more urgent question was "Into whose hands would they fall?" A similar situation obtained at Vladivostok, where enormous importations had been made by the Americans and Japanese. Was all this mass of deadly material to replenish the arsenals of the Central Powers and prolong the war in indefinite slaughter? Ought it even to enable a recreant Government, traitor to the Allies and the avowed foe of every civilized institution, to crush every form of opposition to its absolute sway? These issues arose in the winter of 1917; they became vital even before the Peace of Brest-Litovsk was signed.

The terms of the Treaty made it plain that the blockade of the Central Powers on which such immense naval efforts had been concentrated was to a large extent broken. The Germans obviously had Russia at their disposal. The granaries of the Ukraine and Siberia, the oil of the Caspian, all the resources of a vast continent could, it seemed to us, henceforth be drawn upon to nourish and maintain the German armies now increasing so formidably in the west, and the populations behind them. . . . How far or how soon these reliefs could become effective was uncertain; but the subsidiary arrangements made with the Ukraine revealed the immediate German intention of overrunning that country and drawing from it the largest quantities of supplies. No one at this time saw any prospect of a speedy end to the war, and there seemed no reason to doubt that the German and Austrians would have the time—as they certainly had the power—to draw new life almost indefinitely from the giant Empire prostrated before them. Finally, the Germans were in process of transporting 70 Divisions, comprising more than a million men, and 3,000 guns with all their munitions from the Russian to the Western front. The Austrians had similarly reinforced their Italian front and further reinforcements were moving westward in a continuous stream. The French Army had scarcely recovered from the mutinies of 1917 and the British, in their efforts to take the pressure off the French and secure them a breathing space, had bled themselves white in ceaseless offensives from Arras to Paschendaele. Such was the dark situation on the morrow of the Russian collapse. It was soon to become even graver in the explosion of the greatest battles ever fought.

The reconstruction of an Eastern front against Germany and the withholding of Russian supplies from the Central Powers seemed even from the end of 1917 vital to win the war. The Military Representatives of the Supreme War Council accordingly recommended on December 12 that all national troops in Russia who were determined to continue the war should be supported by every means in our power. In Siberia one ally above all others could act with swiftness and overwhelming power. Japan was near, fresh, strong, ready, and intimately affected. . . . The Japanese showed themselves not unwilling to make exertions. They were prepared to take control of a considerable section of the Siberian railway. But they said that American participation would be unpopular in Japan. . . . The United States expressed themselves averse from either solitary intervention by Japan or combined intervention by America and Japan. The Japanese were offended by this attitude, which the British Government at first felt bound to endorse . . . since the development of hostile German influence on the shores of the Pacific would be a peculiar menace to Japan. The British Government, with the support of the French, at the end of January decided to propose that Japan should be invited to act as the mandatory of the Allies. President Wilson remained adverse to all intervention and especially to isolated action by Japan. The Japanese, on the other hand, stipulated that if Japan were to act as mandatory for the Powers she must receive American aid in gold and steel. . . .

For four precious months a see-saw process between Japan and America continued in which one or the other successively demurred to every variant proposed by the French and British. However, the terrible conflict in France and Belgium and the increasing German exploitation of Russia presented arguments of inexorable force. They were aided from an unexpected quarter. Trotsky was now Minister of War, and with remarkable energy was creating a Red Army to defend alike the Revolution and Russia. On March 28, he informed our Representative at Moscow, Mr. Lockhart, that he saw no objection to Japanese forces entering Russia to resist German aggression if the other Allies cooperated and certain guarantees were given. He asked for a British Naval Commission to reorganize the Russian Black Sea Fleet and for a British officer to control the Russian railways. Lastly, even Lenin was said to be not opposed to foreign intervention against the Germans, subject to guarantees against interference in Russian politics. Every effort was made by the British to obtain a formal invitation from the Bolshevik leaders. This would have been all important in overcoming the reluctance of the United States. Probably the Bolsheviks were only maneuvering to gain a measure of external sanction for their regime in its early days and to baffle and divide the patriotic antagonisms which were arming against them. Something else was needed to clinch the issue and bring the five great Allies into practical agreement. This new incentive was now to be supplied.

There suddenly appeared in Russia a foreign factor, unique in character and origin. On the outbreak of war a number of Czecho-Slovaks resident in Russia had voluntarily entered the Russian army. . . . These soldiers, separated from their homes and families by immense distances, by a world of war and infinite confusion, and finally by the offences they had committed against the Austrian Government, preserved a disciplined comprehension of national and international causes and were entirely immune from all local Russian influence. . . . Professor Masaryk went to Russia, brought about the consolidation of all Czecho-Slovak units in one force, placed them under the red and white flag of Bohemia and procured

for them in Paris the status of an Allied army. From the moment
of the Treaty of Brest-Litovsk they held themselves fully armed at
the disposition of the Allies for the general purposes of the war.
. . .

When the Treaty of Brest-Litovsk ended the Russian resistance
to Germany the Czecho-Slovak Army demanded to be transported
to the Western front. The Bolsheviks were equally anxious that
they should leave Russia. A free exit was promised to the Czechs
by the Bolshevik Commander-in-Chief and embodied in a formal
agreement between the Allies and the Soviet Government in Moscow on March 26. . . .

It was natural that the Germans should view these arrangements
with disapproval. To prevent the manhood of two army corps of
trustworthy troops from being transported round the world to the
Western front became an object of urgent consequence to the
enemy General Staff. Exactly what pressures they put upon the
Soviet authorities is not yet known. At any rate they were effective.
Lenin and Trotsky freed themselves from their engagements to
the Czechs by treachery. . . . On May 26, the first echelon of
Czecho-Slovak artillery arrived at Irkutsk. Their agreement with
the Bolsheviks had left them only 30 carbines and some grenades
for personal self-defence. When the trains steamed into the
station the Czechs found themselves in the presence of a large and
greatly superior force of Red Guards. They were ordered to surrender their few remaining arms within a period of 15 minutes.
While the Czechs, nearly all of whom were unarmed, were discussing the situation on the railway-station platform, a machine
gun fired upon them from the station building. The Czechs did
not succumb. The training of the Red Army at this time had not
progressed beyond a knowledge of Communism, the execution of
prisoners and ordinary acts of brigandage and murder. In a few
minutes with their 30 carbines and hand-grenades the Czechs not
only defeated but captured and disarmed their despicable assailants. Equipped with the captured weapons they overcame a few
days later new forces sent against them by the local Soviet, and
reported what had occurred to their army headquarters.

The whole of the Czech troops thereupon ceased to deliver up
their arms and wherever they stood assumed an attitude of active

self-defence which passed quite rapidly into a vigorous counter-attack. Their very dispersion now became the foundation of an extraordinary power. Eleven thousand had already arrived at Vladivostok, the rest were scattered all along the Trans-Siberian Railway and its subsidiary lines from a hundred miles west of the Ural Mountains to the Pacific Ocean. . . . By the third week of July an immense area of Russia, several hundred miles broad and 3,000 miles long, including the backbone connections from the Volga River almost to Lake Baikal, was in the effectual possession of these strangers thus foully attacked when seeking to leave the country in virtue of signed agreements. The pages of history recall scarcely any parallel episode at once so romantic in character and so extensive in scale.

We may anticipate the culmination of this effort. Those Czechs who had already reached and made themselves masters of Vladivostok determined to return to the rescue of their compatriots cut off in Central Siberia, and by about the middle of September, 1918, railway communication had again been established along the whole Trans-Siberian route. Thus, through a treacherous breach of faith, by a series of accidents and chances which no one in the world had foreseen, the whole of Russia from the Volga River to the Pacific Ocean, a region almost as large as the continent of Africa, had passed as if by magic into the control of the Allies. . . .

\*　\*　\*

These astonishing events as they proceeded were decisive upon the action of the great Allies. On July 2, 1918, the Supreme War Council had made from Versailles a further appeal to President Wilson to agree to the support of the Czech forces. The President thereupon proposed the dispatch of an international force of British, Japanese and United States troops, avowedly to restore and preserve the communications of the Czechs. . . .

Two Japanese divisions, 7,000 Americans and two British Battalions under the command of Colonel Johnson and of Colonel John Ward, a Labour Member of Parliament, 3,000 French and Italians, all under the supreme command of Japan, were set in motion, landed as rapidly as possible at Vladivostok and proceeded

westward along the railway. Concurrently with this an international force of 7,000 or 8,000 men, mainly British and all under
British command, disembarked in June and July at Murmansk and
Archangel. They were welcomed by the inhabitants, who expelled the Bolsheviks and formed a local administration. Agreements were signed between this Northern Government and the
British commander whereby the local authorities undertook to
assist the Allies to defeat German aggression and the Allied Governments became responsible for finance and food.

In Siberia within the widespread picket line—for it was little
more—of the Czecho-Slovaks, an Anti-Bolshevik Russian Government began to organize itself at Omsk. . . .

In the summer of 1918 a provisional Government was formed
at Omsk, aiming primarily at the convocation of a constituent
assembly for all Russia. This Government passed through various
transformations during its tenure. . . . Even before the Armistice
cast its fatal depression upon all anti-Bolshevik movements, the
tide of Siberian fortunes had begun to ebb. The Czechs were
already wearying somewhat in well-doing. Their toils were ceaseless and their dangers increasing. Their own political opinions
were of an advanced character, and accorded ill with White Russian views. They were, moreover, exasperated by constant contact
with Russian instability and mismanagement. Their far-spread
Southern line in October, 1918, had been forcibly contracted by
Red pressure in front and around them.

Already also by September, 1918, there were two governments
functioning side by side at Omsk—one for Siberia and the other
claiming to be an all-Russian body. Meanwhile, Cossack and anti-
Bolshevik officers had been energetically raising armed forces. As
these forces grew in size and influence they overshadowed both
these mushroom administrations. It became increasingly evident
that all would have soon to fight for their lives, and in these straits
the military point of view quickly became predominant. The
original Omsk Government yielded readily to this new pressure;
its brother government, on the contrary, became a hotbed of socialist conspiracy. The rival administrations counter-worked each
other. The futility of these proceedings in the face of impending
slaughter led to a military *coup d'état*. On November 17, a week

after the Armistice, the leaders of the new armies forcibly appropriated one government and arrested the principal members of the other. They decided, probably wisely in the desperate circumstances, to concentrate all power in the hands of one man. They found this man in Admiral Kolchak, the former commander of the Black Sea Fleet.

At the same time, far to the south in the Province of the Don, the Russian Volunteer Army, now under Denikin, had already made itself master of a large and fertile area, and before the end of the year was destined to advance to Ekaterinodar after an operation in which over 30,000 Bolsheviks were made prisoners.

Such was the surprising transformation of the Russian situation which followed the Treaty of Brest-Litovsk. The snows of winter war had whitened five-sixths of Red Russia, but the springtime of Peace, for all others a blessing, was soon to melt it all again.

\* \* \*

The Armistice and the collapse of Germany had altered all Russian values and relations. The Allies had only entered Russia with reluctance and as an operation of war. But the war was over. They had made exertions to deny to the German armies the vast supplies of Russia: but these armies existed no more. They had set out to rescue the Czechs; but the Czechs had already saved themselves. Therefore every argument which had led to intervention had disappeared.

On the other hand, all the Allies were involved physically and morally in many parts of Russia. The British commitments were in some ways the most serious. Twelve thousand British and eleven thousand Allied troops were actually ice-bound in North Russia at Murmansk and Archangel. Whatever was decided, they must stay there until the spring. . . .

Lord Balfour, the Foreign Secretary, in a Memorandum of November 29 set forth to the Cabinet the policy which should be pursued.

> This country [he wrote] would certainly refuse to see its forces, after more than four years of strenuous fighting, dissipated over the huge ex-

panse of Russia in order to carry out political reforms in a State which is no longer a belligerent Ally.

We have constantly asserted that it is for the Russians to choose their own form of government, that we have no desire to intervene in their domestic affairs, and that if, in the course of operations essentially directed against the Central Powers we have to act with such Russian political and military organizations as are favorable to the *Entente*, this does not imply that we deem ourselves to have any mission to establish or disestablish any particular political system among the Russian people.

To these views His Majesty's Government still adhere, and their military policy in Russia is still governed by them. But it does not follow that we can disinterest ourselves wholly from Russian affairs. Recent events have created obligations which last beyond the occasions which gave them birth. The Czechoslovaks are our Allies and we must do what we can to help them. In the South-east corner of Russia, in Europe, in Siberia, in Transcaucasia and Transcaspia, in the territories adjacent to the White Sea and the Arctic Ocean, new anti-Bolshevik administrations have grown up under the shelter of Allied forces. We are responsible for their existence and must endeavor to support them. How far we can do this, and how such a policy will ultimately develop, we cannot yet say. It must largely depend upon the course taken by the associated Powers who have far larger resources at their disposal than ourselves. For us no alternative is open at present than to use such troops as we possess to the best advantage; where we have no troops to supply arms and money; and in the case of the Baltic provinces, to protect as far as we can the nascent nationalities by the help of our Fleet. Such a policy must necessarily seem halting and imperfect to those who on the spot are resisting the invasion of militant Bolshevism, but it is all that we can accomplish or ought in existing circumstances to attempt.

\*     \*     \*

I entered the War Office as Secretary of State on January 14, 1919. . . . Up to this moment I had taken no part of any kind in Russian affairs, nor had I been responsible for any commitment. I found myself in the closest agreement on almost every point with Sir Henry Wilson, the Chief of the Imperial General Staff, and the policy which we advised and, so far as we had the power, pursued to the end, had at any rate the merit of simplicity. Our armies were melting fast. The British people would not supply the men or the money for any large military establishment elsewhere than on the Rhine. It was highly questionable whether any troops raised under compulsion for the war against Germany would consent to fight anybody else in any circumstances, or even to remain long in occupation of conquered territory. We therefore sang one tune in harmony: contract your commitments; select your obligations; and make a success of those to which you are able to adhere.

We then urged the following measures: . . . to discharge our pledges faithfully and fully by arming and equipping the anti-Bolshevik forces from our own immense surplus of munitions, and help them with expert officers and instructors to train efficient armies of their own. Naturally it followed that we should try to combine all the border States hostile to the Bolsheviks into one system of war and diplomacy and get everyone else to do as much as possible. Such was the policy we consistently pursued—and such were its limitations.

But an alternative policy of which there were powerful advocates competed and clashed with these simple contentions.

\* \* \*

Mr. Lloyd George's view is well set forth in the following telegram:

PRIME MINISTER TO MR. PHILIP KERR.

February 16, 1919

See Churchill and tell him . . . I trust he will not commit us to any costly operations which would involve any large contribution either of men or money. . . .

The main idea ought to be to enable Russia to save herself if she desires to do so; and if she does not take advantage of opportunity, then it means either that she does not wish to be saved from Bolshevism or that she is past saving. There is only one justification for interfering in Russia—that Russia wants it. If she does, then Kolchak, Krasnov and Denikin ought to be able to raise much larger force than Bolsheviks. This force we could equip, and a well-equipped force of willing men would soon overthrow Bolshevik army of unwilling conscripts especially if whole population is against them.

If, on the other hand, Russia is not behind Krasnov and his coadjutors, it is an outrage on every British principle of freedom that we should use foreign armies to force upon Russia a Government which is repugnant to its people.

The Prime Minister [demanded] exact estimates of the cost in money of the various alternatives open.

MR. CHURCHILL TO THE PRIME MINISTER.

February 27, 1919

I send you herewith a statement of British assistance given to Russia, which, as you will see, is considerable. The criticism that may be passed is that it is related to no concerted policy, and that while it constitutes a serious drain on our resources it is not backed with sufficient vigor to lead to any definite result. There is no "will to win" behind any of these ventures. At every point we fall short of what is necessary to obtain real success. The lack of any "will to win" communicates itself to our troops and affects their morale: it communicates itself to our Russian allies and retards their organization, and to our enemies and encourages their efforts.

With regard to your complaint that the War Office have not furnished you with information, I must point out to you that the War Cabinet have long been accustomed to deal direct with the Chief of the Staff and other military authorities, and they know as well as I do the difficulties of obtaining precise plans and estimates of cost from military men in regard to this Russian problem. The reason is that all the factors are uncertain and that the military considerations are at every point intermingled with political decisions which have not been given. For instance, to begin with what is fundamental, the Allied Powers in Paris have not decided whether they wish to make war upon the Bolsheviks or to make peace with them. They are pausing midway between these two courses with an equal dislike of either. . . .

And a fortnight later:

MR. CHURCHILL TO THE PRIME MINISTER.

March 14, 1919

The four months which have passed since the Armistice was signed have been disastrous almost without relief for the anti-Bolshevik forces. This is not due to any great increase in Bolshevik strength, though there has been a certain augmentation. It is due to the lack of any policy on the part of the Allies, or of any genuine or effective support put into the operations which are going on against the Bolsheviks at different points in Russia.

. . . The fact that the German troops were commanded to withdraw from the Ukraine without any provision being made to stop the Bolshevik advance, has enabled large portions of this rich territory full of new supplies of food to be overrun, and the Bolsheviks are now very near the Black Sea at Kherson. There are many signs of weakness in Kolchak's forces, and, as you have observed, many Bolshevik manifestations are taking place behind the Siberian front, in one of which the Japanese have had quite severe fighting.

*    *    *

Clemenceau, Lloyd George, President Wilson, Orlando, and the Japanese delegate, Saionji, set forth their views [at last] in a note addressed to Admiral Kolchak.  This document is so important that it must be printed textually.

### NOTE FROM THE SUPREME COUNCIL TO ADMIRAL KOLCHAK
May 26, 1919

The Allied and Associated Powers feel that the time has come when it is necessary for them once more to make clear the policy they propose to pursue in regard to Russia.

It has always been a cardinal axiom of the Allied and Associated Powers to avoid interference in the internal affairs of Russia.  Their original intervention was made for the sole purpose of assisting those elements in Russia which wanted to continue the struggle against German autocracy and to free their country from German rule, and in order to rescue the Czecho-slovaks from the danger of annihilation at the hands of the Bolshevist forces.

Since the signature of the Armistice on November 11th, 1918, they have kept forces in various parts of Russia.  Munitions and supplies have been sent those associated with them at a very considerable cost. . . .

Some of the Allied and Associated Governments are now being pressed to withdraw their troops and to incur no further expense in Russia on the ground that continued intervention shows no prospect of producing an early settlement.  They are prepared, however, to continue their assistance on the lines laid down below, provided they are satisfied that it will really help the Russian people to liberty, self-government, and peace.

The Allied and Associated Governments now wish to declare formally that the object of their policy is to restore peace within Russia by enabling the Russian people to resume control of their own affairs through the instrumentality of a freely-elected constituent assembly, and to restore peace along its frontiers by arranging for the settlement of disputes in regard to the boundaries of the Russian State and its relations with its neighbors through the peaceful arbitration of the League of Nations.

They are convinced by their experience of the last twelve months that it is not possible to attain these ends by dealing with the Soviet Government of Moscow.  They are therefore disposed to assist the government of Admiral Kolchak and his associates with munitions, supplies, and food to establish themselves as the government of all Russia, provided they receive from them definite guarantees that their policy has the same object in view as the Allied and Associated Powers.

In the first place as soon as they reach Moscow that they will summon a constituent assembly elected by a free, secret, and democratic franchise, as the supreme legislature for Russia, to which the government of Russia must be responsible, or, if at that time order is not sufficiently restored, they will summon the Constituent Assembly, elected in 1917, to sit until such time as new elections are possible.

Secondly—that throughout the areas which they at present control they will permit free elections in the normal course for all free and legally constituted assemblies, such as municipalities, Zemstvos, etc.

Thirdly—that they will countenance no attempt to revive the special privilege of any class or order in Russia. The Allied and Associated Powers have noted with satisfaction the solemn declaration made by Admiral Kolchak and his associates, that they have no intention of restoring the former land system. They feel that the principles to be followed in the solution of this and other internal questions must be left to free decision of the Russian Constituent Assembly. But they wish to be assured that those whom they are prepared to assist stand for the civil and religious liberty of all Russian citizens and will make no attempt to re-introduce the regime which the revolution has destroyed. . . .

Seventhly—that as soon as a government for Russia has been constituted on a democratic basis, Russia should join the League of Nations and co-operate with other members in the limitation of armaments and military organization throughout the world.

Finally—that they abide by the declaration made by Admiral Kolchak on November 27th, 1918, in regard to Russia's national debt.

The Allied and Associated Powers will be glad to learn as soon as possible whether the government of Admiral Kolchak and his associates is prepared to accept these conditions, and also whether in the event of acceptance they will undertake to form a single government and army command as soon as the military situation makes it possible.

G. CLEMENCEAU.
LLOYD GEORGE.
ORLANDO.
WOODROW WILSON.
SAIONJI.

Naturally Kolchak did not delay his reply. "I should not retain power one day longer than required by the interests of the country; my first thought at the moment when the Bolsheviks are definitely crushed will be to fix the date of the election of the Constituent Assembly. . . . I shall hand over to it all my power in order that it may freely determine the system of government; I have, moreover, taken the oath to do this before the Supreme Russian Tribunal, the guardian of legality. All my efforts are aimed at concluding the civil war as soon as possible by crushing Bolshevism in order to put the Russian people in a position to express its free will." He then proceeded to answer satisfactorily all the specific questions which the Council of Five had asked.

This answer was dated June 4, and on June 12 Lloyd George, Wilson, Clemenceau, and the representative of Japan, welcomed the tone of the reply which seemed to them "to be in substantial agreement with the proposition they had made, and to contain satisfactory assurances for the freedom and self-government of the

Russian people and their neighbors." They were therefore "willing to extend to Admiral Kolchak and his Associates the support set forth in their original letter."

If this far-reaching and openly proclaimed decision was wise now in June, would it not have been wiser in January?  No argument existed in June not obvious in January: and half the power available in January was gone by June.  Six months of degeneration and uncertainty had chilled the Siberian Armies and wasted the slender authority of the Omsk Government.  It had given the Bolsheviks the opportunity of raising armies, of consolidating their power and of identifying themselves to some extent with Russia. It had provided enough opposition to stimulate and not enough to overcome the sources of their strength.  The moment chosen by the Supreme Council for their declaration was almost exactly the moment when that declaration was certainly too late.

*    *    *

During the year 1919 there was fought over the whole of Russia a strange war; a war in areas so vast that considerable armies, armies indeed of hundreds of thousands of men, were lost—dispersed, melted, evaporated; a war in which there were no real battles, only raids and affrays and massacres, as the result of which countries as large as England or France changed hands to and fro; a war of flags on the map, of picket lines, of cavalry screens advancing or receding by hundreds of miles without solid cause or durable consequence; a war with little valor and no mercy.  Whoever could advance found it easy to continue; whoever was forced to retire found it difficult to stop.  On paper it looked like the Great War on the Western and Eastern fronts.  In fact it was only its ghost: a thin, cold, insubstantial conflict in the Realms of Dis. Kolchak first and then Denikin advanced in what were called offensives over enormous territories.  As they advanced they spread their lines ever wider and wider and ever thinner.  It seemed that they would go on till they had scarcely one man to the mile.  When the moment came the Bolsheviks lying in the center, equally feeble but at any rate tending willy-nilly constantly towards compression, gave a prick or a punch at this point or that.  Thereupon the balloon burst and all the flags moved back and the cities changed hands and found it convenient to change opinions, and horrible vengeances were wrecked on helpless people, vengeances per-severingly paid over months of fine-spun inquisition.    Mighty natural or strategic barriers, like the line of the Volga River or the line of the Ural Mountains, were found to be no resting places, no strategic consequences followed from their loss or gain.   A war of few casualties and unnumbered executions!   The tragedy of each Russian city, of loyal families, of countless humble households might fill libraries of dreary volumes. . . .

Moscow held the controls of Russia; and when the cause of the Allies burnt itself out in victory, there were no other controls: just chatter and slaughter on a background of Robinson Crusoe toil. The ancient capital lay at the center of a web of railroads radiating to every point of the compass.   And in the midst a spider!   Vain hope to crush the spider by the advance of lines of encircling flies! Still I suppose that twenty or thirty thousand resolute, compre-hending, well-armed Europeans could, without any serious diffi-culty or loss, have made their way very swiftly along any of the great railroads which converged on Moscow; and have brought to the hard ordeal of battle any force that stood against them.   But twenty or thirty thousand resolute men did not exist or could not be brought together.   Denikin's forces foraged over enormous areas. . . . But there never was a thrust; no Napoleon eagle-swoop at the mysterious capital; only the long thin lines wending on ever thinner, weaker and more weary.   And then finally when the Bolsheviks in the center of the circle were sufficiently concentrated by the mere fact of retirement, they in their turn advanced and found in front of them—nothing!—nothing but helpless popula-tions and scores of thousands of compromised families and indi-viduals.

The fitful and fluid operations of the Russian armies found a counterpart in the policy, or want of policy, of the Allies.   Were they at war with Soviet Russia?   Certainly not; but they shot Soviet Russians at sight.   They stood as invaders on Russian soil.   They armed the enemies of the Soviet Government.   They blockaded its ports, and sunk its battleships.   They earnestly desired and schemed its downfall.   But war—shocking! Interference—shame!

It was, they repeated, a matter of indifference to them how Russians settled their own internal affairs. They were impartial—Bang! And then—at the same time—parley and try to trade.

The reader might well have supposed that the decision of the Big Five to support Kolchak, which was finally taken in June, marked the end of doubt and vacillation. They could send no troops; they could not spend much money. But they could give a steady aid in surplus munitions, in moral countenance and in concerted diplomacy. Had they acted together simply and sincerely within these limitations, they might have reached a good result. But their decisions to support Kolchak, and later to support Denikin, represented only half a mind. The other half had always been, and was throughout the summer of 1919, uncertain of itself, sceptical about the prospects of the anti-Bolsheviks, ill-informed about the true nature of the Soviet Government and the Third International, and anxious to see whether the extremists in Moscow would not respond to the exercise of reason and patience.

*  *  *

[All] this must be brought into relation with the general situation of Europe. I cannot do this better than by reprinting a letter which I wrote to Mr. Lloyd George on starting for a brief Easter holiday in France.

MR. CHURCHILL TO THE PRIME MINISTER.
March 29, 1920

I write this as I am crossing the Channel to tell you what is in my mind. Since the Armistice my policy would have been "Peace with the German people, war on the Bolshevik tyranny." Willingly or unavoidably, you have followed something very near the reverse. Knowing the difficulties, and also your great skill and personal force—so much greater than mine—I do not judge your policy and action as if I could have done better, or as if anyone could have done better. But we are now face to face with the results. They are terrible. We may well be within measurable distance of universal collapse and anarchy throughout Europe and Asia. Russia has gone into ruin. What is left of her is in the power of these deadly snakes. But Germany may perhaps still be saved. I have felt with a great sense of relief that we may be able to think and act together in harmony about Germany: that you are inclined to make an effort to rescue Germany from her frightful fate—which if it overtakes her may well overtake others. If so, time is short and action must be simple. You ought to tell France that we will make a defensive alliance with her against Germany if, *and only if*, she entirely alters her treatment of Germany and loyally accepts a British policy of help and friendship towards Germany. Next you should send a great man to Berlin to help consolidate the anti-Spartacist anti-Ludendorff elements into a strong left center block. For this task you have two levers: firstly, food and credit, which must be generously accorded in spite of our own difficulties (which otherwise will worsen); secondly, early revision of the Peace Treaty by a conference to which New Germany shall be invited as an equal partner in the rebuilding of Europe.[1] Using these levers it ought to be possible to rally all that is good and stable in the German nation to their own redemption and to the salvation of Europe. I pray that we may not be "too late."

As a part of such a policy I should be prepared to make peace with Soviet Russia on the best terms available to appease the general situation, while safeguarding us from being poisoned by them. I do not of course believe that any real harmony is possible between Bolshevism and present civilization. But in view of the existing facts a cessation of arms and a promotion of material prosperity are inevitable: and we must trust for better or for worse to peaceful influences to bring about the disappearance of this awful tyranny and peril. . . .

*　*　*

---

[1] This of course referred to the economic and financial clauses.—W.S.C.

III

# WORLD REVOLUTION
# AND NATIONAL INTEREST

# THE OCTOBER REVOLUTION AND TROTSKY'S THEORY OF PERMANENT REVOLUTION*

BY

## JOSEPH STALIN

[1924]

### THE INTERNAL AND EXTERNAL SETTING FOR THE OCTOBER REVOLUTION

Three circumstances of an external nature determined the comparative ease with which the proletarian revolution in Russia succeeded in breaking the chains of imperialism and thus overthrowing the rule of the bourgeoisie.

First: The circumstance that the October Revolution began in a period of desperate struggle between the two principal imperialist groups, the Anglo-French and the Austro-German; at a time when, engaged in mortal struggle between themselves. these two groups had neither the time nor the means to devote serious attention to the struggle against the October Revolution. This circumstance was of tremendous importance for the October Revolution, for it enabled it to take advantage of the fierce conflict within the imperialist world to strengthen and organize its own forces.

Second: The circumstance that the October Revolution began during the imperialist war, at a time when the laboring masses, exhausted by the war and thirsting for peace, were, by the very logic of events, led to the proletarian revolution as the only way out of the war. This circumstance was of extreme importance for the October Revolution, for it put into its hands the mighty weapon of peace, furnished the opportunity of connecting the Soviet revolution with the ending of the hated war, and thus created mass sympathy for it both in the West, among the workers, and in the East, among the oppressed peoples.

*From "The October Revolution and the Tactics of the Russian Communists" in *Leninism* by Joseph Stalin, copyright 1942 by International Publishers. Reprinted by permission.

Third: The existence of a powerful working-class movement in Europe and the fact that a revolutionary crisis was maturing in the West and in the East, brought on by the protracted imperialist war. This circumstance was of inestimable importance for the revolution in Russia, for it secured the revolution faithful allies outside Russia in its struggle against world imperialism.

But in addition to circumstances of an external nature, there were also a number of favorable internal conditions which facilitated the victory of the October Revolution.

The following conditions must be regarded as the principal ones:

First: The October Revolution enjoyed the most active support of the overwhelming majority of the working class in Russia.

Second: It enjoyed the undoubted support of the poor peasants and of the majority of the soldiers, who were thirsting for peace and land.

Third: It had at its head, as its guiding force, a party so tried and tested as the Bolshevik Party, strong not only by reason of its experience and years of discipline, but also by reasons of its vast connections with the laboring masses.

Fourth: The October Revolution was confronted by enemies who were comparatively easy to overcome, such as the rather weak Russian bourgeoisie, a landlord class which was utterly demoralized by peasant "revolts," and the compromising parties (the Mensheviks and Socialist-Revolutionaries), which had become utterly bankrupt during the war.

Fifth: It had at its disposal the vast expanses of the young state, in which it was able to maneuver freely, retreat when circumstances so required, enjoy a respite, gather strength, etc.

Sixth: In its struggle against counter-revolution, the October Revolution could count upon sufficient resources of food, fuel and raw materials within the country.

The combination of these external and internal circumstances created that peculiar situation which determined the comparative ease with which the October Revolution won its victory.

This does not mean, of course, that there were no unfavorable features in the external and internal setting of the October Revolution.  Think of such an unfavorable feature as, for example, the isolation, to some extent, of the October Revolution, the absence near it, or bordering on it, of a Soviet country on which it could rely for support.  Undoubtedly, the future revolution, for example, in Germany, will be in a much more favorable situation in this respect, for it has in close proximity so powerful a Soviet country as our Soviet Union.  I might also mention so unfavorable a feature of the October Revolution as the absence of a proletarian majority within the country.

But these unfavorable features only emphasize the tremendous importance of the peculiar external and internal conditions of the October Revolution of which I have spoken above. . . .

## Two Peculiar Features of the October Revolution—Or the October Revolution and Trotsky's Theory of Permanent Revolution

There are two peculiar features of the October Revolution which must be understood first of all if we are to comprehend the inner meaning and the historical significance of that revolution.

What are these peculiar features?

First, the fact that the dictatorship of the proletariat was born in our country as a power which came into existence on the basis of an alliance between the proletariat and the laboring masses of the peasantry, the latter being led by the proletariat.  Second, the fact that the dictatorship of the proletariat became established in our country as a result of the victory of socialism in one country— a country with capitalism still little developed—while capitalism was preserved in other countries more highly developed in the capitalist sense.  This does not mean, of course, that the October Revolution has no other peculiar features.  But it is these two peculiar features that are important for us at the present moment, not only because they distinctly express the essence of the October Revolution, but also because they fully reveal the opportunist nature of the theory of "permanent revolution."

Let us briefly examine these peculiar features.

The problem of the laboring masses of the petty bourgeoisie, both urban and rural, the problem of winning these masses to the side of the proletariat, is of exceptional importance for the proletarian revolution. Whom will the laboring people of town and country support in the struggle for power, the bourgeoisie or the proletariat; whose reserve will they become, the reserve of the bourgeoisie or the reserve of the proletariat—on this depend the fate of the revolution and the stability of the dictatorship of the proletariat. The revolutions in France in 1848 and 1871 came to grief chiefly because the peasant reserves proved to be on the side of the bourgeoisie. The October Revolution was victorious because it was able to deprive the bourgeoisie of its peasant reserves, because it was able to win these reserves to the side of the proletariat, and because in this revolution the proletariat proved to be the only guiding force for the vast masses of the laboring people of town and country.

He who has not understood this will never comprehend the character of the October Revolution, or the nature of the dictatorship of the proletariat, or the peculiar characteristics of the internal policy of our proletarian power.

The dictatorship of the proletariat is not simply a governing upper stratum "skillfully" "selected" by the careful hand of an "experienced strategist," and "judiciously relying" on the support of one section or another of the population. The dictatorship of the proletariat is a class alliance between the proletariat and the laboring masses of the peasantry for the purpose of overthrowing capital, for achieving the final victory of socialism, on the condition that the guiding force of this alliance is the proletariat.

Thus, it is not a question of "slightly" underestimating or "slightly" overestimating the revolutionary potentialities of the peasant movement, as certain diplomatic advocates of "permanent revolution" are now fond of expressing it. It is a question of the nature of the new proletarian state which arose as a result of the October Revolution. It is a question of the character of the proletarian power, of the foundations of the dictatorship of the proletariat itself.

> The dictatorship of the proletariat [says Lenin] is a special form of class alliance between the proletariat, the vanguard of the toilers, and the numerous non-proletarian strata of toilers (the petty bourgeoisie, the small

proprietors, the peasantry, the intelligentsia, etc.), or the majority of
these; it is an alliance against capital, an alliance aiming at the complete
overthrow of capital, at the complete suppression of the resistance of the
bourgeoisie and of any attempt on their part at restoration, an alliance
aiming at the final establishment and consolidation of socialism. (V. I.
Lenin, *Collected Works*, Russian ed., Vol. XXIV, p. 311.)

And further on:

If we translate the Latin, scientific, historical-philosophical term "dictatorship of the proletariat" into more simple language, it means just the following: Only a definite class, namely, that of the urban workers and industrial workers in general, is able to lead the whole mass of the toilers
and exploited in the struggle for the overthrow of the yoke of capital, in
the process of this overthrow, in the struggle to maintain and consolidate
the victory, in the work of creating the new, socialist social system, in
the whole struggle for the complete abolition of classes. (V. I. Lenin,
*Selected Works*, Vol. IX, p. 432.)

Such is the theory of the dictatorship of the proletariat given by
Lenin.

One of the peculiar features of the October Revolution is the
fact that this revolution represents the classic application of Lenin's
theory of the dictatorship of the proletariat.

Some believe that this theory is a purely "Russian" theory,
applicable only to Russian conditions. That is wrong. It is absolutely wrong. In speaking of the laboring masses of the non-
proletarian classes which are led by the proletariat, Lenin has in
mind not only the Russian peasants, but also the laboring elements
of the border regions of the Soviet Union, which until recently
were colonies of Russia. Lenin constantly reiterated that without
an alliance with these masses of other nationalities the proletariat
of Russia could not achieve victory. In his articles on the national
problem and in his speeches at the congresses of the Communist
International, Lenin repeatedly said that the victory of the world
revolution was impossible without a revolutionary alliance, a revolutionary bloc, between the proletariat of the advanced countries
and the oppressed peoples of the enslaved colonies. But what are
colonies if not the oppressed laboring masses, and, primarily, the
laboring masses of the peasantry? Who does not know that the
question of emancipating the colonies is *essentially* a question of
emancipating the laboring masses of the non-proletarian classes
from the oppression and exploitation of finance capital?

But from this it follows that Lenin's theory of the dictatorship of the proletariat is not a purely "Russian" theory, but a theory which applies to all countries. Bolshevism is not only a Russian phenomenon. *"Bolshevism,"* says Lenin, is *"a model of tactics for all."* (V. I. Lenin, *Selected Works,* Vol. VII, p. 183.)

Such are the characteristics of the first peculiar feature of the October Revolution.

How do matters stand with regard to Trotsky's theory of "permanent revolution" in the light of this peculiar feature of the October Revolution? . . .

Let us take Trotsky's "Preface" to his book *The Year 1905,* written in 1922. Here is what Trotsky says in this "Preface" concerning "permanent revolution":

> It was precisely during the interval between January 9 and the general strike of October 1905 that the views on the character of the revolutionary development of Russia which came to be known as the theory of "permanent revolution" crystallized in the author's mind. This abstruse term represented the idea that the Russian revolution, whose immediate objectives were bourgeois in nature, would not, however, stop when these objectives had been achieved. The revolution would not be able to solve its immediate bourgeois problems except by placing the proletariat in power. And the latter, upon assuming power, would not be able to confine itself to the bourgeois limits of the revolution. On the contrary, precisely in order to ensure its victory, the proletarian vanguard would be forced in the very early stages of its rule to make deep inroads not only into feudal property but into bourgeois property as well. In this it would come into *hostile collision* not only with all the bourgeois groupings which supported the proletariat during the first stages of its revolutionary struggle, *but also with the broad masses of the peasants* who had been instrumental in bringing it into power. The contradictions in the position of a workers' government in a backward country with an overwhelming majority of peasants can be solved *only* on an international scale, in the arena of world proletarian revolution. (My italics.—J.S.)

This is what Trotsky says about his "permanent revolution."

One need only compare this quotation with the above quotations from Lenin's works on the dictatorship of the proletariat to perceive the great chasm that lies between Lenin's theory of the dictatorship of the proletariat and Trotsky's theory of "permanent revolution."

Lenin speaks of the alliance between the proletariat and the laboring strata of the peasantry as the basis of the dictatorship of the proletariat. Trotsky sees a *"hostile collision"* between "the proletarian vanguard" and "the broad masses of the peasants."

Lenin speaks of the *leadership* of the toiling and exploited masses by the proletariat. Trotsky sees *"contradictions* in the position of a workers' government in a backward country with an overwhelming majority of peasants."

According to Lenin, the revolution draws its strength primarily from among the workers and peasants of Russia itself. According to Trotsky, the necessary strength can be found only "in the arena of the world proletarian revolution."

But what if the world revolution is fated to arrive with some delay? Is there any ray of hope for our revolution? Trotsky sees no ray of hope, for "the contradictions in the position of a workers' government . . . can be solved *only* . . . in the arena of the world proletarian revolution." According to this plan, there is but one prospect left for our revolution: to vegetate in its own contradictions and rot away while waiting for the world revolution. . . .

"Permanent revolution" is not a mere underestimation of the revolutionary potentialities of the peasant movement. "Permanent revolution" is an underestimation of the peasant movement which leads to the repudiation of Lenin's theory of the dictatorship of the proletariat. . . .

This is how matters stand with regard to the first peculiar feature of the October Revolution.

What are the characteristics of the second peculiar feature of the October Revolution?

In his study of imperialism, especially in the period of the war, Lenin arrived at the law of the uneven, spasmodic economic and political development of the capitalist countries. According to this law, the development of enterprises, trusts, branches of industry and individual countries proceeds not evenly—not according to an established order of rotation, not in such a way that one trust, one branch of industry or one country is always in advance of the others, while other trusts or countries keep regularly one behind the other—but spasmodically, with interruptions in the development of some countries and leaps ahead in the development of others. Under these circumstances the "quite legitimate" striving of the countries that have slowed down to hold their old positions and the equally "legitimate" striving of the countries that have leapt ahead to seize new positions lead to a situation in which armed clashes among the imperialist countries are inevitable. Such was the case, for example, with Germany, which half a century ago was a backward country in comparison with France and England. The same must be said of Japan as compared with Russia. It is well known, however, that by the beginning of the twentieth century Germany and Japan had leapt so far ahead that Germany had succeeded in overtaking France and had begun to press England hard on the world market, while Japan was pressing Russia. As is well known, it was from these contradictions that the recent imperialist war arose.

This law proceeds from the following:

1. "Capitalism has grown into a world system of colonial oppression and of the financial strangulation of the overwhelming majority of the population of the world by a handful of 'advanced' countries" (V. I. Lenin, Preface to French edition of *Imperialism, Selected Works,* Vol. V, p. 9);

2. "This 'booty' is shared between two or three powerful world marauders armed to the teeth (America, Great Britain, Japan), who involve the whole world in *their* war over the sharing of *their* booty" (Ibid.);

3. In consequence of the growth of contradictions within the world system of financial oppression and of the inevitability of armed clashes, the world front of imperialism becomes easily vulnerable to revolution, and a breach in this front in individual countries becomes probable;

4. This breach is most likely to occur at those points, and in those countries, where the chain of the imperialist front is weakest, that is to say, where imperialism is least protected and where it is easiest for a revolution to expand;

5. In view of this, the victory of socialism in one country, even if this country is less developed in the capitalist sense, while capitalism is preserved in other countries, even if these countries are

more highly developed in the capitalist sense—is quite possible and probable.

Such, in a nutshell, are the foundations of Lenin's theory of the proletarian revolution.

What is the second peculiar feature of the October Revolution?

The second peculiar feature of the October Revolution lies in the fact that this revolution represents a model of the practical application of Lenin's theory of the proletarian revolution.

He who has not understood this peculiar feature of the October Revolution will never understand either the international nature of this revolution, or its colossal international might, or its peculiar foreign policy.

> Uneven economic and political development [says Lenin] is an absolute law of capitalism. Hence, the victory of socialism is possible first in several or even in one capitalist country, taken singly. The victorious proletariat of that country, having expropriated the capitalists and organized its own socialist production, would stand up *against* the rest of the world, the capitalist world, attracting to its cause the oppressed classes of other countries, raising revolts in those countries against the capitalists, and in the event of necessity coming out even with armed force against the exploiting classes and their states. [For] the free union of nations in socialism is impossible without a more or less prolonged and stubborn struggle by the socialist republics against the backward states. (V. I. Lenin, *Selected Works*, Vol. V, p. 141.)

The opportunists of all countries assert that the proletarian revolution can begin—if it is to begin anywhere at all, according to their theory—only in industrially developed countries, and that the more highly developed these countries are industrially the more chances are there for the victory of socialism. Moreover, according to them, the possibility of the victory of socialism in one country, and in a country little developed in the capitalist sense at that, is excluded as something absolutely improbable. As far back as the period of the war, Lenin, taking as his basis the law of the uneven development of the imperialist states, opposed to the opportunists his theory of the proletarian revolution of the victory of socialism in one country, even if that country is less developed in the capitalist sense.

It is well known that the October Revolution has fully confirmed the correctness of Lenin's theory of the proletarian revolution.

How do matters stand with Trotsky's "permanent revolution" in the light of Lenin's theory of the proletarian revolution? . . .

Let us examine another pamphlet written by Trotsky, his *Program of Peace*, which appeared before the October Revolution of 1917 and has now (1924) been reprinted in his book *The Year 1917*. In this pamphlet Trotsky criticizes Lenin's theory of the proletarian revolution and the victory of socialism in one country and opposes to it the slogan of a United States of Europe. He asserts that the victory of socialism in one country is impossible, that the victory of socialism is possible only as a victory in several of the principal states of Europe (England, Russia, Germany), which should combine into a United States of Europe; otherwise it is not possible at all. He says quite plainly that "a victorious revolution in Russia or in England is inconceivable without a revolution in Germany, and vice versa."

> The only more or less concrete historical argument [says Trotsky] advanced against the slogan of a United States of Europe was formulated in the Swiss *Sotsial-Demokrat* [at that time the central organ of the Bolsheviks—J.S.] in the following sentence: "Uneven economic and political development is an absolute law of capitalism." From this the *Sotsial-Demokrat* drew the conclusion that the victory of socialism is possible in one country, and that, therefore, there is no point in making the creation of a United States of Europe a condition for the dictatorship of the proletariat in each separate country. That capitalist development in different countries is uneven is an absolutely incontrovertible argument. But this unevenness is itself extremely uneven. The capitalist level of England, Austria, Germany or France is not identical. But in comparison with Africa and Asia all these countries represent capitalist "Europe," which has grown ripe for the social revolution. That no single country should "wait" for others in its own struggle is an elementary idea which it is useful and necessary to repeat in order to prevent the substitution of the idea of expectant international inaction for the idea of simultaneous international action. Without waiting for the others, we begin and continue our struggle on our national soil, confident that our initiative will give an impetus to the struggle in other countries; but if that does not happen, it will be hopeless, in the light of historical experience and in the light of theoretical reasoning, to think that a revolutionary Russia, for example, could hold its own in the face of a conservative Europe, or that a socialist Germany could remain isolated in a capitalist world.

As you see, we have before us the same theory of the simultaneous victory of socialism in the principal countries of Europe which, as a rule, excludes Lenin's theory of revolution about the victory of socialism in one country.

It goes without saying that for the *complete* victory of socialism, for *complete* security against the restoration of the old order, the united efforts of the proletarians of several countries are necessary. It goes without saying that, without the support given to our revolution by the proletariat of Europe, the proletariat of Russia could not have held its own against the general onslaught, just as without the support the revolution in Russia gave to the revolutionary movement in the West the latter could not have developed at the pace at which it has begun to develop since the establishment of the proletarian dictatorship in Russia. It goes without saying that we need support. But what does support of our revolution by the West-European proletariat imply? Is not the sympathy of European workers for our revolution, their readiness to thwart the imperialists' plans of intervention—is not all this support? Is this not real assistance? Of course it is. If it had not been for this support, if it had not been for this assistance, not only from the European workers but also from the colonial and dependent countries, the proletarian dictatorship in Russia would have been in a tight corner. Has this sympathy and this assistance, coupled with the might of our Red Army and the readiness of the workers and peasants of Russia to defend their socialist fatherland to the last— has all this been sufficient to beat off the attacks of the imperialists and to win us the necessary conditions for the serious work of construction? Yes, it has been sufficient. Is this sympathy growing stronger, or is it ebbing away? Undoubtedly, it is growing stronger. Hence, have we favorable conditions, not only to push on with the organization of socialist economy, but also, in our turn, to give support to the West-European workers and to the oppressed peoples of the East? Yes, we have. This is eloquently proved by the seven years' history of the proletarian dictatorship in Russia. Can it be denied that a mighty wave of labor enthusiasm has already risen in our country? No, it cannot be denied.

After all this, what does Trotsky's assertion that a revolutionary Russia could not hold its own against a conservative Europe signify?

It can signify only this: first, that Trotsky does not appreciate the inherent strength of our revolution; secondly, that Trotsky does not understand the inestimable importance of the moral support which is given to our revolution by the workers of the West and the peasants of the East; thirdly, that Trotsky does not perceive the internal cancer which is eating at the heart of imperialism today. . . .

But perhaps this pamphlet too has become out of date and has ceased for some reason or other to correspond to Trotsky's present views? Let us take his later works, written after the victory of the proletarian revolution in *one country,* in Russia. Let us take, for example, Trotsky's "Postscript" to the new edition of his pamphlet *A Program of Peace,* which was written in 1922. Here is what he says in this "Postscript":

> The assertion, repeated several times in *A Program of Peace,* that a proletarian revolution cannot be carried through to a victorious conclusion within the boundaries of one country may appear to some readers to have been refuted by the almost five years' experience of our Soviet republic. But such a conclusion would be groundless. The fact that the workers' state has maintained itself against the whole world in one country, and in a backward country at that, bears witness to the colossal might of the proletariat, which in other countries, more advanced, more civilized, will be capable of performing real miracles. But, although we have held our ground in the political and military sense as a state, we have not yet undertaken or even approached the task of creating a socialist society. . . . As long as the bourgeoisie remains in power in the other European countries, we will be compelled, in our struggle against economic isolation, to strive for agreement with the capitalist world; at the same time it may be said with certainty that these agreements may at best help us to mitigate some of our economic ills, to take one or another step forward, but that a genuine advance of socialist economy in Russia will become possible *only after the victory* [My italics.—J.S.] of the proletariat in the most important countries of Europe.

Thus speaks Trotsky, plainly sinning against reality and stubbornly trying to save his "permanent revolution" from final shipwreck.

It appears, then, that, twist and turn as you like, we have not only "not undertaken" the task of creating a socialist society but we have "not even approached" it. It appears that some people have been hoping for "agreements with the capitalist world," but it also appears that nothing will come of these agreements, for, twist and turn as you like, a "genuine advance of socialist economy" will not be possible until the proletariat has been victorious in the "most important countries of Europe."

Well, then, since there is still no victory in the West, the only "choice" that remains for the revolution in Russia is: either to rot away or to degenerate into a bourgeois state.

It is no accident that Trotsky has been talking for two years now about the "degeneration" of our party.

It is no accident that last year Trotsky predicted the "doom" of our country. . . .

How can this "permanent" hopelessness be reconciled . . . with the following words of Lenin's:

> As a matter of fact, the power of state over all large-scale means of production, the power of state in the hands of the proletariat, the alliance of this proletariat with the many millions of small and very small peasants, the assured leadership of the peasantry by the proletariat, etc.—is not this all that is necessary in order to build a complete socialist society from the co-operatives, from the co-operatives alone, which we formerly treated as huckstering and which from a certain aspect we have the right to treat as such now, under N.E.P.? Is this not all that is necessary for the purpose of building a complete socialist society? This is not yet the building of socialist society, but it is all that is necessary and sufficient for this building. (V. I. Lenin, *Selected Works*, Vol. IX, p. 403.)

It is plain that these two views cannot be reconciled. Trotsky's "permanent revolution" is the negation of Lenin's theory of the proletarian revolution; and, conversely, Lenin's theory of the proletarian revolution is the negation of the theory of "permanent revolution."

Lack of faith in the strength and capabilities of our revolution, lack of faith in the strength and capabilities of the Russian proletariat—that is what lies at the root of the theory of "permanent revolution." . . .

Of late our press has begun to teem with rotten diplomats who try to palm off the theory of "permanent revolution" as something compatible with Leninism. . . .

Honeyed speeches and rotten diplomacy cannot hide the yawning chasm which lies between the theory of "permanent revolution" and Leninism. . . .

# THE PERMANENT REVOLUTION*

BY

## LEON TROTSKY

[1930]

As this book goes to press in the English language, the whole thinking part of the international working class, and in a sense, the whole of "civilized" humanity, listens with particularly keen interest to the reverberations of the economic turn taking place on the major part of the former czarist empire. The greatest attention in this connection is aroused by the problem of collectivizing the peasant holdings. And no wonder: in this sphere the break with the past assumes a particularly clear-cut character. But a correct evaluation of collectivization is unthinkable without a general conception of the socialist revolution. And here on an even higher plane, we are again convinced that everything in the field of Marxian theory is bound up with practical activity. The most remote, and it would seem, "abstract" disagreements, if they are thought out to the end, will sooner or later be expressed in practise, and the latter allows not a single theoretical mistake to be made with impunity. . . .

There are two distinct, and in the final analysis, directly opposed theoretical conceptions of socialism. Out of these flow basically different strategy and tactics.

Two principle variants are possible: (a) the course described [as] the economic entrenchment of the proletarian dictatorship in one country until further victories of the international proletarian revolution (the viewpoint of the Left Opposition); (b) the course towards the construction of an isolated national socialist society and that "in the shortest historical time" (the present official viewpoint). . . .

Let us recall . . . that the theory of socialism in one country was first formulated by Stalin in the fall of 1924, in complete contra-

---

*Selected and arranged from the Preface to the American Edition of *The Permanent Revolution* by Leon Trotsky, translated by Max Shachtman. Published by Pioneer Publishers.

diction not only to all the traditions of Marxism and the school of Lenin, but even to what Stalin wrote in the spring of the same year. . . .

Marxism proceeds from world economy, not as a sum of national parts, but as a mighty, independent reality, which is created by the international division of labor and the world market, and, in the present epoch, predominates over the national markets. The productive forces of capitalist society have long ago grown beyond the national frontier. The imperialist war was an expression of this fact. In the productive-technical respect, socialist society must represent a higher stage compared to capitalism. To aim at the construction of a *nationally isolated* socialist society means, in spite of all temporary successes, to pull the productive forces backward even as compared to capitalism. To attempt, regardless of the geographic, cultural and historical conditions of the country's development, which constitutes a part of the world whole, to realize a fenced-in proportionality of all the branches of economy within national limits, means to pursue a reactionary utopia. If the heralds and supporters of this theory nevertheless participate in the international revolutionary struggle (with what success is a different question) it is because as hopeless eclectics, they mechanically combine abstract internationalism with reactionary utopian national socialism. The consummate expression of this eclecticism is the program of the Comintern adopted by the Sixth Congress.

To expose completely one of the main theoretical mistakes, lying at the base of the national socialist conception, we can do nothing better than to quote the recently published speech of Stalin, devoted to the internal questions of American Communism.* "It would be wrong," says Stalin against one of the American factions, "not to take into consideration the specific peculiarities of American capitalism. The Communist party must consider them in its work. But it would be still more wrong to base the activity of the Communist party on these specific features, for the foundation of the activity of every Communist party, the American included, on

---

*This speech was delivered on May 6, 1929, was first published at the beginning of 1930, and under such circumstances that it acquires a "programmatic" significance.

which it must base itself, are the *general features* of capitalism, which are essentially the *same for all countries,* but not the specific features of *one* country. *It is precisely on this that the internationalism of the Communist parties rests.* The specific features are merely *supplementary* to the general features." (*Bolshevik,* No. 1, 1930, page 8. Our emphasis.)

These lines leave nothing to be desired in the way of clarity. Under the guise of an economic motivation for internationalism, Stalin in reality presents a motivation for national socialism. It is false that world economy is simply a sum of similar national parts. It is false that the specific features are *"merely supplementary* to the general features," like warts on the face. In reality, the national peculiarities are a unique combination of the basic features of the world process. This originality can be of decisive significance for revolutionary strategy for a number of years. It is sufficient to recall the fact that the proletariat of a backward country has come to power many years before the proletariat of the advanced countries. This historic lesson alone shows that in spite of Stalin, it is absolutely wrong to base the activity of the Communist parties on some "general features," that is, on an abstract type of national capitalism. It is radically wrong to contend that this is what the "internationalism of the Communist parties rests upon." In reality, it rests on the inconsistency of a national state, which has long ago outlived itself and acts as a brake on the development of the productive forces. National capitalism cannot be conceived of, let alone reconstructed, except as a part of world economy.

The economic peculiarities of different countries are in no way of a subordinate character: It is enough to compare England and India, the United States and Brazil. But the specific features of national economy, no matter how great, enter as component parts, and in increasing measure into the higher reality, which is called world economy, and on which alone, in the final analysis, the internationalism of the Communist parties rests.

Stalin's characterization of the national peculiarities as a simple "supplement" to the general type, is in crying and yet not accidental contradiction to Stalin's understanding (that is, his lack of understanding) of the law of the uneven development of capitalism. This law, as is known, is proclaimed by Stalin as the most fundamental, most important and universal. With the help of the law of uneven development, which he has converted into an abstraction, Stalin attempts to solve all the riddles of existence. But it is astounding: He does not notice that *national peculiarity is the most general product of unevenness of historical development, its final result, so to say.* It is only necessary to understand this unevenness correctly, to consider it to its full extent, and also to extend it to the pre-capitalist past. A faster or slower development of productive forces; the expanded, or on the contrary, the contracted character of whole historical epochs—for example, of the middle ages, the guild system, enlightened absolutism, parliamentarism; the uneven development of the different branches of economy, different classes, different social institutions, different fields of culture—all these lie at the base of these national "peculiarities." . . . The October revolution is the grandest manifestation of the unevenness of the historic process. . . .

Stalin resorted to the law of uneven development not in order to forsee in time the seizure of power by the proletariat of a backward country, but in order, after the fact, in 1924, to foist upon the already victorious proletariat the task of constructing a national socialist society. But it is precisely here that the law of uneven development has nothing to do with the matter, for it does not replace nor does it abolish the laws of world economy; on the contrary, it is subordinated to them.

By making a fetish of the law of uneven development, Stalin proclaims it a sufficient basis for national socialism, not as a type, common to all countries, but exceptional, Messianic, purely Russian. To construct an independent socialist society is possible, according to Stalin, only in Russia. By this alone he raises the national peculiarities of Russia not only above the "general features" of every capitalist nation, but also above world economy as a whole. This is just where the fatal flaw begins in the whole Stalin conception. The peculiarity of the U.S.S.R. is so immense that it makes possible the construction of its own socialism within its limits, regardless of what happens with the rest of humanity.

As for other countries to which the Messianic seal has not been affixed, their peculiarities are only "supplementary" to the general features, only a wart on the face. "It would be wrong," Stalin teaches, "to base the activities of the Communist parties on these specific features." This moral holds good for the American Communist Party, the British, South African and Serbian, but . . . not for the Russian, whose activity is based not on the "general features" but precisely on the "peculiarities." From this flows the thoroughly discordant strategy of the Comintern: while the U.S.S.R. "liquidates the classes" and builds national socialism, the proletariat of all the other countries, completely independent of actual national conditions, is obligated to uniform action according to the calendar. . . . Messianic nationalism is complemented by bureaucratically abstract internationalism. This discordance runs through the whole program of the Comintern, and deprives it of any principled significance.

If we take England and India as the opposite poles of capitalist types, we must state that the internationalism of the British and Indian proletariat does not at all rest on the *similarity* of conditions, tasks, and methods, but on their inseparable *interdependence*. The successes of the liberation movement in India presuppose a revolutionary movement in England, and the other way around. Neither in India, nor in England is it possible to construct an independent socialist society. Both of them will have to enter as parts into a higher entity. In this and only in this rests the unshakable foundation of Marxian internationalism.

Only recently, on March 8, 1930, *Pravda* expounded Stalin's unhappy theory anew, in the sense that "socialism, as a social-economic formation," that is, as a definite form of productive relations, can be absolutely realized "on the national scale of the U.S.S.R." "The *complete victory of socialism* in the sense of a guarantee against the intervention of capitalist encirclement," is quite another matter—such a complete victory of socialism "actually demands the triumph of the proletarian revolution in several advanced countries." What abysmal decline of theoretical thought was required for such sorry scholasticism to be expounded in a learned guise on the pages of the central organ of Lenin's party!

If we should assume for a minute the possibility of realizing social-ism as a finished social system in the isolated framework of the U.S.S.R., then what would be the "complete victory"—what inter-vention could even be talked of then? The socialist order of society presupposes high levels of technique, culture and solidarity of the population. Since the U.S.S.R., at the moment of complete construction of socialism, will have, it must be assumed, a popu-lation of from 200,000,000 to 250,000,000, then we ask: What intervention could be talked of then? What capitalist country, or coalition of countries would dare think of intervention under these circumstances? The only conceivable intervention could be on the part of the U.S.S.R. But would it be needed? Hardly. The example of a backward country, which in the course of several "five year plans" constructed a mighty socialist society with its own forces would mean a death blow to world capitalism, and would reduce to a minimum, if not to zero, the costs of the world prole-tarian revolution. This is why the whole Stalinist conception actually leads to the liquidation of the Communist International. . . .

The passing of power from the hands of czarism and the bour-geoisie into the hands of the proletariat, abolishes neither the processes, nor the laws of world economy. It is true that for a certain time after the October revolution, the economic ties be-tween the Soviet Union and the world market were weakened. But it would be a monstrous mistake to generalize a phenomenon which was merely a short stage in the dialectical process. The international division of labor and the supranational character of modern productive forces, not only retain, but will increase two-fold and tenfold their significance for the Soviet Union, depending upon the degree of its economic ascent.

Every backward country that has become a part of capitalism has gone through various stages of decreasing or increasing depend-ence upon the other capitalist countries, but in general the tendency of capitalist development leads towards a colossal growth of world ties, which is expressed in the growth of foreign trade, including, of course, capital export as well. . . .

In the process of its development, and consequently in the

struggle with its internal contradictions, every national capitalism turns in ever increasing measure to the reserves of the "external market," that is, of world economy. The uncontrollable expansion growing out of the permanent internal crisis of capitalism, constitutes its progressive force until it becomes fatal.

The October revolution inherited from old Russia, besides the internal contradictions of capitalism, no less profound contradictions between capitalism as a whole and the pre-capitalist forms of production. These contradictions had and still have, a material character, that is, they are contained in the material relations between the city and country in definite proportions or disproportions of various branches of industry and national economy in general, etc. Some of the roots of these contradictions lie directly in the geographic and demographic conditions of the country, that is, they are nurtured by the surplus or the shortage of one or the other natural resource, and the historically created distribution of the masses of the people, etc. The strength of Soviet economy lies in the nationalization of the means of production and in their planned direction. The weakness of Soviet economy, on the other hand, besides the backwardness inherited from the past, lies in its present post-revolutionary isolation, that is, in its inability to gain access to the resources of world economy, not only on a socialist but even on a capitalist basis, that is, in the form of normal international credits, and "financing" in general, which plays such a decisive role for backward countries. However, the contradictions of its capitalist and pre-capitalist past not only do not disappear of themselves, but on the contrary, rise out of the twilight of the years of decline and destruction, revive and are accentuated simultaneously with the growth of Soviet economy, and in order to be overcome or even mitigated, demand at every step contact with the resources of the world market.

To understand what is happening now in the vast territory which the October revolution awakened to new life, we must always clearly picture to ourselves that to the old contradictions recently revived by the economic successes, there has been added a new and enormous contradiction between the concentrated character of Soviet industry, which opens up the possibility of an unprecedented tempo of development, and the isolation of Soviet economy, which excludes the possibility of a normal utilization of the reserves of world economy. The new contradiction, bearing down upon the old ones, leads to the fact that alongside of the exceptional successes, painful difficulties arise. The latter find their most immediate and strongest expression, felt daily by every worker and peasant, in the fact that the conditions of the toiling masses do not keep step with the general rise of economy, but even grow worse at present as a result of the food difficulties. The sharp crises of Soviet economy are a reminder that the productive forces created by capitalism are not adapted to a national framework and can be socialistically coordinated and harmonized only on an international scale. In other words, the crises of Soviet economy are not merely the maladies of growth, a sort of infantile sickness, but something immeasurably more significant—precisely that severe check of the world market, the very one "to which," in Lenin's words, "we are subordinated, with which we are bound up, and from which we cannot escape" (at the Eleventh Congress of the party, March 27, 1922). . . .

The seizure of power by the international proletariat cannot be a single, simultaneous act. The political superstructure—and a revolution is part of "superstructure"— has its own dialectic, which peremptorily interrupts the process of world economy, but does not abolish its deep-seated laws. The October revolution is "legitimate" as *the first stage in the world revolution,* which inevitably extends over decades. The interval between the first and the second stage has turned out to be considerably longer than we had expected. Nevertheless, it remains an interval, without being converted into an epoch of the self-sufficient construction of a national socialist society. . . .

A realistic program of an isolated workers' state cannot set itself the aim of achieving "independence" from world economy, much less of constructing a national socialist society in the "shortest time." The task is not to accomplish the abstract maximum, but the most favorable tempo under the circumstances, that is, those that flow from internal and world economic conditions, strengthen the positions of the proletariat, prepare the *national elements* of the future international socialist society, and at the same time, and above all, systematically improve the living level of the proletariat, strengthening its union with the non-exploiting masses of the village. This perspective remains in force for the whole preparatory period, that is, until the victorious revolution in the advanced countries liberates the Soviet Union out of its present isolated position. . . .

The considerations brought out above are sufficient, let us hope, to reveal the whole significance of the struggle of principles that was carried on in recent years, and is carried on now in the form of contrasting two theories: *socialism in one country* and the *permanent revolution*. . . .

# DOCUMENTS ON THE QUESTION OF UNITED STATES RECOGNITION OF THE SOVIET UNION

1. NOTE FROM SECRETARY OF STATE (COLBY) TO THE ITALIAN AMBASSADOR (AVEZZANO) (AUG. 10, 1920)

Excellency:

The agreeable intimation which you have conveyed to the State Department, that the Italian Government would welcome a statement of the views of this government on the situation presented by the Russian advance into Poland, deserves a prompt response, and I will attempt without delay a definition of this Government's position, not only as to the situation arising from Russian military pressure upon Poland but also as to certain cognate and inseparable phases of the Russian question viewed more broadly.

This Government believes in a united, free and autonomous Polish State, and the people of the United States are earnestly solicitous for the maintenance of Poland's political independence and territorial integrity. From this attitude we will not depart, and the policy of this Government will be directed to the employment of all available means to render it effectual.

The Government, therefore, takes no exception to the effort apparently being made in some quarters to arrange an armistice between Poland and Russia, but it would not, at least for the present, participate in any plan for the expansion of the armistice negotiations into a general European conference, which would in all probability involve two results, from both of which this country strongly recoils, viz., the recognition of the Bolshevist regime and a settlement of the Russian problem almost inevitably upon the basis of a dismemberment of Russia. . . .

The United States maintains unimpaired its faith in the Russian people, in their high character and their future. That they will overcome the existing anarchy, suffering and destitution we do not entertain the slightest doubt. The distressing character of Russia's transition has many historical parallels, and the United States is confident that restored, free and united Russia will again take a leading place in the world, joining with the other free nations in upholding peace and orderly justice.

Until that time shall arrive the United States feels that friendship and honor require that Russia's interests must be generously protected, and that, as far as possible, all decisions of vital importance to it, and especially those concerning its sovereignty over the territory of the former Russian Empire, be held in abeyance. By this feeling of friendship and honorable obligation to the great nation whose brave and heroic self-sacrifice contributed so much to the successful termination of the war, the Government of the United States was guided in its reply to the Lithuanian National Council, on October 15, 1919, and in its persistent refusal to recognize the Baltic States as separate nations independent of Russia. The same spirit was manifested in the note of this Government of March 24, 1920, in which it was stated, with reference to certain proposed settlements in the Near East, that no final decision should or can be made without the consent of Russia. . . .

These illustrations show with what consistency the Government of the United States has been guided in its foreign policy by a loyal friendship for Russia. We are unwilling that while it is helpless in the grip of a non-representative Government, whose only sanction is brutal force, Russia shall be weakened still further by a policy of dismemberment conceived in other than Russian interests.

With the desire of the Allied Powers to bring about a peaceful solution of the existing difficulties in Europe this Government is, of course, in hearty accord, and will support any justifiable steps to that end. It is unable to perceive, however, that a recognition of the Soviet regime would promote, much less accomplish, this object, and it is therefore adverse to any dealings with the Soviet regime beyond the most narrow boundaries to which a discussion of an armistice can be confined.

That the present rulers of Russia do not rule by the will or the consent of any considerable proportion of the Russian people is an incontestable fact. Although nearly two and one-half years have passed since they seized the machinery of government, promising to protect the Constituent Assembly against alleged conspiracies against it, they have not yet permitted anything in the way of a popular election. At the moment when the work of creating a popular representative government, based upon universal suffrage, was nearing completion, the Bolsheviki, although in number an inconsiderable minority of the people, by force and cunning seized the powers and machinery of government, and have continued to use them with savage oppression to maintain themselves in power.

Without any desire to interfere in the internal affairs of the Russian people or to suggest what kind of government they should have, the Government of the United States does express the hope that they will soon find a way to set up a government representing their free will and purpose. When that time comes, the United States will consider the measures of practical assistance which can be taken to promote the restoration of Russia, provided Russia has not taken itself wholly out of the pale of the friendly interest of other nations by the pillage and oppression of the Poles.

It is not possible for the Government of the United States to recognize the present rulers of Russia as a government with which the relations common to friendly Governments can be maintained. This conviction has nothing to do with any particular political or social structure which the Russian people themselves may see fit to embrace. It rests upon a wholly different set of facts. These facts, which none disputes, have convinced the Government of the United States, against its will, that the existing regime in Russia is based upon the negation of every principle of honor and good faith and every usage and convention underlying the whole structure of international law—the negation, in short, of every principle upon which it is possible to base harmonious and trustful relations, whether of nations or of individuals.

The responsible leaders of the regime have frequently and openly boasted that they are willing to sign agreements and undertakings with foreign powers while not having the slightest intention of observing such undertakings or carrying out such agreements. This attitude of disregard of obligations voluntarily entered into they base upon the theory that no compact or agreement made with a non-Bolshevist Government can have any moral force for them. They have not only avowed this as a doctrine, but have exemplified it in practice.

Indeed, upon numerous occasions the responsible spokesmen of this power and its official agencies have declared that it is their understanding that the very existence of Bolshevism in Russia, the maintenance of their own rule, depends, and must continue to depend, upon the occurrence of revolutions in all other great civilized nations, including the United States, which will overthrow and destroy their Governments and set up Bolshevist rule in their stead. They have made it quite plain that they intend to use every means, including, of course, diplomatic agencies, to promote such revolutionary movements in other countries.

It is true that they have in various ways expressed their willingness to give "assurances" and "guarantees" that they will not abuse the privileges and immunities of diplomatic agencies by using them for this purpose. In view of their own declarations, already referred to, such assurances and guarantees cannot be very seriously considered.

Moreover, it is within the knowledge of the Government of the United States that the Bolshevist Government is itself subject to the control of a political faction with extensive international ramifications through the Third International, and that this body, which is heavily subsidized by the Bolshevist Government from the public revenues of Russia, has for its openly avowed aim the promotion of Bolshevist revolutions throughout the world. The leaders of the Bolsheviki have boasted that their promises of non-interference with other nations would in no way bind the agents of this body.

There is no room for reasonable doubt that such agents would receive the support and protection of any diplomatic agencies the Bolsheviki might have in other countries. Inevitably, therefore, the diplomatic service of the Bolshevist Government would become a channel for intrigues and the propaganda of revolt against the institutions and laws of countries with which it was at peace, which would be an abuse of friendship to which enlightened Governments cannot subject themselves.

In the view of this Government, there cannot be any common ground upon which it can stand with a power whose conceptions of international relations are so entirely alien to its own, so utterly repugnant to its moral sense. There can be no mutual confidence or trust, no respect even, if pledges are to be given and agreements made with a cynical repudiation of their obligations already in the minds of one of the parties. We cannot recognize, hold official relations with, or give friendly reception to the agents of a Government which is determined and bound to conspire against our institutions; whose diplomats will be the agitators of dangerous revolt; whose spokesmen say that they sign agreements with no intention of keeping them.

To summarize the position of this Government, I would say, therefore, in response to your Excellency's inquiry, that it would regard with satisfaction a declaration by the allied and associated powers that the territorial integrity and true boundaries of Russia shall be respected. These boundaries should properly include the whole of the former Russian Empire, with the exception of Finland proper, ethnic Poland, and such territory as may by agreement form a part of the Armenian State.

The aspirations of these nations are legitimate. Each was forcibly annexed and their liberation from oppressive alien rule involves no aggression against Russia's territorial rights and has received the sanction of the public opinion of all free peoples. Such a declaration presupposes the withdrawal of all foreign troops from the territory embraced by these boundaries, and in the opinion of this Government should be accompanied by the announcement that no transgression by Poland, Finland, or any other power, of the line so drawn will be permitted.

Thus only can the Bolshevist regime be deprived of its false but effective appeal to Russian nationalism and compelled to meet the inevitable challenge of reason and self-respect which the Russian people, secure from invasion and territorial violation, are sure to address to a social philosophy that degrades them and a tyranny that oppresses them.

The policy herein outlined will command the support of this Government.

Accept, Excellency, the renewed assurances of my highest consideration.

BAINBRIDGE COLBY

His Excellency,
Baron Cammillo Romano Avezzano,
Ambassador of Italy

## 2. Note from People's Commissar for Foreign Affairs (Chicherin) to the Secretary of State (Colby) (Oct. 4, 1920)

Secretary of State Bainbridge Colby's note to the Italian Ambassador contains an attack upon Soviet Russia's policy and her political system. Soviet Russia cannot leave unheeded these false and malicious accusations of a character quite unusual in diplomacy, and desires to bring them before the bar of public opinion. . . .

. . . The condition precedent for Mr. Colby's friendship towards Russia is that her Government should not be a Soviet Government. As a matter of fact any other Government at present would be a *bourgeois* or capitalist government, which in view of the present economic unity of the world, would mean a government identified with the interests of the world's dominating financial groups. The most powerful among the latter, as a consequence of the world war, are the North American financial groups. The condition upon which Mr. Colby would extend American friendship to Russia is therefore that her regime should be such as to permit of the domination of the American financial groups in Russia. Mr. Colby displays in his note a strong friendly feeling towards the Russian Government of 1917, *i.e.*, towards the Russian Government which coerced Russia's working masses to bleed in the world war on the side of the allied and associated powers, which was fought for the interests of financial capital; of that Russian Government which under the cloak of a pretended democratic regime supported the domination of the *bourgeoisie* in Russia, *i.e.*, of the capitalist system, and in the last resort the domination of the world's leading financial interests over Russia. . . . The Soviet Government unwaveringly upholds the right of national self-determination of the working people of every nationality, including the right of secession and of forming separate states. This is the cornerstone on which it wishes to establish friendly relations with the new border states. This system, represented by the Soviet Government, under which the working masses govern themselves and determine their own fate is the only present day challenge to the domination of the exploiting interests of the leading groups of world's capi-

structure, to establish proper, peaceful and friendly relations between them.    The Russian Soviet Government is convinced that not only the working masses, but likewise the far-sighted business men of the United States of America will repudiate the policy which is expressed in Mr. Colby's note and is harmful to American interests and that in the near future normal relations will be established between Russia and the United States.

CHICHERIN

# RECOGNITION OF RUSSIA AND WORLD PEACE*

### BY

## COLONEL RAYMOND ROBINS

### [1926]

It is now nearly eight years since I left Russia, having served there in the American Red Cross, military and diplomatic missions of the United States. Several months of the Provisional government and some eight months of the Soviet power had passed under my observation. Being sufficiently close to the outdoor realities to know, when the Bolshevik revolution culminated on the seventh of November, 1917, that this was the end of the Kerensky regime, I began immediately to deal with the Soviets then under the leadership of Lenin, Trotsky and their associates. For eight months I tested the will and the power of these leaders and the dominion of Soviet control.

Returning to the United States in June, 1918, and reporting to our government at Washington, I advised against military intervention and urged American cooperation with the Russian people struggling to find their way to a long delayed freedom. I gave evidence to prove that Lenin and Trotsky were sincere and trusted leaders of the conscious Russian masses—however wrong might be their political and economic theories; that the Bolsheviks were fundamentally opposed to the German military autocracy; and that the Soviets would probably hold power for the period of the war and possibly much longer. I recommended the sending to Russia of a competent diplomatic and business mission to negotiate a modus vivendi for diplomatic and economic relations between the United States and Russia. For these views there was generous denunciation here and in other lands. These critics, claiming a superior knowledge of the Russian situation, declared that Lenin and Trotsky were thieves, murderers and German agents; that the

---

*From "The United States in Relation to the European Situation," *Annals of the American Academy*, No. 126, July 1926. Reprinted by permission.

Bolshevik revolution was a German-directed conspiracy against the Allies; and that the Soviet power must fall within a few weeks.

Now after nearly eight years Lenin's tomb is the scene of the daily pilgrimage of simple Russian folk, who regard him as their great liberator, Trotsky shares in the highest offices of the Russian government, and the Soviet power is known by all informed, intelligent and disinterested persons to be the most stable social control in Europe. Today Russia is governed by the oldest continuous party cabinet in the Old World.

Alone and outlawed, after the most appalling sacrifices in the great war, followed by the even greater sacrifices due to civil conflict, famine, pestilence and the production-destroying theories of Communism, Russia has now stabilized the most fundamental economic revolution of history, and is under a system of limited capitalism and state socialism approaching prewar production in many of the essentials of civilized life. Her working people enjoy the best labor standards in Europe, she has adopted the most comprehensive program for general popular education ever accepted by a responsible government, and the most humane provisions for the welfare of women and children yet legalized in the Old World.

Despite the heavy handicap of non-recognition—without embassy or consulates—American business men are successfully operating important concessions and Russian trade in cotton alone has brought some one hundred million dollars into the United States during the last two years. America is the only first-class power that has not recognized the Soviet government. Is our government less stable and are our people less immune from the virus of Communism than the governments and peoples of the Old World? Every student knows that the exact opposite is true. Communism has made and will make less headway in these United States than in any other land. Why should American business and trade be longer handicapped by a futile non-intercourse policy with the greatest potential market for our manufactures and certain raw materials remaining on this earth?

If we were as realistic as the British or the French I would recommend immediate recognition of the Soviet government of

Russia by the Government of the United States. In doing this, we would not approve of that government, nor of its methods, moral, economic or political. The fact is so well settled by the principles and precedents of international law that I decline to stress it. But the long sustained propaganda against and misrepresentation of Soviet Russia has doubtless made this forthright action politically impossible for us. Therefore, as a practical method I recommend that we send a competent diplomatic and business mission to Russia, authorized to confer with the proper representatives of the Soviet government regarding the debts due the United States, the settlement of claims due our citizens for the confiscation of their property in Russia, and general provisions for intercourse, trade and commerce between America and Russia. Such an effort for re-establishment of normal relations between Russia and the United States is demanded by the following considerations:

First. Non-recognition is a sort of continuous *casus belli* between the two countries. It seems to justify propaganda for and against such recognition in both lands. It feeds the passion of international hatred, and promotes bitterness and misunderstanding. Such a policy is in direct conflict with our international action for more than a hundred years. Our historic policy has always been to recognize the *de facto* government and having made provisions for intercourse and trade, to refuse any alliance that would bind our future relationships. Under this policy Washington recognized the revolutionary government of France in its worst form. Under this policy we kept out of the affairs of Europe, and became the strongest government and the most prosperous people in the world. Under this policy of normal and friendly intercourse and trade with all nations—but alliance with none—we won the esteem of the people of all lands, and opened all the markets of the world for the commerce of the United States.

Second. Recognition of Russia has been opposed by those persons who fear that such recognition would result in an increase of communist propaganda in this country. Is it not more reasonable to believe that recognition would have just the opposite effect? With a Russian ambassador at Washington and an American am-

bassador in Moscow we could protest much more effectively
against any communist propaganda from Russian sources. As it
is now, communist propaganda in America is of no moment in
Moscow, and then its suppression would be a matter of economic
concern to the Soviet government. I am not greatly excited about
this propaganda. This is not because of the efficiency of the
"bomb squads," but rather because of my conviction that communist institutions are alien to the genus of our political and
economic nature, while democratic institutions are in harmony
with that nature. None the less I would like to quiet the terrible
unrest of some of our witch-hunters, who are otherwise sane and
useful citizens. Class hatred and materialistic Communism are
diseases engendered by the class-poisoned conditions of the Old
World. They wither and die in the atmosphere of free religious,
political and economic institutions. To be fearful of the stability
of American social control because of the patter of the communist
soap-boxer is treason to the strength of our government, and unworthy of any mind capable of understanding the foundations of
our social order.

Third. There can be no real disarmament nor assurance of
international peace so long as our policy of isolating Russia is continued. The economic burden of vast armaments and the threat
of war are the heaviest and most durable curses of the modern
world. Every effort toward disarmament and guaranty of lasting
peace is doomed to failure so long as Russia has one of the largest
standing armies in Europe and remains isolated from the fellow-
ship of nations.

Fourth. The economic stabilization of Europe cannot be effectively maintained until the natural resources of Russia and the
consumption power of the Russian people for imports from other
lands, once again plays its normal part in the currents of world
economic life. Soviet Russia embraces nearly one-seventh of the
earth's surface and contains some one hundred and forty millions
of people. Within her boundaries are more untilled fertile acres,
more untouched forests of valuable timber and more unmined
mineral resources than is possessed by any other nation.

Fifth. The Russian market is potentially the greatest unde-

veloped economic resource now left in this world. Already our
foreign trade has begun to slow down. The need of foreign
markets for our surplus products grows in urgency and importance
from month to month. Russia contains vast stores of gold, man-
ganese, oils and timber and she has a practical monopoly of flax,
furs and platinum. She needs our tractors, machinery, motors,
metals, chemicals, typewriters and cotton. American capital and
technical ability are indispensable for the adequate development
in any near future of Russian resources and trade. The opportunities of this market should be open to American labor and
capital on the best terms. Such concessions as have been secured
by bona fide American business men have been profitable and the
relations with the Soviet authorities have been satisfactory—despite the burdensome conditions of non·recognition. Why should
American business continue to suffer this handicap in securing
our share of Russian trade?

Sixth. There is no principle that justifies our recognition of
the present Italian government that would nòt justify our recognition of the present Russian government. Mussolini is as con-
temptuous of constitutional forms and democratic methods as was
Lenin. His black-shirts are in principle the same ruthless domination by force of the helpless masses of the people as was ever
charged against Lenin's Red guard. His dictatorship in Italy is
the same thing in method as the dictatorship of Lenin in Russia.
The argument used by the eminent international banker, Mr.
Thomas W. Lamont, in justification of Mussolini's regime, in
which he said: "As to the matter of liberalism, the question seems
to me, to be liberal enough to let Italy have the sort of government
she seems to want," I believe to be the true American doctrine
and we invoke it on behalf of the Russian people and the Soviet
government.

Seventh. The Russian people have a special and notable genius
and are capable of a high place in the intellectual and moral leadership of mankind. Their character and geographical position
give them a dominant place in the Far East. Cooperation between
Russia and America is the key to the solution of every international
problem in the Orient. To force Russia into an Oriental trium-

virate inimical to the Occidental nations is colossal diplomatic folly. To be indifferent to the injury to world civilization that can result from the continued effort by America to isolate Russia, is to confess ignorance of these potencies as well as moral bankruptcy in international affairs.

Let us speak frankly. There are individuals and groups in this country and other lands that oppose the recognition of Russia by the United States because of selfish interests, and there are individuals and groups that favor such recognition for the same ulterior reasons. Neither group is entitled to our consideration in the settlement of this momentous question.

Except in the splendid service of the American Relief Administration, under the wise and courageous leadership of Colonel Haskell, our past policy in relations to the Soviet government of Russia has been a tragedy of errors. We have aided in stamping Bolshevism in instead of stamping it out. In obedience to an official diplomatic view, largely the product of the tea-table chatter of emigrés and the propaganda of groups having a selfish interest in the hoped-for return of the old order in Russia, we shared in a costly and futile military intervention that sent American boys to die uselessly in Siberia and north Russia. We participated in a savage embargo that brought privation and death to innocent women and children. We have been brutal and ruthless in dealing with helpless immigrants, while under the sweep of panic fears and prejudices aroused to fever heat by propaganda lies. To bolster this mistaken policy we published under the seal of the United States the feeble forgeries known as the Sisson documents, that had been rejected as stupidly false by the Allied Secret Service in Russia.

After eight years of this furtive and futile policy, during which the Soviet government has been doomed to die daily, that government is more stable and powerful now than at any other hour of its existence. Is it not time to substitute sanity and common sense for hysteria and lying propaganda in dealing with the Russian question? Let our government send to Russia a competent diplomatic and business mission and let them sit down at a table with the representatives of the Russian government. Then if that government declines a reasonable settlement of the debt due our government, to compensate those of our citizens whose property was confiscated and to give reasonable guaranties against official support of communist propaganda in this country, let this commission return and report the facts to the government and the people of the United States, and we will keep the door closed against Russia, and prepare for the next war. If on the other hand the Soviet government does that which I have reason to believe it has been ready to do for the past eight years, *i.e.*, make a satisfactory settlement on all these points, then we can proceed to formal recognition and the establishment of normal intercourse and trade between Russia and America. In that hour we will have returned to our traditional foreign policy that has made this nation prosperous at home and respected abroad, and the cornerstone upon which international peace and economic stabilization can be founded will have been laid.

# THE SOVIET UNION:
# THE QUESTION OF RECOGNITION*

BY

## JOHN SPARGO

[1930]

In the protracted contest between the ideals and institutions of communist-sovietism and those which for convenience we will designate capitalist civilization there has been thus far no single event of greater or more far-reaching importance than the refusal of the government of the United States to recognize the Russian Soviet government. It is agreed by the best minds on both sides that a contrary decision in 1920 would have changed the whole course of international politics during the decade just ended.

Intrinsically, the note which Secretary of State Colby addressed to the Italian Ambassador in Washington on August 10, 1920, stating the position of the United States toward the Russian Soviet government, is one of the most important diplomatic documents in our history . . . .

The armies of Soviet Russia had invaded Poland and seemed likely to subjugate that newly reconstructed nation. The Italian Ambassador in Washington inquired what the attitude of the government of the United States was, both toward the Russian-Polish conflict itself and toward certain efforts that were being made to effect an armistice between the two powers. Secretary Colby replied to the specific question as follows: The United States desired "the maintenance of Poland's political independence and territorial integrity," and took no exception "to the effort apparently being made in some quarters to arrange an armistice between Poland and Russia." At the same time the United States was opposed to "the expansion of the armistice negotiations into a general European conference," the reasons for this opposition being that such a conference would involve recognition of the

---

* From *Current History,* September 1930, Vol. 32. Reprinted by permission.

Soviet regime and a settlement of problems of vital importance to
Russia upon the basis of her dismemberment. "From both of these
results," said the note, "this country strongly recoils."

The reply to the question of the Italian Ambassador was con-
cise, ample and free from ambiguity. It gave notice to the powers
that the policy of the United States was opposed equally to any
dismemberment of either Russia or Poland and also to the recognition of the Soviet regime at that time. Had the note stopped
there it would have met the requirements of the moment well
enough. It would have been a conventionally proper and technically correct diplomatic note, and nothing more.

What gives the Colby note its historical importance and pre-
eminence among the diplomatic papers of our time is the trenchant
and fearless exposition of the reasons why the United States could
not give recognition to the Soviet government, unless and until the
latter divested itself of those inherent characteristics which distinguish it from all other governments, past or present. The note
emphasized the fact that the government of the United States did
not concern itself with any feature of the political or economic
structure which had been set up in Russia by the Bolsheviki. It
did not object to either the Soviet form of government or communism as an economic system. The right to establish either or
both of these is inherent in Russian sovereignty. Denial of recognition was based upon the conviction that there was in the regime
something fundamental to its existence which made it impossible
for the United States to hold with that regime the relations common to friendly governments and logically ensuing from recognition.

It was an impossible thing. There was no matter for argument
or adjustment. The biological impossibility of mating a humming
bird with a hippopotamus was not greater than the impossibility
of friendly relations between powers so infinitely remote from
each other. In language the severity of which is unparalleled in
the history of modern diplomacy Secretary Colby set forth the indictment upon which he based his conclusion that "in the view
of this government there cannot be any common ground upon
which it can stand with a power whose conceptions of international

relations are so entirely alien to its own, so utterly repugnant to its moral sense."

Publication of the note caused a sensation. It was realized that here was no mere statement of momentary policy, another move in the diplomatic game. Here was finality itself, the irrevocable. It was made manifest to all mankind that the United States had measured the Soviet regime, examined its philosophy and principles, and, having reached an inexorable conclusion, had deliberately challenged it. Secretary Colby had placed the United States in the position of foremost defender and champion of the principles and usages upon which international order and comity are founded. Incidentally he established for himself a place among the greatest of our Secretaries of State and as a diplomat whose work was of epochal importance.

Mr. Harding, then a candidate for the Presidency, had declared publicly that if elected he would reverse the entire foreign policy of President Wilson. Privately he had said that he would recognize the Soviet government. "No American statesman," said a high European official, "will dare attempt that for a generation to come upon any terms less than the complete surrender of the Soviet regime to the American position. The note of Secretary Colby is one of those rare declarations which all subsequent statesmen have to accept as unchangeable."

Ten years have passed. Woodrow Wilson has been succeeded by Warren G. Harding, Calvin Coolidge and Herbert Hoover, while Secretaries Hughes, Kellogg and Stimson have succeeded Secretary Colby. The position taken by Colby has been stoutly and ably maintained to the last letter by his successors. So strongly did Secretary Hughes emphasize that position, reiterating his objections and arguments, that the policy came to be widely spoken of as "the Hughes policy." From time to time there have been flurries of agitation in favor of a reversal of the policy and recognition of the Soviet regime, but such a reversal is less likely today than at any time during the ten years that have elapsed since Secretary Colby's declaration rang like a clarion call through the chancelleries of the world. The opposition to the policy in this country is negligible in quantity and quality alike, especially the latter. A few self-styled intellectuals join with scattered political malcontents in a futile protest against the irrevocable, but the policy is buttressed by the incontestable sanctions of the nation, our self-respect and our strength.

Most impressive of all the tributes to the strength of the American position is the pitifully weak case which its opponents have set up. The foremost leaders and spokesmen of the Soviet regime, admittedly among the ablest and adroitest of controversialists, have devoted their talents to the task of discrediting the Colby note and our policy of non-recognition. Yet a dispassionate survey of the pro-Soviet arguments assailing our policy throughout the decade can convey to a thoughtful mind no other impression than one of incredible weakness. Despite the care and precision with which Secretary Colby, in terms understandable and incapable of misinterpretation, stated our position that our refusal to accord recognition to the Soviet government has nothing to do with any feature of any of its domestic institutions, scarcely an argument appears on the Soviet side which does not assail the American policy upon the ground that our refusal to recognize the Soviet government is due to our disapproval either of the Soviet form of government or of communism. If this argument is sincerely advanced, in the belief that it is valid, then the lack of intelligence is most pitiful. The only alternative is to hold the argument in contempt as a studied and cynical affront to our national intelligence.

In our foreign relations we can recognize and hold relations with monarchies, dictatorships and republics, with slave states and free nations, with every variety of race and cultural development. No American statesman would dare to make the political form of any government or the economic system of any nation the basis of a denial of diplomatic recognition and intercourse. Secretaries Hughes and Kellogg were as careful as Secretary Colby to emphasize that our policy involved no such infantile innovation in world politics. Russia can adhere to the Soviet form of government, if it so pleases, and it can develop communism to its ultimate limits, if it so pleases, and still gain recognition. All that it has to do is to abandon its avowed hostility to other nations, including our own, which do not desire, and will not have thrust upon them, either sovietism or communism.  Let the Soviet government abandon its policy of promoting world-wide revolution, either directly or through the instrumentality of the Communist International, let it manifest the international good-will which has invariably been the requisite condition for admission into the family of nations and recognition will be accorded to it.

In the words of Elihu Root, "recognition means that each government accepts the implied assurance of the other that it will maintain true friendship, true respect, true observance of the obligations of good neighborhood. . . . The fundamental doctrine of the men who govern Russia is that it is their mission in the world to overturn and destroy the government of the United States, of England, of France, of all the civilized nations of the Western World. . . . The act of recognition would be a formal and a solemn lie, a false pretense of accepting the obligations of the Bolshevist rulers of Russia to observe friendship to the g. vernment and people of the United States."

That is the essence of the matter.  To enter upon such an agreement with the Soviet government is incompatible with our national self-respect.  The case is without precedent, for there has never before in the history of civilization been a government which on the one hand openly proclaimed its intent and purpose to be the overturning and destruction of the social and political institutions and the economic systems of other nations, while on the other hand it demanded that the governments of those other nations accord it recognition as a friendly power, grant it diplomatic privileges and advantages which are universally reserved for friendly powers and universally withdrawn from any power which commits unfriendly acts.  It is futile and vain to argue the matter; recognition of Soviet Russia would be shameful self-abasement.

With amazing effrontery, or amazing stupidity—it is hard to decide which—the pro-Soviet advocates tell us that, even if the Soviet leaders are hostile to our institutions, and even if the Soviet regime does inspire and direct propaganda in other nations for the overthrow of their economic and political institutions, and would do so in this country through abuse of diplomatic privileges if these were granted to them, the United States ought, nevertheless, to grant recognition to the Soviet government and accord it those opportunities. Failure to do this, they say, is evidence of a lack of faith in the stability of our own institutions, a sense of weakness and fear that propaganda will destroy our political and economic system. It is a curious argument. It does not require answer from a statesman; any psychiatrist can explain it. Our scientific culture, our sanitary and medical forces and resources are ample to enable us to cope with an outbreak of bubonic plague, let us say. Is that any reason why we should admit people suffering from the disease through our seaports to spread infection? Must we say that the danger of a great epidemic is small because we have the means to deal with the epidemic before it becomes great? To state the question clearly is to expose its absurdity.

Our refusal to recognize the Soviet government arose from our consciousness of strength, not from consciousness of weakness or from fear. In one country after another statesmen have expressed their admiration and envy of a policy they dared not emulate because of internal weakness in their own countries. Our Communist movement is a negligible quantity. It has no political significance. Our labor movement, led by the American Federation of Labor, and incomparably the most efficient of all the national labor movements, has from the first been a strong bulwark against Bolshevist propaganda in this country. It is not involved politically as the labor movement is in all the leading countries of Europe, nor compelled by the nature of politics to compromise and placate extremist minorities. When the Colby note was written the United States was the only great power which was in a position to shape its policy with a sole regard to international order and well-being, to be guided by the highest and best traditions and principles of international law and the comity of nations.

We have not attempted to apply to Soviet Russia any new principle. We have not required of the Soviet government, as a condition prerequisite to its recognition, any act or undertaking which is not implicit in every act of recognition of a foreign power in our history and, what is more significant, is clearly and universally recognized as the requisite condition for the continuance of diplomatic relationships however long established.

Suppose that Mr. Ramsay MacDonald and his principal associates in the British Cabinet belonged to a political organization similar in character to the Communist International, which not only claimed but actually exercised the power to control and direct the action and policies of the Cabinet. Suppose this organization were international in scope with branches in many countries, including our own, over which the central organization claimed and exercised the same jurisdiction and control as over the Cabinet. Suppose, further, that Mr. MacDonald, Mr. Henderson, Mr. Thomas, Lord Passfield and other important members of the Cabinet also held important positions in the councils of the international organization; that this organization by formal resolutions and published proclamations declared its hostility to this country and its institutions, avowed its intention of promoting revolution here, and called upon its members in this country, some of them out own citizens, to institute agitation and strikes for revolutionary purposes and to incite conflicts between the white and colored races for the same purpose. That would be a state of affairs exactly parallel to that which obtains in the case of the Soviet government.

Now suppose that Mr. MacDonald and his associate Ministers, while adopting a perfectly correct manner toward our government when speaking in Parliament and in formal communications, nevertheless, in their capacity as members and officials of the international organization, acted in accordance with its policy as above described, does anybody believe that we should maintain diplomatic relations with Great Britain upon any terms less than the complete severance of the British government from the international organization, and the unreserved repudiation of that organization and its hostile policies by the British government? The President of the United States who dared tolerate such an affront and failed to dismiss the British Ambassador would be impeached as fast as our constitutional procedure permitted.

We are told that conditions have changed since 1920 to such an extent as to render obsolete the policy based upon the then prevailing conditions. That argument is advanced, in varied formulas, by all who favor recognition of the Soviet regime, no matter for what reason. There have been changes in conditions since 1920, both in Russia and in the world at large. The Soviet regime has outlasted all expectations and predictions—even those of its own greatest leaders. Contrary to the expectation of its followers and its foes alike, the regime has managed to exist and to function despite the non-appearance of the world revolution upon which it was supposed to be completely dependent and without which, friends and foes believed, it could not exist. So much may be admitted while retaining a sense of proportion and without accepting the fairy stories of propagandists on either side. There is undoubtedly less anarchy in the government than in 1920. There is also greater technological efficiency.

If the matter were in the least degree pertinent to our discussion, instead of being wholly irrelevant, we might profitably devote some time and space to the discounting of some of the romantic nonsense that has lately been published in the famous "Five-Year Program" of the Soviets. The naive assumption that mere multiplication of factories and railroads shows economic growth and progress indicates ignorance of economics that is almost abysmal. During a large part of the eighteenth century Russia under the Czars was the theatre of a colossal program of palace building and dock and harbor construction. That was a program arbitrarily designed by the rulers and imposed upon the nation; it did not develop naturally from the life and needs of the people. A despotic government with slave labor to depend upon had no need to count the cost of anything. Much of the industrialization thus far achieved in connection with the "Five-Year Program" has been of the same uneconomical character as the useless "improvements" of the eighteenth century.

Moreover, thoughtful economists, including many whose sympathies are with the Soviet regime, have been calling attention to the increasingly serious problems arising from the excessive commitments of the Soviet government to its foreign creditors. While thus far it has managed to make the required payments upon its obligations, it is well known in financial circles that the Soviet government is finding payment increasingly difficult. Then, too, there is the serious discrepancy between the officially published exchange rate . . . as on a par basis of two rubles to one dollar, with the fact that the actual exchange in Moscow—effected through "bootleg" channels for the most part—is on the basis of from ten to twelve rubles per dollar. In Berlin and other European capitals the actual exchange rate during July ranged from eight to twelve rubles per dollar.

The sole purpose of these observations upon the romantic accounts of Soviet Russia's economic progress is to suggest caution. Our refusal to grant recognition to the Soviet government was not based upon any theory that it was incapable of efficient functioning, or that it was weak and inherently incapable of developing strength. It was based upon the fact, which no spokesman or apologist for the Soviet regime has questioned or denied, that the central aim and purpose of the Soviet government, avowed by its responsible statesmen, is to promote world revolution and bring about the overthrow of all other governments, including our own. That fact makes it unfit for confidence and trust. Its own choice has placed the Soviet regime beyond the pale. Recognition and the friendly relations which are derived from recognition are impossible between us and a regime which we can never trust and which can never trust us.

True, other nations have recognized the Soviet government. In the main, they have adopted that course because they were compelled to do so by internal political weaknesses from which we were and are happily free. Great Britain would never have recognized Soviet Russia were it not for the fact that its organized labor movement is political in its character, with Communists constituting a disturbing element. That and the Soviet menace to India compelled British recognition, as more than one British statesman has admitted. France, too, with a government politically unstable because of its many political parties and groups, a condition giving to its Communist elements a dangerous power, had to shape her policy according to her inherent weakness.

This view of the causes determining the action of the British and French governments in recognizing the Soviet government may be disputed and rejected, of course, but none can deny that the experience of both nations has amply sustained the contention of the Colby note that the Soviet government is incapable of honorable friendship with the government of any capitalist nation. In both Great Britain and France actual experience has made it necessary to debase diplomatic intercourse as it never has been debased by either nation. . . . There is hardly the pretense that Soviet Ambassadors are trusted as the Ambassadors of other friendly powers are trusted. . . .

Our Russian policy is the product of political realism. We have no romantic illusions. Precisely as any self-respecting individual may buy from or sell to other individuals with whom he refuses to hold friendly social relations, and for whom he has scorn and contempt in social life, so as manufacturers and traders our citizens carry on such trade with Russia, through the existing government, as they find profitable, yet insist upon our own government imposing an effective barrier against the recognition of the Soviet government—a power which we despise as thoroughly as we respect the Russian nation itself. Any departure from our policy in this respect is politically impossible.

# SOVIET FOREIGN POLICY*

BY

MICHAEL T. FLORINSKY

[1934]

## THE PARADOX OF SOVIET FOREIGN RELATIONS

It has often been said that Russia, both Imperial and Communist, is the land of paradoxes, a statement which contains a considerable element of truth. The foreign policies of the Soviet Union for the last ten years present an interesting example of inner contradictions which it is not always easy to reconcile. . . .

The general argument of Marx and Lenin is universally familiar. The inherent contradictions of capitalist and imperialist society bear the germs of its own destruction. They lead to the class struggle within the nations and to international wars between the imperialistic powers. The only salvation for the masses of the exploited is revolution, which will wrest political power from the hands of the oppressors. The national revolutions will merge into the great world revolution which will lead mankind, through the transition period of the dictatorship of the proletariat, to the classless society of the future, a society which will eliminate the exploitation of man by man and put into effect the great communist principle—from each according to his abilities, to each according to his needs. To this scheme of human development, which is based on the Marxian economic interpretation of history, the Communist Party of the Soviet Union, like any other communist party, owes allegiance. It is essentially and avowedly a revolutionary program, which has for its purpose the forcible overthrow of the capitalist system.

The Soviet Union is the first—and so far the only—country of proletarian dictatorship. The Russian Communist Party controls the Soviet Government and is the dominating element in the Third or Communist International, which very properly has its headquarters in Moscow. It would be only natural, therefore, to expect world revolution to be the chief preoccupation of the Kremlin.

---

*From the *Slavonic Review*, Vol. XII, No. 36, April 1934. Reprinted by permission.

And this was undoubtedly true for the first few years of communist rule. But since 1921, and especially since 1924, an unmistakable change has occurred in the foreign policy of the Soviet Union. Far from promoting world revolution, the U.S.S.R. is to be found in the forefront of nations struggling for international cooperation, agitating against international wars, entering into numerous pacts of non-aggression with every nation that cares to do so: in short, doing all in its power to protect the capitalist world against those conflagrations, which, in accordance with the communist doctrine, will lead it to its inescapable doom. This is, indeed, a paradoxical situation: the first country of communist dictatorship working hard for the salvation of capitalism!

## THE EARLY PERIOD

To understand the changing trend of Soviet Foreign relations we must recall the general situation which existed in the world during the first years of Soviet rule. . . .

The establishment of a Bolshevist Government in Petrograd came as a painful shock to Russia's former Allies in the Great War. It was hardly less of a surprise to the new leaders of the country themselves. From the position of an underground party haunted by the police and fighting for its existence they found themselves practically overnight in control of a vast empire. They had no definite concrete policy. . . .

The victory of Lenin and Trotsky was dazzling, but the difficulties they had to face both at home and abroad seemed insurmountable. . . . But if the difficulties were great, even greater were the promises of a brighter future. Were not the nations of Europe exhausted by a long struggle, the reasons for which were never understood by the masses, and, as a matter of fact, could not be properly explained? Did not backward Russia show the real way out to the European proletariat by smashing at one blow not only the age-long institution of Tsardom, but also the rule of the exploiters? World revolution, or at least revolution in the chief European countries, was the logical and inescapable consequence of the unexampled slaughter which imperialism brought in its wake. And it was, moreover, fully in agreement with the Marxian doctrine of class struggle expounded by Lenin in his teaching on imperialism. Zinoviev, the first president of the Communist International, correctly expressed the feeling prevailing among the Bolshevik leaders at that time when he wrote (on May 1, 1919): "Old Europe is dashing at mad speed towards the proletarian revolution. . . . Separate defeats will still occur in the near future. Black will perhaps still win a victory here and there over red. But the final victory will, nevertheless, go to the red; and this in the course of the next months, perhaps even weeks. . . . In a year the whole of Europe will be communist. And the struggle for communism will be transferred to America, perhaps to Asia, and to other parts of the world. . . . Perhaps—for a few years, and side by side with Communist Europe—we shall see American capitalism continue to exist. Perhaps even in England capitalism will continue to exist for a year or two, side by side with communism victorious in the whole of continental Europe. But such a co-existence cannot last long."

These ideas dominated the foreign policy of the Soviet Union . . . until the beginning of 1921. They were, no doubt, stimulated by the openly hostile attitude of the capitalist nations and by Allied intervention. Bolshevist policy found its expression in the intensive propaganda for the immediate overthrow of capitalism supported by all the resources—very limited at the time, it is true—of the Soviet Government. In a sense, it was the logical and fitting counterpart of the domestic policy of war communism. Both were the manifestation of communism in its most aggressive and intolerant mood. . . .

## THE NEW ORIENTATION

The abandonment of the Allied blockade early in 1920, the withdrawal of the Allied troops from various parts of Russian territory, the collapse of the White movement and the termination of the Russo-Polish War . . . confronted the Soviet Government with a new situation. . . : the failure of world revolution, or even of a European revolution. . . . This was a most disturbing thorn in the laurels of Soviet success . . . because it challenged the validity of one of the most important articles of the communist creed, not to mention the personal discomfiture of the communist leaders of whom Zinoviev was merely the most shining example.

Lenin, with that keen sense of realities which distinguished him from the rank and file of his followers and which probably largely explains his unquestionable leadership, rose to the occasion. He outlined the new policy which the Soviet Union was to follow at the tenth congress of the Communist Party, in March, 1921. He pointed out that the revolutionary movement in Europe was undoubtedly making progress, but that this progress was not quite as rapid as was originally hoped.

> We have learned in the course of the last three years (said Lenin) that our stake in international revolution does not mean that we expect it to materialize within a definite period of time, that the pace of development, which is growing more and more rapid, may or may not bring revolution in the spring, and that therefore we must coordinate our activities with the relationships existing among the various classes in our own country and abroad, in order thereby to maintain for a protracted period the dictatorship of the proletariat and to free ourselves, even if gradually, of all the misfortunes and the effects of the crises which have befallen us.

In the parlance of the Washington Government of today this was the announcement of the new deal in both domestic and foreign policy. The intolerable burden of war communism, which resulted in dangerous peasant uprisings and mutinies among the troops, gave place to the relatively liberal regime of the New Economic Policy. In the field of foreign relations the Soviet Government made the first timid steps toward the establishment of a *modus vivendi*, and even of a certain degree of cooperation with the capitalist countries. . . . It was clearly understood, of course, that the policy of world revolution was not to be abandoned. It was simply to be pursued by other methods, more appropriate under the changed condition. . . .

Under the new economic policy the chief preoccupation of the Soviet Government was the economic restoration of the country, which had been reduced to a perfectly shocking condition by the exigencies of the great War, the civil war and the extravaganza of war communism. . . .

## "SOCIALISM IN A SINGLE COUNTRY"

The rapidly increasing interest of the Soviet Government in

questions of economic reconstruction proved fatal to the world revolutionary movement as it was understood by the "Left" leaders of the Communist Party. There is an obvious and irreconcilable contradiction between the Marxian teaching of the economic inter-dependence of the world, its inherent antagonisms and inevitable conflicts and wars, and the practical policy of the Soviet State directed toward a close and effective cooperation with the capitalist nations. . . . The conflict between the supporters and the opponents of the new policy was brought into the fore by an event entirely outside the field of Marxian dialectics, but, nevertheless, one of paramount importance: the death of Lenin, which occurred early in 1924.

The disappearance from the political stage of the recognized leader of the communist movement inevitably raised the question of his successor. It was followed by a bitter struggle between the outstanding personalities of the Communist Party which soon reduced itself to a duel between Stalin and Trotsky. . . .

A close process of dialectic reasoning led Trotsky to the con-clusion that, although a socialist revolution begins on the national soil, it cannot reach its successful conclusion within national fron-tiers. The dictatorship of the proletariat in an isolated country must necessarily be provisional; it is bound to lead to internal and external antagonisms, and it is doomed to destruction unless a victorious social revolution in the advanced countries comes to its rescue. "A national revolution is not a self-contained unit," said Trotsky, "it is just a link in the international chain. The inter-national revolution is a permanent process, in spite of the temporary setbacks and the ebbing of the tide." The practical international implications of this theory are clear and inevitable. Any attempt to establish a national Communist State is not only treason to the cause of communism, but, ignoring the economic and political interdependence of the world, it is also fundamentally fallacious, unsound, and doomed to failure.

Until 1924 these views of Trotsky were never seriously chal-lenged, although they provoked a certain amount of discussion in 1905-06, 1915, and 1921. In 1924 the whole question was re-opened by the enunciation of Stalin's doctrine of "socialism in a single country." It became the center of a heated controversy which raged for about three years and resulted in the complete defeat of Trotsky, and his exile first to Alma Ata and then to Turkey. . . .

The fundamental argument of Stalin's doctrine is engagingly simple. It maintains that a country with a large population, extensive territory and vast natural resources has all the elements which are necessary and sufficient for building up an integral socialist system within its borders. Thus the victory of socialism in a country like the U.S.S.R. is quite possible, but it is not yet a *final* victory, because an isolated Socialist State lives in the hostile environment of capitalist nations. There is always the danger of foreign intervention. To make the victory of socialism final, capitalism in other countries must be destroyed. But while a considerable period of time may elapse before the final victory is achieved, nothing keeps the first country of proletarian dictatorship from proceeding in the meantime with the organization of a complete Socialist State. . . .

The issue of the debate was by no means an idle academic matter. As Stalin pointed out, it determined the very vital question whether the Soviet Union could proceed with its plans for socialist reconstruction. So long as there was no assurance that this was feasible, it would have been impossible to ask the country to make the immense sacrifices which it involved. The acceptance of Stalin's doctrine by the Communist Party gave that assurance and determined the course of Soviet policies, both at home and abroad. At home they took the shape of the first and second Five Year plans. And as the fulfillment of the vast program of industrialization demanded cooperation with the capitalist world—imports of machines and materials being conditioned by the volume of Soviet exports—it also determined the course of Soviet foreign policy. . . .

## RECENT TREND IN FOREIGN RELATIONS

For the last ten years there has been an unmistakable change in the trend of Soviet foreign policy, although, of course, there is no sharp dividing line from the past. In 1923-1927 the Chinese revolution loomed large in the preoccupations of Moscow, and

Michael Borodin became for a time an important factor in the Chinese situation. But revolution in China failed, just as it did in Hungary, Bavaria, and Germany. There were setbacks to the improvement of relations with foreign countries, such as the rupture of diplomatic relations with Great Britain from May, 1927, to October, 1929, and with China between 1929 and 1932. In spite of these unfortunate developments it seems difficult to deny that the Soviet Union was working hard and not without success for the resumption of Russia's place among the great powers.

This policy proceeded along two main lines: the establishment of closer economic ties with the capitalist nations and the prevention of imperialistic wars. The underlying principle of the policy of economic cooperation was clearly stated in a resolution of the fifteenth congress of the Communist Party held in December, 1927.

> We must base our policy on the idea of a maximum development of our economic relations with foreign countries so far as such relations (expansion of foreign trade, foreign credits, concessions, employment of foreign technical advisers, etc.) contribute to the economic strength of the Union. We must make it more independent of the capitalist world, and broaden the socialist foundation for further industrial expansion of the Union.

The second pillar of Soviet foreign policy is the prevention of imperialistic wars. In accordance with Lenin's theory of imperialism, imperialistic wars necessarily grow out of the contradictions of modern capitalist society. In the earlier period of the Soviet rule, when it was believed that imperialistic wars inevitably lead to revolutions, and when international revolution was still the chief *immediate* object of the Soviet Union, the Moscow Government naturally took no special interest in the advancement of peace. But this is no longer the case since the economic reconstruction of the country—a reconstruction, to repeat, which is being carried on with the assistance of the capitalist world—assumed precedence over all other questions. An outbreak of hostilities between the great powers would necessarily interfere with the flow of foreign trade on which the success of the Five Year Plan largely depends. And then the experience of 1914-1918 would seem to indicate that the limits of the expansion of a major armed conflict are entirely unpredictable. One must also keep in mind that the Red Army, whose parades in the Red Square are so much admired, has not yet received its baptism of fire in a war against a first-rate power and is, strictly speaking, an unknown quantity. The Soviet Government, therefore, has been greatly interested since the beginning of the new economic policy, and especially since the adoption of Stalin's doctrine, in postponing the evil day until the U.S.S.R. shall have made real progress in the building up of its socialist system. . . . Imperialistic wars are no longer represented as an important and essential link in the chain of historical development which is to lead to the final victory of the proletariat. They are pictured now as sinister conspiracies on the part of the capitalist powers to strangle and destroy the first country of proletarian dictatorship. Practically every event in the field of international affairs, including such perfectly innocuous agreements as the Pact of Paris, are uniformly interpreted in Moscow as the preparation of a new intervention, a new attack upon the Soviet Union. To stress the peaceful intentions of the Soviet Union in contrast to the aggressive policies of the capitalist nations has been and still remains, the *leit-motiv* of the Soviet press and of the pronouncements of the Soviet leaders. But they never fail to emphasize the point that, while the Soviet Union is only too anxious to preserve peace, it is also determined to defend its territory from foreign invasion. . . . [This] idea was forcibly stated by Stalin at the seventeenth congress of the Communist Party in January, 1934.

> Our foreign policy is plain. We want peace and friendly relations with everyone. We do not think of threatening anyone, still less of attacking them; but we do not fear threats, and we are ready to give blow for blow to those who try to inflame war. Those who have business relations with us will always find support in us, but those who attack us will get such a decisive blow in return that they will learn in future to keep their swinish snouts out of our potato patch.

These remarks, reports Mr. Walter Duranty, the able Moscow correspondent of *The New York Times*, "fired Mr. Stalin's hearers to the greatest applause given during his entire speech." They are likely to be seen on the posters in the Red Square for the next few months.

The statement that peace has been the keynote of Soviet foreign policy for the last decade is fully supported by an even cursory examination of Moscow's diplomatic activities. . . . On February 6,

1933, M. Litvinov, speaking before the Disarmament Conference
in Geneva, offered a new definition of the aggressor which considerably extended the scope of non-aggression agreements. *Izvestia*,
commenting editorially on Litvinov's statement, described it as
"the people's charter of rights to security and independence." The
official organ of the Soviet Government also remarked that "Litvinov's declaration not only is aimed against intervention in a
country where there is a revolution, but in the name of the U.S.S.R.
it undertakes the obligation not to intervene in a country where
there is a counter-revolution." This sounds very much like an
avowed renunciation of Soviet leadership in the international
revolutionary movement. . . .

## THE THIRD INTERNATIONAL

But if the outline of Soviet foreign policy given above be correct and the Moscow Government is fully absorbed in problems of
economic reconstruction and is striving for peace, the question
arises, what has happened to the doctrine of world revolution, that
alpha and omega of militant communism? And what has happened to the Third International, which has for its purpose the
carrying into effect of the policies of world revolution?

The Third or Communist International, it will be remembered,
was founded by Lenin and held its first congress in March, 1919.
"The Communist International," says its statute, "has for its purpose the struggle by all available means, including armed force,
for the overthrow of the international bourgeoisie and the creation
of an international Soviet republic as a transition stage to the
complete abolition of the State." And a manifesto issued by the
second congress of the International added that, "the international
proletariat will not lay down its sword until Soviet Russia has
become a link in the federation of the Soviet republics of the
world." The official policy of the Soviet Government has always
been to deny any connection between itself and the Third International. . . . The undeniable fact is that the Russian Communist
Party controls the Soviet Government and completely dominates
the Third International. It is therefore not surprising to find a
fairly close correlation between their policies. The first and the
second congresses of the Third International held in 1919 and

1920 met at a time when world revolution was still the order of the day, and in their debates and resolutions they had no difficulty in living up to the provisions of the statute. The third congress, in 1921, the fourth, in 1922, and the fifth, in 1924, in accordance with the changed attitude of the Russian communists, concerned themselves with laying the foundation for a protracted proletarian struggle. There was a significant interval of four years before the sixth congress met in 1928. It will be remembered that it was during this period that Stalin's "socialism in a single country" gained official recognition. Zinoviev, Trotsky, and their friends had in the meantime disappeared from the political stage. The sixth congress was entirely dominated by Stalin and Bukharin (who has since also suffered a temporary eclipse), and it had for its purpose to incorporate the doctrine of "socialism in a single country" within the body of communist articles of faith. This was achieved in the program of the Communist International, which was duly voted by the congress and for which Stalin and Bukharin are responsible. The program, while preserving the whole of the revolutionary phraseology of the *Communist Manifesto* of 1848 and of the revolutionary writings of Marx, Engels, and Lenin, nevertheless introduced some fundamental changes in the general teaching of communism. The most important of these changes was the strong emphasis put on the part played by the U.S.S.R. as a revolutionizing element in the world. International revolution, of course, was the final aim of the Third International, but its immediate purposes were defined as follows: the prevention of imperialistic wars, the defense of the U.S.S.R. against capitalist aggression, the struggle against foreign intervention in China, the defense of Chinese revolution and of colonial uprisings. But it was the defense of the Soviet Union which was the chief concern of the sixth congress. From the general staff of the world revolution the Third International had been changed for all practical purposes, if not in theory, into an international labor organization for the defense of the Soviet Union. . . .

## STILL A PARADOX

In spite of the important revision of the communist doctrine in the program of the Third International, the foreign policy of the

Soviet Union still remains a paradox. It is undeniable that the Soviet Government is fully engrossed in its grandiose and absorbing task of building from the backward agricultural Empire of the Tsars the great industrialized commonwealth of the future; that it has to a certain extent adapted the teaching of communism to this purpose; that foreign affairs, except for the denunciation of imperialist conspiracies, are given practically no space in the Soviet press; that the Third International . . . has been reduced to the position of a mere government department and leads an obscure existence; that Soviet policy has been consistently directed to the maintenance of international peace. But it is also true that world revolution through the forcible overthrow of the capitalist system and the dictatorship of the proletariat remains an integral part of the communist teaching; that the Third International has the advancement of the world revolution as its ultimate task; that it continues to exist in Moscow and that its seventh congress has been announced for the autumn of 1934. . . .

The truth of the matter seems to be that there is still a fundamental contradiction between the doctrine of world revolution and the practical policy of the Soviet Union. In my opinion, the Soviet Government has sacrificed much of the Marx-Lenin theory on the altar of expediency and *Realpolitik*. The shell of phraseology of the *Communist Manifesto* remains, but its revolutionary content is gone. World revolution is now something of a communist dogma to which one pays merely lip service. This is by no means an unprecedented situation in the history of the human race. The contempt for earthly riches is a generally accepted principle of the Christian religion. The truth of the statement that it is easier for a camel to pass through a needle's eye than for a rich man to enter the Kingdom of Heaven has never been challenged. Nevertheless, few would maintain that it has exercised any undue influence upon the conduct of either devout churchmen or of the churches themselves. Our capacity for compromise with ideas is, indeed, amazing. A new example of it is offered by the paradox of Soviet foreign relations.[1]

---

[1] I am indebted to my publishers, the Macmillan Company of New York, for permission to use again here some of the material which appeared in my book, *World Revolution and the U.S.S.R.*

IV

# ASPECTS OF
# THE THEORY OF COMMUNISM:
# PRO AND CON

# DIALECTICAL AND HISTORICAL MATERIALISM*

BY

## JOSEPH STALIN

[1938]

. . . Dialectical and historical materialism constitute the theoretical basis of Communism, the theoretical foundations of the Marxist party, and it is the duty of every active member of our Party to know these principles and hence to study them.

What, then, is

1) Dialectical materialism?
2) Historical materialism?

Dialectical materialism is the world outlook of the Marxist-Leninist party. It is called dialectical materialism because its approach to the phenomena of nature, its method of studying and apprehending them, is *dialectical,* while its interpretation of the phenomena of nature, its conception of these phenomena, its theory, is *materialistic.*

Historical materialism is the extension of the principles of dialectical materialism to the study of social life, an application of the principles of dialectical materialism to the phenomena of the life of society, to the study of society and its history . . . .

Dialectics comes from the Greek *dialego,* to discourse, to debate. In ancient times dialectics was the art of arriving at the truth by disclosing the contradictions in the argument of an opponent and overcoming these contradictions. There were philosophers in ancient times who believed that the disclosure of contradictions in thought and the clash of opposite opinions was the best method of arriving at the truth. This dialectical method of thought, later extended to the phenomena of nature, developed into the dialectical method of apprehending nature, which regards the phenomena

---

*From the *History of the Communist Party of the Soviet Union (Bolsheviks),* edited by a Commission of the Central Committee of the C.P.S.U. (B). Authorized by the Central Committee of the C.P.S.U. (B.). Copyright 1939 by International Publishers Co., Inc., New York. Reprinted by permission. This chapter was written by Stalin for the *History* in 1938.

of nature as being in constant movement and undergoing constant change, and the development of nature as the result of the development of the contradictions in nature, as the result of the interaction of opposed forces in nature.

In its essence, dialectics is the direct opposite of metaphysics.

1) The principal features of the Marxist *dialectical method* are as follows:

a) Contrary to metaphysics, dialectics does not regard nature as an accidental agglomeration of things, of phenomena, unconnected with, isolated from, and independent of, each other, but as a connected and integral whole, in which things, phenomena, are organically connected with, dependent on, and determined by, each other.

The dialectical method therefore holds that no phenomenon in nature can be understood if taken by itself, isolated from surrounding phenomena . . . and that, vice versa, any phenomenon can be understood and explained if considered in its inseparable connection with surrounding phenomena, as one conditioned by surrounding phenomena.

b) Contrary to metaphysics, dialectics holds that nature is not a state of rest and immobility, stagnation and immutability, but a state of continuous movement and change, of continuous renewal and development, where something is always arising and developing, and something always disintegrating and dying away.

The dialectical method therefore requires that phenomena should be considered not only from the standpoint of their interconnection and interdependence, but also from the standpoint of their movement, their change, their development, their coming into being and going out of being. . . .

c) Contrary to metaphysics, dialectics does not regard the process of development as a simple process of growth, where quantitative changes do not lead to qualitative changes, but as a development which passes from insignificant and imperceptible quantitative changes to open, fundamental changes, to qualitative changes; a development in which the qualitative changes occur not gradually, but rapidly and abruptly, taking the form of a leap from one state to another; they occur not accidentally but as the natural result of an accumulation of imperceptible and gradual quantitative changes . . . .

Describing dialectical development as a transition from quantitative changes to qualitative changes, Engels says:

> In physics . . . every change is a passing of quantity into quality, as a result of quantitative change of some form of movement either inherent in a body or imparted to it. For example, the temperature of water has at first no effect on the liquid state; but as the temperature of liquid water rises or falls, a moment arrives when this state of cohesion changes and the water is converted in one case into steam and in the other into ice. . . . A definite minimum current is required to make a platinum wire glow; every metal has its melting temperature; every liquid has a definite freezing point and boiling point at a given pressure, as far as we are able with the means at our disposal to attain the required temperatures; finally, every gas has its critical point at which, by proper pressure and cooling, it can be converted into a liquid state. . . .

d) Contrary to metaphysics, dialectics holds that internal contradictions are inherent in all things and phenomena of nature, for they all have their negative and positive sides, a past and a future, something dying away and something developing; and that the struggle between these opposites, the struggle between the old and the new, between that which is dying away and that which is being born, between that which is disappearing and that which is developing, constitutes the internal content of the process of development, the internal content of the transformation of quantitative changes into qualitative changes.

The dialectical method therefore holds that the process of development from the lower to the higher takes place not as a harmonious unfolding of phenomena, but as a "struggle" of opposite tendencies which operate on the basis of these contradictions. . . .

Such, in brief, are the principal features of the Marxist dialectical method.

It is easy to understand how immensely important is the extension of the principles of the dialectical method to the study of social life and the history of society, and how immensely important is the application of these principles to the history of society and to the practical activities of the party of the proletariat.

If there are no isolated phenomena in the world, if all phenomena are interconnected and interdependent, then it is clear that every social system and every social movement in history must be evaluated not from the standpoint of "eternal justice" or some other preconceived idea, as is not infrequently done by historians, but from the standpoint of the conditions which gave rise to that system or that social movement and with which they are connected.

The slave system would be senseless, stupid and unnatural under modern conditions. But under the conditions of a disintegrating primitive communal system, the slave system is a quite understandable and natural phenomenon, since it represents an advance on the primitive communal system.

The demand for a bourgeois-democratic republic when tsardom and bourgeois society existed, as, let us say, in Russia in 1905, was a quite understandable, proper and revolutionary demand, for at that time a bourgeois republic would have meant a step forward. But now, under the conditions of the U.S.S.R., the demand for a bourgeois-democratic republic would be a meaningless and counter-revolutionary demand, .for a bourgeois republic would be a retrograde step compared with the Soviet republic.

Everything depends on the conditions, time and place.

It is clear that without such a *historical* approach to social phenomena, the existence and development of the science of history is impossible, for only such an approach saves the science of history from becoming a jumble of accidents and an agglomeration of most absurd mistakes.

Further, if the world is in a state of constant movement and development, if the dying away of the old and the upgrowth of the new is a law of development, then it is clear that there can be no "immutable" social systems, no "eternal principles" of private property and exploitation, no "eternal ideas" of the subjugation of the peasant to the landlord, of the worker to the capitalist.

Hence the capitalist system can be replaced by the Socialist system, just as at one time the feudal system was replaced by the capitalist system.

Hence we must not base our orientation on the strata of society which are no longer developing, even though they at present constitute the predominant force, but on those strata which are developing and have a future before them, even though they at present do not constitute the predominant force.

In the eighties of the past century ... the proletariat in Russia constituted an insignificant minority of the population, whereas the individual peasants constituted the vast majority of the population. But the proletariat was developing as a class, whereas the peasantry as a class was disintegrating. And just because the proletariat was developing as a class the Marxists based their orientation on the proletariat. And they were not mistaken, for, as we know, the proletariat subsequently grew from an insignificant force into a first-rate historical and political force.

Hence, in order not to err in policy, one must look forward, not backward.

Further, if the passing of slow quantitative changes into rapid and abrupt qualitative changes is a law of development, then it is clear that revolutions made by oppressed classes are a quite natural and inevitable phenomenon.

Hence the transition from capitalism to Socialism and the liberation of the working class from the yoke of capitalism cannot be effected by slow changes, by reforms, but only by a qualitative change of the capitalist system, by revolution.

Hence, in order not to err in policy, one must be a revolutionary, not a reformist.

Further, if development proceeds by way of the disclosure of internal contradictions, by way of collisions between opposite forces on the basis of these contradictions and so as to overcome these contradictions, then it is clear that the class struggle of the proletariat is a quite natural and inevitable phenomenon.

Hence we must not cover up the contradictions of the capitalist system, but disclose and unravel them; we must not try to check the class struggle but carry it to its conclusion.

Hence, in order not to err in policy, one must pursue an uncompromising proletarian class policy, not a reformist policy of harmony of the interests of the proletariat and the bourgeoisie, not a compromisers' policy of "the growing of capitalism into Socialism."

Such is the Marxist dialectical method when applied to social life, to the history of society.

As to Marxist philosophical materialism, it is fundamentally the direct opposite of philosophical idealism.

2) The principal features of Marxist philosophical *materialism* are as follows:

a) Contrary to idealism, which regards the world as the embodiment of an "absolute idea," a "universal spirit," "consciousness," Marx's philosophical materialism holds that the world is by its very nature *material,* that the multifold phenomena of the world constitute different forms of matter in motion, that interconnection and interdependence of phenomena, as established by the dialectical method, are a law of the development of moving matter, and that the world develops in accordance with the laws of movement of matter and stands in no need of a "universal spirit. . . ."

b) Contrary to idealism, which asserts that only our mind really exists, and that the material world, being nature, exists only in our mind, in our sensations, ideas and perceptions, the Marxist materialist philosophy holds that matter, nature, being, is an objective reality existing outside and independent of our mind; that matter is primary, since it is the source of sensations, ideas, mind, and that mind is secondary, derivative, since it is the source of sensations, ideas, mind, and that mind is secondary, derivative, since it is a reflection of matter, a reflection of being; that thought is a product of matter which in its development has reached a high degree of perfection, namely, of the brain, and the brain is the organ of thought; and that therefore one cannot separate thought from matter without committing a grave error. . . .

c) Contrary to idealism, which denies the possibility of knowing the world and its laws, which does not believe in the authenticity of our knowledge, does not recognize objective truth, and holds that the world is full of "things-in-themselves" that can never be known to science, Marxist philosophical materialism holds that the world and its laws are fully knowable, that our knowledge of the laws of nature, tested by experiment and practice, is authentic knowledge having the validity of objective truth, and that there are no things in the world which are unknowable, but only things which are still not known, but which will be disclosed and made known by the efforts of science and practice. . . .

Such, in brief, are the characteristic features of the Marxist philosophical materialism.

It is easy to understand how immensely important is the extension of the principles of philosophical materialism to the study of social life, of the history of society, and how immensely important is the application of these principles to the history of society and to the practical activities of the party of the proletariat.

If the connection between the phenomena of nature and their interdependence are laws of the development of nature, it follows, too, that the connection and interdependence of the phenomena of social life are laws of the development of society, and not something accidental.

Hence social life, the history of society, ceases to be an agglomeration of "accidents," and becomes the history of the development of society according to regular laws, and the study of the history of society becomes a science.

Hence the practical activity of the party of the proletariat must not be based on the good wishes of "outstanding individuals," not on the dictates of "reason," "universal morals," etc., but on the laws of development of society and on the study of these laws.

Further, if the world is knowable and our knowledge of the laws of development of nature is authentic knowledge, having the validity of objective truth, it follows that social life, the development of society, is also knowable, and that the data of science regarding the laws of development of society are authentic data having the validity of objective truths.

Hence the science of the history of society, despite all the complexity of the phenomena of social life, can become as precise a science as, let us say, biology, and capable of making use of the laws of development of society for practical purposes. . . .

Hence the bond between science and practical activity, between theory and practice, their unity, should be the guiding star of the party of the proletariat.

Further, if nature, being, the material world, is primary, and mind, thought, is secondary, derivative; if the material world represents objective reality existing independently of the mind of

men, while the mind is a reflection of this objective reality, it follows that the material life of society, its being, is also primary,
and its spiritual life secondary, derivative, and that the material
life of society is an objective reality existing independently of the
will of men, while the spiritual life of society is a reflection of this
objective reality, a reflection of being.

Hence the source of formation of the spiritual life of society,
the origin of social ideas, social theories, political views and
political institutions, should not be sought for in the ideas, theories,
views and political institutions themselves, but in the conditions of
the material life of society, in social being, of which these ideas,
theories, views, etc., are the reflection.

Hence, if in different periods of the history of society different
social ideas, theories, views and political institutions are to be
observed; if under the slave system we encounter certain social
ideas, theories, views and political institutions, under feudalism
others, and under capitalism others still, this is not to be explained
by the "nature," the "properties" of the ideas, theories, views and
political institutions themselves but by the different conditions of
the material life of society at different periods of social development. . . .

It does not follow from Marx's words, however, that social
ideas, theories, political views and political institutions are of no
significance in the life of society, that they do not reciprocally
affect social being, the development of the material conditions of
the life of society.  We have been speaking so far of the *origin* of
social ideas, theories, views and political institutions, of *the way
they arise,* of the fact that the spiritual life of society is a reflection
of the conditions of its material life.  As regards the *significance*
of social ideas, theories, views and political institutions, as regards
their *role* in history, historical materialism, far from denying them,
stresses the role and importance of these factors in the life of
society, in its history.

There are different kinds of social ideas and theories.  There
are old ideas and theories which have outlived their day and
which serve the interests of the moribund forces of society.  Their
significance lies in the fact that they hamper the development, the

progress of society. Then there are new and advanced ideas and theories which serve the interests of the advanced forces of society. Their significance lies in the fact that they facilitate the development, the progress of society; and their significance is the greater the more accurately they reflect the needs of development of the material life of society.

New social ideas and theories arise only after the development of the material life of society has set new tasks before society. But once they have arisen they become a most potent force which facilitates the carrying out of the new tasks set by the development of the material life of society, a force which facilitates the progress of society. It is precisely here that the tremendous organizing, mobilizing and transforming value of new ideas, new theories, new political views and new political institutions manifests itself. New social ideas and theories arise precisely because they are necessary to society, because it is *impossible* to carry out the urgent tasks of development of the material life of society without their organizing, mobilizing and transforming action. Arising out of the new tasks set by the development of the material life of society, the new social ideas and theories force their way through, become the possession of the masses, mobilize and organize them against the moribund forces of society, and thus facilitate the overthrow of these forces which hamper the development of the material life of society. . . .

That is the answer historical materialism gives to the question of the relation between social being and social consciousness, between the conditions of development of material life and the development of the spiritual life of society.

It now remains to elucidate the following question: what, from the viewpoint of historical materialism, is meant by the "conditions of material life of society" which in the final analysis determine the physiognomy of society, its ideas, views, political institutions, etc.?

What, after all, are these "conditions of material life of society," what are their distinguishing features?

There can be no doubt that the concept of "conditions of material life of society" includes, first of all, nature which surrounds society, geographical environment, which is one of the indispensable and constant conditions of material life of society and which, of course, influences the development of society. What role does geographical environment play in the development of society? Is geographical environment the chief force determining the physiognomy of society, the character of the social system of men, the transition from one system to another?

Historical materialism answers this question in the negative.

Geographical environment is unquestionably one of the constant and indispensable conditions of development of society and, of course, influences the development of society, accelerates or retards its development. But its influence is not the *determining* influence, inasmuch as the changes and development of society proceed at an incomparably faster rate than the changes and development of geographical environment. In the space of three thousand years three different social systems have been successively superseded in Europe: the primitive communal system, the slave system and the feudal system. In the eastern part of Europe, in the U.S.S.R., even four social systems have been superseded. Yet during this period geographical conditions in Europe have either not changed at all, or have changed so slightly that geography takes no note of them. . . .

It follows from this that geographical environment cannot be the chief cause, the *determining* cause of social development, for that which remains almost unchanged in the course of tens of thousands of years cannot be the chief cause of development of that which undergoes fundamental changes in the course of a few hundred years. . . .

What, then, is the chief force in the complex of conditions of material life of society which determines the physiognomy of society, the character of the social system, the development of society from one system to another?

This force, historical materialism holds, is the *method of procuring the means of life* necessary for human existence, *the mode of production of material values*—food, clothing, footwear, houses, fuel, instruments of production, etc.—which are indispensable for the life of development of society.

In order to live, people must have food, clothing, footwear, shelter, fuel, etc.; in order to have these material values, people must produce them; and in order to produce them, people must have the instruments of production with which food, clothing, footwear, shelter, fuel, etc., are produced; they must be able to produce these instruments and to use them.

The *instruments of production* wherewith material values are produced, the *people* who operate the instruments of production and carry on the production of material values thanks to a certain *production experience and labor skill*—all these elements jointly constitute the *productive forces* of society.

But the productive forces are only one aspect of production, only one aspect of the mode of production, an aspect that expresses the relation of men to the objects and forces of nature which they make use of for the production of material values. Another aspect of production, another aspect of the mode of production, is the relation of men to each other in the process of production, men's *relations of production*. Men carry on a struggle against nature and utilize nature for the production of material values not in isolation from each other, not as separate individuals, but in common, in groups, in societies. Production, therefore, is at all times and under all conditions *social* production. In the production of material values men enter into mutual relations of one kind or another within production, into relations of production of one kind or another. These may be relations of cooperation and mutual help between people who are free from exploitation; they may be relations of domination and subordination; and lastly, they may be transitional from one form of relations of production to another. But whatever the character of the relations of production may be, always and in every system, they constitute just as essential an element of production as the productive forces of society. . . .

Consequently, production, the mode of production, embraces both the productive forces of society and men's relations of production, and is thus the embodiment of their unity in the process of production of material values.

*One of the features* of production is that it never stays on one point for a long time and is always in a state of change and development, and that, furthermore, changes in the mode of production inevitably call forth changes in the whole social system, social ideas, political views and political institutions—they call forth a reconstruction of the whole social and political order. At different stages of development people make use of different modes of production, or, to put it more crudely, lead different manners of life. In the primitive commune there is one mode of production, under slavery there is another mode of production, under feudalism a third mode of production, and so on. And, correspondingly, men's social system, the spiritual life of men, their views and political institutions also vary.

Whatever is the mode of production of a society, such in the main is the society itself, its ideas and theories, its political views and institutions.

Or, to put it more crudely, whatever is man's manner of life, such is his manner of thought.

This means that the history of development of society is above all the history of the development of production, the history of the modes of production which succeed each other in the course of centuries, the history of the development of productive forces and people's relations of production.

Hence the history of social development is at the same time the history of the producers of material values themselves, the history of the laboring masses who are the chief force in the process of production and who carry on the production of material values necessary for the existence of society.

Hence, if historical science is to be a real science, it can no longer reduce the history of social development to the actions of kings and generals, to the actions of "conquerors" and "subjugators" of states, but must above all devote itself to the history of the producers of material values, the history of the laboring masses, the history of peoples.

Hence the clue to the study of the laws of history of society must not be sought in men's minds, in the views and ideas of society, but in the mode of production practised by society in any given historical period; it must be sought in the economic life of society.
. . .

*A second feature* of production is that its changes and development always begin with changes and development of the productive forces, and, in the first place, with changes and development of the instruments of production. Productive forces are therefore the most mobile and revolutionary element of production. First the productive forces of society change and develop, and then, *depending* on these changes and *in conformity with them,* men's relations of production, their economic relations, change. This, however, does not mean that the relations of production do not influence the development of the productive forces and that the latter are not dependent on the former. While their development is dependent on the development of the productive forces, the relations of production in their turn react upon the development of the productive forces, accelerating or retarding it. In this connection it should be noted that the relations of production cannot for too long a time lag behind and be in a state of contradiction to the growth of the productive forces, inasmuch as the productive forces can develop in full measure only when the relations of production correspond to the character, the state of the productive forces and allow full scope for their development. Therefore, however much the relations of production may lag behind the development of the productive forces, they must, sooner or later, come into correspondence with—and actually do come into correspondence with—the level of development of the productive forces, the character of the productive forces. Otherwise we would have a fundamental violation of the unity of the productive forces and the relations of production within the system of production, a disruption of production as a whole, a crisis of production, a destruction of productive forces.

An instance in which the relations of production do not correspond to the character of the productive forces, conflict with them, is the economic crises in capitalist countries, where private capitalist ownership of the means of production is in glaring incongruity with the social character of the process of production, with the character of the productive forces. This results in economic crises, which lead to the destruction of productive forces. Furthermore, this incongruity itself constitutes the economic basis of social revolution, the purpose of which is to destroy the existing relations of production and to create new relations of production corresponding to the character of the productive forces.

In contrast, an instance in which the relations of production completely correspond to the character of the productive forces is the Socialist national economy of the U.S.S.R., where the social ownership of the means of production fully corresponds to the social character of the process of production, and where, because of this, economic crises and the destruction of productive forces are unknown. . . .

While the state of the productive forces furnishes an answer to the question—with what instruments of production do men produce the material values they need?—the state of the relations of production furnishes the answer to another question—who owns the *means of production* (the land, forests, waters, mineral resources, raw materials, instruments of production, production premises, means of transportation and communication, etc.), who commands the means of production, whether the whole of society, or individual persons, groups, or classes which utilize them for the exploitation of other persons, groups or classes? . . .

Five *main* types of relations of production are known to history: primitive communal, slave, feudal, capitalist and Socialist.

The basis of the relations of production under the primitive communal system is that the means of production are socially owned. This in the main corresponds to the character of the productive forces of that period. Stone tools, and, later, the bow and arrow, precluded the possibility of men individually combating the forces of nature and beasts of prey. In order to gather the fruits of the forest, to catch fish, to build some sort of habitation, men were obliged to work in common if they did not want to die of starvation, or fall victim to beasts of prey or to neighboring societies. Labor in common led to the common ownership of the means of production, as well as of the fruits of production. . . . Here there was no exploitation, no classes.

The basis of the relations of production under the slave system is that the slave owner owns the means of production; he also owns the worker in production—the slave, whom he can sell, purchase, or kill as though he were an animal. . . . Instead of stone tools, men now have metal tools at their command; instead of the wretched and primitive husbandry of the hunter, who knew neither pasturage, nor tillage, there now appear pasturage, tillage, handicrafts, and a division of labor between these branches of production. There appears the possibility of the exchange of products between individuals and between societies, of the accumulation of wealth in the hands of a few, the actual accumulation of the means of production in the hands of a minority, and the possibility of subjugation of the majority by a minority and their conversion into slaves. Here we no longer find the common and free labor of all members of society in the production process—here there prevails the forced labor of slaves, who are exploited by the non-laboring slave owners. . . .

Rich and poor, exploiters and exploited, people with full rights and people with no rights, and a fierce class struggle between them —such is the picture of the slave system.

The basis of the relations of production under the feudal system is that the feudal lord owns the means of production and does not fully own the worker in production—the serf, whom the feudal lord can no longer kill, but whom he can buy and sell. . . . Further improvements in the smelting and working of iron; the spread of the iron plough and the loom; the further development of agriculture, horticulture, viniculture and dairying; the appearance of manufactories alongside of the handicraft workshops—such are the characteristic features of the state of the productive forces.

The new productive forces demand that the laborer shall display some kind of initiative in production and an inclination for work, an interest in work. The feudal lord therefore discards the slave, as a laborer who has no interest in work and is entirely without initiative, and prefers to deal with the serf, who has his own husbandry, implements of production, and a certain interest in work essential for the cultivation of the land and for the payment in kind of a part of his harvest to the feudal lord.

Here private ownership is further developed. Exploitation is nearly as severe as it was under slavery—it is only slightly mitigated.   A class struggle between exploiters and exploited is the principal feature of the feudal system.

The basis of the relations of production under the capitalist system is that the capitalist owns the means of production, but not the workers in production—the wage laborers, whom the capitalist can neither kill nor sell because they are personally free, but who are deprived of means of production and, in order not to die of hunger, are obliged to sell their labor power to the capitalist and to bear the yoke of exploitation. . . . In place of the handicraft workshops and manufactories there appear huge mills and factories equipped with machinery. . . .

The new productive forces require that the workers in production shall be better educated and more intelligent than the downtrodden and ignorant serfs, that they be able to understand machinery and operate it properly.   Therefore, the capitalists prefer to deal with wage workers who are free from the bonds of serfdom and who are educated enough to be able properly to operate machinery.

But having developed productive forces to a tremendous extent, capitalism has become enmeshed in contradictions which it is unable to solve.   By producing larger and larger quantities of commodities, and reducing their prices, capitalism intensifies competition, ruins the mass of small and medium private owners, converts them into proletarians and reduces their purchasing power, with the result that it becomes impossible to dispose of the commodities produced.   On the other hand, by expanding production and concentrating millions of workers in huge mills and factories, capitalism lends the process of production a social character and thus undermines its own foundation, inasmuch as the social character of the process of production demands the social ownership of the means of production; yet the means of production remain private capitalist property, which is incompatible with the social character of the process of production.

These irreconcilable contradictions between the character of the productive forces and the relations of production make themselves felt in periodical crises of overproduction, when the capitalists, finding no effective demand for their goods owing to the ruin of the mass of the population which they themselves have brought about, are compelled to burn products, destroy manufactured goods, suspend production, and destroy productive forces at a time when millions of people are forced to suffer unemployment and starvation, not because there are not enough goods, but because there is an overproduction of goods.

This means that the capitalist relations of production have ceased to correspond to the state of productive forces of society and have come into irreconcilable contradiction with them.

This means that capitalism is pregnant with revolution, whose mission it is to replace the existing capitalist ownership of the means of production by Socialist ownership.

This means that the main feature of the capitalist system is a most acute class struggle between the exploiters and the exploited.

Such is the picture of the development of men's relations of production in the course of human history.

Such is the dependence of the development of the relations of production on the development of the production forces of society, and primarily, on the development of the instruments of production, the dependence by virtue of which the changes and development of the productive forces sooner or later lead to corresponding changes and development of the relations of production. . . .

Speaking of historical materialism as formulated in *The Communist Manifesto,* Engels says:

> Economic production and the structure of society of every historical epoch necessarily arising therefrom constitute the foundation for the political and intellectual history of that epoch; . . . consequently ever since the dissolution of the primeval communal ownership of land all history has been a history of class struggles, of struggles between exploited and exploiting, between dominated and dominating classes at various stages of social evolution; . . . this struggle, however, has now reached a stage where the exploited and oppressed class (the proletariat) can no longer emancipate itself from the class which exploits and oppresses it (the bourgeoisie), without at the same time forever freeing the whole of society from exploitation, oppression and class struggles. (Preface to the German edition of *The Communist Manifesto*—Karl Marx, *Selected Works,* Vol. I, pp. 192-93.)

*A third feature* of production is that the rise of new productive forces and of the relations of production corresponding to them does not take place separately from the old system, after the disappearance of the old system, but within the old system; it takes place not as a result of the deliberate and conscious activity of man, but spontaneously, unconsciously, independently of the will of man. It takes place spontaneously and independently of the will of man for two reasons.

First, because men are not free to choose one mode of production or another, because as every new generation enters life it finds productive forces and relations of production already existing as the result of the work of former generations, owing to which it is obliged at first to accept and adapt itself to everything it finds ready made in the sphere of production in order to be able to produce material values.

Secondly, because, when improving one instrument of production or another, one element of the productive forces or another, men do not realize, do not understand or stop to reflect what *social* results these improvements will lead to, but only think of their everyday interests, of lightening their labor and of securing some direct and tangible advantage for themselves. . . .

This, however, does not mean that changes in the relations of production, and the transition from old relations of production to new relations of production proceed smoothly, without conflicts, without upheavals. On the contrary, such a transition usually takes place by means of the revolutionary overthrow of the old relations of production and the establishment of new relations of production. Up to a certain period the development of the productive forces and the changes in the realm of the relations of production proceed spontaneously, independently of the will of men. But that is so only up to a certain moment, until the new and developing productive forces have reached a proper state of maturity. After the new productive forces have matured, the existing relations of production and their upholders—the ruling classes—become that "insuperable" obstacle which can only be removed by the conscious action of the new classes, by the forcible acts of these classes, by revolution. Here there stands out in bold relief the *tremendous role* of new social ideas, of new political institutions, of a new political power, whose mission it is to abolish by force the old relations of production. Out of the conflict between the new productive forces and the old relations of production, out of the new economic demands of society there arise new social ideas; the new ideas organize and mobilize the masses; the masses become welded into a new political army, create a new revolutionary power, and make use of it to abolish by force the old system of relations of production, and firmly to establish the new system. The spontaneous process of development yields place to the conscious actions of men, peaceful development to violent upheaval, evolution to revolution. . . .

Here is the brilliant formulation of the essence of historical materialism given by Marx in 1859 in his historic Preface to his famous book, *Critique of Political Economy*:

> In the social production which men carry on they enter into definite relations that are indispensable and independent of their will; these relations of production correspond to a definite stage of development of their material forces of production. The sum total of these relations of production constitutes the economic structure of society—the real foundation, on which rises a legal and political superstructure and to which correspond definite forms of social consciousness. The mode of production in material life determines the social, political and intellectual life process in general. It is not the consciousness of men that determines their being, but, on the contrary, their social being that determines their consciousness. * * *

Such is Marxist materialism as applied to social life, to the history of society.

Such are the principal features of dialectical and historical materialism. . . .

# THE MATERIALIST CONCEPTION OF HISTORY*

BY

## KARL FEDERN

[1939]

### Marx's Theory of History

In the Introduction to the *Criticism of Political Economy*, by Karl Marx, we find the following propositions:

(1) In the course of social economic production men enter into certain relations, and certain conditions are formed by them, of necessity and independently of their will. These conditions of production correspond to a certain stage of development of the material forces of production.

(2) Conditions of production, taken as a whole, constitute the economic structure of society—this is the material basis on which a superstructure of laws and political institutions is raised and to which certain forms of political consciousness correspond.

(3) The political and intellectual life of a society is determined by the mode of production, as necessitated by the wants of material life.

(4) It is not men's consciousness that determines the forms of existence, but, on the contrary, the social forms of life that determine the consciousness. . . .

We may look upon these propositions, which have become famous, as the basis of Historical Materialism. They were written in London in the year 1859. Marx says, however, that as early as 1841, when writing a criticism of Hegel's *Philosophy of the Law,* he had become aware of the truth that "constitutions and laws, and the whole organization of society, cannot be explained by the so-called development of human intellect, but are rooted in the forms of material life." . . .

Marx offered no proofs for his theses; he was satisfied with

---

*Selected and arranged from *The Materialist Conception of History* by Karl Federn. Copyright 1939 by Macmillan and Co., Limited, London, and St. Martin's Press, Inc., New York. Reprinted by permission.

enunciating them. We shall, however, have to examine not only the theses but also the proofs which other writers have since tried to furnish. . . .

. . . Marx informs us in the first proposition of the two facts, namely, that the conditions of production which form the economic structure of society, are "necessary and independent of human will," and that they correspond to a certain development of the productive forces. . . .

The development of the productive forces is indeed—according to this theory—the *causa causans* in history. The fate and development of mankind are determined by them.

We shall, therefore, have first to examine the truth of this proposition.

## THE PRODUCTIVE FORCES

What are productive forces? How do they come into existence and how do they develop? Are they really the last, or rather the first cause, the primary agency in the economic development of mankind and therewith, according to Historical Materialism, of all history?

Productive forces are the forces employed in economic production by man, the fertile qualities of the soil, the special properties of metals, the mechanical and chemical forces of nature, solar heat, steam power, electricity, as well as the forces of animals and of man himself.[1]

Now, all these productive powers, heat, fertility, water and steam power, all the manifold forces of nature, upon the combina-

---

[1] . . . The question arises whether the intellectual forces of man belong to the productive forces or not. We do not see how they can well be excluded, considering that they are the sole forces which play an active part in the process of economic production. Yet, for this very reason, their mode of operation being different from that of all other forces, it would be difficult to include them in the same category. Marx and his followers do not seem to have paid much attention to this important question. Marx certainly did not include them among the productive forces mentioned in his theses, for in this case he would have had to change the latter entirely, and the whole theory would have crumbled. He and his adherents relegate all intellectual activities to the "ideological superstructure."

tion of which economic production depends, are always there; they have existed from time immemorial. It was only necessary to discover them and to find out in what manner they could be put to use.

Magnetism, for instance, and electricity, which play such a conspicuous part in modern economic production, did always exist; but no intelligent human being had discovered them and found out how they might be employed for man's use. There are, no doubt, many undiscovered forces and phenomena in nature which might be of unsuspected value to human economics, waiting to be discovered by man.

Discovering a new productive force, as well as finding out a method of applying it, are mental acts. . . . Probably no one would contend that the discovery and use of productive forces, from the construction of primitive tools, the domestication of animals, the beginning of agriculture, up to the use of steam and electricity, have been unconscious acts and were not brought about by what we call mind, imagination, reasoning and will, in short, the intellectual activities of man. People may not always be conscious of the importance and of the consequences of their discoveries, but every discovery, the most primitive contrivance as well as the most surprising invention, was made by the imaginative and reasoning forces of the human mind. If these forces were lacking, men would live and act like animals; the productive forces of nature would remain undiscovered, and there would be neither development nor civilization. Discoveries and inventions may be necessary, which is to say that they are in no wise exempt from the inter-dependency of cause and effect, but they are due to man's intellect.

We shall have to examine their causation as well as their consequences in order to understand their part in the development of mankind. Before doing this, however, we have to consider an objection which might be raised at this point. Men, one might say, had natural wants; they stood in need of food, shelter, clothing, etc. Chance made a savage in such need break a bough from a tree, lift a sharp-edged stone from the earth, and make use of them; by pure chance another savage found the art of kindling a fire; by chance he tamed the first animal, just as chance would that, in later ages, a civilized man observed and was struck by the effect of steam-power. The discovery once made, the development of the productive force and of the different ways in which it could be used, followed quite naturally. . . .

. . . Yet, even when looked at from this point of view, it is only the experience that was due to chance, whereas it was due to the person's particular bent or quality of mind that the fact struck him as peculiar and that he drew important conclusions from it. . . . Millions of boughs grew on the trees or were lying on the ground, capable of serving as levers or palisades, there were plenty of sharp stones that might be used as knives or axes; steam lifted the tea-pot's lid a hundred thousand times; yet not until a sufficiently intelligent savage decided to make use of the bough or the stone, and not until a gifted man saw that the steam which lifted the teapot's lid, might serve for much greater purposes, was the discovery possible. . . .

The adherents of the Marxist theory, claiming to explain the course of history, say that it is the development of the productive forces which produces all other phenomena and developments. . . . Even if it were, how is the development of the productive forces to be accounted for? . . .

We have seen that all productive forces are discovered, developed and put to use by the human intellect. In like manner, the substitution in some branch of industry of machinery for manufacture by hand, the transition of a tribe from cattle-breeding to agriculture or the reverse, the expansion of industry and commerce in a country where the people hitherto lived chiefly on agriculture, are contrived by the human intellect. Intelligent and enterprising persons are the first to see which new methods promise better results than the old ones gave; they will be the first to apply them, and other people will follow their lead. The more human intelligence develops, the more frequently some persons will be able to forsee that a certain branch or mode of production is going to become unprofitable and that it would be advisable to replace it in time by some better method or to proceed to the production of another kind of commodities. On the other hand, it is a fact of frequent occurrence to see the population of some town or village with a once flourishing industry suffer economic ruin because they cannot be induced to change their customary ways. . . .

Whenever the importance of human intellect in production and economics is pointed out to the adherents of the Materialist Conception of History, they invariably make answer that they know it well, that all their authors . . . gave their attention to the fact, and that it has long been stated by them that intellectual phenomena are more or less important intermediate links in the different historical processes, but being of an ideological nature, they are rooted in the economic system and are ultimately created and determined by the conditions of production. In saying this, they have in view the so-called superstructure, political opinions, philosophy, science, etc. What they completely overlook is the fact that, as we have seen, the human mind plays the decisive part in the *basis,* in economics and production itself. As soon as we become aware of this, the whole theory crumbles, for the division into an economic basis and an intellectual superstructure becomes untenable. . . .

. . . History is the record of the continuous changes in men's relations to each other and to nature as well as of their moral and intellectual developments. The problem of which we are seeking the solution, is the causation of these changes. And with regard to this we can but repeat that, however important the part played by the productive forces may be, they are certainly not the primary agency by which these changes are brought about.

## THE CONDITIONS OF PRODUCTION AND THE IDEOLOGICAL SUPERSTRUCTURE

The essential part [of Marx's theory] is, however, the second [proposition]. . . . The truth of [this] is not dependent on that of the first [proposition]. It may be maintained as an independent theory and, if it could be proved, would be of decisive importance.

To the beginning, there can be no objection: "The conditions of production as a whole constitute the economic structure of society." This is in fact only a paraphrase; the same object is given another name. It is the second part of proposition 2 that contains the main issue of the matter: "The conditions of production are the material basis on which is raised a superstructure of laws and political institutions, and to which certain forms of political consciousness correspond." Proposition 3, "The social, political and intellectual life of a given society depends on the mode of production as necessitated by the wants of material life," is again only a paraphrase, an elucidation perhaps, of the previous sentence; and proposition 4, "It is not man's consciousness that determines the form of existence, but it is, on the contrary, the social forms of life which determine men's consciousness," is in reality only another paraphrase of the same thought, couched in·terms of the current philosophy of the time.

In a limited sense, Marx's theory might be accepted. If we understand his words to imply that human society could not exist without economic production, or as he terms it, the "production of material life," then it is perfectly true. There cannot be the slightest doubt that society depends upon production as its "real basis."

But even though Marx says in another place, "Men must be able to live in order to be able to make history. And to live one needs meat and drink, lodging, clothing and some other things," his words are not so intended. He did not merely wish to imply that society depends on production for its existence. No one, in this case, would have contested his theory, but everyone would have replied: We knew this long ago; man must live in order to be able to think and he must eat in order to be able to live. People who die of starvation are incapable of leading a political or intellectual life. What Marx wanted to say was not only that production is necessary, but that the mode of production is decisive; that laws, constitutions, science, art and religion depend on the mode of production and are determined by it, and when the mode of production changes, everything else changes.

Air is also an essential condition of life; we cannot make laws or write books if we are unable to breathe. If, however, some scientist should succeed in proving that the composition of the atmosphere has a decisive influence on our institutions and opinions, it would be a very important discovery. The problem we have to face is, therefore, whether the mode of economic production really has a definite and unmistakable influence on men's political and intellectual life, or not. That it has some influence cannot be denied, because everything that touches our life and existence in an important manner will, as a rule, have some effect on our opinions and actions; but that is not the question. In the philosophical fourth proposition, Marx stated his meaning with perfect clarity; translated into the language of our time, it would read as follows: economic activity and the social order do not result from man's intelligence, from their thoughts and feelings, rather are their thoughts and feelings determined by their economic activity and the ensuing social order. . . .

The propagation and diffusion of the Christian religion offers an excellent opportunity to apply, so to speak, a crucial test to the truth of the Marxist theory of history.

The diffusion of Christianity in the Old World was accomplished, approximately, in the time from the middle of the first century to the twelfth century, that is, more than a thousand years.

It must be said, in the first place, that the economic misery which, it is asserted, was one of the sources from which the Christian religion derived its origin, did not exist. The larger part of the population of the Roman Empire were at no time so well off and happy as during the first two centuries after the fall of the Republic. Never before had the ancient world enjoyed such a long and unbroken period of peace; the imperial governors were not allowed by the emperors to exploit and oppress the provinces, as the Roman aristocracy had done under the republican regimen, and riches and general well-being increased accordingly. During this time, the Christian religion expanded slowly and gradually over the Empire.

About the end of the second century after Christ, this general prosperity began to decline. Continuous civil wars brought about increasing misery, made worse by invasions of barbaric tribes. . . . The civil population of the Empire was, at this period, perhaps more miserable than ever afterwards. Yet the diffusion of Christianity proceeded with unabated force.

The uncivilized or half-civilized German tribes conquered the Empire, divided it and established new feudal kingdoms in its stead, whose laws, customs and economics were widely different from those of the Ancient World. The diffusion of the new religion, however, continued unimpaired.

It spread in times of peace and opulence as well as in centuries of war, misery and decay; it spread in periods of high civilization, among a refined and sceptical aristocracy, as well as among rude peasants and slaves. . . .

The Christian religion spread in times of highly developed economic systems—for the period of its origin was one of large estates, great industry and a complicated financial system, a period which may well be called one of capitalism—and it spread in times of natural economy among savage warriors and rude peasants.

If, therefore, the mode of production were indeed to be considered as the real basis determining the whole "superstructure" and religion as a part of the superstructure, we should be forced to conclude, on the one hand, that the most different modes of production cause exactly the same spiritual movements and, on the other hand, that the same mode of production gives origin to the most different institutions and opinions. We might ask what strange causes these are whose effects are so uncertain and incalculable? Or should we rather not say that there obviously exists no inter-dependency of cause and effect between the conditions of production and religion, and that those who asserted its existence, did so regardless of logic as well as of history? For so much is clear: either a historical movement of such importance as the diffusion of Christianity was altogether independent of the economic system and had nothing whatever to do with it, or if economics had any influence upon it, this influence was modified and counterbalanced by others to such an extent as to make its effect on the movement appear insignificant.[2]

---

[2] In the light of these facts Marx's utterance on the Christian faith in *Capital*, vol. i, p. 85, seems equally rash and extravagant. He says: "Christianity, treating man as an abstract being, is indeed the religion befitting the bourgeois society that lives on producing saleable goods."
Marx might have said that the comprehension and interpretation of Christianity is different in different times and states of civilization, and that

Marx says: "The social, political and intellectual life of a society depends on the mode of production, that is, on the entire complex of the existing conditions of production." . . .

. . . Is the proposition acceptable that, given a certain mode of production, all other social and intellectual phenomena in the same society invariably result from it?

. . . When a barbarous German tribe conquered a Roman province, dispossessed the landowners of the soil, yet forced them to go on cultivating it for their new lords' benefit, we cannot call the new order a new mode of production, because the mode of production is exactly the same as before, whereas the conditions of production are fundamentally changed. In Marxist literature the two terms are regularly employed as synonymous. Now, according to Marx's theory, the new conditions of production should have been brought about by some new productive force. Are we to understand that this was the brutal force of the ancient Germans? Certainly, this force, by destroying valuable goods and artistic treasures by the million, effected a fundamental change of the conditions of production in the civilized countries of antiquity, but it does not, on this account, seem advisable to call it a productive force.

From whatsoever point of view we may examine the theory of Marx, it does not prove conformable with reality.

Nobody will deny that civil as well as penal law, be it in primitive or in civilized times, is largely framed for the purpose of protecting existing economic conditions, as expressed in rights of property and of succession, in contracts and obligations. It is, however, just as undeniable that many, and not the least important, laws derive their origin from sexual or religious motives, or from motives of personal fear, from the need of the individual to be protected from physical violence and moral constraint. Now all these considerations are in no immediate, and often not even in a distant, connection with economic matters. It is further undeniable that many considerations of a non-economic nature did, in many

---

religious practice will always become more or less adapted to the social and intellectual status of the people who have accepted its dogmas. It is, on the other hand, equally certain that the social and intellectual status of a people is deeply influenced and modified by religion.

cases, influence laws and customs in the economic sphere. We need only mention medieval laws against interest and usury, a good many matrimonial laws, large sections of canonical law, and many other instances.

We shall, however, admit that, law and order being a condition required for the existence of society, they belong, in a broad interpretation of the term, to the conditions of what Engels called the "production and reproduction of material life." But that does not imply that his and Marx's theory accounts in any way for the various legal systems in force in different ages and among different nations.

Much less does it explain their religions and philosophies, their arts and sciences, in short, what is termed by Marx the ideological superstructure.

We did not need Marx's theory to tell us that the intellectual life of a period is to a large extent determined by the prevailing conditions, including economic conditions; we knew that anything that is of importance in men's lives will occupy their thoughts and their imaginations, and that environment influences their opinions. It stands to reason and needs no explanation that an untravelled Englishman does not share the habits and opinions of an Indian, nor a Malay those of a Greenlander. These are truisms.

The question raised by Marx is whether the environment, the *milieu*, and the conditions of production in particular, exert such an exclusive influence on the entire social and intellectual life of the different strata as well as of the single individuals of any society that, given the environment, their intellectual life is bound to take a predetermined form and must go on developing in a predetermined manner? Or are there other factors to influence and to determine it? . . .

We . . . find that the opinions of men belonging to the same class, and brought up under exactly the same conditions, are nevertheless quite different. How is it that from the same class of the Roman Optimates there arose men like Scipio and Opimius who advocated aristocratic rule and interest, and men like the Gracchi? That in the French nobility of the Ancien Régime we find conservative, liberal and revolutionary members? How is it—the question has often been put—that the founders of Socialism and the leaders of the modern labor movement have for long years come almost without exception from the bourgeoisie, that is, from an environment which, if there were any truth in the theory, would necessarily have implanted in them directly opposite views? . . .

If anybody should say that these are but exceptions, we should reply that where there are exceptions, there is no law in the scientific sense of the word, least of all when the exceptions are so frequent as to be noticeable everywhere and every day. We shall see, too, that it is these exceptions which are of the greatest, and even of the only real, importance in the evolution of mankind. If environment did determine their ideology, all men living in the same environment would necessarily have the same ideas and pursue the same ends. It would be impossible that from the same class, the same set and even the same family, there should arise, by the side of brothers and sisters who follow the common track, some original and revolutionary thinker. Either environment determines ideology or does not determine it, but an environment that in some cases determines men's ideology and in other cases fails to do so, is either no causal factor at all, or else there must needs exist other factors which suspend or counteract its effects in numerous cases. . . .

. . . There are individuals in whom the intellect of mankind manifests itself, as it were, in concentrated form. Here, Marx's theory of history is found to be hopelessly at fault. The appearance of those men who opened new outlooks to their generation or who successfully took the lead in some critical situation, is in nowise connected with, or dependent on, the conditions of production. If anybody would contend that it was owing to the development of the productive forces and to the existing conditions of production that such men as Kant and Newton, Rousseau and Mirabeau, Goethe and Napoleon were born, men whose influence extended over a great part of the earth and far into the unknown depth of time, he is bound to prove it and to demonstrate why and how the conditions of production caused the birth of these men at this particular time; otherwise his assertion is idle talk and nothing but an arbitrary hypothesis.

We might have expected that the authors who wrote on the Materialist Conception of History, should at least have made an attempt to do this. But what they say on the subject is indeed idle talk. Cunow informs us that men of genius are influenced by their environment and by prevailing opinions, which is not to the point, being as natural as it is uninteresting. It is what is new in the man's gifts, the qualities by which he distinguishes himself from his fellow men, all that he does not owe to environment, that interests us in a man of genius. If he had no extraordinary qualities, if environment had made him exactly like all the rest, we would not call him a man of genius nor be interested in his personality. . . .

The relation between economic conditions and what Marx calls the economic superstructure resembles that between the soil and the plants, growing on a field that we see for the first time. We know that the plants sprang from the soil and that if there was no soil there would be no plants, but we do not know who sowed them, nor where the seeds came from, nor do we know just why these plants grew here and none other. Yet we may say from long experience that many causes beside the soil had to cooperate to make these plants grow.

From all these accumulated considerations it is evident that the second, the third and the fourth propositions in Marx's formula must be untenable. We may let the second pass in a restricted sense, admitting that the economic system of a society is the real basis of all legal, political and intellectual phenomena, in so far as these phenomena cannot exist independent of it; we may even call them a superstructure upon the economic system, just as we may call the plants a superstructure upon the soil, but not in the sense in which Marx and his followers wish it to be understood. As the plants are created *out* of the soil but not *by* the soil, so the ideological superstructure is *erected upon* the economic system but not *created by* it. We may also admit that *some* of the forces of social consciousness correspond to a certain mode of production, but by no means all of them. Only those forms of social consciousness that are directly connected with production, assume a special character which corresponds to it. They constitute, however, only a part of the cultural and intellectual life of a period, and not always the essential and decisive part. Within these limits the second proposition may be accepted. If, however, the words "superstructure" and "forms of consciousness" are understood in the comprehensive sense in which Marx clearly wished them to be accepted, then the proposition is false. It is practically impossible to demonstrate the dependence of all intellectual life on the conditions of production, because no serious scientific investigation of the intricate phenomena and of the countless causal inter-connections in life and history is possible. But whereas it is impossible to prove the theory, it is very easy to refute it, and in numerous cases to prove the non-existence of any such dependence.

The third proposition would have to be altered in so far as "the mode of production of real life" is a condition of social, political and intellectual life; we shall even admit that it influences the latter to a large extent, but it is false to say that it is its determining cause. Since the same intellectual and other phenomena are compatible with different modes of production and, on the other hand, the greatest differences in intellectual and political life are found, notwithstanding identical mode of production, the latter cannot be the sole determining cause of the former. A causality that is not cogent is no causality at all.

As to the fourth proposition: "It is not man's consciousness that determines his economic and social activity, but it is, on the contrary, his economic system that determines his consciousness," we have shown that in the general form in which Marx enunciated it, it is false. . . . Like the productive forces and the conditions of production, man's consciousness and his economic activity influence one another; there exists a reciprocal inter-dependency between economics and consciousness. That is no new discovery. . . .

It has been our object in this chapter to examine the relations between what is called the economic basis and what is comprised in the term "ideological superstructure." It may, however, be advisable to note at once that the development of the economic basis itself—the changes in the mode of production—has been left unexplained by Marx. Any Marxist historian would tell us that the different state of civilization in which Romans and Germans lived, say, at Caesar's time, was due to the difference in the mode and conditions of production prevailing among the two races. If, however, we should ask for the reason why these two kindred races who once had lived under exactly similar conditions of production, nevertheless developed economic and social systems so widely different, if we should ask for the causes determining this divergent evolution, we should receive no answer. It is true that in *German Ideology* Marx—or Engels—derides those who "still cherish the old illusion that it depends only on men's good intentions to change the existing conditions," adding that "any change in men's consciousness is itself produced by the existing conditions and is a part of them." This is clearly no explanation, but one of the tautologies in which Marxism abounds. Evidently anything that is new, follows from what already exists. We knew that long ago. What we want to know is, how and why the particular new fact is produced. . . .

\* \* \*

. . . While the productive forces are considered to be the basic element in history, and the conditions of production as a form of development of these forces, whereas all the rest is nothing but an ideological superstructure and, as such, a consequence of the conditions of production, class war is the method or the form in which the historical evolution of mankind is accomplished. We read in the first paragraph of the *Communist Manifesto*: "The history of all societies that existed up to our time, is the history of class struggles; free men and slaves, patricians and plebians, barons and serfs, masters and companions of a guild, in short, oppressors and oppressed, lived in constant opposition to one another, and in uninterrupted warfare against one another, a war which at certain times was latent and at other times became open strife, and which every time ended either in a revolutionary transformation of the whole society or in the extinction of both classes."

We do indeed find class struggles or at least class differences in nearly all countries and times since civilization began. It was Plato who wrote, "There are two states in the state, one is that of the rich, the other that of the poor." In Athens and in Rome class struggles went on for centuries. They play a conspicuous part in all medieval countries and towns as well as in modern times; and now, at present, since the classes have become conscious of the struggle and since there exists a theory of it, it plays an even greater part than ever before.

Nevertheless, the way in which history is declared to be merely a record of class struggles, is open to objection. . . .

However great the importance of class struggles may have been, their influence was by no means the only one that shaped society, and it cannot even be said that they are the most important fact in history, unless seen from a class standpoint. He who studies history with an unbiased mind, will find that wars between nations certainly played no less a part. We may even say that, as a rule, they were more frequent, more violent, caused much more bloodshed and were certainly more effective in deciding the fate and the development of the peoples of the earth than domestic struggles. . . . Even in our time, the national feeling, the consciousness of belonging to the same country, proves in foreign wars, with very few exceptions, to be stronger than all class differences. All through history ruling classes and subject classes, rich and poor, fought as co-nationals side by side against foreign enemies. It is immaterial whether the reason was an "antiquated ideology," a "lack of class consciousness," the "suggestion of patriotism," or a natural feeling of belonging to those to whom they were bound by the same blood, the same language, and many common interests. . . .

This holds good especially with regard to religious discords. Though it happened that a certain class was particularly affected by a religious movement, as when in the beginning of the Reformation in some countries the nobility became protestant, in others the townships, and in some regions the peasant population, such a state of things did not last. Soon all classes in Catholic countries or provinces were fanatic partisans of Rome, whereas in others they stood with equal zeal for the Reformation. . . . Supposing it to be true and demonstrable, that the true causes of the Reformation were of an economic nature, the fact would remain that the poor people, who from class interest ought to have acted quite differently, fought, for the sake of religion, with fanatic zeal by the side of princes and nobles of their creed, against handicrafts-men, workmen and peasants of the opposite persuasion who for similar reasons took the side of their lords. . . . In general, members of all classes either took the side of the Roman Church or were against it.  If anybody should object that they were not suf-ficiently enlightened and did not know their class interests, we would reply that this only serves to prove that ideology is decisive, and that neither class interest nor conditions of production are suf-ficient to produce a certain determined ideology.  It proves further that struggles of such world-wide importance as the religious wars for and against the Reformation, which went on for two centuries, were not class struggles and only in a few exceptional cases took the form of, or coincided with, class struggles. . . .

The history of mankind is a history of struggles and fighting of every kind.  In these struggles the weaker side is beaten, and the path of mankind is marked by oppression and exploitation of the vanquished.  It is quite natural that these constant struggles, and the suffering that is their consequence, create a great longing for peace, and that the oppressed and exploited hope for deliverance. Whether these hopes and this longing will ever be fulfilled, and which may be the right path towards fulfilment, is very uncertain. Up to our time, mankind has been similar to the city of which Dante sang:

> Thou shalt behold thyself as woman sick
> Who on her pillow finds no rest at night,
> And seeks to ease her pain by turning quick.

* * *

## HISTORICAL DIALECTICS

There is in all our philosophy, in historical, and to a certain extent even in natural, science a strong residue of scholasticism. Thinkers are still liable to mistake words for the facts denoted by them, to confound the sphere of thought with that of empirical investigation; they frequently believe themselves to be treating of facts while they are only displacing words. Thus Marx and Engels were the dupes of mere words. What they called the "dialectical" development of society is the development from one social system to another which is considered to be contradictory to it, as, for instance, from Feudalism to Capitalism, from Capitalism to Socialism. They quite lost sight of the fact that terms like "Capitalism," "Socialism," "Revolution," etc., are but sophisticated and artificial expedients to denote a multitude of the most various real facts and processes by one single comprehensive or collective word. They are a kind of spoken stenography. . . .

The word "Feudalism" for instance, is intended to denote millions of facts, events and institutions which in reality existed in many countries through centuries, which differed widely in the various regions, and yet had a few features in common. The word "Feudalism" is meant, at one time, to call up these common features in the hearer's mind whereas, at another time, it is used with the intention of evoking a vague image of the life of those past times. We cannot dispense with these collective terms, we should be absolutely unable to reason without them, and provided we remain conscious of their being mere symbols denoting a multitude of facts, we may even reach results which are not utterly false. Marx and Engels, however, and their followers, by taking such words as Feudalism, Capitalism, Socialism, for realities, and founding their dialectics upon them, opened a back door to metaphysics, which they believed they had excluded from their system, without being in the least aware of it. . . .

We are not only free to choose certain facts or phenomena from among those of a certain period and denote them by some comprehensive term, but it also depends entirely on our point of view which phenomena of another period we shall consider as contradictory to the former, in short, which group or set of facts, opinions and institutions we shall oppose to one another. If, for instance, we comprehend a certain class of political opinions and institutions by the word "Democracy," we may consider that class of opinions and institutions which we call by a collective word "Aristocracy," as contradictory to it. We may, however, from another point of view or under the impression of different events consider those aspects which we denote by the word "Dictatorship" as the "negation" of Democracy. We shall certainly prefer to do so at present under the influence of contemporary events, owing to which the main issue at this moment seems to be between Democracy and Dictatorship. We might, however, at another time have regarded "Liberalism" and "Democracy" as opposed to each other. Several authors have certainly done so. Our choice will depend on what particular current in the entire evolution seems at a given time most important to us, and on the course which this current seems to take. What will "of necessity" be the future development of democracy depends solely on the writer's opinion, and his opinion will probably be determined by the fact that certain conflicting currents make themselves particularly felt at the moment. Thinkers generally succumb to the illusion that these currents are permanent phenomena, that the evolution of mankind will proceed in the same direction in which it now seems to tend, and that the same conflicting opinions which agitate the present generation, will upset mankind a thousand years hence. Yet no more than a few decades later, the same currents will present a very different aspect from now, other conflicts will seem important and other contradictory phenomena have come to the fore. . . .

But the whole conception of dialectical development is untenable. It is false that historical evolution invariably proceeds through a series of contradictions. When we compare the principal currents and tendencies in European history since the end of Antiquity—the economic development, the expansion of Christianity and the rise of the Church, the intellectual and artistic development of the race, the continuous struggle between freedom and authority, revolution and reaction—we shall find that the evolution in every single sphere of life proceeds, now by a transition from one state or one tendency to its opposite, and now in an unbroken and straight line; now at a rapid pace and sometimes very slowly, now gradually and peacefully and at other times through a series of violent conflicts and catastrophes. At times the entire evolution seems to come to a standstill, and conditions remain almost identical for a long period, whereas at other times they change at a feverish speed. . . .

One thing is certain, and it is perhaps the only fact we are sure of in this respect, namely, that this world of man is liable to change, that this change is uninterrupted and is what we call life. It is also indisputable that the change is sometimes slow and gradual and sometimes violent, taking the form of conflict and strife of all sorts.  By choosing suitable distances and by selecting those changes and events which seem to be opposed to each other, we shall always be able to state a dialectical contradiction and a dialectical development.  The result will be the surer as it is of our own making.  It is as if a man should, from the regular series of numbers, select the numbers 1, 4, 9, 16, 25, 36, 49, etc., and then proclaim his discovery that numbers progress by squares. If we select other phenomena less distant from one another, we may find that development proceeds in a straight line. . . .

Therefore, what Marx says in *The Poverty of Philosophy*, "No progress without contradiction, that is the law which civilization has obeyed up to this day," is a law put forward arbitrarily; his assertion is undemonstrable and at bottom meaningless, because no one can decide at what moment the new period with its asserted contradiction actually began. History passes on as an uninterrupted ceaseless stream, of which no one knows either the beginning or the end, nor are any man's eyes sharp enough to discover any partition or interruption in its course.  The usual divisions into historical periods are artificial and subjective, absolutely extraneous to the events themselves, invented for expediency's sake by one historian and adopted by others, because our intellect, unable to grasp the whole, cannot dispense with divisions and classifications. . . .

. . . Marx's doctrine offers an instance of an inadmissible combination or rather confusion of science and politics.  In order to disguise the fact that the demand for a more just and humane distribution of the goods of this earth is a moral demand, that socialism, in short, is a moral end, they declare it to be a logical necessity and their political theory is called "scientific" socialism.  Now, theoretical knowledge and practical activity are essentially different and realize themselves on different planes.  Science is theoretical, politics practical, activity.  A man may found his political activity on scientific experience or make use of scientific knowledge in his political activity; but scientific experience belongs of necessity to the past and all knowledge is based on past experience; nobody can base his political theory on future experience which has not yet been made. . . .

. . . According to the materialist conception of history, the next stage that, of necessity and inevitably, follows on middle-class domination, is socialism. This necessity, however, is not capable of proof. A socialist system has indeed been established in a vast territory, but this was the region in which the "necessary" previous stage of middle-class predominance and capitalism was less developed than in any other part of the civilized world, which was nearer to what Marxists are wont to call the feudal state of society. Socialism realized itself in Russia in direct contradiction to the theory.

There are persons who demand socialism for moral reasons and because they are of opinion that the system is more adequate to the real needs of mankind and to the very exigencies of production by modern technical means. The adherents of Marx, however, refuse to adduce moral reasons. On the contrary, they generally have a dread of ethics akin to that which medieval Catholics had of the devil; their invariable reasoning is that socialism is inevitable and necessary, that it will come according to a "historical law." They add, however, and Marx himself was of this opinion, that these historical laws are of a different kind and operate differently from the laws of nature.[3] This is perfectly true, for these so-called historical laws are in fact only assertions or assumptions made on the strength of insufficient and uncertain observations. They are, moreover, uncontrollable because history never repeats itself and because experiments under definite and chosen conditions are impossible in history.

If, however, such laws did exist, and if socialism were bound to come according to a law, then it would be quite unnecessary and in a sense impossible to demand what is bound to come to pass of necessity; if socialism really were the inevitable next stage in the

---

[3] Engels, who, as we have repeatedly pointed out, is apt to reason in a very naive manner, says somewhere that historical laws "appear and disappear." But who is to tell us whether a law that has the habit of appearing and disappearing, is still in force or not?

evolution of society, there would be no need of a socialist theory and still less of a socialist party. Nobody is likely to found a party to bring about spring or summer.

Feeling, however, or we might even say, knowing, though they do not own up to it, that their theory is false, knowing moreover, from practical experience that very few human actions are automatic, that they are generally brought about by some previous mental or psychic process, they adopt a different method. Being perfectly aware that in order to erect a socialist system of economy on the basis of certain existing conditions of production, men must first be imbued with a socialistic ideology, they display an indefatigable activity in propagating this ideology, though, if their theory were true, they might spare themselves their pains. Nobody ever made any propaganda for the capitalistic order of society, and yet it came; and nobody knew beforehand that it was necessary and would come.

That a past event was necessary stands to reason; to know this is not to have any special knowledge. To know that a future event which is not of regular occurrence is necessary, is to be a prophet. Now, prophecy and belief may be highly important elements of human life and history, yet they do not belong to the sphere of science. . . .

Future historical development is hidden from our sight and from our knowledge. We do not know whether a socialist or communist order of society will be introduced in many countries or in all; and we know still less whether this new society will be durable. That there should ever be a time in which there will be no contradictory opinions, interests and systems, no conflicts between men and no parties, is something which we can hardly imagine, nor do we know whether such a state would be desirable. For the small grain of truth in the doctrine of historical dialectics is that, from the conflict of contradictory opinions and interests and from their discussion, there result new knowledge in the theoretical and new institutions in the practical sphere. The latter are invariably the result of conflicting forces, though this does not imply that they in all cases represent a solution of existing contradictions. That, however, is an age-old experience; the fact is in

striking analogy to a well-known law of physical science, but has
nothing whatever to do with dialectics. Whether human nature
will change to such a degree that these conflicts will in some future
time be decided, as Adolf Goldscheid said, "no longer by the edge
of the sword but by the acumen of the intellect," is unknown to us.
It has often been tried and will again be tried whenever circumstances seem favorable, but no one can say whether it will ever be
the general rule. . . .

# IMPERIALISM—THE HIGHEST STAGE OF CAPITALISM*

BY

## V. I. LENIN

[1916]

### IMPERIALISM AS A SPECIAL STAGE OF CAPITALISM

Imperialism emerged as the development and direct continuation of the fundamental attributes of capitalism in general. But capitalism only became capitalist imperialism at a definite and very high stage of its development, when certain of its fundamental attributes began to be transformed into their opposites, when the features of a period of transition from capitalism to a higher social and economic system began to take shape and reveal themselves all along the line. Economically, the main thing in this process is the substitution of capitalist monopolies for capitalist free competition. Free competition is the fundamental attribute of capitalism, and of commodity production generally. Monopoly is exactly the opposite of free competition; but we have seen the latter being transformed into monopoly before our very eyes, creating large-scale industry and eliminating small industry, replacing large-scale industry by still larger-scale industry, finally leading to such a concentration of production and capital that monopoly has been and is the result: cartels, syndicates and trusts, and merging with them, the capital of a dozen or so banks manipulating thousands of millions. At the same time monopoly, which has grown out of free competition, does not abolish the latter, but exists over it and alongside of it, and thereby gives rise to a number of very acute, intense antagonisms, friction and conflicts. Monopoly is the transition from capitalism to a higher system.

If it were necessary to give the briefest possible definition of imperialism we should have to say that imperialism is the monopoly stage of capitalism. Such a definition would include what is

---

* Copyright 1939 by International Publishers Co., Inc. Reprinted by permission.

most important, for, on the one hand, finance capital is the bank capital of a few big monopolist banks, merged with the capital of the monopolist combines of manufacturers; and, on the other hand, the division of the world is the transition from a colonial policy which has extended without hindrance to territories unoccupied by any capitalist power, to a colonial policy of monopolistic possession of the territory of the world which has been completely divided up.

But very brief definitions, although convenient, for they sum up the main points, are nevertheless inadequate, because very important features of the phenomenon that has to be defined have to be especially deduced. And so, without forgetting the conditional and relative value of all definitions, which can never include all the concatenations of a phenomenon in its complete development, we must give a definition of imperialism that will embrace the following five essential features:

1) The concentration of production and capital developed to such a high stage that it created monopolies which play a decisive role in economic life.

2) The merging of bank capital with industrial capital, and the creation, on the basis of this "finance capital," of a "financial oligarchy."

3) The export of capital, which has become extremely important, as distinguished from the export of commodities.

4) The formation of international capitalist monopolies which share the world among themselves.

5) The territorial division of the whole world among the greatest capitalist powers is completed.

Imperialism is capitalism in that stage of development in which the dominance of monopolies and finance capital has established itself; in which the export of capital has acquired pronounced importance; in which the division of the world among the international trusts has begun; in which the division of all territories of the globe among the great capitalist powers has been completed.
. . .

In this matter of defining imperialism, however, we have to enter into controversy, primarily, with K. Kautsky, the principal Marxian theoretician of the epoch of the so-called Second International—that is, of the twenty-five years between 1889 and 1914.

Kautsky, in 1915 and even in November 1914, very emphatically attacked the fundamental ideas expressed in our definition of imperialism. Kautsky said that imperialism must not be regarded as a "phase" or stage of economy, but as a policy; a definite policy "preferred" by finance capital; that imperialism cannot be "identified" with "contemporary capitalism"; that if imperialism is to be understood to mean "all the phenomena of contemporary capitalism"—cartels, protection, the domination of the financiers and colonial policy—then the question as to whether imperialism is necessary to capitalism becomes reduced to the "flattest tautology"; because, in that case, "imperialism is naturally a vital necessity for capitalism" and so on. The best way to present Kautsky's ideas is to quote his own definition of imperialism, which is diametrically opposed to the substance of the ideas which we have set forth. . . .

Kautsky's definition is as follows:

> Imperialism is a product of highly developed industrial capitalism. It consists in the striving of every industrialist capitalist nation to bring under its control and to annex increasingly big *agrarian* (Kautsky's italics) regions irrespective of what nations inhabit those regions. . . .

Imperialism is a striving for annexations—this is what the *political* part of Kautsky's definition amounts to. It is correct, but very incomplete, for politically, imperialism is, in general, a striving towards violence and reaction. For the moment, however, we are interested in the *economic* aspect of the question, which Kautsky *himself* introduced into *his* definition. The inaccuracy of Kautsky's definition is strikingly obvious. The characteristic feature of imperialism is *not* industrial capital, *but* finance capital. It is not an accident that in France it was precisely the extraordinarily rapid development of *finance* capital, and the weakening of industrial capital, that, from 1880 onwards, gave rise to the extreme extension of annexationist (colonial) policy. The characteristic feature of imperialism is precisely that it strives to annex *not only* agricultural regions, but even highly industrialized regions (German appetite for Belgium; French appetite for Lorraine), because 1) the fact that the world is already divided up obliges those contemplating a *new* division to reach out for *any kind* of territory, and 2) because an essential feature of imperialism is the rivalry between a number of great powers in the striving for hegemony, *i.e.,* for the conquest of territory, not so much directly for themselves as to weaken the adversary and undermine *his* hegemony. (Belgium is chiefly necessary to Germany as a base for operations against England; England needs Bagdad as a base for operations against Germany, etc.) . . .

Kautsky's definition is not only wrong and un-Marxian. It serves as a basis for a whole system of views which run counter to Marxian theory and Marxian practice all along the line. . . . The fact of the matter is that Kautsky detaches the politics of imperialism from its economics, speaks of annexations as being a policy "preferred" by finance capital, and opposes to it another bourgeois policy which, he alleges, is possible on this very basis of finance capital. According to his argument, monopolies in economics are compatible with non-monopolistic, non-violent, non-annexationist methods in politics. According to his argument, the territorial division of the world, which was completed precisely during the period of finance capital, and which constitutes the basis of the present peculiar forms of rivalry between the biggest capitalist states, is compatible with a non-imperialist policy. The result is a slurring-over and a blunting of the most profound contradictions of the latest stage of capitalism, instead of an exposure of their depth; the result is bourgeois reformism instead of Marxism. . . .

Kautsky writes: "from the purely economic point of view it is not impossible that capitalism will yet go through a new phase, that of the extension of the policy of cartels to foreign policy, the phase of ultra-imperialism," *i.e.,* of a super-imperialism, a union of world imperialisms and not struggles among imperialisms; a phase when wars shall cease under capitalism, a phase of "the joint exploitation of the world by internationally combined finance capital."

Is "ultra-imperialism" possible "from the purely economic point of view" or is it ultra-nonsense? . . .

Compare . . . the vast diversity of economic and political conditions, the extreme disparity in the rate of development of the various countries, etc., and the violent struggles of the imperialist states, with Kautsky's silly little fable about "peaceful" ultra-imperialism. Is this not the reactionary attempt of a frightened philistine to hide from stern reality? Are not the international cartels which Kautsky imagines are the embryos of "ultra imperialism" . . . an example of the division and the *re-division* of the world, the transition from peaceful division to non-peaceful division and vice versa? Is not American and other finance capital, which divided the whole world peacefully, with Germany's participation for example, in the international rail syndicate, or in the international mercantile shipping trust, now engaged in *re-dividing* the world on the basis of a new relation of forces, which has been changed by methods *by no means* peaceful?

Finance capital and the trusts are increasing instead of diminishing the difference in the rate of development of the various parts of world economy. When the relation of forces is changed, how else, *under capitalism,* can the solution of contradictions be found, except by resorting to violence. . . ?

Capitalism is growing with the greatest rapidity in the colonies and in overseas countries. Among the latter, *new* imperialist powers are emerging (*e.g.,* Japan). The struggle of world imperialism is becoming more acute.

It is well known that the development of productive forces in Germany, and especially the development of the coal and iron industries, has been much more rapid during this period than in England—not to mention France and Russia. In 1892, Germany produced 4,900,000 tons of pig iron and Great Britain produced 6,800,000 tons; in 1912, Germany produced 17,600,000 tons and Great Britain 9,000,000 tons. Germany, therefore, had an overwhelming superiority over England in this respect. We ask, is there *under capitalism* any means of removing the disparity between the development of productive forces and the accumulation of capital on the one side, and the division of colonies and "spheres of influence" for finance capital on the other side—other than by resorting to war? . . .

The imperialism of the beginning of the twentieth century completed the division of the world among a handful of states, each of which today exploits (*i.e.,* draws super-profits from) a part of the world only a little smaller than that which England exploited in 1858. Each of them, by means of trusts, cartels, finance capital, and debtor and creditor relations, occupies a monopoly position in the world market. Each of them enjoys to some degree a colonial monopoly. (We have seen that out of the total of 75,000,000 sq. km. which comprise the *whole* colonial world, 65,000,000 sq. km., or 86 per cent, belong to six great powers; 61,000,00 sq. km., or 81 per cent, belong to three powers.) . . .

Embryonic imperialism has grown into a dominant system; capitalist monopolies occupy first place in economics and politics; the division of the world has been completed. On the other hand, instead of an undisputed monopoly by Great Britain, we see a few imperialist powers contending for the right to share in this monopoly, and this struggle is characteristic of the whole period of the beginning of the twentieth century. . . .

## The Critique of Imperialism

By the critique of imperialism, in the broad sense of the term, we mean the attitude toward imperialist policy of the different classes of society as part of their general ideology.

The enormous dimensions of finance capital concentrated in a few hands and creating an extremely extensive and close network of ties and relationships which subordinate not only the small and medium, but also even the very small capitalists and small masters, on the one hand, and the intense struggle waged against other national state groups of financiers for the division of the world and domination over other countries, on the other hand, cause the wholesale transition of the possessing classes to the side of imperialism. The signs of the times are a "general" enthusiasm regarding its prospects, a passionate defence of imperialism, and every possible embellishment of its real nature. . . .

Bourgeois scholars and publicists usually come out in defence of imperialism in a somewhat veiled form, and obscure its complete domination and its profound roots; they strive to concentrate attention on partial and secondary details and do their very best to distract attention from the main issue by means of ridiculous schemes for "reform," such as police supervision of the trusts and banks,

etc.  Less frequently, cynical and frank imperialists speak out and
are bold enough to admit the absurdity of the idea of reforming
the fundamental features of imperialism. . . .

The question as to whether it is possible to reform the basis of
imperialism, whether to go forward to the accentuation and deepening of the antagonisms which it engenders, or backwards, towards allaying these antagonisms, is a fundamental question in
the critique of imperialism.  As a consequence of the fact that the
political features of imperialism are reaction all along the line, and
increased national oppression, resulting from the oppression of the
financial oligarchy and the elimination of free competition, a petty-
bourgeois-democratic opposition has been rising against imperialism in almost all imperialist countries since the beginning of the
twentieth century. . . .

In the United States, the imperialist war waged against Spain
in 1898 stirred up the opposition of the "anti-imperialists," the
last of the Mohicans of bourgeois democracy.  They declared this
war to be "criminal"; they denounced the annexation of foreign
territories as being a violation of the Constitution, and denounced
the "Jingo treachery" by means of which Aguinaldo, leader of the
native Filipinos, was deceived (the Americans promised him the
independence of his country, but later they landed troops and
annexed it).  They quoted the words of Lincoln:

> When the white man governs himself, that is self-government; but when
> he governs himself and also governs another man, that is more than self-
> government—that is despotism.

But while all this criticism shrank from recognizing the indis-
soluble bond between imperialism and the trusts, and, therefore,
between imperialism and the very foundations of capitalism; while
it shrank from joining up with the forces engendered by large-
scale capitalism and its development—it remained a "pious wish."

. . . Here is an example of Kautsky's economic criticism of imperialism.  He takes the statistics of the British export and import
trade with Egypt for 1872 and 1912.  These statistics show that
this export and import trade has developed more slowly than
British foreign trade as a whole.  From this Kautsky concludes
that:

> We have no reason to suppose that British trade with Egypt would have
> been less developed simply as a result of the mere operation of economic
> factors, without military occupation. . . . The urge of the present-day
> states to expand . . . can be best promoted, not by the violent methods of
> imperialism, but by peaceful democracy.

. . . Kautsky departed from Marxism by advocating what is, in
the period of finance capital, a "reactionary ideal," "peaceful
democracy," "the mere operation of economic factors," for *objectively* this ideal drags us back from monopoly capitalism to the
non-monopolist stage, and is a reformist swindle.

Trade with Egypt (or with any other colony or semi-colony)
"would have grown more" *without* military occupation, without
imperialism, and without finance capital. What does this mean?
That capitalism would develop more rapidly if free competition
were not restricted by monopolies in general, by the "connections"
or the yoke (*i.e.,* also the monopoly) of finance capital, or by the
monopolist possession of colonies by certain countries?

Kautsky's argument can have no other meaning; and *this* "meaning" is meaningless. But suppose, for the sake of argument, free
competition, without any sort of monopoly, *would* develop capitalism and trade more rapidly. Is it not a fact that the more rapidly
trade and capitalism develop, the greater is the concentration of
production and capital which *gives rise* to monopoly? And monopolies have *already* come into being—precisely *out of* free competition! Even if monopolies have now begun to retard progress, it
is not an argument in favor of free competition, which has become
impossible since it gave rise to monopoly.

Whichever way one turns Kautsky's argument, one will find
nothing in it except reaction and bourgeois reformism.

Even if we modify this argument and say . . . that the trade of
the British colonies with the mother country is now developing
more slowly than their trade with other countries, it does not save
Kautsky; for it is *also* monopoly and imperialism that is beating
Great Britain, only it is the monopoly and imperialism of another
country (America, Germany). It is known that the cartels have
given rise to a new and peculiar form of protective tariffs, *i.e.,*
goods suitable for export are protected (Engels noted this in Vol.
III of *Capital*). It is known, too, that the cartels and finance

capital have a system peculiar to themselves, that of "exporting goods at cut-rate prices," or "dumping," as the English call it: within a given country the cartel sells its goods at a high price fixed by monopoly; abroad it sells them at a much lower price to undercut the competitor, to enlarge its own production to the utmost, etc.  If Germany's trade with the British colonies is developing more rapidly than that of Great Britain with the same colonies, it only proves that German imperialism is younger, stronger and better organized than British imperialism, is superior to it.  But this by no means proves the "superiority" of free trade, for it is not free trade fighting against protection and colonial dependence, but two rival imperialisms, two monopolies, two groups of finance capital that are fighting.  The superiority of German imperialism over British imperialism is stronger than the wall of colonial frontiers or of protective tariffs.  To use this as an argument *in favor* of free trade and "peaceful democracy" is banal, is to forget the essential features and qualities of imperialism, to substitute petty-bourgeois reformism for Marxism. . . .

Kautsky's theoretical critique of imperialism has nothing in common with Marxism and serves no other purpose than as a preamble to propaganda for peace and unity with the opportunists and the social-chauvinists, precisely for the reason that it evades and obscures the very profound and radical contradictions of imperialism: the contradictions between monopoly and free competition that exist side by side with it, between the gigantic "operations" (and gigantic profits) of finance capital and "honest" trade in the free market, the contradictions between cartels and trusts, on the one hand and non-cartelised industry, on the other, etc.

The notorious theory of "ultra-imperialism," invented by Kautsky, is equally reactionary. . . .

> Cannot the present imperialist policy be supplanted by a new, ultra-imperialist policy, which will introduce the common exploitation of the world by internationally united finance capital in place of the mutual rivalries of national finance capital?  Such a new phase of capitalism is at any rate conceivable.  Can it be achieved?  Sufficient premises are still lacking to enable us to answer this question.

. . . The only objective, *i.e.*, real, social significance Kautsky's

"theory" can have, is that of a most reactionary method of con-
soling the masses with hopes of permanent peace being possible
under capitalism, distracting their attention from the sharp antagonisms and acute problems of the present era, and directing it
towards illusory prospects of an imaginary "ultra-imperialism" of
the future.   Deception of the masses—there is nothing but this in
Kautsky's "Marxian" theory.

Indeed, it is enough to compare well-known and indisputable
facts to become convinced of the utter falsity of the prospects
which Kautsky tries to conjure up before the German workers (and
the workers of all lands).   Let us consider India, Indo-China and
China.   It is known that these three colonial and semi-colonial
countries, inhabited by six to seven hundred million human beings,
are subjected to the exploitation of the finance capital of several
imperialist states: Great Britain, France, Japan, the U.S.A., etc.
We will assume that these imperialist countries form alliances
against one another in order to protect and extend their possessions, their interests and their "spheres of influence" in these
Asiatic states; these alliances will be "inter-imperialist" or "ultra-
imperialist" alliances.   We will assume that *all* the imperialist
countries conclude an alliance for the "peaceful" division of these
parts of Asia; this alliance would be an alliance of "internationally
united finance capital."   As a matter of fact, alliances of this kind
have been made in the twentieth century, notably with regard to
China.   We ask, is it "conceivable," assuming that the capitalist
system remains intact—and this is precisely the assumption that
Kautsky does make—that such alliances 'would be more than
temporary, that they would eliminate friction, conflicts and struggle in all and every possible form?

This question need only be stated clearly enough to make it
impossible for any other reply to be given than that in the negative; for there can be *no* other conceivable basis under capitalism
for the division of spheres of influence, of interests, of colonies,
etc., than a calculation of the *strength* of the participants in the
division, their general economic, financial, military strength, etc.
And the strength of these participants in the division does not
change to an equal degree, for under capitalism the development

of different undertakings, trusts, branches of industry, or countries cannot be *even*. Half a century ago, Germany was a miserable, insignificant country, as far as its capitalist strength was concerned, compared with the strength of England at that time. Japan was similarly insignificant compared with Russia. Is it "conceivable" that in ten or twenty years' time the relative strength of the imperialist powers will have remained *un*changed? Absolutely inconceivable.

Therefore, in the realities of the capitalist system . . . no matter what form they may assume, whether of one imperialist coalition against another, or of a general alliance embracing *all* the imperialist powers, are *inevitably* nothing more than a "truce" in periods between wars. Peaceful alliances prepare the ground for wars, and in their turn grow out of wars; the one is the condition for the other, giving rise to alternating forms of peaceful and non-peaceful struggle out of *one and the same* basis of imperialist connections and the relations between world economics and world politics. . . .

Kautsky's toning down of the deepest contradictions of imperialism, which inevitably becomes the embellishment of imperialism, leaves its traces in this writer's criticism of the political features of imperialism. Imperialism is the epoch of finance capital and of monopolies, which introduce everywhere the striving for domination, not for freedom. The result of these tendencies is reaction all along the line, whatever the political system, and an extreme intensification of existing antagonisms in this domain also. Particularly acute becomes the yoke of national oppression and the striving for annexations, *i.e.*, the violation of national independence (for annexation is nothing but the violation of the right of nations to self-determination). Hilferding justly draws attention to the connection between imperialism and the growth of national oppression.

> In the newly opened up countries themselves, [he writes] the capitalism imported into them intensifies contradictions and excites the constantly growing resistance against the intruders of the peoples who are awakening to national consciousness. This resistance can easily become transformed into dangerous measures directed against foreign capital. The old social relations become completely revolutionized. The age-long agrarian incrustation of "nations without a history" is blasted away, and they are

drawn into the capitalist whirlpool. Capitalism itself gradually procures for the vanquished the means and resources for their emancipation and they set out to achieve the same goal which once seemed highest to the European nations: the creation of a united national state as a means to economic and cultural freedom. This movement for national independence threatens European capital just in its most valuable and most promising fields of exploitation, and European capital can maintain its domination only by continually increasing its means of exerting violence.

To this must be added that it is not only in newly opened up countries, but also in the old, that imperialism is leading to annexation, to increased national oppression, and, consequently, also to increasing resistance. . . . Let us suppose that a Japanese is condemning the annexation of the Philippine Islands by the Americans. Will many believe that he is doing so because he has a horror of annexations as such, and not because he himself has a desire to annex the Philippines? And shall we not be constrained to admit that the "fight" the Japanese are waging against annexations can be regarded as being sincere and politically honest only if he fights against the annexation of Korea by Japan, and urges freedom for Korea to secede from Japan?*

Kautsky's theoretical analysis of imperialism, as well as his economic and political criticism of imperialism, are permeated *through and through* with a spirit, absolutely irreconcilable with Marxism, of obscuring and glossing over the most profound contradictions of imperialism. . . .

## THE PLACE OF IMPERIALISM IN HISTORY

We have seen that the economic quintessence of imperialism is monopoly capitalism. This very fact determines its place in his-

---

*"[This] pamphlet . . . was written in Zurich in the spring of 1916 . . . with an eye to the tsarist censorship. . . .

"In order to show, in a guise acceptable to the censors, how shamefully the capitalists and the social-chauvinist deserters (whom Kautsky opposes with so much inconsistency) lie on the question of annexations, in order to show with what cynicism they *screen* the annexations of *their* capitalists, I was forced to quote as an example—Japan! The careful reader will easily substitute Russia for Japan, and Finland, Poland, Courland, the Ukraine, Khiva, Bokhara, Estonia or other regions peopled by non-Great Russians, for Korea." —quoted from Lenin's "Preface to the Russian Edition," written in Petrograd, April 26, 1917.

tory, for monopoly that grew up on the basis of free competition, and precisely out of free competition, is the transition from the capitalist system to a higher social-economic order. We must take special note of the four principal manifestations of monopoly capitalism, which are characteristic of the epoch under review.

Firstly, monopoly arose out of the concentration of production at a very advanced stage of development. This refers to the monopolist capitalist combines, cartels, syndicates and trusts. We have seen the important part that these play in modern economic life. At the beginning of the twentieth century, monopolies acquired complete supremacy in the advanced countries. And although the first steps towards the formation of the cartels were first taken by countries enjoying the protection of high tariffs (Germany, America), Great Britain, with her system of free trade, was not far behind in revealing the same basic phenomenon, namely, the birth of monopoly out of the concentration of production.

Secondly, monopolies have accelerated the capture of the most important sources of raw materials, especially for the coal and iron industries, which are the basic and mostly highly cartelised industries in capitalist society. The monopoly of the most important sources of raw materials has enormously increased the power of big capital, and has sharpened the antagonism between cartelised and non-cartelised industry.

Thirdly, monopoly has sprung from the banks. The banks have developed from modest intermediary enterprises into the monopolists of finance capital. Some three or five of the biggest banks in each of the foremost capitalist countries have achieved the "personal union" of industrial and bank capital, and have concentrated in their hands the disposal of thousands upon thousands of millions which form the greater part of the capital and income of entire countries. A financial oligarchy, which throws a close net of relations of dependence over all the economic and political institutions of contemporary bourgeois society without exception —such is the most striking manifestation of this monopoly.

Fourthly, monopoly has grown out of colonial policy. To the numerous "old" motives of colonial policy, finance capital has added the struggle for the sources of raw materials, for the export of capital, for "spheres of influence," *i.e.*, for spheres for profitable deals, concessions, monopolist profits and so on; in fine, for economic territory in general.  When the colonies of the European powers in Africa, for instance, comprised only one-tenth of that territory (as was the case in 1876), colonial policy was able to develop by methods other than those of monopoly—by the "free grabbing" of territories, so to speak.  But when nine-tenths of Africa had been seized (approximately by 1900), when the whole world had been divided up, there was inevitably ushered in a period of colonial monopoly and, consequently, a period of particularly intense struggle for the division and the redivision of the world.

The extent to which monopolist capital has intensified all the contradictions of capitalism is generally known.  It is sufficient to mention the high cost of living and the oppression of the cartels.  This intensification of contradictions constitutes the most powerful driving force of the transitional period of history, which began from the time of the definite victory of world finance capital.

Monopolies, oligarchy, the striving for domination instead of striving for liberty, the exploitation of an increasing number of small or weak nations by an extremely small group of the richest or most powerful nations—all these have given birth to those distinctive characteristics of imperialism which compel us to define it as parasitic or decaying capitalism.  More and more prominently there emerges, as one of the tendencies of imperialism, the creation of the "bondholding" (rentier) state, the usurer state, in which the bourgeoisie lives on the proceeds of capital exports and by "clipping coupons."  It would be a mistake to believe that this tendency to decay precludes the possibility of the rapid growth of capitalism.  It does not.  In the epoch of imperialism, certain branches of industry, certain strata of the bourgeoisie and certain countries betray, to a more or less degree, one or other of these tendencies.  On the whole, capitalism is growing far more rapidly than before.  But this growth is not only becoming more and more uneven in general; its unevenness also manifests itself, in particular, in the decay of the countries which are richest in capital (such as England). . . .

# IMPERIALISM AND CAPITALISM*

BY

## JOSEPH A. SCHUMPETER

[1919]

A purely capitalist world . . . can offer no fertile soil to imperialist impulses. The competitive system absorbs the full
energies of most of the people at all economic levels. Constant
application, attention, and concentration of energy are the conditions of survival within it, primarily in the specifically economic
professions, but also in other activities organized on their model.
There is much less excess energy to be vented in war and conquest
than in any precapitalist society. What excess energy there is flows
largely into industry itself, accounts for its shining figures—the
type of the captain of industry—and for the rest is applied to art,
science, and the social struggle. In a purely capitalist world, what
was once energy for war becomes simply energy for labor of every
kind. Wars of conquest and adventurism in foreign policy in
general are bound to be regarded as troublesome distractions,
destructive of life's meaning, a diversion from the accustomed and
therefore "true" task. . . .

That does not mean that [a capitalist world] cannot still maintain an interest in imperialist expansion. We shall discuss this
immediately. The point is that its people are likely to be essentially
of an unwarlike disposition. Hence we must expect that anti-
imperialist tendencies will show themselves wherever capitalism
penetrates the economy and, through the economy, the mind of
modern nations—most strongly, of course, where capitalism itself
is strongest, where it has advanced furthest, encountered the least
resistance, and pre-eminently where its types and hence democracy
—in the "bourgeois" sense—come closest to political dominion.

---

* Selected and arranged from "The Sociology of Imperialisms" in *Imperialism
and Social Classes* by Joseph A. Schumpeter, translated by Heinz Norden, edited
by Paul M. Sweezy. Published by Augustus M. Kelley, Inc., N. Y. Copyright
1951 by the Trustees under the Will of Elizabeth Boody Schumpeter. Reprinted
by permission.

We must further expect that the types formed by capitalism will actually be the carriers of these tendencies. Is such the case? The facts that follow are cited to show that this expectation, which flows from our theory, is in fact justified.

1. Throughout the world of capitalism and specifically among the elements formed by capitalism in modern social life, there has arisen a fundamental oposition to war, expansion, cabinet diplomacy, armaments, and socially-entrenched professional armies. This opposition had its origin in the country that first turned capitalist—England—and arose coincidentally with that country's capitalist development. . . . True, pacifism as a matter of principle had existed before, though only among a few small religious sects. But modern pacifism, in its political foundations if not its derivation, is unquestionably a phenomenon of the capitalist world.

2. Wherever capitalism penetrated, peace parties of such strength arose that virtually every war meant a political struggle on the domestic scene. . . . That is why every war is carefully justified as a defensive war by the governments involved, and by all the political parties, in their official utterances—indicating a realization that a war of a different nature would scarcely be tenable in a political sense. . . . In former times this would not have been necessary. Reference to an interest or pretense at moral justification was customary as early as the eighteenth century, but only in the nineteenth century did the assertion of attack, or the threat of attack, become the only avowed occasion for war. In the distant past, imperialism had needed no disguise whatever, and in the absolute autocracies only a very transparent one; but today imperialism is carefully hidden from public view—even though there may still be an unofficial appeal to warlike instincts. No people and no ruling class today can openly afford to regard war as a normal state of affairs or a normal element in the life of nations. No one doubts that today it must be characterized as an abnormality and a disaster. True, war is still glorified. But glorification . . . is rare and unleashes such a storm of indignation that every practical politician carefully dissociates himself from such things. Everywhere there is official acknowledgment that peace is an end in itself—though not necessarily an end overshadowing all

purposes that can be realized by means of war.  Every expansionist urge must be carefully related to a concrete goal.  All this is primarily a matter of political phraseology, to be sure.  But the necessity for this phraseology is a symptom of the popular attitude. And that attitude makes a policy of imperialism more and more difficult—indeed, the very word imperialism is applied only to the enemy, in a reproachful sense, being carefully avoided with reference to the speaker's own policies.

3.  The type of industrial worker created by capitalism is always vigorously anti-imperialist.  In the individual case, skillful agitation may persuade the working masses to approve or remain neutral—a concrete goal or interest in self-defense always playing the main part—but no initiative for forcible policy of expansion ever emanates from this quarter.  On this point official socialism unquestionably formulates not merely the interests but also the conscious will of the workers.  Even less than peasant imperialism is there any such thing as socialist or other working-class imperialism.

4.  Despite manifest resistance on the part of powerful elements, the capitalist age has seen the development of methods for preventing war, for the peaceful settlement of disputes among states.  The very fact of resistance means that the trend can be explained only from the mentality of capitalism as a mode of life. It definitely limits the opportunities imperialism needs if it is to be a powerful force.  True, the methods in question often fail, but even more often they are successful.  I am thinking not merely of the Hague Court of Arbitration but of the practice of submitting controversial issues to conferences of the major powers or at least those powers directly concerned—a course of action that has become less and less avoidable.  True, here too the individual case may become a farce.  But the serious set-backs of today must not blind us to the real importance or sociological significance of these things.

5.  Among all capitalist economies, that of the United States is least burdened with precapitalist elements, survivals, reminiscences, and power factors.  Certainly we cannot expect to find imperialist tendencies altogether lacking even in the United States,

for the immigrants came from Europe with their convictions fully formed, and the environment certainly favored the revival of instincts of pugnacity. But we can conjecture that among all countries the United States is likely to exhibit the weakest imperialist trend. This turns out to be the truth. The case is particularly instructive, because the United States has seen a particularly strong emergence of capitalist interests in an imperialist direction —those very interests to which the phenomenon of imperialism has so often been reduced, a subject we shall yet touch on. Nevertheless the United States was the first advocate of disarmament and arbitration. It was the first to conclude treaties concerning arms limitations (1817) and arbitral courts (first attempt in 1797)— doing so most zealously, by the way, when economic interest in expansion was at its greatest. Since 1908 such treaties have been concluded with twenty-two states. In the course of the nineteenth century, the United States had numerous occasions for war, including instances that were well calculated to test its patience. It made almost no use of such occasions. Leading industrial and financial circles in the United States had and still have an evident interest in incorporating Mexico into the Union. There was more than enough opportunity for such annexation—but Mexico remained unconquered. Racial catch phrases and working-class interests pointed to Japan as a possible danger. Hence possession of the Philippines was not a matter of indifference—yet surrender of this possession is being discussed. Canada was an almost defenseless prize—but Canada remained independent. Even in the United States, of course, politicians need slogans—especially slogans calculated to divert attention from domestic issues. Theodore Roosevelt and certain magnates of the press actually resorted to imperialism—and the result, in that world of high capitalism, was utter defeat, a defeat that would have been even more abject, if other slogans, notably those appealing to anti-trust sentiment, had not met with better success.[1]

---

[1] It is an interesting fact, by the way, that while the peace policy is certainly not rooted in the capitalist upper class, some of the most eminent exponents of the political interests of the trusts are among the most zealous promoters of the peace movement.

These facts are scarcely in dispute.[2]   And since they fit into the
picture of the mode of life which we have recognized to be the
necessary product of capitalism, since we can grasp them adequately
from the necessities of that mode of life and industry, it follows
that capitalism is by nature anti-imperialist.   Hence we cannot
readily derive from it such imperialist tendencies as actually exist,
but must evidently see them only as alien elements, carried into
the world of capitalism from the outside, supported by non-capitalist factors in modern life. . . .

The capitalist world . . . suppresses rather than creates [im-
perialist] attitudes.   Certainly, all expansive interests within it are
likely to ally themselves with imperialist tendencies flowing from
non-capitalist sources, to use them, to make them serve as pretexts,
to rationalize them, to point the way toward action on account of
them.   And from this union the picture of modern imperialism is
put together; but for that very reason it is not a matter of capitalist
factors alone.   Before we go into this at length, we must understand the nature and strength of the economic stake which capitalist society has in a policy of imperialism—especially the
question of whether this interest is or is not inherent in the nature
of capitalism—either capitalism generally, or a special phase of
capitalism.

It is in the nature of a capitalist economy—and of an exchange
economy generally—that many people stand to gain economically
in any war.   Here the situation is fundamentally much as it is with
the familiar subject of luxury.   War means increased demand at
panic prices, hence high profits and also high wages in many parts
of the national economy.   This is primarily a matter of money incomes, but as a rule (though to a lesser extent) real incomes are
also affected.   There are, for example, the special war interests,
such as the arms industry.   If the war lasts long enough, the circle
of money profiteers naturally expands more and more—quite
apart from a possible paper-money economy.   It may extend to

---

[2]Rather, imperialist and nationalist literature is always complaining vociferously about the debility, the undignified will to peace, the petty commercial
spirit, and so on, of the capitalist world.   This in itself means very little, but
it is worth mentioning as confirming a state of affairs that can be established
from other indications.

every economic field, but just as naturally the commodity content of money profits drops more and more, indeed, quite rapidly, to the point where actual losses are incurred. The national economy as a whole, of course, is impoverished by the tremendous excess in consumption brought on by war. It is, to be sure, conceivable that either the capitalists or the workers might make certain gains as a class, namely, if the volume either of capital or of labor should decline in such a way that the remainder receives a greater share in the social product and that, even from the absolute viewpoint, the total sum of interest or wages becomes greater than it was before. But these advantages cannot be considerable. They are probably, for the most part, more than outweighed by the burdens imposed by war and by losses sustained abroad. Thus the gain of the capitalists as a class cannot be a motive for war—and it is this gain that counts, for any advantage to the working class would be contingent on a large number of workers falling in action or otherwise perishing. There remain the entrepreneurs in the war industries, in the broader sense, possibly also the large landowner—a small but powerful minority. Their war profits are always sure to be an important supporting element. But few will go so far as to assert that this element alone is sufficient to orient the people of the capitalist world along imperialist lines. At most, an interest in expansion may make the capitalists allies of those who stand for imperialist trends.

It may be stated as being beyond controversy that where free trade prevails *no* class has an interest in forcible expansion as such. For in such a case the citizens and goods of every nation can move in foreign countries as freely as though those countries were politically their own—free trade implying far more than mere freedom from tariffs. In a genuine state of free trade, foreign raw materials and foodstuffs are as accessible to each nation as though they were within its own territory.[3] Where the cultural backwardness of a

---

[3] The stubborn power of old prejudices is shown by the fact that even today the demand for the acquisition of colonies is justified by the argument that they are necessary to supply the demand for food and raw materials and to absorb the energies of a vigorous, rising nation, seeking world outlets. Since the flow of food and raw materials from abroad is only impeded by tariffs at home, the justification has no rhyme or reason even in our world of high protective tariffs, especially since, in the event of war, traffic with colonies is subject to the same perils as traffic with independent countries. . . .

region makes normal economic intercourse dependent on colonization, it does not matter, assuming free trade, which of the "civilized" nations undertakes the task of colonization. Dominion of
the seas, in such a case, means little more than a maritime traffic
police. Similarly, it is a matter of indifference to a nation whether
a railway concession in a foreign country is acquired by one of its
own citizens or not—just so long as the railway *is* built and put
into efficient operation. For citizens of any country may use the
railway, just like the fellow countrymen of its builder—while in
the event of war it will serve whoever controls it in the military
sense, regardless of who built it. It is true, of course, that profits
and wages flowing from its construction and operation will accrue,
for the greater part, to the nation that built it. But capital and
labor that go into the railway have to be taken from somewhere,
and normally the other nations fill the gap. It is a fact that in a
regime of free trade the essential advantages of international intercourse are clearly evident. The gain lies in the enlargement of the
commodity supply by means of the division of labor among nations, rather than in the profits and wages of the export industry
and the carrying trade. . . . Not even monopoly interests—if they
existed—would be disposed toward imperialism in such a case.
For under free trade only *international* cartels would be possible.
Under a system of free trade there would be conflicts in economic
interests neither among different nations nor among the corresponding classes of different nations. . . .

Protective tariffs alone . . . do not basically change this situation
as it affects interests. True, such barriers move the nations economically farther apart, making it easier for imperialist tendencies
to win the upper hand; they line up the entrepreneurs of the different countries in battle formation against one another, impeding
the rise of peaceful interests; they also hinder the flow of raw
materials and foodstuffs and thus the export of manufactures, or
conversely, the import of manufactures and the export of raw
materials and foodstuffs, possibly creating an interest in—sometimes forcible—expansion of the customs area; they place
entrepreneurs in a position of dependence on regulations of governments that may be serving imperialist interests, giving these

governments occasion to pervert economic relations for purposes of sharpening economic conflicts, for adulterating the competitive struggle with diplomatic methods outside the field of economics, and, finally, for imposing on peoples the heavy sacrifices exacted by a policy of autarchy, thus accustoming them to the thought of war by constant preparation for war. Nevertheless, in this case the basic alignment of interests remains essentially what it was under free trade. . . . Colonial possessions acquire more meaning in this case, but the exclusion from the colonies of aliens and foreign capital is not altogether good business since it slows down the development of the colonies. . . . Thus an aggressive economic policy on the part of a country with a unified tariff—with preparedness for war always in the background—serves the economy only seemingly rather than really. Actually, one might assert that the economy becomes a weapon in the political struggle, a means for unifying the nation, for severing it from the fabric of international interests, for placing it at the disposal of the state power. . . .

A protectionist policy, however, does facilitate the formation of cartels and trusts. And it is true that this circumstance thoroughly alters the alignment of interests. . . . Union in a cartel or trust confers various benefits on the entrepreneur—a saving in costs, a stronger position as against the workers—but none of these compares with this one advantage: a monopolistic price policy, possible to any considerable degree *only* behind an adequate protective tariff. Now the price that brings the maximum monopoly profit is generally far above the price that would be fixed by fluctuating competitive costs, and the volume that can be marketed at that maximum price is generally far below the output that would be technically and economically feasible. Under free competition that output *would* be produced and offered, but a trust cannot offer it, for it could be sold only at a competitive price. Yet the trust *must* produce it—or approximately as much—otherwise the advantages of large-scale enterprise remain unexploited and unit costs are likely to be uneconomically high. The trust thus faces a dilemma. Either it renounces the monopolistic policies that motivated its founding; or it fails to exploit and expand its plant, with resultant high costs. It extricates itself from this dilemma by producing the full output that is economically feasible, thus securing low costs, and offering in the protected domestic market only the quantity corresponding to the monopoly price—insofar as the tariff permits; while the rest is sold, or "dumped," abroad at a lower price, sometimes (but not necessarily) *below* cost.

What happens when the entrepreneurs successfully pursue such a policy is something that did not occur in the cases discussed so far—a conflict of interests between nations that becomes so sharp that it cannot be overcome by the existing basic community of interests. Each of the two groups of entrepreneurs and each of the two states seeks to do something that is rendered illusory by a similar policy on the part of the other. In the case of protective tariffs *without* monopoly formation, an understanding is sometimes possible, for only a few would be destroyed, while many would stand to gain; but when monopoly rules it is very difficult to reach an agreement for it would require self-negation on the part of the new rulers. All that is left to do is to pursue the course once taken, to beat down the foreign industry wherever possible, forcing it to conclude a favorable "peace." This requires sacrifices. The excess product is dumped on the world market at steadily lower prices. Counterattacks that grow more and more desperate must be repulsed on the domestic scene. The atmosphere grows more and more heated. Workers and consumers grow more and more troublesome. Where this situation prevails, capital export, like commodity export, becomes aggressive, belying its ordinary character. A mass of capitalists competing with one another has no means of counteracting the decline in the interest rate. . . . But *organized* capital may very well make the discovery that the interest rate can be maintained above the level of free competition, if the resulting surplus can be sent abroad and if any foreign capital that flows in can be intercepted and—whether in the form of loans or in the form of machinery and the like—can likewise be channeled into foreign investment outlets. Now it is true that capital is nowhere cartelized. But it is everywhere subject to the guidance of the big banks which, even without a capital cartel, have attained a position similar to that of the cartel magnates in industry, and which are in a position to put into effect similar policies. It is necessary to keep two factors in mind. In the first place, everywhere except, significantly, in England, there has come into being a close alliance between high finance and the cartel magnates, often going as far as personal identity. . . . Leading bankers are often leaders of the national economy. Here capitalism has found a central organ that supplants its automatism by conscious decisions. In the second place, the interests of the big banks coincide with those of their depositors even less than do the interests of cartel leaders with those of the firms belonging to the cartel. The policies of high finance are based on control of a *large* proportion of the national capital, but they are in the actual interest of only a *small* proportion and, indeed, with respect to the alliance with big business, sometimes not even in the interest of capital as such at all. The ordinary "small" capitalist foots the bills for a policy of forced exports, rather than enjoying its profits. He is a tool; his interests do not really matter. . . .

In . . . a struggle among "dumped" products and capitals, it is no longer a matter of indifference who builds a given railroad, who owns a mine or a colony. Now that the law of costs is no longer operative, it becomes necessary to fight over such properties with desperate effort and with every available means, including those that are not economic in character, such as diplomacy. The concrete objects in question often become entirely subsidiary considerations; the anticipated profit may be trifling, because of the competitive struggle—a struggle that has very little to do with normal competition. What matters is to gain a foothold of some kind and then to exploit this foothold as a base for the conquest of new markets. This costs all the participants dear—often more than can be reasonably recovered, immediately or in the future. Fury lays hold of everyone concerned—and everyone sees to it that his fellow countrymen share his wrath. Each is constrained to resort to methods that he would regard as evidence of unprecedented moral depravity in the other.

It is not true that the capitalist system as such must collapse from immanent necessity, that it necessarily makes its continued existence impossible by its own growth and development. . . . Nevertheless, the situation that has just been described is really untenable both politically and economically. Economically, it amounts to a *reductio ad absurdum*. Politically, it unleashes storms of indignation among the exploited consumers at home and the threatened producers abroad. Thus the idea of military force readily suggests itself. Force may serve to break down foreign customs barriers and thus afford relief from the vicious circle of economic aggression. If that is not feasible, military conquest may at least secure control over markets in which heretofore one had to compete with the enemy. In this context, the conquest of colonies takes on an altogether different significance. Nonmonopolist countries, especially those adhering to free trade, reap little profit from such a policy. But it is a different matter with countries that function in a monopolist role *vis-à-vis* their colonies. There being no competition, they can use cheap native labor without its ceasing to be cheap; they can market their products, even in the colonies, at monopoly prices; they can, finally, invest capital that would only depress the profit rate at home and that could be placed in other civilized countries only at very low interest rates. And they can do all these things even though the consequence may be much slower colonial development. . . .

Thus we have here, within a social group that carries great political weight, a strong, undeniable, economic interest in such things as protective tariffs, cartels, monopoly prices, forced exports (dumping), an aggressive economic policy, an aggressive foreign policy generally, and war, including wars of expansion with a typically imperialist character. . . .

Yet the final word in any presentation of this aspect of modern economic life must be one of warning against overestimating it. The conflicts that have been described, born of an export-dependent monopoly capitalism, may serve to submerge the real community of interests among nations; the monopolist press may drive it underground; but underneath the surface it never completely disappears. Deep down, the normal sense of business and trade usually prevails. Even cartels cannot do without the custom of their foreign economic kin. Even national economies characterized by export monopoly are dependent on one another in many respects. . . . Furthermore, if a policy of export monopolism is to be driven to the extremes of forcible expansion, it is necessary to win over all segments of the population—at least to the point where they are halfway prepared to support the war; but the real interest in export monopolism as such is limited to the entrepreneurs and their ally, high finance. Even the most skillful agitation cannot prevent the independent traders, the small producers who are not covered by cartels, the "mere" capitalists, and the workers from occasionally realizing that they are the victims of such a policy. . . .

This countermovement against export monopolism, within capitalism rather than opposed to it, would mean little if it were merely the political death struggle of a moribund economic order which is giving way to a new phase of development. If the cartel with its policy of export aggression stood face to face with non-cartelized factory industry, as that industry once faced handicraft industry, then even the most vigorous opposition could scarcely change the ultimate outcome or the fundamental significance of the process. But it cannot be emphasized sharply enough that such is not the case. Export monopolism does *not* grow from the inherent laws of capitalist development. The character of capitalism leads to large-scale production, but with few exceptions large-scale production does *not* lead to the kind of unlimited concentration that would leave but one or only a few firms in each industry. On the contrary, any plant runs up against limits to its growth in a given location; and the growth of combinations which would make sense under a system of free trade encounters limits of organizational efficiency. Beyond these limits there is no tendency toward combination inherent in the competitive system. In particular, the rise of trusts and cartels—a phenomenon quite different from the trend to large-scale production with which it is often confused —can never be explained by the automatism of the competitive system. This follows from the very fact that trusts and cartels can attain their primary purpose—to pursue a monopoly policy—only behind protective tariffs, without which they would lose their essential significance. But protective tariffs do not automatically grow from the competitive system. They are the fruit of political action—*a type of action that by no means reflects the objective interests of all those concerned* but that, on the contrary, becomes impossible as soon as the majority of those whose consent is necessary realize their true interests. To some extent it is obvious, and for the rest it will be presently shown, that the interests of the minority, quite appropriately expressed in support of a protective tariff, do not stem from capitalism as such. It follows that *it is a basic fallacy to describe imperialism as a necessary phase of capitalism, or even to speak of the development of capitalism into imperialism.* We have seen before that the mode of life of the capitalist world does not favor imperialist attitudes. We now see that the alignment of interests in a capitalist economy—even the interests of its upper strata—by no means points unequivocally in the direction of imperialism. We now come to the final step in our line of reasoning.

Since we cannot derive even export monopolism from any tendencies of the competitive system toward big enterprise, we must find some other explanation. A glance at the original purpose of tariffs provides what we need. Tariffs sprang from the financial interests of the monarchy. They were a method of exploiting the trader which differed from the method of the robber baron in the same way that the royal chase differed from the method of the poacher. They were in line with the royal prerogatives of safe conduct, of protection for the Jews, of the granting of market rights, and so forth. From the thirteenth century onward this method was progressively refined in the autocratic state, less and less emphasis being placed on the direct monetary yield of customs revenues, and more and more on their indirect effect in creating productive taxable objects. In other words, while the protective value of a tariff counted, it counted only from the viewpoint of the ultimate monetary advantage of the sovereign. . . . Every customs house, every privilege conferring the right to produce, market, or store, thus created a new economic situation which deflected trade and industry into "unnatural" channels. All tariffs, rights, and the like became the seed bed for economic growth that could have neither sprung up nor maintained itself without them. Further, all such economic institutions dictated by autocratic interest were surrounded by manifold interests of people who were dependent on them and now began to demand their continuance—a wholly paradoxical though at the same time quite understandable situation. The trading and manufacturing bourgeoisie was all the more aware of its dependence on the sovereign, since it needed his protection against the remaining feudal powers; and the uncertainties of the times, together with the lack of great consuming centers, impeded the rise of free economic competition. Insofar as commerce and manufacturing came into being at all, therefore, they arose under the sign of monopolistic interest. Thus the bourgeoisie willingly allowed itself to be molded into one of the power instruments of the monarchy, both in a territorial and in a national sense. . . .

Trade and industry of the early capitalist period thus remained strongly pervaded with precapitalist methods, bore the stamp of autocracy, and served its interests, either willingly or by force. With its traditional habits of feeling, thinking, and acting molded along such lines, the bourgeoisie entered the Industrial Revolution. It was shaped, in other words, by the needs and interests of an environment that was essentially noncapitalist, or at least precapitalist—needs stemming not from the nature of the capitalist economy as such but from the fact of the coexistence of early capitalism with another and at first overwhelmingly powerful mode of life and business. Established habits of thought and action tend to persist, and hence the spirit of guild and monopoly at first maintained itself, and was only slowly undermined, even where capitalism was in sole possession of the field. Actually capitalism did not fully prevail *anywhere* on the Continent. Existing economic interests, "artificially" shaped by the autocratic state, remained dependent on the "protection" of the state. The industrial organism, such as it was, would not have been able to withstand free competition. Even where the old barriers crumbled in the autocratic state, the people did not all at once flock to the clear track. They were creatures of mercantilism and even earlier periods, and many of them huddled together and protested against the affront of being forced to depend on their own ability. They cried for paternalism, for protection, for forcible restraint of strangers, and above all for tariffs. . . .

These are facts of fundamental significance to an understanding of the soul of modern Europe. . . . The social pyramid of the present age has been formed, not by the substance and laws of capitalism alone, but by two different social substances, and by the laws of two different epochs. Whoever seeks to understand Europe must not forget this and must concentrate all attention on the indubitably basic truth that one of these substances tends to be absorbed by the other and thus the sharpest of all class conflicts tends to be eliminated. Whoever seeks to understand Europe must not overlook that even today its life, its ideology, its politics are greatly under the influence of the feudal "substance," that while the bourgeoisie can assert its interests everywhere, it "rules" only in exceptional circumstances, and then only briefly. The bourgeois outside his office and the professional man of capitalism outside his profession cut a very sorry figure. Their spiritual leader is the rootless "intellectual," a slender reed open to every impulse and a prey to unrestrained emotionalism. The "feudal" elements, on the other hand, have both feet on the ground, even psychologically speaking. Their ideology is as stable as their mode of life. . . .

The bourgeoisie . . . did not take the state over from the sovereign as an abstract form of organization. The state remained a special social power, confronting the bourgeoisie. In some countries it has continued to play that role to the present day. It is in the *state* that the bourgeoisie with its interests seeks refuge, protection against external and even domestic enemies. The bourgeoisie seeks to win over the state for itself, and in return serves the state and state interests that are different from its own. Imbued with the spirit of the old autocracy, trained by it, the bourgeoisie often takes over its ideology. . . . Because the sovereign needed soldiers, the modern bourgeois—at least in his slogans—is an even more vehement advocate of an increasing population. Because the sovereign was in a position to exploit conquests, needed them to be a victorious warlord, the bourgeoisie thirsts for national glory. . . . Because pugnacious sovereigns stood in constant fear of attack by their equally pugnacious neighbors, the modern bourgeois attributes aggressive designs to neighboring peoples. All such modes of thought are essentially noncapitalist. Indeed, they

vanish most quickly wherever capitalism fully prevails. They are
survivals of the autocratic alignment of interests, and they endure
wherever the autocratic state endures on the old basis and with the
old orientation, even though more and more democratized and
otherwise transformed. They bear witness to the extent to which
essentially imperialist absolutism has patterned not only the economy of the bourgeoisie but also its mind—in the interests of
autocracy and against those of the bourgeoisie itself. . . .

Here we find that we have penetrated to the historical as well
as the sociological sources of modern imperialism. It does not
*coincide* with nationalism and militarism, though it *fuses* with
them by supporting them as it is supported by them. It too is—
not only historically, but also sociologically—a heritage of the
autocratic state, of its structural elements, organizational forms,
interest alignments, and human attitudes, the outcome of pre-
capitalist forces which the autocratic state has reorganized, in part
by the methods of early capitalism. It would never have been
evolved by the "inner logic" of capitalism itself. This is true even
of mere export monopolism. It too has its sources in absolutist
policy and the action habits of an essentially precapitalist environment. That it was able to develop to its present dimensions is
owing to the momentum of a situation once created, which continued to engender ever new "artificial" economic structures, that
is, those which maintain themselves by political power alone. In
most of the countries addicted to export monopolism it is also
owing to the fact that the old autocratic state and the old attitude
of the bourgeoisie toward it were so vigorously maintained. But
export monopolism, to go a step further, is not yet imperialism.
And even if it had been able to arise without protective tariffs, it
would never have developed into imperialism in the hands of an
unwarlike bourgeoisie. If this did happen, it was only because the
heritage included the war machine, together with its socio-psycho-
logical aura and aggressive bent, and because a class oriented
toward war maintained itself in a ruling position. This class clung
to its domestic interest in war, and the pro-military interests among
the bourgeoisie were able to ally themselves with it. This alliance
kept alive war instincts and ideas of overlordship, male supremacy,

and triumphant glory—ideas that would have otherwise long since died. . . .

This diagnosis also bears the prognosis of imperialism. The precapitalist elements in our social life may still have great vitality; special circumstances in national life may revive them from time to time; but in the end the climate of the modern world must destroy them. This is all the more certain since their props in the modern capitalist world are not of the most durable material. Whatever opinion is held concerning the vitality of capitalism itself, whatever the life span predicted for it, it is bound to withstand the onslaughts of its enemies and its own irrationality much longer than essentially untenable export monopolism—untenable even from the capitalist point of view. Export monopolism may perish in revolution, or it may be peacefully relinquished; this may happen soon, or it may take some time and require desperate struggle; but one thing is certain—it *will* happen. This will immediately dispose of neither warlike instincts nor structural elements and organizational forms oriented toward war—and it is to their dispositions and domestic interests that, in my opinion, much more weight must be given in every concrete case of imperialism than to export monopolist interests, which furnish the financial "outpost skirmishes"—a most appropriate term—in many wars. But such factors will be politically overcome in time, no matter what they do to maintain among the people a sense of constant danger of war, with the war machine forever primed for action. And with them, imperialisms will wither and die.

It is not within the scope of this study to offer an ethical, esthetic, cultural, or political evaluation of this process. Whether it heals sores or extinguishes suns is a matter of utter indifference from the viewpoint of this study. It is not the concern of science to judge that. The only point at issue here was to demonstrate, by means of an important example, the ancient truth that the dead always rule the living.

V

RUSSIA AND THE EAST

# GEOK-TEPE. WHAT IS ASIA TO US?*

## FEODOR DOSTOIEVSKY

[1881]

Geok-Tepe[1] is captured. The Turkomans are defeated, and although they are not yet quite pacified, our victory is indubitable. Society and the press are jubilant. But was it long ago that society, and partly also the press, took a most indifferent attitude toward this affair? . . . "Why should we go there? What is Asia to us?— So much money has been expended, whereas we have a famine, diphtheria, we have no schools, etc." . . . One can hardly maintain that our society has a clear conception of our mission in Asia— what specifically she means to us now and in the future. Generally speaking, our whole Russian Asia, including Siberia, still exists to Russia merely in the form of some kind of an appendix in which European Russia has no desire to take any interest. "We are Europe"—it is implied.—"What is our business in Asia!" There even sounded very harsh voices: "Oh, this Russian Asia of ours! We are even unable to establish order and settle properly in Europe, and here we have to meddle with Asia! Why Asia is quite super-fluous to us! How can we get rid of her!" Even in our day such opinions are expressed by our wiseacres—of course, out of their great wisdom.

Skobelev's victory resounded all over Asia to her remotest cor-ners: "Another fierce and proud orthodox people bowed before the White Czar!" And let this rumor echo and re-echo. Let the conviction of the invincibility of the White Czar and of his sword grow and spread among the millions of those peoples—to the very borders of India and in India herself. . . .

---

*From *The Diary of a Writer,* Vol. II, by Feodor Dostoievsky, translated
and annotated by Boris Brasol. Copyright 1949 by Charles Scribner's Sons.
Reprinted by permission of the publisher.
[1]Geok-Tepe—a former fortress of the Turkomans in Central Asia. In December, 1880, General Skobelev at the head of 6,000 Russian troops at-tacked the fortress and carried it by storm although the defenders numbered 25,000.

What for? What future? What is the need of the future seizure of Asia? What's our business there?

This is necessary because Russia is not only in Europe but also in Asia; because the Russian is not only a European but also an Asiatic. Moreover, Asia, perhaps, holds out greater promises to us than Europe. In our future destinies Asia is, perhaps, our main outlet!

I anticipate the indignation with which this reactionary suggestion of mine will be read. To me, however, it is an axiom. Yes, if there is one of the major roots which has to be rendered healthy, it is precisely our opinion of Asia. We must banish the slavish fear that Europe will call us Asiatic barbarians, and that it will be said that we are more Asiatics than Europeans. This fear that Europe might regard us as Asiatics has been haunting us for almost two centuries. It has particularly increased during the present nineteenth century, reaching almost the point of panic. . . . This erroneous fright of ours, this mistaken view of ourselves solely as Europeans, and not Asiatics—which we have never ceased to be—this shame and this faulty opinion have cost us a good deal in the course of the last two centuries, and the price we have had to pay has consisted of the loss of our spiritual independence, of our unsuccessful policies in Europe, and finally of money—God only knows how much money—which we spent in order to prove to Europe that we were Europeans and not Asiatics.

However, Peter's shock which pushed us into Europe, at first necessary and salutary, proved too strong, and for this we cannot be fully blamed. And was there a limit to our efforts to make Europe recognize us as *hers*, as Europeans, solely as Europeans, and not Tartars! Continually and incessantly we have annoyed Europe, meddling with her affairs and petty business. Now, we scared her with our strength, dispatching our armies "to save the kings," now we bowed before Europe—which we shouldn't have done—assuring her that we were created solely for the purpose of serving her and making her happy. In 1812, having driven Napoleon out of Russia, we did not make peace with him, as certain perspicacious Russians advised us to do, but moved into Europe as a solid wall in order to make her happy and to liberate her from her aggressor.

Of course, this was a lustrous picture: on the one hand was the despot and the aggressor, while on the other—the peace-maker and the resurrector. Still, in those days our political fortune consisted not in the picture, but in the fact that that aggressor had been placed, for the first time during his whole career, in a position where he would have made peace with us—a sincere, lasting peace, maybe, forever. On condition that we should not hinder him in Europe, he would have given us the East, so that our present Eastern problem—the menace and calamity of our present and of our future—would have been settled long ago. The aggressor later said it himself, and surely he did not lie, since he could have done nothing better than to be our ally on condition that the East should be ours, and the West—his. Then he certainly would have mastered the European nations, whereas the latter, including England, were then still too weak to stop us in the East. Subsequently, Napoleon, or his dynasty after his death, would, perhaps, have fallen, but the East nevertheless would have been ours. (Then we should have had access to the sea, and we could have met England on the seas.) But we gave all this up for a little show. What was the result?—All these nations we liberated, before they had even dispatched Napoleon, began to look on us with most obvious malevolence and the bitterest suspicion. At the Congresses at once they all united against us, as a solid wall, grabbing everything for themselves. And not only did they leave nothing to us, but they exacted from us certain obligations—true, these were voluntary obligations—which, however, subsequently proved to be very costly ones.

Later, despite this lesson—what did we do throughout the subsequent years of our century, up to this very day? Didn't we contribute to the consolidation of the German states? Didn't we strengthen them to such an extent that today they are, perhaps, stronger than we?—Indeed, it is no exaggeration to say that we have contributed to their growth and strength. Didn't we, in answer to their appeals, go to quell their strifes? Didn't we protect their rear when calamities threatened them? And now, contrariwise, didn't they threaten our rear when we were faced with a calamity, or didn't they threaten to appear in our rear, when we were menaced with other danger? It came to the point where everybody in Europe, every tribe and every nation, held in their bosom a stone stored against us long ago, merely waiting for the first conflict. This is what we have gained in Europe by serving her.—Nothing but her hatred! . . .

But why this hatred against us? Why can't they all, once and for all, start trusting us and become convinced of our harmlessness? Why can't they believe that we are their friends and good servants, and that our whole European mission is to serve Europe and her welfare? (For is it not so? Haven't we been acting so throughout this century? Have we done or achieved anything for ourselves? —Everything was spent on Europe!) Nay, they cannot place trust in us. The main reason is that they are altogether unable to recognize us as *theirs*.

Under no circumstance will they believe that we can in truth, on an equal basis with them, participate in the future destinies of their civilization. They consider us alien to their civilization; they regard us as strangers and imposters. They take us for thieves who stole from them their enlightenment and who disguised themselves in their garbs. Turks and Semites are spiritually closer to them than we, Aryans. All this has a very important reason: we carry to mankind an altogether different idea than they—that's the reason. And this, despite the fact that our "Russian Europeans" exert their efforts to assure Europe that we have no idea whatsoever, and that we can have none in the future; that Russia is incapable of possessing an idea of her own, being capable of mere imitation; that we shall always imitate, and that we are not Asiatics, not barbarians, but just as they—Europeans.

Europe, however, for once, at least, did not believe our Russian Europeans. On the contrary, in this matter her inferences coincide with those of our Slavophiles, although she knows them not—at best she might have merely heard something about them. The coincidence is precisely that Europe believes, much as the Slavophiles believe, that we have an "idea" of our own—a peculiar, not a European idea; that Russia can have, is capable of possessing, an idea. Of course, as yet, Europe knows nothing about the essence of our idea, since did she know it she would forthwith be pacified and even gladdened. But some day she will unfailingly come to know this idea, precisely when the critical moment in her destiny arrives. At present, however, she does not believe: admitting the fact that we possess an idea, she is afraid of it. Finally, she is quite disgusted with us, even though, at times, she is polite to us. For instance, they readily admit that Russian science can already point to several remarkable workers; that it has to its credit several good works which have even rendered service to European science. But under no circumstance will Europe now believe that not only scientific workers (even though very talented) may be born in Russia, but men of genius, leaders of mankind, such as a Bacon, Kant or Aristotle. This they will never believe, since they do not believe in our civilization, while, as yet, they do not know our future idea. In truth, they are right: we shall have no Bacon, no Newton, no Aristotle so long as we fail to stand on our own road and be spiritually independent. The same is true of all other things—of art and industry: Europe is ready to praise us, to stroke our heads, but she does not recognize us as hers, she despises us, whether secretly or openly; she considers us as an inferior race. At times, she feels aversion to us, especially when we fling ourselves on her neck with brotherly embraces.

However, it is difficult to turn away from "the window to Europe"; here is predestination. Meanwhile Asia may be, in truth, our future outlet! I reiterate this exclamation. And if we could only take cognizance of this idea, even though partially, what a root would be rendered whole! Asia, our Asiatic Russia—why, this is also our sick root, which has to be not only refreshed but resurrected and transformed! A principle, a new principle, a new vision of the matter—this is what we need.

*　*　*

"What for? What for?"—irritated voices will sound.—"Our Asiatic affairs even now continually require from us troops and unproductive expenditures. And what is Asia's industry? What is her merchandise? Where shall we find there consumers for our goods? And you suggest, no one knows why, that we should forever turn away from Europe!"

"Not forever," I continue to insist—"for the time being, and not altogether: hard as we may try we shall never completely tear ourselves away from Europe. We should not abandon Europe completely. Nor is this necessary. . . . Europe, even as Russia, is our mother, our second mother. We have taken much from her; we shall again take, and we shall not wish to be ungrateful to her. . . . Even so, we have the right to take care of our re-education and of our exodus from Egypt, since we ourselves created out of Europe something on the order of our spiritual Egypt."

"Wait,"—I shall be interrupted—"in what way will Asia contribute to our independence? There, we'll fall asleep in an Asiatic fashion, but we shall not become independent!"

"You see," I continue, "when we turn to Asia, with our new vision of her, in Russia there may occur something akin to what happened in Europe when America was discovered. Since, in truth, to us Asia is like the then undiscovered America. With our aspiration for Asia, our spirit and forces will be regenerated. The moment we become independent, we shall find what to do, whereas during the two centuries with Europe we lost the habit of any work; we became chatterers and idlers."

"Well, how are you going to arouse us for the Asiatic venture, if we are idlers? Who's going to be aroused first even if it were proved, as by two times two, that our happiness lies there?"

"In Europe we were hangers-on and slaves, whereas we shall go to Asia as masters. In Europe we were Asiatics, whereas in Asia we, too, are Europeans. Our civilizing mission in Asia will bribe our spirit and drive us thither. It is only necessary that the movement should start. Build only two railroads: begin with the one to Siberia, and then—to Central Asia—and at once you will see the consequences."

"Indeed, yours is a modest desire!"—people will tell me laughingly.—"Where are the funds? And what shall we get in return? —Nothing but a loss to us!"

"First, had we in the last twenty-five years set aside only three million rubles annually (and three million rubles, at times, simply slip through our fingers)—by now we should have built seventy-five million rubles' worth of Asiatic roads, i.e., over one thousand versts, no matter how you reckon. Then you speak about losses. Oh, if instead of us Englishmen or Americans inhabited Russia, they would show you what losses mean! They would certainly discover our America! Do you know that in Asia there are lands which are less explored than the interior of Africa? And do we know what riches are concealed in the bosom of these boundless lands? Oh, they would get at everything—metals and minerals, innumerable coal fields; they would find and discover everything —and they would know how to use these materials. They would summon science to their aid; they would compel the earth to yield fifty grains to one—that same earth about which we here still think that it is nothing but a steppe naked as our palm. Corn would attract people; production, industry, would come into existence. Don't you worry: consumers would be found, and the road to them would be discovered; they would be found in the depths of Asia, where millions of them are slumbering now; to reach them new roads would be constructed!"

"Well, here you are eulogizing science, and at the same time you urge us to renounce science and enlightenment; you are suggesting that we become Asiatics!"

"There, we shall need science all the more"—I exclaim—"since what are we in science now?—Half-educated men and dilettanti. But there we shall become workers: necessity itself will compel us to it the moment the independent, enterprising spirit arises. In science, too, we shall become masters and not hangers-on, as we now are all too often. But the main thing is that our civilizing mission in Asia will be understood and learned by us from the very first steps—this cannot be doubted. It will lift our spirit; it will convey to us dignity and self-consciousness, which at present we either lack altogether or possess in a trifling degree. . . . And don't you worry: Russia will not be depopulated: the thing will start gradually. At first, only a few men will go, but after a while news from them will be received which will attract others. Even so, to the Russian Sea this will be imperceptible. . . . Only a neg-ligible percentage of the population will drift thither, so that the migration will remain unnoticed. Over there, however, it will be quite noticeable! Wherever a 'Uruss' settles in Asia, the land will forthwith become Russian land. A new Russia will arise which in due time will regenerate and resurrect the old one and will show the latter the road which she has to follow. This, however, requires a new principle and a turn. These would necessitate the least destruction and commotion. Let it be only slightly fathomed (but fathomed) that Asia is our future outlet, that our riches are there, that there is our ocean; that when in Europe, because of the overcrowded condition alone, inevitable and humiliating communism is established, communism which Europe herself will loathe; when whole throngs will crowd around one hearth, and gradually individual economies will be ruined, while families will forsake their homes and will start living in collective communes; when children (three quarters of them foundlings) will be brought up in foundling institutions—then we shall still have wide expanses, meadows and forests, and our children will grow up in their parents' homes, not in stone barracks—amidst gardens and sowed fields, beholding above them clear, blue skies.

"Yes, Asia holds out to us many a promise, many an opportunity, the full scale of which we here cannot clearly conceive. . . ."

"Wait,"—I hear a voice—". . . we are in no position to brush everything aside. Take, to begin with, the Eastern question: it remains pending. How are we going to evade it?"

"On the Eastern question at this time I would say: At this minute, in our political spheres there is, perhaps, not even one political mind which would consider it common sense that Constantinople must be ours (save in some remote, enigmatic future). If, so, what is there to wait for?—At this minute the essence of the Eastern problem comes down to an alliance of Germany with Austria, plus the Austrian seizures in Turkey which are encouraged by Prince Bismarck. We can and, of course, do protest only in some extreme cases. However, so long as these two nations are united, what can we do without incurring very grave risks? Please observe that the Allies are waiting only until, at length, we should grow angry. However, as heretofore, we may love the Slavic nations, encourage them at times, even extend our help to them. Besides, they will not perish within a short time. And the term is likely to expire very soon. Let it suffice to say that we shall make it appear that we do not intend to meddle with European affairs, as heretofore; bereft of us, they will quarrel among themselves all the sooner. Indeed, Austria will never believe that Germany fell in love with her solely because of her beautiful eyes. Austria knows only too well that in the long run Germany must incorporate the Austrian Germans into the German union. But for no price will Austria cede her Germans—not even if Constantinople were offered her for them—so highly she values them. Therefore pretexts for discords are present there. And, on top of that, Germany is faced with the same insoluble French problem which, to her, has now become an eternal problem. Besides, Germany's unification itself appears to be incomplete and is apt to be undermined. It also appears that European socialism not only is not dead but continues to constitute a very grave menace.

"In a word, let us only wait and refrain from meddling—even if we are invited to meddle. Just as soon as their discord comes to a crash, 'political equilibrium' will crack, and then the Eastern question will at once be solved. We should only have to choose the opportune moment, even as at the time of the Franco-Prussian slaughter, and we should suddenly declare, as we then declared concerning the Black Sea: 'We do not wish to recognize any Austrian seizures in Turkey!'—and all seizures will instantly vanish, perhaps, together with Austria herself. In this way we shall catch up with everything which ostensibly, for the time being, we let slip."

"What about England? You overlook England. When she observes our Asiatic aspirations, she will instantly grow alarmed."

"Paraphrasing the proverb, I retort: 'If one fears England one should sit at home and move nowhere.' Besides, nothing new is going to alarm her since she is also alarmed with the same old thing at present. On the contrary, now we are holding her in confusion and ignorance concerning the future, and she is expecting from us the worst things. When, however, she comes to understand the true character of all our moves in Asia, perhaps some of her apprehensions will be toned down. . . . Well, I concede: she will not tone them down; she is too far from this frame of mind. Still, I repeat: 'If one fears England, one should sit at home and move nowhere!' Therefore, let me exclaim once more: 'Long live the Geok-Tepe victory! Long live Skobelev and his good soliders!' Eternal memory to those valiant knights who 'were eliminated from the rolls.' We shall record them on our rolls."

# THE RUSSIAN ADVANCE*

BY

ALBERT J. BEVERIDGE

[1904]

Everybody will recall how the triumph of China was universally predicted when the war between that country and Japan broke out [in 1894]. China was big, everybody said; her reserve strength was so enormous, her resources so inexhaustible, and so forth. Japan might win at first. It would take much time to arouse the giant of the Asiatic mainland. Yes, but once China was aroused, impertinent little Japan would be crushed. This was the belief of even the English Foreign Office. It seems incredible that the British ministry should have had no better information and reached no wiser conclusion than that of the rumor-fed crowd on the streets; but such appears, even to the warmest friend of England, to have been the fact. . . .

On the contrary, in this great Asiatic crisis (world crisis it might properly be called) the intelligent, patient (her enemies say unscrupulous) work of Russia's bureaus of information throughout the Orient bore golden fruit. Russia knew that Japan would win. She reasoned that Japan would probably demand the cession of some portion of Chinese territory, most likely the lower part of Manchuria, which commands Korea; and on Manchuria Russia had long looked with desiring eyes. With that celerity and address which make Russia's foreign statesmanship as much superior to that of other nations as her internal and economic statesmanship previous to Witte's administration had been inferior, the government of the Czar prepared for the result. . . .

The end came. China was defeated. . . . Li Hung Chang, representing China, and that extraordinary intellect, Marquis Ito, representing Japan, met at Shimonoseki, and concluded the famous treaty of peace which bears that name. By this treaty Port Arthur,

---

*From *The Russian Advance* by Albert J. Beveridge; published by Harper & Brothers, 1904.

Talienhwan*, and the entire Liao-Toung peninsula were ceded to
Japan.  It was not only a war indemnity to Japan, but it secured
the very points of the Korean controversy which were the origin
of the war itself.

But now, when Japan was in the full flower of her well-earned
success, when the world applauded the diplomatic ability which
had concluded one of the most ably conducted conflicts in history
(little, though, that war was); now, when Japan stepped forth
from the smoke of battle, amid the applause of nations, to her
place among the powers of the world—a place earned by her civil
and industrial revolutions at home and confirmed by glorious conduct in war by sea and by land: now, when China was prostrate,
humiliated, disgraced—at this supreme and psychic hour Russia
made her carefully prepared play, which in an instant deprived
Japan of the material fruits of her victory and the glory of her
achievement, apparently rescued the Manchu dynasty from certain
ruin, and bound it by the consideration of gratitude and every form
of obligation to Russia.

A joint note of the Russian, the French, and the German governments was addressed to Japan, telling her, in the politest of
terms, and with the cleverest of arguments, why the peace of the
Orient would be permanently endangered by her retaining possession of the Chinese territory ceded to her, and expressing the hope
of these "friendly" governments that the wise, the peace-loving,
and the humane Mikado would save the situation by surrendering
what his generals' skill and his soldiers' blood had won.

At the same time there were gathering ships of war between
Japan and her prey.  French ships came from the south, Russian
ships came from the north, German ships hovered near.  The Japanese navy was overmatched.  The attitude of the Russians was
that of immediate and determined action.  Steam was kept up,
decks cleared for battle, and every dramatic effect of war was introduced and employed with the skill of accomplished performers. . . .

The Japanese nation clamored for war; but Japanese statesmen
knew that war at this moment, without powerful aid, meant defeat,
and defeat ruin.  Therefore, the little empire broke her sword,

*Now known as Dairen.

submitted to her fate, and, with her hand held in the mailed fingers of the alliance which Russia had constructed, wrote the historic withdrawal of her claim to and authority over the territory China had ceded to her.

It was but two days after the ratification of the treaty by which Japan became the owner of the southern shores of Manchuria that she was forced to give them up, with such swift effect did the triple alliance strike.   Apparently, in willing response to the note of the three powers, but in reality under duress of the alternative of war, the Japanese government issued to the world her withdrawal from every foot of land she had wrested from China. . . .

> We recently, at the request of the Emperor of China, appointed plenipotentiaries for the purpose of conferring with the ambassadors sent by China, and of concluding with them a treaty of peace between the two empires. Since then the governments of the two empires of Russia and Germany, and of the French Republic, considering that the permanent possession of the ceded districts of the Feng-t'ien peninsula by the Empire of Japan would be detrimental to the lasting peace of the Orient, have called, in a simultaneous recommendation to our government, to refrain from holding these districts permanently.
>
> Earnestly desirous, as we always are, for the maintenance of peace, nevertheless we were forced to commence hostilities against China for no other reason than our sincere desire to secure for the Orient an enduring peace.  The governments of the three powers are, in offering their friendly recommendations, similarly actuated by the same desire, and we, out of our regard for peace, do not hesitate to accept their advice.  Moreover, it is not our wish to cause suffering to our people or to impede the progress of the national destiny by embroiling the empire in new complications, and thereby imperilling the situation and retarding the restoration of peace.
>
> China has already shown, by the conclusion of the treaty of peace, the sincerity of her repentance for her breach of faith with us, and has made manifest to the world our reasons and the object we had in waging war with that empire.
>
> Under these circumstances, we do not consider that the honor and dignity of the empire will be compromised by resorting to magnanimous measures and by taking into consideration the general situation of affairs.
>
> We have, therefore, accepted the advice of the friendly powers, and have commanded our government to reply to the government of the three powers to that effect.

[Russia's] next move in the game was to secure from China authority to extend the Siberian railroad across Manchuria. . . .

The enemies of Russia say that it was in anticipation of the difficulties, diplomatic and others, involved in such a grant of powers that the Russian government (and, if true, it shows how superb their resource is in foreign affairs) caused the famous Russo-Chinese Bank to be incorporated. . . .

This bank, therefore, secured from the Chinese government a contract by which to extend the Siberian railroad across Manchuria, the Chinese government giving the necessary authority. . . .

Under concessions granted by the Chinese government to the Russo-Chinese Bank, this financial arm of the Russian government organized, under Russian laws, the East China Railway Company. This company is the builder of the road. It had a capital of 5,000,000 rubles ($2,500,000), practically all controlled by the Russo-Chinese Bank. But the actual capital for construction was raised by an issue of bonds guaranteed by the Russian government. Most of these bonds, it is believed, are held by the Russian Government itself, either directly or through the instrumentality of government banks. Thus the money to build the road comes out of the Russian imperial treasury directly. . . .

It thus appears that for all practical purposes the work is the direct work of the Russian government, and that the Russo-Chinese Bank and the railway company are nothing but agents.

The following are a few of the traffic and operating provisions of the railway agreement. . . .

First. The gauge of the railway must be the same as that of Russian railways (five feet).

Second. If the Manchuria railway becomes inadequate to care for the traffic turned over to it by the Siberian and Ussuri railways or Russian shiplines, it shall increase its capacity upon notification of the railway named. If the Manchurian and Siberian railways disagree about this, the Russian Minister of Finance shall decide the question, and if the Manchurian Railway Company has not enough money to make the improvements, the Russian Minister of Finance may supply the funds, if he think wise.

Third. Freight, passenger, and all other kinds of trains running upon the Trans-Baikal Siberian and Ussuri railway lines shall be received by the Manchurian railway as if these separate systems were one system, in full complement, without delay of any kind. The same rate of speed shall be maintained on the Manchurian lines as is maintained by the Siberian railways. . . .

It is thus seen that in the contract itself the railroad is made for all purposes a mere extension of the Siberian system. . . .

Finally, it is provided by this contract that the Chinese government may purchase the road from this railway company at the end of thirty years, and at the end of eighty years the whole property shall revert to the Chinese government without payment of any kind. . . .

And so it is that the Russian statesmen are extending their network of power over Asia with a far-sightedness not exhibited in the foreign diplomacy of any other nation of the present day, except, perhaps, Germany. So it is that England may find herself helpless in the presence of accomplished facts and a series of impregnable diplomatic positions. So it is that quietly, plausibly, skilfully, and by the lasting methods of material constructiveness, Russia has achieved the first of her plans for the capture of the only remaining uncaptured markets of the world. So it is that, while England and America have been wasting time on academic argumentations about unsubstantial theories, Germany has been forging ahead towards the position of the first maritime power of the twentieth century, and Russia has been placing on the future the mortgage of her material dominion.

"Yes," said a Russian, "you may be stronger now, richer now, than we are, but we shall be stronger tomorrow than you—yes, and all the world; for the future abides with the Slav!" Such expressions you may hear again and again from young Russian gentlemen who have not become government haters. For example, take from another young Russian the following, which is striking: "Would you know another name for Russia? Very well, then, call her 'the Inevitable.'"

* * *

Preparedness is the secret of most successes in this world. Fate seldom makes league with the unequipped. Events come marching into every century, into every day, crying aloud for the nation or the man who is prepared. Russia's foreign statesmanship, admittedly the ablest of the present day, as her internal development has been admittedly the most backward, consists largely in reasoning out possible events from existing conditions, and then preparing for them. Her bloodless triumph over Japan, after Japan's bloody triumph over China, is an illustration of this. When the future of Manchuria looked most hopeless for Russia, she was in reality winning her right to build her railway and creating opportunities for permanent occupation, should that ever appear desirable. But the right to build the railway did not include the right to occupy the two coveted ports on the open and ice-free waters on the south Manchurian coast—Port Arthur and Talienhwan. She had merely secured the right to build her railway across Manchuria to her superb harbor of Vladivostock, which, however, is open to commerce during the winter months only by aid of ice-breaking devices. It was Russia's desire to secure ports where ice did not chain the feet of her commerce. It is believed that for decades her intentions have been firmly fixed on the two excellent Manchurian ports above mentioned.

Indeed, some outlet on the open oceans has been the determination of the Russian for centuries.

From the time of Peter the Great—he whom statesmen-for-a-day called mad, but whose vision embraced all future Russian policy, so far as the eye of man can now discern it—from the time of this marvelous mind and will till now, one vast purpose of Russia has become so fixed as to be almost a religion, and that is the determination of the Slav to reach the seas where summer skies await him and over whose waters the winds of commerce blow. There is something pathetic about the patient effort of the Rusian to reach the oceans of the globe—to sail the seas that other men sail, to make the ports that his brothers make, and to meet his fellows face to face in all the harbors of the world. There is something that wins our sympathy in the Russian's almost instinctive attempts to escape from his vast and mighty cage, unequalled in its own extent though that cage may be.

For Russia is a cage and has always been a cage—the prison of a race. On the west, millions of gathering bayonets of Germany and all Europe, menacing the Slav with the perpetual possibility of war; on the south, the Turk turning Russia backward from the Mediterranean and the common highways of mankind; on the north, the frozen Arctic; on the east, the savage and remorseless tribes of Asia; and, later in time and farther in distance, India disciplined, armed, and fortified by England against the Russian's progress towards the Oriental seas. On the east, again, and farther south, between Siberia and India, the ancient empire of the Son of Heaven, mighty in its day, but now in the period of its decline and falling in pieces, yet forbidden to the Russian by the masterful policy and power of England in former days, and later by the jealousies and fears of other nations. Turn where he would, the Slav could discern in the far distance the world's common oceans, which he felt to be his common right as well as the right of other peoples, but from which man and nature had conspired to bar him.

And so, for this priceless privilege of the seas, the Slav has for centuries been battling, until by sheer experience in the concentration of his energies and thoughts on foreign policy he has become the most finished diplomat in the history of negotiation, and the first in foreign affairs among the statesmen of the nineteenth and twentieth centuries. . . .

Remember, then, that the original railway agreement by which Russia began to throw her lines across Manchuria did not include that branch that has since become the trunkline itself, running hundreds of miles through central Manchuria to Port Arthur and Talienhwan. But the Slav was on the ground. He was already building railroads, as contemplated in the initial agreement. He had already rescued China from its conqueror; he had already made the Manchu dynasty his debtor. Now he patiently built his railroad towards Vladivostock; and while he built he patiently awaited the development of events.

And events did not disappoint him. Once more the ancient tale was told of fate conspiring with him who is prepared. Some time before two German missionaries had been wantonly murdered in the province of Shan-Tung. Germany demanded reparation. . . . Finally, the German Emperor landed marines at Tsing-Tau, the port of Kiaochou, seized the latter town and the entire bay. . . .

Confronted at last by the display of actual force, which most European statesmen believe to be the only thing the Asiatic anywhere understands, the Manchu Emperor made a definite grant to Germany of the entire bay of Kiaochou, including the city and port, and a coast boundary of land surrounding it. . . .

When Germany seized Kiaochou, Russia was not long in acting.
Russia reasoned thus: Here was a seizure of territory by an empire
which is already one of the great powers, and which has declared
ambitions to become the first and chiefest power among the
nations. Here was Germany throwing her influence across the path
of Russian intentions in Asia, as she has so effectively thrown her
financial and commercial power across the path of Russia, and of
England too, in Turkey and Asia Minor. And here was this seizure
of territory, an extension of physical and material influence into
the very breast of China, sanctioned by the Chinese government.

The event for which Russia was prepared had occurred at last.
Very clearly, if the seizure of a portion of Chinese territory by
Japan, as her price of peace in closing her war with China, was a
menace to the permanent peace of the Orient, Germany's seizure
of territory in the very center of the Chinese coast was equally a
menace. True that Germany, Russia, and France had protested
against Japan's occupation of a portion of Chinese territory; true
that Germany's seizure of Kiaochou and the extension of German
railways into one of China's great provinces was inconsistent with
the allies' protest against Japan's occupation of southern Manchuria; true that the implied understanding as to the integrity of
China, necessarily involved in the allies' protest to Japan, had been
broken.

But, said, in effect, the Russian statesmen, it was not Russia that
had broken it. It was not Russia that had changed these conditions.
Apparently, so far as the letter of the implied agreement was concerned, Russia had been faithful to the understanding. But now
conditions were changed, and through no fault of Russia. She was
justified in protecting her interests, then. Nobody could find any
fault with that. She would protect her interests therefore. If
Germany received a port, so should Russia receive a port. If Germany occupied Kiaochou, Russia should occupy Port Arthur and
Talienhwan. So reasoned Russian statesmen. Such was her rep-
resentation to China. Such was her case before the public opinion
of the world. Like lightning, she carried this determination into
effect. The German lease was dated March 6, 1898.

On March 27th of the same year a treaty was signed by the representatives of the Chinese and Russian governments, leasing Port Arthur and Talienhwan to the Czar, and extending all railroad construction rights from where the line of the road crosses north-central Manchuria on its way to Vladivostock southward to these ports.

And because the Russian lease . . . is fundamental, because it . . . is an historical and political landmark, from which the beginning of the disintegration of China, in a physical, tangible, and material sense, may be reckoned, if that break-up ever occurs, it is here set out almost in full:

Article I.—It being necessary for the due protection of her navy in the waters of north China that Russia should possess a station she can defend, the Emperor of China agrees to lease to Russia Port Arthur and Talienhwan, together with the adjacent seas, but on the understanding that such lease shall not prejudice China's sovereignty over this territory. . . .

Article III.—The duration of the lease shall be twenty-five years from the day this treaty is signed, but may be extended by mutual agreement between Russia and China.

Article IV.—The control of all military forces in the territory leased by Russia, and of all naval forces in the adjacent seas, as well as of the civil officials in it, shall be vested in one high Russian official, who shall, however, be designated by some title other than Governor-General (Tsung-tu) or Governor (Hsun-fu). All Chinese military forces shall, without exception, be withdrawn from the territory. . . .

Article VI.—The two nations agree that Port Arthur shall be a naval port for the sole use of Russian and Chinese men-of-war, and be considered as an unopen port so far as the naval and mercantile vessels of other nations are concerned. As regards Talienhwan, one portion of the harbor shall be reserved exclusively for Russian and Chinese men-of-war, just like Port Arthur, but the remainder shall be a commercial port, freely open to the merchant vessels of all countries.

Article VII.—Port Arthur and Talienhwan are the points in the territory leased most important for Russian military purposes. Russia shall, therefore, be at liberty to erect forts at her own expense, and to build barracks and provide defences at such places as she desires.

Article VIII.—China agrees that the procedure sanctioned in 1896, regarding the construction of railroads by the Board of the Eastern China Railway Company, shall, from the date of the signature of this treaty, be extended so as to include the construction of a branch line to Talienhwan, or, if necessary, in view of the interests involved, of a branch line to the most suitable point on the coast between New-Chwang* and the Yalu River. Further, the agreement entered into in September, 1896, between the Chinese government and the Russo-Chinese Bank shall apply with

---

*Now known as Antung.

equal strength to this branch line. The direction of this branch line and the places it shall touch shall be arranged between Hsu Tajen and the Board of Eastern Railroads. The construction of this line shall never, however, be made a ground for encroaching on the sovereignty of China.

It will be observed that Russia's lease of Port Arthur and Talienhwan is for the period of twenty-five years. But note also that the first article states that the lease is made because it is necessary for the due protection of Russia's navy in the waters of north China that Russia *shall possess* a station she can defend.

Also note, as with Germany in Shan-Tung, authority is given to *fortify;* and note, most of all, that Russia has acted upon this authority. The harbor at Port Arthur is deep and narrow and not over large, and is surrounded by high, almost mountainous hills. With all speed, day and night, Russia instantly began planting impregnably her power on these eminences. At the time the writer reached Port Arthur, at the end of the journey of investigation through Manchuria, work was still in progress. Trench and earthwork and guns—not frowning guns, but guns that hide their menace—and all the incidents of modern fortification were being perfected over this maritime terminus of her railroad. With the foundation of her physical authority planted deeply, even to the hearts of the everlasting hills, it is not likely that Russia will ever depart, at least from Port Arthur and Talienhwan. It is the last and most conclusive piece of evidence to sustain the proposition that she intends to remain in Manchuria, and permanently. . . .

And so it appears improbable that Russia will withdraw from Manchuria. Her railroad is there, her ships are there, her mines are there. Coal, iron, silver, gold, and other treasures of mineral wealth—all Russia's under her railway agreement—are there. Soil which will grow any vegetable in the temperate zones and some of those of the semi-tropic countries are there. (You may see wheat, barley, oats, tobacco, potatoes, Indian corn, beans, millet growing in fields that look like miniature American farms, or, rather, like overgrown American gardens, in all the inhabited portions of Manchuria. The soil is so rich that many crops were seen, in the summer of 1901, already beginning to grow in the same fields from which the first crop had been gathered only a fortnight be-

fore.)   All these are there.   And, most of all, the command of all
China, the point from which the sceptre of the Russian Autocrat
may be extended over all the East, is there.   The throne of the
future of the Orient appears to be planted now upon the eminence
that lifts above the waters of Port Arthur, and above it already
floats the Russian flag.

*　　*　　*

There is but one agency which might dislodge the Russian from
Manchuria; that agency is the swordlike bayonets of the soldiers
of Japan, the war-ships of Japan, the siege-guns of Japan, the
embattled frenzy of a nation stirred to its profoundest depths by
the conviction that the Czar has deprived the Mikado of the
greatest victory and the richest prize in all the history of the Island
Empire—a history which reaches back not through centuries, but
through millenniums.   And that Japan is determined that Russia
shall withdraw from Manchuria no careful student on the ground
can doubt.   No thoughtful student of geography can doubt it.

War between Russia and Japan is a serious probability.   It is
believed by the best informed that it would be raging now if Japan
had the money.   It came near breaking out in February, 1901, in
spite of the Mikado's poverty.   Only the financial situation muz-
zles the artillery of the England of the Orient.   And Russia's
financial situation is almost as bad.   And so it is that both Russia
and Japan will hesitate to give the other a *casus belli*.   All statesmen are obliging, conciliatory, reasonable when confronted with
the grim alternative of armed conflict before they are ready for it.
But, however long the want of actual cash may postpone this conflict, it is hard to see how it is to be avoided in the end.   If it is
put off for five years, the causes for it will still remain; if it is put
off for ten years, yet will those causes persist; if it is put off for a
quarter of a century, nevertheless the elements of conflict will continue.   What then are those enduring causes which time itself, as it
now appears, cannot remove?

Look at your map.   Just above Japan, within hardly more than
a day's sail, is Vladivostock, one of the finest harbors for naval

and military purposes in the world, and one whose only defect is its three months of ice. It is the Gibraltar of the East. And it is Russian. In its waters the Russian war-ships lie safe from all attack. From its wharves Russian railways run northward through Russian wheatfields to the Russian capital of east Siberia.

Cross now, southward, a peninsula and reach the sea; and travel, still south, the shores of the sea till you come to the mate of Vladivostock, Port Arthur, of which so much already has been said. Here, again, the war-ships of Russia are within instant touch of Japan. Here, again, they lie in safety, secure from all attack. Again, from the wharves of this southern Vladivostock the Russian railway lines run northward; and though the territory through which these railway lines run is still nominally Chinese, the facts here presented show that, for all practical purposes, it may, in the future, become Russian, if the Russian wills it so.

North of this peninsula, then are Russian ports, Russian ships, and Russian guns; a Russian railway, Russian commerce, the Russian people. Back of this peninsula, again, are Russian railways, Russian commerce, and Russian bayonets. South of this peninsula, again, are Russian harbors, Russian guns, Russian commerce, and Russian railways.

And this peninsula, running out from these Russian environments, almost touches Japan itself. As a Japanese statesman said, in speaking of this peninsula, "It is like an arrow, with the point aimed at our heart."

This peninsula is Korea, and it is inevitable that Korea shall become either Russian or Japanese. And if it be Japanese, it will be a powerful factor in preventing Manchuria from ever becoming Russian.

Let us listen again to the Japanese publicist just quoted: "The absorption," said he, "of Manchuria by the Russians, if completed, renders the position of Korea precarious. And Korea is a matter of first and last importance to us. Korea is life or death to Japan."

"Yes," said another Japanese publicist, of high intelligence, "if I were a Russian I might insist on Korea becoming Russian; but as I am a Japanese, for the safety of my country, I insist that it shall become Japanese, and upon that insistence every subject of the Mikado is willing to lay down his life." . . .

This is fervid language; but talks with merchants, with guides, with even the common people of Japan, will convince you that this Japanese diplomat's Oriental eloquence is quite within the limits of the truth.

Here, then, is reason enough, and there are other reasons still more profound. Japan is already seriously crowded for living-room for her people. During the past ages of her history, the birth rate was, no doubt, as great as now, but the death rate also was almost equally great. And so her population, during many centuries, was very steady, just as China's is today. But in recent years Japan has become a modern hygenic nation. The science of medicine has made no such progress anywhere in the Orient as in this island-empire. Indeed, comparing her ignorance of the healing art, even in recent years, with the high position she occupies today, her medical progress is the greatest, relatively speaking, in the world. . . .

The result, of course, will occur to any one. The birth rate continues as great as formerly, and in only two or three places in the world is it greater than in Japan; but the death rate daily decreases. The population of Japan, therefore, steadily and rapidly increases. Japan has no method of relieving this accession of numbers by emigration as Germany has, so we find her in the condition in which Germany would find herself if the millions of Germans who have come to America and the other millions who have gone elsewhere throughout the world had all been kept at home. So Japan is looking for some place to plant her surplus millions. This was one of the three or four great reasons for acquiring Formosa; it is one of the vital reasons for ultimately occupying Korea. Manchuria, with its comparatively scanty population, and climatic conditions like those of Japan, would have been an ideal spot for the planting of a Japanese empire with the surplus Japanese population.

On the other hand, in addition to the other reasons given why Russia considers Manchuria desirable, is the fact that she, also, feels that the natural pressure of her population requires Russian occupation of Manchuria. It is not a matter of future speculation, but only of simple arithmetic and of near-by certainty, that Siberia will be as thickly peopled as Russia itself. When that occurs, the overflow can go no place but southward, through the fertile valleys of Manchuria.

Still another fundamental reason for this conflict is that which gave rise to the triple alliance, whose diplomacy and menace drove Japan from southern Manchuria after her war with China. This is the fear entertained by every Russian, German, and French statesman, in common with every student of Oriental affairs, that Japan intends to undertake the reorganization of the Chinese Empire; and that Japan regards this as her "destiny" no one who has gone over the ground will deny. The reasons for it are powerful. They grow out of the elements of race and geography. The Japanese and Chinese are both Asiatics. Their written language is very similar, and for practical purposes the same; some of their religions are identical; their modes of thought are so much alike that the Japanese may be said to be the only people who understand the Chinese. In this, it is true, the Russian is a close second to the Japanese. Furthermore, they are so close together that they may be said to be physically in elbow touch. . . .

Indeed, an entire chapter might be written, and upon respectable authority, describing the ultimate intentions which Japan entertains as to China. It sometimes seems that her statesmen do not take very much pains to conceal them. There is no doubt that up to the present she has earnestly hoped that she might be aided in this, her high dream of Oriental dominion, by an alliance with England and America; and although such an alliance would rob her of most of the fruit of her statesmanship, she would be only too glad to make the division for the invaluable aid of these two powers. It is believed, however, that she has abandoned hope of such a far-reaching, hard-and-fast compact, and that she has finally come to the consciousness that she must go it alone.

Of course, if Japan should thus become the dominant influence in China, her merchants and manufacturers would capture the lion's share of the vast future commerce of the Flowery Kingdom. Such Japanese predominance in China would also make of China a far more powerful barrier against Russian advance than Japan itself now is.

It is thus easy to see that the Japanese conception of the Oriental "destiny" of Japan and the Russian conception of the Oriental "destiny" of Russia come into a face-to-face conflict. On the one hand, Russia would be deprived of the markets which she hopes in the future (perhaps not for a century or two) to be able to as perfectly control physically as she now controls those of her own dominions; on the other hand, a halt would be called to the march of her alleged national ideal of setting up the cross over China's myriads of millions. . . . Even if Japan's program were carried out with the cooperation of England and the United States, the effect upon Russia would be precisely the same. So it appears that this dispute, whose springs are deep in the rocks and soil of circumstances, seemingly beyond the control of any human statesmanship, may have to be settled, in the final analysis, by trial of battle.

And if war does come, there are more contradictory elements of strength, more contradictory conditions, more premises upon which wagers for either side might be reasonably made than in any war of modern times—the Japanese navy, the Russian navy; Japanese preparedness, Russian preparedness; the Japanese soldier, the Russian soldier; the skill, valor, the staying powers of the flower of the people of the Orient, against the slowest, most undeveloped, but yet the most tenacious and most unexhausted race of the Occident. It will be a great drama, and when the curtain falls on its last desperate act the destiny of the East, and in a certain sense the future of the world, will be forecast by the flag which flies in triumph over the carnage of that final conflict. . . .

# SOME ASPECTS OF THE FAR EASTERN CRISIS*

BY

ANDREI LOBANOV-ROSTOVSKY

[1938]

There has been much discussion as to the true reasons which induced Japan to embark on her present adventure in China. Various causes have been given: Japan, over-populated and small in area, needs territory for the overflow of her population; as a great industrial power she needs raw materials for her industries, and in addition she is seeking control of the Chinese market particularly for her silk exports; she is stamping out Communism in China.

These three arguments may be briefly refuted: With regard to territory for colonization, she already possessed a considerable colonial empire prior to her conquest of Manchukuo in 1931. After the Russo-Japanese War, with an eye to the coming annexation of Korea, an ambitious plan was drawn up for the settlement of a million Japanese a year on the mainland of Asia. In actual fact, in the following two decades less than one million Japanese settled in the Japanese overseas possession. As for Manchuria, it has been the Chinese and not the Japanese who have flowed in to colonize it.

With regard to the second argument, it might have been valid prior to the conquest of Manchukuo, but not afterwards. In Manchuria Japan found for her industrial needs a reserve of timber estimated at 200,000,000 tons; coal estimated in the Hsin mine alone at 600,000,000 tons; and in all Manchuria and Inner Mongolia 2,500,000,000 tons; iron deposits estimated at 1,200,000,000 tons; shale oil conservatively estimated at 350,000,000 tons; agricultural fertilizers, soda magnesium, aluminum and agricultural products such as oats, millet, koaliang and soya. These estimates, as given in the Tanaka Memorial, are said to be those of the South

* From *The Slavonic and East European Review*, April 1938. Reprinted by permission.

Manchurian Railway and of the Japanese General Staff. Whether these figures are correct or not, is irrelevant. Suffice it to say that had Japan concentrated her energies on the development of Manchukuo instead of dispersing them in all her subsequent conquests, Manchukuo to a great extent could have solved her problem with regard to the need of raw materials for her industries. Similarly, the question of controlling the Chinese market might have been solved more profitably by winning the friendship of the Chinese people and by bolstering up the growing prosperity of China, instead of plunging that country into a ruinous war and assuming the role of the arch-enemy of the Chinese people.

Further, it must be remembered that the misery, destruction and famine caused by this war in China not only ruins trade but also serves as an excellent breeding ground for the very Communism which Japan is purporting to fight. . . .

We find China for the first time unified. In the past China had grown to be less and less of a nation and more and more of a loose federation of peoples held together solely by a common civilization or, more exactly, by a common outlook on life. Hence the spirit of independence shown by the various provinces, the deep cleavage between North and South, and the facility with which provincial governors and war-lords betrayed the Central government. Today, in striking contrast, we find a nation unified in spirit, presenting a common front to the enemy; and there can be little doubt that this change was brought about by the menace of Japan.

Thus we may say that two novel elements have appeared in Chinese life within the past decade which, for lack of better words, we may qualify as militarism and nationalism. Assuming that these are not passing trends and that they are liable to be further strengthened by the increasing pressure of Japan on China, it may well be that the future destinies of Asia will be molded by them. Indeed, in projecting the growth of these trends into the future, we have to face two possibilities: Japan is victorious and conquers China, or Japan fails in her task and breaks down. In the first case China may undergo the fate of Poland; but the example of that nation shows that a nation which keeps its national spirit and civilization alive cannot be destroyed. Moreover, how much more difficult it would be for Japan to hold China than it was for the three combined mighty empires of Europe to hold a relatively smaller and weaker Poland! If on the other hand, Japan fails in her effort to subdue China and breaks down, or—what would be tantamount to it—gets involved with other powers so that the struggle becomes general, the result will be the emergence of a nationally awakened China welded together by the fire of martyrdom—the perennial manifestation of the Phoenix rising from its ashes. And what will the triumph of Chinese nationalism mean to the world at large?

The story of all nationalisms has been the same, be it Italian, German, Polish, Russian or even Japanese. First, a weak country oppressed or menaced by powerful neighbors; then the national awakening and struggle against the oppressor, with the war of liberation becoming the symbol of national courage and inspiration for the patriotism of future generations; then the hour of triumph, the gradual overflow of national aspirations beyond the borders of the newly unified or liberated state; the appearance of theories of national or race superiority, the concept of some great historic mission which leads in turn to conquests, to oppression of neighboring peoples, and possibly war with other nations and once more defeat. The France of Louis XIV and Napoleon, the Russia of Catherine II and Nicholas I, Germany from Jena to 1914, Italy from Mazzini to Mussolini have all gone through or are going through this cycle. What would stop China from following the same path? . . .

There is a widespread tendency to overlook the resiliency shown by nations after great national catastrophes. Many were those who in the dismal years following the advent of Soviet power in Russia in the face of civil war, terror, epidemics and famine, predicted the complete disintegration of Russia in a wave of anarchy. Similarly, today many observers are predicting the death of China and the destruction of her age-long civilization at the hands of Japan. But the record of progress shown by China in the past decade, as well as the unleashing of national energies as revealed by the present struggle, give a reasonable basis for the assumption that the end of this struggle will be followed by a period of development similar to the one witnessed in Soviet Russia under the various five-year plans, and very much for the same reasons. A backward nation, having learned by the bitter lesson of war the cost of neglecting its economic and technical development, strains its energy, as a means of survival, to overtake more advanced nations. In the relatively improbable contingency of Japan's succeeding in transforming China into a colony, the effect would be very much the same, though in a slower and more indirect way; the story of all colonizations has revealed that the colonized nation uses to its own advantage the lessons imparted by its colonizers. There remains however one prerequisite for this, namely, the survival of an ardent national spirit and the urge for survival in the face of defeat; if the lessons of the present struggle are correctly read, it would appear that the Chinese people have exchanged their past Sybaritic passivity for a new dynamic energy, just as every nation has done under similar circumstances.

Turning to Soviet Russia, we may trace the appearance of similar trends under somewhat similar conditions. It is hardly possible to speak of Russian history as being pacific. Indeed, Professor Sorokin, in his comparative study of wars throughout history, points out that the percentage of war years for Russia throughout the course of her history is 46 per cent, as compared to 50 per cent for France and 56 per cent for England, with other European countries lagging behind. But notwithstanding this high percentage of wars, the Russian people have in common with the Chinese a fundamentally non-warlike psychology. Wars were fought by Russia either in self-defense or in pursuit of a national policy such as the drive toward the sea, or the obvious rounding off of national frontiers, or, again, the support of fellow Slav peoples. Such policies were dictated by the government and, with the exception of the governing bureaucracy and portions of the nobility which were inspired by patriotism and a sense of nationalism, the people at large went to war because such was the command of the Tsar. Religion and a primitive elemental sense of nationality were the nearest equivalents to nationalism one could find in pre-War Russia. Moreover, the immensity of the country and the remoteness of the border made for a strong sense of regionalism and a lack of any hostile discrimination against one particular foreign nation. Neither Japan nor Germany were really hated during the hostilities against them in the last two wars preceding the Revolution.

All the more remarkable is therefore the change taking place today, ironically, within the framework of Soviet ideology. The rise of what we may term Soviet nationalism is as remarkable as the corresponding rise of Chinese nationalism. It originated in the segregation of Russia from other nations during the early period of the Revolution. Regarded with unmitigated horror by the Western nations and driven into economic and moral isolation, the Soviet Russia of the early twenties had to find support within herself for her moral and economic rehabilitation and develop a psychology of superiority, based upon her own Messianic ideology. She had to build up a powerful army and an industrial equipment which today form an inseparable element of military power. She also had to mobilize the national spirit. Partly for its own propaganda purposes and partly for this mobilization of spirit, the Soviet government began instilling into the people, as the Five Year Plan was nearing completion, a pride of achievement. The "We and You" attitude toward capitalist nations was gradually being changed into a pride in "our Socialist Fatherland" and a stress on the jealousy of other nations. It will be noticed that the Japanese war menace appeared just at this time, that is to say, toward the end of the first Five-Year Plan. Here was a tangible proof of the menace of the outside world which was anxious not to allow Russia to develop peacefully at home, or at least such is the interpretation given for internal consumption; and when the rise of Hitler completed this picture on the Western border, all the elements for the rise of an exacerbated feeling of nationalism were ripe. True, this new nationalism is not Russian in the sense of glorification of the Russian nationality, but Soviet, putting more stress on the glorification of the system and of the community of races living within the Soviet border; yet that is a difference which matters little with regard to the effect this phenomenon will have on the outside world. Furthermore the changed attitude of the Kremlin toward the Russian past, the reinstatement of Peter the

Great as a national hero and even more strikingly of St. Alexander Nevsky, is proof that the movement is not only growing in strength but is narrowing itself to a more and more Russian national ideology.

Thus if present Russia shows the rise, in an ever increasing degree of the glorification of the military, and an appearance of a proud spirit of nationalism, both these trends may be directly credited to Japan's actions. Both in China and in Russia Japan has so far accomplished a moral revolution of tremendous significance for the future of Asia. But she has done even more: she has succeeded in bringing the two nations once more together.

That the two revolutionary movements should have looked to each other for mutual support in the earlier stages of their development was easily understandable. China looked to Russia for badly needed assistance in technical advice and war equipment, whereas Soviet Russia, after the failure of a direct Communist drive upon Western Europe, turned to Asia as a field for a flanking attack on European capitalism. Already the Congress of Baku in 1920 had succeeded in bringing the various Asiatic revolutionary movements under the co-ordinated guidance of Moscow; and subsequent events showed China to be a particularly fruitful field for Soviet endeavor. Indeed, Sun Yat-sen in dying had left a famous testament recommending close co-operation between the Kuomintang and the Soviet government. There was only the necessity of slightly modifying the interpretations of the three principles which Sun Yat-sen had laid down as the basic character of the Chinese revolution, in order to bring them into accord with the demands of the Third International.

The period between 1924 and 1927 marked the high-water mark of Russian influence in China. Not only was the Kuomintang under the direct control of the Soviet agent, Borodin and his mission, but the Chinese nationalist forces in South China were effectively reorganized under Russian guidance. However, the moderate wing of the Kuomintang party not only feared the impact of Communism on the Chinese masses but held to the slogan "China for the Chinese." Headed by Chiang-Kai-shek and the powerful financial interests of the Soong family this group not only succeeded in driving the Russian Soviets out of China but ever since has been waging a bitter struggle against the Chinese Communists. As a result of six campaigns fought against the Chinese Communists, General Chiang Kai-shek succeeded in localizing their influence to the more remote parts of China, particularly to the upper reaches of the Yangtse Kiang. It would therefore have been logical for the Japanese, who have proclaimed as one of their major goals in China the stamping out of Communism, to have given full support to Chiang Kai-shek instead of undermining his power and then directly attacking him. Even in the earlier periods of Japanese aggression in Manchukuo and Jehol, Chiang Kai-shek was still concentrating on the struggle with Communism. When it became apparent that Japanese aggression would not stop short of a conquest of China proper, the inevitable happened. As a result of the mysterious kidnapping of Chiang Kai-shek at Sianfu in December 1936, a peace compromise was made between the Nationalist Generalissimo and the commanders of the Chinese Red Army, which eventually was transformed into the Eighth Route Army and, by one of those mysteries of Chinese politics, found itself at the opportune moment located in a position to operate on the flank of the advancing Japanese in Shansi and Shensi. The next step was just as logical: finding nothing but desultory support from the League of Nations and the Western Powers, the Nanking government came to an agreement with Soviet Russia. "A drowning man will clutch a snake," said the Turkish diplomat Reis Effendi, when under relatively similar circumstances in 1833 Turkey appealed to Russia for aid against Mehemet Ali, the rebellious Viceroy of Egypt. Whether the future will see a Soviet China in close union with Soviet Russia, is a question which it would be dangerous to attempt to answer at this juncture; but the mere fact that the question has come within the realm of plausibility is a striking testimony to the fact that here again Japan has succeeded in achieving the exact opposite of what she had set out to do. There is little doubt that the knowledge of the Sianfu transactions between Chiang Kai-shek and the Communists hastened the Japanese advance in China last July; but again it must be stated that it was Japan's earlier actions which made such a transaction possible.

The evolution of parallel moods in China and in Russia is not the sole result of the Far Eastern crisis. Something even more tangible may be noticed in the resulting shifts of population, which tend to bring the two countries physically closer to each other. Let us examine the case of Russia first. It has been said that when any particular part of the human body is ailing, the blood and the vital energies tend to stream to that particular point. Something similar takes place in the body politic, and in the past Russia has given striking evidences of this phenomenon. The menace of invasions by the Crimean Tartars led to the founding, in the 16th century, of the belt of cities in the south central steppe area such as Voronezh and Orel. A century later, the menace of Sweden led to the rise of St. Petersburg and the cities around the Gulf of Finland. Similarly, the Turkish wars of Catherine II saw the founding and rise of cities of the Black Sea region: Odéssa, Sebastopol, Ekaterinoslav, Rostov and others. In each case a semi-desert region was not only studded by new cities of strategic value but transformed by rapid colonization and the rise of agriculture and industries.

Something similar is taking place today in the Russian Far East, as a result of the Japanese menace. The Soviets, it is true, had taken over from Tsarist Russia a land already opened up by earlier colonization, but . . . Eastern Siberia and the Russian Maritime Province remained a fallow land awaiting energetic pioneer development. The attempts to develop it in the period following the building of the Chinese Eastern Railway remained artificial, and this was one reason for the failure of the Tsarist Far Eastern policy. Why should it have been artificial? Because the region east of the Baikal could not be colonized before Western Siberia had been developed, just as in the United States any attempts to develop California and the Pacific Coast would have remained unsuccessful until the corresponding rise of the Middle West had occurred. The fact that Russian history has been a movement of colonization going west-east need not be stressed here. Suffice it to say that the present center of population is moving steadily eastwards, and that it has been calculated that the center of population, when the Eurasian plain will be fully populated, will be located East of the Ural Mountains. . . .

But under normal circumstances it may have been expected that Eastern Siberia would lag behind awaiting the further development of Western Siberia. If this order has now been reversed, the cause is to be found primarily in the Japanese war menace: the whole driving power and energy of the Soviet Government has been increasingly canalized to bolster up Russia's Pacific empire. . . . The double tracking of the Transsiberian Railway, the building of the Baikal-Amur Railway, a pioneer line over virgin land, the construction of strategic highways, not to mention the development of air lines, and intensive exploitation of natural resources for army needs—all these inevitably will become milestones of progress even though at present they are serving only military purposes.

The second important result is the rise of Soviet Russia's power on the Pacific which, after an interval of a quarter of a century, has resumed the trend which was initiated in the nineties of the last century. The assembling of an airfleet, officially estimated by Japanese sources at 1,500 airplanes, and the corresponding rise of Soviet naval power, so far represented by a fleet of submarines, again estimated at from 50 to 100, and bolstered up by recently announced plans for construction of capital and other large ships, have brought about the renascence of Russia as a factor in the balance of naval power on the Pacific Ocean.

Moreover, if the comparison with blood flowing to the affected part of the human body holds good in the case of Russia, it is also applicable to the case of Japan. Manchuria and later Manchukuo, just because it has been the "Tinder Box of Asia," to use the title of a recent work, has thereby been transformed from a semi-desert into one of the most highly developed and populous regions of the Far East. Just as in the case of Russia, the efforts of Japan to strengthen its military position in Manchukuo, such as, for example, the building of a vast network of strategic railways and other works of engineering, will eventually result in further developing the country, regardless of who may become its future possessor. Thus the parallel development of the Soviet Far East and Manchukuo for rival purposes is bound to lead in the long run to a rise of new trade routes and to other important developments in the field of economic and cultural interrelations. If we

function.  But this would require a period of decades, possibly centuries, and the Russian factor has to be considered in the meantime.

Assuming that Russia in her turn meets with defeat, either at the hands of Japan alone or as a result of a combined onslaught from the west and the east, what would happen?  The loss of the Transbaikal region, and (let us hypothetically add) of Ukraine in the West, would result in the compression of Russia but not her destruction.  The vitality and youthful vigor of the Russian people have not been sapped by the present Revolution; the evidences are very much to the contrary.  One of the outstanding features of Russian history has been the tenacity with which the Russians have regained lost territories or tended to solve other frontier problems.  The long struggle of Muscovy with Lithuania and Poland from the 15th to the 18th century, the century and a half struggle with Sweden for the Baltic seaboard, and twelve wars with Turkey testify to the persistence of Russia's foreign policy notwithstanding the internal transformations of the country.  Thus one can reasonably expect that the loss of Eastern Siberia would open a similar period of long struggle which would drain the forces of Japan and not permit her to settle down.  Furthermore, the compression of Russia might make her bulge out elsewhere and Russia might overflow into North Western China, transforming that country into a battle-ground between the two neighboring imperialisms and once more hindering Japan in her attempt to consolidate her gains.

The possibility of other powers becoming involved in the present struggle and the forming of some kind of a coalition against Japan, though at present relatively remote, must not be overlooked, for this has been the solution found by history in previous cases of over-expansion of one state, from the France of Louis XIV down to the Germany of the World War.  Needless to say, it would produce the same effect on the respective positions of China and Russia as, in mechanics, the division of forces previously applied at one particular point relieves the strain on that point.

The last and perhaps less remote possibility of a Japanese defeat or breakdown, which might or might not be followed by a revolution in Japan, would naturally be welcomed in Russia, for it would remove a dangerous menace. Should, furthermore, revolution follow defeat, there would open up the possibility of a co-operation between the three great revolutionary movements of Asia which might lead to the increase of Soviet influence over the whole of Far Eastern Asia in the spirit of the principles established at the Congress of Baku.

It would therefore appear to be in the better interests of Soviet Russia at present to wait and let events mature. So long as Japan does not invade Siberia proper or Outer Mongolia and so long as the Japanese conquest, following the coastline of China, has veered off into the interior menacing the Yangtse valley and the region of Canton, the position of Soviet Russia is not only secure but extremely profitable. Japan is spending herself in an effort which apparently she underestimated, and the chances of the great maritime powers being involved become greater. Russia is able to play the same role that Japan played in the World War, when Japan at a small cost of personal expenditure reaped the benefits of a struggle which ruined her competitors and rivals.

As for Japan, whatever the outcome of the struggle, one thing is becoming apparent: there is too great a disparity between the means that Japan is able to marshal and the immensity of the goal set. It is probable therefore that the outcome of the present crisis will be very different from what the Japanese military leaders had conceived when they were planning their moves. If this outcome results in the strengthening of Russia's position in Asia and in the rise of a new great power, a unified China, modernized and strong, the present events will overshadow in importance the World War and will open a new chapter in world history.

# ON THE PEOPLE'S DEMOCRATIC DICTATORSHIP *

BY

MAO TSE-TUNG

[1949]

This date, the first of July 1949, shows that the CCP [Chinese Communist Party] has passed through twenty-eight years. Like a man, it has its childhood, youth, manhood, and old age. The CCP is no longer a child, nor is it a youth in his teens; it is an adult. When a man reaches old age he dies; it is the same with a political party. When classes are eliminated, all the instruments of class struggle, political parties and the state apparatus, will, as a result, lose their functions, become unnecessary and gradually wither away; and their historical mission accomplished, mankind will move to a higher plan of human society. We are just the opposite of the political parties of the bourgeoisie. They are afraid to talk of the elimination of classes, state authority, and party, while we openly declare that we struggle hard precisely for the creation of prerequisites which will achieve the elimination of these things. The CP and the state authority of the people's dictatorship constitute such prerequisites. Anyone who does not recognize this truth is no Communist. Young comrades who have just joined the Party and have not read Marxism-Leninism may not yet understand this truth. They must understand this truth before they can have a correct world outlook. They must understand that all mankind have to go through the process of eliminating classes, state authority, and party; the question is only one of time and conditions. The Communists in the world are more intelligent than the bourgeoisie in that respect. They understand the law governing the existence and development of things. They

* Reprinted from *A Documentary History of Chinese Communism,* by Conrad Brandt, Benjamin Schwartz, and John K. Fairbank. Copyright, 1952, by Harvard University Press. Reprinted by permission. The original source is an English translation of New China News Agency published in the *China Digest* (Hong Kong), Vol. VI, No. 7, July 13, 1949.

understand dialectics and thus see farther ahead. The bourgeoisie do not welcome this truth because they do not want to be overthrown by the people. To be overthrown—as in the case of the KMT [Kuomintang (The Nationalist Party of China)] reactionaries who are being overthrown by us at present or of Japanese imperialism which was overthrown by us along with peoples of various countries in the past—is painful and is inconceivable to the persons overthrown. But for the working class, laboring people, and Communists, the question is not one of being overthrown but of working hard and creating conditions for the natural elimination of classes, state authority, and political parties, so that mankind will enter the era of universal fraternity. We have here touched on the perspectives of the progress of mankind in order to explain the following questions. . . .

After China's defeat in the Opium War of 1840, progressive Chinese underwent countless tribulations seeking for the truth from the Western countries. . . . At that time, all Chinese who sought for progress read every book that contained any fresh Western teaching. The number of students sent to Japan, England, America, France, and Germany was staggering. Great efforts were made to learn from the West: in the nation the imperial examination system was abolished and schools established, [such measures] multiplying like bamboo shoots after rain. What I learned in my youth consisted of such things. These constituted the culture of Western bourgeois democracy, or so-called new school of learning, which included social doctrines and natural sciences of that time as opposed to the culture of China's feudalism, or so-called old school of learning. For quite a long time people who learned the new knowledge were confident that it was sure to save China. . . .

Imperialist aggression shattered the Chinese dream of learning from the West. They wondered why the teachers always practiced aggression against their pupils. The Chinese learned much from the West, but what they learned could not be put into effect. Their ideals could not be realized. Meanwhile, conditions in the country worsened day by day, and the environment was such that the people could not live. Doubt sprang up, it grew and developed. The First World War shook the whole world. The Russians carried out the October Revolution, creating the first socialist country in the world. Under the leadership of Lenin and Stalin the revolutionary energy of the great Russian proletariat and laboring people, which had lain hidden and could not be seen by foreigners, suddenly erupted like a volcano. The Chinese and all mankind then began to look differently at the Russians. Then, and only then, did there appear for the Chinese an entirely new era both in ideology and in living. The Chinese found the universal truth of Marxism-Leninism which holds good everywhere, and the face of China was changed.

It was through the introduction of the Russians that the Chinese found Marxism. Before the October Revolution the Chinese not only did not know Lenin and Stalin, but also did not know Marx and Engels. The gunfire of the October Revolution sent us Marxism-Leninism. The October Revolution helped the progressive elements of the world and of China to use the world outlook of the proletariat as the instrument for perceiving the destiny of the country, and for reconsidering their own problems. Travel the road of the Russians—this was the conclusion. In 1919, the May Fourth movement took place in China, and the CCP was formed in 1921. In his moment of despair Sun Yat-sen came across the October Revolution and the CCP. He welcomed the October Revolution, welcomed Russian help to China, and welcomed the cooperation of the CCP. Sun Yat-sen died [March 1925] and Chiang Kai-shek came into power. During the long period of twenty-two years [since 1927] Chiang Kai-shek has dragged China into hopeless straits.

During this period the anti-fascist Second World War, with the Soviet Union as its main force, defeated three big imperialist powers, weakened two other big imperialist powers, leaving only one imperialist country in the world—the United States of America, which suffered no loss. However, the domestic crisis in America is very grave. She wants to enslave the entire world and she aided Chiang Kai-shek with arms to slaughter several millions of Chinese. Under the leadership of the CCP, the Chinese people, after having driven away Japanese imperialism, fought the people's

war of liberation for three years and gained a basic victory.   Thus
the civilization of the Western bourgeoisie, the bourgeois democracy, and the pattern of the bourgeois republic all went bankrupt
in the minds of the Chinese people.   Bourgeois democracy has
given way to the people's democracy under the leadership of the
proletariat, and the bourgeois republic has given way to the
people's republic.   A possibility has thus been created of reaching socialism and Communism through the people's republic, of
attaining the elimination of classes and universal fraternity. . . .
The bourgeois republic has existed in foreign countries but cannot
exist in China, because China is a country oppressed by imperialism.   The only way for us is to travel the road of the people's
republic under the leadership of the proletariat and attain the
elimination of classes and universal fraternity. . . .

Having learned Marxism-Leninism after the October Revolution, the vanguard of the Chinese proletariat established the CCP.
Following this, it entered into the political struggle and had to
travel a zigzag path for twenty-eight years before it could gain a
basic victory.   From the experiences of twenty-eight years, just as
from the "experiences of forty years," as Sun Yat-sen said in his
will, a common conclusion has been reached, namely: "The firm
belief that to attain victory we must awaken the masses of the
people and unite ourselves in a common struggle with those peoples
of the world who treat us on the basis of equality" [quoted from
Sun's famous testament].   Sun Yat-sen had a different world
outlook from us, and started out from a different class standpoint
in observing and dealing with problems, but in the twenties of the
twentieth century, on the problem of how to struggle against imperialism, he arrived at a conclusion which was fundamentally in
agreement with ours.

Twenty-four years have elapsed since Sun Yat-sen's death, and
under the leadership of the CCP, Chinese revolutionary theory and
practice have made big forward strides, fundamentally changing
the realities of China.   Up to the present, the Chinese people have
gained the following two major and basic lessons of experiences:
(1) We must awaken the masses in the country.   This is to unite
the working class, the peasant class, the petty bourgeoisie, the

national bourgeoisie into a national united front under the leadership of the working class, and develop it into a state of the people's democratic dictatorship led by the working class with the alliance of workers and peasants as its basis. (2) We must unite in a common struggle with those nations of the world who treat us on the basis of equality and with the people of all countries. This is to ally ourselves with the Soviet Union, to ally ourselves with all the New Democratic countries, and to ally ourselves with the proletariat and the broad masses of the people in other countries, to form an international united front.

"You lean to one side." Precisely so. The forty years' experience of Sun Yat-sen and the twenty-eight years' experience of the CCP have taught us to believe that in order to win and to consolidate the victory we must lean to one side. The experiences of forty years and twenty-eight years, respectively, show that, without exception, the Chinese people either lean to the side of imperialism or to the side of socialism. To sit on the fence is impossible; a third road does not exist. We oppose the Chiang Kai-shek reactionary clique who lean to the side of imperialism; we also oppose the illusion of a third road. Not only in China but also in the world, without exception, one either leans to the side of imperialism or to the side of socialism. Neutrality is mere camouflage and a third road does not exist.

"You are too provocative." We are talking of dealing with domestic and foreign reactionaries; that is, imperialists and their running dogs, and not of any other people. With regard to these people [foreign and domestic reactionaries], the question of provocation does not arise, for whether we are provocative or not makes no difference to their being reactionaries. Only by drawing a clear line between reactionaries and revolutionaries, only by exposing the designs and plots of the reactionaries, arousing vigilance and attention within the revolutionary ranks, and only by raising our own morale while subjugating the arrogance of the enemy—can the reactionaries be isolated, conquered, or replaced. In front of a wild beast you cannot show the slightest cowardice. We must learn from Wu Sung. . . . To Wu Sung, the tiger on the Chingyang ridge would eat people all the same whether they were provocative or not. You either kill the tiger or are eaten by it; there is no third choice.

"We want to do business." Entirely correct. Business has to be done. We only oppose domestic and foreign reactionaries who hamper us from doing business, and do not oppose any other people. It should be known that it is no other than imperialists and their lackeys—the Chiang Kai-shek reactionary clique—who hinder our doing business with foreign countries and even hinder our establishing diplomatic relations with foreign countries. Unite all forces at home and abroad to smash the domestic and foreign reactionaries and then there will be business, and the possibility of establishing diplomatic relations with all foreign countries on the basis of equality, mutual benefits, and mutual respect of territorial sovereignty.

"Victory is also possible without international assistance"—this is an erroneous conception. In the era when imperialism exists, it is impossible for the true people's revolution of any country to win its own victory without assistance in various forms from the international revolutionary forces, and it is also impossible to consolidate the victory even when it is won. The great October Revolution was thus won and consolidated, as Stalin has told us long ago. It was also in this way that the three imperialist countries were defeated and the new democratic countries established. This is and will be the case with the People's China at present and in the future. Let us think it over; if the Soviet Union did not exist, or there had been no victory in the anti-fascist Second World War, and especially for us, no defeat of Japanese imperialism, if the various new democratic countries had not come into being, and no rising struggles of the oppressed nations in the East, if there had been no struggles of the masses of people in the United States, Britain, France, Germany, Italy, Japan, and other capitalist countries against the reactionary cliques ruling over them, and if there were no sum-total of these things, then the reactionary forces bearing down on us would surely be many times greater than they are at present. Could we have won victory under such circumstances? Obviously not; it would also be impossible to consolidate the victory even when it was won. The Chinese people have had much experience in this matter. The remark made by Sun Yat-sen before his death, that alliance must be made with the international revolutionary forces, reflected this experience long ago.

"We need the assistance of the British and American governments." This is also a childish idea at the moment. At present the rulers in Britain and the United States are still imperialists. Would they extend aid to a people's state? If we do business with these countries or suppose these countries would be willing in the future to lend us money on terms of mutual benefit, what would be the reason for it? It would be because the capitalists of these countries want to make money and the bankers want to earn interest to relieve their own crisis; that would be no aid to the Chinese people. The Communist Parties and progressive parties and groups in these countries are now working to bring about business relations, and even to establish diplomatic relations with us. This is well meant; it means to help us, and it cannot be regarded in the same light as the acts of the bourgeoisie in these countries. During his lifetime Sun Yat-sen repeatedly appealed to the imperialist countries for aid. The outcome was futile, and instead he met with merciless attacks. In his lifetime Sun Yat-sen received international aid only once, and that was from the U.S.S.R. The reader can refer to the will of Dr. Sun Yat-sen, in which he did not ask the people to look and hope for aid from imperialist countries, but earnestly bade them "to unite with those peoples of the world who treat us on the basis of equality." Dr. Sun had had the experience; he had been duped. We must remember his words and not be duped again. Internationally we belong to the anti-imperialist front headed by the U.S.S.R., and we can look for genuine friendly aid only from that front, and not from the imperialist front.

"You are dictatorial." Dear sirs, you are right; that is exactly what we are. The experience of several decades, amassed by the Chinese people, tells us to carry out the people's democratic dictatorship. That is, the right of reactionaries to voice their opinions must be abolished and only the people are allowed to have the right of voicing their opinions.

Who are the "people"?    At the present stage in China, they are the working class, the peasant class, the petty bourgeoisie, and national bourgeoisie.    Under the leadership of the working class and the CP, these classes unite together to form their own state and elect their own government so as to carry out a dictatorship over the lackeys of imperialism—the landlord class, the bureaucratic capitalist class, and the KMT reactionaries and their henchmen representing these classes—to suppress them, allowing them only to behave properly and not to talk and act wildly.    If they talk and act wildly their action will be prohibited and punished immediately.    The democratic system is to be carried out within the ranks of the people, giving them freedom of speech, assembly, and association.    The right to vote is given only to the people and not to the reactionaries.    These two aspects, namely, democracy among the people and dictatorship over the reactionaries, combine to form the people's democratic dictatorship.

Why should it be done this way?    Everybody clearly knows that otherwise the revolution would fail, and the people would meet with woe and the State would perish.

"Don't you want to eliminate state authority?"    Yes, but we do not want it at present, we cannot want it at present.    Why?    Because imperialism still exists, the domestic reactionaries still exist, and classes in the country still exist.    Our present task is to strengthen the apparatus of the people's state, which refers mainly to the people's army, people's police, and people's courts, for the defence of the country and the protection of the people's interests; and with this as a condition, to enable China to advance steadily, under the leadership of the working class and the CP, from an agricultural to an industrial country, and from a New Democratic to a Socialist and Communist society, to eliminate classes and to realize the state of universal fraternity.    The army, police, and courts of the state are instruments by which classes oppress classes.    To the hostile classes the state apparatus is the intrument of oppression.    It is violent, and not "benevolent."    "You are not benevolent."    Just so.    We decidedly will not exercise benevolence towards the reactionary acts of the reactionaries and reactionary classes.    Our benevolence applies only to the people, and not to the reactionary acts of the reactionaries and reactionary classes outside the people.

The function of the people's state is to protect the people.   Only when there is the people's state, is it possible for the people to use democratic methods on a nation-wide and all-round scale to educate and reform themselves, to free themselves from the influence of reactionaries at home and abroad (this influence is at present still very great and will exist for a long time and cannot be eliminated quickly), to unlearn the bad habits and ideas acquired from the old society and not to let themselves travel on the erroneous path pointed out by the reactionaries, but to continue to advance and develop towards a Socialist and Communist society accomplishing the historic mission of completely eliminating classes and advancing towards a universal fraternity.

The methods we use in this field are democratic; that is, methods of persuasion and not coercion.   When people break the law they will be punished, imprisoned, or even sentenced to death. But these are individual cases and are different in principle from the dictatorship over the reactionary class as a class.

After their political regime is overthrown the reactionary classes and the reactionary clique will also be given land and work and a means of living; they will be allowed to re-educate themselves into new persons through work, provided they do not rebel, disrupt, or sabotage. If they are unwilling to work, the people's state will compel them to work. Propaganda and educational work will also be carried out among them, and, moreover, with care and adequacy, as we did among captured officers. This can also be called "benevolent administration," but we shall never forgive their reactionary acts and will never let their reactionary activity have the possibility of a free development.

Such re-education of the reactionary classes can only be carried out in the state of the people's democratic dictatorship.   If this work is well done the main exploiting classes of China—the landlord and bureaucratic capitalist classes—will be finally eliminated. Of the exploiting classes there remain the national bourgeoisie among many of whom appropriate educational work can be carried out at the present stage.   When socialism is realized, that is, when the nationalization of private enterprises has been carried out, they can be further educated and reformed. The people have in their hands a powerful state apparatus and are not afraid of the rebellion of the national bourgeois class.

The grave problem is that of educating the peasants. The peasants' economy is scattered. Judging by the experience of the Soviet Union, it requires a very long time and careful work to attain the socialization of agriculture. Without the socialization of agriculture, there will be no complete and consolidated socialism. And to carry out the socialization of agriculture a powerful industry with state-owned enterprises as the main component must be developed. The state of the people's democratic dictatorship must step by step solve this problem of the industrialization of the country. . . .

The foreign reactionaries who vilify us for carrying out "dictatorship" and "totalitarianism" are in fact the very people who are carrying out dictatorship and totalitarianism of one class, the bourgeoisie, over the proletariat and other people. They are the very people referred to by Sun Yat-sen as the bourgeois class in countries of modern times who oppress the common people. Chiang Kai-shek's counter-revolutionary dictatorship was learned from these reactionary fellows. . . .

The revolutionary dictatorship and the counter-revolutionary dictatorship are opposite in nature. The former learns from the latter. This process of learning is very important, for if the revolutionary people do not learn the methods of ruling over counter-revolutionaries, they will not be able to maintain their regime, which will be overthrown by the reactionary cliques at home and abroad. The reactionary cliques at home and abroad will then restore their rule in China and bring woe to the revolutionary people.

The basis of the people's democratic dictatorship is the alliance of the working class, peasant class, and the urban petty-bourgeois class, and is mainly the alliance of the working class and the peasant class because they constitute eighty to ninety per cent of the Chinese population. It is mainly through the strength of these two classes that imperialism and the KMT reactionary clique were overthrown. The passing from New Democracy to Socialism mainly depends on the alliance of these two classes.

The people's democratic dictatorship needs the leadership of the working class, because only the working class is most far-sighted, just and unselfish and endowed with revolutionary thoroughness. The history of the entire revolution proves that without the leadership of the working class, the revolution is bound to fail, and with the leadership of the working class, the revolution is victorious. In the era of imperialism no other class in any country can lead any genuine revolution to victory. This is clearly proved by the fact that the Chinese national bourgeoisie has led the revolution many times and each time had failed.

The national bourgeoisie is of great importance at the present stage. Imperialism is still standing near us and this enemy is very fierce. A long time is required for China to realize true economic independence and become free from reliance on imperialist nations. Only when China's industries are developed, and she no longer depends economically on powerful nations, can there be real independence. The proportion of China's modern industry in the entire national economy is still very small. There are still no reliable figures at present, but according to certain data it is estimated that modern industry only occupies about ten per cent of the total productive output in the national economy of the whole country. To cope with imperialist oppression, and to raise our backward economic status one step higher, China must utilize all urban and rural factors of capitalism which are beneficial and not detrimental to the national economy and the people's livelihood, and unite with the national bourgeoisie in a common struggle. Our present policy is to restrict capitalism and not to eliminate it. But the national bourgeoisie cannot be the leader of the revolutionary united front and should not occupy the main position of state power. This is because the social and economic status of the national bourgeoisie has determined its feebleness; it lacks foresight, lacks courage, and in large part fears the masses.

Sun Yat-sen advocated "awakening the masses" or "helping the peasants and workers." Who is to awaken and help them? Sun Yat-sen meant the petty bourgeoisie and the national bourgeoisie.

But this is in fact not feasible.    Sun Yat-sen's forty years of revolutionary work was a failure.    Why?    The reason lies precisely here, in that in the era of imperialism it is impossible for the bourgeoisie to lead any true revolution towards success.

Our twenty-eight years are entirely different.    We have plenty of invaluable experience.    A party with discipline, armed with the theories of Marx, Engels, Lenin, and Stalin, employing the method of self-criticism, and linked up closely with the masses; an army led by such a party; a united front of various revolutionary strata and groups led by such a party; these three are our main lessons of experience.    They all mark us off from our predecessors.    Relying on these three things, we have won a basic victory. . . .

In the twenty-eight long years of the Party we have done only one thing, and that is, we have won the basic victory.    This is worth celebrating, because it is the people's victory and a victory in a large country like China.    But there is plenty of work before us, and, as on a march, what work has been done in the past is like the first step on a ten-thousand-mile long march.    Remnants of the enemy have still to be wiped out, and the grave task of economic reconstruction still lies before us.    Some of the things with which we are familiar will soon be laid aside, and we are compelled to tackle things with which we are unfamiliar.    This means difficulty.    The imperialists are positive that we are incapable of tackling our economic work.    They look on and wait for our failure.

We must overcome difficulties, and must master what we do not know.    We must learn economic work from all who know the ropes no matter who they are.    We must acknowledge them as our teachers, and learn from them respectfully and earnestly.    We must acknowledge our ignorance, and not pretend to know what we do not know, nor put on bureaucratic airs.    Stick to it, and eventually it will be mastered in a few months, one or two years, or three or five years.    At first some of the Communists in the U.S.S.R. also did not know how to do economic work, and the imperialists also waited for their failure.    But the CP of the Soviet Union won.    Under the leadership of Lenin and Stalin they not only could do revolutionary work but also reconstruction work.

They have already built up a great and brilliant socialist state. The CP of the U.S.S.R. is our best teacher from whom we must learn. . . . We can rely wholly on the weapon of the people's democratic dictatorship to unite all people throughout the country, except the reactionaries, and advance steadily towards the goal.

# LET A HUNDRED FLOWERS BLOOM*

BY

## MAO TSE-TUNG

[1957]

Our general subject is the correct handling of contradictions among the people. . . . Although reference will be made to contradictions between ourselves and our enemies, this discussion will center mainly on contradictions among the people. . . .

### Two Different Types of Contradictions

If we are to have a correct understanding of these two different types of contradictions, we must first of all make clear what is meant by "the people" and what is meant by "the enemy."

The term "the people" has different meanings in different countries, and in different historical periods in each country. Take our country for example. During the Japanese aggression, all those classes, strata and social groups which opposed aggression belonged to the category of the people, while the Japanese imperialists, Chinese traitors and the pro-Japanese elements belonged to the category of enemies of the people. During the war of liberation, the United States imperialists and their henchmen, the bureaucrat-capitalists and landlord class, and the Kuomintang reactionaries, who represented these two classes, were the enemies of the people, while all other classes, strata and social groups which opposed these enemies belonged to the category of the people. At this stage of building socialism, all classes, strata and social groups that approve, support and work for the cause of Socialist construction belong to the category of the people, while those social forces and

---

* From a speech given at a closed session of the Supreme State Conference of Communist China on February 27, 1957. Reprinted from *Let a Hundred Flowers Bloom. The Complete Text of "On the Correct Handling of Contradictions Among the People"* by Mao Tse-tung. With notes and an introduction by G. F. Hudson. Published by *The New Leader*, 1957.

groups that resist the Socialist revolution and are hostile to and try to wreck Socialist construction, are enemies of the people.

The contradictions between ourselves and our enemies are antagonistic ones. Within the ranks of the people, contradictions among the working people are nonantagonistic, while those between the exploiters and the exploited classes have, apart from their antagonistic aspect, a nonantagonistic aspect. Contradictions among the people have always existed, but their content differs in each period of the revolution and during the building of socialism.

In the conditions existing in China today what we call contradictions among the people include the following:

Contradictions within the working class, contradictions within the peasantry, contradictions within the intelligentsia, contradictions between the working class and the peasantry on the one hand and the intelligentsia on the other; contradictions between the working class and other sections of the working people on the one hand and the national bourgeoisie on the other; contradictions within the national bourgeoisie, and so forth. Our people's Government is a Government that truly represents the interests of the people and serves the people, yet certain contradictions do exist between the Government and the masses. These include contradictions between the interests of the state, collective interests and individual interests; between democracy and centralism; between those in positions of leadership and the led, and contradictions arising from the bureaucratic practices of certain state functionaries in their relations with the masses. All these are contradictions among the people; generally speaking, underlying the contradictions among the people is the basic identity of the interests of the people.

In our country, the contradiction between the working class and the national bourgeoisie is a contradiction among the people. The class struggle waged between the two is, by and large, a class struggle within the ranks of the people; this is because of the dual character of the national bourgeoisie in our country. In the years of the bourgeois-democratic revolution, there was a revolutionary side to their character; there was also a tendency to compromise with the enemy—this was the other side. In the period of the socialist revolution, exploitation of the working class to make profits is one side, while support of the Constitution and willingness to accept Socialist transformation is the other. The national bourgeoisie differs from the imperialists, the landlords and the bureaucrat-capitalists. The contradiction between exploiter and exploited which exists between the national bourgeoisie and the working class is an antagonistic one. But, in the concrete conditions existing in China, such an antagonistic contradiction, if properly handled, can be transformed into a nonantagonistic one and resolved in a peaceful way. But if it is not properly handled, if say, we do not follow a policy of uniting, criticizing and educating the national bourgeoisie, or if the national bourgeoisie does not accept this policy, then the contradictions between the working class and the national bourgeoisie can turn into an antagonistic contradiction as between ourselves and the enemy.

Since the contradictions between ourselves and the enemy and those among the people differ in nature, they must be solved in different ways. To put it briefly, the former is a matter of drawing a line between us and our enemies, while the latter is a matter of distinguishing between right and wrong. It is, of course, true that drawing a line between ourselves and our enemies is also a question of distinguishing between right and wrong. For example, the question as to who is right, we or the reactionaries at home and abroad—that is, the imperialists, the feudalists and bureaucrat-capitalists—is also a question of distinguishing between right and wrong, but it is different in nature from questions of right and wrong among the people. . . .

Our dictatorship is known as the people's democratic dictatorship, led by the working class and based on the worker-peasant alliance. That is to say, democracy operates within the ranks of the people, while the working class, uniting with all those enjoying civil rights, the peasantry in the first place, enforces dictatorship over the reactionary classes and elements and all those who resist Socialist transformation and oppose Socialist construction. By Civil Rights we mean, politically, freedom and democratic rights.

But this freedom is freedom with leadership and this democracy is democracy under centralized guidance, not anarchy. Anarchy does not conform to the interests or wishes of the people.

Certain people in our country were delighted when the Hungarian events took place. They hoped that something similar would happen in China, that thousands upon thousands of people would demonstrate in the streets against the People's Government. Such hopes ran counter to the interests of the masses and therefore could not possibly get their support. In Hungary, a section of the people, deceived by domestic and foreign counter-revolutionaries, made the mistake of resorting to acts of violence against the People's Government, with the result that both the state and the people suffered for it. The damage done to the country's economy in a few weeks of rioting will take a long time to repair.

There were other people in our country who took a wavering attitude toward the Hungarian events because they were ignorant about the actual world situation. They felt that there was too little freedom under our people's democracy and that there was more freedom under Western parliamentary democracy. They ask for the adoption of the two-party system of the West, where one party is in office and the other out of office. But this so-called two-party system is nothing but a means of maintaining the dictatorship of the bourgeoisie; under no circumstances can it safeguard the freedom of the working people. As a matter of fact, freedom and democracy cannot exist in the abstract, they only exist in the concrete.

In a society where there is class struggle, the exploiting classes are free to exploit the working people while the working people have no freedom from being exploited; where there is democracy for the bourgeoisie there can be no democracy for the proletariat and other working people. . . .

While we stand for freedom with leadership and democracy under centralized guidance, in no sense do we mean that coercive measures should be taken to settle ideological matters and questions involving the distinction between right and wrong among the people. Any attempt to deal with ideological matters or questions involving right and wrong by administrative order or coercive measures will not only be ineffective but harmful. We cannot abolish religion by administrative orders; nor can we force people not to believe in it. We cannot compel people to give up idealism any more than we can force them to believe in Marxism. In settling matters of an ideological nature or controversial issue among the people, we can only use democratic methods, methods of discussion, of criticism, or persuasion and education, not coercive, high-handed methods. . . .

Many dare not acknowledge openly that there still exist contradictions among the people which are the very forces that move our society forward. Many people refuse to admit that contradictions still exist in a Socialist society, with the result that when confronted with social contradictions they become timid and helpless. They do not understand that Socialist society grows more united and consolidated precisely through the ceaseless process of correctly dealing with and resolving contradictions. . . .

## The Suppression of Counter-revolution

The question of suppressing counter-revolutionaries is a question of the struggle of opposites in the contradiction between ourselves and the enemy. Within the ranks of the people, there are some who hold somewhat different views on this question. There are two kinds of persons whose views differ from ours. Those with a rightist way of thinking make no distinction between ourselves and the enemy and mistake our enemies for our own people. They regard as friends the very people the broad masses regard as enemies. Those with a leftist way of thinking so magnify contradictions between ourselves and the enemy, and regard as counter-revolutionaries persons who really are not. Both these views are wrong. . . .

After liberation, we rooted out a number of counter-revolutionaries. Some were sentenced to death because they had committed serious crimes. This was absolutely necessary; it was the demand of the people; it was done to free the masses from long years of oppression by counter-revolutionaries and all kinds of local tyrants; in other words, to set free the productive forces. If we had not done so, the masses would not have been able to lift their heads.

Since 1956, however, there has been a radical change in the situation.   Taking the country as a whole, the main force of counter-revolution has been rooted out.   Our basic task is no longer to set free the productive forces but to protect and expand them in the context of the new relations of production.   Some people do not understand that our present policy fits the present situation and our past policy fitted the past situation; they want to make use of the present policy to reverse decisions of great success we achieved in suppressing counter-revolution.   This is quite wrong, and the people will not permit it.

As regards the suppression of counter-revolution, the main thing is that we have achieved successes, but mistakes have also been made. . . .

Steps have been or are being taken to correct mistakes which have already been discovered in the work of suppressing counter-revolutionaries.   Those not yet discovered will be corrected as soon as they come to light.   Decisions on exoneration and rehabilitation should receive the same measure of publicity as the original mistaken decisions.   We promise that a comprehensive review of the work of suppressing counter-revolution will be made this year or next to sum up experience and foster a spirit of righteousness and combat unhealthy tendencies.

## The Question of Industrialists and Businessmen

The year 1956 saw the transformation of privately owned industrial and commercial enterprises into joint state-private enterprises as well as the organization of cooperatives in agriculture and handicrafts as part of the transformation of our social system. The speed and smoothness with which this was carried out are closely related to the fact that we treated the contradiction between the working class and the national bourgeoisie as a contradiction among the people.   Has this class contradiction been resolved completely?   No, not yet.   A considerable period of time is still required to do so.   However, some people say that the capitalists have been so remolded that they are now not much different from the workers and that further remolding is unnecessary.   Others go so far as to say that the capitalists are even a bit better than the workers.   Still others ask, if remolding is necessary, why does not the working class undergo remolding? Are these opinions correct? Of course, not.

In building a Socialist society, all need remolding, the exploiters as well as the working people. Who says the working class does not need it? Of course, remolding of the exploiters and that of the working people are two different types of remolding. The two must not be confused. In the class struggle and the struggle against nature, the working class remolds the whole of society, and at the same time remolds itself. It must continue to learn in the process of its work and step by step overcome its shortcomings. It must never stop doing so. Take us who are present here for example. Many of us make some progress each year; that is to say, we are being remolded each year. I myself had all sorts of non-Marxist ideas before. It was only later that I embraced Marxism. I learned a little Marxism from books and so made an initial remolding of my ideas, but it was mainly through taking part in the class struggle over the years that I came to be remolded. And I must continue to study if I am to make further progress, otherwise I shall lag behind. Can the capitalists be so clever as to need no more remolding?

Some contend that the Chinese bourgeoisie no longer has two sides to its character, but only one side. Is this true? No. On the one hand, members of the bourgeoisie have already become managerial personnel in joint state-private enterprises and are being transformed from exploiters into working people living by their own labor. On the other hand, they still receive a fixed rate of interest on their investments in the joint enterprises, that is, they have not yet cut themselves loose from the roots of exploitation. Between them and the working class there is still a considerable gap in ideology, sentiments and habits of life. How can it be said that they no longer have two sides to their character? Even when they stop receiving their fixed interest payments and rid themselves of the label "bourgeoisie," they will still need ideological remolding for quite some time. If it were held that the bourgeoisie no longer has a dual character, then such study and remolding for the capitalist would no longer be needed.

But it must be said that such a view does not tally with the actual circumstances of our industrialists, businessmen, nor with what most of them want.   During the last few years, most of them have been willing to study and have made marked progress.   Our industrialists and businessmen can be thoroughly remolded only in the course of work; they should work together with the staff and workers in the enterprises, and make the enterprises the chief centers of remolding themselves.   It is also important for them to change certain of their old views through study.   Study for them should be optional.   After they have attended study groups for some weeks, many industrialists and businessmen on returning to their enterprises find they speak more of a common language with the workers and the representatives of state shareholdings, and so work better together.   They know from personal experience that it is good for them to keep on studying and remolding themselves. The idea just referred to, that study and remolding are not necessary, does not reflect the views of the majority of industrialists and businessmen.   Only a small number of them think that way.

### The Question of Intellectuals

Contradictions within the ranks of the people in our country also find expression among our intellectuals.   Several million intellectuals who worked for the old society have come to serve the new society.   The question that now arises is how they can best meet the needs of the new society and how we can help them to do so.   This is also a contradiction among the people.

Most of our intellectuals have made marked progress during the past seven years.   They express themselves in favor of the Socialist system.   Many of them are diligently studying Marxism, and some have become Communists.   Their number, though small, is growing steadily. . . .

Since the social system of our country has changed and the economic basis of bourgeois ideology has in the main been destroyed, it is not only necessary but also possible for large numbers of our intellectuals to change their world outlook.   But a thorough change in world outlook takes quite a long time, and we should go about it patiently and not be impetuous.   Actually, there are bound to be some who are all along reluctant, ideologically, to accept Marxism-Leninism and communism.   We should not be too exacting in what we expect of them; as long as they comply with the requirements of the state and engage in legitimate pursuits, we should give them opportunities for suitable work. . . .

It seems as if the Marxism that was once all the rage is not so much in fashion now.   This being the case, we must improve our ideological and political work. . . .

Not to have a correct political point of view is like having no soul.   Ideological remolding in the past was necessary and has yielded positive results.   But it was carried on in a somewhat rough-and-ready way and the feelings of some people were hurt— this was not good.   We must avoid such shortcomings in the future. . . .

### On 'Letting a Hundred Flowers Blossom' and 'Letting a Hundred Schools of Thought Contend'

"Let a hundred flowers blossom," and "Let a hundred schools of thought contend"; how did these slogans come to be put forward?

They were put forward in the light of the specific conditions existing in China, on the basis of the recognition that various kinds of contradictions still exist in a Socialist society, and in response to the country's urgent need to speed up its economic and cultural development.

The policy of letting a hundred flowers blossom and a hundred schools of thought contend is designed to promote the flourishing of the arts and the progress of science; it is designed to enable a Socialist culture to thrive in our land.   Different forms and styles in art can develop freely and different schools in science can contend freely.   We think that it is harmful to the growth of art and science if administrative measures are used to impose one particular style of art or school of thought and to ban another.   Questions of right and wrong in the arts and sciences should be settled through free discussion in artistic and scientific circles and in the course of practical work in the arts and sciences.   They should not be settled in summary fashion.   A period of trial is often needed to determine whether something is right or wrong.   In the past, new and correct things often failed at the outset to win recognition from the majority of people and had to develop by twists and turns in struggle. Correct and good things have often at first been looked upon not as fragrant flowers but as poisonous weeds. The Copernicus theory of the solar system and Darwin's theory of evolution were once dismissed as erroneous and had to win through over bitter opposition. Chinese history offers many similar examples. In Socialist society, conditions for the growth of new things are radically different from and far superior to those in the old society. Nevertheless, it still often happens that new, rising forces are held back and reasonable suggestions smothered.

The growth of new things can also be hindered, not because of deliberate suppression, but because of lack of discernment. That is why we should take a cautious attitude in regard to questions of right and wrong in the arts and sciences, encourage free discussion, and avoid hasty conclusions. We believe that this attitude will facilitate the growth of the arts and sciences.

Marxism has also developed through struggle. At the beginning, Marxism was subjected to all kinds of attacks and regarded as a poisonous weed. It is still being attacked and regarded as a poisonous weed in many parts of the world. However, it enjoys a different position in the Socialist countries. . . .

The proletariat seeks to transform the world according to its own world outlook, so does the bourgeoisie. In this respect, the question whether socialism or capitalism will win is still not really settled. Marxists are still a minority of the entire population as well as of the intellectuals. . . .

Ideological struggle is not like other forms of struggle. Crude, coercive methods should not be used in this struggle, but only the method of painstaking reasoning. Today, socialism enjoys favorable conditions in the ideological struggle. The main power of the state is in the hands of the working people led by the proletariat. The Communist party is strong and its prestige stands high. . . .

People may ask: Since Marxism is accepted by the majority of the people in our country as the guiding ideology, can it be criticized?  Certainly it can.  As a scientific truth, Marxism fears no criticism.  If it did, and could be defeated in argument, it would be worthless. . . .  Marxists should not be afraid of criticism from any quarter.  Quite the contrary, they need to steel and improve themselves and win new positions in the teeth of criticism and the storm and stress of struggle.  Fighting against wrong ideas is like being vaccinated—a man develops greater immunity from disease after the vaccine takes effect.  Plants raised in hothouses are not likely to be robust.  Carrying out the policy of letting a hundred flowers blossom and a hundred schools of thought contend will not weaken but strengthen the leading position of Marxism in the ideological field.

What should our policy be toward non-Marxist ideas?  As far as unmistakable counter-revolutionaries and wreckers of the social-ist cause are concerned, the matter is easy; we simply deprive them of their freedom of speech.  But it is quite a different matter when we are faced with incorrect ideas among the people.  Will it do to ban such ideas and give them no opportunity to express them-selves?  Certainly not. . . .

In the political life of our country, how are our people to deter-mine what is right and what is wrong in our words and actions? Basing ourselves on the principles of our Constitution, the will of the overwhelming majority of our people and the political pro-grams jointly proclaimed on various occasions by our political parties and groups, we believe that, broadly speaking, words and actions can be judged right if they:

1.  Help to unite the people of our various nationalities, and do not divide them;

2.  Are beneficial, not harmful, to Socialist transformation and Socialist construction;

3.  Help to consolidate, not undermine or weaken, the people's democratic dictatorship;

4.  Help to consolidate, not undermine or weaken, democratic centralism;

5.  Tend to strengthen, not to cast off or weaken, the leadership of the Communist party;

6.  Are beneficial, not harmful, to international Socialist soli-darity and the solidarity of the peace-loving peoples of the world.

Of these six criteria, the most important are the Socialist path and the leadership of the party. These criteria are put forward in order to foster, and not hinder, the free discussion of various questions among the people. . . .

Naturally, in judging the truthfulness of scientific theories or assessing the æsthetic value of works of art, other pertinent criteria are needed, but these six political criteria are also applicable to all activities in the arts or sciences. In a Socialist country like ours, can there possibly be any useful scientific or artistic activity which runs counter to these political criteria?

All that is set out above stems from the specific historical conditions in our country. Since conditions vary in different Socialist countries and with different Communist parties, we do not think that other countries and parties must or need to follow the Chinese way.

# NEW PHASE OF MAO'S REVOLUTION *

BY

## G. F. HUDSON

[1958]

A Shanghai repair shop in former days is said to have proudly displayed a placard in English reading: "Any mortal thing can do." With suitable adaptation to the jargon of modern Communist boast-and-boost propaganda, the phrase might well be taken to express the spirit of the new phase of the Chinese Communist revolution initiated by the special "second session" of the Eighth Party Congress of the CPC held in May 1958 (the original session having been convened in September 1956). The opening of the Congress on May 5 coincided with the publication in the party organ *Jen-min jih-pao* of the tirade against Tito which launched the new drive against the Yugoslav heresy in the Communist world, and the proceedings of the Congress (in so far as they were reported, which was only partially) were marked by a combination of invective against revisionism (and its Chinese equivalent, "bourgeois rightism") and demands for "leaping progress" in economic expansion.

The two themes were linked together by the contention that revisionism, at least in its indirect influence, was to blame for the slow development of production: the creative urge of the masses, craving the opportunity to forge ahead at high speed, was being thwarted and frustrated by the faint-hearted caution of officials and managers who underestimated the productive potential of the Chinese people. The task of the party cadres was now not so much to stimulate the masses to greater efforts as to break down the obstacles, ultimately of an ideological character, which were "restricting the forces of production" already operative. Mao

---

* From *Problems of Communism*, Vol. VII, No. 6, November-December 1958, published by the United States Information Agency, Washington, D.C. Reprinted by permission.

Tse-tung was quoted as declaring that "the liberation of the productive force of the laboring people has the same effect as the smashing of the nucleus of an atom."

The new phase of Chinese communism must be viewed in relation to the situation which confronted the leadership during the first four months of 1958. There were signs that this situation was considered far from satisfactory, whether from the political or from the economic angle. Politically, the period of the "hundred flowers" had been extremely disturbing and demoralizing. Although we cannot know even now quite what was going on in the seats of power in Peiping when the policy was tried out, it seems better to regard it as an experiment in relaxation which got out of control rather than as a cleverly laid trap to bring concealed opponents out into the open. No regime, even with the intention of operating as an *agent provocateur,* could really have wanted the blasts of only too telling criticism to which the institutions and policies of Communist China were exposed, by license from itself, in the spring of 1957. The dangerous thoughts were, indeed, quickly driven underground again, and the critics vilified and humiliated, but immense damage had already been done. The seeds of doubt had been sown everywhere, and the work of years of indoctrination and propaganda suddenly upset, by a few weeks of free speech. The intensity of the campaign against revisionism, which continued in growing volume after all public antagonism to the regime had been silenced, was evidence of the wide circulation of the ideas expressed during the interlude of toleration, and of the seriousness with which the Communist leadership regarded this opposition.

Moreover, at the same time that the party had to cope with the political disarray resulting from its ill-judged attempt to combine an ideological dictatorship with a measure of intellectual liberty, it was also confronted with alarming difficulties on the economic front. Having collectivized agriculture and virtually expropriated the remaining private sectors of industry during 1955-56, the regime now found itself directly responsible for all branches of the national economy and discovered that in many of them its administration had been unequal to the task. The press was filled

with complaints of bottlenecks and shortages, of targets unattained
and work held up for lack of essential supplies.

In most cases there is no reason to suppose that these muddles
and failures were due to anything but the inexperience and incompetence to be expected in the early stages of a planned economy,
but the unsettling and bewildering effects of the unleashing of
criticism in 1957 may also have been an important factor adverse
to the single-minded zeal required for a great production drive.
Mao Tse-tung at any rate appears to have viewed the shortcomings
in the economic field as largely the outcome of a political inade-
quacy, and to have decided to overcome the economic obstacles
by a new political campaign. Instead of concluding from the
failure to reach set targets that these had been too high, he inferred
that they had been too low, and the planners were charged with
the political sin of insufficient faith in the capacities of the people.
The officials of the Ministry of Coal, who had failed to keep factories properly supplied, were told that they had been "suppressing
rather than encouraging the initiative of the masses," and were
ordered to increase production by 40 percent in the coming year.
All production targets were revised upwards, often drastically, and
any suggestions that they were impossible of fulfilment were now
attributed not to any honest technical misgivings (which might
be well- or ill-founded), but to a basic ideological defect tending toward revisionist heresy and liable to end in counterrevolution.

The whole idea of gradual economic progress now fell under
a ban; progress should be by "leaps." Nothing was impossible
for China's vast population, and officials in charge of production
must cease to obstruct its wonder-working "initiative." Whether
the masses really had any such initiative outside the minds of Mao
and his associates was not a question which could be discussed; it
had to be accepted as an article of faith, and the masses themselves
had to conform to the Communist picture of them, for if anyone
were to resist or oppose the imposition of increased tasks decreed
by the popular will, he would be clearly marked by such an attitude
as a counterrevolutionary. Thus, while the Communist leaders
were representing themselves as merely deferring to a mass initia-

tive, they were at the same time preparing to justify a great campaign of repression and coercion in the name of removing impediments to the will of the people.

## THE ROLE OF THE "COMMUNES"

It soon became apparent that the new effort at economic expansion was no ordinary production drive, but a new stage of the revolution, in which a further transformation of society was to be carried out concurrently with a decisive breakthrough in the process of industrializing China. All difficulties were to be overcome by taking the offensive, by a relentless attack carried out with what used to be called, in the days of Stalin's first Five-Year Plan, "Bolshevik firmness." To maximize the productive force of the masses and operate it with a minimum of capital equipment and virtually without incentives in the form of immediate improvements in standards of living, a new form of social organization was needed, and this was to be provided by so-called "communes." These institutions were sprung quite suddenly on the Chinese people; mass propaganda for them began only in July. But once started, they multiplied at high speed during August and September, and it probably was not altogether a coincidence that this same period witnessed the deliberate creation by Peiping of the international crisis over Quemoy.

The significance of the communes can be studied on two levels —the practical and the theoretical. To consider the practical first, the commune appears intended as an appropriate answer to a number of difficulties which have confronted the Communists in their attempt to carry out "socialist construction" in China. One of the most formidable of these has been the government's failure to control the movement of labor between the countryside and the towns. Of course, the industrialization of China required in any case that large numbers of workers be drawn from the rural areas into industry, but owing to the frequent revisions of plans and the difficulties of estimating labor requirements, there has been a tendency for peasants attracted by hopes of better conditions of life than in the villages, to migrate to the towns in numbers far greater than have been needed, resulting in large-scale urban unemployment. To cope with these uncontrolled movements of labor, the Communists have worked out schemes for labor brigades which can be directed to work either in the country (including the construction of dikes and canals as well as agriculture) or in the local town, as planning requires. Since, in the average commune, an urban centre will be combined with surrounding villages in a single economic unit, it should be easier to regulate and harness the available labor force within the commune than if various industrial enterprises have to bid for labor from the collective farms.

The commune also has its advantages for a policy which seeks to combine a decentralized socialist economy with central political control. In their moves to end the excessive concentration of industry and make fuller use of a dispersed workshop production in various branches of the economy, including peasant handicrafts, the Chinese Communists have certainly been following the Soviet example to some extent, but they have also been responding to special conditions in China, among which the still serious poverty of communications and transport is the most important. But it is the natural tendency of the totalitarian state to centralize and concentrate, and if the economy is to be more dispersed and localized, a serious problem of control at once arises; moreover, when the control problem is compounded by a recent collectivization of agriculture, the situation obviously can be very formidable for the ruling party. In Russia, where the Soviet power has existed for four decades and collective farms for nearly three, and where, moreover, there was a tradition of strong centralized administration from before the Bolshevik Revolution, the difficulties are less acute than in China, where effective centralized rule has only recently been established for the first time and the total numbers of peasants brought into the collectives are nearly three times as great. In such circumstances there is a real danger that the central government may be defeated by the sheer multiplicity of the rural economic units it has to administer, and their amalgamation into fewer and larger entities offers considerable administrative advantages.

## MILITARY AND SOCIAL SIGNIFICANCE

Military considerations also have undoubtedly played a part, in both the USSR and China, in schemes for economic decentralization. The chances for any power to survive a nuclear war depend largely on the degree of peacetime dispersal of industry and administrative services; a socialist economy is especially vulnerable if it is directed from a warren of offices in a capital city which can be knocked out at one blow. From the outset Peiping has laid emphasis on the military functions of the communes; it has declared that the same organization which will be used to mobilize labor for whatever purpose it is needed can be used also for defense in time of war. It appears, indeed, that the communes are to be run on semi-military lines and that their members will form militia units available either for partisan resistance in the event of foreign invasion or for the suppression of local disturbances.

Finally, the design of economic life in the communes is aimed at breaking down what the Communists regard as the principal obstacle to the attainment of their ends—the cohesion of the family as the traditional basis of Chinese society. The principle of collective work is to be carried out thoroughly; not only are young children to be cared for in crêches so that women can work on the land or in mines and factories, but all meals are to be taken, if possible, in canteens, and household cleaning, sewing and mending will be done by squads going from house to house, so that there will be virtually nothing left to be done privately in the home; in this way it is apparently hoped that the family, already weakened by the setting of children against their parents and by the encouragement of informing to the party or the police against close relatives, will lose all significance as a social unit, since the individual will pass almost his whole life in the wider group activities of the commune.

It is primarily in this connection that the new policies in Communist China appear to be ideologically, and not just practically, significant, for they bear an imprint of utopian extremism which goes beyond anything currently practiced in Soviet Russia. In the USSR, the early visions of a perfect society without personal private property, family ties or the use of money have faded with the passing of time; in China, on the contrary, there is still a fanatical faith in the early attainment of the utopian paradise of primitive Marxism. The present drive for "leaping progress" is no doubt genuinely intended to bring about enormous increases in production, and the communes may contribute to this end: but the new, intensive attack on individualism is also conceived as an end in itself and might be continued even if it were to prove economically a mistake. The propaganda of the current campaign has been full of a quasi-religious exhortation to collectivist virtue. People are urged to forget their private interests and devote themselves to the common task with utter selflessness; they must not think about their wages or conditions of work, but only about producing "more, better, faster and more thriftily"; they must "surrender their hearts" and "break out from the small world of individualism into the big world of communism." The Chinese people is being driven harder than ever before; at the same time, it is being led to expect the millennium in the near future and is being urged to an absolute break, not only with the social class order of the past, but also with all the habitual ways of living.

## QUEMOY AND THE NEW LINE

Such pressure for total change necessarily involves high emotional tensions and strains in the population, with risks of resistance and revolt, and it is not in any way surprising that the rulers of Communist China should seek to rally popular support and close the ranks by appealing to patriotic passions against an external enemy. There is in any case the patriotic motive of making China great and powerful through industrialization and of wiping out the backwardness and humiliations of the last century. But a more immediate stimulus is also needed to forge national unity and arouse patriotic enthusiasm to its highest pitch. The Chinese nation must be rallied against "imperialism," which to Peiping means against America. There must be an apparent threat of attack, but not real danger of a major war; the external tension must be such that the government can gain prestige and make tangible gains by a strong policy in a situation verging on but not reaching large-scale belligerency.

The conditions for a policy of this kind are not easy to arrange, and any reckless adventure might well have fatal consequences for the regime. A Communist state is highly vulnerable when in the throes of a major economic reconstruction, and for this reason many political commentators have regarded big programs of economic development in Communist countries as guarantees of peace. Their rulers, it is held, will want to avoid complications in foreign affairs when they have their hands full with internal problems. On the other hand, it is just when a Communist government is pressing hardest on its people that it has most need of an external enemy to stir up patriotic emotions and provide a pretext for discrediting opponents as agents of a foreign power.

During the period of the Soviet first Five-Year Plan, it was too dangerous for the Soviet Union, isolated as it then was, to pursue an aggressive policy or provoke external conflicts, but the myth of an impending imperialist attack was continually projected and was dramatized by means of the Ramzin and other show trials. Later in the 1930's, when Stalin was faced with a real menace from the expansionist policies of Germany and Japan, he made full use of it in framing the Old Bolsheviks. China today is in a happier position than Russia formerly was in that she can avail herself of Soviet protection if she gets into trouble by provocations in foreign policy. Indeed, this was clearly demonstrated in the Korean war, when Communist China was able to send an army to fight against the United Nations in the Korean peninsula without suffering any retaliation on her own territory because of Western concern that any widening of hostilities might involve war with Russia.

In precipitating the crisis over the offshore islands, it seems probable that Peiping counted on the anticipated reluctance of the United States' NATO allies to back a policy of defending the islands at the risk of war, so that there was a good possibility for Communist China, with Soviet backing, to confront an isolated America in a brink-of-war crisis. The deliberate manner in which the offensive against Quemoy was launched, less than a month after Khrushchev's visit to Peiping and just after the commencement of the nationwide propaganda drive for the establishment of the communes, indicates that it was a step planned very consciously and with a careful calculation of risks. The crisis was at once used to whip up patriotic enthusiasm and fresh hatred against America, to justify mobilization of the militia, and to commend the communes as pillars of national defense. . . .

It is noteworthy in this connection that Chinese Communist propaganda systematically endeavors to deny the Nationalists any reality as a political force and to represent them simply as American puppets. The Chinese Communists always speak of the Americans as "occupying" Formosa and thus as having actually seized Chinese territory, not as merely protecting the residue of the former governing power in China. This line of propaganda not only keeps continually before the minds of the Chinese on the mainland the picture of America as an aggressive enemy always looking for an opportunity to strike at People's China, but also identifies the Nationalist regime with foreign domination. The fact is that the Nationalist government on Formosa represents a serious political threat to Peiping just because it *is* a Chinese government and administration on Chinese territory and not a mere aggregate of exiles in scattered foreign countries like the refugees from the Communist regimes of the Soviet Union, Poland or Hungary. The Nationalists maintain a state and an economy "in being" which offer a Chinese alternative to the Communist system, and the political attraction of this alternative is likely to increase in proportion to the aggravation of conditions on the mainland as the masses are made to suffer for the sake of high-speed industrialization and enforced collectivism. In deciding to step up the pressure of their revolution, therefore, it was a necessity for the Communist leaders to do something to discredit, humiliate, demoralize and, if possible, liquidate the Nationalist regime concurrently with "leaping progress" in the domestic field. . . .

PEIPING AND ANTI-REVISIONISM

A foreign policy of accentuated conflict with the strongest of the Western powers, however, involves reliance on the solidity of Communist China's military alliance with the Soviet Union and on the cohesion of the Communist bloc as a whole. Logically, therefore, it must be of special importance for Peiping to denounce and discredit any ideological tendencies in the Communist world which threaten that cohesion, and to oppose any inclinations on the part of the Soviet Union itself towards a relaxation of tension in its relations with the West. Hence the initiative taken ·by Communist China in launching the new campaign of Marxist-Leninist orthodoxy against Tito. From the Chinese point of view, the unforgivable sin of Yugoslav communism was its neutralism in foreign policy, its ostentatious aloofness from the Warsaw Pact and impartial condemnation of military blocs, those among Communist states no less than those of the Western powers. On the score of domestic policy, Yugoslavia was far more respectable than Poland; Tito firmly maintained the single-party system and had shown by the imprisonment of Djilas that no fundamental criticism of Communist rule would be tolerated in Yugoslavia. But Yugoslav neutralism was a crying scandal, and if it were not vigorously denounced and condemned, it might influence other Communist countries. After all, the Hungarian insurgents, in demanding the withdrawal of Hungary from the Warsaw Pact in October 1956, had only followed the Yugoslav example.

However, Khrushchev, through his gamble of reconciliation with Tito in 1955, had so deeply committed himself personally to the hope of bringing Tito ultimately back into the Communist bloc that he was extremely reluctant to face the fact of permanent Yugoslav recalcitrance. . . . It therefore fell to China to take the lead in the political onslaught against Tito. . . . Moscow followed it up, but with less asperity and with vacillations which suggested that even at the eleventh hour Khrushchev was still hoping for Tito's acceptance of some formula which could be represented as a recantation. There was no response, however, from Tito's side, and finally a line of blood was drawn between the Soviet Union and Yugoslavia and a stern warning given to all revisionists in Eastern Europe by the execution of Nagy and other leaders of the Hungarian revolt, who had left the asylum of the Yugoslav Embassy in Budapest with a Soviet safe-conduct. There is no direct evidence that the Chinese Communists had anything to do with the executions, but the glee with which the news was announced in the Chinese press indicated that the action had the entire approval of the Peiping leadership.

The Chinese compulsion to strengthen the Communist bloc as a united power in world affairs did not stop at merely combatting tendencies towards neutralism; it extended to an endeavor to obtain formal recognition of the leadership of the Soviet Union in the common cause of communism.  The need for such an avowal arose particularly from the attitude of Poland, where anti-Soviet feeling had produced an unwillingness not only to defer to Soviet "experience" in domestic matters but also to conform to Soviet requirements in matters of foreign policy.  The Chinese Communist view was in agreement with that of the Poles on the right of each Communist state to frame its internal policy according to its special problems and conditions, but Peiping insisted that policies in the international field must be coordinated and that this could be done only by accepting the leadership of a single power, which had to be the Soviet Union.  At first sight it may seem strange to find China—which might be expected to be jealous, considering its great size, population and traditional pride, of any Soviet preeminence in the fraternity of Communist states—not merely failing to oppose, but even actively promoting, Moscow's supremacy.  In part this may be regarded as a *quid pro quo* for the support which Peiping claimed from Moscow for its own purposes.  But, more fundamentally, it appears to reflect the Chinese conception of the requirements of "proletarian internationalism" —a belief that the Communist bloc cannot be effective internationally unless it has a recognized controlling leadership, and that only the Soviet Union, with its great preponderance of industrial and military power, is capable of performing this function.

Mao Tse-tung, not unreasonably, saw a danger that too much Polish independence might bring dissension and disunity to the bloc in a time of crisis, and he considered that China's part was to help in persuading the Poles to accept a certain degree of subordination to Moscow in return for Mao's moral backing of Gomulka for that part of the latter's program which involved Poland's right to manage her internal affairs.  Already when Chou En-lai visited Warsaw in January 1957, it was reported that he tried to get

Gomulka to acknowledge Soviet international leadership in the joint communique they were to issue, but received the reply that the state of public feeling in Poland at that time made such a gesture out of the question.

Ten months later, when the leaders of the governing Communist parties of the world gathered in Moscow to celebrate the fortieth anniversary of the Bolshevik Revolution, the Chinese renewed their persuasion of the Poles and this time succeeded in inducing them to put their signature to the 12-party declaration which recognized the preeminent position of the Soviet Union at the same time that it denounced revisionism as the greatest current danger to the Communist cause. In Poland, the more liberal-minded of Gomulka's followers had earlier been enthusiastic about Mao's expositions of the "hundred flowers" principle and the methods of resolving contradictions among the people, and for a while there had been talk of a "Warsaw-Peiping axis" to check the domination of the Soviet Union in the Communist world. There was correspondingly bitter disappointment when China appeared to desert Poland and throw her weight on the side of Moscow.

### THE IRON LAW: PARTY SUPREMACY

But the policies of the Chinese Communist leadership over the past three years should not be regarded as merely the result of a fickle opportunism. They have reflected rather an adaptation to facts which have been discovered to be different from what they were thought to be. Between the beginning of 1956 and the middle of 1957, the outlook of the ruling circles in Peiping, and particularly of Mao himself, was colored by an exaggerated optimism with regard to the popular support enjoyed by the Communist Party and the prospects of China's smooth and rapid achievement of large-scale industrialization on a socialist basis. From this Mao drew the conclusion that a milder and more relaxed policy could be pursued without in any way endangering the political supremacy of the party and the progress of socialist construction. There is no reason to doubt that he preferred to lighten the burden of the regime if he could, and that the events in Hungary confirmed him in his belief that the greatest danger for the party in China lay in the tendency to lose contact with the masses and become identified with an oppressive bureaucratic system.   Hence his endeavors both to give more freedom of thought and criticism to the intelligentsia and to provide some scope for the expression of discontent among the people, even to the extent of tolerating strikes and minor disturbances which might represent harmless contradictions between the government and the governed.   But always there was the reservation that the whole apparatus of repression and coercion must be called into play again if it should prove that the relaxation was endangering the foundations of the regime.

A change of policy back from soft to hard need not involve any reversal of principle, for the party always remained, in Mao's theory, the sole judge of whether criticisms of itself were permissible and whether any particular conflict was to be regarded as a non-antagonistic one "among the people" or as an antagonistic one "with the enemy."   The party, indeed, must be the judge of how much violence or intolerance is needed in order to maintain its monopoly of power, and this is a matter of weighing the various elements and possibilities in a given concrete situation. The only fixed principles are those of maintaining the rule of the party and of building socialism.

The reaction in China, the turn from relaxation and indulgence to ferocious persecution and intransigence, has resulted from the discovery that Mao was not loved as much as he thought he was. Undoubtedly he wishes to be loved by his people, and it is always fatally easy for a dictator, who has dragooned a society by suppressing opposition and rigging elections, to believe in the reality of the universal praise and adulation that surround him.   The shock is all the greater when an over-confident raising of the lid suddenly discloses the disaffection hitherto kept underground. But for a Marxist-Leninist who is convinced that history is on his side and that the mission of the proletarian vanguard cannot be affected by any blindness of the masses, the revelation of unpopularity cannot be a reason for the abandonment of power or a modification of social objectives, but only for the adoption of sterner measures and greater vigilance against the enemy.   Any relaxation of Communist rule leads sooner or later to the point where the process either must dissolve the party dictatorship and inaugurate a genuine political liberty, or else must be reversed so that the crumbling monopoly of power may be restored.    The more radical revisionists in Europe, such as Djilas and Kolakowski, are ready for the former alternative, but the Communist rulers everywhere have seen the danger signals and since the middle of 1957 have been endeavoring to tighten up once more the bonds of totalitarian control.    The only difference in China is that the swing of the pendulum has been greater than anywhere else. Today the "hundred flowers" are dead and the Chinese Communists are advancing under a banner which might well bear the slogan, "Forward to Stalinism!"

VI

# IDEOLOGY AND THE BALANCE OF POWER

# THE COMINTERN

## The Twenty-one Conditions of Admission into the Communist International

*(Adopted at the Second Congress of the Communist International held in Moscow, July 17th to August 7th, 1920)*

The First Inaugural Congress of the Communist International did not draw up precise conditions for the admission of separate parties to the Third International. At the time the First Congress was convened there were only Communist *trends* and *groups* in the majority of countries.

The Second World Congress of the Communist International has met under different conditions. There are now in most countries not only Communist trends and tendencies, but Communist *Parties* and *organizations*.

The Communist International is now more and more often receiving applications from parties and groups which, but a short time ago, belonged to the Second International and now desire to join the Third International, but which have not really become Communist organizations. The Second International has completely collapsed. The intermediary parties and groups of the "Center," realizing that the Second International is utterly hopeless, are trying to lean upon the Communist International, which is growing ever stronger; at the same time, however, they hope to preserve such "autonomy" as would enable them to pursue their former opportunist or "Centrist" policy. The Communist International is, to a certain degree, becoming the fashion.

The desire of some of the leading groups of the "Center" to join the Third International is an indirect confirmation of the fact that the Communist International has gained the sympathy of the overwhelming majority of the class-conscious workers of the whole world, and that it is becoming a greater and greater force every day.

Under certain circumstances, the Communist International may be threatened with the danger of dilution by wavering, vacillating groups that have not yet abandoned the ideology of the Second International.

Moreover, in some of the large parties (Italy, Sweden, Norway, Yugoslavia and others) the majority of whose members adopt the Communist point of view, there still remains a considerable reformist and social-pacifist wing, which is only waiting for the opportune moment to lift its head to begin an active sabotage of the proletarian revolution, and thus help the bourgeoisie and the Second International.

No Communist should forget the lessons of the Hungarian Soviet Republic. The alliance between the Hungarian Communists and the so-called "Left" social-democrats cost the Hungarian proletariat dear.

Hence, the Second World Congress of the Communist International considers it necessary to lay down the most precise conditions for the admission of new parties, and also to point out to those parties which have already been accepted as members of the Communist International, the obligations that rest upon them.

The Second Congress of the Communist International resolves that the conditions for membership in the Communist International shall be as follows:

1. The daily propaganda and agitation must bear a truly Communist character and correspond to the program and all the decisions of the Third International. All the organs of the press that are in the hands of the Party must be edited by reliable Communists who have proved their loyalty to the cause of the proletarian revolution. The dictatorship of the proletariat should not be spoken of simply as a current hackneyed formula; it should be advocated in such a way that its necessity should be apparent to every rank-and-file working man and woman, each soldier and peasant, and should emanate from the facts of everyday life systematically recorded by our press day after day.

The periodical and non-periodical press and all Party publishing organizations must be wholly subordinate to the Central Committee of the Party, irrespective as to whether the Party as a whole, at the given moment, is legal or illegal. That publishing organizations, abusing their autonomy, should pursue a policy that does not completely correspond to the policy of the Party, cannot be tolerated.

In the columns of the newspapers, at public meetings, in the trade unions, in the co-operative societies—wherever the adherents

of the Third International gain access, they must systematically and
mercilessly denounce not only the bourgeoisie, but also its assist-
ants, the reformists of every shade.

2. Every organization desiring to belong to the Communist
International must steadily and systematically *remove* from all responsible posts in the Labor movement in the Party organization,
editorial boards, trade unions, parliamentary fractions, co-operative
societies, municipalities, etc., all reformists and followers of the
"Center," and have them replaced by Communists even at the cost
of replacing at the beginning, "experienced" leaders by rank-and-
file working-men.

3. The class struggle in almost all the countries of Europe and
America is entering the phase of civil war. Under such conditions
the Communists can have no confidence in bourgeois law. They
must *everywhere* create a parallel illegal apparatus which at the
decisive moment could assist the Party in performing its duty to
the revolution. In all countries where, in consequence of martial
law or exceptional laws, the Communists are unable to carry on
all their work legally, a combination of legal and illegal work is
absolutely necessary.

4. The obligation to spread Communist ideas includes the particular necessity of persistent, systematic propaganda in the army.
Wherever such propaganda is forbidden by exceptional laws, it
must be carried on illegally. The abandonment of such work
would be equivalent to the betrayal of revolutionary duty and is
incompatible with membership in the Third International.

5. It is necessary to carry on systematic and steady agitation in
the rural districts. The working class cannot consolidate its victory
without the backing of at least part of the agricultural laborers and
the poorest peasants, and without having neutralized, by its policy,
a part of the rest of the rural population. Communist work in the
rural districts is acquiring a predominant importance during the
present period. It should be carried on in the main, by revolutionary Communist workers of both city and country only, who have
connections with the rural districts. To refuse to do this work or
to transfer such work to untrustworthy half-reformists is equal to
renouncing the proletarian revolution.

6. Every party that desires to belong to the Third International

must expose, not only open social patriotism, but also the falsity and hypocrisy of social-pacifism; it must systematically demonstrate to the workers that without revolutionary overthrow of capitalism, no international arbitration courts, no disarmament, no "democratic" reorganization of the League of Nations will save mankind from new imperialist wars.

7. The Parties desiring to belong to the Communist International must recognize the necessity of a complete and absolute rupture with reformism and the policy of the "Center," and they must carry on propaganda in favor of this rupture among the broadest circles of the party membership. Otherwise a consistent Communist policy is impossible.

The Communist International unconditionally and peremptorily demands that this split be brought about *with the least delay*. The Communist International cannot reconcile itself to the fact that such avowed reformists, as Turatti, Kautsky, Hilferding, Hillquit, Longuet, MacDonald, Modigliani, and others should be entitled to consider themselves members of the Third International. This would make the Third International resemble, to a considerable degree, the late Second International.

8. On the question of the colonies and oppressed nationalities an especially distinct and clear line must be taken by the parties in those countries where the bourgeoisie possesses colonies or oppresses other nations. Every party desirous of belonging to the Third International must ruthlessly denounce the methods of "their own" imperialists in the colonies, supporting, not in words, but in deeds, every independence movement in the colonies. It should demand the expulsion of their own imperialists from such colonies, and cultivate among the workers of their own country a truly fraternal attitude towards the toiling population of the colonies and oppressed nationalities and carry on systematic agitation in its own army against every kind of oppression of the colonial population.

9. Every party that desires to belong to the Communist International must carry on systematic and persistent Communist work in the trade unions, in workers' and industrial councils, in the co-operative societies, and in other mass organizations. Within these organizations it is necessary to create Communist groups, which by means of practical and stubborn work must win over the trade

unions, etc., for the cause of Communism. These cells should constantly denounce the treachery of the social-patriots and the vacillations of the "Center," at every step. These Communist groups should be completely subordinate to the Party as a whole.

10. Every party that belongs to the Communist International must carry on a stubborn struggle against the Amsterdam "International" of yellow trade unions. It must persistently propagate among the organized workers the necessity of a rupture with the yellow Amsterdam International. It must give all the support in its power to the incipient international alliance of the Red trade unions affiliated to the Communist International.

11. The parties desiring to belong to the Third International must overhaul the membership of their parliamentary fractions, eliminate all unreliable elements from them, to control these fractions, not only verbally but in reality, to subordinate them to the Central Committee of the Party, and demand from every Communist member of parliament that he devote his entire activities to the interest of really revolutionary propaganda and agitation.

12. Parties belonging to the Communist International must be built up on the principle of democratic *centralism*. At the present time of acute civil war, the Communist Party will only be able fully to do its duty when it is organized in the most centralized manner, if it has iron discipline, bordering on military discipline, and if the Party center is a powerful, authoritative organ with wide powers, possessing the general trust of the party membership.

13. The Communist parties of those countries where the Communists' activity is legal shall make periodical cleanings (re-registration) of the members of the Party organizations, so as to systematically cleanse the party from the petty-bourgeois elements who inevitably attach themselves to it.

14. Every party that desires to belong to the Communist International must give every possible support to the Soviet Republics in their struggle against all counter-revolutionary forces. The Communist parties should carry on a precise and definite propaganda to induce the workers to refuse to transport munitions of war intended for enemies of the Soviet Republics, carry on legal or illegal propaganda among the troops, which are sent to crush the workers' republics, etc.

15. The parties which up to the present have retained their old Social-Democratic programs must in the shortest possible time overhaul these programs and draw up a new Communist program in conformity with the special conditions of their respective countries and in accordance with resolutions of the Communist International. As a rule, the program of every party that belongs to the Communist International must be ratified by the next Congress of the Communist International or by the Executive Committee. In the event of the Executive Committee of the Communist International failing to ratify the program of a particular party, that party has the right to appeal to the Congress of the Communist International.

16. All decisions of the Congresses of the Communist International, as well as the decisions of its Executive Committee, are binding on all parties affiliated to the Communist International. The Communist International, operating in the midst of most acute civil war, must have a far more centralized form of organization than that of the Second International. At the same time, the Communist International and its Executive Committee must, of course, in all their activities, take into consideration the diversity of the conditions under which the various parties have to work and fight and should issue universally binding decisions only on questions on which the passing of such decisions is possible.

17. In connection with all this, all parties desiring to join the Communist International must change their names. Every party that desires to join the Communist International must bear the name: *Communist Party* of such-and-such country (Section of the Third Communist International). This question as to name is not merely a formal one, but a political one of great importance. The Communist International has declared a decisive war against the entire bourgeois world and all the yellow, Social-Democratic parties. Every rank-and-file worker must clearly understand the difference between the Communist Parties and the old official "Social-Democratic" or "Socialist" parties which have betrayed the cause of the working class.

18. All the leading Party organs of the press in all countries must publish all the chief documents of the Executive Committee of the Communist International.

19. All parties belonging to the Communist International, or

having made an application to join it, must, in the shortest possible period, but not later than four months after the Second Congress of the Communist International, call special Party congresses, for the purpose of discussing these obligations. In this connection, the Central Committees must take measures to enable all the local organizations to become acquainted with the decisions of the Second Congress of the Communist International.

20. The parties that would now like to join the Third International but which have not yet radically changed their former tactics, must, before joining, take steps to ensure that their Central Committees and all most important central bodies of the respective parties, shall be composed, to the extent of at least two-thirds, of such comrades as even prior to the Second Congress of the Communist International have openly and definitely declared for joining the Third International. Exceptions may be made with approval of the Executive Committee of the Third International. The Executive Committee of the Communist International also has the right to make exceptions of the representatives of the "Center" mentioned in point 7.

21. *Members of the Party who reject the conditions and theses of the Communist International, on principle, must be expelled from the party.*

This applies also to the delegates to the special Party Congresses.

# THE ORGANIZATION OF PEACE*

## MAXIM LITVINOV

[1934]

I would like my first words to be the expression of my sincere thanks to you, Mr. President, for the very kind way in which you have greeted the first appearance here of the Soviet delegation. I would extend my gratitude to all those delegations on whose invitation, and as a result of whose votes, we have come here today. It is also my pleasant duty to record with gratitude the initiative by the French Government actively supported by the Governments of the United Kingdom and Italy, and the sincere efforts made by the French delegation, and personally by the esteemed Foreign Minister of the French Republic, M. Barthou, and the President of the Council, Dr. Benes, in the furtherance of this initiative.

The telegram of invitation to my Government, and the vote taken by the Council and the Assembly, convince me that all delegations, with very few exceptions, realize the importance of the arrival in this hall of a delegation from the Soviet State, as well as the favourable results to be expected from this event. It derives its significance not merely from the formal act of our joining the League, but also from the circumstances in which this takes place, and the evolution of the relations between the Soviet Government and the League of Nations which led up to it. I should like to dwell briefly upon this evolution, even if this should involve my making—for the last time, I hope—a swift excursion to a past that has been by no means altogether pleasant. This seems to me the more necessary in that the past has been touched upon in another place, and that the entry into the League, in the fifteenth year of its

---

*From the speech of Maxim Litvinov, Commissar for Foreign Affairs of the Soviet Union, at the League of Nations Assembly on the entry of the Soviet Union into the League of Nations, September 18, 1934. From *Soviet Documents on Foreign Policy,* Volume III, selected and edited by Jane Degras. Oxford University Press, 1953. Reprinted by permission.

existence, of one of the greatest States in the world does undoubtedly call for some explanation.

I will speak with that frankness and moderation which many of you, knowing me of old, will, I am sure, grant me, and which can only be helpful to our mutual understanding and our future co-operation.

We represent here a new State—new, not geographically, but new in its external aspects, its internal political and social structure, and its aspirations and ideals. The appearance in the historical arena of a new form of State has always been met with hostility on the part of old State formations. It is not surprising that the phenomenon of a new State with a social-political system radically different from any heretofore known should come up against intense hostility from without and manifested by literally all other countries in the world. This hostility has been not merely theoretical, but has found expression even in military action, assuming the form of prolonged externally organized attempts to interfere in the internal affairs of the new State for the purpose of getting it back to the old lines. At the time when the League of Nations was being formed to proclaim the organization of peace, the people of our country had as yet not been enabled to enjoy the blessings of peace. They still had to defend their internal peace with arms, and to contend for long their right to internal self-determination and their external independence. Even after the most extreme forms of intervention in the affairs of our State were over, the hostility of the outer world continued to be manifested in the most varying degrees and forms.

All this makes it quite obvious that the relations between the Soviet State and the League of Nations could not be other than those existing between itself and the States belonging to the League. Not only this, but the people of the Soviet Union naturally feared that these nations united in the League might give collective expression to their hostility towards the Soviet Union and combine their anti-Soviet activities. It can hardly be denied that at that time, and even very much later, there were still statesmen who thought, or at least dreamed, of such collective action. On the one hand they were inclined to underrate the internal powers of resistance of the new State, and, on the other hand, to overrate that harmony of political and economic interests in the other States which, it seemed to them, the League should have embodied. They continued to believe that the last world war would be the last war in the world, and that the order established by it was immutable and secure against any attempts at alteration by force. They dreamed of establishing at least temporary peace, which would, however, by no means have been extended to the new Soviet State. The history of the last ten years, the history of the League of Nations itself, the increasing conflicts of international interests, the prolonged economic crisis, and, finally the development of the Soviet State, have shown the world how Utopian were these dreams and aspirations.

Today we are happy to be able to state that the exponents of those Utopias and the advocates of the policy of ignoring and isolating the Soviet Union are no longer to be met among broad-minded statesmen, among the representatives of the more important States moulding international life who think on realistic lines and understand the needs of the present day, but must be searched for among narrow-minded politicians unable to rise above their petty political passions and strong prejudices and deriving their knowledge of countries and people from muddied sources. It remains only to pity such people and to wish them a speedy enlightenment and a return to more reliable sources of information.

I take this opportunity of expressing my conviction that, in the meantime, the League will see to it that such people have nothing to do with the settlement of affairs affecting the interests of the Soviet State, in which impartial judgment and at least an elementary understanding of world events are necessary. . . .

In order to make our position quite clear, I should like further to state that the idea in itself of an association of nations contains nothing theoretically inacceptable for the Soviet State and its ideology. The Soviet Union is itself a league of nations in the best sense of the word, uniting over 200 nationalities, thirteen of which have a population of not less than one million each, and others, such as Russia and the Ukraine, a population running into scores of millions. I will make so bold as to claim that never before have so many nations coexisted so peacefully within a single State, never before have so many nations in one State had such free cultural development and enjoyed their own national culture as a whole and the use of their own language in particular. In no other country are all manifestations of race and national prejudice so resolutely put down and eradicated as in the Soviet Union.

Here, as regards equality of rights, are neither national majorities nor minorities, since no nation, either in theory or practice, has less rights and fewer opportunities for cultural and economic development than another. Many nationalities which seemed to have been doomed to die out altogether have received a fresh lease of life and begun to develop anew, and this on territories where, before the Soviet regime, all nationalities except the dominating Russian were being stamped out by violence and oppression.

At the present time the periodical Press in the Soviet Union comes out in fifty languages. The national policy of the Soviet Union and the results of this policy have received their due both from friends and foes visiting the Soviet Union and studying the national question on the spot.

All the nationalities in our Union are, of course, united by a common political and economic regime and by common aspirations towards a single ideal, for the attainment of which they vie among themselves. The Soviet State has, however, never excluded the possibility of some form or other of association with States having a different political and social system, so long as there is no mutual hostility and if it is for the attainment of common aims. For such an association it considers that the essential conditions would be, first, the extension to every State belonging to such an association of the liberty to preserve what I might call its State personality and the social-economic system chosen by it—in other words, reciprocal non-interference in the domestic affairs of the States therein associated; and, secondly, the existence of common aims.

As to the first condition which we have named, the peaceful coexistence of different social-political systems at a given historical stage, we have advocated it again and again at international conferences. We have managed to get it recognized by inclusion in some of the resolutions of these conferences. But further developments were necessary before this principle was able to gain for itself wider recognition. The invitation to the Soviet Union to join the League of Nations may be said to represent the final victory of this principle. The Soviet Union is entering into the League today as representative of a new social-economic system, not renouncing any of its special features, and—like the other States here represented—preserving intact its personality.

With regard to common aims, these have long ago been establish in many spheres. Workers in the fields of science, art and social activities in the Soviet Union have long been co-operating fruitfully with representatives of other States, both individually and on organized lines, in all spheres of science and culture and on problems of a humanitarian nature.

The co-operation of the Soviet Union with other States within the framework of the League of Nations has also long ago shown itself to be both desirable and possible in the sphere of economics. Soviet delegations have taken part in the Committee of Enquiry for European Union, which occupied itself chiefly with economic questions; in both Economic Conferences, and in other Conferences of a lesser range. It will not be out of place here to remark that at all these Conferences proposals were put forward by the Soviet delegations with a view to the utmost reduction of the existing chaos in international economic relations and in the interests common to all concerned.

The Soviet Government has also not abstained from co-operation of a political nature whenever some alleviation of international conflicts and increase of guarantees of security and consolidation of peace might reasonably be expected from such co-operation. I will only mention the active part taken by the Soviet delegation in the Preparatory Commission of the Disarmament Conference and in the Conference itself, when, on behalf of the Soviet Government, it declared its readiness for any degree of disarmament, taking its stand on far-reaching proposals for the ensuring of peace, some of which have received worldwide recognition and even application. In this respect, I remember, not without pride, the Soviet definition of aggression, which has been made the basis of innumerable international acts.

It needed however, one great dominating common aim to prove incontestably to all nations, including those of the Soviet Union, the desirability—nay, the necessity—for closer co-operation between the Soviet Union and the League of Nations, and even for the entry of the Soviet Union into the League. The discovery of such a common aim has been greatly facilitated by the events of the last two or three years.

Thirty delegations to the Assembly, comprising most of the Members of the League, and representing all the big States and those of importance in international life, declared in their address to the Soviet Union that the mission of the League was the organization of peace, and that the success of this mission demanded the co-operation of the Soviet Union. They knew that the State which they were addressing had not spared, throughout the seventeen years of its existence, its efforts for the establishment of the best possible relations with its own neighbours, on the most solid foundations, for *rapprochement* with all States desiring this, thus making itself a powerful factor for international peace.

For its part, the Soviet Government, following attentively all developments of international life, could not but observe the increasing activity in the League of Nations of States interested in the preservation of peace and their struggle against aggressive militarist elements. More, it noted that these aggressive elements themselves were finding the restrictions of the League embarrassing and trying to shake them off. All this could not be without its influence on the attitudes towards the League of Nations of the Soviet Government, ever searching for further means for the organization of peace, for co-operation in which we have been invited to come here.

The organization of peace! Could there be a loftier and at the same time more practical and urgent task for the co-operation of all nations? The words used in political slogans have their youth and their age. If they are used too often without being applied, they wear themselves out and end by losing potency. Then they have to be revived and instilled with new meaning. The sound and the meaning of the words "organization of peace" ought now to be different from their sound and meaning twelve or fifteen years ago. Then, to many Members of the League of Nations, war seemed to be a remote theoretical danger, and there seemed to be no hurry as to its prevention. Now, war must appear to all as the threatening danger of tomorrow. Now, the organization of peace, for which so far very little has been done, must be set against the extremely active organization of war. Then, many believed that the spirit of war might be exorcised by adjurations, resolutions and declarations. Now, everybody knows that the exponents of the idea of war, the open promulgators of the refashioning of the map of Europe and Asia by the sword, are not to be intimidated by paper obstacles. Members of the League of Nations know this by experience. We are now confronted with the task of averting war by more effective means.

The failure of the Disarmament Conference, on which formerly such high hopes were placed, in its turn compels us to seek more effective means. We must accept the incontestable fact that, in the present complicated state of political and economic interests, no war of any serious dimensions can be localized, and any war, whatever its issue, will turn out to have been but the first of a series. We must also tell ourselves that sooner or later any war will bring misfortune to all countries, whether belligerents or neutrals. The lesson of the world war, from the results of which both belligerents and neutrals are suffering to this day, must not be forgotten. The impoverishment of the whole world, the lowering of living standards for both manual and brain workers, unemployment, robbing all and sundry of their confidence in the morrow, not to speak of the fall in cultural values, the return of some countries to medieval ideology—such are the consequences of the world war, even now, sixteen years after its cessation, which are making themselves acutely felt.

Finally, we must realize once and for all that no war with political or economic aims is capable of restoring so-called historical justice, and that all it could do would be to substitute new and perhaps still more glaring injustices for old ones, and that every new peace treaty bears within it the seeds of fresh warfare. Further, we must not lose sight of the new increase in armaments going on under our very eyes, the chief danger of which consists in its qualitative still more than in its quantitative increase, in the vast increase of potential destruction. The fact that aerial warfare has with such lightning speed won itself an equal place with land and naval warfare is sufficient corroboration of this argument.

I do not consider it the moment to speak in detail about effective means for the prevention of impending and openly promulgated war. One thing is quite clear for me, and that is that peace and security cannot be organized on the shifting sands of verbal promises and declarations. The nations are not to be soothed into a feeling of security by assurances of peaceful intentions, however often they are repeated, especially in those places where there are grounds for expecting aggression or where, only the day before, there have been talk and publication about wars of conquest in all directions, for which both ideological and material preparations are being made. We should establish that any State is entitled to demand from its neighbours, near and remote, guarantees for its security, and that such a demand is not to be considered as an expression of mistrust. Governments with a clear conscience and really free from all aggressive intentions, cannot refuse to give, in place of declarations, more effective guarantees which would be extended to themselves and give them also a feeling of complete security.

Far be it from me to overrate the opportunities and means of the League of Nations for the organization of peace. I realize, better perhaps than any of you, how limited these means are. I am aware that the League does not possess the means for the complete abolition of war. I am, however, convinced that, with the firm will and close co-operation of all its Members, a great deal could be done at any given moment of the utmost diminution of dangers of war, and this it a sufficiently honourable and lofty task, the fulfillment of which would be incalculable advantage to humanity. The Soviet Government has never ceased working at this task throughout the whole period of its existence. It has come here to combine its efforts with the efforts of other States represented in the League. I am convinced that in this, our common work, from now on the will to peace of the Soviet Union with its 170 million inhabitants— peace for itself and for other States—will make itself felt as a powerful factor. I am convinced that, as we observe the fruitful consequences of this stream of fresh forces in the common cause of peace, we shall always remember with the utmost satisfaction this day, as one occupying an honourable place in the annals of the League.

# WORLD COMMUNISM*

BY

## FRANZ BORKENAU

[1939]

A few years ago there would have been little point in writing a history of the Communist International. As recently as 1933 there was not a single country outside Russia where the communists counted as a political force. But since 1934 the Communist International has evolved a new policy, has claimed to defend democracy, has sought alliances of the closest kind with the democratic parties of various countries, and has, during this latest period, increased very considerably in strength. Today it is again important to know the Communist International. . . .

Some believe that the Communist International will save the world; others, that it is the shape of the devil in our present time; some, and among them this author, that it is neither the one nor the other, but simply a failure. . . .

The history of the Communist International, as it has unfolded itself between 1919 and the present day, is certainly a puzzling phenomenon. It is difficult to find a central point in the story around which to group the whole. There is no climax. The events seem to pass one after another, without any very close link between them. The history of the Comintern can be summed up as a series of hopes and disappointments. Ever and again Russia and the communist parties abroad imagined that in this or that country revolution was approaching, victory near. The front of the bourgeoisie would be broken, and through the gap world revolution would make its way. Then, instead of success, there was always failure. Progress made by the various communist parties during difficult years of struggle, won at the price of heavy sacrifices, vanished into nothing within a few days, as in Germany in 1923, in England in 1926, in China in 1927. The communists hunted a

*From *World Communism* by F. Borkenau. Copyright 1939 by W. W. Norton & Company, Inc. Reprinted by permission.

phantom which deceived them continually: the vain phantom of social revolution such as Marx had seen it. This history of the Comintern contains many ups and downs. It contains no steady progress, not a single lasting success.

But against this disappointing reality there stand the firm hopes of the communists. They are convinced, every single time they enter on a new policy, an attack on a new country, that this time it will be different from what it was before, that now they have found the true method, that this time advance will not end in a complete rout. The basic conviction of communism is that it needs only a truly "Bolshevist" party, applying the appropriate tactics, in order to win. Therefore every defeat—and the history of the Comintern consists of defeats—brings about a change both of leadership and of policy. One day the Comintern tries a policy to the "right"; then the importance of democracy is emphasized, collaboration is sought with the other sections of the labor movement, care is taken to participate in the day-to-day struggles of the workers and of the lower classes in general, the communist parties grow, both in membership and in influence. Everything seems to be smooth going till the decisive moment when an attempt is made to leap out of the preparatory stage into revolutionary action. Then, suddenly, the parties feel somehow unable to make the jump and break down. The communists are convinced that the failure was due only to wrong ideology. In taking account of the pacifist and constitutional "prejudices" of the masses the communists have imbued themselves with them, have themselves become "opportunists"; that is the view of the orthodox. A turn to the left is effected. Often armed insurrection, which was not undertaken at the height of communist mass influence, is launched when the decisive moment is over and the party has lost all influence or at least every chance of victory; thus in Bulgaria in 1923, and in China in 1927, to mention only two outstanding examples. But even when no sudden rising takes place the turn to the left implies a wholesale change of policy. Suddenly the communists refuse to acknowledge any difference between democracy on the one hand and autocracy and Fascism on the other. All contacts with the democratic mass parties are broken off. Attempts are made to split

the trade unions.  Bona fide participation in the day-to-day struggles of the masses is decried as "opportunism."  Propaganda of
revolution takes the place of every other sort of propaganda.  And
the parties are rigidly purged of all "opportunist" elements.  But
if the policy of the "right" wing has led to defeat at the decisive
moment that of the "left" wing reduces the party to the exiguity
and the lack of influence of a sect, until the decline is patent and
the policy of the "right" is given a new trial.  And so forth in
endless rotation. . . .

Only one thing the communists seem unable to acquire through
all the shiftings of their policy: a sense of the adequacy of means
and ends.  During the rapid swings from right to left and from
left to right there is generally one short moment when communist
policy moves along a middle line: as when, lately, in 1934, the
communists veered round to defend democracy together with all
other democratic forces.  But those are only points of transition
between opposite extremes.

From a description of this basic law of the evolution of the
Comintern evolves at once one important result: it would be a grave
mistake to overestimate the role of Russia, or, more correctly, to
regard the basic character of the communist parties simply as
a result of "orders from Moscow."  Moscow's influence upon world
communism, rooted both in its prestige and its financial power, of
late even in the control the Russian G.P.U. exerts over all communist parties, is strong indeed.  But this domination of Moscow
over the Comintern is much more the result than the cause of the
evolution of Communism outside Russia.  As long as there were
relatively strong revolutionary movements outside Russia, these
movements, in spite of all the prestige of the Russian revolution,
did not accept orders from Moscow. . . . No other section of the
Comintern has ever had so much independence as the Chinese
Soviets, and only when their vigor was broken by Chiang Kai-
shek's "annihilation drives" did they become simple instruments
of Russian foreign policy, which during the last year decided to
dissolve them altogether.  When the Comintern was founded, during the year 1919, at the height of the post-war revolutionary crisis,
it ought to have had tremendous authority.  In reality, precisely

during that year 1919, it was quite an insignificant force because the revolutionary movements of other countries did not care to take orders from Moscow.

The Comintern as an organization under the sway of Moscow is itself a product of defeat. When in 1920 it became clear that the post-war revolutionary wave was ebbing away, the star of Moscow rose. The ideas of Bolshevism, the dogma that the labor movement must be purged thoroughly of all unorthodox elements before being able to win, was only now accepted by the defeated left wing of the Continental socialist parties, and the split inaugurated by the second world-congress of the Comintern started from that assumption. Only this split led to the formation of communist mass parties. The new communist parties, believing that with the creation of a communist party the chief condition of success was fulfilled, threw themselves into battle, only to learn in the German disaster of March 1921 that they had been entirely mistaken and that the existence of a communist mass party could not make up for the lack of revolutionary impetus in the masses. When the Comintern was born the revolution in the West was already at an end.

The coincidence of these two events was not a matter of chance. Before the war, no revolutionary socialist had conceived the idea that the proletariat could win in a state of disunion. Yet already the outbreak of the war had brought about precisely such a state. The majority of the labor parties all over the world had buried the ideals of the class-struggle precisely at the moment when these ideals, for the first time for many decades, would have had practical revolutionary implications. The revolutionary minority, which stood firm to its convictions, cried treason. But this is a moral point of view and its acceptance depends on the conviction that it is the duty of a decent man to be a revolutionary. The majority of the workers and their leaders, however, had thought at that moment that it was their duty to defend home and country. The national allegiance had proved to be much stronger than the social one. It was a long time before the revolutionaries accepted this verdict of history. Even in 1919 Lenin and Sinoviev imagined that it was sufficient to raise the banner of the new, revolutionary International for the workers to gather swiftly round it. But this was not the case and so the split, with its twenty-one points, grew from an incident to a lasting reality. The twenty-one points, with their stipulations about repeated purges, started from the implicit assumption that a large section of the labor movement, not to mention the other sections of the lower classes, would always remain reformist, as long as the capitalist regime existed. But if this was so, how was a proletarian revolution to succeed? By the very act of its creation as a mass organization, by the perpetuation of the split which it implied, the Comintern signed the death warrant for the proletarian revolution to which it was pledged and which had never had many chances.

What followed was again natural enough. In matters of organization and finance the communist parties, who had only a relatively small following of their own, had to rely on help from Moscow, on which they became thus dependent. But more important still was the ideological dependence on Russia. The further real chances of revolution recede into the background the more the adoration of the accomplished revolution in Russia takes their place. Every defeat of revolution in the West and in the East is accompanied by an increase of admiration for Russia. During the first years of the Comintern there is still a very serious concern for the possible chances of revolution abroad. There are constant attempts to square these interests with the interests of Russia as a state, but these attempts gradually change in character. On the one hand, Russia leaves its own revolution further behind. Precisely because revolution in Russia is an established fact, the revolutionary impetus of Russia abroad fades out. At the same time, revolution recedes further into the background everywhere, at least that sort of revolution which the Russians regard as desirable.

The defeat of the Chinese revolution is the turning-point in this respect. During the year 1925 the dissensions in Russia had begun to influence the Comintern considerably. Now the chances of the left wing of the Chinese revolutionaries are really spoiled by Moscow. In all other cases the revolutionary chances existed only in the heads of the communists. In Germany in 1921 and 1923, in Britain in 1926, there could not have been a revolution. But the Chinese revolution was in fact ruined by the interference of Moscow, which tried to square its interests with the interests of the revolutionaries, which proved to be impossible. The defeat of the Chinese revolution destroys the last serious chance of the Comintern in all the world. Henceforth the Comintern, which has no longer a serious task of its own, becomes a plaything in the hands of the ruling group at Moscow. The left extremism of 1929-34 is largely a maneuver of Stalin in his factional fight against the right of Bukharin and Rykov in Russia.

The situation changes once more with the advent of Hitler. Moscow for the first time since 1921 feels itself seriously menaced and feels its revolutionary past as a handicap in its defence. The Comintern must stop its extremist talk, which might hamper Russia's attempts at finding suitable alliances, and by doing so becomes automatically an instrument of Russian foreign policy, which it had not before primarily been.

*Thus, three periods can be clearly distinguished. During the first period the Comintern is mainly an instrument to bring about revolution. During the second period it is mainly an instrument in the Russian factional struggles. During the third period it is mainly an instrument of Russian foreign policy.* The boundary lines between these three periods are naturally not rigid. But one thing remains clear: for the true communist this whole evolution can only be the result of an immense betrayal. Leon Trotsky fills the world with his accusations that the German, the French, the Spanish, the Belgian, and what not revolution had been possible, had only Stalin not betrayed. In reality it is the other way round. The evolution of the Comintern and partly even that of Russia are due to the fact that that international proletarian revolution after which the Bolsheviks originally hunted was a phantom. After many disappointments they had indirectly to acknowledge it by their deeds, and take things as they were. This change of the function of the Comintern is the real trend of its evolution behind the welter of shifts to the right and to the left which constitute its surface.

This change could not possibly remain without effect on the structure of the communist parties themselves. This structure did not from the beginning correspond at all to the ideas which the communists held about their own party.  In Russia the Bolshevik party had really been, to a great extent, what Lenin wanted it to be: a select community, a sort of religious order of professional revolutionaries, crusaders of a materialistic faith, a selection of the most self-sacrificing, the most decided and active among the revolutionary intelligentsia.  But the structure of the communist parties of the West and the East never corresponded to this idea.  They consisted essentially of shifting elements, which came and went.  This character of the membership explains to a great extent the rapid changes of policy.  Such contradictory policies as those followed by the various communist parties could not have been carried out one after another by the same men.  The complete lack of tradition has the same source.  Russian Bolshevism was conscious of having its roots in the deeds of the revolutionaries of a century before, and the membership kept a close memory of the history of the party, until Stalin ordered the reading of a revolutionary history entirely of his own invention.  The membership in the Western and Eastern parties, however, is a new one every five years and ready to believe anything the newest version of official communism tells it about the past of the party.  Serious studies of party history are not encouraged.  But this lack of consistency and of tradition has still more important consequence: with the shifting of the membership the social character of the communist parties shifts too.  There was a moment, after the second world-congress, in 1921, when the more important communist parties were really working-class parties.  But this has changed long since.  With the shifting of the membership the communist parties tended to attract, more and more, *déclassé* elements: young intellectuals with Bohemian leanings on the one hand, unemployed on the other.  During the period of left extremism between 1929 and 1934 most communist parties consisted primarily of these elements.  Today an even more radical change announces itself.  In China the Communist Party is a party of the peasants and the Red army, in Spain it is a party of all classes except the urban proletariat, in Britain and U.S.A. it is mostly a party of young intellectuals. . . .

In this slow transformation of the social structure of the Communist International we strike again one of the roots of its history. The proletarian revolution, in which Marx and Lenin believed, seems to be incompatible with the real labor movement as it is. Certain elements of Marx's and Lenin's revolutionary predictions have proved only too true. It is true that the "capitalist" society of private ownership and private initiative is unable to cope with the problems of our period. It is true, as Marx has predicted, that at a certain stage of its development it enters on a cycle of gigantic economic crises for which, as most experts are agreed today, there is no remedy but state control, state interference, and planning. It is true, moreover, that economic crises bring with them tremendous social dislocations and political convulsions. Only one thing is certainly not true: the idea that, at the height of such a crisis, the proletariat will rise and, throwing all the propertied classes into the dust, will take the lead of society, abolish private property in the means of production, and create a regime where there are no more classes. This leading role of the proletariat in the upheavals of our time has proved to be the Utopian element of Marxism. In Russia, not the proletariat, but a quasi-religious order of professional revolutionaries of the intelligentsia took the lead, with the help of the peasants, the peasant soldiers, and the workers. In the West, where there was neither such an order nor masses willing to follow it, the idea of a proletarian revolution proved to be a complete illusion.

There are many reasons for this, reasons which have little or nothing to do with a betrayal. Had all the socialist leaders sided with the revolutionaries the majority of the proletariat would simply have left them for some more moderate party. For the idea of the proletariat opposing, victoriously, all other classes of a complex modern society is a fantastic one. In the West there are no revolutionary peasants such as in Russia. Moreover, in Russia there existed that absolute cleavage between the people and the ruling classes which is completely absent in the West. The old civilization of the West has given its seal, not only to an alleged workers' aristocracy, but to all strata of the working classes, who all have something to lose, who all share with the upper classes their chief loyalties and beliefs. If somebody wants to express this in Marxist terms he may say that in the most developed modern countries all classes and groups are much too "bourgeois" to make a proletarian revolution a practical proposition.

Therefore, in the West only two solutions for the crisis of the existing social regime remained: in some countries a revolutionary party coming from all classes and taking a stand above them all has curbed the class struggle with iron hand and subordinated all group antagonisms within the nation to the violent struggle for domination of their own nation over all others. Such is Fascism. In other countries, and this is the second possibility, all classes, by a tradition of cooperation and compromise, have hitherto managed to hold the inevitable social antagonisms within bounds and cooperate in the gradual bringing about of a new type of society: this is typical of a progressive and evolutionary democracy. There is no third solution in the conditions of highly developed modern industrial countries. Industrially backward countries such as Russia, Spain, South America, China, are a different matter.

The labor movement of the West, moreover, knows very well why, by instinct and conviction, it holds to democracy. The achievements of the dictatorships may be ever so brilliant; but not from the end of the crisis in Germany, nor from the colonial expansion of Italy, nor from the Five-Year Plan of Russia, have the masses had more than the slightest advantages. Liberty of movement for the working-class organizations, notably the trade unions, is the primary condition for the workers to share in the fruits of the economic and political successes of their nation. But the liberty of the trade unions depends on liberty as a basic principle of the political regime. To this liberal and constitutional spirit of the Western labor movement the communists could only either submit, and then the Comintern would have dissolved itself, or they could fight the bulk of the labor movement, which they did. But in doing so they gradually severed their ties with the real proletariat. The possibility of such a severance was contained in Lenin's basic assumption when he formed the Bolshevik Party: the revolutionary party must not be an agent of the proletariat, but a separate group, only knitted with it by its convictions. The Western labor parties are the labor movement itself, are identical with it. The communist parties were only linked with it. But what is linked can be severed.

The communists wanted to lead the proletariat along their road. But their own rule, the dictatorship of the Communist Party, was their primary aim from the beginning. When the Western proletariat proved not to be responsive it was only natural for the communists to seek support elsewhere. The fight for the power of the party and the International was and remained the central point. It was not a result of any betrayal, therefore, but the most logical result of their basic assumptions that, in due course of time, the communists became a classless party, held together by the worship of their totalitarian state—Russia—and their *voshd,* their Führer, the leader-superman, Stalin. . . .

Much of what the Comintern does today is conscious and intentional imitation of Fascism: the Führer-worship of the leader of every communist party, the nationalism, the appeal to youth, the military atmosphere. But: "Si duo idem faciunt non est idem." The Germans worship Hitler, who is a German. The French workers cannot worship Stalin, who is a Russian. German Fascism is sincerely nationalist and aggressive for its own nation. But a Fascism aggressive on behalf of a foreign nation is a preposterous idea. With all their beliefs in Russia, the French, British, and other workers cannot be Russian nationalists. The idea of a nationalist international is perhaps not contradictory in itself if movements rooted in their respective countries join in it. But a movement whose loyalty is split between its home country and a foreign country can never have the convincing force which the genuine Fascist movements have had in their respective countries. It was impossible for Russia to transfer its revolution abroad. It will prove equally impossible for it to spread its totalitarian regime.

Besides, it is very doubtful whether Moscow at present really wants the communist parties to win power in any country. The imposition of a nationalist dictatorship implies no less a revolution than the social upheaval wrought in Russia in 1917. Russia, in its obvious desire to remain allied with Czechoslovakia, France, and China and to become allied to Britain and to the United States, cannot at present wish any deep upheaval in those countries, not even one which might conceivably bring the communists into power. Communist policy is therefore self-contradictory. To launch a policy full of Fascist or semi-Fascist elements, and not even to want to win with it, is a strange attempt, indeed. Yet this is what is actually taking place.

It is the more surprising, in view of this basic wish of Russia for the political stability of her allies, that the new moderate policy was originally initiated under the lure of very sanguine hopes. But then the Russian communists have never been very subtle in their appreciation of the effects and implications of communist policy abroad. Their aim doubtless was to unite with the democratic socialists all over the world, to permeate the whole labor movement, to link it closely in "popular front" movements with the other parties of the left, to create a very strong international left-wing current, and thus finally to control the policy of all non-Fascist European countries for the benefit of Russia. But this plan failed. With the exception of those in France and Spain, the democratic labor movements refused to be permeated, and no "popular front" movement of any appreciable strength was formed outside these two countries. . . .

From the point of view of the countries in which communism is active all this presents a factor not to be neglected. Russian policy and communist aims have become much more modest than before. It is nonsense for the anti-Comintern powers to denounce present-day communism as an attempt to destroy property, family, and religion, as if we were still in the year 1917; with these contentions those powers only cover their own unavowable aims. But communism has not become less dangerous for that; on the contrary. The revolutionary menace for which communism seemed to stand in 1917 was never much more than a phantom in which visionary revolutionaries and frightened employers believed in common. In the West communism hardly ever was more than a big nuisance for the police. And Trotskyism, which still keeps to the principles of 1917, is not even that and could hardly ever be. But if communism as a revolutionary force was something infinitely more futile than its fervent adversaries would be ready to admit, the same thing need not apply to present-day non-revolutionary communism with its narrower aims. The fact is that in many countries today Moscow disposes of forces strong enough to influence national policy, forces loyal and moderate as long as the policy of their respective countries suits Russia, but threatening wrecking and rebellion as soon as this is no longer the case. This may not matter very much in peaceful times but must matter enormously in moments of tension, when relatively small forces may upset the balance. Numerous mass movements completely at the orders of a foreign power, and bound by no other interests and considerations, are a symptom of disintegration of the political system of those countries in which such movements exist. But the movements are there and the task of dealing with them ought not to be underrated.

It is true that the appeal of present-day non-revolutionary communism is a strange psychological phenomenon. It is not due to a revolutionary program, because the communists are no longer revolutionary; it is not due to a moderate program, because there is no lack of moderate parties of old standing. It is due, however, to the strange merging of an utterly unrevolutionary and antirevolutionary policy with the belief in the myth that paradise on earth has already been achieved over "one-sixth of the earth's inhabitated surface." At home, the masses which vote communist would never fight against democracy, for revolution. It is only the more gratifying, therefore, to adore the dictatorship in Russia and to indulge, in its service, in all those impulses of violence, of vilification and extermination of one's adversaries, which cannot be satisfied at home. Present-day communism is essentially the belief in a savior abroad; for this very reason it is a serious symptom of the decay of liberalism and democracy. For the essence of both is a belief in the capacity to manage politics without a savior, by the forces of the politically emancipated people themselves. The communists may perorate about the defence of democracy and liberty; in fact, the basic impulses upon which their appeal relies are diametrically opposed to both. Nor can this strange combination of moderation at home and worship of violence and horror abroad continue indefinitely. At present, in most countries, the real "toilers" are hardly touched by communist propaganda. If these real "toilers" at any time should lose their faith in liberty and democracy under some very severe stress and look out for a savior, the happy smile on the photos of Stalin would give them no consolation. They would then turn to a savior, not abroad but at home, as they did in Germany. And, again as in Germany, many thousands who have been communists would then become Fascists. In those countries where Fascism has not yet had any opportunity, communism, in its present form, supplies that belief in a savior which is essential to Fascism; but its savior is more remote, as is suitable, in a situation less tense, for social groups far away from practical possibilities of action. Yet the effect, the slow sapping of the democratic and liberal spirit, is there. As the constant interference of communist forces in the foreign policy of their respective countries sometimes constitutes a serious nuisance in matters of international policy, so communist ideals represent a constant menace to the basic forces of the European polity. It is not that the communists want to overthrow this polity at present; on the contrary, few men are so intensely interested in the strength and fighting power of the democratic countries as is Stalin, though this interest will change to the contrary the very day that Russia finds it suitable to change her foreign policy. Whether Stalin wants an alliance with the democratic countries or not is immaterial, however. The effect of communist ideals is to menace liberty and democracy; and in the end, in all likelihood, the effect of communist propaganda will have been to strengthen Fascism.

From the point of view of the democratic powers the question naturally arises whether there exist means to check these effects of communist activities. . . . Democratic powers cannot use the means of repression which are customary in Italy, Germany, and Russia, and it would obviously be very bad policy to evolve a system of pin-pricks, which would only be apt to create exasperation without being efficient. But the question remains, whether, from the point of view of Moscow, the Comintern is so valuable an asset as appears at first sight.

There can be little doubt, in fact, that the superficial advantages derived from the existence of communist parties abroad are balanced by very heavy liabilities for Russian foreign policy. With all its efforts to be a great military power, and with all the pains taken to drown its revolutionary past in a sea of blood, Russia, up to now, has not won a single reliable ally; not even Chiang Kai-shek, in his desperate straits, can be regarded as such. At one time France seemed likely to become a very close ally of Russia, but on second thoughts drew much nearer to Britain than to her eastern partner. One of the chief reasons for this reluctance on the part of all powers to combine with Russia is the existence of the Comintern. At the same time, the Comintern provides the Fascist powers with their best pretext of aggression, and it is the existence of the Comintern which is invoked by those parties of the right which, in democratic countries, favor cooperation with Germany in preference to cooperation with Russia. The dubious and limited influence Russia exerts in the political game of various democratic countries through its communist parties is certainly not worth the price paid for it. There is every chance that, in case of a large-scale international conflict, the Comintern will prove almost powerless, but will contribute to the isolation of Russia and to the grouping against it of many forces which might have remained neutral. To allay these consequences it will not be sufficient to cut off as many heads of ancient communists as are available. The very existence of the Comintern, in public opinion at large, rouses anxieties deriving from the aims it originally pursued. And there is no saying that, in a final emergency, the Comintern may not return in fact to its original methods. As long as the Comintern exists the average citizen and even the average politician in the West will judge Russia more after the revolution of 1917 than after the execution of Sinoviev and Bukharin. It would therefore be in the interest of Russia itself to dissolve the Comintern and to prove, by scrupulous abstention from interference abroad, that it can be treated on an equal footing with those democratic powers whose ideals it professes to share. Closer cooperation between the great democratic powers and Russia would become a practical proposition as the result, and the mere possibility of such closer cooperation would be a powerful contribution to the maintenance of peace and the prevention of aggression.

Whether such a solution will come about will mainly depend on the psychology of the leaders at Moscow. Unfortunately, precisely the attitude of Stalin and his staff is one of the sorest spots of international politics. Comprehension of the West, its views, impulses, and driving forces has never been the strong point of Russian Bolshevism, and this has led already to more than one miserable failure. Moreover, a naive sort of Machiavellism has been adopted in Russia, with metaphysical thoroughness. Lenin and the original Bolsheviks were already actuated by the conviction that all capitalist promises are deceptions and all ideals cheats. Under Stalin this view has evolved into a real all-round belief in human wickedness. Both in Russian home politics and in the activities of the Comintern double-dealing has been carried to such a degree as to defeat, very often, its own ends. Stalin, the man who could not allow a single one of his old companions to live, is the last man to believe in the possibility of sincere collaboration in the international field. A man such as Stalin cannot be brought to reason by argument. There is, however, just a small chance that events will teach him, and then when finally given the choice of complete isolation or a genuine dissolution of the Comintern, he will choose the latter. It would be highly desirable from the angle of those ideals to which he and his Comintern are paying continual lip-service: to the causes of liberty, democracy, peace, and to the integrity and greatness of the Russian people.

# WE STAND FOR PEACE*

BY

## JOSEPH STALIN

[1939]

Comrades, five years have elapsed since the Seventeenth Party Congress. No small period, as you see. During this period the world has undergone considerable changes. States and countries, and their mutual relations, are now in many respects totally altered.

What changes exactly have taken place in this period in the international situation? In what way exactly have the foreign and internal affairs of our country changed?

For the capitalist countries this period was one of very profound perturbations in both the economic and political spheres. In the economic sphere these were years of depression, followed, from the beginning of the latter half of 1937, by a period of new economic crisis, of a new decline of industry in the United States, Great Britain and France—consequently, these were years of new economic complications. In the political sphere they were years of serious political conflicts and perturbations. A new imperialist war is already in its second year, a war waged over a huge territory stretching from Shanghai to Gibraltar, and involving over five hundred million people. The map of Europe, Africa and Asia is being forcibly redrawn. The entire postwar system, the so-called peace regime, has been shaken to its foundations.

For the Soviet Union, on the contrary, these were years of growth and prosperity, of further economic and cultural progress, of further growth of political and military might, of struggle for the preservation of peace throughout the world.

Such is the general picture.

Let us now examine the concrete data illustrating the changes in the international situation.

---

*From the Report to the 18th Congress of the Communist Party of the Soviet Union on the Work of the Central Committee, March 10, 1939.

## 1. NEW ECONOMIC CRISIS IN THE CAPITALIST COUNTRIES

The economic crisis which broke out in the capitalist countries in the latter half of 1929 lasted until the end of 1933. After that the crisis passed into a depression, and was then followed by a certain revival, a certain upward trend of industry. But this upward trend of industry did not develop into a boom, as is usually the case in a period of revival. On the contrary, in the latter half of 1937 a new economic crisis began which seized the United States first of all and then England, France and a number of other countries.

The capitalist countries thus found themselves faced with a new economic crisis before they had even recovered from the ravages of the recent one.

This circumstance naturally led to an increase of unemployment. The number of unemployed in capitalist countries, which had fallen from 30,000,000 in 1933 to 14,000,000 in 1937, has now again risen to 18,000,000 as a result of the new crisis.

A distinguishing feature of the new crisis is that it differs in many respects from the preceding one, and, moreover, differs for the worse and not for the better.

Firstly, the new crisis did not begin after an industrial boom, as was the case in 1929, but after a depression and a certain revival, which, however, did not develop into a boom. This means that the present crisis will be more severe and more difficult to cope with than the previous crisis.

Further, the present crisis has broken out not in time of peace, but at a time when a second imperialist war has already begun; when Japan, already in the second year of her war with China, is disorganizing the immense Chinese market and rendering it almost inaccessible to the goods of other countries; when Italy and Germany have already placed their national economies on a war footing, squandering their reserves of raw material and foreign currency for this purpose; and when all the other big capitalist powers are beginning to reorganize themselves on a war footing. This means that capitalism will have far less resources at its disposal for a normal way out of the present crisis than during the preceding crisis.

Lastly, as distinct from the preceding crisis, the present crisis is not universal, but as yet involves chiefly the economically powerful countries which have not yet placed themselves on a war economy basis. As regards the aggressive countries, such as Japan, Germany and Italy, who have already reorganized their economies on a war footing, they, because of the intense development of their war industry, are not yet experiencing a crisis of overproduction, although they are approaching it. This means that by the time the economically powerful, nonaggressive countries begin to emerge from the phase of crisis the aggressive countries, having exhausted their reserves of gold and raw material in the course of the war fever, are bound to enter a phase of very severe crisis.

. . . For what does placing the economy of a country on a war footing mean? It means giving industry a one-sided, war direction; developing to the utmost the production of goods necessary for war and not for consumption by the population; restricting to the utmost the production and, especially, the sale of articles of general consumption—and, consequently, reducing consumption by the population and confronting the country with an economic crisis.

Such is the concrete picture of the trend of the new economic crisis in the capitalist countries.

Naturally, such an unfavorable turn of economic affairs could not but aggravate relations among the powers. The preceding crisis had already mixed the cards and sharpened the struggle for markets and sources of raw materials. The seizure of Manchuria and North China by Japan, the seizure of Abyssinia by Italy—all this reflected the acuteness of the struggle among the powers. The new economic crisis was bound to lead, and is actually leading, to a further sharpening of the imperialist struggle. It is no longer a question of competition in the markets, of a commercial war, of dumping. These methods of struggle have long been recognized as inadequate. It is now a question of a new redivision of the world, of spheres of influence and colonies, by military action.

Japan tried to justify her aggressive actions by the argument that she had been cheated when the Nine-Power Pact was concluded and had not been allowed to extend her territory at the expense of China, whereas Britain and France possess vast colonies.

Italy recalled that she had been cheated during the division of the spoils after the first imperialist war and that she must recompense herself at the expense of the spheres of influence of Britain and France. Germany, who had suffered severely as a result of the first imperialist war and the Peace of Versailles, joined forces with Japan and Italy and demanded an extension of her territory in Europe and the return of the colonies of which the victors in the first imperialist war had deprived her.

Thus the bloc of three aggressive states came to be formed.

A new redivision of the world by means of war became imminent.

## 2. INCREASING ACUTENESS OF THE INTERNATIONAL POLITICAL SITUATION

Here is a list of the most important events during the period under review which marked the beginning of the new imperialist war. In 1935 Italy attacked and seized Abyssinia. In the summer of 1936 Germany and Italy organized military intervention in Spain, Germany entrenching herself in the north of Spain and in Spanish Morocco, and Italy in the South of Spain and in the Balearic Islands. In 1937, having seized Manchuria, Japan invaded North and Central China, occupied Peking, Tientsin, and Shanghai and began to oust her foreign competitors from the occupied zone. In the beginning of 1938 Germany seized Austria, and in the autumn of 1938 the Sudeten region of Czechoslovakia. At the end of 1938 Japan seized Canton, and at the beginning of 1939 the Island of Hainan.

Thus the war, which has stolen so imperceptibly upon the nations, has drawn over five hundred million people into its orbit and has extended its sphere of action over a vast territory, stretching from Tientsin, Shanghai and Canton, through Abyssinia, to Gibraltar.

After the first imperialist war the victor states, primarily Britain, France and the United States, had set up a new regime in the relations between countries, the post-war peace regime. The main props of this regime were the Nine-Power Pact in the Far East, and the Versailles and a number of other treaties in Europe. The

League of Nations was set up to regulate relations between countries within the framework of this regime, on the basis of a united front of states, of collective defence of the security of states. However, three aggressive states, and the new imperialist war launched by them, upset the entire system of this post-war peace regime. Japan tore up the Nine-Power Pact, and Germany and Italy the Versailles Treaty. In order to have their hands free, these three states withdrew from the League of Nations.

The new imperialist war became a fact.

It is not so easy in our day to suddenly break loose and plunge straight into war without regard for treaties of any kind or for public opinion. Bourgeois politicians know this quite well. So do the fascist rulers. That is why the fascist rulers decided, before plunging into war, to mould public opinion to suit their ends, that is, to mislead it, to deceive it.

A military bloc of Germany and Italy against the interests of England and France in Europe? Bless you, do you call that a bloc? "We" have no military bloc. All "we" have is an innocuous "Berlin-Rome axis"; that is, just a geometrical equation for an axis. (*Laughter.*)

A military bloc of Germany, Italy and Japan against the interests of the United States, Great Britain and France in the Far East? Nothing of the kind! "We" have no military bloc. All "we" have is an innocuous "Berlin-Rome-Tokyo triangle"; that is, a slight penchant for geometry. (*General laughter.*)

A war against the interests of Britain, France, the United States? Nonsense! "We" are waging war on the Comintern, not on these states. If you don't believe it, read the "anti-Comintern pact" concluded between Italy, Germany and Japan.

That is how Messieurs the aggressors thought to mould public opinion, although it was not hard to see how preposterous this whole clumsy game of camouflage was; for it is ridiculous to look for Comintern "hotbeds" in the deserts of Mongolia, in the mountains of Abyssinia, or in the wilds of Spanish Morocco. (*Laughter.*)

But war is inexorable. It cannot be hidden under any guise. For no "axes," "triangles" or "anti-Comintern pacts" can hide the fact that in this period Japan has seized a vast stretch of territory in China, that Italy has seized Abyssinia, that Germany has seized

Austria and the Sudeten region, that Germany and Italy together have seized Spain—and all this in defiance of the interests of the nonaggressive states. The war remains a war; the military bloc of aggressors remains a military bloc; and the aggressors remain aggressors.

It is a distinguishing feature of the new imperialist war that it has not yet become universal, a world war. The war is being waged by aggressor states, who in every way infringe upon the interests of the nonaggressive states, primarily Britain, France and the U.S.A., while the latter draw back and retreat, making concession after concession to the aggressors.

Thus we are witnessing an open redivision of the world and spheres of influence at the expense of the nonaggressive states, without the least attempt at resistance, and even with a certain connivance, on their part.

Incredible, but true.

To what are we to attribute this one-sided and strange character of the new imperialist war?

How is it that the nonaggressive countries, which possess such vast opportunities, have so easily and without resistance abandoned their positions and their obligations to please the aggressors?

Is it to be attributed to the weakness of the nonaggressive states? Of course not! Combined, the nonaggressive, democratic states are unquestionably stronger than the fascist states, both economically and militarily.

To what then are we to attribute the systematic concessions made by these states to the aggressors?

It might be attributed, for example, to the fear that a revolution might break out if the nonaggressive states were to go to war and the war were to assume world-wide proportions. The bourgeois politicians know, of course, that the first imperialist world war led to the victory of the revolution in one of the largest countries. They are afraid that the second imperialist world war may also lead to the victory of the revolution in one or several countries.

But at present this is not the sole or even the chief reason. The chief reason is that the majority of the nonaggressive countries, particularly England and France, have rejected the policy of collective security, the policy of collective resistance to aggressors and have taken up a position of nonintervention, a position of "neutrality."

Formally speaking the policy of nonintervention might be defined as follows: "Let each country defend itself against the aggressors as it likes and as best it can. That is not our affair. We shall trade both with the aggressors and with their victims." But actually speaking, the policy of nonintervention means conniving at aggression, giving free rein to war, and, consequently, transforming the war into a world war. The policy of nonintervention reveals an eagerness, a desire not to hinder the aggressors in their nefarious work: not to hinder Japan, say, from embroiling herself in a war with China, or, better still, with the Soviet Union; not to hinder Germany, say, from enmeshing herself in European affairs, from embroiling herself in a war with the Soviet Union; to allow all the belligerents to sink deeply into the mire of war, to encourage them surreptitiously in this, to allow them to weaken and exhaust one another; and then, when they have become weak enough, to appear on the scene with fresh strength, to appear, of course, "in the interests of peace," and to dictate conditions to the enfeebled belligerents.

Cheap and easy!

Take Japan for instance. It is characteristic that before Japan invaded North China all the influential French and British newspapers shouted about China's weakness and her inability to offer resistance, and declared that Japan with her army could subjugate China in two or three months. Then the European and American politicians began to watch and wait. And then, when Japan seriously started military operations, they let her have Shanghai, the vital center of foreign capital in China; they let her have Canton, a center of Britain's monopoly influence in South China; they let her have Hainan, and they allowed her to surround Hongkong. Does not this look very much like encouraging the aggressor? It is as though they were saying: "Embroil yourself deeper in war; then we shall see."

Or take Germany, for instance. They let her have Austria, despite the undertaking to defend her independence; they let her have the Sudeten region; they abandoned Czechoslovakia to her fate, thereby violating all their obligations; and then they began to lie vociferously in the press about "the weakness of the Russian army," "the demoralization of the Russian air force," and "riots" in the Soviet Union, egging on the Germans to march farther east, promising them easy pickings, and prompting them: "Just start war on the Bolsheviks, and everything will be all right." It must be admitted that this too looks very much like egging on and encouraging the aggressor.

The hullabaloo raised by the British, French and American press over the Soviet Ukraine is characteristic. The gentlemen of the press there shouted until they were hoarse that the Germans were marching on Soviet Ukraine, that they now had what is called the Carpathian Ukraine, with a population of some seven hundred thousand, and that not later than this spring the Germans would annex the Soviet Ukraine, which has a population of over thirty million, to this so-called Carpathian Ukraine. It looks as if the object of this suspicious hullabaloo was to incense the Soviet Union against Germany, to poison the atmosphere and to provoke a conflict with Germany without any visible grounds.

It is quite possible, of course, that there are madmen in Germany who dream of annexing the elephant, that is, the Soviet Ukraine, to the gnat, namely, the so-called Carpathian Ukraine. If there really are such lunatics in Germany, rest assured that we shall find enough strait jackets for them in our country. (*Thunderous applause.*) But if we ignore the madmen and turn to normal people, is it not clearly absurd and foolish to seriously talk of annexing the Soviet Ukraine to this so-called Carpathian Ukraine? Imagine: The gnat comes to the elephant and says perkily: "Ah, brother, how sorry I am for you. Here you are without any landlords, without any capitalists, with no national oppression, without any fascist bosses. Is that a way to live? As I look at you I can't help thinking that there is no hope for you unless you annex yourself to me. (*General laughter.*) Well, so be it: I allow you to annex your tiny domain to my vast territories." (*General laughter and applause.*)

Even more characteristic is the fact that certain European and American politicians and pressmen, having lost patience waiting for "the march on the Soviet Ukraine," are themselves beginning to disclose what is really behind the policy of nonintervention.

They are saying quite openly, putting it down in black on white, that the Germans have cruelly "disappointed" them, for instead of marching farther east, against the Soviet Union, they have turned, you see, to the west and are demanding colonies. One might think that the districts of Czechoslovakia were yielded to Germany as the price of an undertaking to launch war on the Soviet Union, but that now the Germans are refusing to meet their bills and are sending them to Hades.

Far be it from me to moralize on the policy of nonintervention, to talk of treason, treachery and so on. It would be naive to preach morals to people who recognize no human morality. Politics are politics, as the old, case-hardened bourgeois diplomats say. It must be remarked, however, that the big and dangerous political game started by the supporters of the policy of nonintervention may end in serious fiasco for them.

Such is the true face of the now prevailing policy of nonintervention.

Such is the political situation in the capitalist countries.

## 3. THE SOVIET UNION AND THE CAPITALIST COUNTRIES

The war has created a new situation with regard to the relations between countries. It has enveloped them in an atmosphere of alarm and uncertainty. By undermining the postwar peace regime and overriding the elementary principles of international law, it has cast doubt on the value of international treaties and obligations. Pacifism and disarmament schemes are dead and buried. Feverish arming has taken their place. Everybody is arming, small states and big states, including primarily those which practise the policy of nonintervention. Nobody believes any longer in the unctuous speeches which claim that the Munich concessions to the aggressors and the Munich agreement opened a new era of "appeasement." They are disbelieved even by the signatories to the Munich agreement, Britain and France, who are increasing their armaments no less than other countries.

Naturally, the U.S.S.R. could not ignore these ominous developments. There is no doubt that any war, however small, started by the aggressors in any remote corner of the world constitutes a danger to the peaceable countries. All the more serious then is the danger arising from the new imperialist war, which has already drawn into its orbit over five hundred million people in Asia, Africa and Europe. In view of this, while our country is unswervingly pursuing a policy of maintaining peace, it is at the same time working very seriously to increase the preparedness of our Red Army and our Red Navy.

At the same time, in order to strengthen its international position, the Soviet Union decided to take certain other steps. At the end of 1934 our country joined the League of Nations, considering that despite its weakness the League might nevertheless serve as a place where aggressors can be exposed, and as a certain instrument of peace, however feeble, that might hinder the outbreak of war. The Soviet Union considers that in alarming times like these even so weak an international organization as the League of Nations should not be ignored. In May 1935 a treaty of mutual assistance against possible attack by aggressors was signed between France and the Soviet Union. A similar treaty was simultaneously concluded with Czechoslovakia. In March 1936 the Soviet Union concluded a treaty of mutual assistance with the Mongolian People's Republic. In August 1937 the Soviet Union concluded a pact of nonaggression with the Chinese Republic.

It was in such difficult international conditions that the Soviet Union pursued its foreign policy of upholding the cause of peace.

The foreign policy of the Soviet Union is clear and explicit.

1. We stand for peace and the strengthening of business relations with all countries. That is our position; and we shall adhere to this position as long as these countries maintain like relations with the Soviet Union, and as long as they make no attempt to trespass on the interests of our country.

2. We stand for peaceful, close and friendly relations with all the neighboring countries which have common frontiers with the U.S.S.R. That is our position; and we shall adhere to this position as long as these countries maintain like relations with the Soviet Union, and as long as they make no attempt to trespass, directly or indirectly, on the integrity and inviolability of the frontiers of the Soviet state.

3. We stand for the support of nations which are the victims of

aggression and are fighting for the independence of their country.

4. We are not afraid of the threats of aggressors, and are ready to deal two blows for every blow delivered by instigators of war who attempt to violate the Soviet borders.

Such is the foreign policy of the Soviet Union. (*Loud and prolonged applause.*)

In its foreign policy the Soviet Union relies upon:

1. Its growing economic, political and cultural might;

2. The moral and political unity of our Soviet society;

3. The mutual friendship of the nations of our country;

4. Its Red Army and Red Navy;

5. Its policy of peace;

6. The moral support of the working people of all countries, who are vitally concerned in the preservation of peace;

7. The good sense of the countries which for one reason or another have no interests in the violation of peace.

\* \* \*

The tasks of the Party in the sphere of foreign policy are:

1. To continue the policy of peace and of strengthening business relations with all countries;

2. To be cautious and not allow our country to be drawn into conflicts by warmongers who are accustomed to have others pull the chestnuts out of the fire for them;

3. To strengthen the might of our Red Army and Red Navy to the utmost;

4. To strengthen the international bonds of friendship with the working people of all countries, who are interested in peace and friendship among nations.

# DOCUMENTS ON RUSSIA AS A NEUTRAL

1. TREATY OF NON-AGGRESSION BETWEEN GERMANY AND THE UNION OF SOVIET SOCIALIST REPUBLICS (AUGUST 23, 1939) *

The Government of the German Reich and the Government of the Union of Soviet Socialist Republics, desirous of strengthening the cause of peace between Germany and the U.S.S.R., and proceeding from the fundamental provisions of the Neutrality Agreement concluded in April 1926 between Germany and the U.S.S.R., have reached the following agreement:

ARTICLE I. Both High Contracting Parties obligate themselves to desist from any act of violence, any aggressive action, and any attack on each other, either individually or jointly with other powers.

ARTICLE II. Should one of the High Contracting Parties become the object of belligerent action by a third power, the other High Contracting Party shall in no manner lend its support to this third power.

ARTICLE III. The Governments of the two High Contracting Parties shall in the future maintain continual contact with one another for the purpose of consultation in order to exchange information on problems affecting their common interests.

ARTICLE IV. Neither of the two High Contracting Parties shall participate in any grouping of powers whatsoever that is directly or indirectly aimed at the other party.

ARTICLE V. Should disputes or conflicts arise between the High Contracting Parties over problems of one kind or another, both parties shall settle these disputes or conflicts exclusively through friendly exchange of opinion or, if necessary, through the establishment of arbitration commissions.

*From *Nazi-Soviet Relations, 1939-1941*, U. S. Department of State Publication 3023, Government Printing Office, Washington, D. C.

Article VI. The present treaty is concluded for a period of ten years, with the proviso that, in so far as one of the High Contracting Parties does not denounce it one year prior to the expiration of this period, the validity of this treaty shall automatically be extended for another five years.

Article VII. The present treaty shall be ratified within the shortest possible time. The ratifications shall be exchanged in Berlin. The agreement shall enter into force as soon as it is signed.

Done in duplicate, in the German and Russian languages. Moscow, August 23, 1939

For the Government
of the German Reich:
v. Ribbentrop

With full power of the
Government of the U.S.S.R.:
V. Molotov

## SECRET ADDITIONAL PROTOCOL

On the occasion of the signature of the Nonaggression Pact between the German Reich and the Union of Socialist Soviet Republics the undersigned plenipotentiaries of each of the two parties discussed in strictly confidential conversations the question of the boundary of their respective spheres of influence in Eastern Europe. These conversations led to the following conclusions:

1. In the event of a territorial and political rearrangement in the areas belonging to the Baltic States (Finland, Estonia, Latvia, Lithuania), the northern boundary of Lithuania shall represent the boundary of the spheres of influence of Germany and the U.S.S.R. In this connection the interest of Lithuania in the Vilna area is recognized by each party.

2. In the event of a territorial and political rearrangement of the areas belonging to the Polish state the spheres of influence of Germany and the U.S.S.R. shall be bounded approximately by the line of the rivers Narew, Vistula, and San.

The question of whether the interests of both parties make desirable the maintenance of an independent Polish state and how such a state should be bounded can only be definitely determined in the course of further political developments.

In any event both Governments will resolve this question by means of a friendly agreement.

3. With regard to Southeastern Europe attention is called by the Soviet side to its interest in Bessarabia. The German side declares its complete political disinterestedness in these areas.

4. This protocol shall be treated by both parties as strictly secret.

Moscow, August 23, 1939

| | |
|---|---|
| For the Government of the German Reich: v. Ribbentrop | Plenipotentiary of the Government of the U.S.S.R., V. Molotov |

## 2. STATEMENT OF V. M. MOLOTOV ON THE MEANING OF THE SOVIET-GERMAN NON-AGGRESSION PACT (AUGUST 31, 1939)*

Comrades: Since the third session of the Supreme Soviet the international situation has shown no change for the better. On the contrary, it has become even more tense. The steps taken by various governments to put an end to this state of tension have obviously proved inadequate. They met with no success. This is true of Europe.

Nor has there been any change for the better in East Asia. Japanese troops continue to occupy the principal cities and a considerable part of the territory of China. Nor is Japan refraining from hostile acts against the U.S.S.R. Here, too, the situation has changed in the direction of further aggravation.

In view of this state of affairs, the conclusion of a pact of non-aggression between the U.S.S.R. and Germany is of tremendous positive value, eliminating the danger of war between Germany and the Soviet Union. In order more fully to define the significance of this pact, I must first dwell on the negotiations which have taken place in recent months in Moscow with representatives of Great Britain and France. As you know, Anglo-French-Soviet negotiations for conclusion of a pact of mutual assistance against aggression in Europe began as far back as April.

---

*An address before the joint sitting of the Council of the Union and the Council of Nationalities of the Supreme Soviet of the U.S.S.R. Reprinted from *The Strategy and Tactics of World Communism*, Supplement I, U. S. Government Printing Office, Washington, D. C.

True, the initial proposals of the British Government were, as you know, entirely unacceptable. They ignored the prime requisites for such negotiations—they ignored the principle of reciprocity and equality of obligations. In spite of this, the Soviet Government did not reject the negotiations and in turn put forward its own proposals. We were mindful of the fact that it was difficult for the Governments of Great Britain and France to make an abrupt change in their policy from an unfriendly attitude towards the Soviet Union which had existed quite recently to serious negotiations with the U.S.S.R. based on the condition of equality of obligation.

However, the subsequent negotiations were not justified by their results. The Anglo-French-Soviet negotiations lasted four months. They helped to elucidate a number of questions. At the same time they made it clear to the representatives of Great Britain and France that the Soviet Union has to be seriously reckoned with in international affairs. But these negotiations encountered insuperable obstacles. The trouble, of course, did not lie in individual "formulations" or in particular clauses in the draft of the pact. No, the trouble was much more serious.

The conclusion of a pact of mutual assistance against aggression would have been of value only if Great Britain, France and the Soviet Union had arrived at agreement as to definite military measures against the attack of an aggressor. Accordingly, for a certain period not only political but also military negotiations were conducted in Moscow with representatives of the British and French armies. However, nothing came of the military negotiations.

They encountered the difficulty that Poland, which was to be jointly guaranteed by Great Britain, France and the U.S.S.R., rejected military assistance on the part of the Soviet Union. Attempts to overcome the objections of Poland met with no success. More, the negotiations showed that Great Britain was not anxious to overcome these objections of Poland, but on the contrary encouraged them. It is clear that, such being the attitude of the Polish Government and its principal ally towards military assistance on the part of the Soviet Union in the event of aggression, the Anglo-French-Soviet negotiations could not bear fruit. After this it became clear to us that the Anglo-French-Soviet negotiations were doomed to failure.

What have the negotiations with Great Britain and France shown? The Anglo-French-Soviet negotiations have shown that the position of Great Britain and France is marked by howling contradictions throughout. Judge for yourselves.

On the one hand, Great Britain and France demanded that the U.S.S.R. should give military assistance to Poland in case of aggression. The U.S.S.R., as you know, was willing to meet this demand, provided that the U.S.S.R. itself received like assistance from Great Britain and France. On the other hand, precisely Great Britain and France brought Poland on the scene, who resolutely declined military assistance on the part of the U.S.S.R. Just try under such circumstances to reach an agreement regarding mutual assistance, when assistance on the part of the U.S.S.R. is declared beforehand to be unnecessary and intrusive.

Further, on the one hand, Great Britain and France offered to guarantee the Soviet Union military assistance against aggression in return for like assistance on the part of the U.S.S.R. On the other hand, they hedged around their assistance with such reservations regarding indirect aggression as could convert this assistance into a myth and provide them with formal legal excuse to evade giving assistance and place the U.S.S.R. in a position of isolation in the face of the aggressor. Just try to distinguish between such a "pact of mutual assistance" and a pact of more or less camouflaged chicanery.

Further, on the one hand Great Britain and France stressed the importance and gravity of negotiations for a pact of mutual assistance and demanded that the U.S.S.R. should treat the matter most seriously and settle very rapidly all questions relating to the pact. On the other hand, they themselves displayed extreme dilatoriness and an absolutely light-minded attitude towards the negotiations, entrusting them to individuals of secondary importance who were not invested with adequate powers. . . .

Such are the intrinsic contradictions in the attitude of Great Britain and France towards the negotiations with the U.S.S.R. which led to their breakdown.

What is the root of these contradictions in the position of Great

Britain and France? In a few words, it can be put as follows: On the one hand, the British and French governments fear aggression, and for that reason they would like to have a pact of mutual assistance with the Soviet Union provided it helped strengthen them, Great Britain and France.

But, on the other hand, the British and French governments are afraid that the conclusion of a real pact of mutual assistance with the U.S.S.R. may strengthen our country, the Soviet Union, which, it appears, does not answer their purpose. It must be admitted that these fears of theirs outweighed other considerations. Only in this way can we understand the position of Poland, who acts on the instructions of Great Britain and France.

I shall now pass to the Soviet-German Non-Aggression Pact.

The decision to conclude a non-aggression pact between the U.S.S.R. and Germany was adopted after military negotiations with France and Great Britain had reached an impasse owing to the insuperable differences I have mentioned. As the negotiations had shown that the conclusion of a pact of mutual assistance could not be expected, we could not but explore other possibilities of ensuring peace and eliminating the danger of war between Germany and the U.S.S.R. If the British and French governments refused to reckon with this, that is their affair. It is our duty to think of the interests of the Soviet people, the interests of the Union of Soviet Socialist Republics. (*Prolonged applause.*) All the more since we are firmly convinced that the interests of the U.S.S.R. coincide with the fundamental interests of the peoples of other countries. (*Applause.*) But that is only one side of the matter.

Another circumstance was required before the Soviet-German Non-Aggression Pact could come into existence. It was necessary that in her foreign policy Germany should make a turn towards good-neighborly relations with the Soviet Union.

Only when this second condition was fulfilled, only when it became clear to us that the German Government desired to change its foreign policy so as to secure an improvement of relations with the U.S.S.R. was the basis found for the conclusion of a Soviet-German Non-Aggression Pact. Everybody knows that during the last six years, ever since the National-Socialists (Nazis) came into power, political relations between Germany and the U.S.S.R. have been strained.   Everybody also knows that despite the differences of outlook and political systems, the Soviet Government endeavored to maintain normal business and political relations with Germany. . . .

I must, however, recall the explanation of our foreign policy given several months ago at the Eighteenth Party Congress. Speaking of our tasks in the realm of foreign policy, Stalin defined our attitude to other countries as follows:

1. To continue the policy of peace and of strengthening business relations with all countries;

2. To be cautious and not to allow our country to be drawn into conflicts by warmongers who are accustomed to have others pull the chestnuts out of the fire for them.

As you see, Stalin declared in conclusion that the Soviet Union stands for strengthening business relations with all countries. But at the same time Stalin warned us against warmongers who are anxious in their own interests to involve our country in conflicts with other countries.

Exposing the hullabaloo raised in the British, French, and American press about Germany's "plans" for the seizure of the Soviet Ukraine, Stalin said:

> It looks as if the object of this suspicious hullabaloo was to incense the Soviet Union against Germany, to poison the atmosphere and to provoke a conflict with Germany without any visible grounds.

As you see, Stalin hit the nail on the head when he exposed the machinations of the Western European politicians who were trying to set Germany and the Soviet Union at loggerheads.

It must be confessed that there were some short-sighted people even in our own country who, carried away by oversimplified antifascist propaganda, forgot about this provocative work of our enemies.   Mindful of this, Stalin even then suggested the possibility of other, unhostile, good-neighborly relations between Germany and the U.S.S.R.   It can now be seen that on the whole Germany correctly understood these statements of Stalin and drew practical conclusions from them. (*Laughter.*) The conclusion of the Soviet-German Non-Aggression Pact shows that Stalin's historic pre-vision has been brilliantly confirmed. (*Loud applause.*) . . .

Voices are now being heard testifying to the lack of understanding of the most simple reasons for the improvement of political relations between the Soviet Union and Germany which has begun. For example, people ask with an air of innocence how the Soviet Union could consent to improve political relations with a state of a fascist type. "Is that possible?" they ask. But they forget that this is not a question of our attitude towards the internal regime of another country but of the foreign relations between the two states. They forget that we hold the position of not interfering in the internal affairs of other countries and, correspondingly, of not tolerating interference in our own internal affairs. Furthermore, they forget the important principle of our foreign policy which was formulated by Stalin at the Eighteenth Party Congress as follows:

> We stand for peace and the strengthening of business relations with all countries. That is our position; and we adhere to this position as long as these countries maintain like relations with the Soviet Union, and as long as they make no attempt to trespass on the interests of our country.

The meaning of these words is quite clear: the Soviet Union strives to maintain friendly relations with all non-Soviet countries, provided that these countries maintain a like attitude towards the Soviet Union. In our foreign policy towards non-Soviet countries, we have always been guided by Lenin's well-known principle of the peaceful coexistence of the Soviet state and of capitalist countries. . . .

It is true that it is not a pact of mutual assistance that is in question, as in the case of the Anglo-French-Soviet negotiations, but only of a non-aggression pact. Nevertheless, conditions being what they are, it is difficult to over-estimate the international importance of the Soviet-German pact. . . .

The Non-Aggression Pact between the U.S.S.R. and Germany marks a turning point in the history of Europe, and not only of Europe. Only yesterday the German fascists were pursuing a foreign policy hostile to us. Yes, only yesterday we were enemies in the sphere of foreign relations. Today, however, the situation has changed and we are enemies no longer.

The art of politics in the sphere of foreign relations does not consist in increasing the number of enemies for one's country. On the contrary, the art of politics in this sphere is to reduce the number of such enemies and to make the enemies of yesterday good neighbors, maintaining peaceable relations with one another. (*Applause.*)

History has shown that enmity and wars between our country and Germany have been to the detriment of our countries, not to their benefit. Russia and Germany suffered most of all countries in the war of 1914-1918. Therefore the interests of the peoples of the Soviet Union and Germany stand in need of peaceable relations. The Soviet-German Non-Aggression Pact puts an end to enmity between Germany and the U.S.S.R. and this is in the interests of both countries. The fact that our outlooks and political systems differ must not and cannot be obstacles to the establishment of good political relations between both states, just as like differences are not impediments to good political relations which the U.S.S.R. maintains with other non-Soviet capitalist countries. Only enemies of Germany and the U.S.S.R. can strive to create and foment enmity between the peoples of these countries. We have always stood for amity between the peoples of the U.S.S.R. and Germany, for the growth and development of friendship between the peoples of the Soviet Union and the German people. (*Loud and prolonged applause.*)

The importance of the Soviet-German Non-Aggression Pact lies in the fact that the two largest states of Europe have agreed to put an end to the enmity between them, to eliminate the menace of war and live at peace one with the other, making narrow thereby the zone of possible military conflicts in Europe. Even if military conflicts in Europe should prove unavoidable, the scope of hostilities will now be restricted. Only the instigators of a general European war can be displeased by this state of affairs, those who under the mask of pacifism would like to ignite a general conflagration in Europe.

The Soviet-German Pact has been the object of numerous attacks in the English, French and American press. . . . Attempts are being made to spread the fiction that the signing of the Soviet-

German Pact disrupted the negotiations with England and France on a mutual assistance pact. . . .

In reality, as you know, the very reverse is true. The Soviet Union signed the Non-Aggression Pact with Germany, for one thing, in view of the fact that the negotiations with France and England had run into insuperable differences and ended in failure through the fault of the ruling classes of England and France. . . .

In all this, we find fresh corroboration of Stalin's warning that we must be particularly cautious with warmongers who are accustomed to have others pull chestnuts out of the fire for them. We must be on guard against those who see an advantage to themselves in bad relations between the U.S.S.R. and Germany, in enmity between them, and who do not want peace and good neighborly relations between Germany and the Soviet Union.

We can understand why this policy is being pursued by out-and-out imperialists. But we cannot ignore such facts as the especial zeal with which some leaders of the Socialist Parties of Great Britain and France have recently distinguished themselves in this matter. And these gentlemen have really gone the whole hog, and no mistake. (*Laughter.*) These people positively demand that the U.S.S.R. get itself involved in war against Germany on the side of Great Britain. Have not these rabid warmongers taken leave of their senses? (*Laughter.*) Is it really difficult for these gentlemen to understand the purpose of the Soviet-German Pact, on the strength of which the U.S.S.R. is not obligated to involve itself in war either on the side of Great Britain against Germany or on the side of Germany against Great Britain? Is it really difficult to understand that the U.S.S.R. is pursuing and will continue to pursue its own independent policy, based on the interests of the people of the U.S.S.R. and only their interests? (*Prolonged applause.*)

If these gentlemen have such an uncontrollable desire to fight, let them do their own fighting without the Soviet Union. We would see what fighting stuff they are made of.

In our eyes, in the eyes of the entire Soviet people, these are just as much enemies of peace as all other instigators of war in Europe. Only those who desire a grand new slaughter, a new holocaust of nations, only they want to set the Soviet Union and Germany at loggerheads, they are the only people who want to destroy the incipient restoration of good-neighborly relations between the peoples of the U.S.S.R. and Germany.

The Soviet Union signed a pact with Germany, fully assured that peace between the peoples of the U.S.S.R. and Germany is in the interests of all peoples, in the interests of universal peace. Every sincere supporter of peace will realize the truth of this. This pact corresponds to the fundamental interests of the working people of the Soviet Union and cannot weaken our vigilance in defense of these interests. This pact is backed by firm confidence in our real forces, in their complete preparedness to meet any aggression against the U.S.S.R. (*Loud applause.*)

This pact, like the unsuccessful, Anglo-French-Soviet negotiations, proves that no important questions of international relations, and questions of Eastern Europe even less, can be settled without the active participation of the Soviet Union, that any attempts to shut out the Soviet Union and decide such questions behind its back are doomed to failure.

The Soviet-German Non-Aggression Pact spells a new turn in the development of Europe, a turn towards improvement of relations between the two largest states of Europe. This pact not only eliminates the menace of war with Germany, narrows down the zone of possible hostilities in Europe, and serves thereby the cause of universal peace: it must open to us new possibilities of increasing our strength, of further consolidation of our position, of further growth of the influence of the Soviet Union on international developments.

There is no need to dwell here on the separate clauses of the pact. The Council of People's Commissars has reason to hope that the pact will meet with your approval as a document of cardinal importance to the U.S.S.R. (*Applause.*)

The Council of People's Commissars submits the Soviet-German Non-Aggression Pact to the Supreme Soviet and proposes that it be ratified. (*Loud and prolonged applause. All rise.*)

* * *

On the conclusion of Molotov's statement, the joint sitting of the Council of the Union and the Council of Nationalities of the

Supreme Soviet of the U.S.S.R. unanimously adopted the following resolution:

Having heard the statement of Comrade V. M. Molotov, the Chairman of the Council of People's Commissars, and People's Commissar of Foreign Affairs, on the ratification of the Non-Aggression Pact between the U.S.S.R. and Germany, the Supreme Soviet of the U.S.S.R. resolves:

1. To approve the foreign policy of the government.

2. To ratify the Non-Aggression Pact between the U.S.S.R. and Germany, concluded in Moscow, August 23, 1939.

# THE SOVIET NEMESIS*

BY

## WINSTON S. CHURCHILL

[1948]

[In the Spring of 1939] we reached the period when all relations between Britain and Germany were at an end. We now know, of course, that there never had been any true relationship between our two countries since Hitler came into power. He had only hoped to persuade or frighten Britain into giving him a free hand in Eastern Europe; and Mr. Chamberlain had cherished the hope of appeasing and reforming him and leading him to grace. However, the time had come when the last illusions of the British Government had been dispelled. The Cabinet was at length convinced that Nazi Germany meant war, and the Prime Minister offered guarantees and contracted alliances in every direction still open, regardless of whether we could give any effective help to the countries concerned. To the Polish guarantee was added a Rumanian guarantee, and to these an alliance with Turkey. . . .

The British Government had to consider urgently the practical implications of the guarantees given to Poland and to Rumania. Neither set of assurances had any military value except within the framework of a general agreement with Russia. It was, therefore, with this object that talks at last began in Moscow on April 15 [1939] between the British Ambassador and M. Litvinov. Considering how the Soviet Government had hitherto been treated, there was not much to be expected from them now. However, on April 16 they made a formal offer, the text of which was not published, for the creation of a united front of mutual assistance between Great Britain, France, and the U.S.S.R. The three Powers, with Poland added if possible, were furthermore to guarantee those states in Central and Eastern Europe which lay under the menace of German aggression. The obstacle to such an agreement was the

* From *The Second World War*, Vols. I, III, and IV. Copyright 1948, 1950, by Houghton Mifflin Company. Reprinted by permission.

terror of these same border countries of receiving Soviet help in the shape of Soviet armies marching through their territories to defend them from the Germans, and incidentally incorporating them in the Soviet-Communist system of which they were the most vehement opponents. Poland, Rumania, Finland, and the three Baltic States did not know whether it was German aggression or Russian rescue that they dreaded more. It was this hideous choice that paralyzed British and French policy.

There can, however, be no doubt, even in the after light, that Britain and France should have accepted the Russian offer, proclaimed the Triple Alliance, and left the method by which it could be made effective in case of war to be adjusted between allies engaged against a common foe. In such circumstances a different temper prevails. Allies in war are inclined to defer a great deal to each other's wishes; the flail of battle beats upon the front, and all kinds of expedients are welcomed which, in peace, would be abhorrent. It would not be easy in a grand alliance, such as might have been developed, for one ally to enter the territory of another unless invited.

But Mr. Chamberlain and the Foreign Office were baffled by this riddle of the Sphinx. When events are moving at such speed and in such tremendous mass as at this juncture, it is wise to take one step at a time. The alliance of Britain, France, and Russia would have struck deep alarm into the heart of Germany in 1939, and no one can prove that war might not even then have been averted. The next step could have been taken with superior power on the side of the Allies. The initiative would have been regained by their diplomacy. Hitler could afford neither to embark upon the war on two fronts, which he himself had so deeply condemned, nor to sustain a check. It was a pity not to have placed him in this awkward position, which might well have cost him his life. Statesmen are not called upon only to settle easy questions. These often settle themselves. It is where the balance quivers and the proportions are veiled in mist, that the opportunity for world-saving decisions presents itself. Having got ourselves into this awful plight of 1939, it was vital to grasp the larger hope. . . .

On May 4, I commented on the position in these terms:

Above all, time must not be lost. Ten or twelve days have already passed since the Russian offer was made. The British people, who have now, at the sacrifice of honored, ingrained custom, accepted the principle of compulsory military service, have a right, in conjunction with the French Republic, to call upon Poland not to place obstacles in the way of a common cause. Not only must the full cooperation of Russia be accepted, but the three Baltic States, Lithuania, Latvia, and Esthonia, must also be brought into association. To these three countries of war-like peoples, possessing together armies totalling perhaps twenty divisions of virile troops, a friendly Russia supplying munitions and other aid is essential.

There is no means of maintaining an Eastern Front against Nazi aggression without the active aid of Russia. Russian interests are deeply concerned in preventing Herr Hitler's designs on Eastern Europe. It should still be possible to range all the states and peoples from the Baltic to the Black Sea in one solid front against a new outrage or invasion. Such a front, if established in good heart, and with resolute and efficient military arrangements, combined with the strength of the Western Powers, may yet confront Hitler, Goering, Himmler, Ribbentrop, Goebbels and Company with forces the German people would be reluctant to challenge. . . .

\* \* \*

The negotiations had come to a seemingly unbreakable deadlock. The Polish and Rumanian Governments, while accepting the British guarantee, were not prepared to accept a similar undertaking in the same form from the Russian Government. A similar attitude prevailed in another vital strategic quarter—the Baltic States. The Soviet Government made it clear that they would only adhere to a pact of mutual assistance if Finland and the Baltic States were included in a general guarantee. All four countries now refused, and perhaps in their terror would for a long time have refused, such a condition. Finland and Esthonia even asserted that they would consider a guarantee extended to them without their assent as an act of aggression. On the same day, May 31, Esthonia and Latvia signed non-aggression pacts with Germany. Thus Hitler penetrated with ease into the frail defenses of the tardy, irresolute coalition against him. . . .

A renewed effort to come to an arrangement with Soviet Russia was made by the British and French Governments. It was decided to send a special envoy to Moscow. Mr. Eden, who had made useful contacts with Stalin some years before, volunteered to go.

This generous offer was declined by the Prime Minister. Instead, on June 12, Mr. Strang, an able official but without any special standing outside the Foreign Office, was entrusted with this momentous mission. This was another mistake. The sending of so subordinate a figure gave actual offense. It is doubtful whether he was able to pierce the outer crust of the Soviet organism. In any case all was now too late. Much had happened since . . . August, 1938. Munich had happened. Hitler's armies had had a year more to mature. His munition factories, reinforced by the Skoda Works, were all in full blast. The Soviet Government cared much for Czechoslovakia; but Czechoslovakia was gone. Benes was in exile. A German Gauleiter ruled in Prague.

On the other hand, Poland presented to Russia an entirely different set of age-long political and strategic problems. Their last major contact had been the Battle of Warsaw in 1920, when the Bolshevik armies under Ensign Krylenko had been hurled back from their invasion by Pilsudski aided by the advice of General Weygand and the British Mission under Lord D'Abernon, and thereafter pursued with bloody vengeance. During these years Poland had been a spearpoint of anti-Bolshevism. With her left hand she joined and sustained the anti-Soviet Baltic States. But with her right hand, at Munich-time, she had helped to despoil Czechoslovakia. The Soviet Government were sure that Poland hated them, and also that Poland had no power to withstand a German onslaught. They were, however, very conscious of their own perils and of their need for time to repair the havoc in the High Commands of their armies. In these circumstances, the prospects of Mr. Strang's mission were not exuberant.

The negotiations wandered around the question of the reluctance of Poland and the Baltic States to be rescued from Germany by the Soviets; and here they made no progress. . . . All through July the discussions continued fitfully, and eventually the Soviet Government proposed that conversations should be continued on a military basis with both French and British representatives. The British Government, therefore, dispatched Admiral Drax with a mission to Moscow on August 10. These officers possessed no written authority to negotiate. The French Mission was headed by General Doumenic. On the Russian side, Marshal Voroshilov officiated. We now know that at this same time the Soviet Government agreed to the journey of a German negotiator to Moscow. The military conference soon foundered upon the refusal of Poland and Rumania to allow the transit of Russian troops. The Polish attitude was, "With the Germans we risk losing our liberty; with the Russians our soul."

At the Kremlin in August, 1942, Stalin, in the early hours of the morning, gave me one aspect of the Soviet position. "We formed the impression," said Stalin, "that the British and French Governments were not resolved to go to war if Poland were attacked, but that they hoped the diplomatic line-up of Britain, France, and Russia would deter Hitler. We were sure it would not." "How many divisions," Stalin had asked, "will France send against Germany on mobilization?" The answer was: "About a hundred." He then asked: "How many will England send?" The answer was: "Two and two more later." "Ah, two and two more later," Stalin had repeated. "Do you know," he asked, "how many divisions we shall have to put on the Russian front if we go to war with Germany?" There was a pause. "More than three hundred." I was not told with whom this conversation took place or its date. It must be recognized that this was solid ground, but not favorable for Mr. Strang of the Foreign Office. . . .

On the evening of August 19 [1939], Stalin announced to the Politburo his intention to sign a pact with Germany. On August 22, Marshal Voroshilov was not to be found by the Allied missions until evening. He then said to the head of the French Mission:

> The question of military collaboration with France has been in the air for several years, but has never been settled. Last year, when Czechoslovakia was perishing, we waited for a signal from France, but none was given. Our troops were ready. . . . The French and English Governments have now dragged out the political and military discussions too long. For that reason the possibility is not to be excluded that certain political events may take place. . . .

The next day Ribbentrop arrived in Moscow.

. . . The Non-Aggression Pact and the secret agreement were signed rather late on the night of August 23.

Despite all that has been dispassionately recorded in this chapter, only totalitarian despotism in both countries could have faced the odium of such an unnatural act. It is a question whether Hitler or Stalin loathed it most. Both were aware that it could only be a temporary expedient. The antagonisms between the two empires and systems were mortal. Stalin no doubt felt that Hitler would be a less deadly foe to Russia after a year of war with the Western Powers. Hitler followed his method of "One at a time." The fact that such an agreement could be made marks the culminating failure of British and French foreign policy and diplomacy over several years.

On the Soviet side it must be said that their vital need was to hold the deployment positions of the German armies as far to the west as possible so as to give the Russians more time for assembling their forces from all parts of their immense empire. They had burnt in their minds the disasters which had come upon their armies in 1914 when they had hurled themselves forward to attack the Germans while still themselves only partly mobilized. But now their frontiers lay far to the east of those of the previous war. They must be in occupation of the Baltic States and a large part of Poland by force or fraud before they were attacked. If their policy was cold-blooded, it was also at the moment realistic in a high degree. . . .

This treaty was to last ten years, and if not denounced by either side one year before the expiration of that period, would be automatically extended for another five years. There was much jubilation and many toasts around the conference table. Stalin spontaneously proposed the toast of the Fuehrer, as follows, "I know how much the German Nation loves its Fuehrer, I should therefore like to drink to his health." A moral may be drawn from all this, which is of homely simplicity—"Honesty is the best policy." Several examples of this will be shown in these pages. Crafty men and statesmen will be shown misled by all their elaborate calculations. But this is the signal instance. Only twenty-two months were to pass before Stalin and the Russian nation in its scores of millions were to pay a frightful forfeit. If a Government has no moral scruples, it often seems to gain great advantages and liberties of action, but "All comes out even at the end of the day, and all will come out yet more even when all the days are ended."

*  *  *

. . . According to Hitler's plan, the German armies were unleashed on September 1, 1939, and ahead of them his air force struck the Polish squadrons on their airfields. In two days the Polish air power was virtually annihilated. Within a week the German armies had bitten deep into Poland. Resistance everywhere was brave but vain. . . .

The second week was marked by bitter fighting and by its end the Polish Army, nominally of about two million men, ceased to exist as an organized force. . . .

It was within the claws of the Warsaw pincers that the Polish Army fought and died. . . . On the twentieth, the Germans announced that the battle of the Vistula was "one of the greatest battles of extermination of all times."

It was now the turn of the Soviets. What they now call "Democracy" came into action. On September 17, the Russian armies swarmed across the almost undefended Polish eastern frontier and rolled westward on a broad front. On the eighteenth, they occupied Vilna, and met their German collaborators at Brest-Litovsk. Here in the previous war the Bolsheviks, in breach of their solemn agreements with the Western Allies, had made their separate peace with the Kaiser's Germany, and had bowed to its harsh terms. Now in Brest-Litovsk, it was with Hitler's Germany that the Russian Communists grinned and shook hands. The ruin of Poland and its entire subjugation proceeded apace. Warsaw and Modlin still remained unconquered. The resistance of Warsaw, largely arising from the surge of its citizens, was magnificent and forlorn. After many days of violent bombardment from the air and by heavy artillery, much of which was rapidly transported across the great lateral highways from the idle Western Front, the Warsaw radio ceased to play the Polish National Anthem, and Hitler entered the ruins of the city. Modlin, a fortress twenty miles down the Vistula, had taken in the remnants of the Thorn group, and fought on until the twenty-eighth. Thus, in one month all was over, and a nation of thirty-five millions fell into the merciless grip of those who sought not only conquest but enslavement, and indeed extinction for vast numbers. . . .

The Soviet armies continued to advance up to the line they had settled with Hitler, and on the twenty-ninth the Russo-German Treaty partitioning Poland was formally signed. I was still convinced of the profound, and as I believed quenchless, antagonism between Russia and Germany, and I clung to the hope that the Soviets would be drawn to our side by the force of events. I did not, therefore, give way to the indignation which I felt and which surged around me in our Cabinet at their callous, brutal policy. I had never had any illusions about them. I knew that they accepted no moral code, and studied their own interests alone. But at least they owed us nothing. Besides, in mortal war anger must be subordinated to defeating the main immediate enemy. I was determined to put the best construction on their odious conduct. Therefore, in a paper which I wrote for the War Cabinet on September 25, I struck a cool note.

Although the Russians were guilty of the grossest bad faith in the recent negotiations, their demand, made by Marshal Voroshilov that Russian armies should occupy Vilna and Lemberg if they were to be allies of Poland, was a perfectly valid military request. It was rejected by Poland on grounds which, though natural, can now be seen to have been insufficient. In the result Russia has occupied the same line and positions as the enemy of Poland, which possibly she might have occupied as a very doubtful and suspected friend. The difference in fact is not so great as might seem. The Russians have mobilized very large forces and have shown themselves able to advance fast and far from their pre-war positions. They are now limitrophe with Germany, and it is quite impossible for Germany to denude the Eastern Front. A large German army must be left to watch it. I see General Gamelin puts it at least twenty divisions. It may well be twenty-five or more. An Eastern Front is, therefore, potentially in existence.

In a broadcast on October 1, I said:

Poland has again been overrun by two of the Great Powers which held her in bondage for a hundred and fifty years, but were unable to quench the spirit of the Polish nation. The heroic defence of Warsaw shows that the soul of Poland is indestructible, and that she will rise again like a rock, which may for a time be submerged by a tidal wave, but which remains a rock.

Russia has pursued a cold policy of self-interest. We could have wished that the Russian armies should be standing on their present line as the friends and allies of Poland instead of as invaders. But that the Russian armies should stand on this line was clearly necessary for the safety of Russia against the Nazi menace. At any rate, the line is there, and an Eastern Front has been created which Nazi Germany does not dare assail.
. . .

I cannot forecast to you the action of Russia. It is a riddle wrapped in a mystery inside an enigma; but perhaps there is a key. That key is Russian national interest. It cannot be in accordance with the interest or the safety of Russia that Germany should plant herself upon the shores of the Black Sea, or that she should overrun the Balkan States and subjugate the Slavonic peoples of Southeastern Europe. That would be contrary to the historic life-interests of Russia.

* * *

. . . It was thus with relief and excitement that towards the end of March, 1941, I read an Intelligence report from one of our most trusted sources of the movement and counter-movement of . German armor on the railway from Bucharest to Cracow. This showed that as soon as the Yugoslav Ministers made their submission in Vienna, three out of the five Panzer divisions which had moved through Rumania southward towards Greece and Yugoslavia had been sent northward to Cracow, and secondly, that the whole of this transportation had been reversed after the Belgrade revolution and the three Panzer divisions sent back to Rumania. This shuffling and reversal of about sixty trains could not be concealed from our agents on the spot.

To me it illuminated the whole Eastern scene like a lightning flash. The sudden movement to Cracow of so much armor needed in the Balkan sphere could only mean Hitler's intention to invade Russia in May. This seemed to me henceforward certainly his major purpose. The fact that the Belgrade revolution had required their return to Rumania involved perhaps a delay from May to June. I sent the momentous news at once to Mr. Eden in Athens.

PRIME MINISTER TO MR. EDEN, ATHENS                30 March 41
My reading of the Intelligence is that the bad man concentrated very large armored forces, etc., to overawe Yugoslavia and Greece, and hoped to get former or both without fighting. The moment he was sure Yugoslavia was in the Axis he moved three of the five Panzers towards the

Bear, believing that what was left would be enough to finish the Greek affair. However, the Belgrade revolution upset this picture and caused the northward move to be arrested in transit. This can only mean, in my opinion, the intention to attack Yugoslavia at earliest, or alternatively [to] act against the Turk. It looks as if heavy forces will be used in Balkan Peninsula and that Bear will be kept waiting a bit. Furthermore, these orders and counter-orders in their relation to the Belgrade *coup* seem to reveal magnitude of design both towards southeast and east. This is the clearest indication we have had so far. . . .

I also cast about for some means of warning Stalin. . . . I made the message short and cryptic, hoping that this very fact, and that it was the first message I had sent him since my formal telegram of June 25, 1940, commending Sir Stafford Cripps as Ambassador, would arrest his attention and make him ponder.

PRIME MINISTER TO SIR STAFFORD CRIPPS                          3 April 41
Following from me to M. Stalin, *provided it can be personally delivered by you:*
I have sure information from a trusted agent that when the Germans thought they had got Yugoslavia in the net—that is to say, after March 20—they began to move three out of five Panzer divisions from Rumania to Southern Poland. The moment they heard of the Serbian revolution this movement was countermanded. Your Excellency will appreciate the significance of these facts.

. . . The British Ambassador did not reply till April 12, when he said that just before my telegram had been received he had himself addressed to Vyshinsky a long personal letter reviewing the succession of failures of the Soviet Government to counteract German encroachments in the Balkans, and urging in the strongest terms that the U.S.S.R. in her own interest must now decide on an immediate vigorous policy of co-operation with countries still opposing the Axis in that area if she was not to miss the last chance of defending her own frontiers in alliance with others.

Were I now [he said] to convey through Molotov the Prime Minister's message, which expresses the same thesis in very much shorter and less emphatic form, I fear that the only effect would be probably to weaken impression already made by my letter to Vyshinsky. Soviet Government would not, I feel sure, understand why so short and fragmentary a commentary on facts of which they are certainly well aware, without any definite request for explanation of Soviet Government's attitude or suggestion for action by them, should be conveyed in so formal a manner.

I have felt bound to put these considerations before you, as I greatly fear that delivery of Prime Minister's message would be not merely ineffectual but a serious tactical mistake. If, however, you are unable to share this view, I will, of course, endeavor to arrange urgently for an interview with Molotov.

. . . I was vexed at this and at the delay which had occurred. This was the only message before the attack that I sent Stalin direct. Its brevity, the exceptional character of the communication, the fact that it came from the head of the Government and was to be delivered personally to the head of the Russian Government by the Ambassador, were all intended to give it special significance and arrest Stalin's attention.

PRIME MINISTER TO FOREIGN SECRETARY                16 April 41

I set special importance on the delivery of this personal message from me to Stalin. I cannot understand why it should be resisted. The Ambassador is not alive to the military significance of the facts. Pray oblige me.

And again:

PRIME MINISTER TO FOREIGN SECRETARY                18 April 41

Has Sir Stafford Cripps yet delivered my personal message of warning about the German danger to Stalin? I am very much surprised that so much delay should have occurred, considering the importance I attach to this extremely pregnant piece of information. . . .

PRIME MINISTER TO FOREIGN SECRETARY                30 April 41

When did Sir Stafford Cripps deliver my message to M. Stalin? Will you very kindly ask him to report.

FOREIGN SECRETARY TO PRIME MINISTER                30 April 41

Sir Stafford Cripps sent the message to M. Vyshinsky on April 19, and M. Vyshinsky informed him in writing on April 23 that it had been conveyed to M. Stalin.

I very much regret that, owing to an error, the telegrams reporting this were not sent to you at the time. I attach copies.

These were the enclosures:

SIR STAFFORD CRIPPS, MOSCOW, TO FOREIGN SECRETARY       19 April 41

I have today sent text of message to Vyshinsky, asking him to convey it to Stalin. It was not clear from your telegram whether commentary was to be incorporated in message or added as from myself, and consequently, in view of my letter to Vyshinsky of April 11 and my interview with him yesterday, I felt it preferable to abstain from adding any commentary which could only have been repetition.

SIR STAFFORD CRIPPS, MOSCOW, TO FOREIGN SECRETARY     22 April 41
    Vyshinsky informed me in writing today that message had been conveyed to Stalin.

I cannot form any final judgment upon whether my message, if delivered with all the promptness and ceremony prescribed, would have altered the course of events. Nevertheless, I still regret that my instructions were not carried out effectively. If I had had any direct contact with Stalin I might perhaps have prevented him from having so much of his air force destroyed on the ground.

We know now that Hitler's directive of December 18 had prescribed May 15 as the date for invading Russia, and that in his fury at the revolution in Belgrade this date had on March 27 been postponed for a month, and later till June 22. Until the middle of March the troop movements in the north on the main Russian front were not of a character to require special German measures of concealment. On March 13, however, orders were issued by Berlin to terminate the work of the Russian commissions working in German territory and to send them home. The presence of Russians in this part of Germany could only be permitted up to March 25. In the northern sector strong German formations were already being assembled. From March 20 onward an even heavier massing would take place. . . .

When I awoke on the morning of Sunday, June 22, the news was brought to me of Hitler's invasion of Russia. This changed conviction into certainty. I had not the slightest doubt where our duty and our policy lay. Nor indeed what to say. There only remained the task of composing it. I asked that notice should immediately be given that I would broadcast at nine o'clock that night. . . .

In this broadcast I said:

The Nazi regime is indistinguishable from the worst features of Communism. It is devoid of all theme and principle except appetite and racial domination. It excels all forms of human wickedness in the efficiency of its cruelty and ferocious aggression. No one has been a more consistent opponent of Communism than I have for the last twenty-five years. I will unsay no word that I have spoken about it. But all this fades away before the spectacle which is now unfolding. The past, with its crimes, its follies, and its tragedies, flashes away. ·I see the Russian soldiers standing on the threshold of their native land, guarding the fields which their fathers have tilled from time immemorial. I see them guarding their homes where mothers and wives pray—ah, yes, for there are times when all pray—for the safety of their loved ones, the return of the breadwinner, of their champion, of their protector. I see the ten thousand villages of Russia where the means of existence is wrung so hardly from the soil, but where there are still primordial human joys, where maidens laugh and children play. I see advancing upon all this in hideous onslaught the Nazi war machine, with its clanking, heel-clicking, dandified Prussian officers, its crafty expert agents fresh from the cowing and tying-down of a dozen countries. I see also the dull, drilled, docile, brutish masses of the Hun soldiery plodding on like a swarm of crawling locusts. I see the German bombers and fighters in the sky, still smarting from many a British whipping, delighted to find what they believe is an easier and a safer prey.

Behind all this glare, behind all this storm, I see that small group of villainous men who plan, organize, and launch this cataract of horrors upon mankind. . . .

I have to declare the decision of His Majesty's Government—and I feel sure it is a decision in which the great Dominions will in due course concur—for we must speak out now at once, without a day's delay. I have to make the declaration, but can you doubt what our policy will be? We have but one aim and one single, irrevocable purpose. We are resolved to destroy Hitler and every vestige of the Nazi regime. From this nothing will turn us—nothing. We will never parley, we will never negotiate with Hitler or any of his gang. We shall fight him by land, we shall fight him by sea, we shall fight him in the air, until, with God's help, we have rid the earth of his shadow and liberated its peoples from his yoke. Any man or state who fights on against Nazidom will have our aid. Any man or state who marches with Hitler is our foe. . . . That is our policy and that is our declaration. It follows, therefore, that we shall give whatever help we can to Russia and the Russian people. We shall appeal to all our friends and allies in every part of the world to take the same course and pursue it, as we shall faithfully and steadfastly to the end. . . .

This is no class war, but a war in which the whole British Empire and Commonwealth of Nations is engaged, without distinction of race, creed, or party. It is not for me to speak of the action of the United States, but this I will say, if Hitler imagines that his attack on Soviet Russia will cause the slightest divergence of aims or slackening of effort in the great democracies who are resolved upon his doom, he is woefully mistaken. On the contrary, we shall be fortified and encouraged in our efforts to rescue mankind from his tyranny. We shall be strengthened and not weakened in determination and in resources.

This is no time to moralize on the follies of countries and Governments which have allowed themselves to be struck down one by one, when by united action they could have saved themselves and saved the world from this catastrophe. But when I spoke a few minutes ago of Hitler's blood-lust and the hateful appetites which have impelled or lured him on his Russian adventure, I said there was one deeper motive behind his outrage. He wishes to destroy the Russian power because he hopes that if he succeeds in this he will be able to bring back the main strength of his army and air force from the East and hurl it upon this island, which he knows he must conquer or suffer the penalty of his crimes. His invasion of Russia is no more than a prelude to an attempted invasion of the British Isles. He hopes, no doubt, that all this may be accomplished before the winter comes, and that he can overwhelm Great Britain before the Fleet and air power of the United States may intervene. He hopes that he may once again repeat, upon a greater scale than ever before, that process of destroying his enemies one by one by which he has so long thrived and prospered, and that then the scene will be clear for the final act, without which all his conquests would be in vain—namely, the subjugation of the Western Hemisphere to his will and to his system.

The Russian danger is, therefore, our danger, and the danger of the United States, just as the cause of any Russian fighting for his hearth and home is the cause of free men and free peoples in every quarter of the globe. Let us learn the lessons already taught by such cruel experience. Let us redouble our exertions, and strike with united strength while life and power remain.

\* \* \*

Nemesis personifies "the Goddess of Retribution, who brings down all immoderate good fortune, checks the presumption that attends it . . . and is the punisher of extraordinary crimes."[1] We must now lay bare the error and vanity of cold-blooded calculation of the Soviet Government and enormous Communist machine, and their amazing ignorance about where they stood themselves. They had shown a total indifference to the fate of the Western Powers, although this meant the destruction of that "Second Front" for which they were soon to clamor. They seemed to have no inkling that Hitler had for more than six months resolved to destroy them. If their Intelligence Service informed them of the vast German deployment towards the East, which was now increasing every day, they omitted many needful steps to meet it. Thus they had allowed the whole of the Balkans to be overrun by Germany. They hated and despised the democracies of the West; but the four countries,

---

[1]Oxford English Dictionary.

Turkey, Rumania, Bulgaria, and Yugoslavia, which were of vital interest to them and their own safety, could all have been combined by the Soviet Government in January with active British aid to form a Balkan front against Hitler. They let them all break into confusion, and all but Turkey were mopped up one by one. War is mainly a catalogue of blunders, but it may be doubted whether any mistake in history has equalled that of which Stalin and the Communist chiefs were guilty when they cast away all possibilities in the Balkans and supinely awaited, or were incapable of realizing, the fearful onslaught which impended upon Russia. We have hitherto rated them as selfish calculators. In this period they were proved simpletons as well. The force, the mass, the bravery and endurance of Mother Russia had still to be thrown into the scales. But so far as strategy, policy, foresight, competence are arbiters, Stalin and his commissars showed themselves at this moment the most completely outwitted bunglers of the Second World War.

\* \* \*

In the course of one of my later talks with Stalin I said, "Lord Beaverbrook has told me that when he was on his mission to Moscow in October, 1941, you asked him, 'What did Churchill mean by saying in Parliament that he had given me warnings of the impending German attack?' I was of course," said I, " referring to the telegram I sent you in April '41" and I produced the telegram which Sir Stafford Cripps had tardily delivered. When it was read and translated to him Stalin shrugged his shoulders. "I remember it. I did not need any warnings. I knew war would come, but I thought I might gain another six months or so." In the common cause I refrained from asking him what would have happened to us all if we had gone down for ever while he was giving Hitler so much valuable material, time, and aid.

# THE DISSOLUTION OF THE COMINTERN*

[1943]

The historic role of the Communist International, which was founded in 1919 as a result of a political union of the great majority of the old pre-war working-class parties, consisted in upholding the principles of the working-class movement, in helping to promote consolidation in a number of countries of the vanguard of the foremost workers in the real working-class parties, and in helping them mobilize workers for the defense of their economic and political interests, and for the struggle against Fascism and the war which the latter was preparing, and for the support of the Soviet Union as the chief bulwark against Fascism.

The Communist International from the first exposed the real meaning of the Anti-Comintern Pact as a weapon for the preparation of war by the Hitlerites. Long before the war it ceaselessly and tirelessly exposed the vicious, subversive work of the Hitlerites, who masked it by their screams about so-called interference of the Communist International in the internal affairs of these states.

But long before the war it became more and more clear that, with increasing complications in internal and international relations of various countries, any sort of international center would encounter insuperable obstacles in solving the problems facing the movement in each separate country.

Deep differences of the historic paths of development of various countries, differences in their character and even contradictions in their social orders, differences in the level and the tempo of their economic and political development, differences finally in the degree of consciousness and organization of workers, conditioned different problems affecting the working class of the various countries.

The whole development of events in the last quarter of a century

---

*The text of the resolution of the Presidium of the Executive Committee of the Communist International, May 22, 1943.

and the experience accumulated by the Communist International convincingly showed that the organizational form of uniting workers, chosen by the First Congress of the Communist International, answered conditions of the first stages of the working-class movement, but it has been outgrown by the growth of this movement and by the complications of its problems in separate countries and has even become a drag on the further strengthening of the national working-class parties.

The World War that the Hitlerites have let loose has still further sharpened the differences in the situation of the separate countries and has placed a deep dividing line between those countries that fell under the Hitlerite tyranny and those freedom-loving peoples who have united in a powerful anti-Hitlerite coalition.

In countries of the Hitlerite bloc the fundamental task of the working class, toilers and all honest people consists in giving all help for the defeat of this bloc by sabotage of the Hitlerite military machine from within and by helping to overthrow the governments guilty of war.

In countries of the anti-Hitlerite coalition, the sacred duty of the widest masses of the people, and in the first place of foremost workers, consists in aiding by every means the military efforts of the governments of these countries aimed at the speediest defeat of the Hitlerite bloc and the assurance of the friendship of nations based on their equality.

At the same time the fact must not be lost sight of that the separate countries that are members of the anti-Hitlerite coalition have their own particular problems. For example, in countries occupied by the Hitlerites that have lost their state of independence the basic task of the foremost workers and of the wide masses of people consists in promoting the armed struggle developing into a national war of liberation against Hitlerite Germany.

At the same time the war of liberation of freedom-loving peoples against the Hitlerite tyranny, which has brought into movement the masses of people, uniting them without difference of party or religion in the ranks of the powerful anti-Hitlerite coalition, has demonstrated with still greater clearness that the general national uprising and mobilization of people for the speediest victory over the enemy can be best of all and most fruitfully carried out by the vanguard of the working-class movement of each separate country, working within the framework of its own country.

Already the Seventh Congress of the Communist International meeting in 1935, taking into account the change that had taken place both in the international situation and in working-class movements that demanded great flexibility and independence of its sections in deciding the problems confronting them, emphasized the necessity for the Executive Committee of the Communist International in deciding all questions of the working-class movement arising from concrete conditions and peculiarities of each country, to make a rule of avoiding interference in the internal organizational affairs of the Communist parties.

These same considerations guided the Communist International in considering the resolution of the Communist party of the United States of America of November, 1940, on its withdrawal from the ranks of the Communist International.

Guided by the judgment of the founders of Marxism and Leninism, Communists have never been supporters of the conservation of organizational forms that have outlived themselves. They have always subordinated forms of organization of the working-class movement, and methods of working of such organization, to the fundamental political interest of the working-class movement as a whole, to peculiarities of the concrete historical situation and to problems immediately resulting from this situation.

They remember the example of the great Marx, who united foremost workers in the ranks of the Working Men's International Association, and when the First International had fulfilled its historical task of laying the foundations for the development of working-class parties in the countries of Europe and America, and, as a result of the matured situation creating mass national working-class parties, dissolved first the International, inasmuch as this form of organization already no longer corresponded to the demands confronting it.

In consideration of the above and taking into account the growth and the political maturity of Communist parties and their leading cadres in separate countries, and also having in view the fact that during the present war some sections have raised the question of the dissolution of the Communist International as the directing center of the international working-class movement, the Presidium of the Executive Committee of the Communist International, in the circumstances of the World War, not being able to convene a Congress of the Communist International, puts forward the following proposal for ratification by the sections of the Communist International:

The Communist International, as the directing center of the international working-class movement, is to be dissolved, thus freeing the sections of the Communist International from their obligations arising from the statutes and resolutions of the Congresses of the Communist International.

The Presidium of the Executive Committee of the Communist International calls on all supporters of the Communist International to concentrate their energies on the whole-hearted support of and active participation in the war of liberation of the peoples and the states of the anti-Hitlerite coalition for the speediest defeat of the deadly enemy of the working-class and toilers—German Fascism and its associates and vassals.

VII

# THE COLD WAR

# THE REAL ISSUE BETWEEN THE UNITED STATES AND THE SOVIET UNION*

BY

## HANS J. MORGENTHAU

[1951]

### 1. THE THREE CHOICES

Three answers are logically possible to the question of what the issues are between the United States and the Soviet Union. One can answer that there is no real issue of a political nature separating the United States and the Soviet Union, and if only suspicion and false propaganda were eliminated, nothing would stand in the way of normal, peaceful relations. Or one can answer that the issue between the United States and the Soviet Union is that of world revolution, an objective to which the Soviet government is irrevocably committed. Or, finally, one can answer that what concerns the United States in its relations with the Soviet Union is Russian imperialism, which uses for its purposes the instrument of world revolution.

These distinctions are not mere hair-splitting. For the choice of one alternative instead of another will of necessity determine our moral and intellectual attitude toward the Soviet Union, and it is obvious that the choice of the policies to be pursued by the United States with regard to the Soviet Union must depend upon which of these three answers is chosen. If one believes that there is no real political issue, policy must concentrate either upon propaganda penetrating the Iron Curtain or upon economic aid to the countries behind it. This aid will narrow the gap in well-being between East and West, and it is this gap which is presumed to create misunderstanding and suspicion. If one believes that what confronts us as long as the Soviet government reigns in Moscow is the threat

*From Hans J. Morgenthau, *In Defense of the National Interest.* Published by Alfred A. Knopf, Inc. Copyright 1950, 1951 by Hans J. Morgenthau. Reprinted by permission.

of world revolution, then there is only one way to meet that threat: extirpate the evil at its roots. If Russian imperialism is assumed to be the problem, the traditional methods of military and political policies can be employed to meet it. In the first alternative, peace can be brought to the world on the strengthened waves of the Voice of America, or can be bought by ten or twenty billion dollars. In the second alternative, the problem is not how to preserve peace but when to go to war, and the idea of a preventive war is a legitimate one. In the third alternative, military preparations must join hands with an accommodating diplomacy, and preparing for the worst while working for a peaceful settlement becomes the order of the day.

The dilemma of these alternatives confronting the United States today is not a new one in the history of the Western world. It arose in the minds of British statesmen in the last decade of the eighteenth century on the occasion of the expansionist policies of revolutionary France. The three-cornered contest among three of the greatest political minds Great Britain or any other country has produced—Edmund Burke, Charles James Fox, and William Pitt—provides us with the most lucid and penetrating exposition of the problem: the expansionism of a great power which is also the seat of a universal political religion. To grasp the contemporary relevance of that debate one needs only to substitute for France, the Soviet Union; for Jacobinism, Communism; for England, the United States; for Napoleon, Stalin.

The concrete issue of that debate was the participation of Great Britain in the war that the European monarchies were waging against revolutionary France. Fox, the leader of one faction of the Whigs, believed that Great Britain was not at all threatened by France or, for that matter, by the principles of the French Revolution, which were a mere domestic concern of France, and that therefore there was no reason for Great Britain to join the coalition against France. While he detested the terror of the Jacobins, he was not willing to support a war for the purpose of eliminating Jacobinism. "He should now show," he said in the House of Commons on February 1, 1793,

> that all the topics to which he had adverted were introduced into the debate to blind the judgment, by arousing the passions,

and were none of them the just grounds of war. . . . What, then, remained but the internal government of France, always disavowed, but ever kept in mind, and constantly mentioned? The destruction of that government was the avowed object of the combined powers whom it was hoped we were to join. . . . He thought the present state of government in France any thing rather than an object of imitation; but he maintained as a principle inviolable, that the government of every independent state was to be settled by those who were to live under it, and not by foreign force. . . .

In contrast to this position, Burke, the leader of another faction of the Whigs, finds the issue in the prinicples of the French Revolution. He looks on the war as a contest between two moral principles, as

the cause of humanity itself. . . . I do not exclude from amongst the just objects of such a confederacy as the present, the ordinary securities which nations must take against their mutual ambition, let their internal constitutions be of what nature they will. But the present evil of our time, though in a great measure an evil of ambition, is not one of common political ambition, but in many respects entirely different. It is not the cause of nation as against nation; but, as you will observe, the cause of mankind against those who have projected the subversion of that order of things, under which our part of the world has so long flourished, and indeed, been in a progressive state of improvement; the limits of which, if it had not been thus rudely stopped, it would not have been easy for the imagination to fix. If I conceive rightly of the spirit of the present combination, it is not at war with France, but with Jacobinism. They cannot think it right, that a second kingdom should be struck out of the system of Europe, either by destroying its independence, or by suffering it to have such a *form* in its independence, as to keep it, as a perpetual fund of revolutions, in the very centre of Europe, in that region which alone touches almost every other, and must influence, even where she does not come in contact. As long as Jacobinism subsists there, in any form, or under any modification, it is not, in my opinion, the gaining a fortified place or two, more or less, or the annexing to the dominion of the allied powers this or that territorial district that can save Europe, or any of its members. We are at war with a *principle,* and with an example, which there is no shutting out by fortresses, or excluding by territorial limits. No lines of demarcation can bound the Jacobin empire. It must be extirpated in the place of its origin, or it will not be confined to that place. In the whole circle of military arrangements and of political expedients, I fear that there cannot be found any sort of *merely defensive plan* of the least force, against the effect of the *example* which has been given in France. That *example* has shown, for the first time in the history of the world, that it is very possible to subvert the whole frame and order of the best constructed states, by corrupting the common people with the spoil of the superior classes. It is by that instrument that the French orators have accomplished their purpose, to the ruin of France; and it is by that instrument that, if they can establish themselves in France (however broken or curtailed by themselves or others), sooner or later, they will subvert every government in Europe. The effect of *erroneous doctrines* may be soon done away; but the example of *successful pillage* is of a nature more permanent, more applicable to use, and a thing which speaks more forcibly to the interests and passions of the corrupt and unthinking part of mankind, than a thousand theories. Nothing can weaken the lesson contained in that example, but to make as strong an example on the other side. The leaders in France must be made to feel, in order that all the rest there, and in other countries, may be made to see that such spoil is no sure possession.

When the war against France had been in progress for seven years, a supporter of Fox asked Pitt, the Prime Minister and leader of the Tories in the House of Commons, what the war was all about. Was Jacobinism not dead, and was Napoleon not indifferent to the principles of the French Revolution? What, then, was Britain fighting for? Here is Pitt's reply, representing the third answer which can be given to our question.

The hon. gentleman defies me to state, in one sentence, what is the object of the war. In one word, I tell him that it is security;—security against a danger, the greatest that ever threatened the world—security against a danger which never existed in any past period of society. This country alone, of all the nations of Europe, presented barriers the best fitted to resist its progress. We alone recognized the necessity of open war, as well with the principles, as the practice of the French revolution. We saw that it was to be resisted no less by arms abroad, than by precaution at home; that we were to look for protection no less to the courage of our forces than to the wisdom of our councils; no less to military effort than to legislative enactment. At the moment when those, who now admit the dangers of Jacobinism while they contend that it is extinct, used to palliate this atrocity, this House wisely saw that it was necessary to erect a double safe-guard against a danger that wrought no less by undisguised hostility than by secret machination.

## 2. The American Choice

The United States has taken all these three positions toward the Soviet Union, either simultaneously or successively. From 1917 to the entrance of the Soviet Union into the Second World War in 1941, the United States looked at the Soviet Union primarily with the eyes of Burke. It saw in it and its adherents in foreign countries a threat to the established moral and social order of the West. What the United States feared and opposed during that period of history was the Soviet Union, the instigator and mastermind of world revolution, not Russia, the great power; for as a great power Russia did not exist during that period, and its potentialities as a great power were hardly recognized by the United States.

From June 1941 to the breakdown of the Yalta and Potsdam agreements in 1946, the Soviet Union appeared to the United States as revolutionary France had appeared to Fox. The Soviet Union was considered to be no threat to the United States either as the fountainhead of world revolution or as a great imperialistic power. There was a widespread tendency to look upon the Soviet leaders as democrats at heart, somewhat ill-mannered democrats, to be sure, but democrats nevertheless, whom circumstances had thus far prevented from living up to their democratic convictions and with whom, therefore, it was possible "to get along." The Soviet Union was supposed to have lost its revolutionary fervor, and as a great power it was believed to possess enough territory to keep it satisfied, and in any case to be so weakened by the devastations of war as to be unable to embark upon imperialistic ventures even if it wanted to.

Since the breakdown of the war and postwar agreements with the Soviet Union, public opinion in the United States has gone to the other extreme and reverted to the pattern established in the years following 1917. To American public opinion the conflict between the United States and the Soviet Union appears first of all as a struggle between two systems of political morality, two political philosophies, two ways of life. Good and evil are linked in mortal combat, and the struggle can only end, as it is bound to end, with the complete victory of the forces of good over the forces of evil. . . .

A simple test will show which of these three conceptions of the East-West conflict are mistaken and which is correct. Let us suppose for a moment that Lenin and Trotsky had died in exile, the unknown members of a Marxist sect, and that the Czar were still reigning over a Russia politically and technologically situated as it is today. Does anybody believe that it would be a matter of indifference for the United States to see the Russian armies hardly more than a hundred miles from the Rhine, in the Balkans, with Russian influence holding sway over China and threatening to engulf the rest of Asia? Is anybody bold enough to assert that it would make all the difference in the world for the United States if Russian imperialism marched forward as it did in the eighteenth and nineteenth centuries, under the ideological banner and with the support of Christianity rather than of Bolshevism?

One can turn that same question around and ask whether anybody in the United States would need to be concerned about the American Communist Party if it were not a tool in the hands of the Kremlin and, hence, the vanguard of Russian imperialism. If the American Communist Party were an independent revolutionary organization, such as the anarchists were at one time and the Trotskyites are now, one could dismiss them as a coterie of crackpots and misfits, not to be taken seriously. It is the power of Russia that gives the American Communists an importance they would not have otherwise, and their importance is that of treason, not of revolution. If American Communism disappeared tomorrow without a trace, Russian imperialism would be deprived of one of its minor weapons in the struggle with the United States, but the issue facing the United States would not have been altered in the least.

The confusion between the issue of Russian imperialism and that of Communism feeds on four sources. First, the public at large tends to view politics, domestic and international, in the simple contrast of black and white, defined in moral terms. Thus the public is always prone to transform an election contest or an international conflict into a moral crusade carried on in the name of virtue by one's own party or one's own nation against the other party or the other nation, which stands for all that is evil in the world. Secondly, this genuine and typical confusion is aggravated by Russian propaganda, which justifies and rationalizes its imperialistic moves and objectives in the universal terms of Marxist dogma. The Western counter-crusade, taking the revolutionary stereotypes of Russian propaganda at their face value, thus becomes a mere counterpoise of that propaganda, its victim, unwittingly taking for the real issue what is but a tactical instrument of imperialistic policies.

The understanding of the real issue between the United States and the Soviet Union is still further obscured by the ambiguity of the terms "Communism" and "Communist Revolution" themselves. If those who proclaim Communism as the real issue have primarily Europe in mind, they have at least a part of the truth; for in no country of Europe outside the Soviet Union has Communism succeeded in taking over the government except as a by-product of conquest by the Red Army and as an instrument for perpetuating Russian power. What has been true in the past in eastern and central Europe is likely to be true for the future in all of the Western world. If the Soviet Union pursues the goal of world revolution, it can attain that goal only by conquering the Western world first and making it Communistic afterwards. In other words, Communist revolution can come to the Western world only in the aftermath of the victory of the Red Army. In the West, then, the opposition to Communism is an integral part of resistance to Russian imperialism, and to oppose Russian imperialism is tantamount to opposing Communist revolution as well.

If those who refer to Communism as the real issue have primarily the revolutions in Asia in mind, they speak of something fundamentally different. While the Communist revolution could not have succeeded and will not succeed in any European country without the intervention of the Red Army, the revolutionary situation in Asia has developed independently of Russian Communism, and would exist in some form, owing to the triumph of Western moral ideas and the decline of Western power, even if Bolshevism had never been heard of. The revolutions in Europe are phony revolutions, the revolutions in Asia are genuine ones. While opposition to revolution in Europe is a particular aspect of the defense of the West against Russian imperialism, opposition to revolution in Asia is counter-revolution in Metternich's sense, resistance to change on behalf of an obsolescent status quo, doomed to failure from the outset. The issue of revolution in Asia is fundamentally different from that in Europe; it is not to oppose revolution as a creature and instrument of Russian imperialism but to support its national and social objectives while at the same time and by that very support preventing it from becoming an instrument of Russian imperialism. The clamor for consistency in dealing with the different revolutions sailing under the flag of Communism is the result of that confusion which does not see that the real issue is Russian imperialism, and Communist revolution only in so far as it is an instrument of that imperialism.

Finally, this confusion is nourished—and here lies its greatest danger for the political well-being of the United States—by a widespread fear not of revolution but of change. The forces that in the interwar period erected the specter of Communist revolution into a symbol of all social reform and social change itself are at work again, unaware that intelligent social reform is the best insurance against social revolution. What these forces were afraid of in the interwar period was not a threat—actually non-existent—to the security of the United States emanating from the power of Russia, but a threat to the social status quo in the United States. That threat did not stem primarily from the Communist Party, nor did it arise from the imminence of Communist revolution, which in the United States has been at all times a virtually negligible contingency. In embarking upon a holy crusade to extirpate the evil of Bolshevism these forces embarked, as they do now, in actuality upon a campaign to outlaw morally and legally all popular movements favoring social reform and in that fashion to make the status quo impregnable to change. The symbol of the threat of a non-existent Communist revolution becomes a convenient cloak, as it was for German and Italian Fascism, behind which a confused and patriotic citizenry can be rallied to the defense of what seems to be the security of the United States, but what actually is the security of the status quo. The fact that such a movement, if it were ever able to determine the domestic and international policies of the United States, would jeopardize not only the security of the United States but also the domestic status quo, only adds the touch of tragic irony to the confusion of thought and action.

What makes the task of American foreign policy so difficult is not only the unprecedented magnitude of the three great revolutions of our age, culminating in the rise of the Soviet Union, but also the necessity for American foreign policy to deal with four fundamental factors that must be separated in thought while they are intertwined in action: Russian imperialism, revolution as an instrument of Russian imperialism, revolution as genuine popular aspiration, and the use of the international crisis for the purposes of domestic reaction.

Whenever we have fallen victim, not only in thought but also in action, to the oversimplification that reduces the variegated elements of the world conflict to the moral opposition of Bolshevism and democracy, our policy has been mistaken and has failed in its objectives, ideological and political. Whenever such oversimplification and confusion has counseled our actions, we have rendered ourselves powerless either to contain Russian imperialism or prevent the spread of Communism. . . .

The greatest danger that threatens us in the immediate future, aside from the military preponderance of the Soviet Union on land, is the confusion of the two great issues of our time: Russian imperialism and genuine revolution. American foreign policy ought not to have the objective of bringing the blessings of some social and political system to all the world or of protecting all the world from the evils of some other system. Its purpose—and its sole purpose—ought to be, as was England's under Pitt, the security of the nation; "security against the greatest danger that ever threatened the world." If we allow ourselves to be diverted from this objective of safeguarding our national security, and if instead we conceive of the American mission in some abstract, universal, and emotional terms, we may well be induced, against our better knowledge and intent, yet by the very logic of the task in hand, to raise the banner of universal counter-revolution abroad and of conformity in thought and action at home. In that manner we shall jeopardize our external security, promote the world revolution we are trying to suppress, and at home make ourselves distinguishable perhaps in degree, but not in kind, from those with which we are locked in ideological combat. . . .

The search for a clear understanding of the real issue between the United States and the Soviet Union, then, is not a mere academic pastime. Misunderstanding and confusion over the real issue results in much that is ambiguous, fallacious, indecisive, and unsuccessful in American foreign policy; intellectual clarity in the matter is the inescapable precondition for success. It is true that intellectual clarity is not all. It makes political success possible, but does not assure it. To a clear understanding of the issues at stake must be joined the correct judgment of means and ends in terms of the power necessary and available, and the will to do what must be done.

# THE INEVITABILITY OF WARS*

BY

## JOSEPH STALIN

[1952]

### QUESTION OF DISINTEGRATION OF UNITED WORLD MARKET AND DEEPENING OF CRISIS OF WORLD CAPITALIST SYSTEM

The most important result of the Second World War in its economic consequences must be considered the disintegration of a united, all-embracing world market. This circumstance determined further the deepening of the general crisis of the capitalist system.

The Second World War was itself born out of this crisis. Each of two capitalist coalitions, which buried their claws in each other during the war counted on breaking the enemy and obtaining world domination. In this they sought a way out from this crisis. The United States of America counted on putting out of action its most dangerous competitors, Germany and Japan, and on seizing foreign markets, world resources of raw materials and obtaining world domination.

However, the war did not justify these hopes. It is true that Germany and Japan were put out of action as competitors of the three chief capitalist countries. But along with these there fell away from the capitalist system China and other people's democracies in Europe, forming together with the Soviet Union a united and powerful Socialist camp, counter-poised to the camp of capitalism. The economic result of the coexistence of the two counter-poised camps was that the united all-embracing world market fell apart, and as a result of this we now have two parallel world markets also counter-poised one to the other.

It is necessary to note that the United States and England with France themselves assisted, of course beyond their own will, in

*Excerpts from a statement, "Economic Problems of Socialism in the U.S.S.R.," published in *Bolshevik* (Moscow), No. 18, September 1952. Reprinted by permission from the *New York Times*, October 4, 1952.

formation and strengthening of a new parallel world market. They subjected to an economic blockade the U.S.S.R., China and the European people's democracies who did not enter into the system of the Marshall Plan, thinking by this token to stifle them. In fact, there resulted not the stifling, but the strengthening of the new world market.

But the basic thing in this is not of course in the economic blockade, but in fact that during the period after the war these countries economically closed ranks and worked out economic co-operation and mutual aid. The experience of this aid shows that not one capitalist country could give such effective and technically skilled help to the people's democracies as the Soviet Union is giving them.

The root of the matter is not only that this assistance is cheap in a maximum degree and technically first class. The root of the matter is that first of all there lies at the basis of this cooperation a sincere desire to help one another and to attain a general economic rise.

As a result, we have high tempos of development of industry in these countries. One can say with conviction that, with such tempos of development of industry, the matter is soon going to arrive at a situation in which these countries not only will not need to import merchandise from the capitalist countries, but themselves will feel the necessity of disposing on the side of surplus merchandise of their own production.

But from this it follows that the sphere of application of the forces of the chief capitalist countries [the United States, England and France] to the world resources will not expand but will contract, that conditions of the world market of sale for these countries will grow worse, and idleness of enterprises in these countries will increase. In this, properly speaking, there consists a deepening of the general crisis of the world capitalist system in connection with the disintegration of the world market.

The capitalists feel this themselves, for it is difficult not to feel the loss of such markets as the U.S.S.R. and China. They try to make up for these difficulties with the Marshall Plan and war in Korea, by an arms race, by militarization of industry. But this is very like a drowning man clutching at straws.

In connection with this situation, there have arisen before economists two questions:

A. Can one affirm that the well-known thesis of Stalin on the relative stability of markets in a general crisis of capitalism stated before the Second World War still remains in force?

B. Can one affirm that the thesis of Lenin—stated by him in the spring of 1916, to the effect that notwithstanding the rotting of capitalism, "as a whole capitalism is growing immeasurably more rapidly than formerly"—still remains in force?

I think that it is impossible to affirm this. In view of new conditions arising in connection with the Second World War, both theses must be considered as having lost their validity.

## Question of the Inevitability of Wars Between Capitalist Countries

Certain comrades affirm that, as the result of the development of new international conditions after the Second World War, wars among capitalist countries have ceased to be inevitable. They consider that the contradictions between the camp of socialism and the camp of capitalism are stronger than the contradictions between capitalist countries; that the United States has sufficiently subjected to itself other capitalist countries in order not to permit them to fight among themselves and weaken each other; that the progressive people of capitalism have been taught sufficiently by the experience of two World Wars, which dealt serious harm to the entire capitalist world, not to permit themselves again to drag the capitalist countries into a war among themselves—that in view of this wars between capitalist countries have ceased to be inevitable.

These comrades are mistaken. They see the outer phenomena twinkling on the surface, but they do not see those deep forces which although they are acting so far unnoticeably, nevertheless will determine the course of events.

Outwardly, everything, as it were, is "satisfactory": The United States has put on rations Western Europe, Japan and other capitalist countries; West Germany, England, France, Japan, which have fallen into the paws of the United States and obediently carry out the orders of the United States. But it would be incorrect to think that this "prosperity" can be maintained "forever and ever," that these countries will suffer without end the domination and oppression of the United States, that they will not try to break out from American slavery and set forth on a path of independent development.

Let us take, first of all, England and France. It is indubitable that these countries are imperialist. It is indubitable that cheap raw material and assured markets for sales have for them first degree importance. Can one suppose that they will suffer without end the present situation when Americans, under the noise of "help" on the line of the "Marshall Plan," are penetrating the economy of England and France, trying to transform them into an appendage of the economy of the United States of America, when American capital is seizing raw materials and markets in the Anglo-French colonies and preparing thus a catastrophe for high profits of the Anglo-French capitalists? Would it not be more true to say that capitalist England and, in her footsteps, also capitalist France, in the end of ends will be forced to tear themselves out from the embraces of the United States and enter into conflict with them in order to secure themselves an independent situation and of course high profits?

Let us proceed to the chief conquered countries—to (West) Germany, to Japan. These countries are squeezing out a pitiful existence under the heel of American imperialism. Their industry and agriculture, their trade, their foreign and internal policy—all their existence—is shackled by the American "regime" of occupation. And it is in particular these countries, which yesterday were still great imperialist powers, who shook the underpinnings of the domination of England, the United States and France in Europe and in Asia. To think that these countries shall not try again to rise on their feet, to break the "regime" of the United States and to break forth on the path of independent development—that means to believe in miracles.

They say that the contradictions between capitalism and social-ism are stronger than the contradictions between the capitalist countries. Theoretically this, of course, is true. It is true not only now, at the present time, but it was true also before the Second World War and this was, more or less, understood by the leaders of the capitalist countries. Yet the Second World War began not with war against the U.S.S.R., but with a war among the capitalist countries. Why?

Because, in the first place, a war with the U.S.S.R., the country of socialism, is more dangerous for capitalism than a war between individual capitalist countries. For if a war between individual capitalist countries raises the question only of the liquidation of certain capitalist countries by other capitalist countries, war with the U.S.S.R. obligatorily must put the question of the very existence of capitalism.

Secondly, the capitalists, although making noises for the sake of propaganda on the "aggressiveness" of the Soviet Union, themselves do not believe in its aggressiveness, since they take into consideration the peaceful policy of the Soviet Union and know that the Soviet Union itself will not attack capitalist countries.

After the First World War, it was also considered that Germany had finally been put out of action, just as certain comrades think now that Japan and Germany have been finally put out of action. Then they also talked about and made noise in their press to the effect that the United States had put Europe on rations, that Germany cannot again stand on her own feet, that from now on wars between capitalist countries must not be. However, notwithstanding this, Germany rose and stood on her feet as a great power some fifteen to twenty years after her defeat, broke out of slavery and set out on the path of independent development.

In this it is typical that it was none other than the United States and England which helped Germany raise herself economically and raise her military and economic potential. Of course the United States and England, helping Germany to rise economically, had in view to direct the risen Germany against the Soviet Union to use it against the country of socialism. However, Germany directed her forces in the first place against the Anglo-American-French bloc, and when Hitlerite Germany declared war against the Soviet Union then the Anglo-American-French bloc not only did not unite with Hitlerite Germany, but on the contrary, was forced to engage in a coalition with the U.S.S.R., against Hitlerite Germany.

Consequently, the struggle of the capitalist countries for markets and their desire to drown their competitors were, as it turned out in practice, stronger than the contradictions between the camp of capitalism and the camp of socialism.

One asks what guarantee is there that Germany and Japan will not rise again on their feet, that they will not attempt to break out from American slavery and live their independent life? I think that there are no such guarantees.

But from this it follows that the inevitability of wars between the capitalist countries remains in force.

They say that Lenin's thesis that imperialism gives rise to wars should be obsolete in view of the powerful forces of people acting in defense of peace against a new world war. This is untrue.

The contemporary movement for peace has as its purpose to raise masses of people in the struggle for the maintenance of peace and for the prevention of a new world war. Consequently, it does not pursue the purpose of overthrowing capitalism and the establishment of socialism—it limits itself to the democratic purposes of struggle for keeping of peace. In this relation, the contemporary movement for peace is distinguished from the movement in the period of the First World War for the transformation of an imperialist war into a civil war, since this latter movement went further and pursued Socialist purposes. It is possible that in a certain concatenation of circumstances the struggle for peace will develop in certain places into a struggle for the overthrow of capitalism.

But it is most probable of all that the contemporary movement for the maintenance of peace, in case of its success, will lead to the prevention of a *given* war, to its temporary postponement, to the temporary maintenance of a *given* peace, to the retirement of a war-like government and the replacement of it with another government prepared to keep the peace temporarily. This, of course, is good.

It is even very good. But all this is insufficient in order to destroy the inevitability of wars in general between the capitalist countries. It is insufficient since, with all these successes of the movement for peace, imperialism nevertheless will continue to remain in force—consequently there remains in force the inevitability of wars.

In order to destroy the inevitability of wars, it is necessary to destroy imperialism.

# THE INTERNATIONAL POSITION
# OF THE SOVIET UNION*

BY

## NIKITA S. KHRUSHCHEV

[1956]

The emergence of socialism from within the bounds of a single country and its transformation into a world system is the main feature of our era. Capitalism has proved powerless to prevent this process of world-historic significance. The simultaneous existence of two opposite world economic systems, the capitalist and the socialist, developing according to different laws and in opposite directions, has become an indisputable fact.

Socialist economy is developing towards the ever-increasing satisfaction of the material and cultural requirements of all members of society, and continuous expansion and improvement of production on the basis of higher techniques, and closer co-operation and mutual assistance between the socialist countries.

The trend of capitalist economy is that of the ever-increasing enrichment of the monopolies, the further intensification of exploitation and cuts in the living standards of millions of working people, particularly in the colonial and dependent countries, of increasing militarization of the economy, the exacerbation of the competitive struggle among the capitalist countries, and the maturing of new economic crises and upheavals. . . .

Comrades, between the Nineteenth and Twentieth Congresses of the Communist Party of the Soviet Union, very important changes have taken place in international relations.

Soon after the Second World War ended, the influence of reactionary and militarist groups began to be increasingly evident in the policy of the United States of America, Britain and France. Their desire to enforce their will on other countries by economic and political pressure, threats and military provocation prevailed. This became known as the "positions of strength" policy. It reflects the

---

* Selections from the *Report of the Central Committee of the Communist Party of the Soviet Union to the 20th Party Congress*, February 14, 1956.

aspiration of the most aggressive sections of present-day imperialism to win world supremacy, to suppress the working class and the
democratic and national-liberation movements; it reflects their
plans for military adventures against the socialist camp.

The international atmosphere was poisoned by war hysteria.
The arms race began to assume more and more monstrous dimensions. Many big U. S. military bases designed for use against the
U.S.S.R. and the People's Democracies were built in countries
thousands of miles from the borders of the United States. "Cold
war" was begun against the socialist camp. International distrust
was artificially kindled, and nations set against one another. A
bloody war was launched in Korea; the war in Indo-China dragged
on for years.

The inspirers of the "cold war" began to establish military
blocs, and many countries found themselves, against the will of
their peoples, involved in restricted aggressive alignments—the
North Atlantic bloc, Western European Union, SEATO (military
bloc for South-East Asia) and the Baghdad pact.

The organizers of military blocs allege that they have united for
defence, for protection against the "communist threat." But that
is sheer hypocrisy. We know from history that when planning a
redivision of the world, the imperialist powers have always lined
up military blocs. Today the "anti-communism" slogan is again
being used as a smokescreen to cover up the claims of one power
for world domination. The new thing here is that the United
States wants, by means of all kinds of blocs and pacts, to secure
a dominant position in the capitalist world for itself, and to reduce
all its partners in the blocs to the status of obedient executors of
its will.

The inspirers of the "positions of strength" policy assert that
this policy makes another war impossible, because it ensures a
"balance of power" in the world arena. This view is widespread
among Western statesmen and it is therefore all the more important
to thoroughly expose its real meaning.

Can peace be promoted by an arms race? It would seem that it
is simply absurd to pose such a question. Yet the adherents of the
"positions of strength" policy offer the arms race as their main
recipe for the preservation of peace! It is perfectly obvious that

when nations compete to increase their military might, the danger of war becomes greater, not lesser.

The arms race, the "positions of strength" policy, the lining up of aggressive blocs and the "cold war"—all this could not but aggravate the international situation, and it did. This has been one trend of world events during the period under review.

But other processes have also taken place in the international arena during these years, processes showing that in the world today monopolist circles are by no means controlling everything.

The steady consolidation of the forces of socialism, democracy and peace, and of the forces of the national-liberation movement is of decisive significance. The international position of the Soviet Union, the People's Republic of China, and the other socialist countries has been further strengthened during this period, and their prestige and international ties have grown immeasurably. The international camp of socialism is exerting ever-growing influence on the course of international events. *(Applause.)*

The forces of peace have been considerably augmented by the emergence in the world arena of a group of peace-living European and Asian states which have proclaimed non-participation in blocs as a principle of their foreign policy. The leading political circles of these states rightly hold that to participate in restricted military imperialist alignments would merely increase the danger of their countries being involved in military gambles by the aggressive forces and draw them into the maelstrom of the arms drive.

As a result, a vast Zone of Peace including peace-loving states, both socialist and non-socialist, of Europe and Asia, has emerged in the world. This zone includes vast areas inhabited by nearly 1,500 million people, that is, the majority of the population of our planet. . . .

The October Socialist Revolution struck a most powerful blow at the imperialist colonial system. Under the influence of the Great October Revolution the national-liberation struggle of the colonial peoples developed with particular force, it continued throughout the subsequent years and has led to a deep-going crisis of the entire imperialist colonial system.

The defeat of fascist Germany and imperialist Japan in the Second World War was an important factor stimulating the liberation struggles in the colonies and dependent countries. The democratic forces' victory over fascism instilled faith in the possibility of liberation in the hearts of the oppressed peoples.

The victorious revolution in China struck the next staggering blow at the colonial system; it marked a grave defeat for imperialism.

India, the country with the world's second biggest population, has won political independence. Independence has been gained by Burma, Indonesia, Egypt, Syria, the Lebanon, the Sudan, and a number of other former colonial countries. More than 1,200 million people, or nearly half of the world's population, have freed themselves from colonial or semi-colonial dependence during the last ten years. *(Prolonged applause.)*

The disintegration of the imperialist colonial system now taking place is a post-war development of history-making significance. Peoples who for centuries were kept away by the colonialists from the high road of progress followed by human society are now going through a great process of regeneration. People's China and the independent Indian Republic have joined the ranks of the Great Powers. We are witnessing a political and economic upsurge of the peoples of South-East Asia and the Arab East. The awakening of the peoples of Africa has begun. The national-liberation movement has gained in strength in Brazil, Chile and other Latin-American countries. The outcome of the wars in Korea, Indo-China and Indonesia has demonstrated that the imperialists are unable, even with the help of armed intervention, to crush the peoples who are resolutely fighting for a life of freedom and independence. The complete abolition of the infamous system of colonialism has now been put on the agenda as one of the most acute and pressing problems. *(Applause.)*

The new period in world history which Lenin predicted has arrived, and the peoples of the East are playing an active part in deciding the destinies of the whole world, are becoming a new mighty factor in international relations. In contrast to the pre-war period, most Asian countries now act in the world arena as sovereign states or states which are resolutely upholding their right to an independent foreign policy. International relations have spread beyond the bounds of relations between the countries inhabited chiefly by peoples of the white race and are beginning to acquire the character of genuinely world-wide relations.

The winning of political freedom by the peoples of the former colonies and semi-colonies is the first and most important prerequisite of their full independence, that is, of the achievement of economic independence. The liberated Asian countries are pursuing a policy of building up their own industry, training their own technicians, raising the living standards of the people, and regenerating and developing their age-old national culture. History-making prospects for a better future are opening up before the countries which have embarked upon the path of independent development.

These countries, although they do not belong to the socialist world system, can draw on its achievements to build up an independent national economy and to raise the living standards of their peoples. Today they need not go begging for up-to-date equipment to their former oppressors. They can get it in the socialist countries, without assuming any political or military commitments.

The very fact that the Soviet Union and the other countries of the socialist camp exist, their readiness to help the underdeveloped countries in advancing their industries on terms of equality and mutual benefit are a major stumbling-block to colonial policy. The imperialists can no longer regard the underdeveloped countries solely as potential sources for making maximum profits. They are compelled to make concessions to them.

Not all the countries, however, have thrown off the colonial yoke. A big part of the African continent, some countries of Asia, Central and South America continue to remain in colonial or semi-colonial dependence. They are still retained as agrarian raw-material appendages of the imperialist countries. The living standard of the population in the dependent countries remains exceedingly low.

The contradictions and rivalry between the colonial powers for spheres of influence, sources of raw materials, and markets are growing. The United States is out to grab the colonial possessions of the European powers. South Viet-Nam is passing from France to the United States. The American monopolies are waging an offensive against the French, Belgian and Portuguese possessions in

Africa. Once Iran's oil riches were fully controlled by the British, but now the British have been compelled to share them with the Americans; moreover, the American monopolies are fighting to oust the British entirely. American influence in Pakistan and Iraq is increasing under the guise of "free enterprise."

The American monopolies, utilizing their dominant position in the Central and South-American countries, have moulded the economies of many of them in a distorted, one-sided way, extremely disadvantageous for the population. They are hampering their industrial development and shackling them with the heavy chains of economic dependence. . . .

To preserve, and in some places also to re-establish their former domination, the colonial powers are resorting to the suppression of the colonial peoples by the force of arms, a method which has been condemned by history. They also have recourse to new forms of colonial enslavement under the guise of so-called "aid" to underdeveloped countries, which brings colossal profits to the colonialists. Let us take the United States as an example. The United States renders such "aid" above all in the form of deliveries of American weapons to the underdeveloped countries. This enables the American monopolies to load up their industry with arms orders. Then the products of the arms industry, worth billions of dollars and paid for through the budget by the American taxpayers, are sent to the underdeveloped countries. States receiving such "aid" in the form of weapons, inevitably fall into dependence; they increase their armies, which leads to higher taxes and a decline in living standards.

The monopolists are interested in continuing the "positions of strength" policy; the ending of the "cold war" is to their disadvantage. Why? Because the fanning of war hysteria is used to justify imperialist expansion, to intimidate the masses and dope their minds in order to justify the higher taxes which then go to pay for war orders and flow into the safes of the millionaires. Thus, the "cold war" is a means for maintaining the war industry at a high level and for extracting colossal profits.

Naturally, "aid" to underdeveloped countries is granted on definite political terms, terms providing for their integration into aggressive military blocs, the conclusion of joint military pacts, and support for American foreign policy aimed at world domination, or "world leadership," as the American imperialists themselves call it.

SEATO and the Baghdad pact are not only aggressive military and political alignments, but also instruments of enslavement, a new form of exploitation, colonial in nature, of the underdeveloped countries. It is obvious that SEATO policy is determined neither by Pakistan or Thailand, nor that of the Baghdad pact by Iraq, Iran, or Turkey.

The establishment of such blocs and the pitting of some countries against others is also one of the means used to divide the economically-underdeveloped countries, and to continue the long-standing colonialist policy of "divide and rule." They try to use the Baghdad pact as a wedge to split the unity of the countries of the Arab East. With the help of SEATO they seek to divide the countries of South-East Asia.

The struggle of the peoples of the Eastern countries against participation in blocs is a struggle for national independence. It is not fortuitous that the overwhelming majority of countries in South-East Asia and the Middle East have rejected the importunate attempts of the Western Powers to inveigle them into closed military alignments.

Despite all the efforts to set the peoples of the underdeveloped countries at loggerheads with each other and with the peoples of the socialist camp, their friendship and co-operation is growing ever stronger. The Bandung Conference of 29 Asian and African countries has strikingly demonstrated the growing solidarity of the Eastern peoples. Its decisions reflected the will of hundreds of millions of people in the East. It struck a powerful blow at the plans of the colonialists and aggressors.

The friendship and co-operation between the Eastern peoples who have thrown off the colonial yoke and the peoples of the socialist countries is growing and strengthening. This was graphically revealed by the visits of the leaders of India and Burma to the Soviet Union and by the visit of the Soviet leaders to India, Burma and Afghanistan. Those visits confirmed the identity of views existing between the Soviet Union and the Republic of India, one of the Great Powers of the world, and between the Soviet

Union, Burma, and Afghanistan, on the fundamental international issue of today: the preservation and consolidation of universal peace and the national independence of all states.

The exceptionally warm and friendly welcome accorded the representatives of the great Soviet people has strikingly demonstrated the deep-rooted confidence and love the broad masses in the Eastern countries have for the Soviet Union. Analyzing the sources of this confidence, the Egyptian *Al Akhbar* justly wrote: "Russia does not try to buy the conscience of the peoples, their rights and liberty. Russia has extended a hand to the peoples and said that they themselves should decide their destiny, that she recognizes their rights and aspirations and does not demand their adherence to military pacts or blocs." Millions of men and women ardently acclaim our country for its uncompromising struggle against colonialism, for its policy of equality and friendship among all nations and for its consistent peaceful foreign policy. *(Stormy, prolonged applause.)*

*       *       *

*The peaceful co-existence of the two systems.* The Leninist principle of peaceful co-existence of states with different social systems has always been and remains the general line of our country's foreign policy.

It has been alleged that the Soviet Union advances the principle of peaceful co-existence merely out of tactical considerations, considerations of expediency. Yet it is common knowledge that we have always, from the very first years of Soviet power, stood with equal firmness for peaceful co-existence. Hence, it is not a tactical move, but a fundamental principle of Soviet foreign policy.

This means that if there is indeed a threat to the peaceful co-existence of countries with differing social and political systems, it by no means comes from the Soviet Union or the rest of the socialist camp. Is there a single reason why a socialist state should want to unleash aggressive war? Do we have classes and groups that are interested in war as a means of enrichment? We do not. We abolished them long ago. Or, perhaps, we do not have enough territory or natural wealth, perhaps we lack sources of raw materials or markets for our goods? No, we have sufficient of all those and to spare. Why then should we want war? We do not want it, as a matter of principle we renounce any policy that might lead to millions of people being plunged into war for the sake of the selfish interests of a handful of multi-millionaires. Do those who shout about the "aggressive intentions" of the U.S.S.R. know all this? Of course they do. Why then do they keep up the old monotonous refrain about some imaginary "communist aggression"? Only to stir up mud, to conceal their plans for world domination, a "crusade" against peace, democracy, and socialism.

To this day the enemies of peace allege that the Soviet Union is out to overthrow capitalism in other countries by "exporting" revolution. It goes without saying that among us Communists there are no supporters of capitalism. But this does not mean that we have interfered or plan to interfere in the internal affairs of countries where capitalism still exists. Romain Rolland was right when he said that "freedom is not brought in from abroad in baggage trains like Bourbons." (Animation.) It is ridiculous to think that revolutions are made to order. We often hear representatives of bourgeois countries reasoning thus: "The Soviet leaders claim that they are for peaceful co-existence between the two systems. At the same time they declare that they are fighting for communism, and say that communism is bound to win in all countries. Now if the Soviet Union is fighting for communism, how can there be any peaceful co-existence with it?" This view is the result of bourgeois propaganda. The ideologists of the bourgeoisie distort the facts and deliberately confuse questions of ideological struggle with questions of relations between states in order to make the Communists of the Soviet Union look like advocates of aggression.

When we say that the socialist system will win in the competition between the two systems—the capitalist and the socialist—this by no means signifies that its victory will be achieved through armed interference by the socialist countries in the internal affairs of the capitalist countries. Our certainty of the victory of communism is based on the fact that the socialist mode of production possesses decisive advantages over the capitalist mode of production. Precisely because of this, the ideas of Marxism-Leninism are more and more capturing the minds of the broad masses of the working people in the capitalist countries, just as they have captured the minds of millions of men and women in our country and the People's Democracies. *(Prolonged applause.)* We believe that all working men in the world, once they have become convinced of the advantages communism brings, will sooner or later take the road of struggle for the construction of socialist society. *(Prolonged applause.)* Building communism in our country, we are resolutely against war. We have always held and continue to hold that the establishment of a new social system in one or another country is the internal affair of the peoples of the countries concerned. This is our attitude, based on the great Marxist-Leninist teaching. . . .

*The possibility of preventing war in the present era.* Millions of people all over the world are asking whether another war is really inevitable, whether mankind which has already experienced two devastating world wars must still go through a third one? Marxists must answer this question taking into consideration the epoch-making changes of the last decades.

There is, of course, a Marxist-Leninist precept that wars are inevitable as long as imperialism exists. This precept was evolved at a time when 1) imperialism was an all-embracing world system, and 2) the social and political forces which did not want war were weak, poorly organized, and hence unable to compel the imperialists to renounce war.

People usually take only one aspect of the question and examine only the economic basis of wars under imperialism. This is not enough. War is not only an economic phenomenon. Whether there is to be a war or not depends in large measure on the correlation of class, political forces, the degree of organization and the awareness and resolve of the people. Moreover, in certain conditions the struggle waged by progressive social and political forces may play a decisive role. Hitherto the state of affairs was such that the forces that did not want war and opposed it were poorly organized and lacked the means to check the schemes of the war-makers. Thus it was before the First World War, when the main force opposed to the threat of war—the world proletariat—was disorganized by the treachery of the leaders of the Second International. Thus it was on the eve of the Second World

War, when the Soviet Union was the only country that pursued an active peace policy, when the other Great Powers to all intents and purposes encouraged the aggressors, and the Right-wing Social-Democratic leaders had split the labour movement in the capitalist countries.

In that period this precept was absolutely correct. At the present time, however, the situation has changed radically. Now there is a world camp of socialism, which has become a mighty force. In this camp the peace forces find not only the moral, but also the material means to prevent aggression. Moreover, there is a large group of other countries with a population running into many hundreds of millions which are actively working to avert war. The labour movement in the capitalist countries has today become a tremendous force. The movement of peace supporters has sprung up and developed into a powerful factor.

In these circumstances certainly the Leninist precept that so long as imperialism exists, the economic basis giving rise to wars will also be preserved remains in force. That is why we must display the greatest vigilance. As long as capitalism survives in the world, the reactionary forces representing the interests of the capitalist monopolies will continue their drive towards military gambles and aggression, and may try to unleash war. But war is not fatalistically inevitable. Today there are mighty social and political forces possessing formidable means to prevent the imperialists from unleashing war, and if they actually try to start it, to give a smashing rebuff to the aggressors and frustrate their adventurist plans. To be able to do this all anti-war forces must be vigilant and prepared, they must act as a united front and never relax their efforts in the battle for peace. The more actively the peoples defend peace, the greater the guarantees that there will be no new war. *(Stormy, prolonged applause.)*

# THE TASK OF SURPASSING
# THE U. S. A.*

BY

## NIKITA S. KHRUSHCHEV

[1957]

The year 1957, which ends in a few days, has been an anniversary year, the 40th year in the life of the Soviet socialist state. It has been rich in events both in the domestic life of our country and in the international arena. This year has been marked by the successful fulfillment of the historic decisions of the 20th Party Congress, which outlined a magnificent program of communist construction.

The celebration of the 40th anniversary of Great October was a great festive occasion not only for the peoples of the Soviet Union but for all progressive mankind, since the October Socialist Revolution, because it initiated the building of a new world on socialist principles, was an event of world significance.

The 40 years of work by the working class, the peasantry and the intelligentsia and by the peoples of the Soviet Union under the leadership of the Communist Party, which was founded by the great Lenin, have been marked by historic victories. The building of socialism and the successful construction of communism is the principal result of our people's labor effort. All our country's successes are a result of the consistent application of the Leninist policy of the Communist Party of the Soviet Union. The unbreakable unity between the Communist Party and the Soviet people is the inexhaustible wellspring of the creative forces of our Soviet motherland, which is advancing to new communist triumphs. (*Prolonged applause.*)

* This speech, given at the Anniversary Session of the Ukraine Republic Supreme Soviet, appeared in *Pravda* and *Izvestia,* December 25, 1957. These selections are from the translation of the complete text in *The Current Digest of the Soviet Press* (New York), Vol. IX, No. 52. Copyright; reprinted by permission.

The enemies of socialism deny the creative abilities of the working class, of the working people, who, having taken power into their own hands, began building life on socialist principles. They advertised in every way the advantages of capitalism over socialism and lauded the merits of "private enterprise," the prime mover of which is profit and gain. But life has refuted their assertions.

The socialist system has proved its great vital force. It has opened up immense possibilities for an economic and cultural upsurge, for development of all the creative forces of the people. As a result of socialist transformations, our country, which before the revolution was backward in comparison with other countries, has been turned into a mighty industrial state in an historically short period of time.

Now even the most diehard enemies of socialism have been obliged to admit that the Soviet Union has scored exceptional successes in the development of industry, agriculture, science and technology, in the technical equipping of the various branches of the national economy and in the training of highly qualified specialists and workers.

The decisions of the 20th Party Congress evoked a fresh surge of energy and creative activity on the part of the working people. All Soviet people are working with tremendous patriotic enthusiasm to realize the Party Congress decisions and to carry out the measures charted by the Communist Party and the Soviet government for the further development of socialist industry, agriculture, science and culture and for increasing the output of consumer goods.

We note with great satisfaction that the period since the 20th Party Congress has been marked by major new successes in the development of our country. (*Applause.*) . . .

All industry in the Soviet Union is on a sharp rise. The reorganization of the management of industry and construction by economic regions, the transfer of the administration of industry and construction to the Union republics, the setting up of economic councils and bringing management into direct, close contact with the enterprises have had a favorable effect on the work of our industry. This is attested to by the work results at enterprises and construction projects throughout the country, and is eloquently attested to by the achievements of the Soviet Ukraine as well. (*Applause.*)

The 1957 plan called for a 7.1% increase in our country's industrial output. The actual growth in industrial output this year will be 10%. (*Applause.*)

It is important to note that in the second half of 1957 industry fulfilled its quotas on a higher level than in the corresponding period of 1956. While last year the third-quarter plan for gross production was fulfilled by 101%, the third-quarter plan for this year was fulfilled by 104%. In October and November of 1956 the plan for industrial output was fulfilled by an average of 103%; the plan for the corresponding period of 1957 was fulfilled by 105%. . . .

Of course, there are still many shortcomings in the work of industry and construction, both in the country as a whole and in the Ukraine. But, contrary to the assertions of the "skeptics," things have gone not worse but much better since the reorganization of the management of industry and construction. (*Applause.*)

The task now is to improve the work of the economic councils, to have them probe more deeply into the work of each enterprise, manage the enterprises effectively, know their needs, and give enterprises and construction projects the necessary assistance in fulfilling national economic tasks. The economic councils have a great deal of work to do in further improving the specialization, integrated mechanization and automation of production, and in improving cooperation among enterprises in order to bring about a substantial rise in labor productivity, expand production and cut unit costs.

A major task of the economic councils is to fill orders from other economic areas promptly and with high-quality goods. It is necessary that our industry fill all orders on time. But the filling of orders for other economic areas must be unflaggingly supervised by the economic councils. We must remember, comrades, that failure to fill these orders on time impedes integration and specialization of industry and harms the planned functioning of the economy. Our industry's fulfillment of all foreign orders promptly and with high-quality goods must be put under the same unflagging supervision.

We are convinced that the heroic working class of the Soviet Union and the workers in the industry of the Ukraine will achieve new and great successes in the continued mighty advance of heavy industry and in the development of all light and food industries. (*Stormy applause.*)

Comrades! Allow me to tell you about certain agricultural problems. It is common knowledge that 1956 was a record year as regards the total grain harvest and grain procurements. This year has been unfavorable because of the drought in a number of areas, particularly in the Volga region, the Urals and some provinces of Kazakhstan. But thanks to the development of the virgin and idle lands, the country has procured approximately as much grain in 1957 as in 1955, while in comparison with 1953 grain procurements have increased 18%, including a 41% increase for wheat. (*Applause.*) . . .

On Dec. 1, 1957, there were 4,200,000 more cattle (including 600,000 more cows), 6,400,000 more pigs and 8,900,000 more sheep on the Soviet Union's collective and state farms than on Dec. 1, 1956.

Along with the growth in the number of livestock, the productivity of animal husbandry has increased markedly; the output of milk, meat, wool and other products has increased.

The Soviet people are gladdened by the agricultural workers' achievements in increasing milk output. . . .

The growth in the output of milk and the considerable rise in the collective and state farms' share of the country's livestock have made it possible to increase milk procurements. The plenary session's decisions called for an increase in milk procurements of no less than 80% in 1960 as compared with 1954. This task has been achieved in three years rather than in six. (*Prolonged applause.*) . . .

All the Union republics have joined in the struggle for a further increase in the output of animal husbandry products. Many collective farms, state farms and entire districts report that they are successfully fulfilling their pledges to obtain 100 or more centners of meat and 400 to 500 centners of milk per 100 hectares of farm land. This attests to the feasibility of our goal and to our agriculture's great potentialities and latent reserves. . . .

The achievements of leading collective farms attest to the fact that the Ukraine has immense latent potentialities for further increasing the production of grain, meat, milk and other farm products. But you also have collective and state farms that are still producing low yields per 100 hectares of land. You pledged to produce not less than 100 centners of meat and 400 centners of milk per 100 hectares of land for the republic as a whole, and not less than 64 centners of meat and 247 centners of milk per 100 hectares for collective farms.

If such results are to be achieved, a great deal of work must still be done, and all collective and state farms must rise to the level of the leading farms. In order to do this it is necessary first of all to improve organizing work in rural areas and to train collective farmers, team and brigade leaders and collective farm chairmen carefully. This must be mentioned since there are still grave shortcomings in your work with people and particularly with the managerial cadres of collective farms. Persistent application of advanced experience and of the discoveries of agricultural science is also necessary.

I wish to say a few words about how the call to overtake the United States in per capita output of animal husbandry products in the next few years should be properly understood. When the Party Central Committee gave its support to the appeal by our leading collective and state farms to overtake the United States in per capita output of animal husbandry products, and in this connection set the task of increasing meat production, for example, by 250%, it had in mind the country as a whole.

But such an average yardstick cannot be applied to the individual republics. Take the Ukraine as an example; collective and state farms and all rural workers must strive to surpass the United States' indices by a considerable margin.

The amount by which the Ukraine must surpass the United States must be calculated. You Ukrainian comrades must not only overtake the United States in the output of animal husbandry products, you must considerably surpass it—perhaps by 100%, or even more. Unquestionably you have every requisite for obtaining much more farm produce per 100 hectares of land than is obtained in the United States. (*Applause.*) . . .

The Party and government express their firm conviction that the glorious collective farm peasantry and all workers in socialist agriculture will continue to struggle selflessly to increase the output of farm products and will make their worthy contribution to the achievement of an abundance of food for the public and raw materials for light industry. (*Stormy applause.*)

There can be no doubt that the collective farmers and Machine and Tractor Stations and state farm employees of the Ukraine, who have often initiated all-Union competition and introduced new work methods in agriculture, will continue to show creative initiative and to march in the front ranks of the struggle for a further advance in agriculture and for full sufficiency of products in the country. (*Stormy applause.*)

Comrades! The Communist Party and the Soviet government have always devoted a great deal of attention to raising the people's living standard. A number of important measures have been taken in recent years to improve the life of the Soviet people and raise the real incomes of workers, employees and collective farmers.

Our country's national income more than doubled between 1950 and 1957. During the same period the number of workers and employees increased by nearly 14,000,000. Real wages of workers and employees and the income of the peasants have grown considerably during this period.

It must be said that an increase in the working people's real earnings can be achieved in essentially two ways: by reducing the retail prices of consumer goods or by increasing monetary wages, pensions, benefits and other cash income.

As is known, between 1947 and 1954 we mainly followed the path of reducing retail prices. Today state retail prices are 2.3 times lower than in 1947 [i.e., they are 43.48% of 1947 prices], while the price of bread, meat, butter and certain other necessities has been cut even more. This year the prices of a number of articles of mass consumption have also been reduced. We will continue to carry out such measures. (*Applause.*)

It is necessary to bear in mind, however, that a reduction of retail prices is of greatest benefit to those who buy the most, i.e., the higher-paid groups of workers and employees, while the lower-paid groups benefit to a lesser extent.

We proceed from the socialist principle of payment according to the quantity and quality of work and, naturally, cannot allow levelling in wages. But the gap in wages between the higher- and lower-paid groups must be reduced; and as time goes on this gap will be progressively narrowed by raising the wages of the lower-paid categories of working people and by increasing pensions. (*Applause.*) . . .

The Communist Party and the Soviet government will continue to strive to raise the people's living standards, will apply the policy of reducing the gap between the maximum and minimum wage levels. We must bear in mind that a rise in the living standard of the working people, an increase in wages and further reduction of prices all depend on the increase in labor productivity. There is direct dependence here, and this must be made clear to workers, employees, collective farmers and all the working people of our country.

In conformity with the resolutions of the 20th Party Congress, enterprises began a conversion to a shorter workday starting with the second half of 1956. Donets Basin coal miners were put on a shorter workday in the fourth quarter of 1956. Workers and employees in the mining, metallurgical and coke and chemical enterprises of ferrous metallurgy are presently being shifted to a shorter workday.

During the Sixth Five-Year Plan all workers and employees will switch over to a seven-hour day, and workers in a number of jobs to a six-hour day. Reducing the workday at a time when we have a growing need for manpower is yet another proof of the unflagging concern of the Party and government for the well-being of our country's working people. . . .

In recent years the collective and state farms have achieved a significant rise in output. As a result, procurements of farm products from collective and state farms have increased, permitting the state to lower the quotas for obligatory deliveries from the households of collective farmers, workers and employees.

You know that the Party Central Committee and the Council of Ministers adopted a resolution freeing all the households of collective farmers, workers and employees from all obligatory deliveries of farm products to the state beginning with 1958. This means that between 17,000,000 and 18,000,000 households of collective farmers, workers and employees will be able to sell their farm products at more advantageous prices through the state and collective farm-cooperative trade networks instead of turning them over to the state in the form of obligatory deliveries; as a result, they will increase their earnings by more than 3,000,000,000 rubles. This measure will also make possible a reduction in the number of employees in the procurement apparatus. . . .

Comrades! The 20th Party Congress set the task of working out a long-range plan for development of the national economy to cover several five-year plan periods. Preliminary estimates by officials of the planning agencies show that within the next 15 years the Soviet Union not only can overtake, but can surpass the present gross output of the most important types of industrial goods in the United States of America. Of course the U.S.A. can also move ahead somewhat, but thanks to the higher rate of growth of our industry, we can still overtake and surpass it.

All the necessary conditions have now been created in the Soviet Union for economic development to proceed at an ever more rapid pace. . . . Our present level of investment in the national economy is 14 times what it was in the years of the First Five-Year Plan, and investment in industry is more than 15 times what it was. . . .

We are moving ahead considerably faster than the capitalist countries. In the 40 years from 1918 to 1957 the average annual rate of increase in industrial output in the U.S.S.R. was 10% while in the United States it was 3.2%, in Britain 1.9% and in France 3.2%.

If we exclude the years of the Civil War, the reconstruction period and the Patriotic War, then in the 22 peaceful years we increased industrial output by an average 16.2% per year, while the United States increased it 2.8%, Britain 3.2% and France 3%. This means that in one year we registered as large a rate of increase as the capitalist countries do in five to six years. (*Applause.*)

Let us take ferrous metallurgy as an example and examine the figures for steel output in the U.S.S.R. and the United States.

In 1913 our country produced 4,200,000 tons of steel, while the United States produced 31,800,000 tons, i.e., more than seven times as much. . . .

In the prewar year of 1940 we produced 18,300,000 tons of steel and the United States produced 60,800,000 tons, i.e., somewhat more than three times as much. As a result of the losses we suffered in the war, our steel output in 1954 dropped to 12,-300,000 tons, while in the United States it stood at 72,300,000 tons, six times as much.

In 1957 the U.S.S.R. will produce 51,000,000 tons of steel and the United States about 106,000,000 tons, i.e., twice as much.

There is every reason to assume that in steel output, just as in the output of other industrial goods, we can overtake and surpass the United States in a very brief historical period. (*Prolonged applause.*)

Thus the successful accomplishment of the basic economic task of the U.S.S.R.—to overtake and surpass the principal capitalist countries in per capita industrial output—is becoming a real actuality. (*Applause.*) . . .

The economy, science and technology have reached a level of development in the Soviet Union that now enables us to develop light industry at a faster pace without impairing the country's defenses and the further expansion of heavy industry, and, in particular, to produce footwear and fabrics for the people in quantities that will make possible the full satisfaction, within the next five to seven years, of the people's growing demand for these goods.

All the Union republics will have to do a great deal of work to accomplish the tasks set forth in the estimates of the long-range plan. We must make considerably better use of available reserves in all branches of the national economy, persistently raise labor productivity, practice the strictest economy, show true thrift in all matters and fight against extravagance and waste.

I wish to stress once again that a steady rise in labor productivity is the main source of the accumulations we need for the further development of industry, agriculture, science and culture; for consolidating the country's defenses and raising the people's living standard. A rise in labor productivity is the fundamental question of the development of a socialist economy and the attention of all our workers must be constantly directed toward it.

In evaluating the work of industrial enterprises, construction projects, M.T.S. and collective and state farms, account must always be taken of how labor productivity is being raised, how the expenditure of labor per unit of output is being reduced, how the unit cost of production is being lowered and how quality is being improved.

Comrades! One of the greatest achievements of our people in the years of Soviet rule is that we showed the entire world that only socialism opens up the widest possibilities for tempestuous and comprehensive development of the spiritual life of society, opens boundless expanses for the development of science, technology, literature and art and for the development of the people's talents and gifts.

As a result of the cultural revolution accomplished in our country, millions of people, formerly deprived of education, enlightenment and knowledge, have in Soviet times been exposed to the great treasure of culture and have become active creators of culture.

The outstanding successes of the Soviet Union in the sphere of culture are most strikingly manifested in the large-scale training of highly qualified specialists.

While Soviet higher educational institutions are graduating 250,000 to 260,000 persons annually, including 70,000 to 75,000 engineers, the United States of America, with about the same size graduating class, graduates only 25,000 to 26,000 engineers, and other countries even fewer.

The pride of our people is the remarkable cadres of Soviet intelligentsia—reared by socialist society and trained by the Communist Party in the spirit of loyalty to Marxism-Leninism and to their socialist motherland and the people.

Our people are rightly proud of the outstanding achievements of Soviet science and technology.   Soviet scientists and industrial personnel have created high-speed computing machines, have elaborated new principles of accelerating elementary particles and have developed powerful accelerators; they have surpassed the scientists of other countries in this important work.

It was in the Soviet Union that the world's first atomic power station was built, the world's first atomic ice-breaker, the "Lenin," was launched, and substantial advances were made in the peaceful uses of atomic energy, and first-rate passenger planes powered by jet and turboprop engines were produced.   The development of an intercontinental ballistic rocket is an outstanding achievement.

The successes of Soviet industry, science and technology are another conclusive demonstration of the great advantage of the socialist system over the capitalism system; they have demonstrated how socialist society brings out the inexhaustible forces and potentialities of the people.

Soviet scientists, designers and workers have performed the greatest of feats, launching the artificial earth satellites.   The launching of the satellites is the work of the Soviet people, who, under socialism, are making fairy tales into reality.   By their heroic labors the people have created a mighty industry, trained remarkable cadres in all spheres of economic and cultural construction, and raised science and technology to unprecedented heights.

Not long ago at all we were considered backward.   How much ink and paper was wasted by bourgeois scribblers!   Many representatives of the capitalist world spouted streams of lies and slander to the effect that there is no freedom of creativity in the Soviet land. Who today will believe these fables when Soviet satellites are circling our planet, proclaiming to all the world what the creative genius of our people, freed from the shackles of capitalism, can do? (*Stormy applause.*)

Not long ago at all the inordinately boastful American reactionaries, loudly advertising their preparations to launch an earth satellite, were prepared to gloat over our backwardness.

But, as the popular saying goes, "Don't cry 'hup' until you've made your jump." (*Animation in the hall, applause.*) But they often cry "hup" and brag ahead of time. This time again they embarrassed themselves before the whole world. . . .

Comrades!

The talented Ukrainian people are making their own notable contribution to our common treasurehouse of socialist science, technology and culture. More than 1,250,000 specialists with a higher or secondary specialized education are presently employed in the Ukraine's national economy.

The culture of the Ukrainian people, national in form and socialist in content, is flourishing. Ukraine writers, artists, sculptors, composers, film makers and men of other creative professions have produced many vivid works that have enriched Soviet and world literature and art.

The Ukraine's unions of writers, artists and composers have demonstrated that they are ideologically stable, close-knit collectives that are fighting consistently to carry out Party policy in literature and the arts. Their principled stand in the struggle against unsound sentiments and tendencies has exerted a great positive influence on raising the level of the ideological and creative life of our writers, artists and composers.

Allow me to express confidence in the fact that Ukraine scientists, cultural figures, writers, artists and composers will gladden our country with remarkable new discoveries and works, and will continue actively to assist our party in its ideological struggle and in the communist education of the Soviet people. (*Prolonged applause.*)

Comrades! The building of communism is now not only our great ideal but a direct, practical task of Soviet society, a task in which are engaged millions and millions of toilers of city and countryside—all the Soviet people, under the leadership of our Leninist Communist Party.

Marching with us are the peoples of the Chinese People's Republic and all the countries of the mighty socialist camp; with us are millions of our friends in all countries and on all the continents.

The working people abroad note with tremendous admiration the historic triumphs that the Soviet Union has achieved in the years of Soviet rule.

Under the leadership of the Communist Party the Soviet people are accomplishing tremendous tasks in building communist society. In the name of achieving this great goal our party is mobilizing the creative efforts of the working class, the collective farm peasantry and the intelligentsia. Our party's general line, expressing the fundamental interests of the people, is embodied in the 20th Party Congress decisions and the subsequent Party and government decrees. Every Soviet man turns with boundless love and warm gratitude to the Communist Party, the experienced leader, inspirer and organizer of communist construction. . . .

In the struggle for the great cause of building communism the Soviet people are rallying even closer around the Communist Party of the Soviet Union and its Central Committee, which carries high the triumphant banner of Marxism-Leninism. (*Stormy applause.*)

In the fifth decade of its existence the Land of the Soviets has entered into the full flower of its mighty forces. The Soviet Union now has every requirement for further rapid development of productive forces, for bettering the people's life and raising their cultural level.

Our successes in economic and cultural construction, in science and technology and in foreign policy are genuinely great, and this causes joy and legitimate pride among Soviet people. But the strength of our party lies in the fact that it constantly looks ahead and mobilizes the people to meet ever new tasks.   That is why in our work conceit, complacency and an uncritical evaluation of our activities cannot be tolerated. . . .

The national economic plan for 1958, approved by the recently concluded session of the U.S.S.R. Supreme Soviet, envisages a new advance of industry and agriculture and a further increase in the people's well-being and culture.   Successful accomplishment of this plan will be an important landmark along the path of communist construction. . . .

# POWER TODAY*

## ITS LOCATION, NATURE, AND GROWTH

### BY

## DEAN ACHESON

### [1958]

Before the present century was two decades old, the system which had provided an international order since Waterloo was mortally stricken. Twenty years later, it had disappeared altogether.

It is true that in the rosy light of retrospect the period after the Congress of Vienna has seemed more peaceful and idyllic than it was. To the men of the time, says a more realistic writer, the period "was one of appalling turmoil. It was an armed peace. Austria's budget, for instance, was so overburdened by expenditure on armaments that it only once avoided a deficit between 1812 and 1848. France was not pacified: on the contrary resentment against the settlement dominated French political life for a generation. The discontent in the victorious countries was almost as great, except where held down—as in Austria—by police tyranny."[1]

All this is true. Nonetheless, the "Concert of Europe" describes a method and a reality. The empires of Europe, controlling hundreds of millions of people in Europe, Asia, and Africa, and decisively affecting the conduct of hundreds of millions more, did keep international conflict limited in scope and minimal in destruction. They did provide an economic system, accepted without protest, and they did establish political coherence unequaled in extent since the Roman Empire. One essential element in all of this was Great Britain's skillful employment of its power to give stability through shifts of its weight from one side to another, much as a gyroscope gives balance to a moving craft. Another essential element was the managerial and material contribution to

---

*From *Power and Diplomacy*, published by Harvard University Press, copyright 1958 by The Fletcher School of Law and Diplomacy, Tufts University. Reprinted by permission.
[1] *Times Literary Supplement* (London), April 26, 1957.

economic development, first, by the British and, later, by Western European industry and finance.

The First World War ended the Austro-Hungarian, German, and Ottoman Empires and the Czarist regime in Russia, unloosed nationalism in Eastern Europe, and gravely weakened the French and British Empires. The Second World War eliminated the empires of Japan and Italy, and the military power of Germany. France, defeated and occupied, lost her position in the Near East and Far East, and only with increasing difficulty maintains herself in Africa, at the expense of power in Europe. Great Britain, economically exhausted and, save for the African colonies, politically and militarily reduced to her island resources, has by her recent budget decision made clear that the security of the United Kingdom lies in association with other states. . . .

The curtain had been rung down upon an era; the stage set for the unfolding of another, which Alexis de Tocqueville, with amazing vision, forecast almost a century and a quarter ago, in his *Democracy in America*:

"There are at the present time two great nations in the world, which started from different points, but seem to tend towards the same end. I allude to the Russians and the Americans. Both of them have grown up unnoticed; and while the attention of mankind was directed elsewhere, they have suddenly placed themselves in the front rank among the nations, and the world learned their existence and their greatness at almost the same time.

"All other nations seem to have nearly reached their natural limits, and they have only to maintain their power; but these are still in the act of growth. All the others have stopped, or continue to advance with extreme difficulty; these alone are proceeding with ease and celerity along a path to which no limit can be perceived. The American struggles against the obstacles that nature opposes to him; the adversaries of the Russian are men. The former combats the wilderness and savage life; the latter, civilization with all its arms. The conquests of the American are therefore gained by the plowshare; those of the Russian by the sword. The Anglo-American relies upon personal interest to accomplish his ends and gives free scope to the unguided strength and common sense of the people; the Russian centers all the authority of society in a single arm. The principal instrument of the former is freedom; of the latter, servitude. Their starting-point is different and their courses are not the same; yet each of them seems marked out by the will of Heaven to sway the destinies of half the globe."[2]

Today even the component elements of the world order which had swayed the destinies of the entire globe have been destroyed; beginnings have been made on two alignments to succeed it.

In one of these alignments, Britain, which once had the training and capability to manage a world system, no longer has the capability. The United States, which has the material capability, lacks the experience and the discipline needed for responsible management. This is said in no spirit of belittling those far-reaching, bold, and imaginative steps which this government and people have taken to stop the disintegration of international society and to build anew. Americans, like all sensible people who have had the good fortune to be spared the desire for expansion abroad and the experience of national catastrophe from foreign attack, are primarily interested in their own absorbing and immensely profitable affairs, and only secondarily interested in the doings and business of distant peoples. To understand the bearing and urgency of these takes time and experience.

The disappearance of a world system and of the power which sustained it, together with the growth of Soviet power and ambitions, means that the nations which wish to preserve independent national identity can do so only if the material strength and the political and economic leadership of the United States are enlisted in the effort. However much all of us may dislike this thought, the requisite power does not reside anywhere else.

Europe, however, remains of great importance. Its population is still the largest aggregation of skilled workers in the world, its resources are many and varied. Its industry is second only to our own, though closely pressed in many fields by the Russians. Its traditions of civilization go back through two and a half millennia. If Europe should, by evil chance, become subject to Soviet domination, the problems of the remainder of the non-communist world

---

[2] Alexis de Tocqueville, *Democracy in America* (Alfred A. Knopf, New York, 1945), I, 434.

would become unmanageable.[3]   The agreement and support of
Western European nations are necessary for any successful foreign
policy and defense arrangement on our part.   One must not dis-
count the importance of Europe.   But the fact remains that Europe
without American strength and leadership can neither preserve its
own independence nor foster an international system in which
anyone's independence will survive.

## GROWTH OF RUSSIAN POWER

In the other alignment, Russian power, which has for two cen-.
turies been great, appears to be towering now.   In part this is so
because it stands out like a great tree in a forest where all around
it have been felled; in part, because it has fed on the surrounding
decay, and grown.   In the past Russian strength lay in its vast
area and its large and disciplined manpower.   The Soviet regime
has added to these assets industrial productive power, which is
today the indispensable basis of military power, economic penetration, and political attraction.   The Soviet regime gives first
importance to its own perpetuation.   A strong second effort goes
to keeping confusion and unrest as widespread as possible outside

---

[3] " . . . Were the United States to stand alone against a Communist world
which contained all Europe and the Soviet Union, its 1953 production of 102
million metric tons of crude steel would be outweighed by the Communist
113 million metric tons.   Our theoretical capacity (112.7 million metric tons
at January 1, 1954) would, however, be equal to that production total.   By
1960, ignoring the changes in policy and effort that would obviously take
place, our anticipated production of 117 million metric tons would be faced
by a combined production of 161.5 million metric tons.   That is to say, our
production now would equal 90 percent of the combined output of our
opponents and in 1960 only 72 percent."—*Trends in Economic Growth, A
Comparison of the Western Powers and the Soviet Bloc,* prepared for the Joint
Committee on the Economic Report by the Legislative Reference Service of
the Library of Congress, 83 Cong., 2 Sess., January 3, 1955 (Government
Printing Office, Washington, 1955), p. 140.

The impact of this is even greater if it is true, as the subsequent JEC Report
believes it is, that "The bulk of it [steel]—perhaps as much steel as in the
United States—is available for production of military goods or for items
conducive to further economic growth.   The same kind of comparisons might
be made for petroleum." *Soviet Economic Growth: A Comparison with the
United States,* prepared for the Subcommittee on Foreign Economic Policy of
the Joint Economic Committee by the Legislative Reference Service of the
Library of Congress, 85 Cong., 1 Sess., July 5, 1957 (Government Printing
Office, Washington, 1957), pp. 11–12.

the communist area, and to frustrating all attempts to build an international system other than a communist one. All this paves the way for the inevitable—so the regime believes—collapse of capitalistic governments and systems, and for the hegemony of the Soviet Union in a communist world. The regime's efforts gain immense vigor, subtlety, and—for the West—deep deceptiveness from the fact that the Soviet is a revolutionary society, repudiating the most fundamental postulates of the established order, and is in the grip of an ideology which imbues it with unquestioning confidence in its superiority and its destined progression to triumph and dominion.

No matter how plainly the Russians talk and act, we simply refuse to believe what they say and to understand the meaning of what they do. President Eisenhower and Secretary Dulles keep insisting that the test must be deeds, not words. Floods of deeds follow, amply explained by torrents of words. Yet our leaders and, indeed, our people cannot believe what they see and hear.

As I write, President Eisenhower tells us that relations between the United States and the Soviet Union might be improved by a visit from Marshal Zhukov. The President recalls that he and the Marshal "had a most satisfactory acquaintanceship and friendship," and remembers having had "a very tough time trying to defend our position" against the Marshal's contention "that their system appealed to the idealistic, and we completely to the materialistic."[4] The President seems to forget that the same satisfactory friend and persuasive debater insisted upon and carried out the bloody liquidation of the Hungarian revolt. The friendliness which underlies American life makes it impossible to believe that congeniality can accompany the most profound hostility to ourselves and all we believe. As Justice Holmes correctly observed, candor is the best form of deception.

"People," Mr. Khrushchev told the East German communist leaders in September of 1955—"People say our smiles are not honest. That is not true. Our smile is real and not artificial. But if anyone believes that our smile means that we have given up the teachings of Marx, Engels and Lenin, they are badly mistaken. Those who are waiting for that to happen can go on waiting until

---

[4] *New York Times*, July 18, 1957.

Easter and Whit Monday fall on the same day. . . . We are honest people and always tell our opponents the truth. We are supporters of peaceful coexistence but also of education for communism. We are supporters of peaceful coexistence only because there happen to be two systems. We do not need a war to ensure the victory of socialism. Peaceful competition itself is enough . . . one cannot stop the course of history."

The object of competition, Khrushchev points out, is the triumph of the Soviet system. He does not *"need"* a war to ensure this victory; but he would quite clearly not reject force if the risks were low, or if, as in Hungary, he felt that the deepest interests of the regime were at stake. Despite all this, we go on seeing in each new move of the Kremlin to divide and weaken us signs that the Russians may at last be "sincere." The very word shows our lack of understanding. The Russians are and have been wholly sincere in what they believe and are pursuing. But their moves and proposals in dealing with other states are coldly and carefully calculated to advance their own purposes, not any common purpose with the West. In this context "sincerity" is a silly and, indeed, a very dangerous word.

Russian industrial production has been growing at a rate as fast as that of any society of which we have record, and greater than most.[5] The technical competence and quality of their heavy industry is no less impressive. For a decade after the Bolshevik revolution in 1917, the period of the consolidation of power, Soviet industry did not equal production under the Czarist regime. This was achieved in 1926; and pre-war production was surpassed in 1928. In the ten years from 1938 to 1948 industrial growth was suspended by the Second World War, preparing for it and recovering from it—a period in which United States production increased enormously; steel production, for instance, by a third. So the Russian achievement has taken place during twenty productive years.

In 1928 their production was a little less than ours at the turn

---

[5] As might be expected, Soviet economic growth has been carefully studied in the United States. What is said here is taken from *Soviet Economic Growth: A Comparison with the United States,* and *Trends in Economic Growth, A Comparison of the Western Powers and the Soviet Bloc,* cited above, note 3.

of the century.[6]   In 1955,[7] within sixteen working years, its was comparable to ours in 1928.[8]   In the interval, again taking steel production for comparison, the Soviets increased theirs twelvefold; that of the United States has doubled.   In 1955 theirs amounted to 43 per cent of ours.   In 1960, so the earlier report to Congress estimates, it will be 51 per cent.   But the later report also warns that these figures underestimate the relative power of the Soviet Union where "only an insignificant proportion of that steel goes into satisfying consumer needs for automobiles, washing machines, refrigerators, etc.   The bulk of it—perhaps as much steel as in the United States—is available for production of military goods or for items conducive to further economic growth."[9]

In 1928 in Russia "the state of technology was generally backward, and labor skilled in modern technology was scarce."[10]   Two years ago the Soviet Union produced more than twice as many bachelors of science as the United States and over two and a half times as many engineers.

This astonishing growth is not hard to understand.   It flows from the nature of Soviet society and the time in history when this growth is taking place.   By forcing deprivation on the Russian people, the dictatorship has been able since the last war to invest up to 40 per cent of production in capital equipment and arms.   In the United States the comparable figure has varied from 25 per cent to 30 per cent.   Civilians in the Soviet Union have been permitted to consume only about 56 per cent, while personal consumption in 1956 was 72 per cent of production in France, 70 per cent in Italy, 69 per cent in Canada, 67 per cent in the United States.   In Germany, significantly, it was 61 per cent.   Then, too, because of the stage of technical development in which this capital investment is being made, Russia has been able to jump from a peasant society to automation without the decades of slow progression through which the Western World had to go in the nineteenth century.

---

[6] *Soviet Economic Growth: A Comparison with the United States*, p. 5.

[7] The last year of reported figures available to me.

[8] *Soviet Economic Growth: A Comparison with the United States*, pp. 23, 36.

[9] *Id.*, p. 11.

[10] *Id.*, p. 3.

This high rate of growth, so the economists tell us, will tend to taper off as Soviet economy reaches a better balance among industrial equipment, population, and resources. Yet I should stress two factors that are likely to upset the economists' predictions. One is the capacity of the regime to restrict the percentage of production which will go to popular consumption to a level below that of the West; the other, the continued and rapid development of automation in industry.

Automation in industry requires large capital investment, which, in turn, requires continuous increase in productivity and savings. For instance, the Ford Motor Company is replacing most of the expensive machines in its Cleveland engine plant with improved ones. This plant, when it was opened in 1951, was a marvel of automation. But in recent months productivity in the United States has been losing ground to more rapid wage and other cost increases. Working hours have been steadily reduced and the claim for reduction is no longer based on grounds of hygiene. The Twentieth Century Fund "on the basis of increased productivity plus the proportion of gains which the American people have in the past given to time off as opposed to more goods, has estimated that the four-day week will be established by 1975. Meanwhile vacations have been extended. A decade ago there were 34 million weeks taken by the working force; the figure is now calculated to be 70 million."[11]

All this suggests that a most important factor in determining the relation between American and Soviet productive power over the next two or three decades may be the amount of work the people of the opposing social systems may be willing to do and what they make. It is quite possible that the rate at which Soviet production is overtaking ours may not slow down as some have expected. For automation in a society in which civilian consumption is severely restricted can have the effect of increasing considerably the savings available for investment in new productive capacity, which in turn could be even more productive. In another society, where automation might be used to increase consumption and leisure, it could check the development of basic industrial

[11] August Heckscher, "Coming Changes in American Life," Address before the National Conference on Higher Education, Chicago, March 3, 1957.

productivity and decrease the relative power of the society.

At all events, regardless of whether Americans continue to be as hard-working as they are now, present trends and common prudence require us to base policy on the hypothesis that, in the absence of a new and vigorous effort on our part, Soviet productive power will approximate that of the United States well before this century is over. Certainly, Mr. Khrushchev is making his plans on that basis. In his Leningrad speech broadcast by the Moscow radio last July he referred to the reorganization of industry and added: "With the improved organization of industrial and building management, with the more skillful use of all the advantages and possibilities of socialist economy we shall be able in a not-too-distant future to solve the problem of catching up with the United States of America in industrial production per capita of population."[12] And recall that the population of the Soviet Union is larger than that of the United States.

## THE NEED FOR GREATER POWER IN THE FREE WORLD

Well, we may say, suppose that Soviet production does become equal to ours, what of it? How does it hurt us economically? From the military point of view, will there be any more wars determined by great industrial potential converted to the production of overwhelming quantities of war material? Won't nuclear attacks destroy industrial capacity, so that the wars of the future will be won or lost by the forces in being at the beginning of the war? Or won't they be limited in area and in the size and nature of forces involved and the type of strategy employed?

. . . There is much sense in these questions. It seems also likely that eventually Russian productive power will approximate ours. Nevertheless, should it do so before a workable and working non-communist world system has been established and has enlisted the

---

[12] *New York Times*, July 7, 1957. Mr. James Reston, in the report of his interviews with Mr. Khrushchev in Moscow, cites the following views of Mr. Khrushchev: " . . . in another forty years the Soviet Union would have surpassed the United States in industrial and agricultural production.

"The Communists, he said, would leave the United States far behind in another forty years and the world would be proceeding with seven-league steps along the road Marx, Engels and Lenin had outlined."—*New York Times*, October 8, 1957.

loyalty of great sections of the world, a most fundamental shift of power would most certainly occur. The Russians understand the necessity for production in their communist area system, and are making great efforts to provide it. They are quite sure that the competition of "peaceful coexistence," if nothing else, will, as Mr. Khrushchev expressed it, "ensure the victory of socialism." The odds would be overwhelmingly against them if under the leadership of the United States, industrial productive power in the non-communist world were also increased to meet unprecedented calls upon it. These calls will be to furnish a military establishment and weapons system more extensive and varied than now exists; to satisfy expanding internal needs; and, in a magnitude not yet understood, to provide foreign investment for those undeveloped areas which are ready and pressing for capital. To many countries this capital would furnish the only alternative to forced saving in the authoritarian style and to dependence for equipment on Soviet industry.

The growth of Soviet power requires the growth of counterpower among those nations which are not willing to concede Soviet hegemony. With this counter-power the future can be faced with hope and confidence, as well as with a sober appreciation of its dangers. Growth of counter-power is needed in our own country, in other industrially developed nations, and in countries only at the beginning of industrial development. There may be a different reason moving each country which objects to Soviet domination. That is unimportant. There will be great differences in their capacity for industrialization. This is important. For help to industrialize (though not subsidy) should be centered in those areas not willing to accept the hegemony of the Sino-Soviet axis and now capable of industrial advance.

The development of these nations will help in two ways to achieve the long-range purposes we have been discussing. In the developed western countries it will stimulate the growth of basic industries which, as we shall see, are needed to produce the military power to safeguard the non-communist world; and it will stimulate the growth of an operating economic system by which those nations capable of achieving higher standards may do so. Both results are needed for political coherence within the area of the system's operation.

As I have suggested, in the nineteenth century an international system of sorts not only kept the peace for a century but also provided highly successful economic working arrangements. It brought about the industrialization of Europe and of many other parts of the world—our own country, for one. It stimulated production of raw materials and led to a great, though unevenly distributed, rise in the standard of living. This was accomplished by the export of capital, primarily by Great Britain, but also by all of Western Europe.

Professor A. K. Cairncross of the University of Glasgow has written impressively of the magnitude of the effort in the extraordinary half century preceding 1914. He calls it symptomatic of this period "that western Europe had invested abroad almost as much as the entire national wealth of Great Britain, the leading industrial country, and a good deal more than the value of the capital physically located in Great Britain." He goes on to say "that Britain herself had invested abroad about as much as her entire industrial and commercial capital, excluding land, and that one-tenth of her national income came to her as interest on foreign investments." Translating these conditions into the circumstances of this decade and applying them to the United States, Professor Cairncross says that an equivalent situation "would imply American investments overseas of no less than $600 billion and an annual return on those investments of some $30 billion. . . ." To sharpen the contrast between what is and what was, he points out that in recent years private investment has not exceeded $1 billion a year and adds that "even this total has only been sustained by very large investments undertaken by the American oil companies." Professor Cairncross then tells us that "if the same proportion of American resources were devoted to foreign investment as Britain devoted . . . in 1913, the flow of investment would require to be thirty times as great. The entire Marshall Plan would have to be carried out twice a year."[13] I am not suggesting that anything approaching these amounts is possible or necessary; but that a system for the export of capital, much greater than our

---

[13] *Home and Foreign Investment 1870–1913* (Cambridge University Press, 1953), p. 3. The Department of Commerce reports the net private investment of the United States for 1956 as $2.8 billion.

present hand-to-mouth efforts, is necessary. The system has been destroyed which expanded the power of Western Europe and permitted industrial development in societies in which individual liberty survived. One to replace it will be devised, managed, and largely (but not wholly) financed by the United States; otherwise, it is likely to be provided by the Soviet Union, under circumstances destructive of our own power and of an international environment in which independent and diverse nations may exist and flourish.

In the Soviet Union the major effort has gone into scientific research and the establishment of a heavy industry based on the production of energy and the fabrication of metals. Since Soviet industry is still inadequate to meet the demands upon it, the production of capital equipment for further development and for armaments will still be the central object. In our own country and in Western Europe on the other hand, light industry and service industries are growing rapidly. Automobile production has been sharply checked by the fact that old cars, like old soldiers, never die, and usually take plenty of time in fading away. True, substantial demand is made on heavy industry for plant expansion and replacement, for road, bridge, and throughway construction, for schools, housing, and so on. But a still larger base is needed to carry the military requirements and those of foreign development.

Military needs will, for as long as it is profitable to look ahead, exceed means available from our national production. Problems of priority of need and of allocation in meeting needs will still be with us. But no one can doubt that more needs can be met with less sacrifice if the nation's heavy industry becomes larger. To aid in bringing this about and, also, in advancing a workable international economic system, there is another demand which requires only to be made effective. This is the demand for industrial equipment by countries having the managerial and technical manpower to use it—countries such as India and Brazil. The amount of equipment needed is not impossibly large, but it is large enough to stimulate expansion of industrial productive power in the West, and larger than countries, ready for capital, can finance from their own savings. It is important that they be aided to expand faster than their own savings will permit.

Urgency is added by the third of the major current trends in world affairs, namely, the two revolutions, one of nationalism in former dependencies; the other, of rising expectations in all undeveloped areas. There was a time when these areas were isolated from knowledge that higher standards existed elsewhere. That day has passed, particularly in countries where the level of education and competence has permitted industrialization to begin and where, if the necessary capital were available, industrial progress could proceed more rapidly.

And it must accelerate, for we are not given unlimited time to create an operating economic system for the non-communist world. Without such a system, there are insufficient ties of economic interest which, together with the attraction of military power and the security which the system would provide, are necessary to political cohesion in the non-communist world.

Foreign investment can provide wider opportunity for use of national energies. This can well enhance pride in national achievement and relieve frustrations among members of the populace now denied opportunity to use their full capabilities and training. This should tend to lessen xenophobia, strengthen social fabric and political stability, and bring new meaning to national independence. Areas outside of and independent of the Soviet system will achieve new industrial productive power—the power which underlies military strength and greatly affects international alignments and political arrangements.

One cannot guarantee all these results. On the other hand, those who insist on basing foreign policy on sure things are likely to end up with no policy at all; the test of success in a foreign policy is whether it turns a desired possibility into a probability. The development of productive power in the non-communist world, with complementary efforts to produce strong military forces and to increase all that makes for political cohesion, is the course most likely to bring about a workable international system and a stable power relationship. The probability of achieving all this, given full endeavor on our part, ranges from fair to excellent.

# RUSSIA'S ECONOMIC PROGRESS*

BY

## GEORGE F. KENNAN

[1958]

Ten years ago I happened to write an article for the American quarterly *Foreign Affairs,* which came to be spoken of as the X-article, and received a good deal more attention at the hands of the press than I am sure it deserved. It was a discussion of the nature of the Soviet regime, and of the problem it posed for Western society.

In recent months many people have asked me how the same problem looks to me today, and whether I could still take the same reassuring view of the prospects for coping with it that I was able to take in 1947. This is a very big question, and I cannot treat it exhaustively in a series of brief talks—I can only touch on certain individual aspects of it. But the moment does seem propitious for such a discussion, and one may hope that even a few cursory reflections will be useful.

What I would like to talk about first is the internal Soviet scene and its implications for us.

Ten years ago, in writing the X-article, I was obliged to draw attention to the handicaps that rested at that time on Soviet economic development: the enormity of the destruction suffered during the war; the physical and spiritual exhaustion of the Soviet people; the uneven development of the Soviet economy to date, and the sad state of Soviet agriculture.

Today I am free to confess that Soviet economic progress in these intervening years, in the face of all these handicaps, has surpassed anything I then thought possible. In the brief space of twelve years the Soviet people have succeeded not only in recovering from the devastations of the war, but in carrying forward a program of industrialization which has made Russia second only to the United States in industrial output generally, and about equal

*From *Russia, the Atom and the West,* published by Harper & Brothers, copyright 1957, 1958 by George F. Kennan. Reprinted by permission.

to her, we are told, in the production of military goods. The recent launching of the earth satellite has been only a dramatization, misleading in some respects, but perhaps revealing in others, of this impressive economic success.

While conceding to the Soviet leaders and the Soviet people all the respect they deserve for this achievement, we must be careful not to exaggerate its significance. This expansion of the Soviet economy has taken place at a time when the economies of other countries have also been expanding rapidly. During this same postwar period the growth in the productive capacity of my own country, for example, has probably actually been greater in absolute terms than that of Russia.

Now it is, of course, true that the comparative rate of growth in Russia from year to year has been greater than in the United States, and if these trends should be continued indefinitely the Russians would, eventually, catch up with us and outproduce us in many respects.

But actually I think it unlikely that the rate of growth of the Soviet economy will be maintained for long at the present level. Russia has been enjoying, up to this point, many of the possibilities for rapid growth that attend a relatively early stage of industrialization. But her economy is now coming into maturity. She is beginning to run up against problems, organizational problems, manpower problems, and others, which are familiar to all the advanced industrial countries. There is no evidence to date that she has better answers to these problems than any of the rest of us.

We must also remember that the general imbalance which has always characterized the development of the Soviet economy has not yet been fully overcome. Soviet economic progress has thus far represented in fact essentially the fulfillment of a program of military industrialization. Its success has been purchased at the cost of the serious neglect, and even exploitation, of other branches of the economy, as well as a continued repression of living standards. Agriculture, in particular, was shamefully neglected and abused throughout the Stalin era, and while Stalin's successors have indeed made efforts to overcome many of these abuses, some of us are not convinced that they have yet arrived at a correct analysis of the problem, or that they are prepared to do the things that would be necessary if they were to meet it. It remains to be demonstrated, in fact, that collectivization, as heretofore practiced in the Soviet Union, is really a feasible and hopeful manner of developing the agricultural resources of a great country. The experience of the satellite area would certainly not seem to indicate that it is. And even in the Soviet Union the collective farm system has now had to be supplemented by what we in America would call "the plowing up of the dust bowl"—a practice we are coming to recognize as shortsighted and undesirable.

Had a normal balance, or what we would consider a normal balance, been observed in the shaping of Russia's economic growth in these last two or three decades, I think it can well be questioned whether the development of its industrial sector alone would have been appreciably more rapid than that of other countries in a comparable stage of industrialization. It is often forgotten that even prior to the revolution Russian industry was already developing very rapidly, but under quite a different system and without the distortions and hardships that have attended its forced growth under Soviet power.

But when all of this is taken into account, the economic progress achieved by Russia in recent years does remain impressive; and I think that we must, barring unforeseeable accidents, expect it to continue into the future, though at a somewhat decreasing rate. . . .

The Soviet Government has, of course, lost no occasion to exploit this sort of achievement for political purposes. It has endeavored at every turn to present itself as participating in an all-out competition with the Western countries for industrial growth and then to interpret every element of its economic progress as a triumph for its own system of economy and a defeat for the Western world. A great many people in my own country, perhaps elsewhere as well, have come unconsciously to accept this Soviet thesis, to believe that every Soviet gain is automatically our loss and to see our salvation as dependent on our ability to outpace Russia in every single phase of her economic progress.

I am bound to say that I cannot see it this way at all. There's nothing unnatural in the fact that Russia is now rapidly industrializing. Her development in past centuries has lagged behind that of the Western peoples; she has a large and vigorous population, rich in talents of every sort; she occupies a territory liberally endowed with the resources which permit successful industrialization everywhere. If, given these facts and the spirit of the modern age, the Russian people were not now rapidly industrializing their country, this, rather than what is occurring today, would be the true wonder.

I cannot find it in my heart to begrudge the Russians this kind of success; nor can I see that we are in any way handicapped by it in our attack on our own problems. If the Soviet Government loves to portray itself as embarked on a desperate economic competition with us, I don't see that we are under any obligation to accept this interpretation. One sometimes has the impression that Mr. Khrushchev sees international life as one great sporting event, where they and we contend for goals which they, not we, have defined, and where the world looks on.

Not a day passes, for example, but what the Soviet press summons the Russian people to catch up with and surpass America in the per capita production of meat, milk and butter. I simply cannot concede that we're engaged in any such competition. We in the United States have enough of these things. Our problem is not to produce more of them. I should hope that the Russian people, too, would soon have all they need of these and other articles of consumption. And whether this is more or less than our per capita production of them seems to me supremely unimportant.

When they do reach this point, I think they're going to discover—as some of us are now discovering—that this is not the final solution to all things, that the most serious problems in modern life only begin with the achievement of material plenty.

When I think of the enthusiasm of people in Moscow today for economic development, it puts me in mind of my own youth in the American Middle West, and of the inordinate pleasure many of us used to take in the headlong economic progress of that region. We Americans were known as the "Babbitts" of the early twentieth century, and I suppose we were. But many of us, at least, became conscious of the shallowness of this outlook, and it was, after all, an American who coined the word for it. The Russians are now the "Babbitts" of the mid-century. But so far, being good materialists, they have shown no awareness of the limitations of this outlook.

It will be a happy day for everyone when they, too, have solved their problems of production, and can join us in grappling with some of the deeper, more subtle, and more significant problems that lie at the end, rather than at the beginning, of the economic rainbow.

Many of my countrymen would reply to these observations by saying: "What you say is all very well, but how about the military aspects of Soviet economic progress? Do they not spell for us the deepest and most terrible sort of danger?" . . . Let me only say at this point that I fail again to understand the frame of mind that sees in every evidence of Soviet economic or scientific progress some new deterioration in Western security. One is moved to wonder, sometimes, how long it will be before people can bring themselves to realize that the ability to wreak terrible destruction on other peoples now rests in a fairly large number of hands in this world, and that the danger is already so great that variations in degree do not have much meaning.

I am not particularly concerned to learn whether our Soviet friends could, if they wished, destroy us seven times over or only four times; nor do I think that the answer to this danger lies in the indefinite multiplication of our own ability to do fearful injury to them. Our problem is no longer to prevent people from acquiring the ability to destroy us—it is too late for that. Our problem is to see that they do not have the will or the incentive to do it. For this, of course, we have to preserve and cultivate our deterrent capacity. But that is a limited task, not an unlimited one, and it does not necessarily imply an endless industrial and scientific race against the Russians.

Again it will be argued by anxious people, "Yes, but if the Russians gain on us in the race for economic development, the peoples of the underdeveloped areas of the world will come to look to them, rather than to us, for economic guidance, and then, where shall we be?" This, too, is something about which I shall have some things to say.

Suffice it to observe here that it strikes me as a dangerous thing for us to assume that our security must depend indefinitely on keeping the Russians from shouldering their part of the responsibility all industrialized nations bear for giving this sort of aid and guidance to the underdeveloped on~s. People have things to learn from Russia, I am sure, as well as from us; there will be many ways in which our economic system, based as it is on the specifics of our legal and commercial tradition, will not be fully relevant to the problems of people elsewhere, and where the Russians may have more to offer than we do. But the same is going to be true conversely. These things must be permitted to find their own level, and when they do I am sure there will be no lack of opportunity and of work for all of us.

The fact is that we in the West are, of course, engaged in a competition with Russia, but it is not the kind of competition the Russians claim it is; we are not pursuing the same objectives, we are not at the same stage of development, our tasks are not similar. The real competition is rather to see which of us moves most rapidly and successfully to the solution of his own particular problems, and to the fulfillment of his own peculiar ideals. To my own countrymen, who have often asked me where best to apply the hand to counter the Soviet threat, I have accordingly had to reply: to our own American failings, to the things that we are ashamed of in our own eyes, or that worry us. To the racial problem, to the conditions in our big cities, to the problems of education and environment for our young people; to the growing gap between specialized knowledge and popular understanding in our country. I imagine that similar answers could be found for any of the other Western countries.

And I would like to add that these are problems which are not going to be solved by anything we or anyone else does in the stratosphere. If solutions are going to be found for these problems it is going to be right here on this familiar earth in the dealings among men and in the moral struggle within the individual human breast. If one had to choose between launching satellites and continuing to give attention to these more homely problems here below, I should a hundred times over choose the latter, for unless we make this sort of progress in our problems on this earth no satellite will ever save us. Whether we win against the Russians is primarily a question of whether we win against ourselves.

* * *

The demands frequently made upon us by the independent countries in part of the world seem to me to run something like this: "We," they say, "are determined to have economic development and to have it at once. For us, this is an overriding aim, an absolute requirement; and we are not much concerned about the method by which it is achieved. You in the West owe it to us to let us have your assistance and to give it to us promptly, effectively, and without conditions; otherwise we will take it from the Russians, whose experience and methods we suspect anyway to be more relevant to our problems." In response to this approach, a great many people in my own country have come to take it for granted that there is some direct relationship between programs of economic aid on the one hand and political attitudes on the other—between the amount of money we are willing to devote to economic assistance in any given year and the amount of progress we may expect to make in overcoming these troublesome states of mind I have been talking about.

This thesis, as well as the reaction to it at home, seems to me to be questionable at every point. I find myself thrown off at the very start by this absolute value attached to rapid economic development. Why all the urgency? If can well be argued that the pace of change is no less important than its nature, and that great damage can be done by altering too rapidly the sociological and cultural structure of any society, even where these alterations may be desirable in themselves. In many instances one would also like to know how this economic progress is to be related to the staggering population growth with which it is associated. Finally, many of us in America have seen too much of the incidental effects of industrialization and urbanization to be convinced that these things are absolute answers to problems anywhere, or that they could be worth *any* sacrifice to obtain. For these reasons I cannot fully share the basic enthusiasm on which this whole thesis is founded.

I must also reject the suggestion that our generation in the West has some sort of a cosmic guilt or obligation vis-à-vis the underdeveloped parts of the world. The fact that certain portions of the globe were developed sooner than others is one for which I, as

an American of this day, cannot accept the faintest moral responsibility; nor do I see that it was particularly the fault of my American
ancestors. I cannot even see that the phenomenon of colonialism
was one which could be regarded as having given rise to any such
state of obligation. The establishment of the colonial relationship
did not represent a moral action on somebody's part; it represented
a natural and inevitable response to certain demands and stimuli of
the age. It was simply a stage of history. It generally took place
with the agreement and connivance of people at the colonial end
as well as in the mother country. Nor were the benefits derived
from this relationship in any way one-sided. The Marxists claim,
of course, that colonialism invariably represented a massive and
cruel exploitation of the colonial peoples. I am sure that honest
study would reveal this thesis to be quite fallacious. Advantages,
injuries and sacrifices were incurred on both sides. Today these
things are largely bygones. We will do no good by scratching
around to discover whose descendants owe the most to the descendants of the other. If we are to help each other in this world,
we must start with a clean slate.

I can well understand that there are instances in which it will
be desirable for us from time to time to support schemes of economic development which are soundly conceived and which give
promise, over the long run, of yielding greater stability and a new
hopefulness for the countries concerned. I trust that we will not
let such demands go unanswered when they arise. There is no
fonder hope in the American breast, my own included, than that
the experience we have had in developing a continent will prove
relevant and helpful to others. Every American would like to see
us take a useful part in solving problems of economic development
elsewhere in the world. But action of this sort can be useful only
if it proceeds on a sound psychological basis. If there is a general
impression in the recipient countries that this aid represents the
paying of some sort of a debt from us to them, then the extension
of it can only sow confusion. The same is true if it is going to be
interpreted as a sign of weakness on our part or of a fear that
others might go over to the Communists, or if it is going to be
widely attacked in the recipient countries as evidence of what the
Communists have taught people to refer to as "imperialism," by

which they seem to mean some sort of intricate and concealed foreign domination, the exact workings of which are never very clearly explained.

Unless such reactions can be ruled out, programs of economic aid are apt to do more harm than good psychologically; and it ought properly to be the obligation of the recipient governments and not of ourself to see that these misinterpretations do not occur. To those who come to us with requests for aid one would like to say: "You tell us first how you propose to assure that if we give you this aid it will not be interpreted among your people as a sign of weakness or fear on our part, or of a desire to dominate you."

These are not the only psychological dangers of foreign aid. There is the basic fact that any form of benevolence, if prolonged for any length of time (even in personal life this is true), comes to be taken for granted as a right and its withdrawal resented as an injury. There is the fact that any program of economic development represents a change in the terms of competition within a country and brings injury to some parties while it benefits the others. It is hard to give aid to any other country economically without its having an effect on internal political realities there—without its redounding to the benefit of one political party and the disadvantage of another.

All these considerations incline me to feel that, desirable as programs of foreign aid may sometimes be from the long-term standpoint, their immediate psychological effects are apt to be at best mixed and uncertain. For this reason, foreign aid, as a general practice, cannot be regarded as a very promising device for combating, over the short term, the psychological handicaps under which Western statesmanship now rests in Asia and Africa.

Finally, I do not think for a moment that the Soviet Union really presents the alternative people seem to think it represents to a decent relationship with the West. Moscow has its contribution to make to what should be a common task of all the highly industrialized countries; and there is no reason why this contribution should not be welcomed wherever it can be really helpful. But Moscow is not exactly the bottomless horn of plenty it is often held to be; and it is rather a pity that it has never been required to respond all at once to the many expectations directed to it. We

ourselves should be the last, one would think, to wish to spare it
this test. The results might be both healthy and instructive.

What, then, is there to be done about these feelings of people
in Asia and Africa? Very little, I am afraid, over the short term,
except to relax, to keep our composure, to refuse to be frightened
by the Communism alternative, to refrain from doing the things
that make matters worse, and to let things come to rest, as in
the end they must, on the sense of self-interest of the peoples
concerned.

VIII

# THE "CAMP OF SOCIALISM": YUGOSLAVIA

# THE SOVIET-YUGOSLAV DISPUTE*

[1948]

CENTRAL COMMITTEE OF COMMUNIST PARTY OF YUGOSLAVIA
TO CENTRAL COMMITTEE OF COMMUNIST PARTY OF SOVIET
UNION (MARCH 20, 1948)

On 18 March General Barskov told us that he had received a
telegram from Marshal Bulganin, Minister of People's Defense
of the U.S.S.R., in which we are informed that the Government
of the U.S.S.R. has decided to withdraw immediately all military
advisers and instructors because they are "surrounded by hostility,"
that is, they are not treated in a friendly fashion in Yugoslavia.

Of course, the Government of the U.S.S.R. can, when it wishes,
recall its military experts, but we have been dismayed by the reason
which the Government of the U.S.S.R. advances for its decision.
Investigating, on the basis of this accusation, the relations of the
junior leading people of our country towards the Soviet military
advisers and instructors, we are deeply convinced that there is no
basis for this reason for their withdrawal, that during their entire
stay in Yugoslavia relations with them were not only good, but
actually brotherly and most hospitable, which is the custom toward
all Soviet people in the new Yugoslavia. Therefore, we are
amazed, we cannot understand, and we are deeply hurt by not being
informed of the true reason for this decision by the Government
of the U.S.S.R.

Secondly, on 19 March 1948, I was visited by the Chargé
d'Affaires Armaninov and informed of the contents of a telegram
in which the Government of the U.S.S.R. orders withdrawal of all
civilian experts in Yugoslavia also. We cannot understand the
reason for this decision and it amazes us. It is true that the
Assistant of Minister Kidric,[1] Srzentic, stated to your commercial
representative Lebedev that, according to a decision of the Gov-

---

* From *The Soviet-Yugoslav Dispute, Text of the Published Correspondence*,
published November 1948, by the Royal Institute of International Affairs, London
and New York.
[1]Boris Kidric, head of the Yugoslav State Planning Commission.

ernment of the FPRY,[1] he has not the right to give important economic information to any one but that for such information the Soviet people should go higher, that is, to the CC of the CPY[2] and the Government.   At the same time Srzentic told Lebedev to approach Minister Kidric for the information which interested him.   Your people were told long ago that the official representatives of the Soviet Government could obtain all important and necessary information direct from the leaders of our country.

This decision was issued on our part because all the civil servants in our Ministries gave information to any one, whether it was necessary or not.   This meant that they gave various people State economic secrets which could, and in some cases did, fall into the hands of our common enemies. . . .

From all this it can be seen that the above reasons are not the cause of the measures taken by the Government of the U.S.S.R., and it is our desire that the U.S.S.R. openly inform us what the trouble is, that it point out everything which it feels is inconsistent with good relations between our two countries.   We feel that this course of events is harmful to both countries and that sooner or later everything that is interfering with friendly relations between our countries must be eliminated.

Inasmuch as the Government of the U.S.S.R. is obtaining its information from various other people, we feel that it should use it cautiously, because such information is not always objective, accurate, and given with good intentions.

Once again, accept the expression of my respect.

President of the Ministerial Council,

20 March 1948     J. B. TITO

LETTER FROM CENTRAL COMMITTEE OF COMMUNIST PARTY OF SOVIET UNION TO COMRADE TITO AND OTHER MEMBERS OF CENTRAL COMMITTEE OF COMMUNIST PARTY OF YUGOSLAVIA (MARCH 27, 1948)

Your answers of 18 and 20 March have been received.

---

[1] Federated People's Republic of Yugoslavia.

[2] Central Committee of the Communist Party of Yugoslavia.

We regard your answer as incorrect and therefore completely unsatisfactory. . . .

In regard to the withdrawal of military advisers, the sources of our information are the statements of the representatives of the Ministry of Armed Forces and of the advisers themselves.   As is known, our military advisers were sent to Yugoslavia upon the repeated request of the Yugoslav Government, and far fewer advisers were sent than had been requested.   It is therefore obvious that the Soviet Government had no desire to force its advisers on Yugoslavia.

Later, however, the Yugoslav military leaders . . . thought it possible to announce that it was essential to reduce the number of advisers by 60 per cent.   They gave various reasons for this; some maintained that the Soviet advisers were too great an expense for Yugoslavia; others held that the Yugoslav army was in no need of the experience of the Soviet army; some said that the rules of the Soviet army were hidebound, stereotyped and without value to the Yugoslav army, and that there was no point in paying the Soviet advisers since there was no benefit to be derived from them. . . .

The sources of our information leading to the withdrawal of Soviet civilian specialists are, for the most part, the statements of the Soviet Ambassador in Belgrade, Lavrentiev, as also the statements of the specialists themselves.   Your statement, that Srzentic allegedly told the trade representative, Lebedev, that the Soviet specialists seeking economic information should direct their requests to higher authorities, namely to the CC of the CPY and the Yugoslav Government, does not correspond to the truth.   Here is the report made by Lavrentiev on 9 March:

> Srzentic, Kidric's assistant in the Economic Council, informed Lebedev, the trade representative, of a Government decree forbidding the state organs to give economic information to any one at all.   Therefore, regardless of earlier promises, he could not give Lebedev the particulars required.   It was one of the duties of the state security organs to exercise control in this matter. Srzentic also said that Kidric himself intended to speak about this with Lebedev.

From Lavrentiev's report it can be seen, that Srzentic did not even mention the possibility of obtaining economic information from the CC of the CPY or the Yugoslav Government. . . .

In your letter you express the desire to be informed of the other facts which led to Soviet dissatisfaction and to the straining of relations between the U.S.S.R. and Yugoslavia. Such facts actually exist, although they are not connected with the withdrawal of the civilian and military advisers. We consider it necessary to inform you of them.

(a) We know that there are anti-Soviet rumors circulating among the leading comrades in Yugoslavia, for instance, that "the CPSU is degenerate," "great-power chauvinism is rampant in the U.S.S.R.," "the U.S.S.R. is trying to dominate Yugoslavia economically" and "the Cominform is a means of controlling the other Parties by the CPSU," etc. These anti-Soviet allegations are usually camouflaged by left phrases, such as "socialism in the Soviet Union has ceased to be revolutionary" and that Yugoslavia alone is the exponent of "revolutionary socialism.". . .

We do not doubt that the Yugoslav Party masses would disown this anti-Soviet criticism as alien and hostile if they knew about it. We think this is the reason why the Yugoslav officials make these criticisms in secret, behind the backs of the masses.

Again, one might mention that, when he decided to declare war on the CPSU, Trotsky also started with accusations of the CPSU as degenerate, as suffering from the limitations inherent in the narrow nationalism of great powers. Naturally he camouflaged all this with left slogans about world revolution. However, it is well known that Trotsky himself became degenerate, and when he was exposed, crossed over into the camp of the sworn enemies of the CPSU and the Soviet Union. We think that the political career of Trotsky is quite instructive.

(b) We are disturbed by the present condition of the CPY. We are amazed by the fact that the CPY, which is the leading party, is still not completely legalized and still has a semi-legal status. Decisions of the Party organs are never published in the press, neither are the reports of Party assemblies.

Democracy is not evident within the CPY itself. . . . Criticism and self-criticism within the Party does not exist or barely exists.
. . .

It is understandable that we cannot consider such an organization of a Communist Party as Marxist-Leninist, Bolshevik. . . .

According to the theory of Marxism-Leninism the Party is considered as the leading force in the country, which has its specific program and which cannot merge with the non-party masses. In Yugoslavia, on the contrary, the People's Front is considered the chief leading force and there was an attempt to get the Party submerged within the Front. In his speech at the Second Congress of the People's Front, Comrade Tito said: "Does the CPY have any other program but that of the People's Front? No, the CPY has no other program. The program of the People's Front is its program." . . .

These are the facts which are causing the dissatisfaction of the Soviet Government and the CC of the CPSU and which are endangering relations between the U.S.S.R. and Yugoslavia.

These facts, as has already been mentioned, are not related to the question of the withdrawal of the military and civilian specialists. However, they are an important factor in the worsening of relations between our countries.

CC of the CPSU

Moscow,
27 March 1948

CENTRAL COMMITTEE OF COMMUNIST PARTY OF YUGOSLAVIA TO CENTRAL COMMITTEE OF COMMUNIST PARTY OF SOVIET UNION (APRIL 13, 1948)

In answering your letter of 27 March 1948, we must first of all emphasize that we were terribly surprised by its tone and contents. We feel that the reason for its contents, that is, for the accusations and attitudes towards individual questions, is insufficient knowledge of the situation here. We cannot explain your conclusions otherwise than by the fact that the Government of the U.S.S.R. is obtaining inaccurate and tendentious information from its representatives, who, because of lack of knowledge, must obtain such information from various people, either from known anti-Party elements or from various dissatisfied persons. . . . In this concrete case, that information had as its aim to cause difficulties for the leadership of our Party, that is, for the new Yugoslavia; to make more difficult the already difficult task of the development of our country; to make the Five Year Plan impossible, and so to make impossible the realization of socialism in our country. . . . We regard the issuing of such information as anti-Party work and anti-State because it spoils the relations between our two countries.

No matter how much each of us loves the land of Socialism, the U.S.S.R., he can, in no case, love his country less, which also is developing socialism—in this concrete case the FPRY, for which so many thousands of its most progressive people fell. We know very well that this is also similarly understood in the Soviet Union. . . .

As for the withdrawal of Soviet military experts, we see no other reason for it than that we decided to reduce their number to the necessary minimum because of financial difficulties. . . . The wages of the Soviet experts were four times as high as the wages of the commanders of our armies and three times as high as the wages of our Federal Ministers. . . . It is understandable that we felt that this was not only a financial burden but also politically incorrect because it led to misunderstanding among our men. . . . However, we consider these matters too insignificant to be allowed to play any part in straining relations between our States. . . .

What is the basis of the allegation in the letter that there is no democracy in our Party? Perhaps information from Lavrentiev? Where did he get this information? We consider that he, as an ambassador, has no right to ask any one for information about the work of our Party. That is not his business. This information can be obtained by the CC of the CPSU from the CC of the CPY. . . .

The letter further mentions the report of Tito to the Second Congress of the People's Front in Yugoslavia. . . .

The CPY has a completely assured leadership in the People's Front because the CPY is the nucleus of the People's Front. Therefore, there is no danger of its dissolving into the People's Front—as is said in the letter. Through the People's Front the CPY gradually realizes its program, which the People's Front voluntarily adopts, considering it as its own program. This is the basis of Tito's statement that the CPY has no other program. . . .

We cannot believe that the CC of the CPSU can dispute the services and results achieved by our Party up to today because we remember that such acknowledgement was given us many times by many Soviet leaders and by Comrade Stalin himself. We are also of the opinion that there are many specific aspects in the social transformation of Yugoslavia which can be of benefit to the revolutionary development in other countries, and are already being used. This does not mean that we place the role of the CPSU and the social system of the U.S.S.R. in the background. On the contrary, we study and take as an example the Soviet system, but we are developing socialism in our country in somewhat different forms. In the given period under the specific conditions which exist in our country, in consideration of the international conditions which were created after the war of liberation, we are attempting to apply the best forms of work in the realization of socialism. We do not do this, in order to prove that our road is better than that taken by the Soviet Union, that we are inventing something new, but because this is forced upon us by our daily life. . . .

On the basis of everything set out above, the plenary session of the CC of the CPY cannot accept as justified the criticisms in your letter about the work of our Party and its leaders. We are deeply convinced that this is the result of a grave misunderstanding, which should not have happened and which must rapidly be liquidated in the interest of matters concerning our Parties.

Our only desire is to eliminate every doubt and disbelief in the purity of the comradely and brotherly feeling of loyalty of our CC of the CPY to the CPSU, to whom we will always remain thankful for the Marxist-Leninist doctrine which has led us until now and will lead us in the future—loyalty to the Soviet Union which has served us and will continue to serve us as a great example and whose assistance to our people we so highly appreciate.

We are convinced that this disagreement can be liquidated only by full mutual explanation between our two Central Committees on the spot, that is, here.

Therefore, we propose that the CC of the CPSU send one or more of its members, who will have every opportunity here of studying every question thoroughly.

In the hope that you will accept our proposal we send you our comradely greetings.

By order of the CC of the CPY

Belgrade,
13 April 1948

TITO

KARDELJ

## LETTER FROM CENTRAL COMMITTEE OF COMMUNIST PARTY OF SOVIET UNION TO CENTRAL COMMITTEE OF COMMUNIST PARTY OF YUGOSLAVIA (MAY 4, 1948)

Your answer and the announcement of the decision of the Plenum of the CC of the CPY of 13 April 1948, signed by Comrades Tito and Kardelj, have been received.

Unfortunately, these documents, and especially the document signed by Tito and Kardelj, do not improve on the earlier Yugoslav documents; on the contrary, they further complicate matters and sharpen the conflict. . . .

Comrades Tito and Kardelj refer to the large expenses in connection with the salaries of the Soviet military advisers, emphasizing that the Soviet generals receive three to four times as much, in dinars, as Yugoslav generals, and that such conditions may give rise to discontent on the part of Yugoslav military personnel.  But the Yugoslav generals, apart from drawing salaries, are provided with apartments, servants, food, etc.  Secondly, the pay of the Soviet generals in Yugoslavia corresponds to the pay of Soviet generals in the U.S.S.R.   It is understandable that the Soviet Government could not consider reducing the salaries of Soviet generals who are in Yugoslavia on official duty. . . .

In their letter of 13 April 1948 Tito and Kardelj wrote: "We consider that he (the Soviet Ambassador) as an ambassador, has no right to ask any one for information about the work of our Party.   That is not his business."

We feel that this statement by Tito and Kardelj is essentially incorrect and anti-Soviet. They identify the Soviet Ambassador, a responsible communist who represents the Communist Government of the U.S.S.R., with an ordinary bourgeois ambassador, a simple official of a bourgeois State, who is called upon to undermine the foundations of the Yugoslav State. It is difficult to understand how Tito and Kardelj could sink so low. Do these comrades understand that such an attitude towards the Soviet Ambassador means the negation of all friendly relations between the U.S.S.R. and Yugoslavia? Do these comrades understand that the Soviet Ambassador, a responsible communist, who represents a friendly power which liberated Yugoslavia from the German occupation, not only has the right but is obliged, from time to time, to discuss with the communists in Yugoslavia all questions which interest them? How can they be suspicious of these simple elementary matters if they intend to remain in friendly relation with the Soviet Union? . . .

We consider that this attitude of the Yugoslav comrades towards the Soviet Ambassador cannot be regarded as accidental. It arises from the general attitude of the Yugoslav Government, which is also the cause of the inability of the Yugoslav leaders to see the difference between the foreign policy of the U.S.S.R. and the foreign policy of the Anglo-Americans. . . .

In this respect, the speech by Comrade Tito in Ljubljana in May 1945 is very characteristic. He said:

> It is said that this war is a just war and we have considered it as such. However, we seek also a just end; we demand that every one shall be master in his own house; we do not want to pay for others; we do not want to be used as a bribe in international barganing; we do not want to get involved in any policy of spheres of interest. . . .

The statement by Tito in Ljubljana that "Yugoslavia would not pay for others," "would not be used as a bribe," "would not be involved in any policy of spheres of interest," was directed not only against the imperialist States but also against the U.S.S.R., and in the given circumstances the relations of Tito towards the U.S.S.R. are no different from his relations towards the imperialist States, as he does not recognize any difference between the U.S.S.R. and the imperialist States. . . .

Tito and Kardelj in their letter proposed that the CPSU should send representatives to Yugoslavia to study the Soviet-Yugoslav differences. We feel this course would be incorrect, since it is not a matter of verifying individual facts but of differences of principle.

As is known, the question of Soviet-Yugoslav differences has already become the property of the CC of the nine Communist Parties who have their Cominform. It would be highly irregular to exclude them from this matter. Therefore, we propose that this question be discussed at the next session of the Cominform.

Moscow,                                         CC of the CPSU
4 May 1948

## COMMUNIQUE OF INFORMATION BUREAU OF THE COMMUNIST PARTIES (JUNE 28, 1948)

During the second half of June, a meeting of the Information Bureau was held in Rumania. . . .

The Information Bureau discussed the situation in the Communist Party of Yugoslavia and unanimously adopted a resolution on this question.

### RESOLUTION

The Information Bureau notes that recently the leadership of the Communist Party of Yugoslavia has pursued an incorrect line on the main questions of home and foreign policy, a line which represents a departure from Marxism-Leninism. In this connection the Information Bureau approves the action of the Central Committee of the CPSU (B), which took the initiative in exposing this incorrect policy of the Central Committee of the Communist Party of Yugoslavia. . . .

The Information Bureau declares that the leadership of the Yugoslav Communist Party is pursuing an unfriendly policy toward the Soviet Union and the CPSU (B). An undignified policy of defaming Soviet military experts and discrediting the Soviet Union, has been carried out in Yugoslavia. . . .

All these and similar facts show that the leaders of the Communist Party of Yugoslavia have taken a stand unworthy of Communists, and have begun to identify the foreign policy of the Soviet Union with the foreign policy of the imperialist powers, behaving toward the Soviet Union in the same manner as they behave to the bourgeois states. . . .

The Information Bureau denounces this anti-Soviet attitude of the leaders of the Communist Party of Yugoslavia, as being incompatible with Marxism-Leninism and only appropriate to nationalists. . . .

The Information Bureau considers that the leadership of the Communist Party of Yugoslavia is revising the Marxist-Leninist teachings about the Party. According to the theory of Marxism-Leninism, the Party is the main guiding and leading force in the country, which has its own specific program, and does not dissolve itself among the non-Party masses. . . .

In Yugoslavia, however, the People's Front, and not the Communist Party, is considered to be the main leading force in the country. The Yugoslav leaders belittle the role of the Communist Party and actually dissolve the Party in the non-party People's Front, which is composed of the most varied class elements (workers, peasants engaged in individual farming, kulaks, traders, small manufacturers, bourgeois intelligentsia, etc.) as well as mixed political groups which include certain bourgeois parties. . . .

The Information Bureau unanimously concludes that by their anti-Party and anti-Soviet views, incompatible with Marxism-Leninism, by their whole attitude and their refusal to attend the meeting of the Information Bureau, the leaders of the Communist Party of Yugoslavia have placed themselves in opposition to the Communist Parties affiliated to the Information Bureau, have taken the path to seceding from the united socialist front against imperialism, have taken the path of betraying the cause of international solidarity of the working people, and have taken up a position of nationalism. . . .

The Information Bureau considers that, in view of all this, the Central Committee of the Communist Party of Yugoslavia has placed itself and the Yugoslav Party outside the family of fraternal Communist Parties, outside the united Communist front and consequently outside the ranks of the Information Bureau.

* * *

The Information Bureau considers that the basis of these mistakes made by the leadership of the Communist Party of Yugoslavia lies in the undoubted fact that nationalist elements, which previously existed in a disguised form, managed in the course of the past five or six months to reach a dominant position in the leadership of the Communist Party of Yugoslavia, and that consequently the leadership of the Yugoslav Communist Party has broken with the international traditions of the Communist Party of Yugoslavia and has taken the road to nationalism.

Considerably overestimating the internal, national forces of Yugoslavia and their influence, the Yugoslav leaders think that they can maintain Yugoslavia's independence and build socialism without the support of the Communist Parties of other countries, without the support of the people's democracies, without the support of the Soviet Union. They think that the new Yugoslavia can do without the help of these revolutionary forces.

Showing their poor understanding of the international situation and their intimidation by the blackmailing threats of the imperialists, the Yugoslav leaders think that by making concessions they can curry favor with the imperialist states. They think they will be able to bargain with them for Yugoslavia's independence and, gradually, get the people of Yugoslavia orientated on these states, that is, on capitalism. In this they proceed tacitly from the well-known bourgeois-nationalist thesis that "capitalist states are a lesser danger to the independence of Yugoslavia than the Soviet Union."

The Yugoslav leaders evidently do not understand or, probably, pretend they do not understand, that such a nationalist line can only lead to Yugoslavia's degeneration into an ordinary bourgeois republic, to the loss of its independence and to its transformation into a colony of the imperialist countries.

The Information Bureau does not doubt that inside the Communist Party of Yugoslavia there are sufficient healthy elements, loyal to Marxism-Leninism, to the international traditions of the Yugoslav Communist Party and to the united socialist front.

Their task is to compel their present leaders to recognize their mistakes openly and honestly and to rectify them; to break with nationalism, return to internationalism; and in every way to consolidate the united socialist front against imperialism.

Should the present leaders of the Yugoslav Communist Party prove incapable of doing this, their job is to replace them and to advance a new internationalist leadership of the Party.

The Information Bureau does not doubt that the Communist Party of Yugoslavia will be able to fulfil this honorable task.

# STALINISM AND THE MEANING
# OF TITOISM[*]

BY

ROY MACRIDIS

[1952]

## I

The Soviet-Yugoslav dispute and the subsequent defection of
the Yugoslav Communist Party from the ranks of the Cominform
early in 1948 took the world by surprise. This surprise was in
itself indicative of our belief that Stalinist control was to be taken
for granted at least in the areas where the local Communist parties
had come to power through direct or indirect help from the Soviet
Union and particularly from the Red Army. Even when no such
help had been given, the ideological affinities of Communist states
and their need of alliances to preserve the Communist power structures would lead, it was believed, to a tightening of relations with
the Soviet Union and to Soviet predominance. In other words, we
tended to accept without question the premises of Stalinism.

Yet a more careful study of the nature of Stalinism in its
domestic aspects as well as in its foreign policy should have led us
to the conclusion that the potentialities of Soviet control were to
be measured not in terms of revolutionary or ideological affinities,
but primarily in terms of power relations between the Soviet Union
and the local Communist parties; and that the nature of these relations was bound to be affected substantially (a) by the inner cohesion, strength, and discipline of the national Communist parties,
(b) by their attitude toward the nationalist ideology of their respective countries and by the intensity of this ideology, and (c) by
the existence of a Marxist anti-Stalinist ideology. The origin and
significance of the Titoist movement in Eastern Europe today can
be understood properly only when put in the context of these three

* From *World Politics*, Vol. IV, No. 2, January 1952. Copyright 1952 by
Princeton University Press. Reprinted by permission.

factors. Paradoxically enough, the first two factors—the organizational discipline and cohesion of the Communist parties and their attitude toward nationalism—were shaped, as we shall see, in accordance with the theory and practice of Stalinism, which we shall have to discuss briefly before we turn to the Soviet-Yugoslav dispute.

(1) The first element of Stalinism is an intense parochialism closely associated with the traditional patterns of Russian history: a fear and suspicion of the West—even with Western Communist parties and socialist regimes—and a belief in the self-sufficiency of the Russian society. The initial internationalist impetus of the Revolution was followed . . . by an intense nationalism. The fruits of the Revolution were to be cherished as something primarily Russian and were to furnish a model to be imitated in a servile manner and never quesioned.

(2) The second element of Stalinism follows from the first. Slowly the idea of world revolution gave place to the idea of Soviet national security, Soviet defense, and Soviet national strategic considerations. The difficulty that emerged at the outset was due to the fact that such considerations were ideologically incompatible with the broader aspirations of the Third International, in which Western Communists were prepared to argue on a footing of equality in favor of socialism and revolution. No doubt concessions were to be made for the protection of the Soviet socialist reality—but the Comintern leaders were not willing to see Stalin appropriate to himself the right of the ultimate decision. A curious dilemma emerged which had to be resolved. The Stalinist leadership was interested in the security of the Soviet system, whereas the Western leaders and many Soviet Communists considered the Soviet experiment to be only the beginning of the road toward world socialism—an unfortunate beginning at that, for unless the West was to become socialist and come to its aid, socialist growth in Russia would be stunted. The way in which the contradiction was resolved is too well known to merit any comment. Gradually the Comintern lost its internationalist orientation and became a tool in the hands of the Communist Party of the Soviet Union. The idea of revolution became subordinated to the exigencies of national security and defense of the Soviet Union.

(3) Again, the third element of Stalinism follows from the second. To be able to shape the policies of the Comintern, direct control of the Communist parties of Europe and the world was necessary. As the contours of common revolutionary ideology became dimmer, the Soviet leaders resorted to organizational discipline and in many cases to direct personal control. Even in countries like France and Italy, countries with a rich background of individualism and liberal nationalism, Communist party discipline and conformity to the ever-changing party line began to bind together an ever-increasing number of people.

(4) Finally, the most significant element of Stalinism both at home and abroad has been the growing centralization of authority and power within the party and the Soviet state and the slow erosion of internal party democracy. The Leninist conception of the party found its ultimate fruition in the years after Lenin's death through the establishment of a small self-perpetuating elite concentrating in its hands all decision-making powers. . . .

There are a number of contradictions in the Stalinist ideological system as outlined here, contradictions which, with the passage of time and under certain conditions, were bound to come into the open and endanger the whole Soviet power edifice. Soviet patriotism was emphasized in the name of socialism and the socialist fatherland, while every effort was made to establish what amounted to an international control of all national Communist parties. But the Soviet appeal to patriotism and the introduction of traditional values particularly immediately after the declaration of the war, could not leave the national Communist parties unaffected. The mentality of their leaders was shaped in parochial and national terms, so that it was inevitable that Stalinist nationalism would sooner or later create analogous forms of Communist nationalism in the individual countries of Europe and Asia. When the Germans occupied the whole of Europe, the contradiction was at least temporarily resolved, since each local Communist Party received what amounted to *carte blanche* to fight its own patriotic war against Germany. In so doing, they were of course fighting for their countries and the Soviet Union as well as for a dimly seen socialist future. But slowly the idea of nationalism and national Communism of the Stalinist type gained ground, until finally, with the victory of the Red Army against Germany in Eastern Europe and the Balkans and the "liberation" of these countries, the contradiction between Soviet-inspired nationalism and Soviet international control came once more into the open far more clearly than ever before in the past. Tito was talking the language that Stalin could understand only too well when he wrote, "No matter how much each of us loves the land of socialism, the USSR, he can in no case love his country less, which is also developing socialism."[1] A great number of Balkan and European Communist leaders expressed the same thought in practically identical words.

This national aspiration on the part of Communist leaders corresponded to a national Communism of the Stalinist type. In fact, it was an inverted form of Stalinism and as such it appeared, at least to the Soviet leaders, a far more potent foe than the prewar regimes in the same areas of Europe. The possibility of a conflict with the Anglo-Saxon countries made it necessary that these Communist parties and countries be brought quickly under control and the Cominform was established for this very purpose. Significantly enough, the Soviet-Yugoslav dispute occurred at this juncture.

Little need be said about another equally significant contradiction in Stalinist policy. By emphasizing centralized party leadership both at home and abroad, Stalinism came to rely almost exclusively upon a small loyal elite of leaders commanding local support and obedience. As long as the reins of Soviet control could be held tightly by manipulating such leadership, there was no serious danger of defection. But if and when—as happened during the war—local party leadership emancipated itself even to a moderate degree from Soviet surveillance, the dangers of successful defection were great.

So, in essence, two of the three factors which account for Titoism—nationalism and the existence of a strong disciplined party leadership—are derived from Stalinist theory and practice. Under propitious conditions such as war or a relaxation of Soviet international control, these forces were bound to come into the open

---

[1] *The Soviet-Yugoslav Dispute: Text of the Published Correspondence*, Royal Institute of International Affairs, London and New York, 1948.

and challenge Soviet nationalism with the very weapons that were prepared for them by Stalin and his followers. The third factor referred to—the existence of anti-Stalinist Communist ideology—would naturally play a prominent role only when the power friction had reached the final stage of open conflict.

## II

The literature on the history of the Titoist movement has adequately covered the popular origins of the resistance movement in Yugoslavia, its national appeal and strength, and its successes. Tito as a national leader would sooner or later have had to face Stalin —we are told in retrospect. One might have gone a step further and said that two national Communist countries were bound to show the same incompatibilities that bourgeois nationalist countries have showed in the past. The student of Marxism probably could have gone even another step further and raised the question that has been haunting the Communist Party of the Soviet Union ever since the expulsion of Trotsky: Might it not be conceivable, in the event of a conflict between two national Communist states, that the weaker of the two would appeal to the hidden store of Marxist literature and revive the two fundamental ideas of Trotskyism—namely, a criticism of Stalinist socialism in the Soviet Union, and a policy of world revolution for the purpose of establishing equality among the socialist nations and developing an economic system consistent with the demands of all the socialist peoples?

As we shall see, Tito and the Yugoslav Communist Party followed a policy which slowly shifted from one position to another. In the years from 1944 until well into 1947, the regime had all the characteristics of Stalinism. It was based on strong party leadership which controlled the People's Front, was imbued with a strong ambition to establish socialism in Yugoslavia and industrialize as fast as possible, it was hostile to the West. After the establishment of the new Constitution . . . there was no doubt whatsoever that the road to national Communism had been definitely traced by the Yugoslav Communist leaders. Yet, despite strong ideological affinities and despite the adulatory tone of the Yugoslav leaders and the Yugoslav press for the Soviet Union and the

Communist Party of the Soviet Union, incompatibilities in the existence of two autonomous Communist states began to appear.

Already in May 1945, Tito had said in a speech at Ljubljana: " . . . We demand that everyone shall be master in his own house; we do not want to pay for others; we do not want to be used as a bribe in international bargaining; we do not want to get involved in a policy of spheres of interest."[2] This speech, though directed primarily against the Western powers, was interpreted by the Soviet leaders as an act of defiance of Soviet foreign policy, and we are told that the Soviet Ambassador raised strong objections.[3] Serious difficulties appeared also during the period of Yugoslav resistance. Out of deference to the Allies, the Soviet government maintained diplomatic relations with the Yugoslav government in exile, delayed recognizing Tito, and forced him to disclaim any socialist ambitions.

If such a policy was motivated by considerations of expediency dictated by the war, particularly for the purpose of alleviating the fears of the Western Allies, no such justification could be seriously advanced after the end of the war. Yet events within the satellite countries gave to Tito and to the leading circles of the Communist Party of Yugoslavia grounds for concern. The line of the Politburo continued to be very cautious. The French Communists had allowed themselves to be disarmed, General de Gaulle was proclaimed the savior and first resistant of France; the same conciliatory attitude was displayed by the Italian Communist Party, the same hesitation about the fate of the Rumanian king. But what was even more important was the Soviet social policy in the countries "liberated" by the Red Army. In these countries, hybrid regimes known as People's Democracies had been established which were advancing very cautiously in matters of social and economic policy. What was ominous was the definition of the nature of these regimes given by the Soviet authors and leaders. A People's Democracy was not considered originally to be a proletarian dictatorship in the Marxian sense. It was not in itself a transitory stage toward socialism, though socialism might be ar-

[2] *The Soviet-Yugoslav Dispute.*
[3] *Ibid.*

rived at peacefully. Though a form superior to the bourgeois
parliamentary form, since the working class was assuming the
leading role and private property was being restricted, it was not
socialist and could not be considered as a dictatorship of the proletariat. It was a social form varying in character according to the
historical conditions of each individual country.

The leaders of the different Eastern European and Balkan countries repeated this theme with many variations: Dimitrov claimed
in September 1946 that in the Bulgarian Republic there would be
no dictatorship of the proletariat. "The functions of government
were to be performed by an enormous majority of people—workers, peasants, craftsmen, and the people's intelligentsia." The
Polish Communist leader Bierut stated that the specific model of
the People's Democracy in Poland was not similar to the Soviet
socialist model—it was a system "best adapted to the social structure created in our country as a result of the changes caused by the
war." A Soviet author wrote that a People's Democracy is not "a
proletarian [socialist] democracy. Proletarian democracy is identical with the dictatorship of the proletariat which does not share
its power with any other class." The idea of "harmony of classes,"
of "cooperation" and "gradualism," was emphasized and re-
emphasized by the Soviet leaders.

There was probably nothing objectionable in this definition of
People's Democracies other than the pretension of the Soviet leaders and authors of maintaining and using arbitrarily the monopoly
of Marxist interpretation. In fact, the theories advanced appeared
to correspond to the Marxist theory of self-determination: here we
had a number of fraternal socialist countries striving to establish
socialism in accordance with their individual historical conditions.
But the truth was somewhat different, for the Soviet definition
gave to the Soviet Union the tactical advantage not only of deciding at will the social and economic policies of these countries, but
also of deciding the fate of the brother Communist parties depending upon its relations with the West. In case relations with the
West deteriorated and the Anglo-Saxon countries showed themselves to be prepared to engage in war, the theory of "harmony"
and "collaboration between classes" would serve the purpose of
sacrificing some of them to the West, thus giving the Soviet Union

an opportunity to prove its pacifist intentions. In the same eventuality, however, the Soviet Union might find it expedient to consolidate its hold upon these countries—an alternative which could hardly be more pleasing to the national Communist leaders. For it meant that such a decision would be made by the Soviet leaders with the following stipulations, which were already being elaborated in theory:

(a) Unswerving allegiance to the Soviet Union.

(b) Realization of the necessity of accepting Soviet military control and economic and political guidance, since by liberating these countries the Red Army had provided the proper conditions for their revolution.

(c) Acceptance of the preponderant role that the "leading socialist nation" or the "largest socialist state"—that is, the Soviet Union—was to play in the consolidation and the economic integration of the socialist world.

(d) Realization that the Soviet form of society, being the most advanced, was the goal towards which each national Communist regime had to strive by following the same path the Soviet Union had followed in the past.

These stipulations were, as has been pointed out already, formulated in theory. By 1947 the Soviet leaders reversed their previous stand in favor of the freedom of each individual country to develop its own way to socialism, and advanced the theory that the Soviet pattern of revolution was to be followed as if it were law. The Soviet experience was to be "binding upon all countries."

Taking the cue, the leaders of the satellite countries also reversed their stands. Dimitrov stated that Bulgaria's People's Democracy was after all a dictatorship of the proletariat corresponding to a transitional stage toward socialism, while the Hungarian Communist leader Rakosi defined Hungary's regime as a "dictatorship of the proletariat without the Soviet form."

These changes in definition corresponded to a shift in Soviet international tactics. By 1947 the Soviet Union had decided to consolidate its power and to launch an appeal for resistance on the part of the Communist parties of the Western powers. The Cominform, founded in September 1947, corresponded to this effort at consolidation of the Soviet sphere; and significantly enough its first act was to accept the confession of the Communist parties of France and Italy of their mistake in allowing themselves to be disarmed and in collaborating with conservative parties. The holy war against all parties, including the Socialists, was launched once more. At the same time, a dictatorship of the proletariat was proclaimed in the satellite countries, the supporting role of the Red Army was underlined in practice, the economic plans of the satellites coordinated with the economy of the "leading socialist nation," and leadership was concentrated in the hands of safe Communist Party members. In the traditional Stalinist way, the revolution was controlled from above; the various parties were to be purged before they were trusted; the Russian Soviet example was to be closely followed until the Soviet form was realized; and the principle of self-determination was to mean solidarity with the progressive proletarian Soviet State. And, looming above all, we find the same suspicion toward the West, the same exclusive reliance upon direct Soviet leadership and control, the same exaltation of one national form at the expense of all others.

## III

It was six months after the establishment of the Cominform that the Yugoslav leaders advanced cautiously into a position which could not mean anything else but an open rift with the Soviet Union. Though maintaining friendship for the Soviet Union, they now asserted the need for autonomy and national independence and refused to be integrated in the Soviet bloc under the direct control of the Soviet Communist Party. From 1948 to November 1949, they adopted a compromising attitude and seemed willing to come to terms on a footing of equality. They showed great reluctance, even after their expulsion from the Cominform on June 28, 1948, to undertake any direct criticism of the Soviet Union, and were satisfied to address their remarks and protestations to the other Cominform members. However, after the second Cominform meeting, held in November 1949, when it was realized that no possibility of *rapprochement* remained, the Yugoslav leaders passed on to their third and final position—a frontal attack on the Soviet Union and Soviet leadership. At this stage, the power conflict between the two national Communist states had to be rationalized by Yugoslavia in terms of an ideological position which was both Marxist and anti-Stalinist.

There is hardly any need here to trace the development of the conflict in its historical or even ideological setting. We shall try rather to analyze the major ideological aspects of the controversy as it appears to have evolved in its present form. The literature is indeed immense and the Yugoslav pamphlets and articles show a freshness and vigor unparalleled since Trotsky's opposition in the years following Lenin's death. They follow the great lines of the "Marxist-Leninist science." Not for a moment is there a wavering or a conscious departure from Marxism.

Two main themes evolved during the controversy and were fully developed by the Yugoslav leaders: the nature of national independence in a socialist revolutionary period, and the nature of Stalinism as compared with genuine Marxian socialism.

Yugoslav leaders assert that their People's Front represents the transitional stage of proletarian dictatorship suitable to the particular conditions of their country, and reject both of the theses developed by the Soviet leadership which have already been discussed. According to them, the People's Front corresponds to the specific historical conditions of the liberation struggle in Yugoslavia, in which the middle-class farmers, the poor farmers, and even members of the bourgeoisie as well as the intellectuals participated. This popular mass—representing, according to Tito, over seven million people—is being led by the Communist Party toward socialism. They furthermore assert that each nation should be free to decide on its own form of proletarian dictatorship without having to imitate the Soviet pattern, and every effort is made to show the differences between conditions prior to the Russian and to the Yugoslav revolutions. Yugoslavia is portrayed as a politically more advanced nation: its agricultural system is based upon small farmers; its intellectuals, it is claimed, joined the liberation struggle and the social revolution. . . . It is maintained, in fact, that the genuineness of the Yugoslav Revolution adds to the socialist experience and provides for new insights which would be lost had one accepted the Soviet allegation that the Soviet experience constitutes a single law that must be followed blindly. Furthermore, the Soviet claim that the proper conditions for the Revolution were created thanks to the intervention of the Red Army is rejected with scorn: the conditions were prepared by the Yugoslav Communist Party and the Yugoslav Liberation Movement.

The arguments presented above assume special significance with reference to the economic policy to be pursued by the individual socialist states. Again the Yugoslav leaders reject the thesis of the "leading socialist nation," of the "largest socialist state," which is to lead the socialist countries and direct the policies of the social-ist world. They advance arguments in favor of autonomy. Each nation, they say, should follow its own road to socialism without interference from outside, though the Soviet state is duty bound to come to the assistance of individual states and help them to build socialism. Needless to say, the first years of economic cooperation disillusioned the Yugoslavs. Every effort was made by the Soviet to retard socialist development: machinery was not delivered; Yugoslavia was asked to concentrate on the extraction of raw materials and the production of foodstuffs, and the exchange ar-rangements between Yugoslavia and the Soviet Union benefited the latter because of its superior economy. So, indirectly at least, surplus value, we are told, was extracted from the Yugoslav work-er by the Soviet state. . . .

The crux of the matter is, of course, the question of national independence in a socialist world. The Yugoslav position is that a socialist state is an independent political entity, free to enter into agreements with other socialist states, to become part of a socialist confederation, or to secede. Tito has been hailed with justice as a nationalist and was in fact accused of a nationalist deviation by the Soviet leaders. The difficulty, however, is that he himself has only too often proclaimed his internationalist leanings: "We are nationalists inasmuch as this is necessary to develop among our people a healthy socialist patriotism, and socialist patriotism in its essence is internationalism." To understand this statement fully, one should be reminded of some of the voluntaristic aspects of Marxism, according to which the genuine development of socialist societies automatically brings about the end of national barriers. Socialist patriotism reaches out for the universal elements of human and social behavior. By cultivating the one, we bring about the other. It has nothing to do with the traditionalist or reactionary nationalism of the Burkian type which insists upon the specificity and uniqueness of the national experience. A Socialist is, at least in Marxian theory, an internationalist in the same sense that the Jacobin zealot fighting for the French Revolution and France was fighting for human kind. This idea of self-determination in a socialist world became, of course, a dogma in the hands of Stalin, who saw only its revolutionary potentialities—primarily among the colonial peoples—according to which self-determination or secession from the socialist fatherland was anti-Marxian, but self-determination and secession from a capitalist country was revolutionary. The principle of self-determination was turned inside out, so to speak, and the Soviet leaders assumed the monopoly of interpreting it to their strategic advantage. It is primarily to this that Tito and the Yugoslav leaders seem to object, and their objection was so well received by the other countries that the Soviet leaders stopped accusing Tito of nationalist deviations. With this, we come to the second major topic of the controversy which, naturally, has gained prominence in the last two years—namely, the study of the nature of Stalinism in contrast to Marxist socialism.

Among the satellite countries, the repercussions of the Yugoslav-Soviet exchange of letters and the Cominform resolution of June 28, 1948, was so serious that no Cominform meeting was held until November 1949. In the course of a year and a half, the Soviet leaders undertook a vast campaign of purging the Communist parties of the satellites to eliminate all dissident elements. In some cases, as in Poland, direct command of military personnel was entrusted to Russians. By the time the second meeting of the Cominform was held, there appeared to be perfect unanimity in branding Tito a Nazi and Anglo-American spy, an imperialist stooge, a new Trotsky, a militarist, etc., etc. It was at this stage that the Yugoslav leaders passed to a study of the nature of socialism which led them to a frontal attack upon Stalinism, in its domestic as well as in its foreign policy. And it was precisely at this stage that one of the greatest protagonists of revolutionary Marxism, whose ghost had been daily slain in the Soviet Union, re-entered the picture. In the very moment of victory and triumph following the war against Germany, Stalin was once more face to face with his lifelong adversary. For the criticism against the Soviet Union that the Yugoslav leaders advanced came almost literally out of Trotsky's *Revolutic i Betrayed* and *The Real Situation in Russia*. The concrete experience they had in their dealings with the Soviet power led them to a position which vindicated, even if twenty years later, the Trotskyite opposition.

The criticism of the Soviet leadership is put succinctly by one of the Yugoslav leaders (Djilas) in a pamphlet called *On New Roads to Socialism*. The indictment is long indeed: unequal relations with and exploitation of the other socialist countries, un-Marxian treatment of the role of the leader, inequality in pay greater than in bourgeois democracies, ideological promotion of Great Russian nationalism and subordination of other peoples, a policy of division of spheres of influence with the capitalist world, monopolization of the interpretation of Marxism, the abandonment of all democratic forms, etc., etc. The conclusion is obvious: Stalinism represents a deviation of Marxism and must be combated as such. It is nothing else but a deviant social form caused by the backward conditions of Russia, and its essence can be summed up in that magic word that Trotsky employed so often: bureaucracy. "The development of dictatorship of the proletariat," writes Djilas, can ". . . go in two directions: in the direction of its own disappearance . . . or in the direction of transformation of the bureaucracy into a privileged caste which lives at the expense of the society as a whole." It is obviously the latter that has happened in the Soviet Union: a bureaucratic control has been established and gradually extended over all other Communist parties of the world. "If one looked for the cause of weakness of the working class movement," writes Tito, "it is certain that a number of symptoms would lead him to those who claim to be infallible." The result is a bureaucratic control which has stamped out all life from the party, in which leadership has been perpetuated with remarkable monotony, in which the repressive machinery of the state has been developed not so much for purposes of defense but for the purpose of internal control and foreign domination and conquest of brother socialist states, a bureaucratic control, finally, which leads the Soviet ruling caste to an internal economic policy inconsistent with the potentialities of the means of production and which pushes them at last into foreign adventures—since the search for a scapegoat is always the surest way of diverting the people's revolutionary inclinations. Under existing conditions, the future of a socialist world composed of politically independent, democratic nations has become an impossibility and the Soviet Union under Stalin has become an obstacle to the very end for which it claims to stand. Hence the ineluctable conclusion is that, under present conditions, a revolution within the Soviet Union and by the working classes of the satellites is desirable and even necessary. This is the Yugoslav position today, and it is needless to repeat that it is identical to the Trotskyist position.

It is a conclusion that is bound to startle the average observer. When is such an objective to be realized? By what means is Tito proposing to bring it about? For how long is his "arrogance" going to be tolerated? Besides, is this demand for revolution a genuine one? Does not Tito's concept of "socialism in Yugoslavia" come dangerously close to the Stalinist idea of "socialism in one country"? If so, won't Tito be constrained ultimately to put Yugoslavia above socialism and revolution, as Stalin put the Soviet Union in the past? Only speculative answers to these questions can be given, since the development of Titoism as a revolutionary philosophy will ultimately depend upon over-all world relations.

Historically, Titoism can be explained in terms of the nature of Tito's national prestige and power. The Yugoslav Communist Party acted for a long time without direct Soviet interference. It developed into a powerful organization, difficult to break, as has happened with the Communist parties of the other satellites. Furthermore, the People's Front of Yugoslavia was far more popular than the regimes established in the other satellite countries by leaders most of whom came in the wake of the Soviet Army. Conceding all this to be true, we must still admit that it does not explain the present ideological trends of Titoism. For Titoism, in advocating a revolution in the socialist sector of the world at least, is restating Trotsky's idea of world revolution—something which appears to be a negation of the national roots to which he owes his very existence. His ideological position, in other words, transcends the narrow sociological roots of his power and pushes him toward a revolutionary position that may lead to his annihilation *or* to the decline of Stalinism in the Soviet Union and the world. And it is precisely at this point that the significance of the factor mentioned earlier—the existence of an anti-Stalinist Communist ideology— becomes apparent. For though Tito and his party have been nourished in Stalinist philosophy, though the roots of their power are to be found in the strong nationalist movement of Yugoslavia, in the cohesion of his party organization, and in the relative autonomy of his party during the war—a coincidence of circumstances which has not as yet occurred elsewhere—he has been forced by the very nature of his position to appeal to a revolutionary ideology which seems to be inconsistent with the nature and source of his power. Isolated from both the East and the West and urgently in need of support, he was forced while maintaining high hopes for a "Titoist" development in China to appeal to the anti-Stalinist Communist forces of Europe and revive the idea of revolution as a strategic weapon and direct it against its main protagonist—the Soviet Union.

Yet this may appear as too optimistic a conclusion. For the exigencies of national power and national security weigh heavily and they constitute concrete realities that cannot be too easily sacrificed. Tito's Stalinist mentality and training, his ambitious plans to develop socialism rapidly in Yugoslavia, the intense nationalism which his movement has generated, are all factors which may in the last analysis outweigh the revolutionary ideology which was evoked by the conflict with the Soviet Union. Such considerations may force Tito into a more definite alliance with the West and may lead him to the same traditionalist concessions that were made by Stalin during World War II.

It is, however, both premature and risky to make any predictions. For Tito has launched a new movement that threatens the ideological and organizational front of the Soviet power and which has demonstrated with unprecedented urgency to the rank and file of the Communists and Socialists of Western Europe the perils of a close alliance with the Soviet Union, particularly in time of victory. And the West might draw its own conclusions from Tito's experience.

# THE "NORMALIZATION" OF SOVIET-YUGOSLAV RELATIONS

[1955]

## A. THE SOVIET APOLOGY TO TITO, MAY 26, 1955.*

The Soviet delegation has come to your country to determine, together with the Yugoslav Government delegation, the roads for further development and consolidation of friendship and cooperation between our peoples, to consider our joint task in the struggle of our countries for prosperity, for reduction of tension, for strengthening peace in general and the security of peoples.

The peoples of our countries are linked by ties of long brotherly friendship and joint struggle against the enemy.   This friendship and militant collaboration were particularly strengthened during the time of difficult trials in the struggle against the Fascist invaders during the Second World War.   During these difficult years all the Soviet people followed with great feeling the heroic struggle of their Yugoslav brothers, headed by the Communists, and hailed with all their hearts the courageous feats in battle of the National Liberation Army of Yugoslavia under the leadership of Marshal Tito. . . .

As we know, the best relations developed during those years between the peoples of the Soviet Union and Yugoslavia, between our states and our parties.   However, later these good relations were destroyed.

We sincerely regret what happened and resolutely reject the things that occurred, one after the other, during that period.   So far as we are concerned, without a doubt, we understood under this the provocative role played in the relations between Yugoslavia and the U.S.S.R. by enemies of the people Beria, Abakumov and others who have been unmasked. [Lavrenti P. Beria, former

---

* Statement read by Nikita S. Khrushchev, Soviet Communist Party Secretary, at the airport in Belgrade, on his arrival with a delegation to discuss re-establishment of normal relations between the Soviet Union and Yugoslavia.   From the *New York Times*, May 27, 1955.

Soviet Minister of Internal Affairs, Viktor S. Abakumov, one of his aides, and others were executed in 1953 and 1954.]

We have thoroughly studied the materials on which the serious charges and insults directed against the leaders of Yugoslavia were based. The facts testify that these materials were fabricated by enemies of the people, agents of imperialism deserving of scorn who entered the ranks of our party by deceitful means.

We are profoundly convinced that this period of the deterioration of our relations has been left behind us. For our part we are ready to do everything necessary to eliminate all obstacles standing in the way of complete normalization of relations between our states, of the consolidation of friendly relations between our peoples. . . .

Following the teachings of the creator of the Soviet state, Vladimir Ilyich Lenin, the Government of the Soviet Union bases its relations with other countries, large and small, on principles of the peaceful coexistence of states, on principles of equality, nonintervention and respect for sovereignty and national independence, on principles of nonaggression and recognition of the impermissibility of some states' encroaching upon the territorial integrity of others.

We hope that the relations between our countries will continue to develop along these principles for the good of our peoples. This will be a new and important contribution to the cause of reduction of international tension, the cause of preservation and consolidation of general peace in the world.

The desire of Yugoslavia to maintain relations with all states both in the West and in the East has met with complete understanding on our part. We consider that the strengthening of friendship and ties between our countries will contribute to . . . consolidation of peace in general. . . .

We would not be doing our duty to our peoples and to the working people of the whole world if we did not do everything possible to establish mutual understanding between the Communist party of the Soviet Union and the Yugoslav Communist League, on the basis of the teachings of Marxism-Leninism. . . .

Long live lasting peace among nations.

Long live fraternal friendship and close cooperation between the peoples of the Soviet Union and Yugoslavia.

Long live the peoples of Yugoslavia.

## B. Belgrade Declaration, June 2, 1955.*

The delegation of the Government of the Federative People's Republic of Yugoslavia . . . and the delegation of the Government of the U.S.S.R. . . . conducted talks in Belgrade and Brioni from May 27 to June 2, 1955. In the course of the talks, which were conducted in a spirit of friendship and mutual understanding, there took place an exchange of opinions on international problems of interest to Yugoslavia and the Soviet Union.

In their consideration of the questions dealt with in the course of the talks and with a view to the strengthening of confidence and cooperation among nations, the two governments have started from the following principles:

The individuality of peace upon which collective security can alone rest; respect for the sovereignty, independence, integrity and for equality among states in their mutual relations and in their relations with other states.

Recognition and development of peaceful coexistence among nations, regardless of ideological differences or differences of social order which presuppose the cooperation of all states in the field of international relations in general, and more particularly in the field of economic and cultural relations.

Compliance with the principle of mutual respect for, and noninterference in, internal affairs for whatever reason whether of an economic, political or ideological nature, because questions of internal organization, or difference in social systems and of different forms of Socialist development, are solely the concern of the individual countries. . . .

Condemnation of all aggression and of all attempts to subject other countries to political and economic domination.

The recognition that the policy of military blocs increases international tension, undermines confidence among nations and augments the danger of war. . . .

Full attention was given to an analysis of the relations between the two countries up to the present and to the prospects of their further development. Bearing in mind that in recent years the mutual relations have been greatly disturbed and that this has been detrimental, both to the parties and to international cooperation.

---

* From the *New York Times*, June 3, 1955.

firmly resolved to conduct their future relations in a spirit of friendly cooperation and on the basis of the principles set forth in the present declaration, the governments of the Federative People's Republic Yugoslavia and of the U.S.S.R. have agreed to the following:

> With regard to the need for strengthening economic ties and expanding economic cooperation between the two countries:
>
> With this aim in view, the two governments have agreed to take the measures necessary to do away with the consequences arising from the disruption of a normal treaty basis in the economic relations between the two countries.
>
> They have also agreed to proceed with the conclusion of the necessary arrangements, designed to regulate and facilitate the development of economic relations in the same direction. . . .

In the spirit of the peace-loving principles set forth in the present declaration and in order to make it possible for the peoples of their countries to become better acquainted and achieve better mutual understanding, the two governments have agreed to assist and facilitate cooperation among the social organizations of the two countries through the establishing of contacts, the exchange of Socialist experiences and a free exchange of opinions. . . .

## C. MOSCOW DECLARATION, JUNE 20, 1956.*

During the official visit of the delegation of the Federal People's Republic of Yugoslavia to the Soviet Union from June 1 to 23, 1956, Josip Broz Tito, Secretary General of the League of Communists of Yugoslavia . . . and Nikita S. Khrushchev, First Secretary of the Central Committee of the Communist Party of the Soviet Union . . . exchanged views in a spirit of comradely sincerity and frankness on relations and cooperation between the League of Communists of Yugoslavia and the Communist Party of the Soviet Union.

During these conversations they agreed upon the following:

1. The Belgrade Declaration of June 2, 1955, placed the relations between the two Socialist countries on sound foundations, and the principles made public in it are finding ever broader application in their mutual cooperation.

---

* From the *New York Times,* June 21, 1956.

2. Cooperation and the general development of relations between the two countries since the Belgrade Declaration, as well as the contact between the political and other social organizations of their peoples, have created favorable political conditions also for cooperation between the League of Communists of Yugoslavia and the Communist party of the Soviet Union. . . .

3. Abiding by the view that the roads and conditions of Socialist development are different in different countries, that the wealth of the forms of Socialist development contributes to their strengthening, and starting with the fact that any tendency of imposing one's own views in determining the roads and forms of Socialist development are alien to both sides, the two sides have agreed that the foregoing cooperation should be based on complete freedom of will and equality, on friendly criticism and on the comradely character of the exchange of views on disputes between our parties.

\*　　\*　　\*

# CRIMES OF THE STALIN ERA *

BY

## NIKITA S. KHRUSHCHEV

[1956]

Comrades! In the report of the Central Committee of the party at the 20th Congress, in a number of speeches by delegates to the Congress, as also formerly during the plenary CC/CPSU [Central Committee of the Communist Party of the Soviet Union] sessions, quite a lot has been said about the cult of the individual and about its harmful consequences.

After Stalin's death the Central Committee of the party began to implement a policy of explaining concisely and consistently that it is impermissible and foreign to the spirit of Marxism-Leninism to elevate one person, to transform him into a superman possessing supernatural characteristics, akin to those of a god. Such a man supposedly knows everything, sees everything, thinks for everyone, can do anything, is infallible in his behavior.

Such a belief about a man, and specifically about Stalin, was cultivated among us for many years. . . .

In addition to the great accomplishments of V. I. Lenin for the victory of the working class and of the working peasants, for the victory of our party and for the application of the ideas of scientific Communism to life, his acute mind expressed itself also in this —that he detected in Stalin in time those negative characteristics which resulted later in grave consequences. Fearing the future fate of the party and of the Soviet nation, V. I. Lenin made a completely correct characterization of Stalin, pointing out that it was necessary to consider the question of transferring Stalin from the position of the Secretary General because of the fact that Stalin is excessively rude, that he does not have a proper attitude toward his comrades, that he is capricious and abuses his power.

---

* Special Report to the 20th Congress of the Communist Party of the Soviet Union, closed session, February 24-25, 1956. From the edition annotated by Boris I. Nicolaevsky for *The New Leader,* reprinted by permission.

In December 1922, in a letter to the Party Congress, Vladimir Ilyich wrote: "After taking over the position of Secretary General, Comrade Stalin accumulated in his hands immeasurable power and I am not certain whether he will be always able to use this power with the required care."

This letter—a political document of tremendous importance, known in the party history as Lenin's "testament"—was distributed among the delegates to the 20th Party Congress. You have read it and will undoubtedly read it again more than once. You might reflect on Lenin's plain words in which expression is given to Vladimir Ilyich's anxiety concerning the party, the people, the state, and the future direction of party policy.

Vladimir Ilyich said: "Stalin is excessively rude, and this defect, which can be freely tolerated in our midst and in contacts among us Communists, becomes a defect which cannot be tolerated in one holding the position of the Secretary General. Because of this, I propose that the comrades consider the method by which Stalin would be removed from this position and by which another man would be selected for it, a man who, above all, would differ from Stalin in only one quality, namely, greater tolerance, greater loyalty, greater kindness and more considerate attitude toward the comrades, a less capricious temper, etc."

This document of Lenin's was made known to the delegates at the 13th Party Congress, who discussed the question of transferring Stalin from the position of Secretary General. The delegates declared themselves in favor of retaining Stalin in this post, hoping that he would heed the critical remarks of Vladimir Ilyich and would be able to overcome the defects which caused Lenin serious anxiety. . . .

.When we analyze the practice of Stalin in regard to the direction of the party and of the country, when we pause to consider everything which Stalin perpetrated, we must be convinced that Lenin's fears were justified. The negative characteristics of Stalin, which, in Lenin's time, were only incipient, transformed themselves during the last years into a grave abuse of power by Stalin which caused untold harm to our party.

We have to consider seriously and analyze correctly this matter in order that we may preclude any possibility of a repetition in any form whatever of what took place during the life of Stalin, who absolutely did not tolerate collegiality in leadership and in work, and who practiced brutal violence, not only toward everything which opposed him, but also toward that which seemed, to his capricious and despotic character, contrary to his concepts.

Stalin acted not through persuasion, explanation and patient co-operation with people, but by imposing his concepts and demanding absolute submission to his opinion. Whoever opposed this concept or tried to prove his viewpoint and the correctness of his position was doomed to removal from the leading collective and to subsequent moral and physical annihilation. This was especially true during the period following the 17th Party Congress, when many prominent party leaders and rank-and-file party workers, honest and dedicated to the cause of Communism, fell victim to Stalin's despotism. . . .

Stalin originated the concept "enemy of the people." This term automatically rendered it unnecessary that the ideological errors of a man or men engaged in a controversy be proven; this term made possible the usage of the most cruel repression, violating all norms of revolutionary legality, against anyone who in any way disagreed with Stalin, against those who were only suspected of hostile intent, against those who had bad reputations.

This concept "enemy of the people" actually eliminated the possibility of any kind of ideological fight or the making of one's views known on this or that issue, even those of a practical character. In the main, and in actuality, the only proof of guilt used, against all norms of current legal science, was the "confession" of the accused himself; and, as subsequent probing proved, "confessions" were acquired through physical pressures against the accused. . . .

The power accumulated in the hands of one person, Stalin, led to serious consequences during the Great Patriotic War. . . .

During the war and after the war, Stalin put forward the thesis that the tragedy which our nation experienced in the first part of the war was the result of the "unexpected" attack of the Germans against the Soviet Union. But, comrades, this is completely untrue. As soon as Hitler came to power in Germany he assigned to himself the task of liquidating Communism. The fascists were saying this openly; they did not hide their plans.

In order to attain this aggressive end, all sorts of pacts and blocs were created, such as the famous Berlin-Rome-Tokyo Axis. Many facts from the prewar period clearly showed that Hitler was going all out to begin a war against the Soviet state, and that he had concentrated large armed units, together with armored units, near the Soviet borders.

Documents which have now been published show that by April 3, 1941, Churchill, through his Ambassador to the USSR, Cripps, personally warned Stalin that the Germans had begun regrouping their armed units with the intent of attacking the Soviet Union.

It is self-evident that Churchill did not do this at all because of his friendly feeling toward the Soviet nation. He had in this his own imperialistic goals—to bring Germany and the USSR into a bloody war and thereby to strengthen the position of the British Empire.

Just the same, Churchill affirmed in his writings that he sought to "warn Stalin and call his attention to the danger which threatened him." Churchill stressed this repeatedly in his dispatches of April 18 and on the following days. However, Stalin took no heed of these warnings. What is more, Stalin ordered that no credence be given to information of this sort, in order not to provoke the initiation of military operations.

We must assert that information of this sort concerning the threat of German armed invasion of Soviet territory was coming in also from our own military and diplomatic sources; however, because the leadership was conditioned against such information, such data was dispatched with fear and assessed with reservation. . . .

Very grievous consequences, especially in reference to the beginning of the war, followed Stalin's annihilation of many military commanders and political workers during 1937-1941 because of his suspiciousness and through slanderous accusations. During these years repressions were instituted against certain parts of military cadres beginning literally at the company and battalion commander level and extending to the higher military centers; during this time the cadre of leaders who had gained military experience in Spain and in the Far East was almost completely liquidated.

The policy of large-scale repression against the military cadres led also to undermined military discipline, because for several years officers of all ranks and even soldiers in the party and Komsomol cells were taught to "unmask" their superiors as hidden enemies. (*Movement in the hall.*) It is natural that this caused a negative influence on the state of military discipline in the first war period.

And, as you know, we had before the war excellent military cadres which were unquestionably loyal to the party and to the Fatherland. Suffice it to say that those of them who managed to survive, despite severe tortures to which they were subjected in the prisons, have from the first war days shown themselves real patriots and heroically fought for the glory of the Fatherland; I have here in mind such comrades as Rokossovsky (who, as you know, had been jailed), Gorbatov, Maretskov (who is a delegate to the present Congress), Podlas (he was an excellent commander who perished at the front), and many, many others. However, many such commanders perished in camps and jails and the Army saw them no more. . . .

Comrades, let us reach for some other facts. The Soviet Union is justly considered as a model of a multinational state because we have in practice assured the equality and friendship of all nations which live in our great Fatherland.

All the more monstrous are the acts whose initiator was Stalin and which are rude violations of the basic Leninist principles of the nationality policy of the Soviet state. We refer to the mass deportations from their native places of whole nations, together with all Communists and Komsomols without any exception; this deportation action was not dictated by any military considerations.

Thus, already at the end of 1943, when there occurred a permanent break-through at the fronts of the Great Patriotic War benefiting the Soviet Union, a decision was taken and executed concerning the deportation of all the Karachai from the lands on which they lived.

In the same period, at the end of December 1943, the same lot befell the whole population of the Autonomous Kalmyk Republic. In March 1944, all the Chechen and Ingush peoples were deported and the Chechen-Ingush Autonomous Republic was liquidated. In April 1944, all Balkars were deported to faraway places from the territory of the Kabardino-Balkar Autonomous Republic and the Republic itself was renamed the Autonomous Kabardian Republic. The Ukrainians avoided meeting this fate only because there were too many of them and there was no place to which to deport them. Otherwise, he would have deported them also. (*Laughter and animation in the hall.*)

Not only a Marxist-Leninist but also no man of common sense can grasp how it is possible to make whole nations responsible for inimical activity, including women, children, old people, Communists and Komsomols to use mass repression against them, and to expose them to misery and suffering for the hostile acts of individual persons or groups of persons. . . .

The willfulness of Stalin showed itself not only in decisions concerning the internal life of the country but also in the international relations of the Soviet Union.

The July plenum of the Central Committee studied in detail the reasons for the development of conflict with Yugoslavia. It was a shameful role which Stalin played here. The "Yugoslav affair" contained no problems which could not have been solved through party discussions among comrades. There was no significant basis for the development of this "affair"; it was completely possible to have prevented the rupture of relations with that country. This does not mean however, that the Yugoslav leaders did not make mistakes or did not have shortcomings. But these mistakes and shortcomings were magnified in a monstrous manner by Stalin, which resulted in a break of relations with a friendly country.

I recall the first days when the conflict between the Soviet Union and Yugoslavia began artificially to be blown up. Once when I came from Kiev to Moscow, I was invited to visit Stalin who, pointing to the copy of a letter lately sent to Tito, asked me, "Have you read this?"

Not waiting for my reply he answered, "I will shake my little finger—and there will be no more Tito. He will fall."

We have dearly paid for this "shaking of the little finger." This statement reflected Stalin's mania for greatness, but he acted just that way: "I will shake my little finger—and there will be no Kossior"; "I will shake my little finger once more and Postyshev and Chubar will be no more"; "I will shake my little finger again—and Voznesensky, Kuznetsov and many others will disappear."

But this did not happen to Tito. No matter how much or how little Stalin shook, not only his little finger but everything else that he could shake, Tito did not fall. Why? The reason was that, in this case of disagreement with the Yugoslav comrades, Tito had behind him a state and a people who had gone through a severe school of fighting for liberty and independence, a people which gave support to its leaders.

You see to what Stalin's mania for greatness led. He had completely lost consciousness of reality; he demonstrated his suspicion and haughtiness not only in relation to individuals in the USSR, but in relations to whole parties and nations. . . .

# DECLARATION OF 12 COMMUNIST PARTIES *

[1957]

Representatives of the Albanian Labor Party, the Bulgarian Communist Party, the Hungarian Socialist Workers' Party, the Working People's Party of Vietnam, the Socialist Unity Party of Germany, the Communist Party of China, the Korean Labor Party, the Mongolian People's Revolutionary Party, the Polish United Workers' Party, the Rumanian Workers' Party, the Communist Party of the Soviet Union and the Communist Party of Czechoslovakia discussed their relations, current problems of the international situation, and the struggle for peace and socialism.

The exchange of opinions showed the Communist and Workers' Parties represented at the conference to have identical views on all the questions examined at the meeting and to be unanimous in their assessment of the international situation. In the course of discussion the conference also touched upon general problems of the international Communist movement. In drafting the declaration the participants in the meeting consulted with representatives of the fraternal parties in the capitalist countries. The fraternal parties not present at this conference will assess and themselves decide what action they should take on the considerations expressed in the declaration.

## I

The main content of our epoch is the transition from capitalism to socialism which was begun by the Great October Socialist Revolution in Russia. Today more than a third of the population of the world—more than 950,000,000 people—has taken the road of socialism and is building a new life. The tremendous

---

* This declaration was issued at a conference of representatives of Communist and Workers' Parties from Socialist countries, held in Moscow, November 14-16, 1957. A delegation from Yugoslavia attended the conference but did not join in the declaration. The text was printed in *Pravda,* November 22, 1957. These excerpts are from the translation of the complete text in *The Current Digest of the Soviet Press* (New York), Vol. IX, No. 47. Copyright; reprinted by permission.

development of the forces of socialism has stimulated tempestuous growth of the anti-imperialist national movement in the postwar period. Besides the Chinese People's Republic, the Democratic Republic of Vietnam and the Korean People's Democratic Republic, more than 700,000,000 people have shaken off the colonial yoke and established national independent states during the past 12 years. The peoples of the colonial and dependent countries, still languishing in slavery, are intensifying the struggle for their national liberation. The development of socialism and of the national-liberation movement has sharply accelerated the disintegration of imperialism. Imperialism has lost its one-time domination over the greater part of mankind. In the imperialist countries society is rent by deep class contradictions and also by sharp antagonisms among these states; the working class of these countries is putting up increasing resistance to the policy of imperialism and the monopolies, fighting for better living conditions, for democratic rights, peace and socialism.

In our epoch world development is determined by the course and results of the competition between two diametrically opposed social systems. In 40 years socialism has demonstrated that it is superior to capitalism as a social system. It has ensured development of the productive forces at a rate unprecedented and impossible for capitalism, and a sharp rise in the living standard and cultural level of the working people. The Soviet Union's great successes in economics, scientific and technical progress and the results achieved by the other socialist countries in socialist construction are convincing evidence of the great vitality of socialism. In the socialist states the masses of the working people enjoy genuine freedom and democratic rights, people's rule ensures political unity of the masses, equality and friendship of nations and a foreign policy aimed at preserving world peace and rendering assistance to oppressed peoples in their struggle for liberation. The world socialist system, growing and becoming stronger, is exerting ever greater influence upon the international situation in the interest of peace, progress and freedom of peoples. . . .

The question of war or peaceful coexistence has become the fundamental problem of world politics. The peoples of all countries must preserve the utmost vigilance toward the war danger created by imperialism.

The forces of peace have now grown so large that there is a real possibility of averting war, as was demonstrated graphically by the failure of the imperialists' aggressive designs in Egypt. Their plans to use counterrevolutionary forces for the overthrow of the people's democratic system in Hungary likewise failed.

The cause of peace is upheld by powerful forces of our times: the invincible camp of socialist states, headed by the Soviet Union; the peace-loving states of Asia and Africa, taking an anti-imperialist stand and forming, together with the socialist countries, a large peace zone; the international working class and, above all, its vanguard, the Communist Parties; the liberation movement of the peoples of the colonies and semicolonies; the mass peace movement of the peoples; the peoples of the European countries who have proclaimed neutrality, the peoples of Latin America and the masses in the imperialist countries themselves, offering determined resistance to the plans for a new war. The alliance of these mighty forces could prevent the outbreak of war, but should the bellicose imperialist maniacs venture, regardless of anything, to unleash a war, imperialism will doom itself to destruction, for the people will no longer tolerate a system that brings them so much suffering and exacts so many sacrifices.

The Communist and Workers' Parties taking part in this conference declare that the Leninist principle of peaceful coexistence of the two systems, which has been further developed in contemporary circumstances in the decisions of the 20th Party Congress, is the firm foundation of the foreign policy of the socialist countries and the reliable foundation of peace and friendship among the peoples. . . .

The Communist Parties regard the struggle for peace as their foremost task. Together with all peace-loving forces, they will do all in their power to prevent war.

## II

The conference considers that strengthening of the unity and fraternal cooperation of the socialist states and of the Communist and Workers' Parties of all countries and closing of the ranks of the international working class, national-liberation and democratic movements take on special importance in the present situation.

The relations among the countries of the world socialist system and among all the Communist and Workers' Parties rest on the principles of Marxism-Leninism, the principles of proletarian internationalism, which have been tested by life. Today the vital interests of the working people of all countries call for their support of the Soviet Union and all the socialist countries, which, pursuing a policy of preserving world peace, are the bulwark of peace and social progress. The working class, the democratic forces and the working people of all countries are interested in tirelessly strengthening fraternal contacts in the interests of the common cause, in defending, against all encroachments by the enemies of socialism, the historic political and social gains effected in the Soviet Union, the first and mightiest socialist power; in the Chinese People's Republic, and in all the socialist countries, in seeing these gains extended and consolidated.

The socialist countries base their relations on the principles of complete equality, respect for territorial integrity and state independence and sovereignty, and noninterference in one another's affairs. These are important principles, but they do not exhaust the essence of relations among the socialist countries. Fraternal mutual aid is an integral part of these relations. The principle of socialist internationalism finds effective expression in this mutual aid.

On a basis of complete equality, mutual benefit and comradely mutual assistance, the socialist states have established among themselves extensive economic and cultural cooperation that plays an important part in strengthening the economic and political independence of each socialist country and in strengthening the entire socialist commmonwealth as a whole. The socialist states will continue to expand and improve economic and cultural cooperation among themselves.

The socialist states also advocate comprehensive expansion of economic and cultural ties with all other countries, provided the latter express a similar desire, on a basis of equality, mutual benefit, and noninterference in internal affairs.

The solidarity of the socialist states is not directed against any other state. What is more, it serves the interests of all peace-loving peoples, restraining the aggressive striving of the bellicose imperialist circles and supporting and encouraging the growing forces of peace. The socialist countries are against division of the world into military blocs. But, in view of the situation that has arisen, with the Western powers refusing to accept the proposals of the socialist countries for mutual abolition of military blocs, the Warsaw Pact organization, which bears a defensive character, serves the security of the peoples of Europe and supports world peace, must exist and be strengthened.

The socialist states are united in a single commonwealth by the fact that they are taking the common socialist road, by the common class essence of their social and economic system and state regimes, by the need of mutual support and aid, by community of interests and aims in the struggle against imperialism and for the victory of socialism and communism, and by the ideology of Marxism-Leninism, common to all of them.

The solidarity and close unity of the socialist countries constitute a reliable guarantee of the national independence and sovereignty of each socialist country. Stronger fraternal relations and friendship among the socialist countries call for a Marxist-Leninist internationalist policy on the part of the Communist and Workers' Parties, for educating all the working people in the spirit of combining internationalism with patriotism, and for a determined struggle to overcome the survivals of bourgeois nationalism and chauvinism. All issues pertaining to relations among the socialist countries can be fully settled through comradely discussion, with strict observance of the principles of socialist internationalism.

### III

\* \* \*

The conference confirmed the unity of views of the Communist and Workers' Parties on the basic questions of the socialist revolution and socialist construction. The experience of the

U.S.S.R. and other socialist countries has fully confirmed the correctness of the tenet of Marxist-Leninist theory that the processes of the socialist revolution and the building of socialism are governed by a number of basic laws applicable in all countries embarking on a socialist path. These laws are manifested everywhere alongside a great variety of historically formed national features and traditions which should be taken into account without fail. . . .

Marxism-Leninism requires a creative application of the general principles of socialist revolution and socialist construction depending on the specific conditions in each country and does not permit mechanical copying of the policies and tactics of the Communist Parties of other countries. V. I. Lenin repeatedly warned about the necessity of correctly applying the basic principles of communism in accord with the specific features of a given nation, a given national state. Disregard of national peculiarities by the proletarian party [dogmatism] inevitably leads to its detachment from reality, from the masses, and is bound to harm the cause of socialism, and, conversely, exaggeration of the role of these peculiarities and departure, under the pretext of national peculiarities, from the universal Marxist-Leninist truth regarding socialist revolution and socialist construction [revisionism] will inevitably harm the socialist cause. The participants in the meeting consider that it is necessary to wage a simultaneous struggle against both these tendencies. The Communist and Workers' Parties of the socialist countries must firmly adhere to the principles of combining the universal Marxist-Leninist truth with the specific practice of revolution and construction in their countries, creatively apply the general laws governing socialist revolution and socialist construction in accordance with the specific conditions in their countries, learn from each other and share experience. . . .

The theoretical basis of Marxism-Leninism is dialectical materialism. This outlook reflects the universal law of the development of nature, society and human thought. This outlook is valid for the past, the present and the future. Metaphysics and idealism are counterposed to dialectical materialism. If a Marxist political party did not proceed from dialectics and materialism in examining questions, this would lead to one-sidedness and subjectivism, stagnation of thought, isolation from practice and loss of ability to make the necessary analysis of things and phenomena, revisionist or dogmatic mistakes and mistakes in policy. . . . Revisionism and dogmatism in the workers' and Communist movement are today, as they have been in the past, of an international nature. Dogmatism and sectarianism hinder the development of Marxist-Leninist theory and its creative application in specific, changing conditions, replace study of the specific situation with quotations and pedantry, and lead to the Party's isolation from the masses. A party that has locked itself up in sectarianism and that has lost contact with the broad masses can by no means bring victory to the cause of the working class.

In condemning dogmatism, the Communist Parties consider the main danger in present-day conditions to be revisionism or, in other words, right-wing opportunism, as a manifestation of bourgeois ideology that paralyzes the revolutionary energy of the working class and demands the preservation or restoration of capitalism. However, dogmatism and sectarianism can also be the main danger at different stages of development of one party or another. Each Communist Party determines what danger is the main danger to it at a given time. . . .

It is necessary to point out that for the working class the conquest of power is only the beginning of the revolution and not its completion. After the conquest of power the working class is faced with the serious tasks of bringing about the socialist transformation of the national economy and laying the economic and technical foundation of socialism. At the same time the overthrown bourgeoisie always seeks restoration; the influence exerted on society by the bourgeoisie, the petty bourgeoisie and their intelligentsia is still great. Hence a fairly long time is required to resolve the question of "who will win"—capitalism or socialism. The existence of bourgeois influence is an internal source of revisionism, while surrender to the pressure of imperialism is the external source.

Present-day revisionism seeks to defame the great teaching of Marxism-Leninism, declares that it is "obsolete" and that it has

allegedly lost its importance for social development.    The revisionists are trying to destroy the revolutionary soul of Marxism, to
undermine the faith of the working class and the working people
in socialism.    They deny the historical necessity of a proletarian
revolution and the dictatorship of the proletariat during the period
of transition from capitalism to socialism, deny the leading role of
the Marxist-Leninist party, deny the principles of proletarian
internationalism, demand abandonment of the Leninist principles
of Party organization and, above all, of democratic centralism and
demand that the Communist Party be transformed from a militant
revolutionary organization into a kind of debating club.

The entire experience of the international Communist movement teaches that resolute defense by the Communist and Workers'
Parties of the Marxist-Leninist unity of their ranks and the ban-
ning of factions and groups that undermine its unity are a necessary guarantee of the successful accomplishment of the tasks of
the socialist revolution and the building of socialism and communism. . . .

## IV

\*   \*   \*

In connection with the profound historic changes and fundamental shifts in the alignment of forces in the international arena
in favor of socialism and as a result of the mounting power of
attraction of the ideas of socialism among the working class, working peasantry and working intelligentsia, more favorable conditions
are being created for the victory of socialism.

The forms of the transition of different countries from capitalism to socialism may vary.    The working class and its vanguard—
the Marxist-Leninist party—seek to bring about socialist revolution
by peaceful means.    Realization of this possibility would accord
with the interests of the working class and of all the people and
with the over-all national interests of the country.

In present-day conditions in a number of capitalist countries
the working class, headed by its vanguard, has the possibility—
on the basis of a workers' and people's front or of other possible
forms of agreement and political cooperation among the different

parties and public organizations—to unite the majority of the people, win state power without civil war and ensure the transfer of the basic means of production to the hands of the people. Relying on the majority of the people and decisively rebuffing the opportunist elements incapable of relinquishing a policy of compromise with the capitalists and landlords, the working class can defeat the reactionary, antipopular forces, win a firm majority in parliament, transform the parliament from an instrument serving the class interests of the bourgeoisie into an instrument serving the working people, develop a broad mass struggle outside the parliament, break the resistance of the reactionary forces and create the necessary conditions for bringing about the socialist revolution peacefully. All this will be possible only by extensive, steady development of the class struggle of the workers, peasant masses and middle urban strata against big monopoly capital, against reaction, for profound social reforms, for peace and socialism.

In conditions in which the exploiting classes resort to violence against the people, it is necessary to bear in mind another possibility—nonpeaceful transition to socialism. Leninism teaches and history confirms that the ruling classes never relinquish power voluntarily. In these conditions the severity and forms of the class struggle will depend not so much on the proletariat as on the resistance of the reactionary circles to the will of the overwhelming majority of the people, on the use of force by these circles at one or another stage of the struggle for socialism.

In each country the real possibility of one or another means of transition to socialism depends on the specific historical conditions. . . .

In the socialist countries, where the working class has taken power into its own hands, the Communist and Workers' Parties, which have obtained all the conditions for establishing close relations with the broadest masses of the people, should in all their activity constantly rely on the masses and make the building and defense of socialism the cause of the millions of working people, who deeply realize that they are the masters of their country. The measures taken in recent years in the socialist states to expand socialist democracy and develop criticism and self-criticism are of great importance for increasing the activeness and creative initiative of the broad masses and their solidarity, for consolidating the socialist system and for intensifying the building of socialism. . . .

Contrary to the absurd assertions of imperialism regarding the so-called "crisis of communism," the Communist movement is growing and becoming stronger. The historic decisions of the 20th Party Congress are not only of great importance for the Communist Party of the Soviet Union and the building of communism in the U.S.S.R.; they have also laid the basis for a new stage in the international Communist movement and contributed to its further development on the basis of Marxism-Leninism. . . .

The participants in the conference unanimously express their firm confidence that, by rallying their ranks and thereby rallying the working class and the peoples of all countries, the Communist and Workers' Parties will undoubtedly surmount all obstacles on the path of progress and hasten great new victories for the cause of peace, democracy and socialism on a world scale.

# THE LOGIC OF ONE-PARTY RULE *

BY

## RICHARD LOWENTHAL

[1958]

To what extent are the political decisions of the Soviet leadership influenced by its belief in an official ideology—and to what extent are they empirical responses to specific conflicts of interest, expressed in ideological terms merely for purposes of justification? The phrasing of the question at issue suggests the two extreme answers which are *prima facie* conceivable—on the one hand, that ideology provides the Kremlin with a ready-made book of rules to be looked up in any situation; on the other, that its response to reality takes place without any reference to ideology. Yet any clear formulation of this vital issue will show that both extremes are meaningless nonsense.

A ready-made book of rules for any and every situation—an unvarying road-map to the goal of communism which the Soviet leaders must predictably follow—cannot possibly exist, both because the situations to be met by them are not sufficiently predictable, and because no government which behaved in so calculable a manner could conceivably retain power. On the other hand, empirical "Realpolitik" without ideological preconceptions can exist as little as can "empirical science" without categories and hypotheses based on theoretical speculation. Confronted with the same constellation of interests and pressures, the liberal statesman will in many cases choose a different course of action from the conservative—and the totalitarian Communist's choice will often be different from that of either. . . .

## THE FUNCTION OF DOCTRINE

Assuming, then, that the Soviet leaders' ideology is relevant to their conduct, the real problem remains to discover which are the actual operative elements in it, and in what way they affect policy

---

* From *Problems of Communism,* Vol. VII, No. 2, March-April 1958, published by the United States Information Agency. Reprinted by permission.

decisions. Clearly it would be folly to expect that Soviet policy could be predicted solely from an exegetic study of the Marxist-Leninist canon. Not only is it impossible for any group of practical politicians to base their decisions on an unvarying book of rules; there is any amount of historical evidence to show that the rules have been altered again and again to fit the practical decisions *ex post facto*. Moreover, there are vast parts of the Communist ideological structure, such as the scholastic refinements of "dialectical materialism" or the labor theory of value, which in their nature are so remote from the practical matters to be decided that their interpretation cannot possibly affect policy decisions. They may be used in inner-party arguments to *justify* what has been decided on other grounds, but that is all.

How, then, are we to distinguish those elements of Soviet ideology which are truly operative politically from those which are merely traditional scholastic ballast, linked to the operative elements by the historical accident of the founding fathers' authorship? The answer is to be found by going back to the original Marxian meaning of the term "ideology"—conceived as a distorted reflection of social reality in the consciousness of men, used as an instrument of struggle. The fundamental, distinctive social reality in the Soviet Union is the rule of the bureaucracy of a single, centralized and disciplined party, which wields a monopoly of political, economic and spiritual power and permits no independent groupings of any kind. The writer proposes as an hypothesis that the operative parts of the ideology are those which are indispensable for maintaining and justifying this state of affairs: "Marxism-Leninism" matters inasmuch as it expresses, in an ideologically distorted form, the logic of one-party rule.

## TOTALITARIAN PARALLELS

There are a few interconnected ideological features which are common to all the totalitarian regimes of our century—whether of the nationalist-fascist or of the Communist variety. We may designate them as the elements of chiliasm, of collective paranoia, and of the representative fiction. Each totalitarian regime justifies its power and its crimes by the avowed conviction, first, that its final victory will bring about the Millennium—whether defined as the final triumph of communism or of the master race—and second, that this state of grace can only be achieved by an irreconcilable struggle against a single, omnipresent and multiform enemy —whether Monopoly Capitalism or World Jewry—whose forms include every particular opponent of the totalitarian power. Each also claims to represent the true will of the people—the *volonté générale*—independent of whether the people actually support it, and argues that any sacrifice may be demanded from the individual and the group for the good of the people and the defeat of its devilish enemies.

The Communist version of these basic beliefs is superior to the Nazi version in one vital respect. Because the appeal of racialism is in its nature restricted to a small minority of mankind, the Nazis' goal of world domination could not possibly have been attained without a series of wars, preferably surprise attacks launched against isolated opponents. Because the appeal of communism is directed to all mankind, it can be linked with the further doctrine of the inevitable victory of the rising forces of socialism over the imperialist enemy, which is disintegrating under the impact of its own internal contradictions. This central ideological difference, and not merely the psychological difference between Hitler and the Soviet leaders, explains why the latter are convinced that history is on their side and that they need not risk the survival of their own regime in any attempt to hasten its final triumph: they believe in violence, revolutionary and military, as one of the weapons of policy, but they do not believe in the inevitability of world war.

## AWKWARD AIMS AND CLAIMS

Yet the Communist version of totalitarian ideology also suffers from some weaknesses and contradictions from which the Nazi and Fascist versions are free. In the first place, its vision of the Millennium has more markedly utopian features—the classless society, the end of exploitation of man by man, the withering away of the state—which make awkward yardsticks for the real achievements of Communist states. Secondly, in a world where nationalism remains a force of tremendous strength, an internationalist doctrine is bound to come into conflict with the interests of any major Communist power, or with the desire of smaller Communist states for autonomy.

Thirdly, by rejecting the "Fuehrer principle" and claiming to be "democratic," Communist ideology makes the realities of party dictatorship and centralistic discipline more difficult to justify; yet because appeal to blind faith is not officially permitted, justification is needed in "rational" terms. It is precisely this continuous need for the pretense of rational argument—the awkward heritage of communism's origin from revolutionary Western democracy—which has led to the far greater elaboration of its ideology compared to that of "irrationalist" right-wing totalitarianism, and which gives its constant interpretation so much greater importance in preserving the cohesion of the party regime. Due to the fictions of democracy and rationality, the morale of party cadres has been made dependent on the appearance of ideological consistency.

The result of these inherent weaknesses of Communist ideology is that the component doctrines—dealing with the "dictatorship of the proletariat," the party's role as a "vanguard" embodying the "true" class consciousness, "democratic centralism," "proletarian internationalism" and the "leading role of the Soviet Union"— become focal points of ideological crises and targets of "revisionist" attacks whenever events reveal the underlying contradictions in a particularly striking way. Yet these are the very doctrines which the regime cannot renounce because they are the basic rationalizations of its own desire for self-preservation.

We can expect, then, that Communist ideology will have an effective influence on the policy decisions of Soviet leaders when, and only when, it expresses the needs of self-preservation of the party regime. We can further expect that ideological changes and disputes within the Communist "camp" will offer clues to the conflicts and crises—the "contradictions"—which are inseparable from the evolution of this, as of any other, type of society. The fruitful approach, in this writer's view, consists neither in ignoring Communist ideology as an irrelevant disguise, nor in accepting it at its face value and treating it as a subject for exegesis, but in using it as an indicator of those specific drives and problems which spring from the specific structure of Soviet society—in regarding it as an enciphered, continuous self-disclosure, whose cipher can be broken by sociological analysis.

## TWO CAMPS—ONE ENEMY

Let us now apply this approach to the doctrine of the "two camps" in world affairs. The "two-camp" concept was not, of course, a Stalinist invention, although this is sometimes supposed. The postwar situation with its alignment of the Communist and Western powers in two openly hostile politico-military blocs merely gave plausibility to a world image which was inherent in Leninism from the beginning, but which attracted little attention in the period when the Communist "camp" was just an isolated fortress with several outposts. Nor has the doctrine disappeared with the post-Stalin recognition of the importance of the uncommitted, ex-colonial nations and of the tactical value of incorporating them in a "peace zone"; it remains one of the basic ideas of the Moscow twelve-party declaration of last November, and one of the fundamental subjects of ideological disagreement between the Soviets and the Yugoslav Communists.

The Yugoslavs can reject the "two camp" doctrine because they admit the possibility of "roads to socialism" other than Communist party dictatorship—"reformist" roads for advanced industrial countries with parliamentary traditions, "national revolutionary" roads for ex-colonial countries. It follows from this view that Communist states have no monopoly on progress, and that alliances have no ultimate ideological meaning.

The Soviets still assert that while there can be different roads to Communist power, and minor differences in the use of power once gained, there is no way of achieving socialism except by the "dictatorship of the proletariat exercised by its vanguard." It follows that tactical agreements with semi-socialist neutrals are not different in kind from the wartime alliance with the Western "imperialists," or the prewar pact with Hitler—maneuvers which are useful in dividing the forces of the "class enemy" but which remain subordinate to the fundamental division of the world into the Communists versus the Rest.

In other words, the "two camp" doctrine is the Communist version of what we have called the element of "collective paranoia" in totalitarian ideology—its need for a single, all-embracing enemy which is assumed to pull the wires of every resistance to the party's power. The term "paranoia" is used here not to imply that the phenomenon in question is due to psychotic processes in either the leaders or the mass following of totalitarian parties, but merely to describe, through a convenient psychological analogy, the ideological mechanism of projection which ascribes the regime's drive for unlimited power to an imagined all-enemy. The essential point is that in the nature of totalitarianism, any independent force—either inside or outside the state—is regarded as ultimately hostile; the concept of "two camps" and that of "unlimited aims" are two sides of the same phenomenon. . . .

### THE SOVIET DILEMMA IN EASTERN EUROPE

If we now turn to interstate and interparty relations within the Communist camp, we seem at first sight to have entered an area where ideology is adapted quite unceremoniously to the changing requirements of practical politics. Lenin, having barely seized power in Russia and looking forward to an early spreading of Communist revolution, could talk airily enough about the sovereign equality and fraternal solidarity of sovereign "socialist" states. Stalin, having determined after the failure of short-term revolutionary hope to concentrate on "socialism in a single country," came to regard international communism as a mere tool of Soviet power, and to believe that revolutionary victories without the backing of Soviet arms were neither possible nor desirable; he wanted no sovereign Communist allies, only satellites, and he got them in postwar Eastern Europe.

The independent victories of the Yugoslav Communists at the end of the war and of the Chinese Communists in 1949 nevertheless posed the problem he had sought to avoid, and thus required a revision of policy and ideology. But, so one argument goes, the stubborn old man had lost the flexibility to accept the situation; he precipitated a needless quarrel with the Yugoslavs and generally prevented the necessary adjustment while he lived. His heirs, however, hastened to correct his mistakes and to put inter-Communist relations back on a basis of sovereign equality and diplomatic give-and-take, not only with China and Yugoslavia but, after some trial and error, with all Communist states. Or did they?

In the above "common sense" account, not only the facts of the final phase are wrong; by deliberately neglecting the ideological aspect, it loses sight of all the real difficulties and contradictions which remain inherent in the situation. Because the Soviet Union is both a great power and a single-party state tied to an international ideology, it cannot be content either to oppress and exploit other Communist states or to come to terms with them on a basis of expediency; it must act in a way that will ensure the ideological unity of the Communist "camp" and its own authority at the center.

Stalin's insistence on making the "leading role of the Soviet Union" an article of the international creed expressed not just the idiosyncrasies of a power-mad tyrant, but his perception of one side of the dilemma—the risk that a recognition of the sovereign equality of other Communist states might loosen the solidarity of the "camp" in its dealings with the non-Communist world, and weaken the ideological authority of the Soviet party leaders, with ultimate repercussions on their position in the Soviet Union itself. His successors disavowed him because his Yugoslav policy had failed, and because they perceived the other side of the dilemma— that rigid insistence on Soviet hegemony might break up the unity of the "camp" even more quickly, and might in particular lead to open conflict with China. But by going to Peiping and Belgrade and admitting the "mistakes" of Stalin's "Great Russian chauvinism" (as well as the "mistakes" of his internal terrorist regime), they precipitated the very crisis of authority which he had feared.

## THE REASSERTION OF SOVIET PRIMACY

Even Khrushchev and his associates, however, never intended to grant effective sovereign equality to the other Communist satellite regimes of Eastern Europe, which in contrast to Yugoslavia and

China had come into being exclusively through the pressure of Soviet power; they merely had planned to make the satellite regimes more viable by reducing Soviet economic exploitation and administrative interference, while maintaining full policy control. In the one case in which not full sovereignty, but at least effective internal autonomy, was in fact granted—the case of Poland—the Soviet leaders were forced to act against their will as a result of open local defiance in a critical international situation. To say that the other East European participants in the Moscow twelve-party meeting of last November, or for that matter the participants from Outer Mongolia and North Korea, represented "governments of sovereign countries" is to mistake the fancies of Communist propaganda for political facts. Nor do the facts bear out the interpretation that the outcome of the conference showed the Soviet leaders' willingness to rely in their future relations with these "sovereign governments" on the give-and-take of diplomacy. Rather, they confirm the view that the need for a single center of international authority is inherent in the Soviet Communist Party's conception of its own role and in its ideology.

The real purpose of that conference was to exploit the recent successes of the Soviet Union as a military and economic power in order to restore the indispensable but lately damaged ideological authority of its leaders in the international Communist movement. The principle of "proletarian internationalism"—*i.e.,* unity in foreign policy—had been recognized by all participants, including for the first time in many years the Yugoslavs, before the conference started. Now Moscow was aiming at the further recognition both of its own leadership role and of the need for doctrinal unity, a joint struggle against "revisionism" on the basis of common principles, abolishing once and for all the heresy of "polycentrism" (*i.e.,* the concept of a plurality of truly autonomous Communist movements).

As it turned out, the Yugoslavs refused both propositions, while the Polish Communists and the nonruling but important Italian Communist Party accepted them only with mental reservations, insisting in practice on their right to decide for themselves how the "common principles" would be applied in their own countries.

As opposed to this partial failure, however, Moscow was successful in winning full acceptance of the new dispensations by the Chinese Communists and the satellites, as well as in getting agreement on a new, elaborate international liaison machinery within the secretariat of the Soviet Communist Central Committee, in implementation of its renewed claim to international authority.

Moscow's partial failure, therefore, does not indicate that the Soviets will be content with less than they demanded, but that conflict continues. The Soviet press has already reactivated its campaign against Polish "revisionist" ideologies, insisting to Mr. Gomulka that revisionism is the chief internal danger in *all* Communist movements, including that of Poland. Moreover, the proposition defending a Communist party's autonomy in deciding its policy—conceded in principle at the time of Khrushchev's Belgrade visit and at the Twentieth CPSU Congress—is now singled out as a "revisionist" heresy; increasingly the example of Imre Nagy is invoked to show how a demand for autonomy led him down a "road" of "betrayal" and finally "counterrevolution." While the methods of Khrushchev remain conspicuously different from those of Stalin, the logic of the one-party regime, which requires insistence on Soviet authority as a precondition for unity both in foreign policy and in ideological principles, has forced the present first secretary to reassert some of the very doctrines he rashly threw overboard in 1955-56.

# THE SOVIET-YUGOSLAV DISPUTE RENEWED

## [1958]

SPEECH BY TITO (APRIL 22, 1958) *

The idea of a crusade against communism is today an ideological foundation for the achievement of various imperialist aims, and especially of new forms of colonial subjugation. This constitutes not only a severe impediment to the solution of present-day international controversies and to peaceful cooperation and coexistence between states with different social systems, but also strongly heightens the permanent danger of war on a world scale.

The division of the world into blocs has been the cause, not of economic integration and fruitful international cooperation in this respect, but of fragmentation of the world's economy, which has led to tremendous damage to nations.

Strategic military bases are being created in Europe, Asia and Africa at the most rapid pace and numerous missile-launching platforms are being set up, a strategic military encirclement thus being forced around the Soviet Union and other Eastern countries.

This policy of military blocs adopted by the United States and other Western powers was particularly affected by the victory of the Chinese revolution. It is necessary to reiterate that this course of the West also was affected by Stalin's inflexible policy, which resulted in the isolation and weakening of the positions of the Soviet Union in the world.

This contributed to the strengthening of the positions of the Western countries, headed by the United States, which vindicated the formation of the Atlantic pact and of the strategic bases precisely by Stalin's power policy and inflexibility, and temporarily

---

* Delivered at the Seventh Congress of the League of Communists of Yugoslavia, Ljubljana. These selections are from the translation of excerpts in *Current History,* July 1958. Reprinted by permission.

won for it the moral support of a great part of international public opinion. Such was the state of affairs in international relations up to 1953.

After Stalin's death, the Soviet Union gradually altered its methods. It took the initiative in foreign policy and endeavored, by negotiation, even at the summit level, to reach any sort of agreement, at least on the settlement, in part, of some international problems.

A relaxation of tension was greatly helped by the extremely significant preliminary measures undertaken by the Soviet Union, such as the beginning of normalization of relations with Yugoslavia and the adoption of the Belgrade Declaration, the settlement of the Austrian issue, the withdrawal of Soviet troops from the territory of China, Austria and Finland, the renunciation of territorial claims against Turkey, the liquidation of mixed companies in China and in the other Eastern countries of People's Democracy and the liberalization of the relations with them, the recognition of the independent position of the young Asian and African countries, and so forth.

This new positive development of Soviet foreign policy, on the one hand, exercised a strong influence on the relaxation of international tension and, on the other, gradually also improved the isolated position of the Soviet Union in the world.

After the arrival of the Soviet delegation in Yugoslavia in 1955, and the visit of our delegation in Moscow in 1956, a fertile atmosphere for very successful progress in the creation of mutual confidence and cooperation [between the Soviet Union and Yugoslavia] was created.

However, clouds in our common sky appeared again. Because of the events in Hungary, a tense situation was again created between us and the Soviet Union, but during our talks with the Soviet leaders in Rumania, in August, 1957, this matter was taken off the agenda. On that occasion, we cleared up some misunderstandings and there remained very little of what could impede our full cooperation and friendly relations.

The important thing is that this is now a thing of the past. It is important that we set out along a new, proper road of cooperation and that we should forget all those past things that could influence the existing and future good, friendly relations.

The essential thing is that between us there is more confidence; that we understand each other; that there exists a friendly and sincere exchange of opinions and experiences on the basis of which broad cooperation is developing.

Certain comrades in the Soviet bloc countries still manifest tendencies of distrust, as well as evidence of wrong estimates of the internal development in our country. Suspicion is expressed with regard to the socialist character of Yugoslavia. There is talk of her anarchist trade union development.

Inside the party it is stressed, and then further spread, that a tactical attitude should be taken in connection with Yugoslavia, that she should be re-educated and again brought into the camp of socialism and so forth.

\*     \*     \*

It would be very useful if these comrades would finally abandon such absurd tendencies, which are only harmful and prevent the proper development of our relations.

We are often accused of not being internationalists, because we are not in the camp. These comrades seem to think that internationalism is conditioned by adherence to the camp and not to the socialist world, in the broader sense. They do not start out from what sort of policy you are conducting, whether you are loyal to the principles of internationalism, which means solidarity with the workers and progressive movements in a universal sense, whether you are building socialism in a way that strengthens socialist ideas, not only inside the country but generally speaking. . . .

Internationalism cannot be divided into narrow and broad areas, into the camp and the non-camp groups, because it is universal in the sense that it develops the science of Marxism and Leninism and increases its practical applications.

Internationalism, then, is practice—not words and propaganda.

This should be borne in mind by those who like to make the classifications internationalists and non-internationalists.

In the period between the Sixth and Seventh Congress of the League of Communists of Yugoslavia, the international workers' movement experienced various phases of the progress, but also of stagnation. . . .

During the last few years of the Stalin period, the workers movement in the world, especially its vanguard, suffered greatly. In this respect, it not only stagnated but even retrogressed. The reasons for this were to be found in the first place, in the dependent policies conducted by the various parties whose leaderships have been accustomed to receiving and implementing directives from outside, regardless of whether these directives were the right ones or not for the country concerned.

This was typical up to the Twentieth Congress of the Communist Party of the Soviet Union. As a result of such policy the growingly frequent failures experienced by the working class in its struggle caused a lack of perspective and apathy, which was most detrimental to the forces of socialism in the world at large. Moreover, the vanguard of the working class was going through the crisis of a split.

But there is no doubt that the pressure on Socialist Yugoslavia, after 1948, was the hardest blow against the working class because, for the first time since the October Revolution, it aroused doubts as to the correctness of the policy conducted by a country that throughout this whole period, was a beacon to the international workers' movement. This resulted in the fact that in the struggle of the working class, the revolutionary blade was blunted, a matter that the enemies of socialism—the international reactionaries—exploited to the utmost.

A significant positive factor and turning point in this respect was the Twentieth Congress of the Communist Party of the Soviet Union, at which the mistakes made during the Stalin period were subjected to sharp criticism, mistakes that were made both in the internal life and development of the Soviet Union and in its foreign policy.

The new course taken by the Soviet leaders, . . . has given rise to new forms of cooperation between Socialist countries, beginning with non-interference in their internal development and the acknowledgement that specific conditions in every country is one of the major factors in the successful building up of socialism.

It is especially important that the old forms of cooperation are being gradually abandoned and that bilateral relations are being adopted. This does not in any way mean that there is a weakening of the Socialist world, or of its unity and effectiveness, but precisely the opposite—this makes possible the mobilization of all the forces of socialism.

In this way there ensues a wealth of new forms and experiences that are placed in the service of socialism because there is a liberation of creative thought that, obstructed by former forms of cooperation, was completely dormant in the present phase of development. Because of this attitude of ours regarding cooperation between Communist parties and progressive movements in the world in general, we could not sign the declaration of the twelve Communist and workers' parties of the Socialist countries, in Moscow.

## Note from the USSR Foreign Ministry to the Yugoslav Embassy in Moscow (May 27, 1958) *

The Ministry of Foreign Affairs of the Union of Soviet Socialist Republics pays its respects to the Embassy of the Federal People's Republic of Yugoslavia and, on the instructions of the U.S.S.R. government, has the honor to address the F.P.R.Y. government in connection with the economic agreements of Jan. 12, 1956, and Aug. 1, 1956. These agreements provide that the Soviet Union will extend credit to Yugoslavia in the period 1957-1964 to finance the construction of an aluminum plant, to pay for equipment for fertilizer plants and other enterprises and also for the work of designing and other work stipulated in the agreement.

---

* This letter and the two that follow were printed in *Pravda* and *Izvestia*, July 1, 1958. Reprinted from the translation of the complete text in *The Current Digest of the Soviet Press* (New York), Vol. X, No. 26. Copyright; reprinted by permission.

It has now become necessary to revise the period for the credits granted Yugoslavia under the above agreements. This necessity has arisen in connection with the decision adopted recently in the Soviet Union to step up the development of the chemical industry, particularly the production of synthetic materials and goods made therefrom, to meet the demands of the population and the needs of the national economy. This will require additional large capital investments in the U.S.S.R. chemical industry during the next few years. Therefore the Soviet government is making some changes in its financial plans for the purpose of ensuring the most effective and economical use of its financial resources.

Due to this circumstance the U.S.S.R. government is faced with the necessity of proposing later dates for the use of the credits extended to Yugoslavia, namely:

Under the agreement of Jan. 12, 1956, in the section concerning the further use of credit, to establish that this credit will be used in the period 1962-1969;

In the agreement of Aug. 1, 1956, to establish that the credit will be used in 1963-1969.

In accord with the above changes in the dates for the use of credits there should also be corresponding changes in the dates for the deliveries of equipment and for the carrying out of the work of designing and the other work provided for by the agreements.

However, if the F.P.R.Y. government so desires, Soviet foreign trade organizations could furnish equipment to Yugoslav organizations and carry out the designing and other work during the periods established by the protocols of July 29, 1957, and supply various equipment in accord with the protocol of Aug. 2, 1956, although not on credit but with payment to be paid for by current trade.

During the delay before the enterprises provided for in the agreements go into operation, including the fertilizer plants, the Soviet side, if the Yugoslav side so desires, could furnish Yugoslavia with a certain quantity of mineral fertilizers and also other industrial products, by agreement of the sides, on terms of mutual exchange of goods.

It is the view of the Soviet government that the proposals set forth above are in accord with the principles of economic co-operation between states and would be advantageous to both sides. The U.S.S.R. government expresses confidence that the F.P.R.Y. government will understand the proposals set forth in this note correctly and will be favorable toward them.

The proposed changes in the agreements of Jan. 12, 1956, and Aug. 1, 1956, could be formalized, depending on the desire of the F.P.R.Y. government, either by an exchange of notes or by the signing of supplementary protocols to these agreements.

The proposal relating to the agreement of Aug. 1, 1956, has been cleared with the government of the German Democratic Republic, which is one of the parties to this agreement.

## NOTE FROM THE YUGOSLAV STATE SECRETARIAT FOR FOREIGN AFFAIRS TO THE USSR EMBASSY IN BELGRADE (JUNE 3, 1958)

The State Secretariat for Foreign Affairs of the Federal People's Republic of Yugoslavia pays its respects to the Embassy of the Union of Soviet Socialist Republics and, on the instructions of the F.P.R.Y. government, has the honor to address the following to the U.S.S.R. government in connection with the May 27, 1958, note from the U.S.S.R. government bearing on the agreements of Jan. 12, 1956, and Aug. 1, 1956, between the two governments.

The F.P.R.Y. government cannot accept the proposals of the U.S.S.R. government set forth in the afore-mentioned note on the establishment of later periods for Yugoslavia's use of credits than those stipulated in the agreement of Jan. 12, 1956, the protocol to this agreement of July 29, 1957, the agreement of Aug. 1, 1956, and the July 29, 1956, protocol to this agreement, just as it cannot accept the proposals for deliveries of equipment to Yugoslav organizations and the conduct of the work of designing and other work to be paid for by current exchange of goods.

In this regard the F.P.R.Y. government wishes to emphasize that the rights and obligations of the two countries in this sphere are clearly defined in the afore-mentioned agreements not only with regard to agreement in principle but also in regard to the stipulation of the means and conditions for the fulfillment of these agreements.

Both the above agreements were the result of a lengthy and comprehensive examination of mutual economic relations, and also of mutual possibilities for fulfilling the obligations deriving from these agreements.

The proposals set forth in the U.S.S.R. government's note of May 27, 1958, would mean a change in the F.P.R.Y.'s current and long-range national economic plans in the sense of a change in the already authorized distribution of the national income, particularly at the expense of investments and, correspondingly, at the expense of the living standards of the population. Moreover, in view of the fact that the construction of certain projects provided for in the above agreements has already been partially begun and that the Yugoslav side has set up an organization which is working toward this, as well as of the fact that considerable forces and resources are engaged there, any postponement of the periods provided for by the agreements would inflict direct damage on Yugoslavia and on the Yugoslav economy.

On the basis of the above and also of the fact that the F.P.R.Y. government is guided in its international relations by consistent respect for and observance of agreements and international obligations and that consequently it has every right to expect the Soviet Union as well to respect its obligations, it cannot give consideration to the reasons given in the U.S.S.R. government's note.

The F.P.R.Y. government cannot forbear mentioning the fact that the Soviet side has already on one occasion raised the question of postponing the periods for the fulfillment of these agreements and that the Yugoslav side at that time, in order to show maximum good will, and despite considerable material loss, even went to extreme limits to meet the wishes of the Soviet side and accepted the proposed postponement.

In its note of May 27 the government of the Soviet Union again proposes, not even a full ten months later, to postpone the dates of fulfillment, which would mean in regard to the initial agreements that there would be a six- to ten-year postponement under one agreement and a seven- to 12-year postponement under the other.

The F.P.R.Y. government should also point out that such actions by the U.S.S.R. government introduce uncertainty into the economic relations between the F.P.R.Y. and the U.S.S.R., which can only be damaging to over-all normal relations between our countries. The F.P.R.Y. government should also call attention to the responsibility which will rest on the U.S.S.R. government for the damage inflicted on the Yugoslav economy should the Soviet government·adhere to its position. In such case the F.P.R.Y. government reserves the right to demand just compensation.

On the basis of the above, the F.P.R.Y. government expects that the U.S.S.R. government will revise its position outlined in its note of May 27, 1958, in favor of strict observance of the obligations it assumed under the afore-mentioned agreements.

The State Secretariat for Foreign Affairs takes advantage of this opportunity to pay its respects to the Embassy of the Union of Soviet Socialist Republics.

NOTE FROM THE USSR FOREIGN MINISTRY TO THE YUGOSLAV EMBASSY IN MOSCOW (JUNE 28, 1958)

The Ministry of Foreign Affairs of the Union of Soviet Socialist Republics pays its respects to the Embassy of the Federal People's Republic of Yugoslavia and, on the instructions of the Soviet government, has the honor to communicate the following in connection with the June 3, 1958, note from the F.P.R.Y. State Secretariat for Foreign Affairs.

In its note of May 27, 1958, the U.S.S.R. government proposed to the F.P.R.Y. government that the periods for fulfillment of the credits granted to Yugoslavia by the Soviet Union under the economic agreements of Jan. 12, 1956, and Aug. 1, 1956, be revised. In its note the U.S.S.R. government set forth the motives which prompted it to make this proposal and expressed confidence that the F.P.R.Y. government would understand this step by the Soviet Union correctly.

However, the F.P.R.Y. government did not even agree to discuss the substance of the Soviet Union's proposal and has taken a position which can only evoke surprise. The content and tone of the June 3 note and also the Yugoslav side's entire approach to this problem, particularly the baseless declaration that the U.S.S.R. has supposedly broken this agreement, represent an attempt to depict the Soviet Union's position on Soviet-Yugoslav economic relations in a false light and at the same time to instill doubts about the Soviet Union's fulfillment of its obligations under international agreements.

It is superfluous to state that the Soviet Union, following a policy aimed at strengthening peace and developing cooperation among all states, carries out its international obligations strictly.

It is also common knowledge that an alteration in particular terms of agreements as a result of negotiations between the sides is not beyond the bounds of the normal, generally recognized practice of states in international agreements and that the fact that agreements have been concluded does not deprive the sides of the right to raise the question of altering certain terms of the agreements.

The Soviet government, in making the afore-mentioned proposal, took into account the interests of the Yugoslav side as well. This is apparent from the fact that in proposing to postpone the dates for the use of the credits and, correspondingly, the dates for the deliveries of equipment and for the work of designing and the other work provided for in the agreements, the Soviet side declared its readiness during the delay before the enterprises go into operation to supply Yugoslavia with the industrial products which are to be produced by these enterprises, with payment to be made through current trade. In this case it is assumed, of course, that these goods would be supplied at mutually advantageous world prices. At the same time—if this should be more acceptable to Yugoslavia —the Soviet government expressed readiness to continue, also on the basis of current trade, deliveries of equipment in the periods specified and to carry out the work of designing and the other work provided in the agreements. This in itself shows that the

Soviet government approached this question in a spirit of good will.

As was stated in the Soviet note of May 27, the Soviet government's proposal to alter the periods for the use of the credits grew out of new demands which have arisen in the Soviet Union for large capital investments to develop the chemical industry. In addition, it also took into account the declarations of the Yugoslav side to the effect that relations between the Soviet Union and the F.P.R.Y. should be based on principles of mutual advantage. The Soviet side proceeds on the assumption that these declarations reflect the reasoned position of the Yugoslav government and its desire to build the economic ties between our countries on the basis of the afore-mentioned principle. Thus, the point in question is that of bringing the terms of the economic agreements between the U.S.S.R. and Yugoslavia closer to the principles on which mutually advantageous agreements between states are usually concluded.

In proposing a postponement of the period in which the credits are to be used, which would in some measure balance the advantages of the agreements for both sides and not for Yugoslavia alone, the Soviet government does not propose to alter the remaining terms of the agreements, although these terms are advantageous for the F.P.R.Y. exclusively and are not applied in cases in which the sides proceed solely from the purely commercial aspects of mutual advantage. This also has to be taken into account in considering the Soviet proposal.

In view of the above, the Soviet government would consider it correct for representatives of both governments to meet in the near future for a businesslike discussion of the questions raised in the Soviet note of May 27, and to reach an agreement on introducing changes in the agreements of Jan. 12, 1956, and Aug. 1, 1956, as proposed by the U.S.S.R. government.

For its part the Soviet government has entrusted the conduct of the negotiations to the State Committee for Foreign Economic Relations.

## Speech by Khrushchev (June 3, 1958) *

I would not like to offend anyone, but at the same time it is impossible not to raise the question which agitates honest Communists everywhere. Why do the imperialist rulers, who aspire to wipe the socialist states from the face of the earth and suppress the Communist movement, nonetheless finance one of the socialist countries and give it easy credit and free handouts? (*Laughter, applause.*) No one really believes that there are two socialisms in the world—one which is fiercely hated by world reaction and one which is acceptable to the imperialists, which has their aid and support. (*Laughter in the hall, applause.*) . . .

When the imperialists decide to "aid" a socialist state, they naturally don't do this in order to strengthen it. The monopolist circles of the United States can in no way be suspected of being interested in strengthening socialism and developing Marxist-Leninist theory. (*Laughter in the hall, applause.*) Representatives of this country claim that we are departing from Marxism-Leninism and that they stand on correct positions. This presents quite a curious situation—the imperialists want to "develop" Marxism-Leninism through this country. (*Laughter in the hall.*) It would be appropriate to recall the words of Bebel: If your enemy praises you, think back on what stupidity you have committed. (*Laughter in the hall, prolonged applause.*) . . .

The Communist Parties preserve and safeguard the unity of their ranks as the apple of their eye. They wage a constant struggle against revisionism and dogmatism. In this struggle the Communist Parties naturally direct their main fire against the revisionists, as scouts of the imperialist camp. The ancient legend of the Trojan horse is well known. When the enemies could not win the city of Troy by siege and attack they "presented" the Trojans with a wooden horse. Inside it they concealed their own people to open the gates of the city by night.

---

* Delivered at the Seventh Congress of the Bulgarian Communist Party, in Sofia, printed in *Pravda,* June 4, 1958. These selections are from the translation of a condensed text in *The Current Digest of the Soviet Press* (New York), Vol. X, No. 22. Copyright; reprinted by permission.

Modern revisionists represent such a Trojan horse. (*Shouts of "That's right!" Applause.*)    The revisionists are trying to bore at the revolutionary parties from within, to undermine their unity and introduce disorder and confusion in Marxist-Leninist ideology.    (*Shouts of "They won't succeed!" Applause.*)

Comrades!    The Communist and Workers' Parties in their historic declaration unanimously condemned revisionism.    They stated that in the present situation it is the chief danger to the international Communist movement.    Revisionism is right-wing opportunism, a manifestation of bourgeois ideology which paralyzes the revolutionary energy of the working class and demands the preservation or restoration of capitalism.    It was quite legitimately emphasized in the declaration that the "existence of bourgeois influence is an internal source of revisionism, while surrender to the pressure of imperialism is its external source."

The Communists of all countries have enthusiastically approved the declaration adopted at the conference of the fraternal parties of the socialist countries and have recognized it as a basic program document of the international Communist movement which gives a profound Marxist-Leninist analysis of the basic general laws of social development in the modern epoch and defines with unusual clarity the tasks of the world Communist movement.

Of all the Communist and Workers' Parties, only one party— the Yugoslav Communist League—expressed disagreement with the declaration, thus counterposing itself to all the Marxist-Leninist parties of the world.    This position of the Yugoslav leaders is expressed most clearly in the Yugoslav Communist League draft program and in the work of its seventh Congress.    All the Communist and Workers' Parties have manifested their complete unity by resolutely condemning the revisionist propositions of the Yugoslav Communist League draft program, propositions contrary to Marxism-Leninism, and the corrupt position taken by the Yugoslav leaders. . . .

Our parties' relations with the Yugoslav Communist League have their own history.    It is necessary to recall at this time some of the important moments in this history.

You know that good relations existed between Yugoslavia and

the Soviet Union up to 1948, relations forged in the common struggle against the fascist invaders in World War II and in the early postwar years. . . . Then there was a deterioration in the relations between the Yugoslav Communist Party and the other fraternal parties.

In 1948 the Information Bureau conference adopted a resolution "On the Situation in the Communist Party of Yugoslavia." This resolution contained legitimate criticism of the work of the Yugoslav Communist Party on a number of questions of principle. It was basically correct and corresponded to the interests of the revolutionary movement. Later, in 1949-1953, conflict arose between the Yugoslav Communist Party and the other fraternal parties. In the course of this struggle mistakes were made and a stratification appeared which damaged our common cause.

With full awareness of its responsibility to our countries and peoples and to the international Communist movement, the Communist Party of the Soviet Union took the initiative in seeking to liquidate this conflict, achieve a normalization of relations between our countries and establish contact and cooperation between the C.P.S.U. and the Yugoslav Communist League on a Marxist-Leninist basis. With this goal and on our initiative, talks were held in May-June, 1955, between representatives of the Soviet Union and Yugoslavia. These talks concluded in the signing of the Belgrade Declaration. It is extremely important to note that during the Belgrade talks Comrade Tito said that our relations should begin on a new basis so as not to resurrect the past. We willingly agreed to this and for our part did everything possible to strengthen friendly relations. In so doing we were aware that there were still ideological differences between our parties on a number of important questions. Much restraint and patience were manifested by our side in order to achieve a unity of views on the basis of principles, on the basis of Marxism-Leninism.

Life has shown, however, that the burden of the past weighed too heavily on the Yugoslav leaders and it turned out that they were not in a position to abandon their erroneous positions and stand firmly on positions of Marxism-Leninism. The Yugoslav leaders, even after relations had been normalized, continued to make anti-Soviet statements and to issue attacks against the socialist camp and the fraternal Communist Parties. The Yugoslav leaders inflicted particularly great damage to the cause of socialism by their public statements and their actions during the Hungarian events. During the counterrevolutionary revolt in Budapest, the Yugoslav Embassy became, in effect, a center for those who began the fight against the people's democratic system in Hungary, a haven for the capitulatory and traitorous Nagy-Losonczy group. Recall the unprecedented speech made by Comrade Tito in Pula, in which the Hungarian rebels were defended, but the U.S.S.R.'s fraternal aid to the Hungarian people was called "Soviet intervention," a speech which contained direct appeals to certain forces in the other socialist countries to follow the so-called "Yugoslav course."

We know very well what this course is, comrades. Let any who so desire follow this course. But parties which really stand on the positions of Marxism-Leninism will not follow it. (*Applause*.) Our socialist countries are resolutely following the Marxist-Leninist compass in moving to communism. (*Prolonged applause*.) . . .

Comrades! I recall one of the conversations I had with the Yugoslav leaders in 1956, when we were exchanging views during a friendly talk. In speaking of our disagreements I called the attention of Comrade Tito at that time to the need for a more profound analysis of the events and of our mutual relations, of correctly appraising the situation that had developed so as to achieve unity of views on a principled basis more rapidly. In doing so I reminded them of the famous expression "Everyone in the company is in step except one soldier" and asked them who should change, the company or the soldier? (*Animation in the hall*.) Koca Popovic, who was present at the conversation, raised the question:

"But who is the company and who is the soldier?"

To this retort I replied: "You think over who is the company and who is the soldier."

"In any case," I said, "every soldier knows that a company is a company and that a soldier is only a part of the company and therefore it is not the company which must get in step with the soldier, but vice-versa. (*Animation in the hall, applause.*) If you take a different stand, then say forthrightly that you are not a soldier of this Communist company, which is marching together in step, guided by Marxism-Leninism.". . .

## SPEECH BY TITO (JUNE 15, 1958) *

Some might think that the present campaign against socialist Yugoslavia was caused by certain theoretical formulations in the Program of the League of the Communists of Yugoslavia and in the reports at the Seventh Congress of the League. This is not so. This campaign has deeper roots. It was organized long before our Congress, when neither the Program nor the reports were known. The Program of the League was only a pretext for the attack on the League of the Communists, and on Yugoslavia. The main reason for this campaign is our refusal to sign the Declaration of the Twelve Parties, issued in Moscow in November, 1957, and our refusal to join the so-called socialist camp for reasons long well-known to everybody and consisting simply in our opposition to the division of the world into camps.

Refusal to sign the Moscow Declaration and to join the socialist camp does not mean that we are not for the greatest cooperation with all socialist countries. It means, on the contrary, that we are for such cooperation in all fields but that in the present tense international situation we believe it is more useful to follow a constructive peace policy, together with other peaceloving countries which also do not belong to either bloc, than to join the bloc and thus still more aggravate a world situation which is tense enough. In accordance with our foreign policy, with the principle of coexistence and the need of cooperation with all countries, that is, in accordance with our peace policy in general, we believe it is necessary to make every effort not to aggravate the world situation and to avoid an armed conflict. We believe that cooperation should be established with all countries instead of a limitation to

---

* Delivered at Labin, Yugoslavia. Reprinted from *Yugoslav Facts and Views*, No. 56, published by the Yugoslav Information Center, New York.

two camps which go on clashing with each other and some day may cause war.

In connection with the Program and the reports at the Seventh Congress, which served as a pretext for starting the violent and hardly comradely campaign against our country and the League of the Communists, I must re-emphasize that the quotations from the Program and the reports used today in the press and speeches in the eastern countries, and especially in China, are inaccurate and sometimes falsified, or taken out of context so as to give an entirely wrong picture of our stands. . . .

In regard to Yugoslav-Soviet relations and cooperation, I said in my report as follows: "Yugoslav-Soviet relations, based on the Belgrade Declaration, are developing today very successfully. Trade is also expanding vastly. A number of agreements has been made, for instance, on the construction of industrial enterprises in Yugoslavia worth 110 million dollars, on commodity credits of 54 million dollars, on scientific-technical cooperation, on a loan in gold or foreign exchange to the amount of 30 million dollars, on cooperation in the field of atomic energy. In addition, a cultural-exchange convention was signed already promoting wide cooperation; also a convention on regulation of dual citizenship; and a special agreement on the construction of an aluminum combine and a fertilizer factory, and so on.

"All this proves that normalization and establishment of good and friendly relations have acquired a material basis in economic cooperation, of great value to both countries."

So that is what I said. Did I attack? I did not. Did I say something that was not true? I did not, for this is true. And what can I do if they are annoyed by my saying that it would be valuable to both countries? One can see from this that I did not minimize Soviet aid or attack the Soviet Union, but that I realistically presented the facts as they were. And I quite rightly said this cooperation benefited both countries. I did not touch upon which country would benefit more. And even now I would not say that we would not have benefited greatly if they had not broken the agreements. We would have. . . .

Evidently we deal here with an attempt to slander our country in an easy way, and that is why only what can mislead and embitter the public of these countries is presented to it. And when people who do not know the reality are served only what is not good, they naturally may sometimes become angry. But I tell you that in almost all these countries the great majority of people no longer believe these bad things, for they say: "In 1948 you did the same and later admitted that you had made a mistake. Who can assure us that now you are not doing the same, and that tomorrow you will not say that it was a mistake again?". . .

At the Seventh Congress of the Communist Party of Bulgaria, recently held in Sofia, comrade Khrushchev came out with a speech in which, among other things, he quite unjustifiably attacked Yugoslavia and the leaders of the League of the Communists of Yugoslavia in terms which have no relation to comradely criticism. He called us a "Trojan horse," with the aid of which western imperialists intend to destroy the socialist countries. In this speech, he denounced not only the Yugoslav leaders but also our peoples. Our people have suffered a good deal because of Stalin's policy of economic and political pressure and therefore we take it very hard when comrade Khrushchev repeats and justifies this today, although at the 20th Congress of the Communist Party of the Soviet Union he sharply condemned this policy.

Speaking of us as an agency of the class enemy in the workers' movement, comrade Khrushchev said in Sofia: "Monopoly circles of the U.S. should by no means be suspected of having an interest in strengthening socialism and in the development of the Marxist-Leninist theory. The representatives of that country (Yugoslavia) claim that we depart from Marxism-Leninism while they (we, the Yugoslavs) maintain correct positions. A rather strange situation arises: the imperialists want to 'develop' Marxism-Leninism through that country (Yugoslavia)."

So, he ironically insinuates that we have a pact with America, which—I agree—doesn't like socialism.

I quite agree that the Americans are not giving us assistance so that socialism may win in Yugoslavia—just as in 1921 and 1922, when during the great calamities and droughts they gave assistance to the Soviet Union, the Americans did not wish to strengthen Soviet power. At that time they were giving great assistance because there was famine in the Soviet Union. The Americans began to furnish aid to us after 1949, not that socialism might win in our country—because they do not like socialism and they do not conceal this—but because, on the one hand we were threatened with famine and, on the other hand, Yugoslavia could thus more easily fight off Stalin's pressures and preserve her independence.

And if perhaps some American circles cherished other hopes, this was not our concern. Stalin's policy of economic blockade and threat inflicted enormous damage on Yugoslavia, amounting in the estimate of experts to about two billion dollars. Therefore the tripartite assistance by the United States, Britain and France was of much benefit to Yugoslavia, then in trouble because of the blockade and Cominform pressure. And by extending this aid, the United States, Britain and France gained a great deal in moral respect in the world.

Comrade Khrushchev often repeats that socialism cannot be built on American wheat. I think that he who knows how, can do it; and he who does not know how, cannot build socialism even on his own wheat. . . .

In his speech in Sofia, comrade Khrushchev said many insulting things about Yugoslavia and her leaders, but most astonishing of all is that he now takes . . . the position of defender of the ill-famed Cominform Resolution—a document which in the history of socialist relations and the international workers' movement will remain a shameful stain. When today one reads this so-called Resolution, one can see on what monstrous inventions and calumnies it was founded to blacken our Party and our country. It is far more surprising that in the present campaign—not discussion—comrade Khrushchev and others should revive this act so disgraceful in socialism. Comrade Khrushchev likes to tell, supposedly as a joke, a Russian proverb which in our language reads: "In a fight, any stick is handy." I think this is a rather poor and discredited weapon in the present so-called discussion or, better, unprincipled campaign against socialist Yugoslavia.

Logically, just as they have pulled out the Cominform Resolution to attack Yugoslavia, we, too, would have to dig into the past and bring out various misdeeds against our country and people in the course of more than four years, and our arguments against Stalin's fabricated charges from 1948 on. But where would this get us?

I am reproached for having spoken in my expose of Stalin's policies as negative and harmful to Yugoslavia, to some small countries and to the Soviet Union itself. However, I believe that I said nothing sharper about Stalin than had been said at the 20th Congress of the Communist Party of the Soviet Union. Besides, the facts I brought out have long been known to the whole world. This is history, the history of Stalin's policy of pressure, his incorrect policy, against Yugoslavia, and we must not, nor do we wish to, permit falsification of history. So, I brought this out only as historic facts, and nothing more. . . .

It seems that our fate is to have to build socialism in our country under incessant blows from all sides. And the heaviest blows come from those who should be our best and most faithful friends. It looks as if history had ordered us on this hard path so that development of socialism may be preserved from degeneration, so that socialism may come out of the present reign of chaos into the world with a moral strength that would assure it the road to final victory. . . .

## SPEECH BY KHRUSHCHEV (JULY 11, 1958) *

The Yugoslavs say that they supposedly stand outside of blocs, condemn the policy of forming blocs, etc. . . .

But what does it mean to stand aside, to ignore the family of socialist countries in our time, when a desperate class struggle is going on on a worldwide scale? To true Communists the maintenance of neutrality under conditions of acute class struggle means

---

* Delivered at the Fifth Congress of the German Socialist Unity Party, printed in *Pravda* and *Izvestia*, July 12, 1958. These selections are from the translation of excerpts in *The Current Digest of the Soviet Press*, Vol. X, No. 28. Copyright; reprinted by permission.

weakening the forces of the revolutionary movement, the forces of socialism, and aiding the enemies of the working class.

The Yugoslav leaders shout until they are hoarse that somebody is encroaching on their independence. But what independence are they talking about? They evidently find fidelity to Marxism-Leninism burdensome and they want to free themselves from it. If so, let them say this straight out; then everything will be clear and in order. (*Applause.*) . . .

The Yugoslav leaders claim that the Soviet Union and the Communist Party of the Soviet Union aspire to some sort of special role, to hegemony, that they want to give orders but that they, the Yugoslavs, won't agree to this. Such declarations are utter lies. It would be understandable if it were the propagandists of the imperialist camp who were trumpeting about this, but when people who call themselves Marxists talk this way, one involuntarily asks how they could sink to such vile slander.

And this slander is not directed at the Soviet Union alone. The authors of these malicious assertions are trying to defile the essence of our revolutionary struggle and defame our communist comradeship and socialist friendship. They distort the concept of the joining of efforts by the working class of all countries in the struggle against the yoke of capital and for the interests of the working people. For the working class consolidation does not mean the sacrifice of their own interests or subordination to someone. The working class of one country unites with the working class of other countries for the purpose of putting an end to capitalism, which has given rise to the policy of diktat, pressure and national oppression. (*Applause.*)

The Yugoslav leaders have chosen as the target of their attacks the section of the Declaration of the Conference of Representatives of the Communist and Workers' Parties of the Socialist Countries which notes the leading role of the Soviet Union and its Communist Party. But the Yugoslav leaders know very well that in the draft declaration, which was in their hands even before the conference, this point was missing. The section on the role of the U.S.S.R. and the Communist Party of the Soviet Union was introduced and approved at the conference itself not by the

C.P.S.U. delegation but by the representatives of the other fraternal parties. (*Applause.*)

What sort of attitude do we Communists of the Soviet Union take toward this matter?

I want to dwell on this because our enemies often employ the "Soviet hegemony" fabrication for their filthy aims and the Yugoslavs are playing into the enemy's hands by inflaming passions. They are setting traps for inexperienced people by playing on national pride and by trying to pound into people's heads the monstrous idea that all the Communist Parties have fallen under the power and control of a single party. We have already become accustomed to such slanderous inventions, since we cannot expect anything else from our enemies. But when people who call themselves Communists talk this way, we cannot but rebuff such assertions. (*Applause.*) . . .

The imperialists calculate that if they succeed in disparaging the Soviet Union's role, they will thereby succeed in disorganizing the international Communist and workers' movement and later in undermining completely the faith of the working class and the Communist Parties of other countries in the Communist Party of the Soviet Union as the vanguard of the international Communist movement and as the bastion of world peace. After that they would concentrate their fire on other Parties, apparently first of all the Chinese Communist Party. As long as the Soviet Union, the Chinese People's Republic and the other socialist countries are strong and as long as they are firmly united the imperialists will give all possible material encouragement to any disruptive activity against the unity of the socialist countries.

The conclusion arrived at by the fraternal Communist Parties concerning the role of the Soviet Union reflects the objective course of the world historic struggle for the victory of socialism and the triumph of Marxist-Leninist ideas. At the same time it is clear evidence of the unity of the Communist Parties of all countries. The enemies of communism and the slanderers have given battle on a very important question, and they should fully bear in mind that the international Communist movement will not permit any discrediting of the Soviet Union and will respond to any slanderous anti-Communist campaign by consolidating the ranks of the revolutionary forces even further. (*Prolonged applause.*)

There can be no question whatsoever of any sort of orders or of the subordination of certain parties or countries to others in the camp of the socialist countries and in the international Communist movement. Indeed there is no need for this; there is not even an agency which could give orders. . . .

## SPEECH BY KHRUSHCHEV (JULY 13, 1958) *

The Yugoslav leaders have been particularly worked up recently over the question of Soviet credits to Yugoslavia. The Soviet government's position and concrete proposals on this matter were set forth in the documents published in the Soviet press.

The Yugoslav leaders interpret our proposals in their own fashion. They declare that we are violating an equitable agreement. But if one of the sides desires to revise the agreement, this indicates that this side is not satisfied. Under pressure of changing circumstances each side has the right to raise the question of revising an agreement. We desire that the agreements with Yugoslavia correspond to the principles of equal rights and mutual advantage, that is, that they be in accord with, not contradictory to, the formula which Comrade Tito expounded in his speech at the Seventh Yugoslav Communist League Congress.

We favor terms which are genuinely mutually advantageous. Who would reject such terms? No one rejects something to his advantage.

The Yugoslav leaders are attempting to exert some kind of pressure on us, insisting that they be granted credits preferential to them and even appealing this matter before the public of the Western countries. The Yugoslav side knows quite well that the terms on which they obtained credits from the Soviet Union were very advantageous to them and at the same time not advantageous to us. So do not try to pressure us, it will do you no good, for

---

* Delivered at a meeting of Muscovites at the Sports Palace, Moscow, printed in *Pravda* and *Izvestia*, July 13, 1958. This selection is from the translation of excerpts in *The Current Digest of the Soviet Press*, Vol. X, No. 28. Copyright; reprinted by permission.

we do not want to enter into agreements whose terms would damage our socialist economy and would be advantageous to the other side only. They demand that we extract funds from our own economy and thereby curtail the possibilities for developing our economy, i.e., damage it in the interests of the other side. What is mutually advantageous about this?

We are amazed by the allegations that our proposals are illegal and that we should pay some sort of forfeit. We ask why they are illegal? Even laws are revised and amended when necessary. Even the marriage contract, which is considered a sacred bond, sometimes has to be dissolved. (*Animation in the hall.*) If one of the sides presents evidence that the other side has not been fulfilling its marital obligations, then even the church recognizes the right to dissolve such a marriage. (*Animation in the hall. Applause.*) It is true that there are some who, after assuming the bonds of matrimony, later break these bonds without even informing the other side of the fact and without paying any forfeit. (*Laughter in the hall.*)

We are prepared to trade and we will trade on the basis of mutual advantage. But the Yugoslavs are apparently striving not to obtain terms on the basis of mutual advantage but to get something outright without giving anything in return. We favor basing relations between socialist countries on mutual aid. But they would like for the socialist countries to grant them everything they need and afterwards declare that their economy is ahead of the economies of the other countries and even term this a result of the so-called special "Yugoslav road" to communism. (*Animation in the hall. Applause.*)

## SPEECH BY TITO (NOVEMBER 23, 1958) *

. . . the interests of our people are not alien to the interests of the peoples of the eastern countries. They are common to all of us. Our whole history has proven that we have very many things in common with them, and not only because we are Slavs

---

* Delivered in the Slovene city of Novo Mesto, Yugoslavia. Reprinted from *Yugoslav Facts and Views*, No. 73, published by the Yugoslav Information Center, New York.

but because we are internationalists. And just because we are internationalists, we have common interests in the construction of socialism and the difference between us, in our opinion, is only in the fact that this end is achieved in each country according to its possibilities, its abilities and its specific conditions. Our common interest, therefore, is the building of socialism, and relations between socialist countries should have proper and firm foundations, and should not be based on camps or on the domination of one party or country by another. We believe relations between socialist countries should be based on equality. . . .

I wish to tell those who may still have some reserves about us and who are not fully acquainted with what we want to achieve, that Yugoslavia will remain faithful to the principles of socialism, that she will gladly extend her hand to anyone who wants to cooperate and maintain friendly relations with her. Therefore, I think that the practice, which is today directed against us, should stop. If there are certain ideological problems, then they cannot be settled by slander and insults in the press and on the radio, but we must meet and discuss the problems concerned. Let them write about the points over which we differ ideologically. Our practice may be different from theirs, but our aim is the same. Our practice is not out of step with the science of Marxism and Leninism, and Marx, Engels and Lenin could not have known what the world would look like today. They, too, were mortal, but life and practice carry with them new elements which enrich their science.

Should we now, because of certain dogmatic interpretations of this science—and in the science and theory of Marxism and Leninism one can always find something that he may interpret in his own way, but this need not necessarily involve any essential points on which we may differ—give up our road to socialism and our practice? We did not agree with the Stalinist practice in the relations between socialist countries, and it is exactly this question, the question of relations between socialist countries, which is the core of this dispute. However, we cannot depart from our policy in this. For, what would be the motive power for the future development of socialist ideology in the world if there were to exist relations such as those which today prevail between our country and the other socialist countries?

This would indeed provide no motive power for the further development of socialism. It would leave us without any prospects whatsoever, people would entirely lose faith in socialism. They would say that it is exactly the same as what we had in the past: those who are stronger oppress those who are weaker. You see, this is exactly the point on which we differ. But, I think the time will come when they will realize that we are right, and that they will therefore give up their futile efforts to make us change our opinions by force, that is, to force us to depart from the line and practice we pursue today. . . .

## IX

# THE "CAMP OF SOCIALISM": HUNGARY

# OUR PEOPLE'S DEMOCRACY*

BY

JOZSEF REVAI

[1949]

I want to speak about a problem, the problem which was mentioned today by Comrade Rakosi[1] . . . the problem of the dictatorship of the proletariat. Comrade Rakosi's statement affirmed that the People's Democracy is a dictatorship of the proletariat, though not in the Soviet form, that our People's Democracy fulfills the functions of the dictatorship of the proletariat.

This problem, Comrades, is a decisively important one, though it must be said before the Central Party Leadership, that it was not given the attention by the Party officials which it deserved. . . .

It is obvious that the statement "the People's Democracy is a specimen of the dictatorship of the proletariat" is not an announcement to make a great fuss about. But if we don't have to make a great fuss about it, we don't need to hide it, to deal with it in secrecy. And the decisive factor is the necessity to make known inside the Party the importance of this statement, of this fact. For, Comrades, we are not speaking about a plain theoretical statement, but about a really practical problem. If we make it known within the Party, in the working class, that the People's Democracy is the dictatorship of the proletariat, then this becomes and should become a further resource of the effort to build Socialism, of the struggle against class enemies, and of the defense against the imperialists.

I believe it is not unnecessary to examine the statement that our People's Democracy, and people's democracies in general, mean the dictatorship of the proletariat though not in the Soviet form. It is obvious that our People's Democracy has not been from the

---

* From Jozsef Revai, "On the Character of Our People's Democracy," originally published in *Tarsadalmi Szemle,* periodical of the Hungarian Workers' Party (Communist), March-April, 1949.
[1]Then Deputy Premier of Hungary.

beginning a dictatorship of the proletariat, but became so during the struggle.

The development of our democracy is nothing else than a struggle which began with the goals of destroying Fascism, of realizing our national independence, and of steadily executing civic democratic tasks, and which was transformed subsequently into a fight against the big fortunes, and then against the whole bourgeoisie; in a fight against capitalism, aiming first at the expulsion of capitalistic elements and of the capitalistic class, and then at their liquidation. Our transformation began as an anti-Fascist, national, civic democratic one, and it became deeper and larger and developed during the struggle into a Socialistic transformation.

Our state, therefore, has not been from the beginning a kind of dictatorship of the proletariat. We should take into consideration the fact that we were for a long time a minority in the government, that until the fall of Ferenc Nagy,[1] the government of the democracy consisted not only of such elements as the kulaks, but of the representatives of the bourgeoisie and the agents of the imperialists as well. Let us take into consideration the fact that the 1944 platform of the Independence Front was in essence only the program of the anti-Fascist, anti-feudalist, anti-German, and bourgeois-democratic transformation and that it pressed only one claim against capitalism: nationalization of the mines, that is, the resources of the earth. Let us take into consideration the fact that in the economy of the People's Democracy, until the year of the transformation, the middle of 1947, the capitalistic elements were dominant in the nationalization of the industry and banks.

The fact that the Hungarian People's Democracy, as a kind of dictatorship of the proletariat, is the result of a development brought about through tough class struggles, is treated also in our Party platform, in spite of the fact that the platform does not mention the dictatorship of the proletariat. According to our platform, with the liberation of the country, and the fall of the power system of the big landlords and big capital, the working class, the whole of the peasantry and therefore the rich peasants as well, and

---

[1] The coalition government headed by Nagy fell in May 1947, at which time the Communists assumed full control in Hungary.

the anti-German faction of the bourgeoisie took over the power. "With the German threat removed, the destruction of feudalism and the resolution, step by step, of the problems raised by the struggle against big capital, during the fight against the reactionaries and with the intensification of international differences, resulted in the ousting from power and from the government of the representatives of the capitalists as well as most of the representatives of the exploiters of the rural districts. Today in Hungary— our platform says—the working class and its ally the working peasantry are in power."

Do you think, Comrades, that our transformation, in its first phase, before it became a Socialistic transformation, was anything else than a bourgeois-democratic transformation? By no means. You know very well that the working class was represented in the government and in the apparatus of power. We were a minority in Parliament and in the government, but at the same time we represented the leading force. We had decisive control over the police forces. Our force, the force of our Party and the working class, was multiplied by the fact that the Soviet Union, and the Soviet Army, were always there to support us with their assistance. In the first phase of our transformation, when we struggled directly and apparently *only* for a steadfast achievement of bourgeois-democratic tasks, we fought as well for the establishment and assurance of the conditions which made possible the Socialist transformation. The change in the development of our People's Democracy into the dictatorship of the proletariat began with the destruction of the right wing of the Smallholders' Party, with the liquidation of the conspiracy and the fall of Ferenc Nagy. Then the kulak became an enemy, then the leading role of our Party and the working class was strengthened. But the struggle for the transformation of Hungary along anti-capitalistic and Socialistic lines was initiated long before, when in the spring of 1946 the Left Wing Bloc, under the leadership of the Communist Party, succeeded in the fight for the nationalization of heavy industry; when, in the fall of 1946, the Third Congress of our Party announced the watchword: "We are constructing the country, not for the capitalists, but for the people." Ferenc Nagy resigned at the end of May 1947, but Comrade Rakosi's address, held in the

Angyalföld district of Budapest, giving the watchword, "Let's make the rich pay," and initiating the struggle, not only for the control, but for the nationalization of the great banks, was held on May 7. Our Three-year Plan, mentioned for the first time before Christmas of 1946 . . . was not directed straightforwardly and openly against capitalism as a whole, the whole bourgeoisie, but it was already connected with the tasks of the struggle against big capital. The Socialistic change of our transformation, the period during which our People's Democracy developed into a kind of dictatorship of the proletariat, extended approximately from May 1947, the fall of Ferenc Nagy, to January 1948. This is the glorious year of the change, when the majority of the working class lined up behind the Communist Party and when at the First National Conference of Party officials, the watchword of the Third Congress, "We are constructing the country not for the capitalists, but for the people," was changed to the new, victorious watchword, "The country is yours, you are constructing it for yourselves." This development, our development into a dictatorship of the proletariat, was crowned and definitely assured in June 1948 by the destruction of the right wing of the Socialist Party and establishment of the unified Workers' Party.

We must ask the question, whether we were able to see clearly, whether we were aware, during the struggle, of the nature and direction of the changes occurring in our people's democracy, in the character of our state. No, comrades, we did not see it clearly. At most we were feeling our way in the right direction. The Party didn't possess a unified, clarified, elaborated attitude in respect to the character of the People's Democracy and its future development. We must point this out, exercising self-criticism. And we must emphasize the fact that we received the decisive stimulation and assistance for the clarification of our future development from the Communist Party of the Soviet Union (Bolshevik), from the teachings of Comrade Stalin. The two sessions of the Cominform, the first in the fall of 1947, the second in the summer of 1948, were of fundamental help for us. The first taught us that a People's Democracy couldn't halt at any but the final stage of its destruction of the capitalistic elements, and the second showed us that the Socialistic transformation couldn't be limited to the towns, but had to be extended to the rural districts and that as regards the fundamental questions of the transformation into Socialism, the Soviet Union is our model and that the way of the People's Democracies differs only in certain external forms, and not in essence, from the way of the Soviet Union.

What were our mistakes in these questions? I think we made the following mistakes:

1. In the first phase of our People's Democracy, when the struggle was not directed straightforwardly against capitalism, when the fight for the consistent performance of bourgeois-democratic tasks was first on the agenda, we said that the People's Democracy was a plebeian, militant, consistent and popular kind of bourgeois democracy. In 1945 when the right wing of the Smallholders' Party wanted to provoke us into fighting the election campaign around the question, "Socialism or bourgeois private property?" we were not mistaken in evading the provocation. I believe we were right when on that occasion we criticized our left wing Socialist comrades, who during the Budapest election announced the watchword: "For a Red Budapest." This action served only our enemies. It was correct at that time to stress that the issue was not a choice between Socialism or bourgeois private property, but rather the following: Should we compromise with the forces of the old system, or should we liquidate them? It was correct that, in the fight against big capital, we did not stress that this was a transition into the struggle for Socialism but that the measures initiated against big capital meant at the same time the protection of small private properties. It was correct not to show our cards, but often even we forgot that the People's Democracy at this time was more than just a plebeian variety of the bourgeois democracy and that it was a step toward the Socialistic transition, which contained even then the elements of development into the dictatorship of the proletariat.

2. The second mistake was the fact that, first of all and overwhelmingly, we emphasized the differences between the development of the Soviet Union and our development into a People's Democracy, instead of stressing the similarity, the substantial identity, of the two developments.

3. As for our third mistake, we concluded from the popular

and, therefore relatively peaceful, character of the development into Socialism, that we could achieve Socialism without a dictatorship of the proletariat. Or—which was only another form of the same mistake—we said that the dictatorship of the proletariat meant the dictatorship of the proletariat in the Soviet Union, while with us in the People's Democracy it was superfluous.

4. It was also a mistake to say that we too needed the dictatorship of the proletariat for the achievement of Socialism, but considered the dictatorship of the proletariat as a form of government, which should follow the People's Democracy and therefore did not consider the People's Democracy a characteristic form of the dictatorship of the proletariat.

5. And finally, Comrades, it was a mistake to see the essence of the People's Democracy in the division of power between the working class and the working peasantry. The dictatorship of the proletariat, as it was defined by Lenin and Stalin, means that power is undivided in the hands of the proletariat and that the working class does not share the power with other classes. Therefore, it does not share its power with the peasantry. . . . Lenin says: "The notion of the dictatorship of the proletariat has meaning . . . only if that class is conscious of its exclusive possession of political power. . . ." According to Stalin, the dictatorship of the proletariat means that that class "does not and cannot exercise power together with other classes. . . ." Furthermore, Stalin adds that "the leader of the dictatorship of the proletariat is but *one* party, the party of the proletariat, the Communist Party, which does not and cannot share leadership with any other parties."

Is this valid for us? With us, there are not only Communists in the government, but also Smallholders' and Peasant Party members. With us, this government, this cabinet, is still a coalition government. Does this coalition of our Party with the Smallholders' and Peasant Parties mean that we exercise leadership together with them, that with us power is divided between the working class and the working peasantry?

As to this, let me cite Stalin once more: "We had been marching October-ward with the slogan of the dictatorship of the proletariat and of the poor peasantry and this in fact was practically achieved in October, inasmuch as we had a bloc with the left wing and a leadership divided with them, although then we already had a proletarian dictatorship in effect, since we Bolsheviks constituted the majority.   The dictatorship of the proletariat and the poor peasantry ceased to exist formally too . . . when the full leadership fell into the hands of one single Party—ours—which does not and cannot share the leadership of the state with other parties."

*Formally*, also with us there are elements of the division of power and leadership.   But *in fact*, Comrades, it is the working class which alone is in power, *in fact* it is our Party alone which runs the state machine.

Of course, the fact that today we still share, though but formally, the leadership with other parties has some significance.   This indicates that the alliance of the working class and of the working peasantry isn't close enough as yet, that we didn't as yet organize the peasantry tightly enough around the working class.

Does the overwhelming and unconditional power of the working class mean the exclusion of the working peasantry from the shaping of its own destiny?   It does not.   The power, the leadership, is undivided, but in certain important realms the working class willingly includes the working peasantry and its representatives in exercising power.   Our state is ruled by the working class alone, but this state is a state of the working people and thus of the peasantry too; consequently this state is being built upon an alliance of the working class and the peasantry.   However, even if the dictatorship of the proletariat is being built upon this class alliance of the working class and the peasantry, it can't be identified with it at all.   Why cannot this power be exercised along with the peasantry?   Because in that case the state would cease to be a weapon with which to realize Socialism.   For the peasantry, even its working part, is halfheartedly for private property and halfheartedly for the cooperatives.   It vacillates.   It should be supported, led, educated and assisted in order that it accept the way to the cooperatives.  This leadership, education and assistance must be given by the state, too, and that is why power cannot be divided with the peasantry.   Furthermore, vacillation concerning the matter of the Socialist progression of the village means at the same time hesitation between capitalism and Socialism, uncertainty in the fight against the kulak, vacillation in the fight against imperialism.  But a state transforming itself into Socialism, a state fighting against the kulak, a state that is to protect itself against imperialism, a power dedicated to oppressing anti-class attitudes, must not vacillate.

That is the reason, Comrades, why we must liquidate the concept that the working class shares its power with other classes.  In this concept we find remnants of a viewpoint according to which a People's Democracy is some quite specific kind of state which differs from the Soviet's not only in its form, but also in its essence and functions.

However, the fact that power is exclusively possessed by the working class isn't to be chattered about everywhere. We do not intend to mislead the peasantry but equally don't wish to strengthen reactionary elements.  Toward the peasantry, we should stress—what is true—that in important fields even the dictatorship of the proletariat includes the working peasantry in wielding power, that the dictatorship of the proletariat is being built upon the close alliance of the working class and the peasantry; of course, not upon any kind of alliance, but upon one building Socialism.

I shall mention briefly what consequences should be drawn from the realization that our People's Democracy is a variation of the dictatorship of the proletariat.

To begin with, the power in possession of the working class must, in the interest of the shaping of Socialism, the oppressing of class enemies and the defense against imperialism be still more decidedly and severely exercised than it has been up to now. "Dictatorship" also means the exercising of force in oppressing enemies.  The realization that the People's Democracy is a variation of the dictatorship of the proletariat arms us with the knowledge that, in fighting this class enemy, those organs destined to apply this force must be rendered more effective and unified than they are.

We are conscious that the dictatorship of the proletariat does not merely consist of the exercise of force; its essential functions also include construction; to conquer allies for the proletariat, and to unite them for Socialist production.  In our case, thanks to the fact that we can rely upon the Soviet Union and so can be spared from a civil war, the foremost function of our dictatorship of the proletariat is a task of economic and cultural construction. However, this does not mean at all that the functions of oppression and violence also appertaining to the dictatorship of the proletariat should be overlooked as secondary.

Rendering innocuous the agents of the imperialists, and the oppression of the class enemy within, are not at all secondary tasks; on the contrary they are conditions of the work of building Socialism. Furthermore, we must also clearly realize that periods may come in our evolution when the chief function of the dictatorship of the proletariat will consist of exercising force against enemies from within and from without. Whoever forgets that commits the crime of pacifism, demobilizes the Party and the working class, and overlooks the building up of our state security organization as well as our Army.

When outlining the tasks which lie ahead, Comrades, we must keep in sight not only the fact that our state is in close kinship with the dictatorship of the proletariat, but also that it is still wearing the eggshells of its origin, remnants from the period of the bourgeois democratic transformation. Our dictatorship of the proletariat isn't as yet a complete, finished achievement—we still have heavy tasks ahead before its final consolidation.

When we say "Our state is a dictatorship of the proletariat, though not in the Soviet form," it must not be meant that there is nothing in the Soviet form of the dictatorship of the proletariat to be studied and applied at home. Of course there is. The organism of our state should get closer to the Soviet-type of the dictatorship of the proletariat: *i.e.*, in reorganizing our administration, putting an end to the dualism of that administration, making the working people cooperate more and more effectively in the administration and in exercising the power of the state. No doubt, even our Parliament has to be reformed, inasmuch as it still wears the remnants of a bourgeois, prattling parliamentarianism, the dualism of the legislative and the executive.

Comrades, on March 21 of this year we shall celebrate the thirtieth anniversary of the proclamation of the first glorious Hungarian dictatorship of the proletariat.[1] For 30 years, we have

---

[1]This refers to the brief Communist regime of Bela Kun.

been cherishing its memory, keeping up its traditions and educating our Party in a spirit of self-criticism exercised upon the faults committed in those early days. Today, in a different way from that of some 30 years ago, in entirely different and much riper circumstances, we have reached the stage where we had to stop working 30 years ago. Then the dictatorship of the proletariat lasted but 131 days; today we are in the fifth year of that People's Democracy, which developed into the dictatorship of the proletariat. In 1919 our innate shortcomings and foes from without brought the dictatorship of the proletariat to an end. This time we will win and build up Socialism.

# DECOMPRESSION IN HUNGARY *

BY

## PAUL KECSKEMETI

[1958]

It is a safe generalization that revolutions do not break out when governmental tyranny is at its peak. As Crane Brinton puts it:

> Nothing can be more erroneous than the picture of the old regime as an unregenerate tyranny, sweeping to its end in a climax of despotic indifference to the clamor of its abused subjects. Charles I was working to "modernize" his government. . . . George III and his ministers were trying very hard to pull together the scattered organs of British colonial government. Indeed, it was this attempt at reform, this desire to work out a new colonial "system," that gave the revolutionary movement in America a start. In both France and Russia, there had been a series of attempted reforms, associated with names like Turgot, Malesherbes, Necker, Witte, and Stolypin. It is true that these reforms were incomplete, that they were repealed or nullified by sabotage on the part of the privileged. But they are on the record, an essential part of the process that issued in revolution in these countries.[1]

To the classic examples cited by Brinton, we may now add that of the Hungarian uprising of October 1956. In trying to explain the Hungarian revolution, the first thing we must bear in mind is that it occurred during a period of "thaw." The second is that this "thaw" did not originate in Hungary but was part of the "decompression" campaign which started in Soviet Russia with Stalin's death and spread over the whole satellite empire. A third essential point that we have to take into account is that, although the relaxation of governmental practices throughout the Communist world followed the same blueprint everywhere, the results varied considerably from one part of the Soviet empire to another.

The main question facing the historian in connection with the Hungarian revolution of 1956 as well as the parallel developments in Poland is surely related to this last point: what we have to

---

* From *The Annals* of The American Academy of Political and Social Science, May 1958. Reprinted by permission.

[1] Crane Brinton, *The Anatomy of Revolution,* revised edition (New York: Prentice-Hall, 1952), p. 41.

explain is, first and foremost, why events took a violent turn in
Budapest and nearly did so in Warsaw when in Prague and the
other satellite capitals everything remained quiet.   In trying to
find the answer, we must look for political factors that were present
in Hungary and Poland but not elsewhere.   One such differentiat-
ing factor can be identified at first glance: it was only in Poland
and Hungary that the top leadership of the Communist party
broke up into two sharply antagonistic factions: the Gomulkaites
vs. the Natolin group in Poland, the Nagy wing vs. the Old Guard
led by Rákosi in Hungary.

The split in the party leadership, however, could not have
developed the way it did if it had not been for a novel factor
introduced into Soviet political life in 1953.   This was the basic
post-Stalin rule forbidding Communist powerholders anywhere to
use police and judiciary terror against Communist rivals and opponents.   There had been some departures from this rule, but
on the whole it had been adhered to up to the October events,
not only in Russia and in those satellite countries where the party
leadership was reasonably homogeneous, but also in Poland and
Hungary where sharply polarized factions emerged within the
leadership.   The rule continued to be observed even when it became apparent that the liberalizing, national-Communist groups
in Poland and Hungary by mobilizing mass support were gaining
strength at the expense of the more orthodox and conservative
wing.

In Hungary, the regime was in open crisis from the Twentieth
Congress of the Soviet Communist party onward.   For months on
end, Budapest presented the astonishing spectacle of a Communist capital where the government and the official party leadership
were denounced day in and day out in newspapers and public
meetings.   Still Moscow did not relax its ban on police and
judiciary terror.   Not that it was neutral as between Rákosi and
his Communist detractors: it backed the former but expected him
to keep, or rather regain, control by means short of terrorism,
relying only on the techniques of the modified totalitarianism of
the post-Stalin era.

The general conclusion that emerges from this preliminary anal-

ysis is that the techniques of political control developed by
the Moscow leadership after Stalin's death did not enable the
Soviet Union to remain on top of political developments in Poland
and Hungary.   How and why post-Stalinist modified totalitarianism came to grief in Hungary will be shown in outline below.
As we shall see, the Soviet leadership manipulated the distribution
of political power in the Hungarian party by fiat, first favoring
Nagy over Rákosi and then throwing its support behind the latter,
but never allowing its favorite of the moment to become all-
powerful.   The idea was to maintain stability by keeping antagonistic forces in balance, but the intraparty struggle got out of
hand and eventually brought the regime down in a violent explosion.

## COLLECTIVE LEADERSHIP

When Stalin died, Mátyás Rákosi was the undisputed boss of
Hungary.   Not content with the position of Secretary General
of the Hungarian Communist party (officially designated as Hungarian Workers' party), he also assumed the office of Prime
Minister in August 1952—up to that time, he had been Vice-
Premier in a number of successive cabinets of varying composition.
Such a cumulation of offices, however, could not endure long after
Stalin's death.   The new Soviet leadership proceeded to dilute
authority at the top: control of the party apparatus was separated
from leadership in the administration.   Hungary, of course, had
to follow suit, but Rákosi was not allowed to redistribute authority
as he saw fit.   It would have been easy for him, if left alone,
to divest himself of part of his offices and fill them with his own
dummies; and this was precisely what he set out to do when
Moscow instructed him to replace "one-man rule" by "collective
leadership."   But the center was in dead earnest about diluting
authority.   In May 1953 Rákosi was summoned to appear in
Moscow *ad audiendum verbum* and to take along, not only his
faithful henchmen Ernö Gerö and Mihály Farkas, but also two
mavericks, Imre Nagy and István Dobi.

This was a straw in the wind.   It indicated that Moscow not
only wanted to replace one-man rule by collegiate government in

Hungary, but also was interested in giving authority within the new governing body to people who did not see eye to eye with Rákosi on certain important matters. The choice of the outsiders whom Rákosi was instructed to take along much against his will was significant. Dobi was not even a member of the Communist inner circle but a former Smallholder party man turned Communist; Nagy, an old party wheelhorse and former émigré in Moscow, had only recently been reinstated as member of the Hungarian Politburo after being under a cloud for Titoist deviations. Both were known to be extremely critical of Rákosi's policy of forced collectivization of peasant holdings. By giving them the nod, the Moscow center intimated its desire for concessions to the peasantry.

Appearing early in June before the Moscow Presidium with his ill-matched companions, Rákosi was forced to listen to a scathing denunciation of his stewardship during the past years. Beria, Malenkov, Molotov, Khrushchev, and Kaganovich took him severely to task. He was told that his attempt to build up a gigantic heavy industry in Hungary under his Five Year Plan of 1950, expanded further in 1951, was unsound, extravagant adventurism. His farm policy, determined in the needs of industrialization, had also been disastrous. It drove hundreds of thousands of peasants from the countryside, swelling the ranks of industrial workers who could only produce at a loss while leaving the land without enough people to work it. The country lacked food and the mood of the people was bitter. If the situation was not remedied, the government would be eventually be "booted out." [2]

## Rákosi Chastised

The Hungarian delegation returned to Budapest with precise instructions. The Central Committee was to meet and condemn

[2] A deliberately vague summary of the Soviet leaders' denunciation of Rákosi's policy is found in *Imre Nagy on Communism* (New York: Frederick A. Praeger, 1957), p. 66. The last remark about the Hungarian government facing the risk of being "booted out" is attributed there to Khrushchev. Nagy also states that at the June meeting, Molotov and not Beria (*sic*) told the Hungarians that there was no objection to permit the dissolution of kolkhozes (*ibid.*, p. 153). The covert meaning of this pointed reference to Beria will become clear as we proceed with our narrative.

Rákosi's policy of overindustrialization and forced collectivization. Rákosi was to abandon the premiership and hand it to Imre Nagy, whose mission was to placate the peasantry by stopping the collectivization drive and to emphasize production of consumer goods at the expense of heavy industry. There were also to be other reforms, notably the relaxation of police terror. At the same time, Rákosi was to remain head of the party apparatus; the party under Rákosi and the administration under Nagy were to work hand in hand to correct the mistakes of the past and create more tolerable conditions.

The Hungarian Communist party did as told: meeting on June 27-28, 1953, the Central Committee duly condemned Rákosi without deposing him as party leader and adopted new policy directives in accordance with Moscow's wishes. On July 4, Nagy was appointed Premier. Presenting himself before the National Assembly on the same day, he announced a bundle of reforms. Peasants, he said, will no longer be forced to join kolkhozes or even to remain in them against their will; the people will be given more consumer goods; police terror will be abolished.

The Hungarians could hardly believe their ears when they heard Nagy's inaugural speech. The more sanguine in the countryside concluded that "Communism was over," and proceeded to restore private property in land. In the cities, there were great expectations; for the first time since the establishment of the Communist one-party state, the country had a government which had a measure of genuine popularity.

CONSEQUENCES OF THE "THAW"

This was the beginning of "decompression" in Hungary. While Rákosi's regime had been, in some respects, the most Stalinist of all, the "thaw" under Nagy was the most sudden and most radical. To be sure, the Hungarian innovations were not unique; but it was only in Hungary that the announcement of the new course created the impression of a substantial change in the nature of the system itself.

The Moscow center neither anticipated nor desired this, and Nagy himself was too orthodox a Communist to conceive his role in such terms.    He neither wanted to change the nature of the system nor aspired to set up a "national Communist" regime independent of Soviet tutelage.    In fact, in all he was doing, he felt he was merely carrying out Moscow's instructions, as implemented by the Hungarian party's Central Committee.    Hence, from Nagy's point of view, there was no reason why Rákosi should not go along with him.    The differences between them concerned only tactics, and the highest party authorities had pronounced his, Nagy's, tactical approach to be the correct one.    As a disciplined Communist, Rákosi had had no choice but to co-operate in putting Nagy's reforms into practice.

## Split in Leadership

Rákosi, however, did no such thing.    Rallying the party apparatus which he still controlled, he gave out the watchword that Nagy's drive was full of danger and must be stopped.    In fact, within a few days after Nagy's speech, the whole countryside was in uproar; the peasants decided to disband the kolkhozes before the harvest rather than wait for the directives which the government promised to issue after it was completed.    This led to many clashes, a situation which Rákosi exploited to discredit Nagy.    At a meeting of the Budapest party organization on July 11, 1953, he sounded the alarm about kulaks moving to destroy the Socialist order.    All those present understood that Rákosi's real target was the Nagy government.    Thus, the beginning of the "thaw" in Hungary also marked the beginning of the split in the Communist leadership.

At first, the split was not a matter of clashing doctrines.    Rákosi did not say that Nagy's reform program was wrong in principle. What Rákosi told his followers was to keep their powder dry; he, Rákosi, would soon be back in Moscow's favor, and the apparatus would then be restored to supreme authority.    There were, indeed, capital developments in Moscow which nourished Rákosi's optimism:    Beria, who had carried the ball at the Moscow conference which condemned him, was liquidated soon afterward.

Even after Beria's fall, however, Rákosi did not make much headway with this master argument which he kept urging in

Moscow.  The center, apparently, was quite happy about things as they were, with the state machinery and the party apparatus locked in stalemate.  Moscow also was far from being dissatisfied with Nagy's reform policy as such, in spite of such initial mishaps as the peasant revolts of the summer of 1953 which Rákosi took such pains to exploit against his rival.  In 1953 and 1954, when Malenkov's authority was at its height, there was not much chance of undermining a policy based upon making concessions to the people and relaxing terrorism.

In May 1954, the Hungarian leaders went on another pilgrimage to Moscow, asking the center to arbitrate their differences. Rákosi trotted out his Beria argument; but was told that Beria, scoundrel though he was, had for once been quite correct in so far as he, Rákosi, was concerned.  This is what Khrushchev, according to Nagy, said on that occasion:

> In June, 1953, we correctly passed judgment on the Hungarian Party's leadership, and that judgment is still entirely correct today.  They can't hide behind Beria as Rákosi is trying to do.  We were there, too, when these errors were ascertained, every one of us!  We were right, and what we decided then is also right today.  This should have been acted on already! [3]

The last cryptic sentence in Khrushchev's speech is particularly revealing.  Nagy does not explain it; this is understandable, since his book is a brief he composed after his exclusion from the party in the fall of 1955, arguing the case for his reinstatement.  To the party audience for which Nagy's text was written, the allusion was perfectly clear.  What Khrushchev had in mind was that the Hungarian party's Third Congress, scheduled to meet on April 18 to elect a new Politburo from which some of Rákosi's followers were to be dropped, had been postponed at Rákosi's urging to give him a chance to plead his case once more in Moscow.  The delay, Khrushchev implied, was totally unnecessary: the prearranged script was not to be changed.  Thus, the pilgrims having returned from Moscow, the Congress convened on May 24; on the 30th, it elected the new Politburo minus the three Rákosites whose elimination Moscow had prescribed.

---

[3] *Ibid.*, p. 143.

### THE FREEING OF POLITICAL PRISONERS

The Moscow meeting of May 1954 also decided in Nagy's favor a policy dispute of long standing between him and the apparatus, a decision which was to have extremely far-reaching consequences in the sequel. The dispute concerned the release of many thousands of political prisoners detained in concentration camps and penitentiaries. In his inaugural speech of July 1953, Nagy had promised to put an end to the system of arbitrary police arrests, to dissolve the concentration camps, and to review the cases of all those who had been incarcerated on political charges during the Rákosi era. Rákosi fought this policy tooth and nail and with considerable success. To be sure, there were no more political arrests after Nagy assumed the government, and many totally innocuous and obscure internees were freed. Rákosi had no objection to this; but he was vitally interested in blocking the review of the cases of hundreds of people, mostly Communists and Social Democrats, who had been arrested, tortured, and sentenced on fictitious charges in the vast purges he had instituted in 1949-52. For about a year, Rákosi had his way, but Nagy continued to press the matter. When the question came up at the May conference, the Soviet leaders expressed displeasure with the dilatory way in which the issue was being handled and ordered the release and rehabilitation of the victims of Rákosi's purges. For Moscow, this was a matter of course. There had been a political amnesty in Soviet Russia the year before; no satellite government could be allowed to follow a different path.

The Hungarian case, however, was not comparable to the Russian. No mass purges had occurred in Russia since before World War II, and the amnesty of 1953 was not calculated to raise grave moral problems among Communists brought face to face with the enormity of synthetic trials and extorted confessions. By contrast, when hundreds of Hungarian Communists and Social Democrats returned from prisons and concentration camps and told their friends what had happened to them, the moral effect was devastating.

These tales, of course, were not published at that time. The public comments made by Nagy and the spokesmen of his regime after the rehabilitation campaign was nearly completed in the fall of 1954 were stern enough but still remained on a general plane. Nagy, for example, wrote in an article in *Szabad Nép* on October 10, 1954:

> The Party's June resolutions[4] have been put into effect by the rehabilitations, by the liberation of unjustly sentenced comrades. . . . In this sphere, too, we must and will liquidate the grave mistakes of the past. This demonstrates the Party's sense of justice and its strength, as well as the wisdom of collective leadership.

There was nothing in this to disturb the peace of mind of the general reader: there had been faults, but the party in its wisdom had seen to it that they should be corrected. At the nerve center of the party, however, the rehabilitations had entirely different repercussions.

Many of the former political prisoners were left-wing intellectuals, writers, and journalists who had always moved in the Budapest literary set and now made it a point to tell all to their erstwhile cronies. Nights were spent going through what had happened—a story of unspeakable, gruesome tortures, revealing the Communist state apparatus as a monster of depravity. The recipients of these confidences wished they were dead, for as Communist writers they had provided a richly orchestrated literary accompaniment to the purges. They had exhausted the remarkable resources of the Hungarian language to vilify the victims and render thanks to their torturers for saving humanity and socialism from harm. Now they felt they had no excuse whatever and began to hate themselves and Communism, the cause of their utter moral degradation. This was one of the decisive impulses behind the revolt of the Communist writers which set the stage for revolution two years later. It must be stated here that the greatest figure among the Communist writers, Tibor Déry, did not need this kind of shock to see the light: he never lent his name to Rákosi's manhunts and was in opposition throughout the latter's reign.

---

[4] The reference is to the Central Committee's resolutions of the previous year (June 1953) which censured Rákosi's policy and spelled out the "New Course." Nagy and the publicists of his regime were constantly invoking the "June resolutions" which, however, were withheld from the general public: Rákosi had succeeded in obtaining a party decision blocking their publication.

Another momentous consequence of the rehabilitations was that many party functionaries who had gone through the inferno of Rákosi's jails and camps were restored to high or middle party offices. The best known of these is János Kádár, one of the architects of the October revolution who was to betray it; he was made First Secretary of the Communist party organization of the Thirteenth District of Budapest, a working-class quarter which early in 1956 became one of the focal points of the intraparty revolt against Rákosi.

## NAGY'S FALL

In October 1954, Nagy's position seemed impregnable and Rákosi appeared to be on his way out. He was absent from the Central Committee meeting of late October which again condemned the forced industrialization policy of the Rákosi era and gave the green light to Nagy for a reorganization of the economy with emphasis upon consumer goods. A few months later, however, Nagy was ousted; and Rákosi was back. The wind suddenly changed in Moscow: Malenkov was forced to resign in February 1955; and on March 9 the Central Committee of the Hungarian Communist party, following instructions from Moscow, condemned Nagy's reform policy as a "rightist deviation." From then on, Nagy's political decline was rapid. On April 14, the Central Committee not only deposed him as Premier but also dropped him from the Politburo; in November he was expelled from the party.

Nagy, as we see, was treated far more rigorously than Rákosi had been when he fell out of favor. The Soviet center, in fact, no matter how displeased with Rákosi's conduct of Hungarian affairs, always viewed him as an insider, an important figure in international Communism, whereas Nagy was expendable. To be sure, after Nagy's fall, Rákosi was not permitted to combine his party office with the premiership; the latter post went to András Hegedüs. But this separation of offices had no real significance: Hegedüs, a nonentity, was completely dominated by Rákosi. Hungary seemed to have returned to one-man rule in substance if not in form.

The main reason for Nagy's fall was that his key policy, the reconversion of industry, was anathema to the anti-Malenkov group which got the upper hand in Moscow. The chief stumbling block was that new capital would have been needed to put reconversion into effect, but Hungary had no money and Moscow firmly refused to foot the bill. It was now Nagy's turn to be criticized for extravagance. He pleaded for an expansion of trade exchanges with the Soviet Union, but Moscow told him that Soviet supplies to Hungary would be cut in half in 1955. He then proposed to increase trade with the "people's democracies," but learned that these were moving toward autarchy. In desperation, Nagy decided to try to finance his experiment by trade with the Western countries.[5] This definitely was the last straw; the idea of financing his domestic schemes by sources outside the "camp of peace and democracy" put Nagy's Communist loyalty in doubt. Rákosi's past crimes were venial by comparison. Nagy had to be dealt with harshly; he had no roots in the apparatus, and he dabbled in heresy.

Nagy's policy appeared costly and dangerous in other ways too. The economic report submitted to the October meeting of the Central Committee admitted that labor productivity in 1954 had dropped 3.3 per cent; this was due to the relaxation of the Rákosi regime's slave-driving methods. That tendency, too, had to be stopped. Whatever the merits of Rákosi's industrial policies had been, Moscow now decided that Hungary had better get along with the industrial plant that was there, forgetting about reconversion and higher standards of living. Rákosi's reinstatement was the logical consequence of this decision.

### Rákosi Regains Power

It would be a mistake to interpret Rákosi's comeback as a return to Stalinism. The *status quo ante* was restored in some respects, notably as regards labor policy; conservatism was the order of the day, and all ambitious reform plans were shelved in the chilly new climate of retrenchment. But wholesale terror was not resumed, no new collectivization drive got under way, and most

---

[5] *Ibid.,* pp. 184 ff.

important, the policy of rehabilitation was not rescinded. Rákosi had to endure the presence in the apparatus of returnees from the camps who thirsted to get even with him. Khrushchev's pet foreign political scheme, the reconciliation with Tito, also was potentially dangerous for him, since Tito was not likely to forget the exceptional viciousness of Rákosi's conduct toward him—and, incidentally, toward Yugoslav minorities and residents in Hungary— during the conflict. Rákosi's enemies in the party could count upon the warm support of Tito whose star was rising in Moscow.

Rákosi, in fact, regained only the shadow rather than the substance of his erstwhile power. The old party bureaucracy continued to back him almost to a man, but the newly reintegrated functionaries back from prison hated him; and the Communist intellectuals, too, now were his fierce enemies. These opponents adopted Nagy as their hero, the man who had attempted to humanize the regime but was brought low by Rákosi's intrigues. It was after his fall that Nagy became the center of a cult among disgruntled Communists.

## OPEN REBELLION

The first symptoms of overt rebellion in the party appeared in the fall of 1955 with a bristling note to the Politburo denouncing the regime's cultural policies and signed by all prominent Communist writers of the country. The Politburo reacted with a sharp resolution verbally castigating the writers, but nobody was arrested; there were only a few disciplinary punishments which the writers shrugged off. In the winter, critical articles began to appear in the official organ of the Writers' Association, the *Literary Gazette*.

These were only isolated incidents. After the Twentieth Congress of the Soviet Communist Party in February 1956, however, all hell broke loose. Khrushchev's secret speech became known overnight. Khrushchev spoke only about Stalin, but his revelations seemed to suit Rákosi to a T; and the latter's foes in the Hungarian party immediately concluded that the new party line, as formulated by Khrushchev, authorized them to denounce the boss openly and in public.

The subsequent press campaign against Rákosi and his system, conducted mainly in the columns of the *Literary Gazette,* has since been described in Western publications, and so has the series of explosive meetings in the Petőfi Circle, a discussion club operating under the auspices of the Communist Youth League.[6] It is less well known that rebellious voices of extreme bluntness were frequently heard in the spring of 1956 at party meetings in various working-class districts of Budapest. The party rebels at first did not know the magnitude of the risks they were taking; they reckoned with the possibility of being arrested. But it soon became clear that there would be no arrests: the police was not permitted to touch Rákosi's critics.

After the Twentieth Congress, the Old Guard was retreating step by step. On March 2, Rákosi publicly admitted that the most prominent victims of his purges, Rajk and the other alleged Titoist conspirators executed with him, had been innocent. This admission gave new impetus to the outcry against the boss. He was now commonly referred to as the "bald-headed murderer"; his authority in the party and in the country sank to zero. Moscow at first sought to keep him in power: the only real alternative, in fact, was Nagy, but the center still regarded him as impossible. In the end, a weak intermediate solution was adopted.

Realizing that Rákosi had outlived his usefulness, Moscow let him go. The axe fell on July 18, but this time there was no pilgrimage to Moscow: instead, Mikoyan came to Budapest. He told the Hungarian party to remove Rákosi as First Secretary and replace him with Ernö Gerö.

This did not appease the critics; Gerö, in fact, had always been closely identified with Rákosi; and he had been one of the driving forces behind Rákosi's Five Year Plan, the source of Hungary's misfortunes. He was in a difficult position. He could not change basic economic policy since Moscow's objections to reforms in this field remained in force. But the people now demanded tangible improvements, and the Poznań riots of June 1956 had shown that violent outbreaks were no longer unthinkable. In his quandary,

---

[6] See United Nations, *Report of the Special Committee on the Problem of Hungary,* New York, 1957, paras. 379-385. The fullest documentation on the intellectuals' revolt is found in a special issue of *Les Temps Modernes,* Paris, Vol. 12, Nos. 129, 130, 131 (January 1957).

Gerö tried to create a better atmosphere by wooing the party opposition. He promised freedom of criticism and sought to improve his position by diverting popular wrath against the political police. The solemn reburial on October 6 of Rajk and some of his covictims was an astonishing spectacle; it was essentially a demonstration under government auspices against the political police. A few days later, Mihály Farkas, the chief torturer of Rajk and his associates, was arrested. But this move could as little save Gerö as Strafford's execution could save Charles I. Nor was Nagy's readmission to the party on October 13 sufficient to stem the rising tide of revolt.

## THE EFFECTS OF THE DECOMPRESSION

This is not the place to go into the revolutionary events themselves; the purpose of the present article was merely to show the working and effects of decompression in Hungary following Stalin's death. What the above analysis suggests above all is that in the special case of Hungary, the policy of decompression which was imposed by the domestic constellation of forces in Soviet Russia raised a number of problems defying solution. This can best be stated in a number of "if" propositions.

The ravages of Rákosi's Five Year Plan might have been mitigated "if" the Soviet Union had been ready to underwrite Nagy's reforms with the necessary funds. This would probably have been less costly in the long run than the course actually followed; the subsidies Russia now must grant the Kádár regime may well be greater than the sums that would have been sufficient to tide Nagy over. But in 1955 fiscal conservatism was the order of the day in Moscow, and Rákosi was able to exploit this in his favor.

Further, the moral crisis of the regime would probably not have become fatal "if" Rákosi had been dropped entirely after the rehabilitations. But this would have involved the complete revamping of the party apparatus, and an operation of such magnitude may well have been infeasible. Also, one of Moscow's guiding principles, collective leadership, militated against a wholesale purge of such radical scope.

Conversely, agitation within the party might have been stopped "if" Rákosi had been allowed to subdue his opponents in the party by police and judiciary terror. In all probability, such measures would not have provoked mass outbreaks. But a number of factors, such as the climate created by the Twentieth Congress and the Soviet Union's need to reconcile Tito, precluded this sharp course. It is also doubtful whether Rákosi, discredited as he was by the dramatic revelation of his past outrages, would have been in a position to impose a new purge even if Moscow had permitted him to do so.

To sum up: revolt in Hungary might well have been forestalled by a consistent evolutionary policy or, failing this, by a recrudescence of terror. Moscow, however, chose to steer a middle course between these alternatives. It had an illusory faith in the unlimited efficacy of manipulation from above and underestimated the moral factor. The Hungarian developments have demonstrated the fallibility of Moscow's concept of manipulative decompression.

# HUNGARY, 1956*

## THE HUNGARIAN STUDENTS' MANIFESTO**

*Students of Budapest!*

The following resolution was born on 22 October 1956, at the dawn of a new period in Hungarian history, in the Hall of the Building Industry Technological University as a result of the spontaneous movement of several thousand of the Hungarian youth who love their Fatherland:

(1) We demand the immediate withdrawal of all Soviet troops in accordance with the provisions of the Peace Treaty.

(2) We demand the election of new leaders in the Hungarian Workers' Party on the low, medium and high levels by secret ballot from the ranks upwards. These leaders should convene the Party Congress within the shortest possible time and should elect a new central body of leaders.

(3) The Government should be reconstituted under the leadership of Comrade Imre Nagy; all criminal leaders of the Stalinist-Rákosi era should be relieved of their posts at once.

(4) We demand a public trial in the criminal case of Mihály Farkas and his accomplices. Mátyás Rákosi, who is primarily responsible for all the crimes of the recent past and for the ruin of this country, should be brought home and brought before a People's Court of Judgment.

(5) We demand general elections in this country, with universal suffrage, secret ballot and the participation of several Parties for the purpose of electing a new National Assembly. We demand that the workers should have the right to strike.

(6) We demand a re-examination and re-adjustment of Hungarian-Soviet and Hungarian-Yugoslav political, economic and

---

* This selection of documents is from the booklet, "The Case of the Toppling Idol: A Case-Study on American Policy and the Hungarian Revolution," ed. Gerald Stourzh. Copyright 1958 by the American Foundation for Political Education; reprinted by permission.

** One form of the 16-point Manifesto, issued October 22, 1956.

intellectual relations on the basis of complete political and economic equality and of non-intervention in each other's internal affairs.

(7) We demand the re-organization of the entire economic life of Hungary, with the assistance of specialists. Our whole economic system based on planned economy should be re-examined with an eye to Hungarian conditions and to the vital interests of the Hungarian people.

(8) Our foreign trade agreements and the real figures in respect of reparations that can never be paid should be made public. We demand frank and sincere information concerning the country's uranium deposits, their exploitation and the Russian concession. We demand that Hungary should have the right to sell the uranium ore freely at world market prices in exchange for hard currency.

(9) We demand the complete revision of norms in industry and an urgent and radical adjustment of wages to meet the demands of workers and intellectuals. We demand that minimum living wages for workers should be fixed.

(10) We demand that the delivery system should be placed on a new basis and that produce should be used rationally. We demand equal treatment of peasants farming individually.

(11) We demand the re-examination of all political and economic trials by independent courts and the release and rehabilitation of innocent persons. We demand the immediate repatriation of prisoners-of-war and of civilians deported to the Soviet Union, including prisoners who have been condemned beyond the frontiers of Hungary.

(12) We demand complete freedom of opinion and expression, freedom of the Press and a free Radio, as well as a new daily newspaper of large circulation for the MEFESZ * organization. We demand that the existing 'screening material' should be made public and destroyed.

(13) We demand that the Stalin statue—the symbol of Stalinist

---

* MEFESZ—League of Hungarian University and College Student Associations.

tyranny and political oppression—should be removed as quickly as possible and that a memorial worthy of the freedom fighters and martyrs of 1848-49 should be erected on its site.

(14) In place of the existing coat of arms, which is foreign to the Hungarian people, we wish the re-introduction of the old Hungarian Kossuth arms. We demand for the Hungarian Army new uniforms worthy of our national traditions. We demand that 15 March should be a national holiday and a non-working day and that 6 October should be a day of national mourning and a school holiday.

(15) The youth of the Technological University of Budapest unanimously express their complete solidarity with the Polish and Warsaw workers and youth in connection with the Polish national independence movement.

(16) The students of the Building Industry Technological University will organize local units of MEFESZ as quickly as possible, and have resolved to convene a Youth Parliament in Budapest for the 27th of this month (Saturday) at which the entire youth of this country will be represented by their delegates. The students of the Technological University and of the various other Universities will gather before the Writers' Union Headquarters tomorrow, the 23rd of this month, at 2:30 P.M., whence they will proceed to the Bem statue, on which they will lay wreaths in sign of their sympathy with the Polish freedom movement. The workers of the factories are invited to join in this procession.

## DECLARATION BY THE GOVERNMENT OF THE USSR, OCTOBER 30, 1956*

The system of people's democracies took shape, grew strong and showed its great vital power in many countries of Europe and Asia . . . after the Second World War and the rout of fascism.

In the process of the rise of the new system and the deep revolutionary changes in social relations, there have been many diffi-

---

* *Pravda*, October 31, 1956. The translation reproduced here is from *The Current Digest of the Soviet Press.* Vol. VIII, No. 40. Reprinted in Paul E. Zinner, ed., *National Communism and Popular Revolt in Eastern Europe*, Columbia University Press, 1957.

culties, unresolved problems, and downright mistakes, including mistakes in the mutual relations among the socialist countries— violations and errors which demeaned the principle of equality in relations among the socialist states.

The 20th Congress of the Communist Party of the Soviet Union quite resolutely condemned these violations and mistakes, and set the task of consistent application by the Soviet Union of Leninist principles of equality of peoples in its relations with the other socialist countries. It proclaimed the need for taking full account of the historical past and peculiarities of each country that has taken the path of building a new life.

The Soviet Government is consistently carrying out these historic decisions of the 20th Congress, which create conditions for further strengthening friendship and cooperation among the socialist countries on the firm foundation of observance of the full sovereignty of each socialist state.

As recent events have demonstrated, it has become necessary to make this declaration of the Soviet Union's stand on the mutual relations of the USSR with other socialist countries, particularly in the economic and military spheres.

The Soviet Government is prepared to discuss together with the governments of other socialist states measures ensuring further development and strengthening of economic ties among the socialist countries in order to remove any possibility of violation of the principles of national sovereignty, mutual benefit, and equality in economic relations.

This principle must also be extended to advisers. It is known that, in the first period of the formation of the new social system, the Soviet Union, at the request of the governments of the people's democracies, sent these countries a certain number of its specialists —engineers, agronomists, scientists, military advisers. In the recent period the Soviet Government has repeatedly raised before the socialist countries the question of recalling its advisers.

In view of the fact that by this time the people's democracies have formed their own qualified national cadres in all spheres of economic and military affairs, the Soviet Government considers it urgent to review, together with the other socialist states, the question of the expediency of the further presense of USSR advisers in those countries.

In the military domain an important basis of the mutual relations between the Soviet Union and the people's democracies is the Warsaw Treaty, under which its members adopted respective political and military obligations, including the obligation to take "concerted measures necessary for strengthening their defense capacity in order to protect the peaceful labor of their peoples, to guarantee the inviolability of their borders and territory, and to ensure defense against possible aggression."

It is known that Soviet units are in the Hungarian and Rumanian republics in accord with the Warsaw Treaty and governmental agreements. Soviet units are in the Polish republic on the basis of the Potsdam four-power agreement and the Warsaw Treaty. Soviet military units are not in the other people's democracies.

For the purpose of assuring mutual security of the socialist countries, the Soviet Government is prepared to review with the other socialist countries which are members of the Warsaw Treaty the question of Soviet troops stationed on the territory of the above-mentioned countries. In so doing the Soviet Government proceeds from the general principle that stationing the troops of one or another state which is a member of the Warsaw Treaty on the territory of another state which is a member of the treaty is done by agreement among all its members and only with the consent of the state on the territory of which and at the request of which these troops are stationed or it is planned to station them.

The Soviet Government considers it necessary to make a statement in connection with the events in Hungary. The course of events has shown that the working people of Hungary, who have attained great progress on the basis of the people's democratic system, are rightfully raising the question of the need to eliminate serious defects in the sphere of economic construction, the question of further improving the living standards of the population, the question of combating bureaucratic distortions in the state machinery. However, this legitimate and progressive movement of the working people was soon joined by the forces of black reaction and counterrevolution, which are trying to take advantage of the dissatisfaction of a part of the working people in order to undermine the foundations of the people's democratic system in Hungary and to restore the old landowner-capitalist ways in that country.

The Soviet Government, like the whole Soviet people, deeply regrets that the development of events in Hungary has led to bloodshed.

At the request of the Hungarian people's government, the Soviet Government has granted consent to the entry into Budapest of Soviet military units to help the Hungarian people's army and the Hungarian agencies of government to bring order to the city.

Having in mind that the further presence of Soviet military units in Hungary could serve as an excuse for further aggravation of the situation, the Soviet Government has given its military command instructions to withdraw the Soviet military units from the city of Budapest as soon as this is considered necessary by the Hungarian Government.

At the same time, the Soviet Government is prepared to enter into the appropriate negotiations with the Government of the Hungarian People's Republic and other members of the Warsaw Treaty on the question of the presence of Soviet troops on the territory of Hungary.

To guard the socialist achievements of people's democratic Hungary is the chief and sacred duty of the workers, peasants, intelligentsia, of all the Hungarian working people at the present moment. . . .

## ADDRESS BY PRESIDENT EISENHOWER, OCTOBER 31, 1956*

In Eastern Europe there seems to appear the dawn of a new day.   It has not been short or easy in coming.

After World War II, the Soviet Union used military force to impose on the nations of Eastern Europe governments of Soviet choice—servants of Moscow.

---

* From an address to the Nation over radio and television.   Reprinted from the Department of State *Bulletin,* November 12, 1956.

It has been consistent United States policy, without regard to political party, to seek to end this situation and to fulfill the wartime pledge of the United Nations that these countries, overrun by wartime armies, would once again know sovereignty and self-government.

We could not, of course, carry out this policy by resort to force. Such force would have been contrary both to the best interests of the Eastern European peoples and to the abiding principles of the United Nations. But we did help to keep alive the hope of these peoples for freedom.

Beyond this, they needed from us no education in the worth of national independence and personal liberty, for, at the time of the American Revolution, many of them came to our land to aid our cause. Recently the pressure of the will of these peoples for national independence has become more and more insistent.

A few days ago, the people of Poland with their proud and deathless devotion to freedom moved to secure a peaceful transition to a new government. And this government, it seems, will strive genuinely to serve the Polish people.

And all the world has been watching dramatic events in Hungary where this brave people, as so often in the past, have offered their very lives for independence from foreign masters. Today, it appears, a new Hungary is rising from this struggle, a Hungary which we hope from our hearts will know full and free nationhood.

We have rejoiced in these historic events.

Only yesterday the Soviet Union issued an important statement on its relations with all the countries of Eastern Europe. This statement recognized the need for review of Soviet policies, and the amendment of these policies to meet the demands of the people for greater national independence and personal freedom. The Soviet Union declared its readiness to consider the withdrawal of Soviet "advisers," who have been the effective ruling force in Soviet-occupied countries, and also to consider withdrawal of Soviet troops from such countries as Poland and Hungary.

We cannot yet know if these avowed purposes will be truly carried out.

But two things are clear.

First, the fervor and the sacrifice of the peoples of these countries, in the name of freedom, have themselves brought real promise that the light of liberty soon will shine again in this darkness.

And second, if the Soviet Union indeed faithfully acts upon its announced intention, the world will witness the greatest forward stride toward justice, trust, and understanding among nations in our generation.

These are the facts.   How has your Government responded to them?

The United States has made clear its readiness to assist economically the new and independent governments of these countries.   We have already—some days since—been in contact with the new Government of Poland on this matter.   We have also publicly declared that we do not demand of these governments their adoption of any particular form of society as a condition upon our economic assistance.   Our one concern is that they be free—for their sake, and for freedom's sake.

We have also, with respect to the Soviet Union, sought clearly to remove any false fears that we would look upon new governments in these Eastern European countries as potential military allies.   We have no such ulterior purpose.   We see these peoples as friends, and we wish simply that they be friends who are free. . . .

## STATEMENT BY IMRE NAGY ANNOUNCING HUNGARIAN NEUTRALITY, NOVEMBER 1, 1956*

People of Hungary:   The Hungarian National Government, imbued with profound responsibility towards the Hungarian people and history, and giving expression to the undivided will of the Hungarian millions, declares the neutrality of the Hungarian

---

* Broadcast over Free Radio Kossuth.   Reprinted from *The Hungarian Revolution,* Melvin J. Lasky (ed.), published for the Congress for Cultural Freedom by Frederick A. Praeger, by permission.

People's Republic.  The Hungarian people, on the basis of independence and equality and in accordance with the spirit of the UN Charter, wishes to live in tru friendship with its neighbors, the Soviet Union and all the peoples of the world.

The Hungarian people desire the consolidation and further development of the achievements of its national revolution without joining any power-blocs.  The century-old dream of the Hungarian people is being fulfilled.  The revolutionary struggle fought by the Hungarian people and heroes has at last carried the cause of freedom and independence to victory.  This heroic struggle has made possible the enforcement, in our people's inter-State relations, of its fundamental national interest: neutrality.  We appeal to our neighbours, countries near and far, to respect the unalterable decision of our people.

It is indeed true that our people are as united in this decision as perhaps never before in their history.  Working millions of Hungary: protect and strengthen—with revolutionary determination, sacrificial work and the consolidation of order—our country, free, independent, democratic and neutral Hungary.

## LETTER TO UN SECRETARY-GENERAL HAMMARSKJOLD FROM IMRE NAGY*

*Budapest, 1 November 1956*

The President of the Council of Ministers of the Hungarian People's Republic as designated Minister for Foreign Affairs has the honour to communicate the following to Your Excellency.

Reliable reports have reached the Government of the Hungarian People's Republic that further Soviet units are entering into Hungary.  The President of the Council of Ministers in his capacity of Minister for Foreign Affairs summoned M. Andropov, Ambassador Extraordinary and Plenipotentiary of the Soviet Union to Hungary, and expressed his strongest protest against the entry of further Soviet troops into Hungary.  He demanded the instant and immediate withdrawal of these Soviet forces.  He informed the Soviet Ambassador that the Hungarian Government immedi-

---

* Reprinted from the Department of State *Bulletin*, November 12, 1956.

ately repudiates the Warsaw Treaty and at the same time declares Hungary's neutrality, turns to the United Nations and requests the help of the four Great Powers in defending the country's neutrality. The Government of the Hungarian People's Republic made the declaration of neutrality on 1 November 1956. Therefore I request Your Excellency promptly to put on the agenda of the forthcoming General Assembly of the United Nations the question of Hungary's neutrality and the defence of this neutrality by the four Great Powers.

I take this opportunity to convey to Your Excellency the expression of my highest consideration.

IMRE NAGY

PRESIDENT OF THE COUNCIL OF MINISTERS OF THE HUNGARIAN PEOPLE'S
REPUBLIC; DESIGNATED MINISTER FOR FOREIGN AFFAIRS

## LETTER TO UN SECRETARY-GENERAL HAMMARSKJOLD FROM IMRE NAGY*

*Budapest, 2 November 1956*

As the President of the Council of Ministers and designated Foreign Minister of the Hungarian People's Republic I have the honour to bring to the attention of Your Excellency the following additional information:

I have already mentioned in my letter of 1 November 1956 that new Soviet military units entered Hungary and that the Hungarian Government informed the Soviet Ambassador in Budapest of this fact, at the same time terminated the Treaty of Warsaw, declared the neutrality of Hungary and requested the United Nations to guarantee the neutrality of the country.

On 2 of November 1956 further and exact information, mainly military reports, reached the Government of the Hungarian People's Republic, according to which large Soviet military units crossed the border of the country, marching towards Budapest. They occupy railway lines, railway stations and railway safety equipment. Reports also have come about that Soviet military

---

* Reprinted from *Official Records of the Security Council,* 11th year, Supplement for October, November, and December 1956.

movements of east-west direction are being observed on the territory of Western Hungary.

On the basis of the above-mentioned facts the Hungarian Government deemed it necessary to inform the Embassy of the USSR and all the other diplomatic missions in Budapest about these steps directed against our People's Republic.

At the same time, the Government of the Hungarian People's Republic forwarded concrete proposals on the withdrawal of Soviet troops stationed in Hungary as well as the place of negotiations concerning the execution of the termination of the Treaty of Warsaw and presented a list containing the names of the members of the Government's delegation. Furthermore, the Hungarian Government made a proposal to the Soviet Embassy in Budapest to form a mixed committee to prepare the withdrawal of the Soviet troops.

I request Your Excellency to call upon the great powers to recognize the neutrality of Hungary and ask the Security Council to instruct the Soviet and Hungarian Governments to start the negotiations immediately.

I also request Your Excellency to make known the above to the members of the Security Council.

IMRE NAGY

PRESIDENT OF THE COUNCIL OF MINISTERS
ACTING MINISTER FOR FOREIGN AFFAIRS

APPEALS FOR HELP, RADIO FREE KOSSUTH (BUDAPEST), NOVEMBER 4, 1956

5:20 A.M. "Attention! attention! Premier Imre Nagy will address the Hungarian people:

"This is Premier Imre Nagy speaking. Today at daybreak Soviet troops attacked our capital with the obvious intent of overthrowing the legal democratic Hungarian government. Our troops are in combat. The government is at its post. I notify the people of our country and the entire world of this fact." [Announcement repeated in English, Russian, Hungarian, and French.]

5:58 A.M. "Imre Nagy, Premier of the national government, appeals to Pal Maleter, Defense Minister, Istvan Kovacs, Chief of the General Staff, and the other members who went to the Soviet Army Headquarters at ten o'clock last night and have not yet returned, to return at once and take charge of their respective offices."

6:08 A.M. Announcement that Imre Nagy has sent the text of his notice of the Soviet attack to UN Secretary-General Dag Hammarskjold.

6:44 A.M. Announcement of an Associated Press report that the UN Security Council has received Hungary's appeal.

7:12 A.M. "Attention, attention, important announcement: The Hungarian government appeals to the officers and men of the Soviet Army not to shoot. Let us avoid bloodshed. The Russians are our friends and will remain our friends."

7:55 A.M. "Report from New York. The Associated Press reported at 7:24 A.M. that the United States early this morning asked the Security Council of the United Nations to hold an emergency meeting on Sunday to discuss the Soviet offensive in Hungary. The request was submitted by American Ambassador Lodge less than an hour after news agencies reported large-scale Soviet attacks in all of Hungary.

"The Security Council had discussed the Hungarian question Saturday night and adjourned the debate until Monday morning. Lodge, however, requested the Council's chairman to hold the meeting earlier should the situation deteriorate. . . ."

7:56 A.M. "Attention, attention. You will now hear the manifesto of the Union of Hungarian Writers:

"This is the Union of Hungarian Writers! To every writer in the world, to all scientists, to all writers' federations, to all science academies and associations, to the intelligentsia of the world! We ask all of you for help and support; there is but little time! You know the facts, there is no need to give you a special report! Help Hungary! Help the Hungarian writers, scientists, workers, peasants, and our intelligentsia!

"Help!  Help!  Help!"

8:24 A.M.  "SOS!  SOS!  SOS! . . ."*

## ANNOUNCEMENT BY FERENC MUNNICH OF FORMATION OF NEW GOVERNMENT, NOVEMBER 4, 1956**

"Open letter to the Hungarian working people: compatriots, our worker and peasant comrades, we the undersigned, Antal Apro, Janos Kadar, Istvan Kossa and Ferenc Munnich, former Ministers in the Imre Nagy government, announce that on November 1, 1956, we broke off our relations with this government, left this government and took the initiative of forming the Hungarian Revolutionary Worker-Peasant Government.

"We were prompted to take this responsible step by the realization that, within the Nagy government, which became impotent under the pressure of the reaction, we could do nothing against the counterrevolutionary danger menacing our People's Republic, the rule of workers and peasants, and our Socialist achievements. . . .

"As members of the government we could no longer watch idly . . . while, under the cover of democracy, counterrevolutionary terrorists and bandits were bestially murdering our worker and peasant brothers and terrorizing our peaceful citizens, dragging our country into anarchy, and putting our entire nation under the yoke of counterrevolution for a long time to come.

"Hungarian workers, compatriots, comrades!  We have decided to fight with all our strength against the threatening danger of Fascism and reaction and its murderous gangs.  We appeal to every loyal son of our People's Democracy, every follower of Socialism—first of all the Communists, workers, miners, the best sons of the peasantry and the intelligentsia, to support every measure of the Hungarian Worker-Peasant Government and its struggle for the liberation of the people."

---

* At 8:25 A.M. Radio Free Kossuth went off the air with a repeated SOS signal.  The station was silent until 9:15 P.M.  When transmission resumed it was in the hands of the Soviet-controlled regime.

** Broadcast on the frequency of the Balaton Szabadi transmitter, probably in Szolnok, 5:05 A.M.

## STATEMENT BY AMBASSADOR LODGE AT THE UN GENERAL ASSEMBLY, NOVEMBER 4, 1956*

At dawn this morning Soviet troops in Hungary opened fire in Budapest and throughout the country. . . . Prime Minister Nagy has appealed to the United Nations for help, and I must say we can understand it. . . .

For the last few days Soviet movements into Hungary have been reported. These reports have been accompanied by Soviet assurances to the United Nations and to the Hungarian Government that Soviet troops in Hungary had not and would not be reenforced. The reported movements were pictured as the redeployment of Soviet forces stationed in the country.

As late as 10 o'clock last night Soviet representatives began negotiations—or what was described as negotiations—with Hungarian representatives ostensibly for the withdrawal of Soviet troops from Hungary pursuant to Hungary's decision to renounce its membership in the Warsaw Pact.

The Soviet Union has made little pretense lately of its urge to dominate Hungary by the power of its military machine. It talked about a new relationship with its satellites based on sovereign equality and independence and nonintervention in internal affairs. It spoke of negotiations under the Warsaw Pact for the withdrawal of its troops from some of these countries, particularly Hungary, where it admitted that the further presence of its army units could "serve as a cause for an even greater deterioration of the situation" —a deterioration which has, of course, so tragically occurred.

What a picture of deception we have had!

Let us not be deceived by this cynical and wanton act of aggression against the Hungarian people and its Government. A small group of Soviet straw men announced their own formation as a government at the moment Soviet troops began their attack. We have seen no passage of governmental authority from one Hun-

---

* The session was called under the Uniting-for-Peace resolution, pursuant to a request by Ambassador Lodge made during an early-morning meeting of the Security Council on November 4, at which the U.S.S.R. had vetoed a U.S. proposal on the situation in Hungary. Reprinted from the Department of State Bulletin, November 19, 1956.

garian government to another, but only the creation of a puppet clique and the overthrow of a liberal socialist government responsive to popular will in their desire to see these troops go. Two hours after the attack began, the new puppet group appealed to the Soviet Union to come to its assistance. It cannot be maintained, therefore, that the Soviet action is undertaken in response to any request for assistance. The "assistance," and I put that in quotes, arrived long before the call.

This is how General Janos Kadar, the Communist puppet installed by Soviet military intervention this morning, spoke of Prime Minister Nagy when the Prime Minister first took over the government: "I am in wholehearted agreement with Nagy, an acquaintance and friend of mine, my esteemed and respected compatriot." Wonderful friend—he was with him up to the hilt.

We must take drastic and decisive action here in this Assembly to answer the appeal of the Hungarian Government. The United States delegation therefore is submitting a draft resolution which we believe should be promptly put to the vote.

## RESOLUTION ADOPTED BY THE GENERAL ASSEMBLY ON NOVEMBER 4, 1956*

*Considering* that the United Nations is based on the principle of the sovereign equality of all its Members,

*Recalling* that the enjoyment of human rights and of fundamental freedom in Hungary was specifically guaranteed by the Peace Treaty between Hungary and the Allied and Associated Powers signed at Paris on 10 February 1947 and that the general principle of these rights and this freedom is affirmed for all peoples in the Charter of the United Nations,

*Convinced* that recent events in Hungary manifest clearly the desire of the Hungarian people to exercise and to enjoy fully their fundamental rights, freedom and independence,

---

* The Resolution is reprinted from the Department of State *Bulletin,* November 19, 1956. The tabulation of the vote on the Resolution is reprinted from United Nations *Record,* General Assembly, Second Emergency Special Session, Plenary Meetings, December 1956.

*Condemning* the use of Soviet military forces to suppress the efforts of the Hungarian people to reassert their rights,

*Noting moreover* the declaration by the Government of the Union of Soviet Socialist Republics of 30 October 1956, of its avowed policy of non-intervention in the internal affairs of other States,

*Noting* the communication of 1 November 1956 of the Government of Hungary to the Secretary-General regarding demands made by that Government to the Government of the Union of Soviet Socialist Republics for the instant and immediate withdrawal of Soviet forces,

*Noting further* the communication of 2 November 1956 from the Government of Hungary to the Secretary-General asking the Security Council to instruct the Government of the Union of Soviet Socialist Republics and the Government of Hungary to start the negotiations immediately on withdrawal of Soviet forces,

*Noting* that the intervention of Soviet military forces in Hungary has resulted in grave loss of life and widespread bloodshed among the Hungarian people,

*Taking note* of the radio appeal of Prime Minister Imre Nagy of 4 November 1956,

1. *Calls upon* the Government of the Union of Soviet Socialist Republics to desist forthwith from all armed attack on the peoples of Hungary and from any form of intervention, in particular armed intervention, in the internal affairs of Hungary;

2. *Calls upon* the Union of Soviet Socialist Republics to cease the introduction of additional armed forces into Hungary and to withdraw all of its forces without delay from Hungarian territory;

3. *Affirms* the right of the Hungarian people to a government responsive to its national aspirations and dedicated to its independence and well-being;

4. *Requests* the Secretary-General to investigate the situation caused by foreign intervention in Hungary, to observe the situation directly through representatives named by him, and to report thereon to the General Assembly at the earliest moment, and as

soon as possible suggest methods to bring an end to the foreign intervention in Hungary in accordance with the principles of the Charter of the United Nations;

5. *Calls upon* the Government of Hungary and the Government of the Union of Soviet Socialist Republics to permit observers designated by the Secretary-General to enter the territory of Hungary, to travel freely therein, and to report their findings to the Secretary-General;

6. *Calls upon* all Members of the United Nations to cooperate with the Secretary-General and his representatives in the execution of his functions;

7. *Requests* the Secretary-General in consultation with the heads of appropriate specialized agencies to inquire, on an urgent basis, into the needs of the Hungarian people for food, medicine and other similar supplies, and to report to the General Assembly as soon as possible;

8. *Requests* all Members of the United Nations, and invites national and international humanitarian organizations to co-operate in making available such supplies as may be required by the Hungarian people.

*A vote was taken by roll call.*

*Romania, having been drawn by lot by the President, was called upon to vote first.*

IN FAVOUR: Spain, Sweden, Thailand, Turkey, Union of South Africa, United Kingdom of Great Britain and Northern Ireland, United States of America, Uruguay, Venezuela, Argentina, Australia, Austria, Belgium, Bolivia, Brazil, Cambodia, Canada, Chile, China, Colombia, Costa Rica, Cuba, Denmark, Dominican Republic, Ecuador, El Salvador, Ethiopia, France, Greece, Guatemala, Haiti, Honduras, Iceland, Iran, Ireland, Israel, Italy, Liberia, Luxembourg, Mexico, Netherlands, New Zealand, Nicaragua, Norway, Pakistan, Panama, Paraguay, Peru, Philippines, Portugal.

AGAINST: Romania, Ukrainian Soviet Socialist Republic, Union of Soviet Socialist Republics, Albania, Bulgaria, Byelorussian Soviet Socialist Republic, Czechoslovakia, Poland.

ABSTAINING: Saudi Arabia, Syria, Yemen, Yugoslavia, Afghanistan, Burma, Ceylon, Egypt, Finland, India, Indonesia, Iraq, Jordan, Libya, Nepal.

*The draft resolution, as amended, was adopted by 50 votes to 8, with 15 abstentions.*

## CONCLUSIONS OF THE UN SPECIAL COMMITTEE*

The mandate given to the Special Committee by the General Assembly was to carry out a full and objective investigation on all aspects of Soviet intervention in Hungary by armed force and by other means and on the effects of such intervention on the political development of Hungary. In carrying out this mandate, the Committee studied a rich documentation supplied by Governments and obtained from other sources, while it closely questioned more than a hundred witnesses, representing every stratum of Hungarian society, whose testimony fills 2,000 pages in the verbatim record. The General Assembly asked that the investigations should be pursued in Hungary also, but the attitude of the Hungarian Government did not allow the Committee to carry out this part of its mandate. The Committee has summarized its conclusions as to the essential facts about the Hungarian uprising under thirteen points. The essence of these conclusions is as follows:

(i) What took place in Hungary was a spontaneous national uprising, caused by long-standing grievances. One of these was the inferior status of Hungary with regard to the USSR;

(ii) The uprising was led by students, workers, soldiers and intellectuals, many of them Communists or former Communists. Those who took part in it insisted that democratic socialism should be the basis of the Hungarian political structure, and that the land reform and other social achievements should be safeguarded. It is untrue that the uprising was fomented by reactionary circles in Hungary or that it drew its strength from "Imperialist" circles in the West;

(iii) The uprising was not planned in advance, but actually

---

* From "Report of the Special Committee on the Problem of Hungary," General Assembly Official Records: 11th Session. The Committee members were representatives of Denmark, Australia, Ceylon, Tunisia, and Uruguay.

took participants by surprise. Its timing was connected with Poland's successful move for greater independence from the USSR and with the disappointment caused by the speech of Ernö Gerö on his return from Yugoslavia on 23 October [1956], when it was hoped that he would adopt a sympathetic attitude towards the popular demands voiced on 22 October by the Hungarian students;

(iv) It would appear that the Soviet authorities had taken steps as early as 20 October to make armed intervention possible. Evidence exists of troop movements, or projected troop movements, from that date on, and Soviet troops from outside Hungary were used even in the first intervention. In Hungary, signs of opposition were evident before 23 October;

(v) The demonstrations on 23 October were at first entirely peaceable and no evidence has been discovered that any demonstrators intended to resort to force. The change was due to the action of the AVH* in opening fire on the people outside the Radio Building and to the appearance of Russian soldiers in Budapest as enemies in combat;

(vi) Mr. Nagy has established that he did not issue any invitation to the Soviet authorities to intervene and the Committee has no evidence as to the circumstances in which an invitation was issued or as to whether such an invitation was issued at all. Similar considerations apply to the alleged invitation by Mr. Kádár's Government for the Soviet troops to intervene on the second occasion. There is abundant evidence that Soviet preparations for this intervention had been under way since the last days of October;

(vii) Mr. Nagy was not at first free to exercise the full powers of the Premiership. By the time the grip of the AVH had been loosened, the real power lay with the Revolutionary and Workers' Councils. Mr. Nagy, seeing that his countrymen were united in their desire for other forms of Government and for the departure of the Soviet troops, threw in his lot with the insurgents;

(viii) During the few days of freedom, the popular nature of the uprising was proved by the appearance of a free press and radio and by general rejoicing among the people;

---

* State Security Authority.

(ix) A number of lynchings and beating by the crowds concerned, in almost all cases, members of the AVH or those who were believed to have co-operated with them;

(x) Steps taken by the Workers' Councils during this period were aimed at giving the workers real control of nationalized undertakings and at abolishing unpopular institutions, such as the production norms. Meanwhile, negotiations were proceeding for the complete withdrawal of Soviet troops and life in Budapest was beginning to return to normal;

(xi) In contrast to demands put forward at this time for the reestablishment of political rights, basic human rights of the Hungarian people were violated by the Hungarian Governments before 23 October, especially up to the autumn of 1955, and such violations have been resumed since 4 November. The numerous accounts of inhuman treatment and tortures by the AVH must be accepted as true. In an attempt to break the revolution, numbers of Hungarians, including some women, were deported to the Soviet Union and some may not have been returned to their homes;

(xii) Since the second Soviet intervention on 4 November there has been no evidence of popular support for Mr. Kádár's Government. Mr. Kádár has proceeded step by step to destroy the power of the workers. Strong repressive measures have been introduced and general elections have been postponed for two years. He refuses in present circumstances to discuss withdrawal of the Soviet troops. Only a small fraction of the 190,000 Hungarians who fled the country have accepted the invitation to return;

(xiii) Consideration of the Hungarian question by the United Nations was legally proper and paragraph 7 of Article 2 of the Charter does not justify objections to such consideration. A massive armed intervention by one Power on the territory of another with the avowed intention of interfering in its internal affairs must, by the Soviet Union's own definition of aggression, be a matter of international concern.

# OUR TRAGEDY*

BY

## JOSIP B. TITO

[1956]

I would like to deal with what is happening today in Hungary and what took place in Poland, so that we may have an accurate idea of those events which are very complicated, notably in Hungary, where it came to this, that a large part of the working class and progressive men were fighting in the streets, with arms in their hands, against the Soviet armed forces. When the Hungarian workers and progressive elements began with demonstrations and then with resistance and armed action against the Rakosi method and against further continuation of that course, I am deeply convinced that one could not then speak of counterrevolutionary tendencies. One can say that it is regrettable and tragic that reaction was able to find highly fertile soil there and gradually to divert matters into its own channels, taking advantage for its own ends of the justified revolt which existed in Hungary.

You are aware, in the main, of the causes which have led to the events in Poland and Hungary. It is necessary that we go back to the year 1948, when Yugoslavia was the first to give an energetic answer to Stalin and when she said that she desired to be independent, that she desired to build her life and socialism in accordance with the specific conditions in her country, and that she was permitting no one to interfere in her internal affairs. Of course, it did not then come to armed intervention, because Yugoslavia was already united. Various reactionary elements were not able to carry out various provocations because we had liquidated their main force already during the People's Liberation War. Second, we had a very strong, united, and monolithic Communist Party, steeled in both the prewar period and during the People's Liberation War. We also had a powerful and steeled Army, and most

---

* *Borba,* November 16, 1956. Reprinted from *National Communism and Popular Revolt in Eastern Europe.* Excerpts from an address before a meeting of the Yugoslav League of Communists at Pula, November 11, 1956.

important, we had the unity of the people which personifies all these things.

Once the truth about our country had been victorious and the period of normalization of relations with the countries which had severed relations with us after the ill-famed resolution had begun, the leaders of Eastern countries expressed the desire that we no longer mention that which had been done to us, that we let bygones be bygones, and we accepted this only in order that relations with those countries might be improved as soon as possible. But you will see later that it is indeed necessary to remind certain people who are again today beginning to slander our country and who stand at the head of Communist Parties in the Eastern countries, and in certain Western countries, of what they had been doing to Yugoslavia during these last four or five years, and even longer, when Yugoslavia had stood entirely alone, face to face with a huge propaganda apparatus, when we had to struggle on all sides to preserve the achievements of our People's Revolution, to preserve that which we had already started to build—the foundations of socialism—in one word, to wipe off the disgrace which they had wanted to inflict upon us by various slanders and to prove where the real truth lay. We should remind them and state that these same men had then accused our country, using every possible means, saying that it was fascist, that we were bloodthirsty men and that we were destroying our people, that our working people were not with us, and so forth. We should remind them, they should remember this and keep this in mind today when they again wish to shift the blame for events in Poland and Hungary onto our shoulders. This perfidious tendency originates in those hard-bitten Stalinist elements in various parties who have still managed to maintain themselves in their posts and who would like to consolidate their rule again and impose those Stalinist leanings upon their peoples and on others. I am going to come back to this later. Just now I wish to tell you only that today we must view the events in Hungary in the light of this whole development.

Because of her desire and on her initiative, we have normalized relations with the Soviet Union. When Stalin died, the new Soviet leaders saw that, thanks to Stalin's madness, the Soviet Union found itself in a very difficult situation, in a blind alley both in foreign and internal policy and in the other countries of people's democracy as well, thanks to his nagging and by forcing his methods on them.    They understood where the main cause of all these difficulties lay and at the 20th Congress they condemned Stalin's acts and his policy up to then, but they mistakenly made the whole matter a question of the cult of personality and not a question of the system.    But the cult of personality is in fact the product of a system.    They did not start the fight against that system, or if they have, they have done so rather tacitly, saying that on the whole everything has been all right but that of late, because Stalin had grown old, he had become a little mad and started to commit various mistakes.

From the very beginning we have been saying that here it was not a question of the cult of personality alone, but of a system which had made possible the creation of that cult, that therein lay the roots, that this is what should be struck at incessantly and tenaciously, and this is the most difficult thing to do.    Where are those roots?    In the bureaucratic apparatus, in the method of leadership and the so-called one-man rule, and in the ignoring of the role and aspirations of the working masses, in different Enver Hoxhas, Shehus, and other leaders of certain Western and Eastern parties who are resisting democratization and the decisions of the 20th Congress and who have contributed a great deal to the consolidation of Stalin's system, and who are today working to revive it and to continue its rule.    Therein lie the roots and this is what must be corrected. . . .

You know that Khrushchev was here for a rest.*    On that occasion, we had talks here and many more in Belgrade.    Since I and comrades Rankovic and Pucar were invited to the Crimea, we went there and continued the talks.**    We saw that it would be rather difficult going for other countries, since the Soviet leaders had a different attitude toward other countries.    They had certain wrong and defective views on relations with these countries, with Poland, Hungary, and others.    However, we did not take this too

---

* Khrushchev arrived in Yugoslavia on September 19, 1956.

** Tito departed for the Soviet Union on September 27 and returned October 5.

tragically, because we saw that this was not the attitude of the entire Soviet leadership, but only of a part which to some degree had imposed this attitude on others.  We saw that this attitude was imposed rather by those people who took and still take a Stalinist position, but that there were still possibilities that within the Soviet leadership those elements would win—through internal evolution—who stand for stronger and more rapid development in the direction of democratization, abandonment of all Stalinist methods, the creation of new relations among socialist states, and the development of foreign policy in this same direction as well. From certain signs and also from the conversations, we saw that these elements were not weak, that they were strong, but that this internal process of development in a progressive direction, in the direction of abandoning Stalinist methods, was also hindered by certain Western countries, which by their propaganda and cease-less repetition of the need for the liberation of these countries were interfering in their internal affairs and hindering a rapid develop-ment and improvement in relations among these countries.   The Soviet Union believes that in view of the fact that this interference in internal affairs has assumed rather extensive proportion through propaganda on the radio, the dispatch of material by balloons, and so forth, unpleasant consequences could result if it left these coun-tries completely and gave them, say, a status such as that enjoyed by Yugoslavia.   They are afraid that reactionary elements might then be victorious in these countries.   In other words, this means that they lack sufficient confidence in the internal revolutionary forces of these countries.   In my opinion, this is wrong, and the root of all later mistakes lies in insufficient confidence in the socialist forces of these peoples. . . .

When we were in Moscow* there also was talk of Poland and Hungary and other countries.   We said that Rakosi's regime and Rakosi himself had no qualifications whatever to lead the Hun-garian state and to bring about inner unity, but that, on the con-trary, their actions could only bring about grave consequences. Unfortunately, the Soviet comrades did not believe us.   They said that Rakosi was an old revolutionary, honest, and so forth.   That

---

\* Reference to Tito's State visit to Russia in June 1956.

he is old, this is granted, but that is not enough. That he is honest—this I could not say, inasmuch as I know him, especially after the Rajk trial and other things. To me, these are the most dishonest people in the world. The Soviet comrades said he was prudent, that he was going to succeed, and that they knew of no one else whom they could rely upon in that country. Just because our policy, both state and Party policy, is opposed to interference in the internal affairs of others, and in order not again to come into conflict with the Soviet comrades, we were not insistent enough with the Soviet leaders to have such a team as Rakosi and Gero eliminated.

When I went to Moscow, there was great surprise that I did not travel via Hungary. It was precisely because of Rakosi that I did not want to do so. I said that I would not go through Hungary even if it would have meant making the journey three times shorter. When increasingly strong dissatisfaction began to rise to the surface in the ranks of the Hungarian Communists themselves, and when they demanded that Rakosi should go, the Soviet leaders realized that it was impossible to continue in this way and agreed that he should be removed. But they committed a mistake by not also allowing the removal of Gero and other Rakosi followers, who had compromised themselves in the eyes of the people. They made it a condition that Rakosi would go only if Gero remained. And this was a mistake, because Gero differed in no way from Rakosi. He pursued the same kind of policy and was to blame just as much as Rakosi was.

Well, comrades, what could we do? We saw that things were not going as they should. When we were in the Crimea, Gero "happened" to be there and we "accidentally" met him. We talked with him. Gero condemned the earlier policy and said that it had been a mistake, that they had slandered Yugoslavia; in short, he heaped ashes on his head and asked that good relations be established, promising that all previous errors would be corrected and that the old policy would never be used again. We wanted to prove that we were not vindictive and that we were not narrow-minded, and so we agreed to have talks with Gero and a delegation of the HWP which was to come to Yugoslavia. We wanted to establish relations with the Hungarian Workers Party because we hoped that by not isolating the Hungarian Party we could more easily influence that country's proper internal development.

However, matters had already gone pretty far, a fact which we did not know, so that Gero's coming to Yugoslavia and our joint declaration could no longer help.  People in Hungary were absolutely against the Stalinist elements who were still in power, they demanded their removal and the adoption of a policy of democratization.  When the Hungarian delegation headed by Gero returned to their country, Gero, finding himself in a difficult situation, again showed his former face.  He called the hundreds of thousands of demonstrators, who at that stage were still only demonstrators, a mob, and insulted nearly the whole nation.  Just imagine how blind he was and what kind of a leader he was.  In such a critical moment, when all was in turmoil and when the whole nation was dissatisfied, he dared to fling the term "mob" at people among whom a huge number, perhaps even the majority, consisted of Communists and youth.  This was enough to ignite the powder keg and to bring about the explosion.  Thus the conflict began.

There is no point now in investigating who fired the first shot. The Army was called out by Gero.  It was a fatal mistake to call the Soviet Army at a time when the demonstrations were still in progress.  It is a great mistake to call in the Army of another country to teach a lesson to the people of that country, even if there is some shooting.  This angered the people even more, and thus a spontaneous revolt broke out in which the Communists found themselves, against their will, together with various reactionary elements. . . .

The question may now be asked whether Soviet intervention was necessary?  The first intervention was not necessary.  The first intervention, coming at the invitation of Gero, was absolutely wrong.  The second mistake consisted in the fact that the men responsible, instead of waiting for the second intervention, did not do at once what they did later on, when the second Soviet intervention took place, that is, form a new Government and issue a declaration. Had they first created a new Government and issued such a declaration, the worker and Communist elements would probably have separated themselves from the reactionary elements and it would have been easier to find a way out of this critical situation. . . .

Many people are now asking why the second Soviet intervention took place. It is clear, and we have said so and will continue to say it, that we are against interference and the use of foreign armed forces. Which was now the lesser evil? There could be either chaos, civil war, counterrevolution, and a new world war, or the intervention of Soviet troops which were there. The former would be a catastrophe and the latter a mistake. And, of course, if it meant saving socialism in Hungary, then, comrades, we can say, although we are against interference, Soviet intervention was necessary. But had they done everything that should have been done earlier, there would not have been any need for military intervention. This error was, unfortunately, a result of their idea that military power solves everything. And it does not solve everything. Just look how a barehanded and poorly armed people offers fierce resistance when it has one goal—to free itself and to be independent. It is no longer interested in the kind of independence it will gain, in whether there will be restored a bourgeois and reactionary system, but only that it should be nationally independent. It was this idea that prevailed among the people. Naturally, I can now say only that the first thing was the worst that could have happened and the second, the intervention of Soviet troops, was also bad, but if it leads to the preservation of socialism in Hungary, that is, to the further building up of socialism in that country, and to peace in the world, then one day this will become a positive thing, provided that the Soviet troops withdraw the moment the situation in that country is settled and quiet.

We said this to the Soviet comrades. We concealed nothing. The Soviet comrades stated that their troops would then leave. It should be borne in mind that the Soviet Union, too, is now in a very difficult situation. Their eyes have now been opened and they realize that not only are the Horthyites fighting but also workers in factories and mines, that the whole nation is fighting. Soviet soldiers go unwillingly, with heavy hearts. Therein lies the tragedy. . . .

It is our tragedy—the tragedy of all of us—that socialism has been dealt such a terrible blow. It has been compromised.

# THE STORM IN EASTERN EUROPE*

BY

## MILOVAN DJILAS

[1956]

With the victory of national Communism in Poland, a new chapter began in the history of Communism and of the subjugated countries of Eastern Europe. With the Hungarian people's revolution, a new chapter began in the history of humanity.

These two events, each in its own way, sharply express the internal condition of the East European countries. If the events in Poland encouraged the aspirations of Communist parties—particularly those of Eastern Europe—for equality with Moscow, the Hungarian Revolution made a gigantic leap and placed on the agenda the problem of freedom in Communism, that is to say, the replacement of the Communist system itself by a new social system. If the former event had encouraged both the people and certain Communist circles, the latter encouraged the popular masses and democratic tendencies.

Between the two events, although they happened almost simultaneously, there lies a whole epoch. The changes in Poland mean the triumph of national Communism, which in a different form we have already seen in Yugoslavia. The Hungarian uprising is something more, a new phenomenon, perhaps no less meaningful than the French or Russian Revolution.

In short, these events have brought to the fore the following new questions: (1) the further possibilities of national Communism; (2) the replacement of Communism by a new system, and, along with this, the right of a people heretofore under Communist rule to choose its own—non-Communist—part of development; (3) the problem of the future foreign (and, in my opinion, internal) policy of the Soviet regime.

* From *The New Leader*, November 19, 1956. Reprinted by permission. For the writing of this article, Mr. Djilas was sentenced by a Yugoslav Court to a three-year prison term.

The experience of Yugoslavia appears to testify that national Communism is incapable of transcending the boundaries of Communism as such, that is, to institute the kind of reforms that would gradually transform and lead Communism to freedom. That experience seems to indicate that national Communism can merely break from Moscow and, in its own national tempo and way, construct essentially the identical Communist system. Nothing would be more erroneous, however, than to consider these experiences of Yugoslavia applicable to all the countries of Eastern Eupore.

Yugoslavia's resistance to Moscow in 1948 was possible, first of all, because the revolution took place in the course of the struggle against foreign occupation; in this revolution, an independent Communist country was formed, and with it a new class, the Communist bureaucracy. Not one of the Eastern European countries had this kind of a class, because their Communists received power from the hands of the Soviet regime. For this reason, a united, autonomous Communist bureaucracy could not have been formed. Therefore, there were and still are essential differences between Yugoslav national Communism and that of the East European countries, even though their common keynote is equality with Moscow.

Yugoslav national Communism was, above all, the resistance to Moscow of the Communist party, that is, of its leaders. Not that the people opposed this resistance, not that they did not support it and benefit from it—quite the contrary. But the interest and initiative of the leaders played a crucial and leading role. The resistance of the leaders encouraged and stimulated the resistance of the masses. In Yugoslavia, therefore, the entire process was led and carefully controlled from above, and tendencies to go farther—to democracy—were relatively weak. If its revolutionary past was an asset to Yugoslavia while she was fighting for independence from Moscow, it became an obstacle as soon as it became necessary to move forward—to political freedom.

In the countries of Eastern Europe, the reverse is true. There, Communist resistance to Moscow resulted from the discontent of the popular masses. There, from the very start, unbridled tendencies were expressed to transcend the bounds of national Commu-

nism itself.   The leaders cannot everywhere control and subjugate
the popular masses; therefore in some cases they try to halt any
further estrangement from Moscow.   That is the case, for example, in Czechoslovakia and Rumania.   In Bulgaria and especially in Albania, further de-Stalinization and the strengthening
of national Communism have been halted—only partially because
of fear of Yugoslav domination, although that plays some role.
Other motives were decisive:   The victory of national Communism
in these countries would probably have meant the beginning of the
end of the existing system.

Yugoslavia, both as an example and through the initiative of its
leaders, played an indispensable and important part at the beginning of the transition of Eastern European countries to national
Communism—but only at the start.   As the price of reconciliation
with Belgrade, Moscow was induced to recognize verbally the
equality of Yugoslavia and its "independent path" to "socialism."
In that way, the deep disaffection of the East European nations
received legal possibilities for expression.   Limited but sanctioned
protests against inequality with Moscow began to turn—and in
Hungary did turn—into protest against the system itself.

Yugoslavia supported this discontent as long as it was conducted
by the Communist leaders, but turned against it—as in Hungary—
as soon as it went further.   Therefore, Yugoslavia abstained in the
United Nations Security Council on the question of Soviet intervention in Hungary.   This revealed that Yugoslav national Communism was unable in its foreign policy to depart from its narrow
ideological and bureaucratic class interests, and that, furthermore,
it was ready to yield even those principles of equality and non-
interference in internal affairs on which all its successes in the
struggle with Moscow had been based.

The Yugoslav experience has thus determined the tendency of
the national Communists in both their internal and external
policies—that is, it has determined the limits to which they are
willing to go.   But wishes are one thing and possibilities another.

In all this, Moscow, with its imperialist appetite, is not a passive
observer but an active participant.   In order to avoid an uprising
in Poland and to gain time, it yielded to national Communism

there.    Gomulka's accession to power was not only the result of
the efforts of the Polish Communists; to a larger extent, it represented a compromise between Moscow and the turbulent masses
of the Polish people.    Given independence from Moscow, Gomulka took a historic step forward.    But with half-hearted reforms
he will soon reach a dilemma—which Moscow had foreseen.    He
will have to choose between internal democracy, which has become
inseparable from complete independence from Moscow, and the
ties with Moscow required to maintain the Communists' monopoly
of power.    The events in Hungary have only accelerated this
dilemma, which Gomulka will not be able to avoid.    The victory
of national Communism in Poland is not the end, but rather the
beginning of further disagreements and conflicts inside the country
and with Moscow.

It is difficult to say whether national Communism in Poland will
choose freedom and independence rather than totalitarian rule and
dependence on Moscow.    But without a doubt many Communists
in Poland will not hesitate to choose their own country and freedom.    Knowing Gomulka, a man who is unusually honest, brave
and modest, I am convinced that he himself will not long hesitate
if he is confronted with such a choice.

In Hungary, however, such internal conflicts are over:    Not
only did the so-called Stalinist set vanish, but the Communist
system as such was repudiated.    Moscow at first tried to cover its
intervention by bringing national Communism to power through
Imre Nagy.    But Nagy could only install national Communism
with the assistance of Soviet bayonets, and this threatened the very
end of Communism.    Having finally arrived at the choice between
Soviet occupation and independence, Nagy courageously decided
to sacrifice the Party and Communist power—which had already
been crushed—for the sake of his country and freedom.    Sensing
Moscow's equivocal game, he asked for the withdrawal of Soviet
troops, declared Hungary's neutrality, and appealed for the protection of the United Nations.    His government, up to that point
insignificant, became overnight the symbol of national resistance.

Moscow could no longer preserve Hungarian Communism; it

now faced the choice of either leaving Hungary or occupying it. Thus, its imperialism dropped its last "socialist" mask.

Had the Hungarian Revolution not only brought political democracy but also preserved social control of heavy industry and banking, it would have exercised enormous influence on all Communist countries, including the USSR. It would have demonstrated not only that totalitarianism is unnecessary as a means of protecting the workers from exploitation (i.e., in the "building of socialism"), but also that this is a mere excuse for the exploitation of the workers by bureaucracy and a new ruling class.

Moscow fought the Hungarian Revolution not only for external but for internal reasons. Just as the Yugoslav revolt revealed Moscow's imperialism with regard to Communist countries, so the Hungarian Revolution threatened to reveal the Soviet internal system as the totalitarian domination of a new exploiting class— the Party bureaucracy.

Had the Hungarian Revolution been saved from Soviet intervention, it would have been difficult indeed for Moscow to obscure its internal conflicts by means of foreign conquests and the "world mission." The Soviet system would soon have been confined to its own national boundaries, and there, too, the citizens would be forced to reflect on their position and their destiny. And not only the citizens, but the leaders. They would have to break up into different groups which could no longer carry out mutual purges within their own closed circle, but would be forced to bid for popular support. Thus, new processes would begin in the Soviet Union, too.

The attack of Israel, Britain and France on Egypt cannot permanently divert attention from the events in Eastern Europe, although it certainly encouraged the most reactionary and aggressive elements in the USSR to settle accounts with the Hungarian people. Human history is changing in Eastern Europe, and that is its center today. The outmoded colonial war in the Middle East will have to be stopped.

Moscow and all the other Communist regimes, each in their own way, now face a dilemma which they never faced before. The

Communist regimes of the East European countries must either begin to break away from Moscow, or else they will become even more dependent. None of these countries—not even Yugoslavia —will be able to avert this choice. In no case can the mass movement be halted, whether it follows the Yugoslav-Polish pattern, that of Hungary, or some new pattern which combines the two.

The view that the movement in Bulgaria and Rumania must be slow because of their undeveloped working classes seems dubious to me. In these countries, the peasantry is deeply nationalistic and, once the process starts, may well play a more important role than it did in Hungary. In Czechoslovakia, despite an advanced working class, no significant movement has yet emerged. But if it does, it is likely to go much farther than that of Hungary.

Nobody can predict precisely what Moscow's ultimate course will be. At the moment, it is playing a dual role: recognizing national Communism verbally, simultaneously undermining it by not renouncing its hegemony and imperialism. Of course, the USSR falsely depicts its intervention and pressure as "aid" to and "security" for Communism as such in the subjugated countries. But that plays only a minor role in its actions. Moscow's policy toward Communist countries clearly reflects a will to resist the breakup of the empire, to preserve the leading role of Soviet Communism—a will demonstrated in its efforts to use national Communism as a means and a mask for its imperialist, expansionist policies.

At the same time, however, all these actions involve Moscow not only in external strife, but in internal conflicts. One can declare with certainty that there is a split within the Soviet leadership, and that even the most reactionary and imperialist (the so-called Stalinist) group is hesitant in its action. The influence of this group prevails today, especially in regard to the East European countries. But that does not mean that the other group is for the independence of these countries. The difference between them lies in their methods: whether to stick to the old army and police methods (Stalinist imperialist methods), or apply new ones in which economic and political elements would be dominant. Attempts at introducing the new methods led to the

Polish case, the return to the old ones led to Hungary. Both methods proved ineffective. From this spring the splits and conflicts in the USSR.

Hesitation, duplicity, ideological and political controversies, inconsistency in the use of methods, reversals of attitude and a consistent and feverish insistence on keeping their own positions—all of these things reveal cleavages and contests among the leading group of the Soviet Union. Further changes in this group seem most plausible, and they will be of great importance both for the USSR and for the rest of the world.

There can be no doubt that the rest of the world—perhaps for the first time since the Bolsheviks took power—can directly and positively influence the direction of these changes. Despite the Soviet repression in Hungary, Moscow can only slow down the processes of change; it cannot stop them in the long run. The crisis is not only between the USSR and its neighbors, but within the Communist system as such. National Communism is itself a product of the crisis, but it is only a phase in the evolution and withering away of contemporary Communism.

It is no longer possible to stop the struggle of the people of Eastern Europe for independence, and only with great effort their struggle for freedom. These two struggles are gradually becoming one. If Moscow's imperialism suffers defeat and is prevented from war adventures, the USSR, too, will have to undergo considerable internal changes. For, just as it is compelled to be national in its forms, in essence Communism is one and the same, with the same historical origins and the same destiny. The events in one Communist country necessarily affect all other Communist countries, as in one and the same living organism. And just as Yugoslav Communism, separating itself from Moscow, initiated the crisis of Soviet imperialism, that is, the inevitable birth of national Communism, in the same way the revolution in Hungary means the beginning of the end of Communism generally.

As in all other great and decisive historic events, the Hungarian fighters for freedom, struggling for their existence and country, may not have foreseen what an epochal deed they had initiated. The world has rarely witnessed such unprecedented unity of the popular masses and such heroism. The unity of the popular masses was so strong that it appears as though there had been no civil strife, as though a ruling class had not been wiped out overnight as if it never existed. And the heroic intoxication was so high that barehanded boys and girls were stopping the tanks of the interventionists who, like the Cossacks of Nicholas I in 1848, tried to suppress their liberty and enslave their country.

This event will probably not be repeated. But the Hungarian Revolution blazed a path which sooner or later other Communist countries must follow. The wound which the Hungarian Revolution inflicted on Communism can never be completely healed. All its evils and weaknesses, both as Soviet imperialism and as a definite system of suppression, had collected on the body of Hungary, and there, like festering sores, were cut out by the hands of the Hungarian people.

I do not think that the fate of the Hungarian Revolution is at all decisive for the fate of Communism and the world. World Communism now faces stormy days and insurmountable difficulties, and the peoples of Eastern Europe face heroic new struggles for freedom and independence.

# SOVIET-HUNGARIAN FRIENDSHIP *

BY

## NIKITA S. KHRUSHCHEV

[1958]

Dear comrades!   Dear class brothers!  . . .

The Hungarian people, without landlords and capitalists, are building their own life on socialist foundations and have made great strides on this path.   But it must be frankly said that in the past former leaders of Hungary made serious mistakes and distortions.   Reaction took advantage of these distortions.   The enemies of the people's democratic system in Hungary, with the support of outside imperialist forces, organized a counterrevolutionary revolt in the autumn of 1956.   Reaction tried to destroy the gains of the working people.   The fascist insurgents organized terrorism against the best people in the working class.

In those days we leaders of the Communist Party of the Soviet Union and the Soviet government were faced with a difficult question—how to act.   We had truth and strength on our side.   Our truth was the truth of the working class, the truth of the working people.   But the difficulty was that certain of the less mature segments of the Hungarian workers had been taken in by the enemy propaganda and were taking part in those disorders brought on by counterrevolution.   The question confronted us—what should we do?   Reason told us that we should help the workers and working people of the Hungarian People's Republic.   But it was one thing to give economic aid, to send metal and grain, to give advice.   To send troops was another matter.   Our hand does not tremble when it comes to repulsing the attacks of an enemy.

---

* From a speech given in the city square, Cegled, Hungary, April 7, 1958, on the occasion of an official visit to Hungary by a Soviet Party and Government Delegation, as reported in *Pravda,* April 8, 1958.   This selection is taken from the translation in *The Current Digest of the Soviet Press* (New York), Vol. X, No. 40.   Copyright; reprinted by permission.

But we saw that a certain segment of the Hungarian population in its political unawareness had become a tool in the hands of the class enemies.

Comrades! Believe me, the decision was difficult, but we considered that we could not stand by indifferently when brazen fascist elements began to brutally attack workers, peasants, Communists and other fine representatives of the Hungarian working people on the streets and squares of Budapest and in other Hungarian cities, when the counterrevolution tried to drown the socialist gains of the Hungarian working people in the blood of the people. We could not reconcile ourselves to the restoration of a fascist regime in Hungary and the conversion of this country into a new hotbed of war.

When we responded to the appeal of the working people of Hungary and the Workers' and Peasants' Government and came to your aid, we knew that the enemies of the working class and imperialist reaction throughout the world would use our action for their own ends. But we believed—we were convinced—that the working class and all the working people of Hungary as well as progressive people in all countries would ultimately take this action in the correct light. . . .

Comrade Hungarians! I think you understand very well that in sending our soldiers and officers to fight against the fascist insurgents, we had no other aim than that of aiding our friends, who were for a time in trouble. (*Applause.*)

When the bourgeois states send their troops to other countries, they have predatory aims; they are trying to tighten their exploitational rule over the working people of these countries. We gave you our aid so that you could defend your interests against a handful of fascist conspirators and uphold the right of the people to build their own life, free from exploiters. In giving aid to the Hungarian people in routing the forces of the counterrevolution, we fulfilled our international duty.

Moreover, after the fascist revolt was put down, so that you could more quickly repair the damage brought on your country by the counterrevolutionary conspirators, we gave Hungary a large amount of economic aid.    The Soviet Union sent coal, metal and grain to Hungary.    (*Applause.*)

It was not only the Soviet Union which gave selfless aid to the Hungarian working people.    All the other socialist countries did so, out of a sincere desire to help, so that the material damage done to the economy of Hungary during the events of October and November, 1956, would not mean a sharp drop in the living standards of the Hungarian people.    A state which was following predatory aims would hardly act in this manner.    (*Applause.*)

And now, when we have come to you at the suggestion of the Hungarian Socialist Workers' Party Central Committee and the government of your republic, at the suggestion of Comrade Gomulka, we come with complete confidence that we will meet with complete understanding from you and that we will look openly and honestly into the eyes of the workers, peasants and working intelligentsia of Hungary.    We have come to you as the most loyal friends and brothers.    (*Applause.*)    And we rejoice that we have not been mistaken in our expectations.    During our stay in people's Hungary we have found the friendliest attitude toward the Soviet Union everywhere.

Comrades!    You remember the terrible clamor raised by international reaction during the 1956 Hungarian events.    What did our enemies not write then!    To confuse the people, they drew an analogy between the 1956 events and the 1849 Hungarian revolution.    Hostile propaganda shouted that the Tsarist government of Russia had sent troops to Hungary in 1848 to suppress the revolutionary movement there, and now, they said, the same thing has happened again: Soviet troops have allegedly once again put down a "people's" revolution.

Only the enemies of our peoples and yours could make such an analogy.    To whom is it not clear that the 1848 Hungarian revolution and the October-November, 1956, counterrevolutionary insurrection of fascist elements, supported by the forces of imperialist reaction, are two completely different things?    The difference is that in 1848 the Tsarist government of Russia, that is, the government of exploiters, went to the aid of the Hungarian government of exploiters.    Hungarians know that in 1848 the

Russian Tsar sent his troops to support the Austro-Hungarian monarchy because the Hungarian revolution threatened the Russian autocracy. The Russian Tsar was the enemy not only of the Hungarian people but also of the Russian people. (*Applause.*) He dealt ruthlessly with progressive Russian leaders and destroyed the Decembrist uprising, killing its leaders.

But, comrades, there was another Russia. The Russia of Herzen and Chernyshevsky upheld the people of Hungary in their uprising against their oppressors. We are the direct heirs of precisely this Russia.

Comrades! I want to say something here that the bourgeois nationalists won't like at all. Some of them are certainly present at this meeting. Hungarian bourgeois nationalists say that we bear responsibility for the actions of the Tsarist government in the past century. But they do not mention that Hungarian troops marched with Hitler's troops into the Soviet Union all the way to Stalingrad. And this was not so long ago—only some 15 years ago. What can the Hungarian bourgeois nationalists say to this? The Soviet people know that the Hungarian working people do not bear responsibility for the action of Horthy's fascist clique. We know that Horthy was an enemy of the Hungarian and the Soviet peoples. (*Applause.*) I think that this question is clear to all the workers, working peasantry and working intelligentsia (*prolonged applause*), and it should be explained to anyone to whom it is not clear. (*Applause.*)

Comrades, when we reported that we were sending a delegation to Hungary but did not specify who would be in the delegation, imperialist reaction began to write in the foreign press that Khrushchev, so they said, would not go to Hungary, that if he did go he would get such a reception that he would never set foot there again. (*Laughter.*) I even received telegrams from nonsocialist countries. In one of them a well-wisher wrote: Mr. Khrushchev, don't go to Hungary, but if you go, take more guards. I advise you to do this, he continued, because I can see that you are a good man and are fighting for peace. (*Laughter, applause.*) Of course we have guards with us, but whatever guards we have brought and however many, if the people do not back up the guards, they are of no use. The people are a great force, they overthrow the thrones of kings and carry out the greatest revolutions. It is hard to foist a foreign will on them if it is counter to their class interests.

We have not come to you with fear, Comrade Hungarians, but as brothers to brothers, and we are glad that we were not mistaken in coming thus. (*Stormy applause.*) . . .

Allow me, dear friends, to express to you our most heartfelt love, gratitude and respect. Our Party and government delegation brings you fraternal greetings from the Soviet people and assurances that you will find no better friends than the peoples of the socialist countries. (*Prolonged applause.*) . . .

# THE EXECUTION OF IMRE NAGY *

[1958]

The organs of justice of the Hungarian People's Republic have completed the trial of the high-ranking group of persons who on October 23, 1956, with the active cooperation of the imperialists, unleashed an armed counterrevolutionary uprising designed to overthrow the lawful regime in the Hungarian People's Republic.

In his indictment the prosecutor general of the Hungarian People's Republic accused Imre Nagy and his accomplices Ferenc Donath, Miklos Gimes, Zoltan Tildy, Pal Maleter, Sandor Kopacsy, Jozsef Szilagy, Ferenc Janosi, and Miklos Vasarhely of organizing a conspiracy aimed at overthrowing the people's democratic state regime in Hungary and, in addition, accused Imre Nagy of treason and Sandor Kopacsy and Pal Maleter of organizing a military uprising. The case against the accused Geza Losonczy was dropped as a result of his death following an illness.

The collegium of the people's court under the H.P.R. Supreme Court on the basis of the testimony of the accused and the interrogations of 29 witnesses, having heard the counsels for the prosecution and the defense and after examining a great number of material exhibits in the case of Imre Nagy and his accomplices, decided:

Imre Nagy and his closest accomplices Geza Losonczy, Ferenc Donath, Miklos Gimes, and Jozsef Szilagy in December, 1955, organized a secret antigovernment conspiracy with the aim of seizing power by force and overthrowing the Hungarian People's Republic. At the trial it was established that Imre Nagy and his accomplices played the leading role in preparing and unleashing the counterrevolutionary uprising in October, 1956. In October, 1956, Zoltan Tildy and Pal Maleter, having learned of the hostile aims of Imre Nagy and his accomplices, expressed their agree-

* From a bulletin of the Ministry of Justice of the Hungarian People's Republic, June 16, 1958, transmitted by the Hungarian Telegraph Agency and printed in *Pravda* and *Izvestia,* June 17, 1958. These excerpts are from the translation in *The Current Digest of the Soviet Press* (New York), Vol. X, No. 24. Copyright; reprinted by permission.

ment with them and took an active part in the counterrevolutionary uprising. The members of the conspiratorial group, heading up the forces of internal reaction and in league with foreign imperialists, carried out their attempt at a putsch aimed at the overthrow of the Hungarian People's Republic. . . .

The infamous demonstration of Oct. 23 was begun at the initiative of Imre Nagy and his group, who used their ties with the Petofi circle and with higher educational institutions for this purpose. For example, at a meeting held at the Polytechnical Institute on the night of Oct. 22, Jozsef Szilagy, on instructions of Imre Nagy, issued a personal appeal for the demonstration. The Oct. 23 demonstration was directed by the Imre Nagy group. . . .

During this period secret meetings of the group of conspirators were held almost every day, and sometimes even several times a day. . . . On the morning of Oct. 23, 1956, a secret meeting was held at the apartment of Geza Losonczy. Present at this meeting, in addition to Imre Nagy, were Miklos Gimes, Miklos Vasarhely, Ferenc Janosi and Sandor Haraszty. A list was drawn up of the members of the government to which the conspirators intended to hand over power after the forcible overthrow of the lawful Hungarian government.

Imre Nagy included himself as Premier in the secret list of government members. The Ministerial portfolios were also distributed among the members of the conspiratorial group.

For direct guidance of the armed uprising, which was unleashed at the same time as, and under cover of, the demonstration, the conspirators created several underground centers. One of these centers was organized in the Budapest Police Department. Sandor Kopacsy, breaking his oath, abusing his office as head of the Budapest Police Department and misleading his subordinates, carried out the tasks worked out by the underground center. In order to arm the forces hostile to the people's democracy and at the same time to disrupt the armed forces, which were loyal to socialism, he ordered the regional police departments not to oppose the rebels but, on the contrary, to hand over their weapons and police buildings to them. In this way Sandor Kopacsy distributed to the rebels more than 20,000 firearms from the police arsenals.

This group worked in close cooperation with another group . . . whose members . . . directed subversive activity in the ranks of the army and at the same time issued regularly to the rebels the military plans of the armed forces which were defending the people's republic.

Long before the October uprising Imre Nagy and his accomplices had established secret ties and held talks with the proponents of a bourgeois restoration, with whom they concluded an alliance for the forcible seizing of power. In the process of these talks, for example, Geza Losonczy and Sandor Haraszty had personally as early as July, 1956, and later through the medium of Istvan Erdei, made an agreement with Anna Kethly that she should participate in the government set up by Imre Nagy. In December, 1955, Imre Nagy decided to revive the old so-called "coalition" parties and together with them to form a government. However, Imre Nagy went a great deal further after he had taken over the post of Premier by force and treachery, relying on counterrevolutionary forces. Knowing no limits, he permitted and made possible, within the few days of counterrevolution, the formation, in violation of the constitution, of 70 different parties and organizations, including such notorious bourgeois and fascist parties—forbidden under the Peace Treaty—as the Hungarian Life Party, the Christian Democratic Party, the Christian Hungarian Party, the Hungarian People's Party, the National Camp, the Christian Front, the Catholic People's Party, the Christian People's Party and, in the city of Gyor, the Arrow Cross Party.

In order to secure its power the conspiratorial group of Imre Nagy concluded an alliance with other extreme reactionary groups as well. It "rehabilitated" even the legally condemned former Cardinal Jozsef Mindszenty and enabled him to come out against the people's republic. After the Imre Nagy group had come to terms with Mindszenty through the mediation of Zoltan Tildy, on Nov. 3, 1956, he broadcast over the radio a plan for the restoration of capitalism. Imre Nagy and his accomplices also came to an agreement with the Hungarian bourgeois-fascist emigration, which is in the employ of the imperialists. This was evidenced by the announcement made Oct. 28, 1956, by Bela Vargas, chairman of the "National Committee," in which he declared: "The members of the committee are in constant contact with the leaders of the Hungarian uprising." Following this announcement Zoltan Tildy made an agreement by phone with Ferenc Nagy, who had arrived in Vienna to support the counterrevolution, to the effect that the emigration would back the Imre Nagy government. . . .

After the dissolution and elimination of the central organs of the people's republic Imre Nagy and his conspiratorial group set about liquidating the local agencies of authority. They dissolved the legal organs of state power, the local councils and the economic administrative agencies, and replaced them with the so-called "revolutionary committees," formed for the most part from bourgeois, fascist elements, and with the so-called workers' councils, designed to deceive the working class.

By means of treasonous and subversive activity, Imre Nagy and his accomplices, having obtained a cease-fire, finally succeeded in paralyzing the armed forces, which were defending the people's republic. At the same time they organized, equipped with arms and ultimately legalized the counterrevolutionary forces of the rebels. They recruited war criminals and criminals against the people, convicts released from prisons, and all possible enemies of the people's republic in their so-called "national guard." After that White terrorism began in Budapest and throughout the country. According to the data released up to this time terrorist units during the short rule of Imre Nagy and his group brutally murdered 234 defenseless citizens. During the same period 3000 progressive citizens devoted to the people's democratic system were thrown into prison, and it was planned that they should be executed within a few days. Moreover, up to Nov. 4 lists were drawn up and the mass murder of more than 10,000 persons was planned.

At the same time that Imre Nagy and his accomplices were gathering around themselves the reactionary, counterrevolutionary forces of the country, they were also establishing broad contact and collaboration with various circles, agencies and representatives of the imperialists. . . .

At the same time certain imperialist circles headed by the American imperialists had for many years been directing their entire propaganda apparatus and intelligence service in support of the Hungarian spokesmen for the counterrevolutionary bent—which they called "national communism"—of the Imre Nagy group. In September, 1956, "Strasbourg University," organ of American intelligence, devised a plan for a counterrevolutionary uprising, which they distributed within the country illegally. During the counterrevolution they smuggled a large quantity of arms into the country along with Red Cross packages. The imperialist press and radio simultaneously unleashed a campaign to popularize Imre Nagy. They emphasized that it would be better for the Western powers if Hungary were torn away from the socialist camp by "a group bearing a Communist title." The notorious Radio Free Europe laid the groundwork for the counterrevolutionary uprising in its Hungarian broadcasts and with the aid of balloons released over Hungary; after the uprising began it guided the rebels and gave them military instructions. The conspiratorial group carried out these instructions.

To accomplish their aims and to open the door wide for imperialist interference, Imre Nagy and his traitorous group tried unlawfully to denounce the Warsaw Pact, a defensive alliance of which the H.P.R. is a member. This attempt was made in a radio broadcast of Nov. 4, 1956, by Imre Nagy; in this broadcast he called on the imperialists to open an armed attack against the Revolutionary Workers' and Peasants' Government and against the Soviet troops called upon by that government for aid.

After the counterrevolutionary armed uprising was crushed, certain groups of conspirators of the Imre Nagy brand sought refuge where they had earlier found support. Bela Kiraly, Anna Kethly, Jozsef Kovago and others who took part in overthrowing the state fled to the West to escape responsibility. Jozsef Mindszenty, as the Hungarian authorities know, hid in the American Embassy. . . . The Imre Nagy group, who had come forth earlier under the pirated banner of "national communism," escaped responsibility by fleeing to the Yugoslav Embassy in Budapest.

It is characteristic that the treacherous conspirators continued to carry on their counterrevolutionary activity without interruption even after the Hungarian people, under the direction of the Revolutionary Workers' and Peasants' Government, had set about reestablishing the lawful regime, ensuring a peaceful life for the people and liquidating the grave damage done by the counter-revolutionaries. Anna Kethly, Bela Kiraly, Jozsef Kovago and their accomplices—from the West—and Imre Nagy, Geza Losonczy and others—from the Yugoslav Embassy—gave instructions on continuing armed resistance, organizing strikes to paralyze the life of the country and reorganizing underground subversive activities.

Thus, for example, Imre Nagy and Geza Losonczy, from the Yugoslav Embassy building, established ties through Miklos Gimes and some of their other accomplices with the "Central Budapest Workers' Council" and with Radio Free Europe and even began publishing a new underground newspaper called October 23. All this was proved by indisputable facts during the investigation conducted later and at the trial.

The evidence obtained during the investigation and trial demonstrated and confirmed that Imre Nagy and his accomplices, in accord with their previous revisionist, bourgeois-nationalist political views, were moving, as would be expected, toward an alliance with the most reactionary, imperialistic forces of the bourgeoisie, toward betrayal of the people's democratic system, the Hungarian working people and the socialist homeland.

At the trial the accused Ferenc Donath, Miklos Gimes, Zoltan Tildy, Sandor Kopacsy, Ferenc Janosi and Miklos Vasarhely, expressing their remorse, made a full confession of their guilt. Imre Nagy, Jozsef Szilagy and Pal Maleter denied their guilt. However, during the course of the trial they were proved guilty by the testimony of their accomplices and of witnesses as well as by material evidence, and in their testimony they partially acknowledged the facts of their crimes.

The collegium of the people's court under the Hungarian People's Republic Supreme Court, considering the seriousness of the crimes and the aggravating and extenuating circumstances, declared on the basis of the materials of the trial that the accused were guilty of the crimes with which they were charged and sentenced Imre Nagy to death, Ferenc Donath to 12 years in jail, Miklos Gimes to death, Zoltan Tildy to six years in jail, Pal Maleter to death, Sandor Kopacsy to life imprisonment, Dr. Jozsef Szilagy to death, Ferenc Janosi to eight years in jail, and Miklos Vasarhely to five years in jail.

The sentence is not subject to appeal.   The death sentences have been carried out.

# THE ROUT OF THE COUNTERREVOLUTION*

BY

## WLADYSLAW GOMULKA

[1958]

Forces inimical to socialism and aggressive imperialist circles take advantage of any opportunity, resorting to any means, in their attempts to weaken the unity of the socialist countries and to sow discord in our country as well. A recent example of this is the propaganda campaign unleashed by these forces against the sentences of the Hungarian court in the case of Imre Nagy and the other defendants. How many deliberately fabricated ravings the Western radio stations have disseminated in this connection, ravings and lies aimed at stirring up the people and sowing discord in our society. These radio stations and the pages of the foreign press have fed public opinion with sensational items like "Gomulka has sent Khrushchev a letter protesting the Hungarian sentences," or, "The Polish United Workers' Party Central Committee has condemned the Nagy trial*** has issued instructions to all Party organizations on this question" or, finally, "Gomulka is resigning his post."

Such, comrades, are the methods employed by reactionary propaganda at the service of aggressive imperialist circles, the methods by which these circles are striving to weaken people's Poland, incite the Polish people against the Soviet Union and weaken the unity of the socialist camp.

The severe sentence of the Hungarian court is an epilogue to the tragic events which took place in Hungary almost two years ago, a sort of completion of the rout of the counterrevolution which occurred at that time in Hungary. It is not our business

---

* Speech delivered June 28, 1958, at the Shipbuilders' Day festival at Gdansk Shipyard. The complete text appeared in *Pravda,* June 30. This selection is from the translation of a condensed text in *The Current Digest of the Soviet Press* (New York), Vol. X, No. 26. Copyright; reprinted by permission.

to evaluate the extent of guilt or the justice of the sentence passed at the Nagy trial. That is Hungary's internal affair.

In recalling the Hungarian events it should be mentioned that at that time the fate of the social system in Hungary was decided. The counterrevolution, which wanted to overthrow the socialist system and introduce the capitalist system, ruthlessly slaughtered the Communists and the defenders of the socialist system and hanged them in the streets. To give you an impression of what went on, let me quote excerpts from a report in the Hungarian press on Nov. 2, 1956. The newspaper *Igasag* wrote: "Yesterday there were lynchings in the city. Inscriptions appeared on the walls: Down with the Communists, down with Party members, destroy the Communists!"

While the counterrevolutionaries in Hungary were hanging Communists, Imre Nagy, as Premier of the Hungarian government, announced over the radio: "No one will be punished for participating in the armed struggle" (*Szabad nep* of Oct. 29, 1956). Imre Nagy, who was a revisionist, under the pressure of the mounting counterrevolutionary wave and of forces inimical to the people's power, moved step by step toward capitulation to the counterrevolution, carried out its assignments and jeopardized the socialist system in Hungary. He announced that Hungary was resigning from the Warsaw Pact, and he turned to the imperialist countries for aid. The whole world is familiar with these facts.

The anti-Soviet and anti-Communist campaign which has been unleashed in the West around Imre Nagy's sentence plays into the hands of aggressive imperialist circles. It always turns out that when these circles are preparing some major venture, their propaganda tries to raise a big commotion in the world around other questions so as to deceive the public and divert its attention. So it was with the aggression against Egypt in 1956 and the campaign of that time over Hungary. Now storm clouds are again gathering on the international horizon. One should not underestimate the dangers from aggressive and adventurist imperialist circles, which have again created a tense situation in the Near East, which continue the arms race and have not discontinued

—despite the example and proposals of the Soviet Union—the atomic and hydrogen weapons tests so dangerous to mankind. The anti-Soviet and anti-Communist campaign organized by these circles in connection with the Hungarian court's sentences is poisoning the international situation, aggravating matters and increasing the danger of war. The policy of West Germany serves these same ends, since under cover of Atlantic pacts and alliances the Bundeswehr is being strengthened and atomic and rocket weapons of destruction are being manufactured for it to the tune of anti-Polish revisionist propaganda.

Therefore only the naive can be deceived by the reactionary propaganda unleashed around the Nagy case.

With this as an example we can see more clearly how correct our party's position was in 1956, in the October days, how correct our political line was. Our party is carrying out a policy which corresponds to the interests of our state and people, a policy which serves the security of our country and its further socialist development. Therefore we have always consolidated and will continue to consolidate our solidarity and fraternal cooperation with our mighty neighbor the Soviet Union and with all the countries of socialism on the basis of internationalism, friendship and equality. In building a system of social justice, the socialist system, we know very well the usefulness of the fraternal cooperation of all countries which are moving toward this common good.

In our time we resolutely rebuffed the forces of reaction in Poland, which were speculating on the "theory of the second stage," building up illusory hopes about the "temporary nature" of our system and the people's regime. We shall act with equal resoluteness today or in the future if any forces aspiring to drag Poland back, to shove her into the abyss, attempt to raise their heads.

Our unshakeable aspiration will be to constantly consolidate socialism and to stabilize our social and political life on the basis of mutual trust between the Party and the entire people, who are united in the Front of National Unity.

The calm and productive labor of each person at his post, con-

sistent implementation of the policy of our party and government—
this is the path along which we are moving forward successfully
and which has opened radiant and fine prospects before us.   We
can look with confidence into the future of our socialist home-
land. . . .

# X

# WHAT GUIDES
# RUSSIAN FOREIGN POLICY?

# RUSSIAN IMPERIALISM OR COMMUNIST AGGRESSION?*

## BY

## MICHAEL KARPOVICH

### [1951]

If we are to examine the roots of Soviet expansion, we must, first of all, reject the notion that any people is by nature warlike, peace-loving, imperialistic, or non-imperialistic. We need not "disprove" this peculiar aspect of "racism." We need only recall that, from the end of the seventeenth to the middle of the nineteenth century, most of Europe regarded the French as highly belligerent and aggressive, and the Germans as peace-loving and hardly able to defend themselves. From 1870 on, the "primordial aggressiveness" of the German people was discovered; French bellicosity passed into the realm of historical legend. Outside Europe, the British were regarded throughout the nineteenth century as inherently imperialistic; now little remains of Britannia's past glories, but there is increasing talk of American imperialism—and not only in Communist countries.

Obviously estimates of the imperialistic or non-imperialistic nature of peoples shift with changes in the relation of international forces. For this reason, the question of Russian imperialism can only be discussed in the light of concrete historical data. And in that light, one is struck first, not by the uniqueness of Russia's development, but rather by how closely it parallels that of the other European countries. . . .

With the formation of the Muscovite empire, the experience of the Russian state not only parallels, but is concurrent with, the growth of national states in the West. The Vassilys and Ivans who unified "the Russian lands" were contemporaries of Ferdinand and Isabella in Spain, Louis XI in France, the Tudors in England.

---

*From *The New Leader*, June 4 and June 11, 1951. Reprinted by permission.

In essence, they all pursued the same methods and sought similar "ideological justifications" for their policies. While the Polish historian Kucharzewski sees something specifically Russian in the aggressiveness, trickery and hypocrisy of the early Muscovite Tsars, Western royal analogies can easily be cited for every example of Tsarist political amorality. In the epoch of Machiavelli, most European rulers employed both cunning and force, violated treaties, were merciless with defeated foes. The Tsars referred to fictitious rights and doubtful historical traditions; West European "legalists" invented similar myths. Certainly the notorious Muscovite messianism has a parallel in the idea of restoring the Roman Empire which captivated the West for so long. The rise of Moscow is a chapter in the modern history of Europe as a whole.

When Europe embarked on a policy of colonial expansion, England, France, Spain and Portugal moved across the Atlantic and Indian Oceans into America and India; Russia moved eastward and gradually conquered northern Asia. Both expansionist processes reveal the same combination of economic and political motives, private initiative and state control, peaceful colonization and violent conquest. . . .

One feature of Russian expansion, it seems to me, has played a large part in producing exaggerated Western notions of it. Russia, always a continental power, never possessed a formidable navy. Unable to establish scattered colonies overseas, the Tsars instead annexed adjoining land. Such expansion is visually more impressive than colonial expansion of the English type. The continuous expanse of Russia, all in one color, cannot be missed on a map; a grasp of the British Empire's dimensions requires a certain mental effort. . . .

The "Russian menace" began to arouse fear rather late in the Western world, toward the end of the eighteenth century—or coincidentally with the emergence of Russia as a European great power. . . .

France was the first great nation to grow alarmed. To the extent that the Tsars' concrete political aims were realized, Turkey, Poland and Sweden were weakened, and the "eastern barrier" which French diplomats had so energetically constructed as part of their struggle against the Hapsburgs was destroyed. When

English and Russian imperial interests began to conflict, at the turn of the century, Great Britain also became uneasy. Russia had reached the Black Sea and was exerting pressure on Turkey; it had consolidated the Caucasus and was trying to bring Turkey under its influence; it had moved through the Trans-Caspian provinces toward Central Asia. In this, it was pursuing isolated concrete aims, unconnected by any "general idea." But to Britain, Russian expansion began to look like a systematic offensive against the British colonial empire. . . .

. . . The inescapable conclusion is that pre-revolutionary Russian imperialism was essentially no different from the imperialism of the other great powers. The Russian empire was a conventional one; its policies were traditional imperialist policies. Neither its emergence nor its expansion needs to be explained by allusions to "Russian messianism" or to peculiar traits of the "Russian character." If there is an illusory identity between pre-revolutionary and Soviet foreign policy, it stems from the fact that the same territories often constitute the objects of expansion. Finland, the Baltic States, Poland, Bessarabia, the Balkans, Constantinople, the Dardanelles, Persia, Chinese Turkestan, Mongolia, Manchuria, Korea—these names stud the pages of Tsarist diplomatic history as they do the newspapers of our own day, creating an impression of historical continuity. But must one fall into geographic fatalism? After all, when one comes down to it, the Soviet Union still occupies the same space as the Russian Empire did before it; its expansionist tendencies can, therefore, be expected to appear in the same neighboring territories. One can hardly conclude from this that the aims, methods and general character of both imperialisms are the same.

For just as the Soviet system, or the modern totalitarian state in general, differs radically from traditional nation-states (whether absolute monarchies, constitutional monarchies or republics), so, too, the foreign policy of such a totalitarian state is something radically and fundamentally new. Postwar Soviet foreign policy's extraordinary territorial scope and dynamism have been referred to often—and rightly so. For it is a "global" policy, persistently seeking to achieve a number of aggressive aims simultaneously in various corners of the earth. This alone sharply distinguishes

Soviet policy from the policy of the Tsars, who, as a rule, pursued limited aims and pursued them in a certain sequence.

Peter quickly gave up his struggle with Turkey to concentrate on the struggle for the Baltic. Catherine contented herself with the conquest of the Black Sea coast and readily pigeonholed the famous "Greek project." At the Congress of Vienna, Alexander I abandoned his original Polish plan when he encountered the opposition of other powers. Diplomatic pressure alone forced Nicholas I to renounce what Russia had gained from Turkey at the Treaty of Unkiar Skelessi. After the Crimean War and the Congress of Berlin, Russian diplomacy instantly drew the appropriate conclusions from its defeat, temporarily "put the Near Eastern question on ice," and concentrated on other problems (in Asia). And after the Russo-Japanese War, Russia divided spheres of influence in the Far East with Japan, concluded an agreement on Central Asian questions with England, and only then moderately and cautiously put forward her Near Eastern aims, attempting to obtain a settlement by negotiation.

This difference between the global activities of the Politburo and the limited activities of the Romanoffs is sometimes explained by the Soviet Union's greater military and economic might. But that might should not be exaggerated, just as, in retrospect, the strength of imperial Russia should not be minimized. In relation to the other great powers, Russia under Peter, Catherine and Alexander I was not militarily weak.

Another explanation seems sounder. This cites the extraordinarily favorable international situation which was created for the Soviet regime at the end of the Second World War. Disruption of the established balance of power and the collapse of existing institutions is always a temptation for expansion. The chaos at the end of the last war was unparalleled in modern times. And thus, it is said, Stalin had opportunities which the Russian emperors never had.

Yet it seems to me that this also fails to explain fully the dynamism of Soviet policy. The difference between Tsarist and Soviet policy is qualitative, not quantitative. The presence of several powerful rivals was not the only reason pre-revolutionary Russian policy lacked global or continental scope. Much more important, pre-Communist Russian policy, in contrast to Soviet diplomacy, had no global *aims*. It did not have these aims because it possessed no *all-embracing political plan*, with an *over-all idea* underlying it. The idea of world revolution underlies an all-embracing Soviet plan, contained in the body of literature the Communists call Marxism-Leninism-Stalinism. The Tsars had no such aims or plans.

Such an assertion conflicts, of course, with the recently developed theory of innate Russian messianism. Putting aside the Russian people for a moment, let us examine the role played by messianism in Russian state policy. The most famous expression of this messianism is the doctrine of "Moscow, the Third Rome," which arose in church circles and which effectively asserted the national identity and independence of Russian Orthodox Christianity. This doctrine also, to some extent, helped mold the ideology of the autocracy. But historians have been unable to show that it exerted any influence whatever on the foreign policy of the Muscovite state. The Moscow regime never asserted its rights to the "Byzantine inheritance," as it did to the "Vladimir" or "Kiev" inheritances. In fact, these rights were stubbornly waved away, even when Western powers, for their own purposes, tried to tempt Moscow with them.

Those who accept the notion of Russian messianism generally make a big jump from the Third Rome to the Pan-Slavism of the nineteenth century and, once again, endow this sporadic, unorganized movement with a significance it never actually possessed. In most cases, Pan-Slavism remained a state of mind; it drew on various ideological sources, many of which had no connection with either the religious idea of the Third Rome or even the romantic historical theories of early Slavophilism. Although there were, at various times, individual Pan-Slavists in diplomatic, military or court circles, Pan-Slavism was never official governmental doctrine. Even at the height of Pan-Slavist agitation (during the Balkan crisis of the 1870s), the Government never identified itself with the movement; on the contrary, it dissociated itself from it and, at times, even penalized it. Nicholas I's hostile attitude toward Pan-Slavism is well known.

The assertion that imperial Russia aspired to European hegemony is equally unfounded. The Holy Alliance, as envisaged by Alexander I, was not an idea for Russian hegemony, but for durable international agreement. As an idea, it played about as great a role in subsequent events as the Atlantic Charter has played in our own time. . . .

The foreign policy of the Tsars was the customary policy of a national state. The Romanoff autocracy, unlike the Soviet Union, was neither an "ideocracy" nor an insurrectionary-totalitarian state, and it is impossible to find a parallel with "Marxism-Leninism-Stalinism" in its foreign policy. Furthermore, the Russian autocracy never had anything at its disposal even remotely suggestive of a Comintern or Cominform. The difference in aims between the Tsars and the Bolsheviks is matched by an equally fundamental difference in methods.

\*     \*     \*

When Western writers today match up selected facts and assert that Tsarist and Soviet diplomacy are continuous, they are essentially doing what apologists for Soviet foreign policy do. These apologists say, "Yes, Russia interferes in the East European countries, but don't America and England do the same in Greece and Iran? Yes, Moscow sends Communist propaganda beyond its frontiers, but doesn't America conduct foreign propaganda, too? Russia is creating puppet governments, but what is America doing in Korea?"

This is the same logic as the matching of pre-revolutionary and Communist foreign policies. The trick in both cases is to tear apparently similar facts out of context, and thus obscure a *basic difference in principle* between two different *systems*. It is a classic example of how a difference in quantity becomes a difference in quality. What in one case was a deviation, in the other becomes a norm. The diplomacy of old Russia was part of a world-wide diplomatic tradition. Soviet diplomacy is hostile to, and consciously violates this tradition; in moments of candor, it justifies the violations on grounds of principle.

Like the Fascist states, the Stalin regime conducts a *diplomacy of civil war*. Its spirit, aims and methods were created by the Bolsheviks during their struggle for power in Russia and against the Russian people; when the opportunity arrived, they were applied on an international scale. The Comintern and Cominform are not in the same class as past instances of internal intervention by foreign states. With the Communist "fifth column," something *fundamentally new* appeared on the historical scene. Anyone who has not fully grasped this is incapable of understanding Soviet foreign policy.

When Western diplomats are piqued at the irascible behavior of Soviet diplomats, they derive consolation from the diaries of foreign tourists in Tsarist Russia. . . . But such comparisons create merely an *illusion* of continuity. For in the final analysis, Tsarist diplomacy spoke the common language of European diplomacy; the Western powers could always reach agreement with pre-Communist Russia by means of a traditional diplomatic pact. An angry Theodore Roosevelt once did write that "Russians always lie," but Tsarist diplomats, following the precept of Talleyrand, lied about as much as the other European diplomats.

The incredible lying of Vishinsky and Malik is something else. It cannot be ascribed to any tradition of general diplomacy or of the Russian nation. Soviet diplomats behave as they do, not because they are Russians, but because they are Communists, because they have special aims which have nothing in common with the aims of pre-Communist Russia. For an explanation of the conduct of Soviet diplomats (and of the diplomats of Red Peking and the "people's democracies"), it is quite sufficient to refer to the history of the Bolshevik party.

More vital to a comparison of Tsarist and Communist expansion are their respective concepts of "security." It appears to me that an appreciation of the unique Soviet concept of "security" will go further toward providing an understanding of Soviet foreign policy, than comparisons with the Tsars.

Traditionally, a nation's external security was guaranteed by political or military agreements, "rectification" of strategic frontiers and, where possible in extreme cases, by spheres of influence or protectorates. From this point of view, Russia's security was amply guaranteed, for example, by the relations established with Czechoslovakia after the last war.

Czechoslovakia made all the political and economic concessions Stalin sought. Benes and Masaryk "voluntarily" ceded the Carpatho-Ukraine, giving the U.S.S.R. direct access to Hungary—a vital "rectification" of the Soviet strategic frontier. The Communists received disproportionate influence in the Government. Moscow vetoed Czech participation in the Marshall Plan. Czechoslovakia was virtually a Soviet protectorate even before the coup of February 1948.

But Stalin needed this coup just the same. He needed it because all he had achieved was still inadequate according to his own concept of "security." For, in contrast to the traditional idea, this Soviet concept aims not at the territorial security of the nation, but at the political security of the regime in power.

Czechoslovakia was a threat to the Soviet regime because, even in 1947, it retained some democratic freedom internally and in its relations with the non-Communist world. And in Communist eyes, nothing is more dangerous than freedom nearby. Fear of freedom is the essence of the Soviet theory of security: The tyranny established in Russia is not secure until the same tyranny is established over the entire world. This so-called "triumph of socialism" is the ultimate aim of the party of Lenin and Stalin. Its immediate task is to "secure" nearby countries which fall under Soviet influence. To provide such "security," these countries must be completely Stalinized. The transition from "people's democracy" to complete Sovietization is an imperative—in Eastern Europe, in China, wherever the Soviets gain a foothold.

The policy based on this concept of "security" is an aggressive one. After stifling freedom in one country, the Politburo must eradicate the threat of freedom in its neighbors. This vicious spiral can only be broken by the world triumph of Communism or the eradication of the Soviet regime.

This is, of course, quite different from the security concept of the Tsars. Nicholas I may have preferred the German monarchies to the constitutional regimes of England and France; Alexander III may have hesitated before allying himself with the Third French Republic. But no Russian diplomat ever imagined that the world triumph of autocracy was needed for Russian security.

We have seen thus far that Russian state policy in the pre-

Communist period was traditional and conventional. This historical fact forces believers in "innate, age-old Russian imperialism"
to link their historical presumptions with theories on "the Russian
soul." Thus the Polish historian Kucharzewski says the Russians
are nomads who cannot create a sufficiently rich and stable culture
on their own soil, and thus must seize the riches amassed by other,
settled peoples. More usually, however, the Russians are called
innately messianistic. Support for this is culled from the utterances
of Russian thinkers from the Slavophiles to Berdyaev. These
prove that messianic tendencies can be found in Russian thought.
But to prove that messianism is the age-old moving force of Russian expansion, one must show that it was widespread among the
Russian people. And this task is, at least as far as history goes, impossible. "Holy Russia" was part of Russian folklore; "Moscow,
the Third Rome" was not. One can hardly assume that the masses
thought much about "the Byzantine inheritance." At times, the
Russians did have a sense of community with their "Slavic brothers" of the same blood and faith. But this feeling hardly represents
the adoption of Pan-Slavism as the political program of the Russian
people.

Among educated circles in Russia, messianism was never too
strong. During the reign of Nicholas I, the Slavophile Aksakov
complained that so many Russian intellectuals in the provinces
supported the "Westerner" Belinsky, and none shared his own
views. A book by Danilevsky, once called "the bible of Pan-
Slavism," enjoyed some success during the reign of Alexander III,
but was completely forgotten by the turn of the century. By that
time, Pan-Slavism had become almost the exclusive property of
nationalist right-wing groups; among most intellectuals, it aroused
little interest.

Messianism, Pan-Slavism and imperialism in general were alien
to most of the Russian intelligentsia from the first quarter of the
nineteenth century; before then, outstanding representatives of
Russian culture did take pride in Russia's foreign gains. (Pushkin
was simultaneously "the bard of empire and liberty.") But after
Pushkin, this attitude steadily declined.

The absence of "imperial consciousness" among the Russian
intelligentsia is a fact. No important work in Russian historical

writing deals with the development of the Russian empire. . . .

Among Russia's liberals and democrats, Paul Miliukov is generally singled out as an imperialist. But his "imperialism" consisted only in a refusal in 1917 to renounce Russian claims to Constantinople and the Straits, which had been conceded by the Western Allies by treaty. . . . Even Miliukov's moderate "imperialism" proved unacceptable to the Russian people in the first months after the democratic revolution of March 1917. The revolutionary government immediately proposed a peace without annexations or indemnities—a program which had strong roots in pre-revolutionary pacifism and anti-imperialism. In judging the state of mind of the Russian people, one should overlook neither the enthusiasm this program evoked, nor the skillful way Lenin exploited it.

History shows that imperialism, like nationalism, never originates among the masses, but seeps down to them from the cultural élite. The pre-Communist Russian intelligentsia was predominantly anti-imperialistic, and it is hard to imagine an imperialist spirit among the popular masses. This heritage quite probably has immunized the Russian people against Communist messianism.

There seems to me no basis for the assertion that the Russian people are burning with the desire to impose Communism on the world. Former Soviet citizens testify to the contrary. Frederick C. Barghoorn, who served in our Moscow Embassy during the war, declares:

> I never met any Soviet people who seemed to take pride in Soviet political or territorial expansion, in Pan-Slavism or in the extension of Communist power.

In the light of historical experience, this seems more like the Russian national tradition than any mythical "innate Russian imperialism." Far from backing Communist aggression abroad, the Russian people yearns for lasting peace, for normal and decent conditions of human life and, above all, for its own liberation from Communist aggression at home.

# THE DRIVING FORCE BEHIND SOVIET IMPERIALISM*

## IS IT A NEW MENACE OR THE OLD BEAR REAWAKENED?

### BY

### PETER MEYER

### [1952]

On June 28, 1951, Secretary of State Dean Acheson, testifying before the House Foreign Affairs Committee, brought to the attention of the American public a question discussed up to then by only a few scholars and isolated groups of emigrés. The question was: are we fighting Russia, or are we fighting Soviet Communism? Does the aggressiveness of Russia's present rulers, with the resulting permanent crisis and threat of war, flow from the very same motives and interests that led the czars to try to expand in more or less the same directions as the Soviets; or is it impelled by an ideology and a system—Communism—international in its character and its aims? That is: do we face Communism dressed as Russian nationalism or Russian nationalism dressed as Communism?

The political consequences of the answer decided on are enormous, as Secretary Acheson well knew, and as the *New York Times* emphasized at the time of his testimony: "Secretary Acheson pointed out that the Soviet rulers have followed the imperialist Russian tradition. . . . The development of the Duchy of Muscovy from a vassal and tribute collector of the Mongol Tartars to an empire which first enslaved the Russian people themselves . . . and then embarked on conquering other nations until it dominates half of Europe and an even larger part of Asia, is part of elementary history. Viewed in the light of this history, there is a peculiar unreality attaching itself to the American policies which

---

*From *Commentary*, March 1952. Copyright 1952 by the American Jewish Committee. Reprinted by permission.

after the First World War opposed any 'dismemberment' of the Russian empire even by nations fighting for their freedom from its rule. . . . Mr. Acheson's statements show that these policies have been replaced by a new realism." . . .

Obviously, the issue is a crucial one, affecting as it does the basic aims of American defense policy in the face of the Soviet challenge, as well as our policy toward the Russian and non-Russian peoples—Ukrainians, Georgians, Uzbeks, etc.—that inhabit the Soviet Union. . . . It is clear that the fate of these peoples constitutes a long-range problem of great significance. It is equally clear, however, that our answer to the question—Is our enemy Russia or Communism?—is of great immediate importance. For the strategy and tactics of the West vis-à-vis the Kremlin must remain hesitant until we arrive at an answer; and it is all-important that it be a correct one. It seems that Secretary Acheson had found the answer to his own satisfaction: our enemy is indeed the same old Russian imperialism *redivivus*, and our policy should be to "contain" it. Since the familiar is always less frightening than the unfamiliar, it would be reassuring if he were right. But is he?

Bolshevik policy has undergone a peculiar evolution since 1917, beginning at an extreme of internationalism and ending at the other extreme of a kind of patriotic xenophobia that regards "cosmopolitanism" as the blackest sin. Lenin would have ridiculed the claim that it was important to preserve and defend the Russian empire, or that Russia and Russian culture were superior to other nations and their cultures. During World War I, he insisted that the only genuine socialist program was that expressed in the slogan of "revolutionary defeatism"—only those who worked for the defeat of their own army and government were true socialists. And no one could be considered a socialist, he added, if he did not fight for the right of all national minorities to full self-determination, including secession.

After the Bolshevik seizure of power, understandably enough, this policy was changed: the Bolsheviks were now for the defense of their "proletarian state." But they were not only for its defense in the geographic or strategic sense: their notion of defense included, when feasible, aggressive warfare to extend socialist rule to other countries. As Lenin had written in 1915: "The victorious proletariat of that country [in which the socialist revolution first takes place], having expropriated the capitalists and organized socialist production at home, will rise against the rest of the capitalist world, attracting the oppressed classes of other countries, raising among them revolts against the capitalists, *launching, in case of necessity, armed forces against the exploiting classes and their states"* (my emphasis). This idea was invoked by the left Communists who opposed the treaty of Brest-Litovsk with Germany in 1918. Did we not always say, they argued, that we would conduct a revolutionary war against capitalist states when we came to power? Lenin agreed this would be most desirable, but he pointed out that it was impossible under the circumstances. The masses did not want to fight, the army had disintegrated. Was it not more reasonable to give the Germans what they demanded and preserve state power for a future comeback?

In this debate and in all Bolshevik discussion in these early years, the idea of "Russia" played no role at all. Both sides were arguing about what was better for "world revolution": to risk a defeat in a glorious struggle against overwhelming odds while trying to arouse the international proletariat by a heroic example— or to preserve a bastion from which the world revolution would strike out in better times. . . .

The final outcome of the discussions of these early days was the decision that, though such aggressive tactics were in principle legitimate, it was inexpedient to adopt them under the circumstances of that time. Rather than risk the loss of Bolshevik control over Russia by launching a revolutionary crusade into Europe, that control was to be consolidated so that Russia could serve as the base and fortress of world revolution. But the result of this decision was, in the end, that Russia was cut off increasingly from Western Europe and forced to develop along lines of her own. These lines were determined by the peculiar conditions of Russia as a historical entity, and—as the power struggles of the 20's decided—by Stalin.

The notion of exporting Communism by force of arms seemed to have been decisively abandoned when Stalin attained exclusive power in the middle 20's on his program of "socialism in one country." Lenin had insisted that, since Russia was a backward country, the Communists could not retain power there for long unless reinforced by victorious proletarian revolutions in the advanced countries of the West. Stalin now claimed that, on the contrary, Russia *was* able to achieve socialism with its own resources. Hearing this, Western statesmen rejoiced and the Communist Left Opposition despaired. For both were convinced that socialism, understood as an economy of plenty, equality, and freedom, would fail in isolated, backward, impoverished Russia. What they did not realize was that Stalin's "socialism" would, by the end of the 20's, mean the centralized exploitation of society by a hierarchy of "administrators" wielding all economic and political power. And such a system, resting on an economy of scarcity instead of plenty, could be established inside one country, and especially a backward one.

How did this new system come into existence? Had Stalin, whatever his original intentions, become transformed, willy-nilly, into a successor of the czars, ruling not only in their place but in their manner, with their motives, and—ultimately—with their policies? In later years it began to look this way, and one should not underestimate the importance of the social and spiritual forces specific to Russia in the transformations that the Bolshevik regime underwent there. But actually it was not the unexpected resurgence of the Slavic soul, but rather the presence of a very specific economic and social situation that led to the total liquidation of socialist hopes.

The Bolsheviks had seized power as a tiny even though highly disciplined and organized minority. The industrial working class in Russia was relatively small, uneducated, and inexperienced in politics. The peasant masses supported the Bolsheviks in the moment of revolution, but could not be relied on after that. This lack of broad social support, plus foreign and civil wars, demanded a thorough centralization of power if Bolshevik rule was to be maintained.

In order to hold on to power, the Bolsheviks sacrificed much of their pre-revolutionary program. Instead of workers' control in the factories, they gave absolute power to directors and managers appointed by the party; instead of equalizing incomes, they introduced high salaries and premiums, first for bourgeois specialists, but later for their own party officials too. The radical democratic program proclaimed by Lenin in *State and Revolution* in the summer of 1917 went overboard: instead of officials elected by, responsible to, and subject to recall by the voters, there were commissars with dictatorial powers, a one-party dictatorship, and terror directed against all opposition.

A centralized, state-owned, planned economy provided, in the absence of democratic checks and balances, a firmer basis for the absolute power of a privileged class than ever capitalism could. This was not an entirely new phenomenon: capitalism is something of an exception in history, and most of the privileged and ruling classes of the past have derived their power from the state, not from private property with the rights that cluster about and extend from it. This is especially true of Asiatic societies, which were ruled, literally for millennia, by despotic hierarchies. In Russia, where such traditions were strong, the evolution toward bureaucratic despotism was easier than it would have been in any other European country.

In the course of two decades, the Stalinist bureaucracy succeeded in completely liquidating the independent peasantry and totally enslaving the urban working class. It became the undisputed master of the country and, having done that, was ready to enter the lists as a competitor for world power—if it got the opportunity. In the Second World War, this opportunity came.

But why are the new rulers of Russia not satisfied to stay at home and exploit the immense natural riches and endless reservoirs of manpower they now possess?

The answer is that they are driven to expansion by the inner conflicts of the new social system they have established. In every modern society there exists some method of regulating the distribution of the means of production and of labor power among the various branches of production. In the free-market countries, the law of supply and demand maintains, even at the cost of recurrent crises, some equilibrium. In Soviet society, this law was superseded by the universal monopoly of the rulers of the state. The distribution of labor and of the national product now depends on their planning. But rational planning and harmonizing of conflicting interests are impossible where free discussion, criticism, timely correction of mistakes by the pressure of public opinion, and democratic bargaining between social groups are outlawed. The omnipotent ruling group tends to sacrifice the various interests of the community to its own appetite for power, and to substitute wishful thinking for economic realities. Their plans, however unrealistic, *must* be fulfilled. . . .

Mistakes in planning are inevitable, and as they cannot be criticized and corrected in time, they swell to colossal proportions. The annals of Soviet economy are full of stories about factories built in impossible locations, machines inoperative for lack of some parts, goods sent back and forth several times through the vastness of Russia, industries left without raw materials, goods rotting for lack of transportation. Often the mistakes are discovered only when the situation approaches disaster. Then a campaign of "self-criticism" breaks loose on orders from above; the resultant purge of scapegoats frequently disorganizes production still more.

The disproportions in planning are not accidental. Their existence is the inevitable result of the absolute rule of bureaucracy. Bureaucracy everywhere inclines to waste, duplication, superfluous paper work, the building of "office empires," and parasitism. It is not difficult to imagine the extent of these abuses where there is no public control and the bureaucrats have the power to jail and execute their critics. . . .

The costs of this bureaucratic machine are tremendous. And if we add the colossal outlays and the diversion of manpower necessary for the maintenance of the army, militia, secret police, etc., we can easily understand why the living standards of Russian workers and kolkhoz peasants are so low. . . .

. . . An economy in which labor is wasted and destroyed on such an immense scale, and which is burdened by such enormous unproductive expenses, remains too unproductive to sustain the accelerated tempo of investment that the bureaucracy demands. Thus Soviet society is plagued by chronic shortages of food, industrial consumption goods, raw materials, machines, skilled labor, manpower in general, and by recurrent economic convulsions.

While there were still strata of the population that were not fully integrated in the totalitarian economy, the crises could be solved at their expense: these classes would be rendered more exploitable by being reduced to the status of immediate serfs of the regime. The best example is the crisis that preceded the collectivization of agriculture. In the early 30's, the tremendous investments in heavy industry did not provide for enough manufactured consumers' goods to give to the peasants in exchange for the food and other things they raised. Offered too little compensation for their products, the peasants "went on strike," cut their production, slowed down their deliveries of food. The answer was the liquidation of the "kulaks" and forced collectivization. At the price of untold atrocities and a famine in which millions perished, the peasants were transformed into serfs of the bureaucracy.

By the end of the 30's, the totalitarian society in Russia had been fully established. There were no more classes to be expropriated, all strata of the population were totally enslaved, and a further intensification of the exploitation of available resources was rapidly reaching the point of diminishing returns. But now resources are present in the countries surrounding the Soviet Union—and would be available to her if organized and exploited in the Soviet way, and under Soviet power. Measured by Russian standards, and seen in the perspective of totalitarian—not capitalist—exploitation, even Poland and Rumania appeared as "have" countries whose "liberation" and integration in the Soviet economic order would be extremely profitable to the latter. And let me point out here that those who believe that the Stalinist regime has occupied neighboring countries or added satellites to its empire for "purely strategic reasons," in order to "protect its borders" and surround itself with a buffer zone of "friendly governments," simply do not understand the workings of the Soviet system. Soviet bureaucracy extends into foreign countries for the same reason that pioneers who "mine the soil" must continually move on—the form of exploitation is so wasteful that new resources are constantly needed.

Soviet expansion thus differs radically from traditional capitalist expansion. Russia obviously does not flood her dependent countries with cheap commodities. Rather her first step is to drain the occupied country of both industrial and agricultural goods; these are expropriated, requisitioned, or simply looted, and then shipped home. Russia usually does not export capital either—rather, she expropriates it as she expropriates goods. Here again the most primitive method of acquisition, the simple appropriation and transfer of capital goods, plays an important role at the beginning of an occupation—billions of dollars worth of industrial equipment, whole factories, whole industries have been removed from Germany and Manchuria and shipped to Russia.

But as soon as their rule in the given country has been stabilized the Soviets begin to exploit the expropriated means of production right on the spot. The forms are diverse. . . . Most [industries] are left formally in the hands of the satellite states, operated under Russian control and supervision, and integrated in Soviet Production plans. . . .

The satellites are required to sell their goods to the Russians at low prices and buy Russian goods in return at prices that are simply dictated: the Russians may then sell satellite products on the world market for huge profits. . . .

Thus the Soviet ruling class has very good economic reasons for seeking to expand its rule. But it has political reasons too—and these not primarily the classical strategic ones such as govern most nations' foreign policies. Quite simply, the existence of any relatively free country, regardless of how weak or small or miserable it may be, is a threat to the rulers of the Soviet Union. Soviet theoreticians have as much as admitted the fact. On August 15, 1951, the Moscow *Bolshevik,* the theoretical organ of the Soviet Communist party, answered a question put by a number of readers: Can we still speak of capitalist encirclement when we now rule, with China and the satellites, a third of the world? The answer begins: *"Capitalist encirclement is a political term. Comrade Stalin has stated that capitalist encirclement cannot be considered a geographic notion."*

The article proceeds to demonstrate that capitalist encirclement will last as long as there are *any* non-Soviet countries at all in the world, and that this is the reason why state power, an army, police, repression, all of which, according to Marx and Lenin, were supposed to "wither away," must be still maintained, even in the period of "complete Communism" that Russia will soon be entering. As long as one country is free, it "encircles" the Soviet world, and the dictatorship must therefore be maintained and strengthened.

This does not mean that the Soviet ruling class consciously in-

vented the notion of "capitalist encirclement" in order to cover its
predatory aims and deceive its subjects. The relation between what
rulers believe and the real motives from which they act is complicated. Like many expansionists before them, Soviet bureaucrats
probably believe just as sincerely in the reality of a worldwide conspiracy against them as they do in their own "civilizing mission."
They must believe this, otherwise they would have to admit and
try to understand that the contradictions of Soviet society which
force it to seek relief by expansion are the necessary consequences
of their own despotic rule. Not only must they refuse to admit
this; it is doubtful whether they can even let themselves understand
it. They cannot acknowledge that economic and social realities
guide and constrain them—as they guide and constrain, *mutatis
mutandis*, the capitalist world too. This is inconceivable to a new
ruling class which having concentrated all economic, political, and
cultural power in its hands, feels that it ought to be able to change
not only social relations but nature itself, and even past history.
The bureaucrats were nurtured in the belief that they had made
the leap from necessity to freedom by virtue of "the Revolution"
and, more importantly, by virtue of the destined role of the class
they represented. They had raised—and believed—such slogans
as "There are no fortresses Bolsheviks cannot storm," or "Cadres
decide everything." . . .

Obviously, the rulers of Soviet Russia have a mentality quite different from that of most statesmen in the West—or even of previous Russian statesmen. They believe that Russia has a superior
social order—but its citizens have to be protected from all contact
with other social orders, even if inferior, because such contact
would corrupt them. They know that Soviet doctrine is the self-
evident truth—but even the mere traces of other doctrines have to
be eradicated because they would confuse and mislead the people.
They boast that the ruling elite is incomparable for its wisdom
and virtue—but every one of the members of that elite may be a
foreign spy; and, as a matter of fact, in the 30's, nine-tenths of the
ruling cadres in Russia were condemned as traitors. The bureau-
crat has to maintain and expand the "classless" society in which
class enemies keep popping up from behind every bush, just as
the greatest world power remains "encircled" so long as one free

country is left.  To defend the Soviet Union, the Stalinist must conquer the globe.

Expansionism is not an accidental feature of Soviet society.  The czars might have felt content with the Straits; not so the present Communist regime, for which limitless expansion is a necessary product of its inner unsolved and unsolvable conflicts, economic, political and psychological.  Two important ideological obstructions stood in the way of the development of a policy of naked Soviet expansionism: (1) the right of the self-determination of nations and (2) the belief in the complete equality of nations and national cultures—both of them hallowed fixtures in the intellectual sanctuary of Bolshevism.

The early Bolsheviks, before seizing power, asserted the right of self-determination to the point of declaring their readiness to permit any nation to secede from the Soviet Union; they did not, of course, look forward to the Balkanization of Russia, but hoped rather that the granting of the right of self-determination would lead to a voluntary union and eventually, after the inevitable world revolution, to the merging of all nations in a common undifferentiated, socialist humanity.  After Bolshevik rule was consolidated, however, the unqualified right of self-determination was given short shrift.

In October 1920, Stalin wrote that Soviet nations "had the inalienable right to secede from Russia," but that actually to do so had become "profoundly counter-revolutionary."  At the tenth party congress in 1921, Stalin said that, since the various nations had joined the federation of Soviet republics "voluntarily," the right to secession "did not arise" any more.  In 1923, at the twelfth party congress, he argued that "besides the right of self-determination there is also the right of the working class to consolidate its power and to this latter right self-determination is subordinate—it cannot be an obstacle to the right of the working class to its dictatorship."  The working class, of course, was represented by its most "conscious" representatives: the party and its Politburo.

The commitment to the equality of nations was harder to dispose of, and a certain degree of cultural freedom remained for the non-Russian minorities after the right of self-determination was interpreted out of existence. But the centralized regime of oppression and exploitation generated dissatisfaction and revolt, which in turn revived old, and created new, national tensions. Ukrainian peasants suffered famine and the atrocities of "de-kulakization" because of policies determined in Moscow. The decline in standards of living after the conquest of Georgia aroused nostalgia for independence and protests against foreign, *i.e.*, Russian rule. Social protest took the form of national resistance, and "nationalist deviations" spread like an epidemic. . . .

These developments finally brought about an official revision of ideology. In a famous speech on May 24, 1945, Stalin declared that the Great Russians were the "most outstanding" nation of the Soviet Union. This sounded innocuous enough, and the apologists for Soviet policies did not fail to interpret it in terms of *primus inter pares*: all nationalities were still equal, the Great Russiaᴌs were merely leading the others on the path of brotherly cooperation. But in the Soviet Union, as well as in Orwell's *Animal Farm*, to say that all animals are equal does not exclude the possibility that some animals are more equal than others. In Communist terminology, to lead means to dictate. The leader acts "in the interest of all," but has to be obeyed. And since, in Soviet Russia, almost any change in present attitudes automatically revises history, the leading role of the Great Russians was projected into the past.

The old czars and their generals again became objects of veneration, especially those among them, like Ivan the Terrible and Peter the Great, who organized, centralized, and expanded Moscovite rule. . . .

In superimposing a Russian on a general Soviet chauvinism, the leaders of the Soviet Union, who after all come from different ethnic groups and are led by the Georgian Stalin, were certainly not motivated by any old-fashioned sentimental nationalist feelings. Almost against their will, the tensions between national groups due to the social antagonisms generated by bureaucratic despotism led them to assert that the Russians were the empire-building, the minorities the empire-threatening, forces. It was not Russian nationalism which created Soviet imperialism. On the contrary: Soviet rule and Soviet imperialism resurrected Russian nationalism to act as a binder, because Russia was central, both in historical and geographical terms, to the complex of nations ruled from Moscow.

We may sum up the evolution of Soviet imperialism by describing three quite distinct, though partly overlapping, periods in its development:

The first period, from 1917 to 1925, saw the seizure of power and the emergence of the new bureaucratic ruling class, which went hand in hand with the substitution of autocratic for democratic methods in dealing with minority peoples and small foreign nations. But the expansion of Bolshevik rule proceeded under the banner of world revolution, to which the interests of the Soviet state were in theory subordinated. The main appeal was to revolutionary internationalism, not to Russian patriotism or nationalism.

In the second period, from 1925 to 1939, the Soviet ruling class secured its totalitarian rule in Russia, avoiding open conflicts with foreign powers but transforming Communist movements everywhere into docile fifth columns. "Defend the Soviet Union!" now became the central slogan; the interests of world revolution were declared identical with—in other words, subordinated to—the defense of Soviet power. Internationalism was replaced by Soviet patriotism.

The third period started in 1939, when a favorable international situation and the consolidation of the new order in Russia made expansion possible on a large scale, and the contradictions of the Soviet system at the same time made it more and more necessary. The new central idea was that of world domination by a hierarchically organized class of rulers directed from Moscow. "Russian nationalism" was revived as an instrument of Soviet imperialism; "world revolution" became a mere synonym for Soviet expansion.

Soviet imperialism is motivated *neither* by the interests of the "Russian nation" *nor* by the interests of "international Communism." Its driving force is *the interest of the Soviet bureaucratic regime*. For this reason, as the experiences of all the satellite countries have shown, the mere expansion of Russia's power and influence is not sufficient—its peculiar social order must be imposed everywhere, replacing previous social forms; only this can satisfy the needs of the Soviet bureaucracy. But, as the Yugoslavs know, the duplication of the Communist order is not enough: it must also be directed from Moscow.

What strategic conclusions flow from this analysis?

Totalitarian imperialism cannot stop expanding. It is a menace to the free world so long as it exists. A policy of containment, therefore, has efficacy only as a prelude, the first necessary condition of a policy whose real aim must be the disintegration of the totalitarian empire. Only by containment *and* disintegration of the totalitarian machine can war be avoided. The undermining of Communist rule is possible. There is no harmony of interests between the Soviet ruling class and the Russian people: imperialist expansion does not ease the oppression weighing on the Great Russians themselves—on the contrary, they pay dearly for militarism and armament. There is a harmony of interest between the Russian people and the subjugated nations of the Russian empire. A sound policy must, in the first place, appeal to this common interest. Both the Russians and the minority nations are potential allies of Western democracy against their present oppressors. And both are entitled to the same treatment and to the same promise: that they will have the right to decide their future for themselves in a democratic way.

The social and national cleavages in the Russian empire can be the driving forces towards its disintegration. These cleavages will begin to be felt strongly when Soviet expansion is stopped; they will gather momentum when its power is rolled back.

# RUSSIA AND THE WEST*

BY

## ARNOLD J. TOYNBEE

[1953]

In the encounter between the world and the West that has been going on by now for four or five hundred years, the world, not the West, is the party that, up to now, has had the significant experience. It has not been the West that has been hit by the world; it is the world that has been hit—and hit hard—by the West.

A Westerner who wants to grapple with this subject must try, for a few minutes, to slip out of his native Western skin and look at the encounter between the world and the West through the eyes of the great non-Western majority of mankind. Different though the non-Western peoples of the world may be from one another in race, language, civilization, and religion, if any Western inquirer asks them their opinion of the West, he will hear them all giving him the same answer: Russians, Moslems, Hindus, Chinese, Japanese, and all the rest. The West, they will tell him, has been the arch-aggressor of modern times, and each will have their own experience of Western aggression to bring up against him. The Russians will remind him that their country has been invaded by Western armies overland in 1941, 1915, 1812, 1709, and 1610; the peoples of Africa and Asia will remind him that Western missionaries, traders, and soldiers from across the sea have been pushing into their countries from the coasts since the fifteenth century. The Asians will also remind him that, within the same period, the Westerners have occupied the lion's share of the world's last vacant lands in the Americas, Australia, New Zealand, and South and East Africa. The Africans will remind him that they were enslaved and deported across the Atlantic in order to serve the European colonizers of the Americas as living tools to minister to their Western master's greed for wealth. The descendants of the aboriginal population of North America will remind him that their ancestors were swept aside to make room for the west European intruders and for their African slaves.

This indictment will surprise, shock, grieve, and perhaps even outrage most Westerners today. Dutch Westerners are conscious of having evacuated Indonesia, and British Westerners of having evacuated India, Pakistan, Burma, and Ceylon, since 1945. British Westerners have no aggressive war on their consciences since the South African War of 1899-1902, and American Westerners none since the Spanish-American War of 1898. We forget all too easily that the Germans, who attacked their neighbors, including Russia, in the first world war and again in the second world war, are Westerners too, and that the Russians, Asians, and Africans do not draw fine distinctions between different hordes of "Franks"— which is the world's common name for Westerners in the mass. "When the world passes judgment it can be sure of having the last word," according to a well-known Latin proverb. And certainly the world's judgment on the West does seem to be justified over a period of about four and a half centuries ending in 1945. In the world's experience of the West during all that time, the West has been the aggressor on the whole; and, if the tables are being turned on the West by Russia and China today, this is a new chapter of the story which did not begin until after the end of the second world war. The West's alarm and anger at recent acts of Russian and Chinese aggression at the West's expense are evidence that, for us Westerners, it is today still a strange experience to be suffering at the hands of the world what the world has been suffering at Western hands for a number of centuries past.

## II

What, then, has been the world's experience of the West? Let us look at Russia's experience, for Russia is part of the world's great non-Western majority. Though the Russians have been Christians and are, many of them, Christians still, they have never been Western Christians. Russia was converted not from Rome, as England was, but from Constantinople; and, in spite of their common Christian origins, Eastern and Western Christendom have always been foreign to one another, and have often been mutually antipathetic and hostile, as Russia and the West unhappily still are today, when each of them is in what one might call a "post-Christian" phase of its history.

This on the whole unhappy story of Russia's relations with the West did, though, have a happier first chapter; for, in spite of the difference between the Russian and the Western way of life, Russia and the West got on fairly well with one another in the early Middle Ages. The peoples traded, and the royal families intermarried. An English King Harold's daughter, for instance, married a Russian prince. The estrangement began in the thirteenth century, after the subjugation of Russia by the Tatars. The Tatars' domination over Russia was temporary, because the Tatars were nomads from the Steppes who could not ever make themselves at home in Russia's fields and forests. Russia's lasting losses as a result of this temporary Tatar conquest were, not to her Tatar conquerors, but to her Western neighbors; for these took advantage of Russia's prostration in order to lop off, and annex to Western Christendom, the western fringes of the Russian world in White Russia and in the Western half of the Ukraine. It was not till 1945 that Russia recaptured the last piece of these huge Russian territories that were taken from her by Western powers in the thirteenth and fourteenth centuries.

These Western conquests at Russia's expense in the late Middle Ages had an effect on Russia's life at home, as well as on her relations with her Western assailants. The pressure on Russia from the West did not merely estrange Russia from the West; it was one of the hard facts of Russian life that moved the Russians to submit to the yoke of a new native Russian power at Moscow which, at the price of autocracy, imposed on Russia the political unity that she now had to have if she was to survive. It was no accident that this new-fangled autocratic centralizing government of Russia should have arisen at Moscow; for Moscow stood in the fairway of the easiest line for the invasion of what was left of Russia by a Western aggressor. The Poles in 1610, the French in 1812, the Germans in 1941, all marched this way. Since an early date in the fourteenth century, autocracy and centralization have been the dominant notes of all successive Russian regimes. This Muscovite

Russian political tradition has perhaps always been as disagreeable for the Russians themselves as it has certainly been distasteful and alarming to their neighbors; but unfortunately the Russians have learned to put up with it, partly perhaps out of sheer habit, but also, no doubt, because they have felt it to be a lesser evil than the alternative fate of being conquered by aggressive neighbors.

This submissive Russian attitude toward an autocratic regime that has become traditional in Russia is, of course, one of the main difficulties, as we Westerners see it, in the relations between Russia and the West today. The great majority of people in the West feel that tyranny is an intolerable social evil. At a fearful cost we have put down tyranny when it has raised its head among our Western selves in the forms of Fascism and National Socialism. We feel the same detestation and distrust of it in its Russian form, whether this calls itself Tsarism or Communism. We do not want to see this Russian brand of tyranny spread; and we are particularly concerned about this danger to Western ideals of liberty now that we Franks find ourselves thrown upon the defensive for the first time in our history since the second Turkish siege of Vienna in 1682-83. Our present anxiety about what seems to us to be a post-war threat to the West from Russia is a well-justified anxiety in our belief. At the same time, we must take care not to allow the reversal in the relation between Russia and the West since 1945 to mislead us into forgetting the past in our natural preoccupation with the present. When we look at the encounter between Russia and the West in the historian's instead of the journalist's perspective, we shall see that, over a period of several centuries ending in 1945, the Russians have had the same reason for looking askance at the West that we Westerners feel that we have for looking askance at Russia today.

During the past few centuries, this threat to Russia from the West, which has been a constant threat from the thirteenth century till 1945, has been made more serious for Russia by the outbreak, in the West, of a technological revolution which has become chronic and which does not yet show any signs of abating.

When the West adopted firearms, Russia followed suit, and in the sixteenth century she used these new weapons from the West to conquer the Tatars in the Volga valley and more primitive peoples in the Urals and in Siberia. But in 1610 the superiority of the Western armaments of the day enabled the Poles to occupy Moscow and to hold it for two years, while at about the same time the Swedes were also able to deprive Russia of her outlet on the Baltic Sea at the head of the Gulf of Finland. The Russian retort to these seventeenth-century Western acts of aggression was to adopt the technology of the West wholesale, together with as much of the Western way of life as was inseparable from Western technology.

It was characteristic of the autocratic centralizing Muscovite regime that this technological and accompanying social revolution in Russia at the turn of the seventeenth and eighteenth centuries should have been imposed upon Russia from above downward, by the fiat of one man of genius, Peter the Great. Peter is a key figure for an understanding of the world's relations with the West not only in Russia but everywhere; for Peter is the archetype of the autocratic Westernizing reformer who, during the past two and a half centuries, has saved the world from falling entirely under Western domination by forcing the world to train itself to resist Western aggression with Western weapons. Sultans Selim III and Mohammed II and President Mustafa Kemal Atatürk in Turkey, Mehemet Ali Pasha in Egypt, and "the Elder Statesmen," who made the Westernizing revolution in Japan in the eighteen-sixties, were, all of them, following in Peter the Great's footsteps consciously or unconsciously.

Peter launched Russia on a technological race with the West which Russia is still running. Russia has never yet been able to afford to rest, because the West has continually been making fresh spurts. For example, Peter and his eighteenth-century successors brought Russia close enough abreast of the Western world of the day to make Russia just able to defeat her Swedish Western invaders in 1709 and her French Western invaders in 1812; but, in the nineteenth-century Western industrial revolution, the·West once more left Russia behind, so that in the first world war Russia was defeated by her German Western invaders as she had been defeated two hundred years earlier, by the Poles and the Swedes. The present Communist autocratic government was able to supplant the Tsardom in Russia in consequence of Russia's defeat by an industrial Western technology in 1914-17; and the Communist regime then set out, from 1928 to 1941, to do for Russia, all over again, what the Tsar Peter had done for her about 230 years earlier.

For the second time in the modern chapter of her history Russia was now put, by an autocratic ruler, through a forced march to catch up with a Western technology that had once more shot ahead of hers; and Stalin's tyrannical course of technological Westernization was eventually justified, like Peter's, through an ordeal by battle. The Communist technological revolution in Russia defeated the German invaders in the second world war, as Peter's technological revolution had defeated the Swedish invaders in 1709 and the French invaders in 1812. And then, a few months after the completion of the liberation of Russian soil from German-Western occupation in 1945, Russia's American-Western allies dropped in Japan an atom bomb that announced the outbreak of a third Western technological revolution. So today, for the third time, Russia is having to make a forced march in an effort to catch up with a Western technology that, for the third time, has left her behind by shooting ahead. The result of this third event in the perpetual competition between Russia and the West still lies hidden in the future; but it is already clear that this renewal of the technological race is another of the very serious difficulties now besetting the relations between these two ex-Christian societies.

### III

Technology is, of course, only a long Greek name for a bag of tools; and we have to ask ourselves: What are the tools that count in this competition in the use of tools as means to power? A power-loom or a locomotive is obviously a tool for this purpose, as well as a gun, an airplane, or a bomb. But all tools are not of the material kind; there are spiritual tools as well, and these are the most potent that Man has made. A creed, for instance, can be a tool; and, in the new round in the competition between Russia and the West that began in 1917, the Russians this time threw into their scale of the balances a creed that weighed as heavily against their Western competitors' material tools as, in the Roman story of the ransoming of Rome from the Gauls, the sword thrown in by Brennus weighed against the Roman gold.

Communism, then, is a weapon; and, like bombs, airplanes, and guns, this is a weapon of Western origin. If it had not been invented by a couple of nineteenth-century Westerners, Karl Marx and Friedrich Engels, who were brought up in the Rhineland and spent the best part of their working lives in London and in Manchester respectively, Communism could never have become Russia's official ideology. There was nothing in the Russian tradition that could have led the Russians to invent Communism for themselves; and it is certain that they would never have dreamed of it if it had not been lying, ready-made, there in the West, for a revolutionary Russian regime to apply in Russia in 1917.

In borrowing from the West a Western ideology, besides a Western industrial revolution, to serve as an anti-Western weapon, the Bolsheviki in 1917 were making a great new departure in Russian history; for this was the first time that Russia had ever borrowed a creed from the West. . . . *But it was a creed* particularly well suited to serve Russia as a Western weapon for waging an anti-Western spiritual warfare. In the West, where Communism had arisen, this new creed was a heresy. It was a Western criticism of the West's failure to live up to her own Christian principles in the economic and social life of this professedly Christian society; and a creed of Western origin which was at the same time an indictment of Western practice was, of course, just the spiritual weapon that an adversary of the West would like to pick up and turn against its makers.

With this Western spiritual weapon in her hands, Russia could carry her war with the West into the enemy's country on the spiritual plane. Since Communism had originated as a product of uneasy Western consciences it could appeal to other uneasy Western consciences when it was radiated back into the Western world by a Russian propaganda. And so now, for the first time in the modern Western world's history since the close of the seventeenth century, when the flow of Western converts to Islam almost ceased, the West has again found itself threatened with spiritual disintegration from inside, as well as with an assault from outside. In thus threatening to undermine Western civilization's founda-

tions on the West's own home ground, Communism has already
proved itself a more effective anti-Western weapon in Russian
hands than any material weapon could ever be.

Communism has also served Russia as a weapon for bringing
into the Russian camp the Chinese quarter of the human race, as
well as other sections of that majority of mankind that is neither
Russian nor Western. We know that the outcome of the struggle
to win the allegiance of these neutrals may be decisive for the outcome of the Russo-Western conflict as a whole, because this non-
Western and non-Russian majority of mankind may prove to hold
the casting vote in a competition between Russia and the West for
world power. Now Communism can make a two-fold appeal to a
depressed Asian, African, and Latin American peasantry when it
is the voice of Russia that is commending Communism to them.

The Russian spokesman can say to the Asian peasantry first;
"If you follow the Russian example, Communism will give you
the strength to stand up against the West, as a Communist Russia
can already stand up against the West today." The second appeal
of Communism to the Asian peasantry is Communism's claim that
it can, and that private enterprise neither can nor would if it could,
get rid of the extreme inequality between a rich minority and a
poverty-stricken majority in Asian countries. Discontented Asians,
however, are not the only public for whom Communism has an
appeal. Communism also has an appeal for all men, since it can
claim to offer mankind the unity which is our only alternative to
self-destruction in an atomic age.

It looks as if, in the encounter between Russia and the West,
the spiritual initiative, though not the technological lead, has now
passed, at any rate for the moment, from the Western to the Russian side. We Westerners cannot afford to resign ourselves to this,
because this Western heresy—Communism—which the Russians
have taken up, seems to the great majority of people in the West
to be a perverse, misguided, and disastrous doctrine and way of
life. A theologian might put it that our great modern Western
heresiarch Karl Marx has made what is a heretic's characteristic
intellectual mistake and moral abberation. In putting his finger
on one point in orthodox practice in which there has been a crying
need for reform, he has lost sight of all other considerations and

therefore has produced a remedy that is worse than the disease.

The Russians' recent success in capturing the initiative from us Westerners by taking up this Western heresy called Communism and radiating it out into the world in a cloud of anti-Western poison gas does not, of course, mean that Communism is destined to prevail. Marx's vision seems, in non-Marxian eyes, far too narrow and too badly warped to be likely to prove permanently satisfying to human hearts and minds. All the same, Communism's success, so far as it has gone, looks like a portent of things to come. What it tells us is that the present encounter between the world and the West is now moving off the technological plane onto the spiritual plane.

# CONTINUITY IN RUSSIAN FOREIGN POLICY*

BY

## R. S. TARN

[1950]

The foreign policies of most countries can be described fairly simply as the process by which they attempt to maintain their national existence, sometimes at the expense of other states, sometimes in peaceful cooperation with them. The policies followed may at times seem suicidal in so far as the end result is concerned, but the ultimate aim remains constant. The foreign policy of the Soviet Union is unlike that of any other modern state in that it combines the nationalist aims constant throughout most of Russian history, with the goal and rules laid down by a world-wide political movement. Marxist-Leninist-Stalinist ideology plays an extremely important role in determining the direction and motivation of Soviet foreign policy, and this feature distinguishes it from that of its Tsarist predecessors, though there are certain overriding factors in *Russian* policy which have remained almost unchanged from the times of Ivan the Terrible. Inherent in this combination of factors is the dualism resulting from the relations of a great power with other countries, and the special position of the Soviet Union resulting from its claim to be the communist motherland.

The feeling is often expressed that Soviet foreign policy is strange and inexplicable. Judged by the standards of the past, it is indeed often puzzling for Westerners. But if its aims and motives are analyzed, there need be no great mystery about it. The feeling which arose after the war that Soviet foreign policy is an enigma, is itself in part due to swallowing too readily wartime hopes that permanent collaboration between the Western powers and the Soviet Union could be continued in peace and in time form the foundation for a solid international structure based on

* From *International Journal*, Autumn 1950. Copyright 1950 by the Canadian Institute of International Affairs. Reprinted by permission.

mutual understanding and friendship, and economic and political cooperation. Many Western leaders firmly believed this was possible, and some were only disabused by the Czech *coup d'etat* in February, 1948, in spite of the mass of evidence to the contrary. The argument is also advanced that the Russians were prepared for friendly cooperation with the Western Powers, but that owing to their own hypersensitivity or other causes, the Soviet leaders quickly reached the conclusion that the Western World was fundamentally hostile and the best course for the Soviet Union was to mend its own fences and prepare for the inevitable conflict.

On the basis of the evidence, however, there can be no real probability that Moscow ever seriously believed friendship between the two camps would be possible or even profitable from its point of view. The preamble to the Soviet Constitution of July 6, 1923, stressed the tremendous gap between the communist and the capitalist worlds; and between these two camps the official Marxist doctrine offered no prospect of permanent peace. The seizure of power in 1917 had been predicated upon a rapid spread of the revolutionary movement to the rest of Europe, China, and South-East Asia. These hopes were not fulfilled, but the Soviet Government continued to be not just the government of Russia, but the possible nucleus for a world federation of Soviet Socialist Republics. The Constitution of 1923 laid down that entry into the U.S.S.R. was open to all Soviet Socialist Republics, both those then existing and those which might arise in the future.

The ultimate aim of the Soviet leaders at that time was world revolution and the formation eventually of a communist state embracing the whole world. In fact Lenin and Trotsky followed Marx closely in believing it would be impossible to establish communism in one state only, because, by the nature of capitalism, the capitalist states would be bound to try to destroy it, and the communists would therefore have to devote so large a proportion of their efforts to preparing for this contingency they would not have sufficient resources left to construct communism.

Since then tactics have been changed from time to time to meet requirements, and Stalin has proclaimed that socialism (and more recently even communism) can be achieved in one state, but essentially the aims of the communist leaders have not changed one iota since 1917. We can make this assertion with some confidence. The evidence goes to show that present day Soviet leaders are still motivated to a very large extent by Marxist-Leninist-Stalinist doctrine. If at times the tactics seem to change that is simply because the Soviet Government does not operate in a vacuum. Like non-communist governments, it is faced with the inevitable divergence between its short-term objectives—security and progress within its own frontiers—and long-term objectives—the expansion of the area dominated by Stalinism.

## THE IDEOLOGICAL BACKGROUND

Much of the bewilderment and irritation that is felt in the Western World at Soviet behavior is due primarily to a failure to realize that the Communist Party leaders approach policy from a fundamentally ideological standpoint. In the Bible of the Soviets, "The Short History of the Communist Party of the Soviet Union," Stalin lays down that: "The power of the Marxist-Leninist theory lies in the fact that it enables the party to find the right orientation in any situation, to understand the inner connection of current events, to foresee their course, and to perceive not only how and in what direction they are developing in the present but how and in what direction they are bound to develop in the future. Only a party which has mastered the Marxist-Leninist theory can confidently advance and lead the working class forward." At the same time Stalin warns that it is not a dogma alone, but also a guide to action.

Soviet policy is by no means arbitrary, irrational and enigmatic, though individual manifestations of it may so appear. It is based to a large extent on an ideological analysis of events and an understanding of it predicates some conception of the Marxist-Leninist ideology which underlies it. The fact that the rigid application of this ideology to contemporary events often results in grotesque miscalculations on the part of the Russians is more or less irrelevant.

It is hardly necessary to go into the details of dialectical and historical materialism, which is the essence of Marxist-Leninist doctrine, but it is obvious from an examination of the writings and statements of Stalin and the other principal Soviet leaders that their general views and policies have been in close accord with these principles. They regard capitalist forces as the decaying and disintegrating forces of modern society, and Communist forces as the rising forces to be speeded to victory. The classes forming a capitalist society they look upon containing in themselves the germs of those social contradictions which are, in effect, irreconcilable and which result in a struggle for power. Capitalism is, in the words of Stalin, "pregnant with revolution, whose mission it is to replace the existing capitalist ownership of the means of production by socialist ownership."

At the same time, Lenin and Stalin have always shown themselves bitter opponents of moderate socialists and trade unionists, who believe in achieving socialism gradually. This opposition is based in part on a theory that development takes place through a struggle of internal contradictions and proceeds by abrupt leaps from slow quantitative changes to qualitative changes. They therefore maintain that the internal contradictions of capitalism must be uncovered and exposed, that the class struggle must be sharpened and carried to its conclusion, and that revolutions are natural and inevitable. As a result, they attack non-revolutionary socialists and trade unionists for helping capitalism to prolong its existence by the advocacy of policies which have the effect of softening capitalist traditions and the struggle between classes. There is also a good tactical reason for the opposition to social democracy in that the latter has been the force in other European countries most likely to prove a rival for the loyalty of the proletariat. That is obviously the principal reason for the intense hatred by the communists of the socialists in France, in the United Kingdom and in Germany. It will be recalled also that it was the unholy alliance of the communists with the Nazis in Germany from 1930 to 1933 which so weakened the Social Democrats that Hitler was able to take power. The only surprising thing is that the moderate socialists of Western Europe labored under the delusion in 1945 that they were better qualified to cooperate with the Russians than the Right Wing parties. Apparently none of them had read, for example, the pronouncements made by the Red Army when it entered Poland and the Baltic States in 1939. It was ordered, above all, to seize the moderate socialist leaders and to exterminate their parties.

Another feature of Soviet ideology which obviously plays an important role in Soviet thinking is the Leninist doctrine that capitalism reaches its highest and decaying state in imperialism, when it is inevitably compelled to try to mitigate its contradictions by extending its domination over sources of raw materials and over the less advanced and developed areas of the world. According to Marxist theory, this ultimately produces a struggle of the colonial peoples against the exploiting foreign capitalists, which proceeds side by side with an intensified struggle by the working masses in individual countries against their own domestic capitalist classes. It also leads to increasing rivalry and periodic wars between capitalist powers for markets and sources of raw material. As recently as February 1946 Stalin repeated this view and implied that he regards further wars as an inevitable consequence of the continuance of the capitalist system.

As mentioned earlier, the strict application of Marxist theory to an examination of world affairs occasionally leads the Soviet leaders to make some extraordinary mistakes, such as their belief in the revolutionary Marxist nature of the world proletariat. The Russians were bitterly disillusioned to discover that the working classes of Germany and the Eastern European countries were by no means either solidly pro-Soviet or the source of power they expected.

Another important miscalculation stemming from the application of Marxist theory has been the Soviet belief in the inevitability of an American economic depression after the war, and the belief that because of the contradictions in capitalism the two principal capitalist powers, the United Kingdom and the United States, would soon fall out. The appreciation in the Kremlin of Marshall Aid was also based on the belief that the United States must acquire new markets in Europe in order to postpone the coming depression in the United States. Even as regards colonial theories, they have had a difficult task in reconciling the peaceful handing over of power by Britain in India and Burma—though Indo-China and Indonesia have provided plentiful ammunition for the Soviet theorists. Finally, a supreme miscalculation has been the failure to gauge properly the continuing force of nationalism, particularly in Eastern Europe.

A brief review of Soviet long-term policy from the standpoint of harmony between Marxist theory and Soviet practice appears to warrant at least two general conclusions. The first is that, in spite of many apparent deviations in their short-term domestic policy, the Soviet leaders have consistently tried to continue and complete the work of the October Revolution of 1917 by developing in the Soviet Union a system of Soviet socialism which they eventually hope to expand and widen into a world-wide system of Soviet communism. The second conclusion is that in foreign affairs the Soviet leaders have always feared that, as long as the Soviet Union was economically weak, the capitalist states might band together to attack her. This view was based not only on the experience of foreign intervention in the civil war, 1918-1920, but also on Marxist theory which could not envisage the capitalist world permitting the communist state to survive unhampered. This has led the Soviet leaders to regard it as their duty to use Soviet power not so much to strengthen socialism in the rest of the world as to try to make use of these forces in the cause of Soviet security and defence. This fear of the capitalist world has prompted a vigorous propaganda campaign calculated, on the one hand, to expose the expected capitalist hostility and machinations, and put them in their proper ideological setting, and on the other, to show that the Soviet Union enjoys the sympathy and support of progressive forces everywhere. The prime aim of Soviet foreign policy during its weak period was to make certain that one corner of the world at least remained as a base for the operation of communism, and on those grounds the territorial sacrifices of the post-1917 period were justified. Similarly today the Soviet leaders have no hesitation in sacrificing the immediate prospects of the Communist Parties of other countries if this serves in some way Russian interests and so in the long run the interests of the whole world proletariat.

## THE TRADITIONAL AIMS OF RUSSIAN FOREIGN POLICY

These appear to be the long-term motives and aims of *Soviet* policy. Combined with them are foreign policy aims which have been constant in Russian councils for four or five centuries. After the principality of Moscow established its primacy in the struggle against the Tartars it began the slow process of expanding and consolidating its own power, as much at the expense of the other Russian principalities as at the expense of the Mongols. Owing to the situation of Moscow in the center of a vast land mass, without well defined strategic frontiers in any direction, and because of the presence of enemies on every side, the advance of Moscow took place in every direction. Sometimes the advance was more clearly marked in the east, against the Mongols, again to the North against the Swedes, at another time to the South against the Tartars and Turks, or again to the West against the Poles and Lithuanians.

This urge towards geographical expansion outwards from the capital city has never really ended. From the time of Ivan the Terrible in the 16th Century, it has seen the small area around Moscow expand to engulf all the area of the Great Russians, the Ukrainians and White Russians, and go on to encompass hundreds of lesser nationalities. The main aim of Ivan the Terrible was to drive the Mongols beyond the Volga, and lessen the danger to Moscow of Polish expansion. Peter the Great's chief aim was to gain an opening on the sea—in St. Petersburg—and to destroy the power of the Swedes who chiefly opposed this. The aim of Elizabeth and Catherine the Great was to acquire an ice-free port on the Baltic in the Livonian principalities, to destroy the Polish and Lithuanian states, and to secure an outlet on the Black Sea. Their successors successfully continued expansion on these fronts, gradually acquiring Finland, most of Poland, and the Black Sea coast. In the meantime the collapse of the Mongols created a huge vacuum to the East into which the Russians pushed until they reached the Pacific Coast.

After the first wave of anti-nationalism which swept the Bolsheviks in 1917, causing them to give up many of the Tsarist possessions, partly in the hope that world revolution would soon make this unimportant, partly because they were not strong enough to resist, one of the main aims of Soviet foreign policy became the desire to re-incorporate these lost areas in the Soviet home-land—and a little more wherever possible. Today this process has been almost completed, with the exception of Finland, and the central area of Poland. To compensate, the southern part of Sakhalin, lost in the war with Japan in 1905, has been regained, and Ruthenia and Northern Bukovina added to the territories of Russia.

However, Tsarist expansion had only been slowed up by 1914, not ended. Ultimate Tsarist aims at the beginning of the century were to ensure a free exit from the Baltic, free egress from the Black Sea, and an ice-free port in the Far East. The first seemed highly unlikely so long as German sea or land power controlled the Baltic, and the latter so long as Turkey controlled the straits. It is obvious that these two aims persist in Soviet strategic thinking today. Both are much nearer achievement. The Soviet position in the Baltic is now relatively far stronger than at any previous time through the elimination of German air and sea power, and through the presence of Soviet troops on the Norwegian Arctic frontier, in Pomerania and East Prussia, and Porkala-Udd, seized from the Finns. In the case of the straits it is not necessary to recapitulate Soviet attempts to secure a foothold on the Bosphorus. The direct thrust having failed, they tried direct intimidation of Turkey in 1946. That having also failed to produce results, they have tried to gain access to the Aegean by establishing a Communist regime in Bulgaria, and by sponsoring its claims to an outlet through Greek Thrace, and by trying to overthrow the anti-communist government in Greece.

Before 1914 Russian expansionism was also manifest in Persia and Afghanistan. In Persia an Anglo-Russian treaty in 1907 had divided the country into two zones of influence. The communists, in 1919, renounced Russian rights in Persia, but since 1942 one of their main aims has been to recover their position there, in part by the threat of force, in part by the attempt to infiltrate through the oil agreement, now happily lapsed by the failure of the Mejlis to ratify it. But obviously Soviet aims remain the same as those of the Tsars: the desire to reach the Indian Ocean through Persia.

Russian expansion into Turkistan brought her to Afghanistan and the borders of India. In the 19th and early 20th century, her lines of communication were too extended to make her a serious direct menace, though her presence across the Himalayas was a constant irritant in Anglo-Russian relations in the 19th century; but since 1945 there has been renewed Soviet interest in these areas which indicate that Russian ambitions in this part of the world have only been dormant.

As soon as Russia started expanding into Siberia, she began to come up against China. The Chinese Empire in the 18th and early 19th centuries was still a mysterious and unknown power whose strength was greatly overestimated. The early Russian explorers who reached the Pacific carried instructions to keep far north of the known Chinese frontiers in order to avoid provoking the Emperor. But gradually Chinese weakness became apparent and the Russians, almost unopposed, pressed down towards Manchuria and eventually reached Vladivostok. All along the enormous frontier from Sinkiang to Korea there were continuous clashes, with effective power passing from Russia to China and back again. This struggle for power along the dividing line between the two countries has continued almost uninterrupted since the Revolution. The Russian communists have spent a good deal of effort on strengthening their economic, military and political situation in the various Soviet Asiatic republics, the native populations of which resemble the peoples across the frontier. The predominant influence in Sinkiang has repeatedly shifted from Russia to China and back again. Tannu Tuva has been finally amalgamated into the Russian SFSR; Outer Mongolia has achieved nominal independence though under strict Soviet control; and Russian and Chinese influence contend for control of Inner Mongolia.

Tsarist Russia did not hesitate to use bribery and intrigue at the Manchu Court to further her diplomacy in the Far East. The communists similarly have used the Chinese Communist Party to further their ends in China. Tsarist policy aimed at neutralizing the Chinese position in Manchuria and its threat to Vladivostok by control of the Chinese Eastern Railway and Dairen and Port Arthur. The Soviet leaders have more than recovered Russian losses in 1905 in the Far East by their return to Port Arthur, the restoration of Southern Sakhalin, and the occupation of Northern Korea.

The Russian communists gave considerable direct support to the Chinese communists from 1918 to 1926, but with the emergence of Chiang Kai-shek as the dominant figure, they made a nominal withdrawal. After the last war, the struggle for power in China was again, as in the past, largely concentrated in Manchuria, where the Russians aided in establishing a dominant position for the

Chinese communists. The victory of communism in China has not finally settled the question of Manchuria, and it still may prove the chief obstacle to good relations between the two great Communist states. In the meantime, however, the two powers have signed a treaty of alliance, and there is no reason to doubt that Soviet power has enormously increased in Asia.

Another feature which the Soviet state shares with the Tsarist state is a deep, almost mystical belief in the special role in world history which the Russians are destined to play. In the 15th century, and particularly after the capture of Constantinople by the Turks, there arose the belief that Moscow was the third Rome, and that from it the true salvation of the world would come. Even after the barriers with the West had been broken down by Peter the Great, and European rationalism seeped into Russia, this belief persisted and was welded into a political force by the Slavophils, who thought that the Slavic race as such was the next great race of peoples that would be called on to play a dominant role in world history. And, of course, Russia was the leader and inspiration of the other Slav peoples.

Today Pan-Slavism still plays an important part in Soviet foreign policy, and has been exploited to the full in Poland, Czechoslovakia, Yugoslavia and Bulgaria. A feeling of Slav solidarity was certainly a not unimportant factor in aligning Czechoslovakia with the U.S.S.R. after the end of the war. The defection of Yugoslavia, however, now makes Pan-Slavism a considerably less effective appeal.

Similarly Moscow has been built up as the spiritual center of world communism, to which all Communists in the world must look for help and guidance. That the Kremlin is regarded in matters of dogma as the supreme power in anything affecting the interpretation of Marxism is now clearly accepted by the non-Russian Communist Parties. One of the striking things that appeared in the Yugoslav-Cominform quarrel was that Yugoslavs did not at first question the *right* of Moscow to pronounce on questions of Marxist theology. They only declared that the information on which the decisions had been taken was false and incomplete. With the persistence of the split, Tito now claims that he represents the true interpretation of Marxism, but this is a position of extreme heresy into which events forced him.

As Max Beloff points out, the marriage between a territorial or ethnic power-complex and an ideology (divine or secular) has always in the past created a formidable combination. Even when the ideological impulse becomes dulled the momentum of such a juggernaut alone can carry it very far. In Beloff's opinion only a successful counter-revolution would suffice to put an end to the Russo-Marxist alliance of 1917, and, of course, he sees no prospect of that.

The dominant role played by ideology in Soviet foreign affairs had the advantage for the Russians of giving them a supreme confidence in their ultimate victory. This continued psychological advantage is enhanced by the extreme flexibility in daily action which they derive from the conviction of their own absolute rightness. It provides them with a dual system of morality which we cannot understand unless we view it in the context of the class struggle. In essence it means that what is permitted to the faithful in the service of the faith is morally reprehensible among the infidels.

## SOVIET TACTICS IN FOREIGN POLICY

As mentioned earlier, apparent deviations from long-run Soviet foreign policy have never in the end proved to be anything more than purely temporary tactical diversions. The principal task of Western diplomacy is therefore to differentiate tactical deviations from long-run policy and to check any gradual wearing away of Western positions because of the often roundabout manner in which the Russians attempt to reach their main objectives.

In tactics the Soviet Union has the advantages of a highly centralized dictatorship, which can be almost impervious to public opinion, assisted by vast fifth columns abroad and an extensive and effective propaganda system within and without the country. It has the disadvantages which stem from a rigid bureaucracy, from the necessity, at least in part, of relating tactical changes to basic ideological aims and motives, and from the peculiarity of the Russian temperament which creates, for example, a highly psychopathic feeling of isolation and suspicion not only of the West in general but of everyone, even friend or neutral, who is not 100 per cent under their control. It was precisely such a motive which, it is thought, played an important part in prompting the Czech *coup d'etat*, and of course the dispute with Tito.

The nature of political developments since 1917 has led the Soviet leaders to use the communist parties abroad not to further communism in their countries but as instruments of Soviet policy. In such a way certainly the French Communist party was ordered into action in the fall of 1947, and again in the spring of 1950, to sabotage the unloading of arms shipments under the North Atlantic Pact, though there seems to be a certain limit to the extent to which foreign communists are prepared to go in sacrificing themselves to the exigencies of Soviet policy. On the other hand, the Soviet view of the possibility of communist revolution appears to have changed radically. While Moscow continues to espouse formally the orthodox Marxist opinion on the inevitability of the October revolution and in theory to claim that it represents the classic type of Communist revolution, in effect the Politburo seems to have accepted the view that it was a unique, non-recurring event. The ideal type of revolution is now considered that of Czechoslovakia where an elite guard takes over the structure of government intact, and where the main factor is the presence of the Red Army. In the Yugoslav-Soviet correspondence, Stalin states bluntly that the Communist Parties in France and Italy could not seize the reins of government only because "unfortunately the Soviet armies could not give the French and Italian Communists assistance."

In Europe Soviet tactics since 1945 have been directed primarily towards creating and consolidating the screen of satellites in Eastern Europe, tightening political and military control and forcing conformity to Soviet practice even at the expense of antagonizing national and religious sentiment and against the opposition of the peasantry. From the Soviet point of view, the basis for the exclusive role the U.S.S.R. plays in this part of the world is the division of Europe into spheres of influence at the Teheran, Yalta and Potsdam Conferences. For a while at any rate the Soviet Government formally observed what it considered to be the tacit assumptions, if not necessarily the explicit stipulations, of the wartime allocation of zones of influence. It is quite probable that the

Russians regarded the post-Potsdam policies of the Western powers as deliberate attempts to reverse this division, in the same way as the West attempted to drive Russia out of Europe after the Congress of Vienna, in 1815, and during the Congress of Berlin in 1878.

The pattern of Eastern European domination by Russia has been badly distorted by the refusal of Marshal Tito tamely to accept the role of a subordinate of Moscow and by the failure of the Greek Communists to capture the Greek Government, or even obtain a foothold in any part of the country. The example of Yugoslavia is peculiarly important in a study of Soviet foreign policy because the published documents present the most revealing insight into the Soviet way of thinking that has so far come to light. For obvious reasons, and even if Tito should not join the Western camp outright, one of the first aims of Soviet diplomacy must be to put an end to this anomalous and humiliating situation. Both Yugoslavia and Greece afford an example, however, of the strength and complexity of Balkan nationalism which even Communism cannot ignore with impunity.

Beyond the Iron Curtain the Communist Parties have more and more come to be used solely as tactical instruments of Soviet foreign policy—at first when communists formed part of the governments in France, Italy and elsewhere, to influence those governments in favor of the U.S.S.R.; later, when ejected from the governments, to sabotage economic and political recovery, and to try to slow up the Marshall plan and the North Atlantic Treaty. Presumably in order better to coordinate communist action abroad, the Comintern, dissolved during the war, was revived in October 1947, under the title of the Cominform, though with a reduced membership. The Comecon, established late in 1948 among the satellites, apparently has a somewhat similar purpose in the economic field.

To go into the question of Soviet tactics in Germany would not be possible in a short study. It is pretty clear that Soviet aims since 1945 have varied enormously from the first primitive urge to revenge, combined with disappointment at the lack of Marxist spirit on the part of the German proletariat, to a desire to drive the western powers out of Berlin and to incorporate the Soviet zone into the Soviet economy of Eastern Europe and finally to a desire to gain a foothold in a United Germany which presumably one day would be communist. The control of all Germany is evidently one of the prime aims of Soviet foreign policy, and indeed the Soviet Union can never regard itself as secure in Europe so long as Germany is outside its control. In this sense Soviet policy in Germany has so far failed.

One important aspect of Soviet foreign policy is found in the Soviet attitude to the United Nations and other international organizations. It is difficult to tell whether or not the Russians signed the San Francisco charter with the intention of seriously cooperating in the work of the United Nations. It is possible that there may have been a stage when the Soviet leaders were seriously considering the possibility of playing a constructive role in the United Nations affairs, but if they ever entertained this possibility they have long since abandoned it. On the basis of the general Soviet approach to international questions, I think it is clear that a genuinely cooperative attitude is at variance with the present Soviet concept of sovereignty which is so rigid as to prevent any serious attempt at its surrender by independent states to an international body not dominated by Moscow. The gulf between the two worlds is not considered bridgeable by the Russians for the reason that any machinery involved must logically demand the sacrifice of sovereignty to a non-communist body which by the nature of things as seen from Moscow must be completely opposed to the U.S.S.R. To inquire, therefore, in what way the "machinery" of international cooperation is deficient, begs the question. If the U.S.S.R. did not join the International Bank or International Monetary Fund, for example, the reason is simple enough. In the U.S.S.R. it is considered a treasonable offense to disclose the gold reserves and the financial status of the Soviet Union. Since practically every item on which information is required successfully to run an international organization, from atomic energy to international aviation, is considered a state secret in the U.S.S.R., it is clear that there is no possibility of cooperating with the Russians on the basis which the West accepts—a partial surrender of sovereignty and the most rudimentary exchange of ideas and information.

At the same time the United Nations serves a useful purpose for the U.S.S.R. in providing a platform from which she can attack the Western world, beguile the naive, and present the Soviet case, as well as prevent positive constructive action being taken. It costs little for the Soviet Union to participate, while the gains are considerable, and it is likely therefore that she will continue to use it for these purposes unless some blow too severe for her pride were struck, in which case she might be prepared to withdraw. An examination of the United Nations agencies which she has joined indicates that she participates only in the work of those where she can do some harm to the West without sacrifice to her own interests, or where she stands to make some positive gain from maintaining her membership, as in the International Telecommunications Union and the World Meteorological Organization.

As early as the first meeting of the Comintern in Moscow in 1923 the Communists agreed that the capitalist system could be attacked with the greatest success at the weakest points, of which one especially singled out for attention was the colonial system. From then on Moscow neglected no portion of the colonial empires of the European powers and commenced the systematic training of Indians, Burmese, Syrians, Malayans, Indo-Chinese, North Africans and Indonesians in preparation for the eventual seizure of their governments. As Mr. Nehru has pointed out on several occasions, the combination of native nationalism with communism is a powerful force in Asia and is Moscow's greatest hope. And it is precisely on this combination in Indo-China and Malaya and other colonial areas that the Russians are likely to concentrate in the next few years.

## CONCLUSION

I have attempted in this article to outline very briefly what appear to me to be the principal aims and motivating factors in the foreign policy of Soviet Russia. I shall not attempt by way of conclusion to launch into speculation as to the direction which the Soviet leaders are likely to take next in the conduct of their country's affairs. One can make guesses, more or less well-informed, but they must remain little better than that.

There is a temptation, however, to think that the spread of communist power and Soviet influence in the Far East is likely to lead the Russians to turn their back on Europe. While Asia would seem to afford them at the moment the most profitable field for exploitation, it would be a grave mistake to think that they have not both the men and the resources to keep up the pressure on all fronts at once, and to take advantage of any weak spot which may appear, no matter in what sector. The Russians have not succeeded in all their aims in Europe indeed, but we must look upon their set-backs as rather a failure to advance further than as "retreat."

There is always a tendency either to underestimate or to overestimate the strength of the Russian colossus. An objective and calm appraisal of Soviet strength is a first prerequisite to an understanding of the problem of our relations with the U.S.S.R. It was with this intention that the above study has been produced.

# RUSSIA'S IMPERIAL DESIGN*

### BY

### EDWARD CRANKSHAW

### [1957]

The concept of imperialism is now so debased that it is almost impossible to discuss it with detachment. This is a pity; imperialism is a useful word, and no other can take its place. It should also be an evolving word, not a term of abuse.

It was designed to express a fact of life: the domination, in the international sphere, of the weak by the strong. This is an enduring fact, and it is much better acknowledged than denied. In the days of the Roman Empire, imperialism stood for the ordering of barbarian tribes by a strong, centralized, highly developed state; for the imposition of the rule of law and the bringing of material progress to dark and backward areas. In the heyday of the British Empire it meant much the same thing. Never in the history of the world has an empire-building course been started and sustained for reasons of altruism; the original motive has always been self-interest.

Self-interest may be diluted, or even transformed, by other motives. But few intelligent Americans, I imagine, would deny that the driving force behind the foreign aid programs of successive United States Administrations, which constitute the most advanced and complex form of imperialism the world has ever seen, was, and remains, self-interest (the response to the threat of Russia), although altruistic motives work to modify and transform the naked self-interest.

Since the days of the Roman Empire, the imperialist dynamic has manifested itself in three broad categories, which overlap: the strategic, the economic, and the missionary. The first is concerned with military security, and sometimes with military glory; the second with mercantile expansion; the third with the salvation of souls and the imposition of what is regarded as a better way of life on what are believed to be inferior cultures. The combinations

---

* From *The Atlantic Monthly*, November 1957. Reprinted by permission.

and variations are infinite and constantly changing. Further, at any given moment in its history, an individual power will exhibit great variations in its own imperialism. The differences of approach on the part of the British to the many parts of their own empire have been wide and sharp. Again, American imperialism shows different faces in different places; the America of the Marshall Plan is identical with the American exploiting, through great business corporations, the backward areas of Latin America. The ways in which dominion can be achieved are also varied and overlapping: through straightforward military occupation, to money lending, to the rule of priests. These categories may also be divided; economic domination, for example, can range from helping foreign peoples to help themselves, so that they may grow into sturdy allies, to subsidizing foreign potentates to keep them on their thrones in face of popular revolt.

To understand Russian imperialism we have to try very hard to put ourselves in the position of the Russians and look at the world through their eyes. The process which brought American dominion to the Pacific coast and beyond was little different from the process which brought Russian dominion to Baku and Vladivostok. Both these processes were similar to the process which took the British to the ends of the earth—the only vital difference being that England, as an island, had to expand across the oceans. Americans were themselves aware of this not so very long ago far more clearly than they are today; it is worth noting that in the nineteenth century, right up to the early days of the twentieth century, American expansionism was taken for granted as a strong and beneficent natural force, and that distinguished Americans regarded Russia as their natural rival.

The first beginnings of what became the Monroe Doctrine may be traced to a speech of Secretary of State John Quincy Adams in 1823: "There can, perhaps, be no better time for saying, frankly and explicitly, to the Russian Government that the future peace of the world, and the interest of Russia herself, cannot be promoted by Russian settlements on any part of the American continent."

Russia, on her side, was disturbed by the American westward drift. In 1860 the Russian ambassador reported: "They have taken California, Oregon, and sooner or later they will get Alaska.

It is inevitable. It cannot be prevented; and it would be better to yield with good grace and cede the territory." In 1866 this was done, and we have a glimpse into the state of a large section of American opinion through a leading article in the New York *Herald*. Referring to Russia and America as "the young giants" of a new world, the writer said: "The young giants are engaged in the same work—that of expansion and progression . . . the colossi having neither territorial nor maritime jealousies to excite the one against the other. The interests of both demand that they should go hand in hand in their march to empire."

But, of course, they did not. Soon there was a new conflict, this time in China. "Eastern Asia," wrote Brooks Adams in 1899, "now appears, without much doubt, to be the only district likely soon to be able to absorb any great manufactures. . . . Whether we like it or not, we are forced to compete for the seat of international exchanges, or, in other words, for the seat of empire."

I have no idea to what extent the heady delights, and the apprehensions, of this early American expansionism are remembered in the United States today. But I know very well that they are remembered in Moscow. "Russia and America may remain good friends until, each having made the circuit of half the globe in opposite directions, they shall meet and greet each other in the regions where civilization first began" (that is, China). These words, written by Secretary of State Seward in 1861, are better remembered in Moscow than the following, from William Woodville Rockhill (1911): "I cannot too emphatically reiterate my conclusion that the sympathetic coöperation of Russia is of supreme importance . . . she can never withdraw from participation in Far Eastern affairs or maintain an attitude of indifference toward them."

When did Russian imperialism begin? It is hard to draw rational lines between the consolidation of a number of principalities into a centralized state, the expansion of the newborn state into contiguous territory for reasons of military security, and the planned or accidental extension of that enlarged and strengthened state to include subject peoples as various as the Eskimos of Yakutia, the nomads of Kazakhstan, the mountaineers of Georgia. But for all practical purposes we are concerned here not with the birth of nations, but with the deliberate attempt to carve empires out of a finite world and to secure markets and bases at the expense of other would-be empire builders. Russia did not embark seriously upon this last course until the nineteenth century. Then, however, she brought to her activities the ingrained habits of a thousand years.

The Czarist Empire was a classic example of the strategic empire. The young Muscovite state had to expand or die. Westward expansion was difficult, in face of highly organized Christian peoples (Lithuanians, Poles, Swedes, Germans). The only objective worth a serious struggle against heavy opposition was an outlet into the Baltic for which Czar after Czar accordingly strove. Expansion eastward, on the other hand, was easy once the power of the Tartar horde had finally been broken by Ivan IV in 1583. And so Russia entered upon her long course of almost unconscious expansion along the line of least resistance—first East, then South. There was nothing to tell her where to stop—nothing until the Pacific coast was reached. And, indeed, it was not safe for her to stop until she had filled up, however thinly, the immense spaces of Eurasia which, sooner or later, would all too easily and willingly have been filled by others. By the time the Pacific was reached, the habit of expansion was so ingrained that it was the most natural thing in the world to cross the Bering Straits into the no man's land of Alaska.

In a century when the modern empire builders were getting into their stride and beginning to carve up Africa, seize bases in the Pacific, and compete for trade in Southeast Asia and Latin America, Russia followed her traditional line: when in doubt, move forward; when you are stopped, try to flow round; when opposition is violent and strong, draw in your horns. The British were in India; the Turkish Empire, with its centuries-old dominion over the Middle East and the lower Danube basin, was breaking up. Poland had been partitioned for the third time among a newly self-conscious Russia, an octopus-like Austria, and the comparatively new state of Prussia with its inordinate ambitions.

In the drive to the East (the Pacific) and the South (the Black Sea) Russia had largely depended on the private initiative of Muscovy traders and Cossack adventurers—just as Britain had once

depended on her exploring merchant adventurers and pirate-
admirals. But now there were tougher nuts to crack. Having
secured her natural Eastern frontier and a warm-water port in the
South, Odessa (which could still be effectively blockaded by any
power controlling Constantinople), Russia sold Alaska to America
and concentrated on a southerly and southwesterly drive, having
for its object an approach to India and a secure outlet, through the
Straits, into the Mediterranean. At the same time, she had her
eye on China and Japan—but more as potential threats to her own
sparsely inhabited hinterland than anything else. In the same
letter of 1860 in which he advised St. Petersburg to give up Alaska
gracefully to the United States, the Russian ambassador to Washington also wrote: "Russia, too, has a manifect destiny on the
Amur, and further South, even in Korea."

Until now the driving power had been almost exclusively strategic. Even the need for an outlet into the Baltic and a warm-
water port on the Black Sea had been more strategic than economic;
that is to say, the Russian Czars needed secure and regular communications with such allies as they might acquire in the outer
world and for the free import of the sinews of war. Even the preoccupation with Constantinople was at first entirely strategic. It
is possible to discuss without end Russia's real intentions in the
matter of the Eastern Question. Did she think of the Straits as a
sally port for her own warships, embarked on further conquests?
Or were they, rather, seen as a danger point, narrows which could
be blocked by enemies to strangle her Odessa trade or to bring
invading armies (as in fact happened in the Crimean War) to the
vulnerable Black Sea coast?

And what about India, a profound interest in which accounted
for Russia's conquest, brutal and highly organized (no longer an
affair of merchant adventurers), of Turkestan? The mad Czar
Paul at one time concocted a crackbrained plot to invade India in
conjunction with the French, a plot which involved a monstrous
portage from the Black Sea to the Caspian. Subsequent Czars kept
the British in a constant state of alarm for the safety of Afghanistan, the Northwest frontier, and Punjab. But it is very much to
be questioned whether any Russian Czar ever seriously contemplated a formal conquest of India—just as it is to be questioned

whether Stalin ever seriously contemplated the conquest of Western Europe. Rather, their own pathological obsession with security (a state of mind readily explained by the vast frontier to be defended and the vulnerability of a hinterland lacking natural lines of defense), together with their inborn and developing technique of the war of nerves (predating Communism by centuries and perhaps springing from their own experiences of Tartar methods), aimed at weakening the concentration, resolution, and unity of real or potential enemies, came before any clearcut imperial ambitions.

For centuries, Russia was separated from the main current of Western culture by her life struggle against the invading Tartars and by the great schism in the Church. While Europe was glorying in the Renaissance, Russia—in Russian eyes—was sacrificing herself as the shield for Europe. The Russians sought consolidation in their isolation by making a virtue of their enforced backwardness. "You may have all sorts of things that we have not got" was the cry ringing down the ages, "but what about your soul? We have preserved our soul. We have suffered and starved and been jeered at. But we have kept our integrity, while you have sold yours—for what? One day Russia will arise to save the world you have betrayed. And then you will see!"

After the fall of Constantinople, Muscovy began to regard herself as the third Rome. The Russians might be materially backward, but spiritually they were a chosen race, and one day they would emerge from their forest gloom and astound the world by their example.

For a long time this brooding impulse was turned inward. But with the defeat of Napoleon and the entry of Russia into the arena as a major power, it began to be turned outward. At the Congress of Vienna, Alexander saw himself as the leading spirit of a guild of Christian monarchs, whose God-given task it was to organize Europe and quell the blind, devouring force of revolution. Russian thinkers began to elaborate the concept of a Russia, backward for so long but with her vital forces husbanded, bringing to a corrupt and bankrupt world a pristine spiritual impulse.

Thus, Russia's historical aspirations toward Constantinople were reinforced by a vision of Russian expansion into the Balkans and rationalized by the proclaimed intention of the Czar to extend his protection to the Christians on the Danube basin and elsewhere still living under Moslem rule. The drive into Southeastern Europe was now in full swing. Its original impulse, strategic and economic, was transformed by a powerful mixture of pure messianic zeal and a new imperial spirit of pan-Russianism to match the jingoism of the times. It was in this spirit, too, that the Russians set about the ruthless subjugation of the Caucasian and Transcaucasian peoples and the lands of what is known now as Soviet Central Asia—populated by numerous peoples who no more resembled the Great Russians of Muscovy than the Hindus and Zulus resembled the British. Here, then, alien peoples were subdued by bloody and sustained assault by organized imperial forces and afterwards run, on colonial lines, from St. Petersburg.

When war broke out in 1914, the Russian Empire, a solid landmass extended from Vladivostok to Warsaw, from Petsamo and Murmansk to the frontiers of India and Persia, from the Baltic to the Amur River. But when, three years later, the Bolsheviks made their *Putsch* against the new government set up after the March Revolution, Lenin denounced the whole concept of Empire and was for the moment ready to concede the independence of all its component parts. But only for the moment. The exigencies of civil war and Western and Japanese intervention made it necessary to carry the Bolshevik revolution to the uttermost possible limits. Soon the supranational Bolsheviks found themselves fighting to retain the conquests of the detested Czars; and there could be no thought of autonomy until the Whites had been driven out and the Reds were in control.

It should be remembered that in the early years of the revolution Lenin still had the idea of a genuine federation of equal peoples, not an empire, in which Bolshevik Russia would be linked amicably, fraternally, and equally with a Bolshevik Ukraine, a Bolshevik Georgia, and above all a Bolshevik Germany. For during the critical years he was expecting—more, he was blindly counting on—successful revolutions elsewhere in Europe, especially in Germany, without which, he was convinced, Bolshevism could never survive in Russia. In the end, the collapse of the revolutionary spirit in Europe and the consequent "capitalist encirclement" of the Soviet Union (the old Russian Empire shorn for the time being of its Baltic and Polish possessions) drove the Russians under Stalin to turn inward once again and to glory in their apartness.

Socialism for the Russians meant building up the Soviet Union in isolation, using what Western help could be obtained without strings, and forcing Russia through her industrial revolution at a breathless and calamitous pace. For a period of eighteen years, from the introduction of Lenin's New Economic Policy in 1921 to the Russo-German nonaggression pact in 1939, the Russians had their hands fully occupied with domestic matters, and, save for an abortive attempt to help the Chinese revolution, removed themselves from the arena of active imperialism—though they were quick to use force and subdue dissident peoples in Turkestan, the Caucasus, and the Ukraine, the remaining assets of the old Czarist imperialism.

In the outside world, apart from China, the only evidence of an aggressive foreign policy was the inconsequent mischief-making of the Comintern, a reversion to the old Czarist habit of trying to sow alarm and despondency with nonexistent threats. Foreign Communists were, to Stalin, as the Christians under Turkish rule had been to the later Czars. Their cause was coldly betrayed, their claims and pretentions ignored, their leaders summoned to Moscow and arrested, just as it suited their master in the Kremlin, who now, like any Czar, had become the leader and slave driver of a reborn Russian state, the Soviet Union. We shall never know what the mature Stalin thought about Communism in the secret corridors of his mind: all we know is that publicly he used it, with perfect cynicism, as an instrument of power—as the Czars had used Christianity; as the early traders had used beads, bright cloth, and firewater.

Then, in 1939, there came a change. The gathering weight of the Soviet Union made itself felt in the outside world. And, with war in the offing, Stalin embarked on a deliberate course of strictly limited expansion which had plainly nothing to do with world revolution, but which was concerned with the securing of definite strategic advantages.

It is not the purpose of this essay to debate the cleverness or the clumsiness of Stalin's policies. All we are concerned with here is what he actually did, and why. And what he actually did, after hesitating a good deal, was to seek an accommodation with Hitler which would postpone a German attack and at the same time secure for the Soviet Union some of the territories lost from the old Czarist Empire, with an immediate eye to making things harder for Germany when the war finally came. It was to this end that in 1939 Stalin invaded and occupied a part of Poland and launched his Finnish War. It was to this end that he infiltrated and then liquidated Estonia, Lithuania, and Latvia (all parts of the old empire) in 1940. What was happening here, disguised by a smoke screen of Communist terminology, was a resurrection of the old Russian strategic imperialism of Ivan the Terrible and Peter the Great. It had, as I have said, a strictly limited aim: defense against a predatory Germany, pushing East.

Nobody who has read the story of the negotiations which culminated in the attack on Finland and continued throughout the course of the Winter War can doubt the fundamentally non-ideological motivation of Stalin's actions. Poland was a pushover: Germany had done the hard work and would have occupied the whole of Poland but for the Soviet stipulation. The three Baltic states were in a hopeless position. But Finland, as always, was a tougher nut to crack, and the Russians knew it.

Stalin did not want the whole of Finland. He was not interested at that time in Bolshevizing the Finns. He simply wanted certain frontier changes which would give him a cushion in front of Leningrad; and he wanted to be able to close the Gulf of Finland to enemy warships by cross fire from the coasts of Finland and Estonia. He would have liked all this without war. And there is every reason to suppose that had Finland been able to agree to an exchange of territory in Karelia and the lease of Hanko on the southwest coast there would have been no war and no further attempt by Stalin to reduce the country. Finland, of course, could not meet these demands and, with wonderful heroism, took on mighty Russia singlehanded.

But the Finnish War showed two things. First, that Stalin's territorial ambitions in 1939 were not unlimited, but had a strictly utilitarian purpose. Second, that once Stalin had set his mind to such a limited aim, nothing would deter him from achieving it— neither the contempt of world public opinion nor considerations of humanity. These two points were important; they showed the world what to expect now that the Soviet Union was beginning to feel her oats as a major power.

These points are still important, as we enter the period which everybody thinks he knows about: the period of Stalinist expansion which culminated in the Berlin blockade and the Korean War. I suppose it is generally taken for granted in the West that during all this period, and even earlier, Stalin was pursuing with fanatical concentration of purpose a single aim: world domination. I question whether he ever held this aim in view.

To argue this matter in detail would require an article by itself. I content myself with simply questioning the general assumption, made as a rule from ignorance of Russian history and based as a rule on meaningless analogies with Hitler. That is why I have tried to show how the Czars got their empire, the spirit behind their expansionism. And I am content to suggest that what happened in Stalinist Russia from 1939, with the conclusion of the nonaggression pact with Germany, until the death of Stalin in 1953 is much better seen as a continuation of the old Russian imperialist dynamic, complicated and reinforced by a distorted Marxism, than as a calculated bid for world dominion or world revolution.

It is generally believed that throughout the war Stalin was plotting to occupy Europe after the war. Anybody who was in Moscow during the two years after the Nazi invasion knows that this is total nonsense. From June, 1941, until, at the earliest, the Stalingrad victory in February, 1943, Stalin was wholly preoccupied in saving the Soviet Union and his own regime. Even much later, when final victory was in sight, Stalin was far more interested in keeping the anti-Nazi coalition alive than in Communist infiltration and revolution. In China he built up Chiang Kai-shek at the expense of Mao Tse-tung; in Yugoslavia he repeatedly snubbed Tito, telling him that the Great Alliance was a matter of life and death and that he was not going to let it be imperiled by Tito's revolutionary zeal.

Stalin also showed himself ready to negotiate with the West about dividing Eastern Europe into old-fashioned spheres of influence, a department welcomed by Churchill but frustrated by

Roosevelt, who was opposed to imperialism in general—except when restricted to islands in the Pacific—and to British imperialism in particular. Even after the war, Stalin was against helping the Greek Communists, so ardently supported by Tito, and poured cold water on the aspirations of Mao Tse-tung—in both cases for reasons of state.

I am not in the least suggesting that during the last decade of Stalin's life Soviet imperialism was not a menace to the world as a whole. Clearly, it was very much a menace. But is was a strictly limited menace, and we in the West played into Stalin's hands by confusing his old-fashioned strategic and economic imperialism, colored now, as I have said, by a distorted Marxism, with an apocalyptic drive to universal revolution. It should have been clear by 1948, when Tito was out-lawed, that Stalin was interested in revolution only insofar as it could be used as an instrument of Russian power. It should have been clear in 1949 that he was seriously concerned over the establishment of a Communist regime in China. But even today too many people go about wondering half fearfully whether Mao Tse-tung may one day "do a Tito"—oblivious of the fact that by his very act of seizing power in China he made himself a Tito. He achieved, that is to say, a Communist revolution in China on his own initiative and with his own arms. The only kind of "revolution" Stalin trusted was one he had made himself with his own agents working under his own detailed and strict directions.

It is time we considered the new complication—what I have called a distorted Marxism—and its effect on the traditional Russian imperialistic drive. Stalin was an adept at using, or abusing, a doctrinaire theory of history as a smoke screen to cover his imperial designs. By this means he gained control of Poland, Czechoslovakia, East Germany, Rumania, Bulgaria, Hungary, half of Austria, Albania, and for a short time Yugoslavia. He was also able to stir up trouble in Southeast Asia and elsewhere. But in the end he overreached himself, unifying and arming a disarmed and disunited West.

It was no doubt the Marxist tincture that caused him to overreach himself. No matter how much or how little Communist ideas appealed to Stalin, his mind was certainly conditioned by the

Marxist-Leninist conception of history. He believed, at least until the last year of his life, that wars between the so-called capitalist powers and the so-called Communist powers were inevitable. He believed that in the end the so-called Communist powers would have things all their own way, being strengthened by every war and its consequent confusion; and he believed that all wars produced in their train revolutionary situations which must be exploited in the interest of the Soviet Union. All that happened after 1945, with Europe in chaos and Asia in revolt, must have confirmed him in these beliefs, with the results we all know.

After him came Malenkov, Khrushchev, and the rest. Malenkov, for a time, behaved like the leader of a great power, almost desperately on the defensive. But with the rise of Khrushchev we began to hear more about the spirit of Leninism, which Khrushchev invoked over the head of his dead master. Stalin was denounced for a variety of sins, but never for imperialism, which would have been in the eyes of Lenin the greatest of all his betrayals. Thus Khrushchev's Leninism has a strong smell of opportunism about it; and my own belief is that for him and his colleagues, Lenin and Leninism serve primarily as a source of authority outside themselves, an authority very necessary at home and otherwise completely lacking.

It seems to me likely that Khrushchev's mind is conditioned pretty thoroughly by what he believes to be Marxism. After all, he was brought up in revolutionary Russia, in the days when the immediate task within the Bolshevik framework was so great that it gave no active man any time to think: born leaders and organizers are not often given to philosophical speculation. It is easy for the present-day youth of Russia to start asking awkward questions; unlike the present Soviet leaders, they have never had to fight a desperate battle against odds and time in Lenin's or Stalin's shadow. I think it likely that Khrushchev takes Leninist theory for granted much as British statesmen of fifty years ago took the parliamentary system for granted, much as American statesmen of today take the American way of life for granted—that is to say, as the best possible way of doing things.

But even Khrushchev at the 20th Party Congress in February, 1956, was at pains to amend the Leninist theses of the inevitability

of major wars and the inevitability of revolution through violence—a revision made, though he did not say so, in the light of
a new fact of life: the H-bomb. It was a revision, moreover, of
the very first importance, though its importance has not been
widely recognized in the West. Stalin, while seeking to avoid
major conflict for reasons of self-interest, believed war was inevitable and that through it Communism, or Russia, would always
grow in strength. Khrushchev no longer holds this simple faith.
The capitalist countries, he has declared—and this declaration has
been written into an official amendment of Leninist theory or
dogma—may now achieve socialism without war and by peaceful
means.

But Khrushchev knows as well as Stalin knew what happens
when countries achieve Communism without the help and guidance of the Soviet Union. To encourage a multiplicity of Yugo-
slavias is no help to Soviet imperialism. And Poland and Hungary
have lately shown what happens to an overgrown and unhomo-
geneous empire when the pressure of police rule is relaxed—and
it has to be relaxed, sooner or later, if the peoples concerned are
to be good for anything.

Once again, therefore, Russian imperialism is at a dead end. It
is not too much to say, I think, that it is now on the retreat. The
Russians may believe that by using every device and trick to disrupt
the Western powers internally and to incite colored or backward
races against Western domination a universal chaos will ensue
from which they alone will profit. Certainly they are behaving as
though they believed this. But their inner councils now must be
muddled. For, again on the long-term view, they know they have
on their own doorstep a most serious threat to meet from China.
There is also Japan.

The Russian leadership are aware of these problems. And, once
more, after the post-war advance into Europe, a very small area,
they are concerned above all with consolidation at home. I have
tried in this essay to treat Soviet imperialism as a natural and understandable phenomenon, which it is. I have tried, all to sketch-
ily, to show that it is not an immediate threat to the outside world;
long-range disruption, designed to weaken and destroy hostile
coalitions, is the real menace now. And in this connection I should

like to conclude with an appeal to the United States, which holds the
present power balance vis-à-vis the Soviet Union.   I should like to
remind all Americans that even if Moscow retreated to the frontiers
of the Soviet Union tomorrow, Russia would still be the greatest
imperial power in the world.   At a time when other imperial
powers are deliberately, and largely for reasons of decency, surrendering their empires, Russia, quite apart from her dominion
over Eastern Europe, which may not last, shows no sign at all of
surrendering her dominion over her own colonial peoples.

The fact that in exploiting these peoples she has brought them
education and machines is neither here nor there:  Britain did the
same before her.   The Caucasus, Transcaucasia, Turkmenistan,
Uzbekistan, Kazakhstan, and the rest are no more part of Russia
than India was of Britain.   The Soviet Union is an empire, not a
country.   And the fact should be remembered.   Roosevelt forgot it
and did the Western coalition in particular and the world in general great harm by this lapse.   The time may come sooner than we
expect when the Soviet Union, presenting herself as a satisfied and
"progressive" land, will make approaches to the United States, as
one anti-imperial power to another.   What will America answer?

The nineteenth-century dream of the two young giants, Russia
and America, coming together in amity to divide and order the
world, was shared by Russians as well as Americans.   There will
always be Russians, under whatever regime, who will believe in
the mighty destiny of their country to save the world from itself
and sweep away the stale effeteness of Western European culture.
There will always be Americans impatient of the endless profitless
bickerings of the smaller powers and the tiny nations and eager to
help the world to perfect itself in America's image.   It is not inconceivable that the nineteenth-century dream might be reborn.
Life would be so much simpler if America and Russia could make
a firm front against China and run the rest of the world between
them.   There will always be Americans whose reaction to the in-
adequacies of smaller powers and tiny countries is to turn their
backs on the whole pack of them and let them stew in their own
juice.   Both arrangements would suit Russia quite well, so long
as she remains an unregenerate imperialist.   "Russia's Imperial
Design"—I wonder if she has one?   But if I were a Russian states-

man, imbued with an invincible belief in the peculiar merits of my own tradition; watching other empires crumble; taking no stock in newfangled ideas about self-determination; filled with a bottomless contempt for the poor dupes, calling themselves Communists, who act as my agents all over the world; perturbed most deeply by the dreadful apparition of an industrialized China, with its hugh population pressing against my vulnerable and sparsely inhabited Eastern lands—if I were a Russian statesman, I should see in America the key to the future.   America must either retreat into isolation, disgusted with the world, and leave free and open a large field of operations for the Soviet Union, or else, sooner or later, America must be persuaded to join with the government of Russia in a major feat of global organization.   Since Russia cannot hope to conquer America, there is no other way.   I wonder how many Americans think of themselves as the potential allies, one way or another, of Russian imperialism?   I wonder what they will do to avoid this situation?

# APPENDIX

# RULERS OF RUSSIA*

## (A.D. 1328-1917)

### GRAND PRINCES OF MOSCOW

| | |
|---|---|
| Ivan I, Kalita | 1328-1341 |
| Simeon, the Proud | 1341-1359 |
| Ivan II, the Red | 1353-1359 |
| Dimitry II | 1359-1362 |
| Dimitry III, Donskoi | 1362-1389 |
| Vasili Dimitrievitch I | 1389-1425 |
| Vasili Vasilievitch II | 1425-1462 |
| Ivan III, the Great | 1462-1505 |
| Vasili, Ivanovitch III | 1505-1533 |

### TSARS

| | |
|---|---|
| Ivan IV, Grozny | 1533-1584 |
| Fyodor Ivanovitch | 1584-1598 |

The period from 1598 to 1613 is called the "Time of Trouble." None of the rulers, including Boris Godunov (1598-1605) who reigned during this time of unrest and anarchy, was fully acknowledged.

## ROMANOV DYNASTY (1613-1917)

### TSARS

| | |
|---|---|
| Michael Fyodorovitch | 1613-1645 |
| Alexei Mikhailovitch | 1645-1676 |
| Fyodor Alexeyevitch | 1676-1682 |
| Ivan V, and Peter I | 1682-1689 |

*From *An Introduction to Russian History and Culture* by Ivar Spector. Copyright, 1949, by D. Van Nostrand Company, Inc. Reprinted by permission.

## EMPERORS AND EMPRESSES

| | |
|---|---|
| Peter I, the Great . . . . . . . . . . . . | 1682-1725 |
| Catherine I . . . . . . . . . . . . . . | 1725-1727 |
| Peter II . . . . . . . . . . . . . . . . | 1727-1730 |
| Anna . . . . . . . . . . . . . . . . | 1730-1740 |
| Ivan VI . . . . . . . . . . . . . . . . | 1740-1741 |
| Elizabeth . . . . . . . . . . . . . . | 1741-1762 |
| Peter III . . . . . . . . . . . . . . | 1762 |
| Catherine II, the Great . . . . . . . . . | 1762-1796 |
| Paul . . . . . . . . . . . . . . . . | 1796-1801 |
| Alexander I . . . . . . . . . . . . . | 1801-1825 |
| Nicholas I . . . . . . . . . . . . . . | 1825-1855 |
| Alexander II . . . . . . . . . . . . . | 1855-1881 |
| Alexander III . . . . . . . . . . . . . | 1881-1894 |
| Nicholas II . . . . . . . . . . . . . . | 1894-1917 |

# CHRONOLOGICAL TABLE*

| | |
|---|---|
| 1147 | Earliest written mention of Moscow. |
| 1220 | First Tartar-Mongol attack in the Caucasus. |
| 1223 | First Mongol invasion; Russians and Polovtsy defeated on the Kalka. |
| 1235-40 | Conquest of the Caucasus by the Tartar-Mongols. |
| 1240 | Capture of Kiev by the Mongols. |
| 1240, July 15 | Alexander Nevsky defeats the Swedes on the Neva. |
| 1242, Apr. 5 | Alexander Nevsky defeats the Teutonic Order at Lake Peipus. |
| 1301-03 | First territorial acquisitions of the Moscow Principality (Kolomna, Pereiaslavl-Zalesski, Mozhaisk). |
| 1360-62 | Struggle between the Muscovite and Suzdal-Novgorod Principalities for the title of Grand Princedom. |
| 1367-68 | First stone fortifications of the Moscow Kremlin. |
| 1378 | Moscow defeats the Tartars on the Vozha. |
| 1380, Sept. 8 | Dimitri Donskoy defeats the Tartars (Mamai) at Kulikovo. |
| 1448 | Election of Jona as Metropolitan of Moscow by the Church Council, confirming independence of the Church of Moscow. |
| 1462-1505 | Ivan III. |
| 1465, 1483, 1499-1500 | First Muscovite campaigns eastward to conquer Yugra, Irtysh and Ob. |
| 1475 | Crimea conquered by the Turks; Crimean Khanate becomes a vassal state of Turkey. |
| 1485-1516 | Building of the new Kremlin in Moscow. |
| 1493 | Ivan III signs an alliance with Denmark. |
| 1496-97 | War with Sweden. |
| 1505-33 | Basil III. |

*All dates cited until January, 1918, are according to the old (Julian) calendar. Abridged from *Russia, Past and Present* by Anatole G. Mazour. Copyright, 1951, by D. Van Nostrand Company, Inc., New York. Reprinted by permission.

| 1507 | Beginning of Crimean raids upon south-Russian territory. |
| 1510 | Incorporation of Pskov in State of Moscow. |
| 1514 | Incorporation of Smolensk territories in State of Moscow. |
| 1520 | Incorporation of Riazan principalities, completing the unification of Russian territories. |
| 1547 | Moscow fire and popular revolt. Ivan IV assumes power; coronation as Tsar. |
| 1553 | Opening of the White Sea route to Russia by Chancellor. |
| 1555-57 | War with Sweden (Gustavus Vasa). |
| 1556 | Capture of the Astrakhan Khanate. |
| 1558-83 | Livonian war. |
| 1571 | Crimean Tartars burn Moscow. |
| 1582 | Truce with Poland. |
| 1583 | Truce with Sweden. |
| 1584-98 | Reign of Feodor Ivanovich. |
| 1585 | Foundation of Archangel. |
| 1587-98 | Boris Godunov as Regent (Lord Protector). |
| 1590-93 | War with Sweden. Treaty of Peace signed, 1595. |
| 1598-1605 | Election of Boris Godunov as Tsar of Russia by the Zemsky Sobor. |
| 1604-13 | Civil wars; "Time of Troubles." |
| 1605-06 | First False Dimitri as Tsar, aided by Poland. |
| 1606-07 | Peasant uprising under the leadership of I. Bolotnikov. |
| 1607-10 | Second False Dimitri. |
| 1610 | Polish invasion; occupation of Moscow. |
| 1611-12 | National uprising led by Minin and Pozharsky; Poles burn Moscow before retreat. |
| 1613 | Election of Michael Romanov as Tsar by the Zemsky Sobor. |
| 1613-45 | Michael Romanov. |
| 1618 | Peace with Sweden (Stolbovo); Moscow loses outlet to the Baltic. Truce with Poland; Smolensk retained by Poland. |

| | |
|---|---|
| 1632-34 | War with Poland. Treaty of Polyanovo. Moscow fails to reconquer Smolensk. |
| 1637 | Capture of Azov by the Don Cossacks. |
| 1645-76 | Alexis I. |
| 1648 | Ukrainian national uprising under the leadership of Bogdan Khmelnitsky against Poland. |
| 1654 | Ukrainian Assembly (Rada) votes in favor of joining Moscow (Jan. 8-9). |
| 1654-67 | Russo-Polish war over the Ukraine; truce of Andrusovo, ceding to Moscow Smolensk, Kiev, and the Ukraine. |
| 1676-80 | War with Turkey and the Crimea. Treaty of Bakhchi-Sarai. |
| 1682-96 | Ivan V. |
| 1682-1725 | Peter I. |
| 1686 | "Permanent peace" with Poland. |
| 1694 | Peter assumes sole political power. |
| 1695 | Beginning of the conquest of Kamchatka; campaign of Vladimir Atlasov. |
| 1695 | First Azov campaign. |
| 1696 | Second Azov campaign; seizure of Azov. |
| 1697-98 | First journey of Peter abroad; negotiations concerning formation of an anti-Turkish coalition. |
| 1703 | Foundation of St. Petersburg. |
| 1705-06 | Astrakhan revolt quelled by B. P. Sheremetev. |
| 1705-11 | Bashkir revolt. |
| 1707-08 | Revolt of K. Bulavin on the Don. |
| 1709 | Battle of Poltava. The Ukraine loses its autonomy. |
| 1710 | Conquest of Livonia, Estonia and Viborg. |
| 1711 | War with Turkey; loss of Azov. |
| 1711 | Discovery of the Kurile Islands by Antsyferov and Kozyrev. |
| 1713-14 | Conquest of Finland. |
| 1717 | Journey of Peter I to Holland and France. |
| 1721 | Treaty of Nystad with Sweden. Acquisition of Livonia, Estonia, Ingria and Karelia. |
| 1721 | Peter I adopts title of Emperor. |

| | |
|---|---|
| 1722-23 | War with Persia. Russian acquisition of the western and southern shores of the Caspian Sea. |
| 1725-27 | Catherine I. |
| 1727-30 | Peter II. |
| 1730-40 | Anna. |
| 1735-39 | War with Turkey; treaty of Belgrade. |
| 1740-41 | Ivan VI. |
| 1741-43 | War with Sweden; treaty of Abo. |
| 1741-61 | Elizabeth. |
| 1746 | Austro-Russian alliance. |
| 1757-61 | Russia's part in the Seven Years' War: Russo-Prussian War. |
| 1759 | Discovery of the Aleutian Islands by Glotov and Ponomarev. |
| 1761-62 | Reign of Peter III. |
| 1762, Apr. 28-<br>1796, Nov. 6 | Catherine II. |
| 1764 | Russo-Prussian alliance and secret convention concerning Poland. |
| 1768-74 | War with Turkey; treaty of Kuchhuk-Kainardji, July 10, 1774, ceding to Russia Black Sea steppes. |
| 1773-74 | Revolt of Pugachev. |
| 1776 | First Russian boat sails to America, sent by G. Shelekhov. |
| 1780 | First "Armed Neutrality" against England. |
| 1781 | Renewal of Austro-Russian alliance aimed against Turkey. |
| 1781-86 | Complete absorption of the Ukraine in the Russian Empire. |
| 1783 | Annexation of Crimea; foundation of Sevastopol. |
| 1783 | Georgian treaty providing Russian protectorship over Eastern Georgia. |
| 1784 | Organization of settlements in Alaska by G. Shelekhov. |
| 1787-91 | War with Turkey; treaty of Jassy, December 29, 1791. |
| 1788-90 | War with Sweden; treaty of Verela. |

| | |
|---|---|
| 1792 | Russian intervention in Poland at the invitation of the Confederates. |
| 1793 | Catherine severs diplomatic relations with France. |
| 1793 | Second partition of Poland. |
| 1794 | Polish rebellion led by Thaddeus Kosciuszko. |
| 1795 | Third partition of Poland. |
| 1796 | War with Persia. |
| 1797 | Formation of the United American and since 1799 Russian-American Company. |
| 1798 | Russia joins the Second Coalition against France. |
| 1799 | Suvorov's campaigns in North Italy and Switzerland. |
| 1800 | Paul I forms alliance with Napoleon; second Armed Neutrality against England. |
| 1801, Mar. 11 | Deposition and murder of Paul I. |
| 1801, Mar. 12- 1825, Nov. 19 | Alexander I. |
| 1801, May 5 | Restoration of diplomatic relations with England. |
| 1801, Oct. 8 | Treaty of peace with France. |
| 1801 | Annexation of Eastern Georgia. |
| 1801-29 | Conquest of Trans-Caucasia. |
| 1803-13 | War with Persia; treaty of Gulistan. Persia recognizes Russian sovereignty over Georgia; northern Azerbeidjan annexed by Russia. |
| 1805 | Third Coalition against France; Austerlitz. |
| 1806-12 | War with Turkey; treaty of Bucharest; annexation of Bessarabia. |
| 1807, June 27 | Treaty of Tilsit. |
| 1807, Oct. 26 | Anglo-Russian diplomatic relations severed; Russia joins the Continental Blockade. |
| 1808-09 | War with Sweden; treaty of Friedrichsham. Annexation of Finland. |
| 1812 | Foundation of the colony Ross in California (existed until 1839). |
| 1812, June-Dec. | Napoleon's campaign and the Patriotic War; Borodino; Moscow burned. |

| 1813-15 | The Grand Alliance. Campaign abroad; capitulation of Paris, March 19, 1814. |
| 1815-25 | Holy Alliance: conclusion of the Alliance, Sept. 14, 1815. Aix-la-Chapelle, Sept. 29-Nov. 22, 1819; Troppau, Oct. 10-Dec. 24, 1820; Laybach, Jan. 11-May 12, 1821; Verona, April 20-Dec. 14, 1822. |
| 1825, Dec. 14 | Decembrist revolt. |
| 1825-55 | Nicholas I. |
| 1826-28 | War with Persia; treaty of Turkmanchai; annexation of Armenia. |
| 1827 | Battle of Navarino; war with Turkey; treaty of Adrianople, Sept. 2, 1829. |
| 1830-31 | Polish rebellion; Warsaw taken by Paskevich, Aug. 26, 1831. |
| 1831-70 | Period of social and political activities of A. I. Herzen. |
| 1833 | Russian landing on the Bosphorus (Feb.-March); treaty of Unkiar-Skelessi, June 26, 1833. |
| 1849 | Russian intervention in Hungary. |
| 1849-50 | Expedition of G. I. Nevelskoi to the Lower Amur River and the Sea of Okhotsk. |
| 1850 | Foundation of Nikolaevsk-on-the-Amur. |
| 1851 | Opening of the Nikolaevsk (now October) railroad between Moscow and St. Petersburg. |
| 1853-56 | The Crimean War; Paris peace, Mar. 18, 1856. |
| 1855-81 | Alexander II. |
| 1858 | Aigun and Tientsin treaties with China; annexation of the Amur and Maritime provinces. |
| 1859 | Surrender of Shamil; conquest of the Caucasus completed, except Circassians, 1864. |
| 1862 | Liquidation of the Russian-American Co. |
| 1863 | Polish rebellion. |
| 1866, Apr. 4 | Attempt at assassination of Alexander II by Karakozov. |
| 1867 | Sale of Alaska and the Aleutian Islands to the United States. |

| | |
|---|---|
| 1872 | Appearance of first translation in Russian of Karl Marx's *Capital*. |
| 1873 | Anglo-Russian Agreement concerning the partition of Central Asia into spheres of influence. |
| 1877-78 | War with Turkey; treaty of San Stefano, Feb. 19, 1878. |
| 1879, Apr. 2 | Attempt at assassination of Alexander II by Soloviev. |
| 1880 | Attempt to blow up the Winter Palace and assassinate Alexander II by Khalturin. |
| 1881, Mar. 1 | Assassination of Alexander II. |
| 1881-94 | Alexander III. |
| 1887, Mar. 1 | Attempt at assassination of Alexander III by Alexander Ulianov (brother of Lenin). |
| 1891 | Beginning of the Trans-Siberian railroad. |
| 1894-1917 | Nicholas II. |
| 1896, May 22 | Sino-Russian defensive alliance against Japan. |
| 1896, Aug. 27 | Sino-Russian Treaty; concession for Chinese-Eastern railway. |
| 1898, Mar. 1-3 | First conference of the Russian Social-Democratic Party in Minsk. |
| 1898, Mar. 15 | Sino-Russian Treaty granting Russia lease on Port Arthur and the Liaotung Peninsula. |
| 1898 | Russian occupation of Port Arthur. |
| 1900 | "Boxer" Rebellion. Russia occupies Manchuria. |
| 1901 | Formation of the Social Revolutionary Party. |
| 1902, Mar. 26 | Sino-Russian agreement concerning evacuation of Russian troops from Manchuria. |
| 1902, Apr. | Assassination of D. S. Sipiagin, Minister of Interior, by S. V. Balmashev, member of the Social Revolutionary Party. |
| 1903, July 17-Aug. 10 | Second conference of the Russian Social-Democratic Party. |
| 1904 Jan. 26 | Japan attacks Russia at Port Arthur without declaration of war; May 14-15: Battle of Tsushima; |

|            | Aug. 23 (Sept. 5 n.s.), 1905: Treaty of Portsmouth. |
| July 15    | Assassination of V. K. Pleve, Minister of Interior, by E. Sazonov, member of the Social-Revolutionary Party. |

1905
| Jan. 1     | Outbreak of the general strike in St. Petersburg. |
| Jan. 9     | "Bloody Sunday." |
| Feb. 4     | Assassination of Grand Duke Sergius by I. P. Kaliaev, member of the Social-Revolutionary Party. |
| June 13-15 | Formation of the first Soviet of Workers' Deputies in Ivanovo-Voznesensk. |
| Oct. 13    | Formation of the St. Petersburg Soviet of Workers' Deputies. |
| Oct. 17    | Manifesto of Nicholas II, summoning a national legislative assembly (Duma), extending suffrage rights, freedom of speech, press, assembly. |
| Nov. 22    | Formation of the Moscow Soviet of Workers' Deputies. |
| Dec. 3     | Arrest of members of the St. Petersburg Soviet. |
| Dec. 9-19  | Moscow uprising. |

1906
| Apr. 27    | Opening of the First Duma. |
| July 8     | Dissolution of the First Duma. Formation of the Stolypin Cabinet. |

1907
| Feb. 20- June 2 | Second Duma. |
| Apr. 30- May 19 | Fifth conference of the Russian Social-Democratic Party. |
| Aug. 18    | Anglo-Russian Agreement dividing spheres of influence in Persia, Afghanistan and Tibet. |
| Nov.- June 1912 | Third Duma. |

1912
| Apr. 22    | First number of the Bolshevik *Pravda* issued. |

Nov. 15-
Feb. 25, 1917 Fourth Duma.

1914

July 19    Germany declares war on Russia.
     24    Austria-Hungary declares war on Russia.

1915

Aug. 26    Nicholas II assumes Supreme Command of the Russian Armies.

1917

Feb. 26    Ukaz of Nicholas II dissolving the Duma; uprising in Petrograd.

     27    Formation of the Soviet of Workers' Deputies in Petrograd; Formation of the Provisional Committee of the Duma. Termination of the Monarchy in Russia.

Mar. 2    Formation of the Provisional government under the chairmanship of Prince G. E. Lvov.

     2    Abdication of Nicholas II from the throne.

June 3-24    First All-Russian Congress of Soviets; June 4: Lenin declares Bolshevik attitude toward Provisional government; June 9: Lenin announces attitude toward war.

July 3-4    Uprising in Petrograd inspired by Bolsheviks; party forced underground.

     24    Formation of a coalition government under the chairmanship of A. F. Kerensky.

Oct. 25-26    Second All-Russian Congress of Soviets in Petrograd; votes in favor of all power to the Soviet.

Oct. 25-
Nov. 2    Uprising in Moscow and establishment of the Soviet regime.

Nov. 2    Armistice signed at Brest-Litovsk.

Dec. 12    Formation of a Ukrainian Soviet government.

Dec. 27    First White organization in the south by Generals L. G. Kornilov and M. V. Alekseev.

1918

Jan.    Rumania occupies Bessarabia.

| Jan. 14 | Introduction of the new (Gregorian) style calendar. |
| Mar. 3 | Signing of the Brest-Litovsk Treaty. |
| 9 | English troops land in Murmansk. |
| 10-11 | National capital transferred from Petrograd to Moscow. |
| 14-16 | Treaty of Brest-Litovsk ratified by the Soviet government. |
| May 25 | Outbreak of the Czechoslovak uprising. |
| July 17 | Execution of the royal family. |
| Aug. 2 | English troops land in Archangel. |
| Nov. 18 | Establishment of the Kolchak government at Omsk. |
| 26-28 | Anglo-French intervention in the South. |

1919

| Mar. 2 | Opening of the First Congress of the Communist International in Moscow. |
| 4 | Beginning of the Kolchak offensive. |
| May 13 | General Yudenich opens campaign against Petrograd. |
| Aug.-Oct. | General Denikin's offensive against Moscow. |

1920

| Feb. 2 | Estonia and Soviet Russia sign peace. |
| Mar. 27 | Capture of Novorossiisk and end of the Denikin's army. |
| Apr. 25 | Poland attacks Soviet Russia. |
| July 12 | Russia and Lithuania sign treaty of peace. |
| Aug. 11 | Russia and Latvia sign peace. |
| Oct. 14 | Russia and Finland sign peace. |
| Nov. 16 | Liquidation of the Crimean front. |

1921

| Mar. 16 | Russia and Turkey sign mutual friendship pact. |
| 18 | Russia and Poland sign Riga treaty of peace. |

1922

| May 16 | Russia and Germany sign Treaty of Rapallo. |
| Dec. 30 | Formation of the Union of Soviet Socialist Republics (USSR). |

1924

| | |
|---|---|
| Jan. 21 | Death of Lenin. |
| Feb. | Great Britain and Italy establish diplomatic relations. |
| May 31 | China and USSR establish diplomatic relations; agreement concerning the management of the Chinese-Eastern railway. |
| Oct. | France establishes relations with the USSR. |

1925

| | |
|---|---|
| Jan. 20 | Japan establishes diplomatic relations with the USSR. |
| Dec. 17 | USSR and Turkey sign neutrality pact. |

1926

| | |
|---|---|
| Apr. 24 | USSR and Germany sign neutrality pact. |

1927

| | |
|---|---|
| Oct. 1 | Expulsion of Trotsky from the Communist Party; victory of Stalin over Trotskyite faction. |

1928

| | |
|---|---|
| Apr. 23-29 | Sixteenth Congress of the Communist Party; adopts the first Five-Year Plan, 1928-33. |

1931

| | |
|---|---|
| | Japanese occupation of Manchuria. |

1933

| | |
|---|---|
| Nov. 16 | Restoration of diplomatic relations between the United States and the USSR. |

1934

| | |
|---|---|
| Sept. 18 | USSR enters the League of Nations. |

1935

| | |
|---|---|
| May 2 | Signing of the Franco-Soviet mutual aid pact. |
| 16 | Signing of the Soviet-Czechoslovak mutual aid pact. |

1936

| | |
|---|---|
| Nov. | Anti-Comintern Pact—Germany and Japan. |
| 1936-38 | Moscow trials. |

1939

| | |
|---|---|
| May 3 | M. Litvinov, Soviet Commissar for Foreign Affairs, resigns; his post assumed by M. Molotov. |
| Aug. 12 | Anglo-French military mission opens negotiations in Moscow. |

| | |
|---|---|
| 23 | Soviet-Nazi pact signed. |
| Sept. 17 | Red army enters Western Ukraine. |
| 29 | Soviet-German treaty of Friendship partitioning Poland. |
| 29 | Soviet-Estonia Mutual Assistance Pact. USSR granted sea- and air-bases. |
| Oct. 5 | Soviet-Latvian Mutual Assistance Pact. USSR granted sea- and air-bases. |
| 10 | Soviet-Lithuanian Mutual Assistance Pact. Vilna ceded to Lithuania. USSR granted sea- and air-bases. |
| 13 | Finnish delegation leaves Moscow after futile negotiations and Soviet demands for Hangö and territory near Leningrad. |
| Nov. 26 | Moscow demands withdrawal of Finnish troops from border territory. |
| 28 | Moscow denounces Soviet-Finnish non-aggression pact. |
| 30 | Finland invaded. |
| Dec. 2 | Finland appeals to the League of Nations. |
| 14 | USSR expelled from the League after mediation declined by Moscow. |
| 1940 | |
| Feb. 15 | Mannerheim Line broken; Red army captures Summa. |
| 22 | Soviet troops occupy islands in Gulf of Finland. |
| Mar. 12 | Soviet-Finnish peace signed in Moscow. |
| June 12 | Soviet ultimatum to Lithuania. |
| 16 | New Lithuanian government formed. |
| 16 | Moscow demands new government in Estonia; accepted on June 22. |
| 16 | Moscow demands new government in Latvia; accepted on June 20. |
| 26 | Soviet ultimatum to Rumania, demanding Bessarabia and Northern Bukovina. |
| 27 | Rumania accepts Soviet ultimatum. |

| July 14 | General elections in Estonia, Latvia, and Lithuania; on July 21 respective assemblies unanimously vote in favor of union with the USSR. |
| Nov. 12-14 | M. Molotov visits Berlin. Negotiations for economic and political collaboration with Axis powers. |
| Dec. 18 | Hitler's Headquarters issues secret "Barbarossa Plan" calling for an attack on the USSR. |

**1941**

| Jan. 10 | Soviet-German trade agreement concluded in Moscow. |
| Apr. 5 | Soviet-Yugoslav pact of friendship and non-aggression signed. |
| 13 | Soviet-Japanese Neutrality Pact signed. |
| May 6 | Stalin replaces M. Molotov as Chairman of Council of Peoples' Commissars. |
| June 22 | Germany invades the USSR. Italy and Rumania declare war on the USSR. |
| 25 | Finland breaks off diplomatic relations with the USSR. Joins in the war against the Soviet Union. |
| 27 | Hungary declares war on the USSR. British military mission arrives Moscow. |
| July 12 | Anglo-Soviet Agreement signed in Moscow: mutual assistance against Hitler and no separate peace. |
| 15 | Churchill declares the Anglo-Soviet agreement "an alliance and the Russian people are now our Allies." |
| 18 | USSR-Czechoslovakia sign agreement in London. Czech contingents to be formed in Russia. |
| 20 | Stalin assumes post of People's Commissar for Defense of the USSR. |
| Sept. 19 | Germans occupy Kiev. |
| Oct. 19 | Stalin declares state of siege in Moscow and pledges that the city "will be defended to the last." |

| Nov. 6 | Announcement of a United States loan to USSR of one billion dollars without interest to finance Lend-Lease supplies. |
| Dec. 10 | Red army takes offensive along entire eastern front. |
| 12 | Moscow declares Germany definitely failed to capture Soviet capital. General von Bock replaced by General List on the Moscow front. |

**1942**

| Mar. 26 | Twenty-Year Anglo-Soviet Treaty signed in London; provides full collaboration during and after the war. |
| June 11 | London announces signature of an Anglo-Soviet treaty concluded on May 26. Understanding reached concerning the creation of "a second front in Europe in 1942." |
| Aug. 16 | Soviet report of military engagements on outskirts of Stalingrad. |
| Sept. 23 | Soviet counteroffensive launched northwest of Stalingrad. |
| Oct. 15 | Moscow approves of allied collective note on punishment of war criminals. Soviet government insists upon necessity to try at once all German leaders who may fall into the hands of Allies during the war. |

**1943**

| Feb. 2 | German forces at Stalingrad capitulate. |
| Mar. 1 | Soviet declares Poland has no claim on Ukraine and White Russia. |
| May 22 | Third International (Comintern) dissolved by declaration from Moscow; decision taken May 15; final action taken on June 10, by Executive Committee of Comintern, after 31 sections consented to dissolution. |
| Nov. 7 | Oumansky, Soviet ambassador to Mexico, declares Russia considers all territory taken from Poland in 1939 as Soviet territory . |

| | |
|---|---|
| 28 | Teheran conference: Stalin, Roosevelt, Churchill. Joint statement signed Dec. 1. Approximate date of invasion of western Europe decided. |

**1944**

| | |
|---|---|
| Jan. 10 | Moscow issues statement on relations with Poland, suggesting new boundary on "Curzon Line." |
| 27 | Complete lifting of Leningrad blockade announced. |
| Mar. 7 | Revealed that Polish government suggested to recognize Curzon Line as *temporary* frontier until after the war; Moscow rejects scheme as inadequate. |
| 17 | Finland rejects Soviet armistice terms. |
| 31 | Soviet-Japanese agreement announced on transfer of North-Sakhalin oil and coal concessions to Russia. |
| Apr. 10 | Odessa recaptured. |
| May 9 | Sevastopol recaptured. |
| 16 | Agreements of the Allies on administration of countries as they are liberated. USSR signatory. |
| June 6 | D-Day. Allied armies land on Northern coast of France between Cherbourg and LeHavre. |
| July 23 | Moscow announces formation of a Committee of National Liberation by the Polish National Council; purpose—to administer liberated Poland. |
| Aug. 23 | Rumania accepts Soviet armistice terms. |
| Sept. 10 | Soviet-Finnish armistice signed. |
| Oct. 9-20 | Third Moscow Conference. Churchill and Eden talk with Stalin; Polish problem discussed. |

**1945**

| | |
|---|---|
| Jan. 5 | Soviet government recognizes Lublin Committee as Provisional Government of Poland. |
| 11 | Russian troops enter Warsaw. |
| 18 | Lublin Provisional Government enters Warsaw. |

| Feb. 4-11 | Yalta Conference: Roosevelt, Churchill, Stalin meet at Yalta to discuss plans for attaining victory and establish lasting peace. |
| Apr. 7 | Russian troops fighting in Vienna; liberated on April 13. |
| 25 | Soviet and United States forces meet at Torgau, on the Elbe River. San Francisco Conference opens. |
| May 2 | Berlin surrenders to First White Russian and First Ukrainian armies. |
| 7 | Unconditional surrender of Germany to Western Allies and Russia. |
| June 17 | Talks in Moscow between M. Molotov, United Kingdom, and US Ambassadors in Moscow, and Polish leaders on formation of a Polish government of National Unity; June 20, agreement reached. |
| 26 | The World Security Charter signed at San Francisco by fifty nations. |
| July 17-<br>Aug. 2 | Potsdam Conference Agreement on Council of Foreign Ministers, on political and economic administration of Germany during occupation, on Poland and on conclusion of peace with the satellite states. |
| 6 | First atomic bomb dropped on Hiroshima. |
| Aug. 8 | Russia declares herself at war with Japan as from midnight. |
| 14 | Announcement at midnight that Japan accepts Allied demand for unconditional surrender. |
| 15 | VJ-Day. |
| 21 | President of the US directs Foreign Economic Administrator to take steps immediately to discontinue all lend-lease operations. |

| | |
|---|---|
| 23 | Stalin announces occupation of all Manchuria, Southern Sakhalin, and of Shimushu and Paramushiro in Kurile Islands. |
| 28 | Occupation of entire Sakhalin Island by Soviet troops completed. |
| Sept. 18 | Report that Marshal Stalin informed US congressional delegation that USSR would like to borrow 6 billion dollars from America for Soviet internal reconstruction. |
| Oct. 2 | The Council of Foreign Ministers meeting since Sept. 11, decides to terminate its session. Serious differences between M. Byrnes and M. Molotov. |
| Dec. 15 | Council of Foreign Ministers meet in Moscow (Byrnes, Bevin, Molotov). |
| 26 | Council of Foreign Ministers ends session. |

1946

| | |
|---|---|
| Feb. 9 | Stalin in a pre-election speech declares to prevent war an equal division of export markets among nations necessary, but this is an impossibility under capitalistic conditions. |
| Mar. 5 | M. Churchill delivers speech at Fulton, Missouri. |
| July 24 | M. Gromyko declares before the Atomic Energy Commission in New York that US proposals for atomic energy development authority and control are unacceptable "either as a whole or in separate parts." No plan can be considered favorably that undermines in any degree the principle of unanimity in the Security Council. |
| Aug. 13 | Note to Turkey of Aug. 8 announced requesting revision of Montreux Convention. |
| 17 | Announced that M. Litvinov had been released from his duties as Deputy Foreign Minister. |
| Sept. 24 | M. Stalin in a questionnaire for the British press states that there can exist a "friendly competition" between western Democracies and the Soviet |

Union; atomic monopoly cannot last; "communism in one country" perfectly possible.

28   Soviet note to Turkey of September 24, published. Maintains international conference on the Straits must be preceded by Soviet-Turkish conversations; complains Turkish rejection of Soviet proposal for joint defense agreement of the Straits.

Oct. 9   US note to Russia maintains that Turkey shall primarily be responsible for the defense of the Straits.

1947
Mar. 12   Announcement of the "Truman Doctrine" to halt the expansion of Communism; Congress requested to aid Greece and Turkey.

25   US State Dept. publishes summaries of unrevealed clauses of agreements at Teheran, Yalta and Potsdam. Among these promise at Yalta of the Kuriles and Southern Sakhalin to the Soviet Union as a condition of Soviet participation in the war against Japan; support admission of Ukraine and White Russia as separate members of the United Nations at Potsdam; recognized that the Montreux Convention be revised because of failure to meet present-day conditions, and that each of the Three Powers have direct conversations with the Turkish Government.

May 22   Greek-Turkish aid bill signed by President Truman.

June 5   M. Marshall speaks at Harvard University on aid to Europe, including Great Britain and the USSR.

16   *Pravda* declares Marshall's plan for European aid nothing less than American dollar pressure and interference in domestic affairs of Europe.

July 11   Moscow reports that 8 countries declined to attend the Paris conference on European economic cooperation. Consider the conference as primarily a plan aimed at formation of a western bloc.

**Oct. 5** Announcement in Moscow that a "Communist Information Bureau" (Cominform) would be set up in Belgrade to coordinate the activities of the Communist parties of Bulgaria, Czechoslovakia, France, Hungary, Italy, Poland, Rumania, USSR and Yugoslavia.

**1948**

**Jan. 23** Soviet government informs UN the Commission on Korea would not be permitted to enter the Soviet zone.

**Feb. 9** Soviet Foreign Office declares the recent US publication of *Nazi-Soviet Relations, 1939-41* (Dept. of State 3023) presents a distorted picture of events and slanders the Soviet Union.

**16** A North Korean "Democratic People's Republic" declared and a "People's Army" announced at Pyongyang.

**25** Communists seize control of the government in Czechoslovakia.

**June 28** Cominform expels Yugoslavia from its membership.

**Dec. 25** Tass announces that Soviet troops completed evacuation from North Korea. President Rhee on Dec. 31, denied that all troops had been withdrawn.

**28** USSR and Yugoslavia sign agreement reducing volume of goods to be exchanged in 1949 to one-eighth of the 1948 total.

**31** Soviet government announces that the unfriendly policy of the Yugoslav government had made large-scale economic cooperation impossible. Belgrade declares reduction of trade result of Yugoslav refusal to accept unfavorable Soviet terms.

**1949**

Jan. 30      Stalin prepared to meet Truman to discuss possibility of conclusion of a world pact. Because of poor health Stalin could not go to the US, but would be willing to meet the President in the USSR, Czechoslovakia, or Poland.

31      White House announces Truman would be glad to welcome M. Stalin in Washington, D. C.

Feb. 4      The Politburo denounces North Atlantic Pact as a "weapon for the preparation of war against the countries of socialism and popular Democracy."

Apr. 4      Atlantic Defense Pact signed in Washington, D.C.

June 2      Yugoslav government protests to Moscow, accusing the Soviet government of hostile action by allowing activities of Yugoslav revolutionary émigrés in the USSR. Moscow replies that it would continue to aid anti-Tito refugees.

July 13      Publication of the Papal ban of excommunication of all communists.

Sept. 23      President Truman announces that an atomic explosion had occurred in recent weeks in the USSR; emphasizes once more the necessity to enforce international control.

Oct. 7      Moscow formally recognizes communist regime in China.

**1950**

Jan. 10      Malik, USSR delegate, offered a resolution requesting immediate expulsion of Dr. Tsiang, representative of Nationalist government of China. After move defeated M. Malik walks out declaring no Soviet delegate will attend Council until Communist China is represented.

Feb. 14      Chinese People's Republic and the USSR sign a 30-year treaty of friendship, alliance and mutual assistance in Moscow.

| | |
|---|---|
| June 25 | North Korean Army crosses the 38th Parallel. |
| 29 | Soviet statement attributes Korean events to the provocation of South Korean troops and asserts that the absence of Communist China from the Security Council prevents it from taking valid decisions. |
| Aug. 1 | J. Malik takes his seat as president of the Security Council for the month of August, thereby ending Soviet boycott. |

**1951**

| | |
|---|---|
| June 23 | J. Malik, Soviet delegate to the UN, suggests the negotiation of a cease-fire agreement by the belligerents in Korea providing for the mutual withdrawal of forces behind the 38th Parallel. |
| July 10 | Beginning of Armistice negotiations in Kaesong. |
| 22 | In Warsaw, Molotov predicts that the Yugoslav people will "eliminate the Tito-Fascist regime." He charges it as having "restored capitalist usages and having converted Yugoslavia into a tool of imperialist powers." |
| 27 | Marshall Tito replies to Molotov's accusations and charges Russia with genocide and mass murder. |
| Sept. 8 | Signing of the Japanese Peace Treaty in San Francisco. The Soviet, Polish, and Czech delegations refuse to sign. |

**1952**

| | |
|---|---|
| Mar. 10 | A Soviet note to the Western powers proposes negotiations on a German Peace Treaty on the basis of the neutralization of Germany. |
| 25 | The Western replies to the Soviet note of March 10 point out that a limitation of Germany's freedom to enter into association with other nations would be a step backward which might jeopardize the new era of co-operation in Europe. |
| May 25 | The "Contractual Agreement" with the German Federal Republic grants it sovereignty. |

|          |                                                                                                                                                                                                                         |
|----------|-------------------------------------------------------------------------------------------------------------------------------------------------------------------------------------------------------------------------|
| 27       | In Paris, the European Defense Community Treaty, including West Germany, is signed.                                                                                                                                      |
| July 2   | A special House of Representatives committee places responsibility on Soviet Russia for the massacre of 4,000 Polish officers at Katyn.                                                                                   |
| Oct. 3   | Russia declares the American ambassador, George F. Kennan, *persona non grata* and demands his recall. On September 19, Kennan had said in Berlin that conditions in Russia reminded him of being interned in Nazi Germany in 1941-42. |
| 5–14     | 19th Congress of the Communist Party of the Soviet Union in Moscow. The main report delivered by G. Malenkov. The Politbureau and the Orgbureau are abolished and replaced by a Presidium of the Central Committee.        |

1953

|          |                                                                                                                                                                                                                         |
|----------|-------------------------------------------------------------------------------------------------------------------------------------------------------------------------------------------------------------------------|
| Jan. 13  | *Tass* announces the discovery of a plot of Jewish doctors to shorten the lives of several Soviet leaders and their confession of being responsible for the death of Zhdanov.                                              |
| Feb. 12  | Russia breaks off diplomatic relations with Israel.                                                                                                                                                                      |
| Mar. 5   | Death of Joseph Stalin.                                                                                                                                                                                                  |
| 6        | Reorganization of leading bodies of Party and Government: Presidium reduced to 10 members; G. Malenkov becomes both Secretary General of the Communist Party and Chairman of the Council of Ministers. Molotov replaces Vyshinsky as foreign minister. |
| 20       | Khrushchev replaces Malenkov as Secretary General of the Party.                                                                                                                                                          |
| Apr. 3   | The release of fifteen doctors is announced and their previous arrest is declared illegal.                                                                                                                               |
| June 17  | Demonstration of workers in East Berlin, leading to intervention of Soviet troops and armored cars.                                                                                                                      |
| July 10  | Dismissal of L. Beria from the Party and the Government. He is called an "international imperialist agent."                                                                                                               |

|        |                                                                                      |
|--------|--------------------------------------------------------------------------------------|
| 19     | Resumption of diplomatic relations with Israel.                                      |
| 27     | Signing of Korean Armistice at Panmunjon.                                            |
| Aug. 20 | *Pravda* announces explosion of a hydrogen bomb.                                    |
| Dec. 23 | Beria and six associates sentenced to death for high treason and shot.              |

## 1954

| Jan. 25– Feb. 18 | Conference of Foreign Ministers of Big Four in Berlin on Germany and Austrian treaty. Only result convocation of a conference to Geneva for discussion of Korea and Indo-China with participation of Communist China. |
|--------|--------------------------------------------------------------------------------------|
| Apr. 26– July 20 | Geneva Conference on Korea and Indo-China, reaches conclusion with the signing of an armistice agreement for Indo-China. |
| May 7 | Fall of Dien Bien Phu in Indo-China. |
| Nov. 22 | Death of A. Vyshinsky, Soviet delegate to the UN. |

## 1955

| Jan. 25 | Russia ends State of War with Germany. |
|--------|--------------------------------------------------------------------------------------|
| Feb. 8 | Resignation of G. Malenkov as Chairman of the Council of Ministers, to be replaced by Marshal Bulganin. |
| 9 | Marshal Zhukov appointed as Defense Minister in succession to Marshal Bulganin. Malenkov appointed Vice-Premier and Minister of Power Stations. |
| Apr. 15 | Conclusion of Austrian-Russian talks in Moscow clearing the way for the Austrian Treaty on condition of Austria's permanent neutrality. |
| May 11–14 | Warsaw Conference of East European states ends with the signing of a twenty-year treaty of mutual alliance, setting up a joint command under Marshal Koniev. |
| 15 | Signing of the Austrian State Treaty in Vienna by the Foreign Ministers of the Big Four. |

| | |
|---|---|
| 26 | A Soviet delegation led by Khrushchev, Bulganin and Mikoyan arrives in Belgrade. Khrushchev blames the "Beria gang" for the breach with Yugoslavia. |
| July 13 | M. Suslov appointed to the Presidium of the Communist Party. |
| 18–23 | Summit meeting in Geneva. |
| Sept. 8–13 | Chancellor Adenauer in Moscow. The establishment of diplomatic relations agreed upon. Adenauer affirms that this does not affect the claim of the Federal Republic to be the only legitimate government of all Germany. |
| 19 | Finnish-Soviet agreement provides for the return of the military base Porkkala to Finland. |
| 20 | Treaty between Russia and East Germany restores East Germany's sovereignty. |
| 27 | Egyptian-Czechoslovak agreement on supply of arms for Egypt concluded. |
| Oct. 27–Nov. 16 | Conference of the Foreign Ministers of the Big Four in Geneva. |
| Nov. 18–Dec. 19 | Bulganin and Khrushchev visit India, Burma and Afghanistan. |

1956

| | |
|---|---|
| Jan. 28 | East Germany included in command of Warsaw Treaty forces. |
| Feb. 14–25 | 20th Congress of the Communist Party of the Soviet Union. It concludes with a secret session where Khrushchev reveals the "Crimes of the Stalin Era" and the evils of the cult of personality. |
| Apr. 18 | The Cominform is dissolved. |
| 18–26 | Bulganin and Khrushchev visit England. |
| June 1 | Molotov replaced as foreign minister by D. Shepilov, on the eve of Marshal Tito's official visit to Moscow. |

20 Moscow Declaration re-establishes close relations between the Communist Parties of Russia and Yugoslavia.

28 Revolt in Poznan, Poland.

Oct. 19 Khrushchev, Molotov, Kaganovich and Mikoyan in Warsaw attempt in vain to prevent the victory of Gomulka in the Polish Communist Party.

23 Beginning of the Hungarian Revolution.

Nov. 1 Hungarian Prime Minister Nagy denounces the Warsaw Pact, announces Hungary's neutrality, and appeals to the UN for help.

4 Soviet troops reoccupy Budapest and break Hungarian resistance; the Soviets set up Janos Kadar as Prime Minister.

1957

Feb. 15 Gromyko replaces Shepilov as Foreign Minister.

May 7 Presentation of Khrushchev's plan for the decentralization of the Soviet economy to the Supreme Soviet.

July 3–4 Malenkov, Molotov, and Kaganovich are expelled from their government posts and, with Shepilov, from the Presidium of the Communist Party as well.

10 Bulganin and Khrushchev arrive in Prague.

Aug. 31 Molotov is designated as Soviet Ambassador to Outer Mongolia.

Oct. 5 The world's first artificial earth satellite is put into orbit by Soviet scientists.

Nov. 2 Marshal Zhukov, charged with promoting his own "cult of the personality," is dismissed as Defense Minister and ousted from the Presidium and the Central Committee of the Communist Party.

3 Firing of second Russian earth satellite.

22 Delegates from 12 Communist countries issue a declaration in Moscow calling for unity against

"imperialism" abroad and "revisionism" within the "camp of socialism." Yugoslavia does not join in the declaration.

**1958**

**Jan. 27–28**   Ferenc Munnich succeeds Janos Kadar as Hungarian premier, but Kadar retains his position as First Secretary of the Hungarian Socialist Workers Party.

**Mar. 27**   Bulganin resigns as premier, succeeded by Khrushchev.

**31**   Bulganin's appointment as Chairman of the State Bank is announced.

**April 2**   Khrushchev arrives in Hungary for an official visit.

**22**   "Observers" from Communist bloc countries walk out of the Yugoslav Party Congress when Tito criticizes the Soviet Union's policies toward Yugoslavia.

**May 15**   The third Russian earth satellite, Sputnik III, weighing 2,925 pounds, is placed in orbit.

**June 17**   The Soviet press reveals the secret trial and execution of Imre Nagy and Pal Maleter, in Hungary, for conspiracy to overthrow the regime.

**July 1**   The Soviet Union reveals that it has informed Yugoslavia that promised credits of $286 million will be postponed for five years or more.

**16**   The UN Special Committee on Hungary denounces the execution of the leaders of the 1956 Hungarian revolution as a violation of the UN Charter.

**Sept. 6**   Announcement that Bulganin, now chairman of an economic council in the northern Caucasus, is no longer a member of the Communist Party Presidium.

**Nov. 10**   Khrushchev calls for an end to the 4-power occupation of Berlin, thereby jeopardizing the position of West Berlin and precipitating a new German crisis.

Nov. 14    Publication of new Seven-Year Plan to surpass the United States in industrial production and give the Soviet people "the world's highest standard of living."

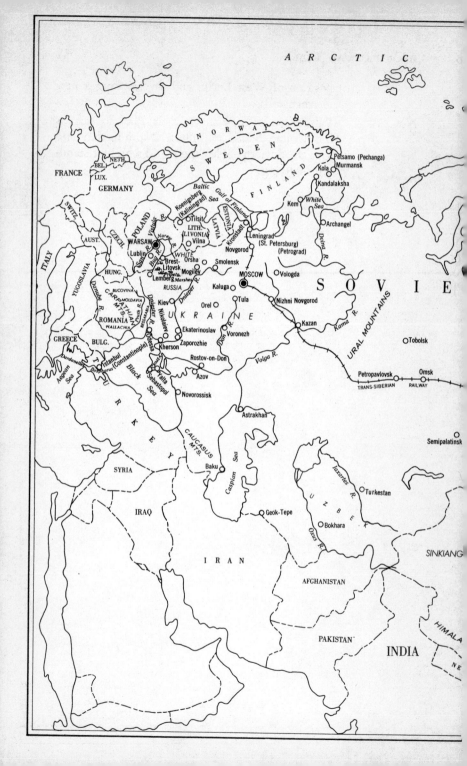

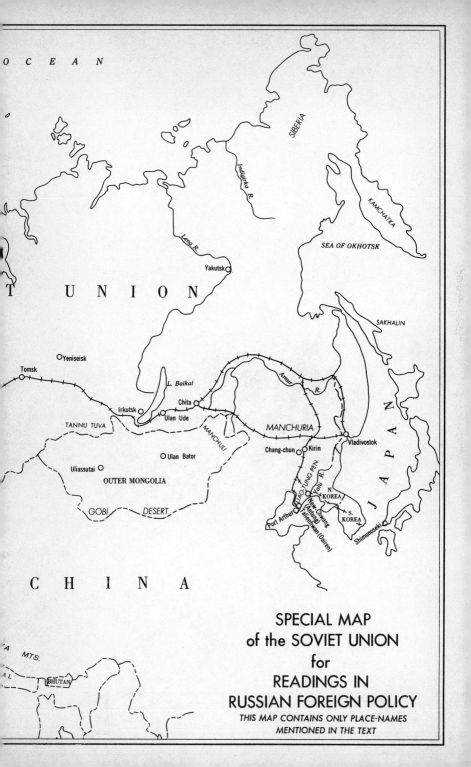

SPECIAL MAP
of the SOVIET UNION
for
READINGS IN
RUSSIAN FOREIGN POLICY
*THIS MAP CONTAINS ONLY PLACE-NAMES
MENTIONED IN THE TEXT*

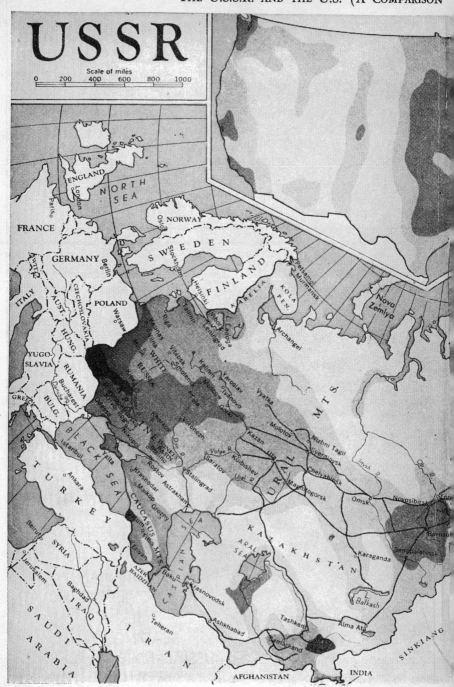

Areas of the United States and the Soviet Union are shown in correct relation.

USSR – 8,300,000 Sq. Mi. (approx.)
US – 3,022,000 Sq. Mi. (approx.)

ALASKA

BERING SEA

ALEUTIAN IS.

KAMCHATKA

SEA OF OKHOTSK

KARAFUTO

SAKHALIN

KURIL IS.

HOKKAIDO

HONSHU

PACIFIC OCEAN

Kolyma R.

Yakutsk

Lena R.

Aldan R.

Bodaibo

Komsomolsk

Khabarovsk

Krasnoyarsk

Lake Baikal

Angara R.

Amur R.

Ulan Ude  Chita

Irkutsk

MANCHURIA

Harbin

Vladivostok

SEA OF JAPAN

Tokyo

SHIKOKU

MONGOLIA

Mukden

LIAOTUNG PENINSULA

Dairen

KOREA

Peiping

YELLOW SEA

KYUSHU

Shanghai

Density of population per square mile

| | |
|---|---|
| ◼ | Over 250 |
| ◼ | 125 – 250 |
| ◼ | 25 – 125 |
| ◻ | 2 – 25 |
| ◻ | Under 2 |

Main railroads
east of the
Urals

# — SOVIET UNION —

INTERNATIONAL BOUNDARY
UNION REPUBLIC BOUNDARIES
CAPITAL OF U.S.S.R. & R.S.F.S.R. ●
CAPITAL OF REPUBLICS ○

SCALE

100  50  0    100    200    300    400    500 MILES

ARMENIA S.S.R.
AZERBAIJAN S.S.R.
BYELORUSSIA S.S.R.
ESTONIA S.S.R.
GEORGIA S.S.R.
KARELO-FINNISH S.S.R.
KAZAKSTAN S.S.R.
KIRGHIZIA S.S.R.

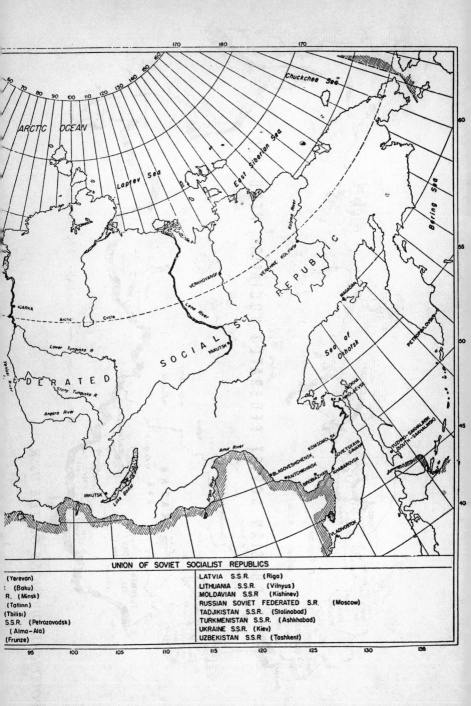

UNION OF SOVIET SOCIALIST REPUBLICS

| ( Yerevan) | LATVIA S.S.R. (Riga) |
| ( Baku) | LITHUANIA S.S.R (Vilnyus) |
| R. (Minsk) | MOLDAVIAN S.S.R (Kishinev) |
| (Tallinn) | RUSSIAN SOVIET FEDERATED S.R. (Moscow) |
| (Tbilisi) | TADJIKISTAN S.S.R. (Stalinabad) |
| S.S.R. (Petrozavodsk) | TURKMENISTAN S.S.R. (Ashkhabad) |
| ( Alma–Ata) | UKRAINE S.S.R. (Kiev) |
| (Frunze) | UZBEKISTAN S.S.R (Tashkent) |

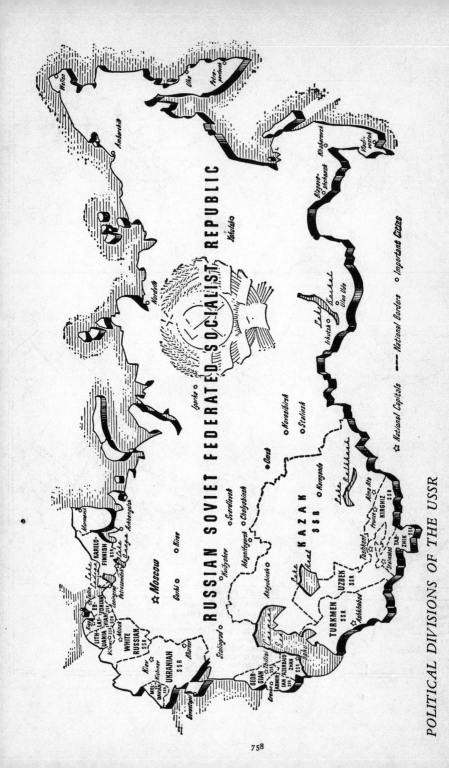

POLITICAL DIVISIONS OF THE USSR

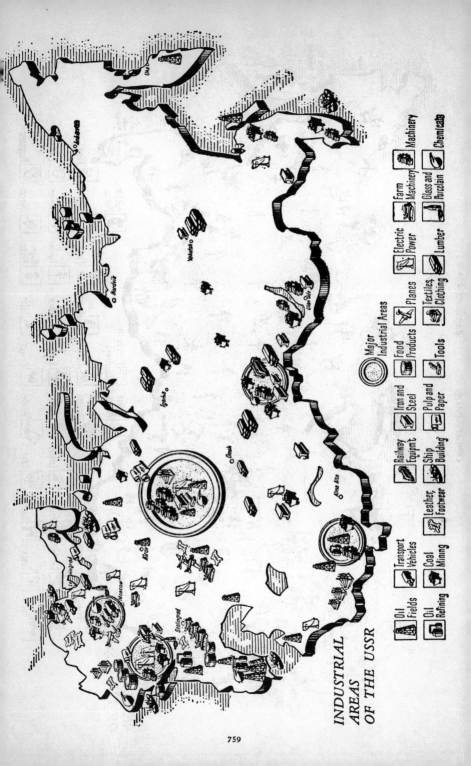

INDUSTRIAL AREAS OF THE USSR

○ Major Industrial Areas

Oil Fields
Oil Refining
Transport Vehicles
Coal Mining
Railway Equip'mt
Leather, Footwear
Iron and Steel
Ship Building
Food Products
Tools
Planes
Textiles, Clothing
Electric Power
Pulp and Paper
Farm Machinery
Lumber
Glass and Porcelain
Chemicals

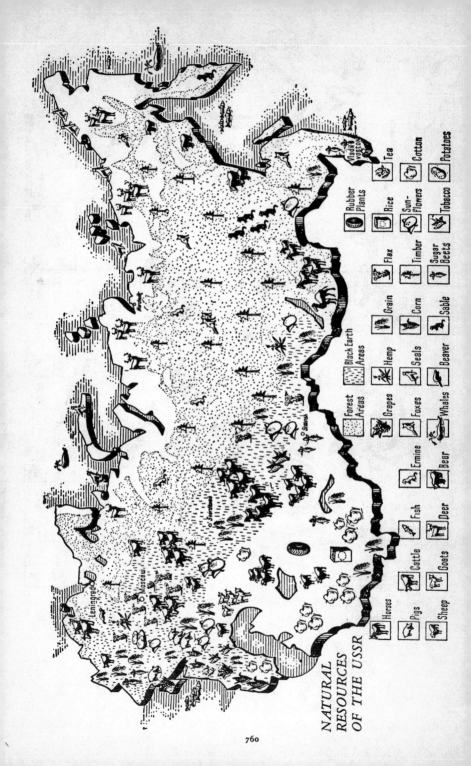

NATURAL RESOURCES OF THE USSR

| | | | |
|---|---|---|---|
| Rubber Plants | Rice | Cotton | Potatoes |
| Flax | Sun-Flowers | Tobacco | Tea |
| Grain | Timber | Sugar Beets | |
| Hemp | Corn | Sable | |
| Seals | Beaver | Black Earth Areas | |
| Grapes | Foxes | Whales | Forest Areas |
| Ermine | Bear | | |
| Fish | Deer | | |
| Cattle | Goats | | |
| Pigs | Sheep | Horses | |

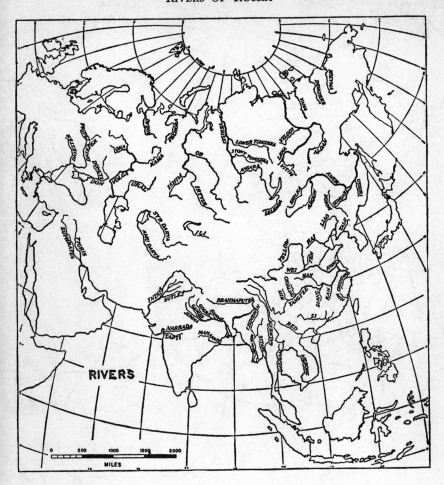

The rivers of the Soviet Union flow either to ice-bound ocean or enter land-locked seas. Five million square miles of interior Eurasia receive so little rainfall that they have no drainage to the ocean.

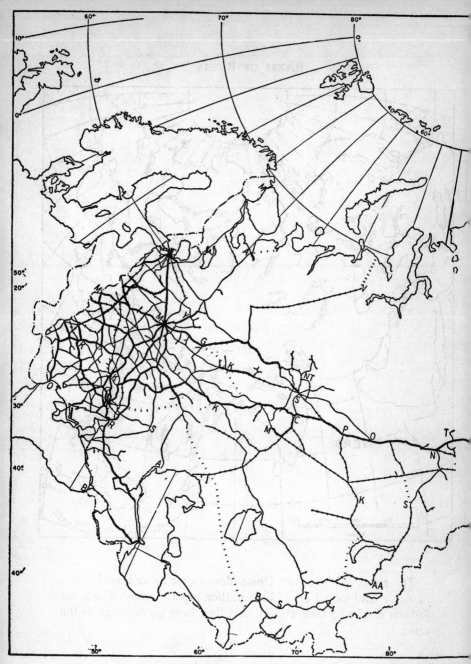

With 62,500 miles of railway in 1940, the U.S.S.R. holds
added under the five year programs. Note the concentration of
Siberia and Middle Asia.

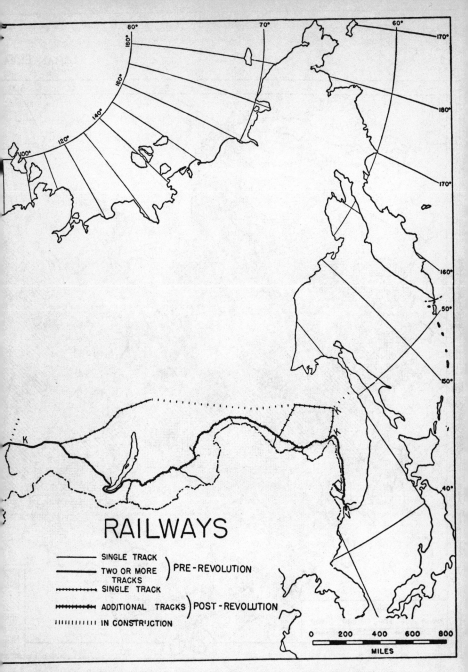

# RAILWAYS

| | | |
|---|---|---|
| ———— | SINGLE TRACK | ) PRE-REVOLUTION |
| ━━━━ | TWO OR MORE TRACKS | |
| ·············· | SINGLE TRACK | |
| ••••••••• | ADDITIONAL TRACKS | ) POST-REVOLUTION |
| ‖‖‖‖‖‖ | IN CONSTRUCTION | |

0   200   400   600   800
MILES

second place in mileage.   A considerable part of this mileage was
railways in a triangular area to the west, and the new lines in

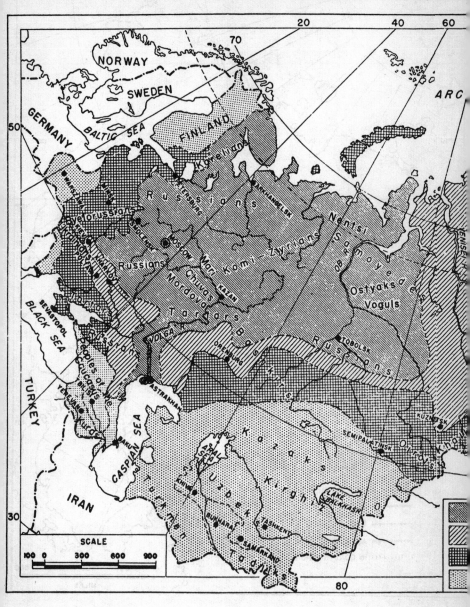

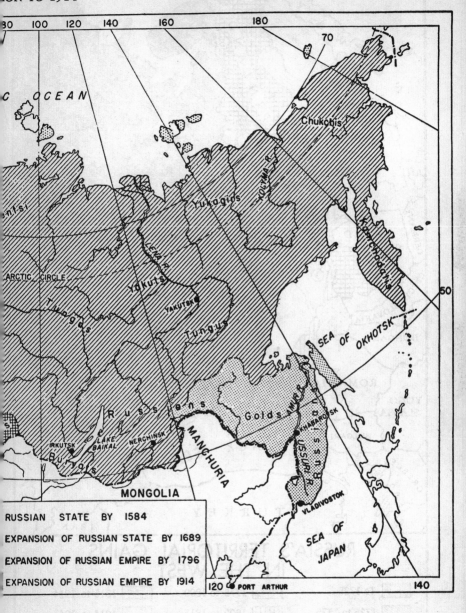

RUSSIAN    STATE    BY    1584

EXPANSION    OF    RUSSIAN    STATE    BY    1689

EXPANSION    OF    RUSSIAN    EMPIRE    BY    1796

EXPANSION    OF    RUSSIAN    EMPIRE    BY    1914

RUSSIA'S TERRITORIAL GAINS
IN THE WEST

| | | |
|---|---|---|
| To 1725 | 1775 to 1800 | 1815 to 1914 |
| 1725 to 1775 | 1800 to 1815 | 1914 to 1947 |

Lost since World War I

Russia's territorial advance toward the west has not been steady or uninterrupted. The map opposite attempts to show schematically the sum of its westward gains to date without indicating the complications of temporary territorial changes. The following summary lists the more important interruptions of Russia's westward advance, and the general regions concerned:

I. FINLAND acquired in 1809; achieved independence after World War I. Rybachi peninsula (A), a section of northern Karelia (B), part of southern Karelia (C), and a section of Finland's Arctic coast including the warm-water port of Petsamo (D) regained by Russia in 1940 after first Russo-Finnish war. At that time Finland leased to Russia the Hangoe peninsula for thirty years at an annual charge of 8 million marks, this peninsula to become a Russian naval and military base.

II. BALTIC STATES—Estonia (E), Latvia (F), and Lithuania (G)—controlled by Russia since the eighteenth century, achieved independence after World War I. Reincorporated into Russia in 1940.

III. Russian acquisitions of Polish territory (H) began with the first partition in 1772 culminating in the creation of the Grand Duchy of Warsaw (I) in the Russian empire in 1815. Russian section of Polish territory lost after World War I upon recreation of an independent Polish state. Eastern Poland occupied by Russia in 1939. The same year Polish White Russia was incorporated into the Byelorussian SSR, and Polish Ukraine into the Ukrainian SSR. Russo-Polish frontier established approximately at the Curzon Line (J) by the Yalta Conference of 1945.

IV. BESSARABIA (K) acquired from Turkey in 1812; occupied by Romania in 1918; regained by Russia in 1940. At the same time Russia obtained from Romania the province of Northern Bukovina, which had been a part of the Austro-Hungarian empire before 1918, when it was taken over by Romania, and had never belonged to the Russian empire.

After World War II Russia, for the first time in its history, acquired a section of Eastern Germany bordering on the Baltic, including the port of Koenigsberg (now Kaliningrad) at the Potsdam Conference of 1945; and Ruthenia (Carpatho-Ukraine), a former province of the Austro-Hungarian empire incorporated after World War I into the new state of Czechoslovakia, from Czechoslovakia under an agreement of June 29, 1945.

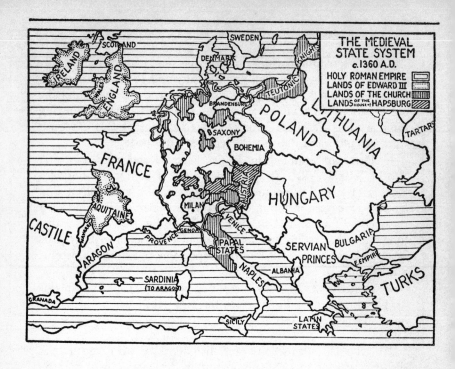

THE MEDIEVAL
STATE SYSTEM
c. 1360 A.D.

HOLY ROMAN EMPIRE
LANDS OF EDWARD III
LANDS OF THE CHURCH
LANDS OF THE HOUSE OF HAPSBURG

SWEDEN
DENMARK
IRELAND
SCOTLAND
ENGLAND
WALES
FRANCE
CASTILE
ARAGON
GRANADA
AQUITAINE
PROVENCE
GENOA
MILAN
SARDINIA (TO ARAGON)
PAPAL STATES
NAPLES
SICILY
BRANDENBURG
SAXONY
AUSTRIA
VENICE
ALBANIA
SERVIAN PRINCES
LATIN STATES
BULGARIA
E. EMPIRE
TURKS
BOHEMIA
POLAND
LITHUANIA
HUNGARY
TARTARS
TEUTONIC

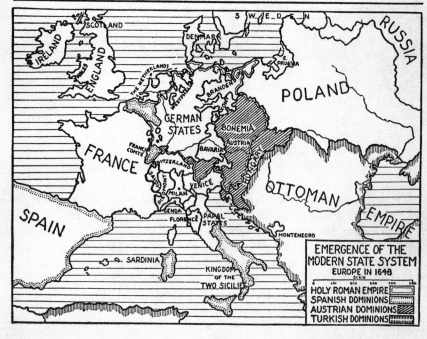

EMERGENCE OF THE
MODERN STATE SYSTEM
EUROPE IN 1648

HOLY ROMAN EMPIRE
SPANISH DOMINIONS
AUSTRIAN DOMINIONS
TURKISH DOMINIONS

SWEDEN
DENMARK
IRELAND
SCOTLAND
ENGLAND
WALES
FRANCE
SPAIN
THE NETHERLANDS
WESTPHALIA
GERMAN STATES
FRANCHE COMTE
SWITZERLAND
SAVOY
PIEDMONT
MILAN
GENOA
FLORENCE
VENICE
PAPAL STATES
SARDINIA
KINGDOM OF THE TWO SICILIES
MONTENEGRO
BRANDENBURG
E. PRUSSIA
BAVARIA
BOHEMIA
AUSTRIA
HUNGARY
POLAND
RUSSIA
OTTOMAN EMPIRE

768

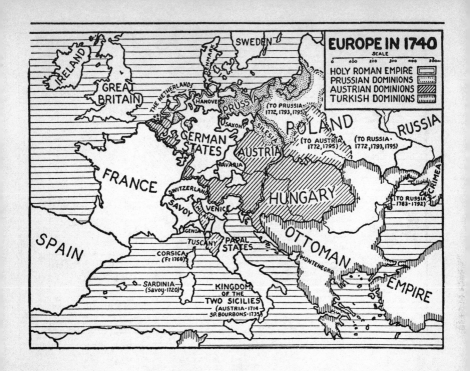

### EUROPE IN 1740

SCALE

| | HOLY ROMAN EMPIRE |
| | PRUSSIAN DOMINIONS |
| | AUSTRIAN DOMINIONS |
| | TURKISH DOMINIONS |

IRELAND

GREAT BRITAIN

SWEDEN

DENMARK

THE NETHERLANDS

HANOVER

PRUSSIA

POLAND

(TO PRUSSIA-1772, 1793, 1795)

RUSSIA

GERMAN STATES

SAXONY

SILESIA

(TO AUSTRIA-1772, 1795)

(TO RUSSIA-1772, 1793, 1795)

FRANCE

BAVARIA

AUSTRIA

HUNGARY

CRIMEA

SWITZERLAND

SAVOY

VENICE

(TO RUSSIA-1783-1792)

GENOA

SPAIN

TUSCANY

PAPAL STATES

OTTOMAN

MONTENEGRO

CORSICA (Fr 1768)

SARDINIA (Savoy-1720)

KINGDOM OF THE TWO SICILIES (AUSTRIA-1714 SP. BOURBONS-1735)

EMPIRE

### THE NAPOLEONIC EMPIRE
#### EUROPE IN 1810

Scale

| | THE FRENCH EMPIRE |
| | DEPENDENCIES of NAPOLEON |
| | TURKISH DOMINIONS |

SWEDEN

DENMARK

GREAT BRITAIN

PRUSSIA

1812

RUSSIAN EMPIRE

GRAND DUCHY OF WARSAW

CONFEDERATION OF THE RHINE

FRENCH EMPIRE

AUSTRIAN EMPIRE

BESSARABIA (TO RUSSIA 1812)

SWITZERLAND

KINGDOM OF ITALY

ILLYRIA

SPAIN

OTTOMAN

MONTENEGRO

EMPIRE

KINGDOM OF NAPLES

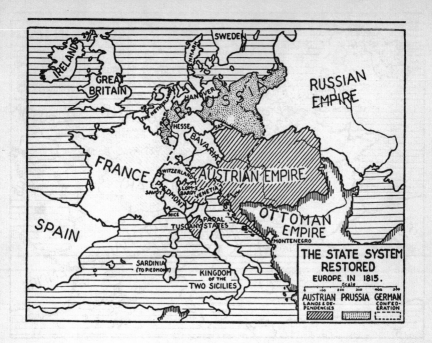

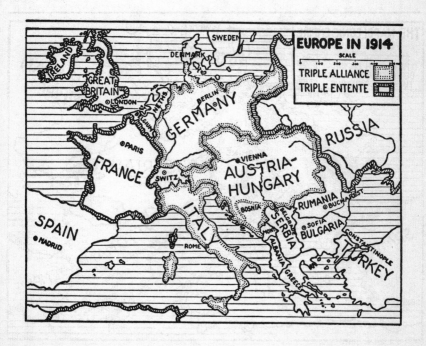

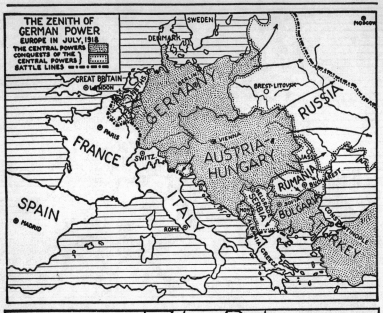

THE ZENITH OF
GERMAN POWER
EUROPE IN JULY, 1918
THE CENTRAL POWERS
CONQUESTS OF THE
CENTRAL POWERS
BATTLE LINES

SWEDEN · DENMARK · MOSCOW · GREAT BRITAIN · LONDON · BERLIN · GERMANY · BREST-LITOVSK · RUSSIA · FRANCE · PARIS · SWITZ. · VIENNA · AUSTRIA HUNGARY · JASSY · RUMANIA · BUCHAREST · SPAIN · MADRID · ROME · ITALY · BELGRADE · SERBIA · MONT. · BULGARIA · SOFIA · ALBANIA · GREECE · CONSTANTINOPLE · TURKEY

EUROPE AFTER VERSAILLES

SCALE
0   100   200   300   400   500 MI.

THE FRENCH BLOC
1919 BOUNDARIES
1914 BOUNDARIES

SMALL STATES
① ANDORRA
② DANZIG
③ LIECHTENSTEIN
④ LUXEMBURG
⑤ MONACO
⑥ SAN MERINO
⑦ VATICAN CITY

NORWAY · SWEDEN · FINLAND · Oslo · Stockholm · Helsingfors · Tallin · ESTONIA · Riga · LATVIA · BALTIC S. · LITHUANIA · IRISH FREE STATE · GREAT BRITAIN · London · NORTH SEA · DENMARK · Copenhagen · E.PRUSSIA (Ger.) · Vilna · Kovno · Moscow · SOVIET UNION · Berlin · GERMANY · Warsaw · POLAND · BELG. · Rhine · Prague · Dnieper · FRANCE · Paris · CZECHOSLOVAKIA · Berne · SWITZ. · Vienna · AUSTRIA · Budapest · HUNGARY · Geneva · RUMANIA · Bukharest · SPAIN · ITALY · JUGOSLAVIA · Belgrade · Rome · BULGARIA · Sofia · BLACK SEA · ALBANIA · GREECE · Angora · TURKEY · Athens · MEDITERRANEAN SEA · ALGERIA · TUNISIA

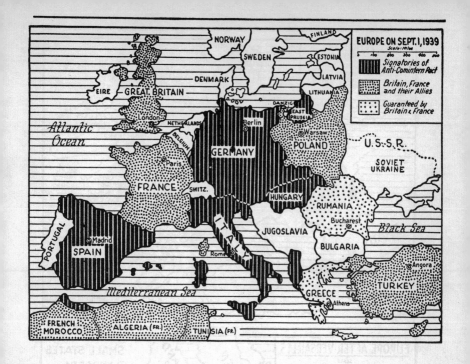

EUROPE ON SEPT. 1, 1939

Scale of Miles

| Signatories of Anti-Comintern Pact |
| Britain, France and their Allies |
| Guaranteed by Britain & France |

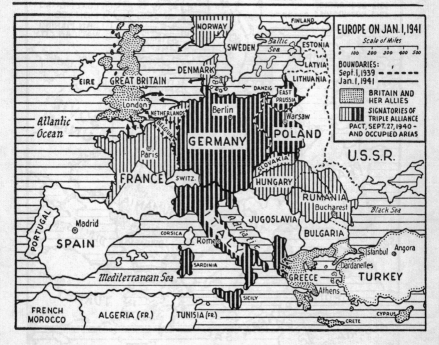

EUROPE ON JAN. 1, 1941

Scale of Miles
0   100   200   300   400   500

BOUNDARIES:
Sept. 1, 1939
Jan. 1, 1941

BRITAIN AND HER ALLIES
SIGNATORIES OF TRIPLE ALLIANCE PACT, SEPT. 27, 1940 — AND OCCUPIED AREAS

# THE ANTI-BOLSHEVIK ARMIES IN RUSSIA, 1919

EAST-CENTRAL EUROPE

▨ Soviet satellite nations.

Ⓐ Part of East Prussia,
now a part of the
Russian Soviet Federated
Republic.

0    MILES    300

From *Current History*, January 1958. Reprinted by permission.

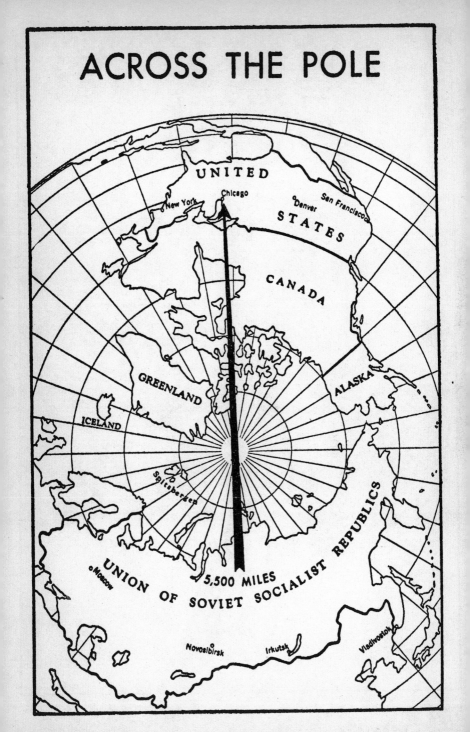

# ACROSS THE POLE

UNITED

New York  Chicago  Denver  San Francisco

STATES

CANADA

GREENLAND

ICELAND

ALASKA

Spitsbergen

5,500 MILES

UNION OF SOVIET SOCIALIST REPUBLICS

Moscow

Novosibirsk  Irkutsk  Vladivostok